lonely planet

San Diego
& Tijuana

Andrea Schulte-Peevers

LONELY PLANET PUBLICATIONS
Melbourne • Oakland • London • Paris

California (USA)
Baja California (MEXICO)

La Rumorosa

El Hongo

Tecate

Valle de
las Palmas

Guadalupe

Ojos Negros

Piedras
Gordas

Villa Juarez

Ensenada

Maneadero

Ejido
Uruapán

Santo Tomás

El Sauzal

San Miguel

Punta Banda

La Bufadora

Islas de
Todos Santos

La Misión

La Fonda

La Salina

Bajamar

Misión del Descanso

Puerto Nuevo

Popotla

Playas de Rosarito

(toll)

La Mesa

National City

San Diego

Coronado

Point Loma

San Diego Bay

Imperial
Beach

San Antonio
del Mar

Otay
Lakes

Tijuana

Islas
Coronados

(Descanso District)

P A C I F I C   O C E A N

50 km

30 miles

25

15

0

0

Elevation

14000ft
12000ft
10000ft
8000ft
6000ft
4000ft
2000ft
Sea Level

San Diego & Tijuana
1st edition – July 2001

Published by
Lonely Planet Publications Pty Ltd ABN 36 005 607 983
90 Maribyrnong St, Footscray, Victoria 3011, Australia

Lonely Planet Offices
Australia Locked Bag 1, Footscray, Victoria 3011
USA 150 Linden St, Oakland, CA 94607
UK 10a Spring Place, London NW5 3BH
France 1 rue du Dahomey, 75011 Paris

Photographs
Many of the images in this guide are available for licensing from
Lonely Planet Images.
email: lpi@lonelyplanet.com.au

Front cover photograph
Longboard skater (Michael Wong/Stone)

ISBN 1 86450 218 5

text & maps © Lonely Planet 2001
photos © photographers as indicated 2001

Printed by The Bookmaker International Ltd
Printed in China

Contents

Contents – Maps

The Author

Andrea Schulte-Peevers

Andrea is a Los Angeles-based writer, editor and translator who caught the travel bug early in life, hitting all continents except Antarctica by the time she turned 18. After finishing high school in Germany, Andrea decided the world was too big to stay in one place and moved first to London, then to Los Angeles. Armed with a degree from UCLA, she managed to turn her wanderlust into a career as a travel writer and may still chase penguins around the South Pole one of these days. Since joining the LP team in 1995, Andrea has authored and/or updated the guides to *Los Angeles*, *Berlin*, *Germany*, *Baja California*, *California & Nevada* and *Spain*.

FROM THE AUTHOR

Even though my name appears as the sole author of this book, my husband David Peevers deserves a huge chunk of the credit. Together we pounded the streets of San Diego and Tijuana, checking hotels and restaurants, bus stations, markets and museums – ending each day with blistered feet but also minds awash with new impressions that make travel so worthwhile. Thank you for being there for me 'on the road' and back at home when long days at the computer surely didn't make me the most fun person to spend a summer with. Thanks also for contributing some of the funniest boxed texts in this book!

In San Diego, we couldn't have done without the generous help of Joe Timko of the San Diego Visitors & Convention Bureau, a master of logistics and a great repository of knowledge about the city. Thank you for making yourself available and for patiently and competently fielding all our requests. Thanks also to Timothy Earp and Beth Binger of The Bristol for their hospitality and insights into the city. Ryan Hurd of Uptown Publications deserves kudos for introducing us to San Diego's gay and lesbian scene. A special mention goes to Sara Harper and Nancy Hirsch, who helped make our stay an extremely pleasant one.

In Tijuana, a heartfelt thank you goes to our 'main man,' Yves Lelevier of Cotuco, who took time to show us around the town and helped us understand what makes it tick. Thanks also to his colleagues Rosario Cázares and Israel Robles Amaro for sharing tips on nightlife, transportation and so much more. A huge round of applause for Armando García Orso and Carlos René Jiménez Rivera of IMAC, who opened our eyes about Tijuana's amazingly fertile cultural scene.

Finally, big fat kudos to everyone at LP Oakland who made this book possible, in particular Mariah Bear for assigning it (thanks also for the Tijuana Bibles idea); Robert Reid for shepherding the project through its various stages with great patience, skill and humor; Elaine Merrill for combing through the text and making it all read smoothly; and Tracey Croom and her team of cartographers for performing another round of miracles with the maps.

This Book

Some of the information in this book appeared before in the 2nd edition of Lonely Planet's *California & Nevada* guide and the 5th edition of the *Baja California* guide. In both cases author Andrea Schulte-Peevers was mainly stealing from her own work (and that of her husband, David Peevers, and *California & Nevada* co-author Marisa Gierlich), which assured that the quality stayed high.

FROM THE PUBLISHER

This 1st edition of *San Diego & Tijuana* is a unique 'twofer,' a groundbreaker for Lonely Planet's Oakland office in that it covers a binational urban area.

The sparkling text of this twin-city special was edited by (almost) twins Elaine Merrill and China Williams, with the wise and witty guidance of Robert Reid and Kate Hoffman. Further editorial help was provided by Vivek 'South of the Border' Waglé, Paul Sheridan, Gabi Knight and freelancer Maureen Klier. Suki Gear and David Zingarelli provided inspiration during the book's briefing, and David Merrill's resident perspective on San Diego was a great boon.

Super-cartographer Ed Turley created the meticulous maps for this book, overseen by Tracey Croom, Annette Olson and Alex Guilbert. Patrick Bock, John Culp, Matthew DeMartini, Mary Hagemann, Christopher Howard, Patrick Huerta and Kat Smith rounded out the mapping team.

Jennifer Steffey designed the psychedelic color pages and the color map section. Josh Schefers labored long and hard on the book's masterful layout. Wendy Yanagihara designed the edgy cover. Susan Rimerman guided the design process with great grace, despite more than once being overheard to mutter, 'those darned *San Diego* people.' Ruth Askevold helped the book make it out the door on schedule.

Illustrations were coordinated by Beca Lafore, who drew on the talents of Hugh D'Andrade, Hayden Foell, Rini Keagy, Justin Marler, Henia Miedzinski, Hannah Reineck, Jennifer 'The Cat in the Hat rocks' Steffey, Jim Swanson and Wendy Yanagihara.

The versatile Margaret Livingston created the index.

Foreword

ABOUT LONELY PLANET GUIDEBOOKS

The story begins with a classic travel adventure: Tony and Maureen Wheeler's 1972 journey across Europe and Asia to Australia. Useful information about the overland trail did not exist at that time, so Tony and Maureen published the first Lonely Planet guidebook to meet a growing need.

From a kitchen table, then from a tiny office in Melbourne (Australia), Lonely Planet has become the largest independent travel publisher in the world, an international company with offices in Melbourne, Oakland (USA), London (UK) and Paris (France).

Today Lonely Planet guidebooks cover the globe. There is an ever-growing list of books, and there's information in a variety of forms and media. Some things haven't changed. The main aim is still to help make it possible for adventurous travelers to get out there – to explore and better understand the world.

At Lonely Planet we believe travelers can make a positive contribution to the countries they visit – if they respect their host communities and spend their money wisely. Since 1986 a percentage of the income from each book has been donated to aid projects and human-rights campaigns.

Updates Lonely Planet thoroughly updates each guidebook as often as possible. This usually means there are around two years between editions, although for more unusual or more stable destinations the gap can be longer. Check the imprint page (following the color map at the beginning of the book) for publication dates.

Between editions, up-to-date information is available in two free newsletters – the paper *Planet Talk* and email *Comet* (to subscribe, contact any Lonely Planet office) – and on our website at www.lonelyplanet.com. The *Upgrades* section of the website covers a number of important and volatile destinations and is regularly updated by Lonely Planet authors. *Scoop* covers news and current affairs relevant to travelers. And, lastly, the *Thorn Tree* bulletin board and *Postcards* section of the site carry unverified, but fascinating, reports from travelers.

Correspondence The process of creating new editions begins with the letters, postcards and emails received from travelers. This correspondence often includes suggestions, criticisms and comments about the current editions. Interesting excerpts are immediately passed on via newsletters and the website, and everything goes to our authors to be verified when they're researching on the road. We're keen to get more feedback from organizations or individuals who represent communities visited by travelers.

> Lonely Planet gathers information for everyone who's curious about the planet – and especially for those who explore it firsthand. Through guidebooks, phrasebooks, activity guides, maps, literature, newsletters, image library, TV series and website, we act as an information exchange for a worldwide community of travelers.

Research Authors aim to gather sufficient practical information to enable travelers to make informed choices and to make the mechanics of a journey run smoothly. They also research historical and cultural background to help enrich the travel experience and allow travelers to understand and respond appropriately to cultural and environmental issues.

Authors don't stay in every hotel because that would mean spending a couple of months in each medium-size city and, no, they don't eat at every restaurant because that would mean stretching belts beyond capacity. They do visit hotels and restaurants to check standards and prices, but feedback based on readers' direct experiences can be very helpful.

Many of our authors work undercover; others aren't so secretive. None of them accept freebies in exchange for positive write-ups. And none of our guidebooks contain any advertising.

Production Authors submit their raw manuscripts and maps to offices in Australia, the USA, the UK or France. Editors and cartographers – all experienced travelers themselves – then begin the process of assembling the pieces. When the book finally hits the shops, some things are already out of date, we start getting feedback from readers and the process begins again....

WARNING & REQUEST

Things change – prices go up, schedules change, good places go bad and bad places go bankrupt – nothing stays the same. So, if you find things better or worse, recently opened or long since closed, please tell us and help make the next edition even more accurate and useful. We genuinely value all the feedback we receive. Julie Young coordinates a well-traveled team that reads and acknowledges every letter, postcard and email and ensures that every morsel of information finds its way to the appropriate authors, editors and cartographers for verification.

Everyone who writes to us will find their name in the next edition of the appropriate guidebook. They will also receive the latest issue of *Planet Talk*, our quarterly printed newsletter, or *Comet*, our monthly email newsletter. Subscriptions to both newsletters are free. The very best contributions will be rewarded with a free guidebook.

Excerpts from your correspondence may appear in new editions of Lonely Planet guidebooks, the Lonely Planet website, *Planet Talk* or *Comet*, so please let us know if you *don't* want your letter published or your name acknowledged.

Send all correspondence to the Lonely Planet office closest to you:

Australia: Locked Bag 1, Footscray, Victoria 3011
USA: 150 Linden St, Oakland, CA 94607
UK: 10a Spring Place, London NW5 3BH
France: 1 rue du Dahomey, 75011 Paris

Or email us at: talk2us@lonelyplanet.com.au

For news, views and updates, see our website: www.lonelyplanet.com

HOW TO USE A LONELY PLANET GUIDEBOOK

The best way to use a Lonely Planet guidebook is any way you choose. At Lonely Planet, we believe the most memorable travel experiences are often those that are unexpected, and the finest discoveries are those you make yourself. Guidebooks are not intended to be used as if they provided a detailed set of infallible instructions!

Contents All Lonely Planet guidebooks follow the same format. The Facts about the Country chapters or sections give background information ranging from history to weather. Facts for the Visitor gives practical information on issues like visas and health. Getting There & Away gives a brief starting point for researching travel to and from the destination. Getting Around gives an overview of the transport options available when you arrive.

The peculiar demands of each destination determine how subsequent chapters are broken up, but some things remain constant. We always start with background, then proceed to sights, places to stay, places to eat, entertainment, getting there and away, and getting around information – in that order.

Heading Hierarchy Lonely Planet headings are used in a strict hierarchical structure that can be visualized as a set of Russian dolls. Each heading (and its following text) is encompassed by any preceding heading that is higher on the hierarchical ladder.

Entry Points We do not assume guidebooks will be read from beginning to end, but that people will dip into them. The traditional entry points are the list of contents and the index. In addition, however, some books have a complete list of maps and an index map illustrating map coverage.

There may also be a color map that shows highlights. These highlights are dealt with in greater detail later in the book, along with planning questions and suggested itineraries. Each chapter covering a geographical region usually begins with a locator map and another list of highlights. Once you find something of interest in a list of highlights, turn to the index.

Maps Maps play a crucial role in Lonely Planet guidebooks and include a huge amount of information. A legend is printed on the back page. We seek to have complete consistency between maps and text, and to have every important place in the text captured on a map. Map key numbers usually start in the top left corner.

Although inclusion in a guidebook usually implies a recommendation, we cannot list every good place. Exclusion does not necessarily imply criticism. In fact, there are a number of reasons why we might exclude a place – sometimes it is simply inappropriate to encourage an influx of travelers.

Introduction

San Diego and Tijuana are two cities joined by a common border. It could be argued that nowhere else in the world is there a greater contrast of cultures, people, economies and environments. And nowhere, either, is there greater symbiosis and cross-fertilization. San Diego and Tijuana essentially grew up together; the first a product of the California land boom of the 1880s, the latter a result of it. For travelers, the region combines a wealth of delights in a visitor-friendly package: Welcome to your 'Two Nation Vacation.'

SAN DIEGO

It's easy to fall in love with San Diego. After all, what's not to like? When much of the US shivers under blankets of rain and snow, San Diegans still picnic outdoors or slice through waves on surfboards. Its downtown skyline stands sentinel over one of the world's great natural harbors. At the foot of the high-rises, the crisply restored historical Gaslamp Quarter offers sophisticated dining and nightlife. Miles of fabulous beaches form its western edge, while the desert playground of Anza-Borrego beckons in the east. Add to that the country's largest urban park and the famous San Diego Zoo and SeaWorld. Not surprisingly, San Diegans are fiercely proud of their hometown and shamelessly, but somehow endearingly, promote it as 'America's Finest City.' So let's ask again, what's not to like?

Detractors have pointed to a certain degree of complacency that all this perfection has inspired. 'Dynamic' and 'San Diego' are rarely mentioned in the same sentence. Still a city shaped by the military, it does lack the urban edge – and energy – of Los Angeles or San Francisco. Just as with these two cities, San Diego has a sizeable immigrant population, but little cosmopolitan flair. Built by visionaries, it now seems mired in a conservative 'no-growth'

and 'no-change' attitude. In the end, though, it's hard to fault San Diego for its contentment. As the saying goes, 'If it ain't broke, don't fix it.' Whether you swim with the Garibaldi in La Jolla, watch the city skyline bathed in the golden glow of the setting sun from Point Loma, or quaff a cold one in Pacific Beach, you'll find that America's Finest City is a mighty fine one indeed.

TIJUANA

Tijuana is a fun city where you can take an easy dip into Mexican border culture. Most people only think of Tijuana as a tawdry booze-and-sex border town, and to some extent that cliché still holds true. But modern Tijuana is not a cultural wasteland: it's a place of increasing sophistication that is no stranger to fine dining, quality shopping and classy arts. Unfortunately, this is not the Tijuana the bulk of visitors gets to experience as they stroll along the tourist corridor that stretches from the border to Avenida Revolución with its tacky souvenir stores, blaring bars and burros painted with zebra stripes.

These days, Tijuana is simultaneously thriving and suffering. The population has grown exponentially as newcomers from impoverished parts of Mexico stream in for job opportunities. Alas, more people also generate more problems. The city is bursting at its seams, and maintaining even basic services such as housing, drinking water and education is a constant challenge.

Nevertheless, for many residents, Tijuana is a city of hope. Thanks in large part to the consumerist appetite of San Diego and the rest of California – and the up to 30 million tourists a year – it is one of Mexico's most prosperous cities. Tijuana's more than a border town, it's a frontier town – still a work in progress, still struggling, still rough on the edges, but also imbued with an energizing spirit of excitement and adventure.

Facts about San Diego

HISTORY
Native Peoples
The earliest residents of the San Diego area were called the Diegueño by the Spanish, but modern anthropologists call them Kumeyaay and further divide them into the Ipai – who inhabited the land north of the San Diego River – and the Tipai to the south. All belonged to the linguistic group of the Yuma. They were hunter-gatherers whose staple food was the acorn – which they ground into flour and made into bread or porridge – as well as shellfish and animals such as rabbits, crows and mice. They used primitive tools made from wood, stone and bone. Most lived in small 'villages' of up to 300 people, in huts made from brush or branches. The men went naked; women covered their privates with woven fibers and animal skins.

With the arrival of the Spanish, the cultural identity of the various native groups was severely compromised by Catholic missionaries who, according to local Native American author and historian Dolan Eargle Jr, 'were more interested in preserving souls than customs.' Today there are 12 Kumeyaay reservations in San Diego, including the Viejas and Barona reservations with their thriving gambling operations. The Museum of Man in Balboa Park has authentic handicrafts made by San Diego's native peoples and excellent exhibits.

European Discovery
Following the conquest of Mexico, the Spanish explored the limits of their new empire. There was much fanciful speculation about a golden island beyond the West Coast, and, before it was actually discovered, California was already named after a mythical island in a Spanish novel. In 1542, the Spanish crown engaged Juan Rodríguez Cabrillo, a Portuguese explorer, to lead an expedition up the West Coast to find the fabled land. He was also to search for the Straits of Anian, an imagined sea route between the Pacific and the Atlantic.

Cabrillo's ships sailed into San Diego Harbor (which he named San Miguel), and he and his crew became the first Europeans to see mainland California. The ships sat out a storm in the harbor and then sailed on, following the coast north. They made a stop on the Channel Islands where, in 1543, Cabrillo fell ill, died and was buried. The expedition continued north as far as Oregon but returned with no evidence of a sea route to the Atlantic, no cities of gold and no islands of spice. The Spanish authorities were unimpressed and showed no interest in California for the next 50 years.

In 1596, the Spanish decided they needed to secure some ports on the Pacific Coast and sent Sebastián Vizcaíno to find them. Vizcaíno's first expedition was a disaster that didn't get past Baja California, but in his second attempt, in 1602, he rediscovered the harbor at San Diego. He entered the bay on the feast day of San Diego de Alcalá and could not resist renaming the place San Diego. He and his crew recorded their findings and moved on.

The Mission Period
Around the 1760s, as Russian ships came to California's coast in search of sea otter pelts, and British trappers and explorers were spreading throughout the West, the Spanish king got worried that they might occupy the various harbors and become a threat to Spain's claim on the land. Also, the Catholic Church was anxious to start missionary work among the native peoples. A combination of Catholic missions and military forts (*presidios*) were founded in the new territory. The Indian converts would live in the mission, learn trade and agricultural skills, and, ultimately, establish *pueblos* that would be like little Spanish towns.

On July 1, 1769, a sorry lot of about 100 missionaries and soldiers, led by the Franciscan priest Junípero Serra and the military commander Gaspar de Portolá, gimped ashore at San Diego Bay. They had just spent several weeks at sea on their journey from Baja California, where Serra had already founded one mission – San Fernando Velicatá. About half of their cohorts had died en route, and many of the survivors were sick or near death.

It was an inauspicious beginning for Mission San Diego de Alcalá, the 'mother' of the chain of 21 northern California missions. Founded on July 16 atop Presidio Hill, the first structure was little more than a brushwood shelter. Around it grew up the presidio to protect the missionaries and to aid them in their efforts at converting the locals. The Kumeyaay didn't exactly roll out the welcome mat, but over time Serra and his fellow Franciscans managed to get the conversion process rolling. Their efforts stalled after the soldiers – presumably restless and bored out of their minds from living in this dusty, isolated outpost – began seriously mistreating the neophytes (converted native peoples; see boxed text 'Conversion & Revenge').

In 1774, the mission moved about 5 miles up the San Diego River to a spot near the Kumeyaay village of Nipaguay, in large part to escape the marauding soldiers but also to be closer to a better water supply and more arable land. Despite some further setbacks, the mission eventually flourished. The missionaries got the Indians to plant wheat and corn and raise livestock, for both subsistence and trade with other tribes. In 1784 they built a solid adobe and timber church and in 1795 started a system of aqueducts to irrigate the fields. In 1797, some 1400 neophytes – more than at any other California mission – cultivated more than 50,000 acres of land and tended to 20,000 sheep, 10,000 cattle and 1250 horses.

Life on the mission was quite harsh and those who broke the rules could count on being flogged or put in the stocks. Unmarried neophytes were locked up at night to prevent 'sinful' behavior. Married couples lived in villages outside the mission.

As missionary activity spread to the north, other missions were established in the San Diego area, including San Luis Rey Francia (1798) and the *asistencias* (satellite missions) of San Antonio de Pala (1815) and Santa Ysabel (1818).

An 1803 earthquake destroyed the original adobe church in San Diego, but by 1813 it was rebuilt. The Mexican defeat of the Spanish in 1821 signaled the mission's decline and foreshadowed its ultimate abandonment in 1834 after Governor Figueroa's Decree of Secularization ended the mission system.

Conversion & Revenge

The first missionaries visited the settlements of the native peoples with gifts and promises, and their first converts were encouraged to move into the mission compound on the presidio, where they lived and worked and contracted European diseases. The Spanish soldiers in the garrison abused the mission neophytes and also raided Indian villages. According to Padre Serra's reports, soldiers would chase their victims on horseback and 'catch an Indian woman with their lassos, to become prey for their unbridled lusts.' So, in 1774, the priests left the presidio and started their new mission near a large Kumeyaay village, well away from the bad influence of the military.

Unfortunately, they were also away from the protection of the military, and in November 1775 the increasingly resentful Kumeyaay made a concerted attack on the mission and burned it to the ground. One of the priests, Luis Jayme, appealed to the attackers with arms outstretched, crying, 'Love God, my children!' He was dragged away and beaten to death, becoming California's first martyr.

The survivors retreated to the presidio, and the Spanish authorities captured, flogged and executed the leaders of the attack. After a few months, the missionaries returned to their site in the valley and built a second mission, with a tiled roof to resist flaming arrows – this became a standard feature of mission architecture.

The Mexican Period

After Mexico won independence from Spain in 1821, San Diego fell under Mexican rule for about a quarter century. The Mexican flag was first raised above the presidio on April 20, 1822. Retired soldiers from the garrison and new settlers began to cultivate and partition the land below Presidio Hill, creating today's Old Town. A plaza was laid out next to Casa Estudillo, home of the pueblo's commandant, Captain Francisco María Ruiz, one of the first to settle down here.

Many citizens of the new nation (ie, Mexico) looked to California to satisfy their thirst for private land. Pretty soon, the various governors were doling out hundreds of free land grants, thus giving birth to the rancho system. One of the first to receive a piece of land in San Diego was Captain Ruiz in 1823; all in all 33 land grants covering 948 sq miles were allocated in the area. The rancheros prospered and quickly became the social, cultural and political fulcrums of California. Their lands, which averaged 16,000 acres, were largely given over to livestock to supply the hide and tallow trade. San Diego played a key role in this new industry, and people from throughout California came to the little town to have the skins cured at the area's many hide houses.

Despite its diminutive size, San Diego was made the unofficial capital of Upper and Lower California in 1825. New settlers brought the population of San Diego to about 600, but it remained a ramshackle village. At the same time, the presidio went into significant decline as more and more of its residents moved down the hill. According to 19th-century writer, seaman and lawyer Richard Henry Dana Jr, in the late 1820s the town was little more than 'about 40 dark brown looking adobe huts…and three or four larger, whitewashed houses' (*Two Years Before the Mast*, 1840).

A series of skirmishes weakened San Diego's role in California, and it lost its capital status in 1831. Four years later, it became a civilian pueblo headed by an elected *alcade* (a combination mayor and magistrate), which had wide powers and dispensed harsh justice to rebellious Indians. The presidio continued to decline and was eventually abandoned in 1837. Another blow came the following year, when San Diego's pueblo status was revoked because its population had dwindled to below 150; until the outbreak of the Mexican-American War in 1846, it was merely a part of the subprefecture of Los Angeles.

Early American Period

In May 1846, the US declared war on Mexico, and US forces quickly occupied all the presidios and imposed martial law. San Diego fell on July 28, when American marines from the USS *Cyane* raised the Stars and Stripes above Old Town's plaza for the first time. By November, Admiral Robert F Stockton had established a fort atop Presidio Hill to prevent Mexican troops from retaking the area.

Such an attempt occurred the following month in what came to be known as the Battle of San Pasqual (near present-day Escondido; see the San Diego Excursions chapter). It pitted American forces under General Stephen Watts Kearny against those of General Andrés Pico, commander of the Californio (Mexican-Californian) army in one of the war's bloodiest battles. The Californios won, but their victory was short-lived as American reinforcements started to arrive by ship.

The Mexican-American War ended on February 2, 1848, with the signing of the Treaty of Guadalupe Hidalgo, which reset the boundaries between the two countries. In California, the new border was moved north to Tijuana, itself little more than a dusty outpost at the time.

The Birth of a City

The 1849 Gold Rush bypassed San Diego, as did the first rail link to Southern California, and by 1855 the population was still only about 800 and dependent on stagecoaches. Nevertheless, in 1850, the year California was granted statehood, San Diego became a city and a county.

The same year, William Heath Davis, a former sea captain and San Francisco property speculator who had married into a San Diego family, bought 160 acres of bay-front land with the dream of building a new city. He erected prefabricated houses, a wharf and warehouses, but did little to attract settlers; even at its peak no more than 250 people lived in Davis' New Town. When a fire at his store in San Francisco wiped out his fortune – said to have amounted to about $700,000 – he had to cut his losses and, in 1857, starting selling off the property for pennies. His ambitious New Town project went down in history as 'Davis' Folly.'

It would only be another decade before another man with the same vision but a better instinct for business picked up where Davis left off. Alonzo Horton, often called the 'Father of Modern San Diego,' arrived in the city by steamer in 1867. A San Francisco-based speculator and businessman, he had heard about the little town located on a perfect natural harbor with mild weather and plenty of open spaces. Horton fell in love at first sight and quickly acquired 960 acres of waterfront land for a mere $265. He divided it into 265 plots and then went back to San Francisco to set up a sales office.

Some of the first lots went for as little as $10, and some lots he gave away for free with the proviso that the buyers build brick houses on them. Soon all of the lots were gone, and people started to move out of Old Town and to build the new city to the south. Meanwhile, property prices had shot up so dramatically that Horton himself had to pay $4000 for another parcel of land, this one measuring a mere 150 acres! The new town prospered, especially after a fire in 1872 wiped out what little was left of Old Town.

Boom and Bust

The discovery of gold in the hills east of San Diego in 1870 in present-day Julian started a frenetic mining boom that lasted until around 1875, by which time more than $2 million worth of gold had been extracted from the mines. A year later, most of them closed, but mining continued on a smaller scale until 1911.

San Diego itself embarked on a roller coaster of growth and decline that lasted well into the 20th century. Despite the efforts of local boosters, the city did not acquire an industrial base in the final decades of the 19th century, and the main economic activity was real estate speculation.

Rumors of the arrival of a railroad connection spurred interest in the city, and when an actual line was completed in 1884, the population quickly exploded to 40,000 (from 2637 in 1880). In 1885, Elisha S Babcock and HL Story bought the peninsula of Coronado for $110,000, reselling the lots to 6000 buyers a year later to turn a profit of $900,000; construction of the Hotel Del Coronado started the same year. Babcock and Story were also instrumental in bringing about the first streetcar system, which began operating in 1886. A year later, sugar magnate John D Spreckels, then based in San Francisco, also jumped on the San Diego real estate bandwagon. Over the years, Spreckels would pump millions of dollars into the small town. In the end, he owned two newspapers, the streetcar network, plus much of Coronado, including the Hotel del Coronado.

All good things must come to an end – a sudden and forceful one in this case. The railroad turned out to be nothing more than a spur line from Los Angeles, which did nothing to boost the local economy. Meanwhile, the big city to the north had grown into Southern California's commerce and transportation hub, with its own new port and intercontinental railroad connections. San Diego limped into the 1890s with a population of merely 16,000. It would take two decades before it would climb back up to 40,000.

Panama-California Exposition

To celebrate the completion of the Panama Canal in 1914, San Francisco hosted the Panama-Pacific International Exposition in Golden Gate Park. San Diego, not to be ignored, held its own exposition in Balboa Park in 1915 and 1916. Planning had begun in 1911 when the city's residents voted in favor of a $1 million bond issue to finance the event; a second vote in 1913 generated another $850,000.

In an effort to give the city a distinctive image, the exposition buildings were deliberately designed in a romantic, Spanish Colonial style. Developers, architects and the public took to this fashion with enthusiasm. San Diego's Mediterranean flair, mission-style architecture and Spanish street names derive more from this conscious image-building than from the city's actual heritage as a small and remote colonial Spanish outpost. By all accounts, the Expo was a huge success and left an architectural legacy that's still the pride of San Diego today.

The Rise of 'Navytown'

More than any other 'industry,' it was the military that stimulated San Diego's growth. In 1910, the federal government first stationed a regiment of Marines on North Island (Coronado), ostensibly to prevent the Mexican Revolution from moving north of the border. After aviation pioneer Glenn Hammond Curtiss' successful seaplane flight over San Diego Bay in January 1911 (the first in world history), he established a flight camp on North Island where he trained military officers as pilots. A year later, the Navy established its first base on North Island and Curtiss' camp evolved into an aviation school.

It was WWI that kick-started the military buildup. San Diego was selected as the site of the Army's Southwest Division, and the Navy chose San Diego Bay as home base for the Pacific Fleet. The federal government bought North Island and created Rockwell Field. Camp Kearny (now Marine Corps Air Station Miramar) was established and construction of a naval hospital approved.

The presence of the military also spurred the creation of the aircraft industry. Ryan Airlines built the *Spirit of St Louis* for Charles Lindbergh's transatlantic flight in 1927, and Reuben H Fleet moved his Consolidated Aircraft (later Convair) from Buffalo, New York, to San Diego. Fleet had already made a name for himself as the organizer of the US airmail service in 1918.

A steady revenue from naval and military bases helped San Diego weather the Great Depression, along with federal projects – through the Work Projects Administration (WPA) projects – such as San Diego State University and the racetrack at Del Mar. Nevertheless, there were still shanty-towns of poor immigrants from the Dust Bowl and from depressed industrial areas around the country.

In 1935, as the Depression eased, San Diego staged another big event, the California-Pacific Exposition, which added even more Hispanic architecture to Balboa Park.

Following the bombing of Pearl Harbor in 1941, the headquarters of the US Pacific Fleet was moved from Hawaii to San Diego. The boom in wartime activity transformed the city: The harbor was dredged and landfill islands were built; vast tracts of instant housing appeared; public spaces became training camps, storage depots and hospitals; and the population doubled in a couple of years. The war, the Marines, the Navy and naval aviators were the subjects of films showcasing San Diego (albeit incidentally) from *Guadalcanal* to the *Sands of Iwo Jima*. Its wartime role, more than anything else, put San Diego on the US map. For details about the military's continued impact, see the boxed text 'San Diego & the Military' in the San Diego Things to See & Do chapter.

Zoom to the Present

Life in San Diego changed after WWII, as it finally grew into a major city. Growth, here as elsewhere in the West, was dependent on the supply of water. In 1944 the Navy had begun with the construction of an aqueduct to bring in water from the Colorado River. The first gallons reached San Diego in 1947.

In many ways the years following WWII provided a dramatic break with the past. The city population swelled, in part because of veterans' deciding to settle here. Buses replaced streetcars in 1949. The tuna fleet, which in 1950 brought in $30 million worth of tuna and kept six canneries busy, fell apart under competition from the Japanese and Chilean fleets. But the plight of the fishermen registered as a mere blip on the

San Diego Stars

Gregory Peck Eldred Gregory Peck was born on April 5, 1916, to a pharmacist father and house-wife mother. He has made some 55 films (so far), including *Moby Dick*, *Roman Holiday* and *To Kill a Mockingbird*, which garnered him an Academy Award as best actor. Peck attended San Diego High School and was a member of the San Diego Rowing Club before enrolling at UC Berkeley. There the pre-med major was tapped by a drama teacher for the role of Starbuck in a stage production of *Moby Dick* – and was promptly bitten by the acting bug. After stints in New York and Hollywood, Peck returned to La Jolla where he cofounded the La Jolla Playhouse in 1947.

Regis Philbin The man who has made 'Is that your final answer?' a new American idiom began his career in San Diego more than 30 years ago. The native New Yorker first got minor behind-the-scenes gigs in Los Angeles before working in San Diego as a news reporter for KSON radio and as a feature reporter, sportscaster and anchor for Channel 8 and Channel 10. His experiences here provided a springboard to a career on the national stage, which culminated in his long-time stint as co-host of *Live! With Regis and Kelly* and as host of *Who Wants to be a Millionaire*.

Robert Duvall Robert Duvall was born January 5, 1931, in San Diego, where his Navy father was stationed at the time – and that's pretty much his entire connection with the city. Duvall grew up in Virginia and attended Principia College in Illinois where he failed all his classes – except acting. He honed his skills in New York at the Neighborhood Playhouse, and went on to a career that spanned 60 movies in 35 years (and still counting). Nominated six times for an Academy Award, he won an Oscar for Best Actor for his portrayal of Mac Sledge in *Tender Mercies* in 1983.

Whoopi Goldberg Whoopi Goldberg, who was born Caryn Johnson in New York in 1949, came to San Diego in 1977 with a little daughter and little money. Life so far had not been kind: growing up with a no-show father, dropping out of school in ninth grade, getting into drugs. During rehab, she fell in love with her counselor and had a child, but then the marriage fell apart in 1974. Pursuing her dream of becoming an actress, Caryn moved to San Diego and stayed for six years, barely surviving on her wages as a dishwasher at the Big Kitchen restaurant. But soon she started getting work with the San Diego Repertory Theater and doing improv comedy here and in Berkeley. She eventually returned to New York, changed her name, was discovered by Mike Nichols – and the rest is history.

radar screen of the economy, which was mostly fueled by the defense and aerospace industries. In the 1960s scientific research emerged as a major new field, led by the Scripps Institution of Oceanography and the Salk Institute in La Jolla. The University of California's San Diego campus began operation in 1964, and high-tech, biotech and communications have all been growing fields ever since.

Its climate and seafront location have also been major factors in the city's growth. Recreation facilities such as Mission Bay help attract visitors, who now contribute a big slice of the county's income. Still,

throughout the postwar era and to this day, San Diego remains dependent on the military as a major engine of its economy. One in five San Diegans gets his or her paycheck from the government. A full fifth of the gross regional product ($16.3 million) is directly or indirectly generated by the military, a figure that may well grow in the future.

GEOGRAPHY & GEOLOGY

San Diego County covers 4260 sq miles, extending about 60 miles from Orange and Riverside counties in the north to the Mexican border in the south, and about

70 miles from the Pacific seashore on the west over the coastal mountain range to the deserts of Anza-Borrego on the east. The area has a great variety of landscapes, a superb coastline and a near-perfect climate. In elevation, it rises from sea level up to 6533 feet (the peak of Hot Springs Mountain).

Geologists divide San Diego County into three regions: the Peninsular Range region (the central mountain range), the Coastal Plain region (west of the Peninsular Range) and the Salton Trough region (east of the Peninsular Range). As the rest of California, San Diego is crisscrossed by several active earthquake faults, including the San Jacinto, Elsinore, La Nación and Rose Canyon faults onshore and the Coronado Bank, San Diego Trough and San Clemente faults offshore. All are related to the great, notorious San Andreas Fault.

Unlike San Francisco and Los Angeles, San Diego has not had to ride out a huge earthquake in recent history. The biggest recorded quake (5.3 on the Richter scale) struck on July 13, 1986 on the Coronado Bank fault, 25 miles off the shore of Solana Beach; a few smaller ones have occurred since.

CLIMATE

One of San Diego's greatest assets is its year-round mild Mediterranean climate. The average temperature is around 70°F (21°C), with summer highs usually in the mid-70s and winter lows in the mid-60s. August is the warmest month, January the coldest. The highest temperature ever recorded was 111°F (43.5°C) in September 1963 and the lowest was 25°F (-4°C) in January 1913.

Out-of-towners are usually surprised to learn that – statistically at least – sunny skies are most likely in winter. The sunniest month, in fact, is November, with sunshine 75% of the time, followed by December (73%), January and February (72%) and March (70%). August is the sunniest summer month (70%), and skies are gloomiest in May and June (58%). This phenomenon is due to persistent coastal fog, which often clears away at midday only to reappear in late afternoon.

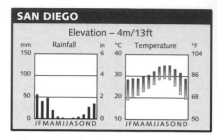

SAN DIEGO
Elevation – 4m/13ft

Paradoxically, San Diego's sunniest months (November to March) are also the wettest and coldest. Of the average 10 inches of rain that fall throughout the year, 8.2 fall during those months. The chance of rain between June and August is practically nil.

ECOLOGY & ENVIRONMENT

San Diego's air quality has consistently improved in recent decades, and in 1999 the county achieved the best air quality on record, with zero exceedances of the federal air pollution standard. By comparison, standards were exceeded on 87 days in 1980. There have been no smog alerts since 1991. Note, though, that these figures are based on federal standards, not the stricter California standards.

This is not to say that San Diego has no air pollution at all. As elsewhere, emissions from vehicles and industry are the main sources of carbon monoxide, nitrogen oxides and particulate matter (PM10). The greatest health hazard, though – especially for people with respiratory problems – is the invisible gas ozone, which forms when sunshine causes nitrogen oxides and organic gases to react.

While most pollutants originate in the coastal plain, ocean breezes blow them inland, causing the county's highest smog levels at the west-facing mountain slopes. Smog is also transported south from the South Coast Air Basin, which encompasses Los Angeles, Orange, San Bernardino and Riverside counties. Because of prevailing winds, Tijuana's polluted air is not a problem in San Diego.

For up-to-date air quality data, consult the daily newspapers or call ☎ 858-565-6626 for a recorded message.

FLORA & FAUNA

San Diego is part of Southern California, an arid region with temperate weather and a mild climate. In the mountains in the eastern county, typical vegetation includes Canyon live oak, with holly-like evergreen leaves and fuzzy acorns; aromatic California laurel, with long slender leaves that turn purple; and Eastwood and Cuyamaca manzanita, tree-like shrubs with intensely red bark and small berries. Almost unique to San Diego is the Torrey pine, *Pinus torreyana*, a species adapted to sparse rainfall and sandy, stony soils.

Within the city, Balboa Park offers the greatest variety of flora with more then 400 tree species, 70 types of palms and many different roses, cacti and tropical flowers. Anza-Borrego Desert State Park has more than 600 naturally occurring species, especially cacti belonging to the genus *Opuntia*, which includes the cholla and prickly-pear cactus.

Many animal species call San Diego County home, especially on the coast and in the thinly populated inland regions. Frequently observed birds include pied-billed grebes, least bitterns, white-tailed kites, red-shouldered hawks, American kestrels and white-winged doves. About 35 pairs of golden eagles are scattered in the foothills and eastern mountain areas, while peregrine falcon nesting sites have been spotted in National City, near the Coronado Bridge, and on Point Loma. Several species of terns (royal, Caspian, elegant) nest near the San Diego Bay salt works, while great blue herons seem to hang around Sea World and the Point Loma submarine base.

Coastal birds include American avocets and black-necked stilts as well as California brown pelicans and cinnamon teals. You'll also easily spot flocks of seagulls, grebes, terns, cormorants, sandpipers and cute little sanderlings chasing waves from the shore.

Good places to observe birds are the estuaries and lagoons, in particular the Tijuana River Estuary in Imperial Beach, Batiquitos Lagoon in Carlsbad, San Elijo Lagoon in Encinitas, Blue Sky Ecological Reserve in Poway and Cuyamaca Rancho State Park

Great blue heron

(see the San Diego Things to See & Do and Excursions chapters for details).

Common reptiles include geckos, snakes and lizards, especially the western whiptail and the zebra-tailed lizard. Mammals you might encounter are bats, moles, coyotes, foxes, mountain lions and bighorn sheep. Sea otters, sea lions and fur seals can be spotted in various areas along the coast, including Children's Pool in La Jolla (see the Downtown La Jolla walking tour in the San Diego Things to See & Do chapter for more on the Children's Pool). Amphibians include salamanders, toads and the California and Pacific tree frogs.

GOVERNMENT & POLITICS

The city of San Diego is governed by a nine-member council: a mayor and eight council members representing one city district each. Council members are nominated and elected by their respective districts, while the mayor is elected citywide. Elections are held every four years. The mayor chairs council meetings but has no veto power. A city manager appointed by the council is in charge of the administration of most municipal departments. Amendments to the city charter that would increase the number of council districts to 10 and give the mayor veto power with a two-thirds council override, are currently under consideration.

In November 2000 Republican Dick Murphy, a former Superior Court judge, was elected mayor of San Diego, narrowly edging out County Board of Supervisors member Ron Roberts with 51.7% of the vote.

The city of San Diego is the largest of the 18 incorporated cities that make up San Diego County. It is divided into five administrative districts, each of which elects a member to the Board of Supervisors, which has vast executive, legislative and quasijudicial powers. County supervisors enact ordinances and resolutions, administer activities of county agencies and departments, and review zoning, planning and land-use matters. They also adopt an annual county budget and establish tax rates. Supervisors are also elected to a four-year term.

ECONOMY

Hobbled by recession in the early 1990s, San Diego has rebounded with vigor, in large part because of aggressive economic restructuring and the overall strong national economy. Between 1993 and 2000, the gross regional product increased from $65.7 billion to an estimated $100 billion. At the same time, unemployment rates plunged from 7.7% in 1993 to around 3% in 1999.

Even though the military and related defense industries still account for a fifth of all jobs, other fields, in particular high-tech and communications, have also started to show an impact. San Diego also prides itself on its concentration of biotech companies, an industry that is supported by several academic institutions at the University of California, San Diego (UCSD), including the Center for Molecular Genetics, the UCSD Cancer Center and the Institute for Bio-Medical Engineering. The fastest growing industry, though, is telecommunications. UCSD's Wireless Communications Research Center and SDU's International Center for Communications are both academic institutions that complement this sector.

POPULATION & PEOPLE

In 2000 about 3 million people lived in San Diego County, an increase of 14.2% since 1990. San Diego itself has about 1.2 million

inhabitants, making it the sixth largest city in the nation, closely followed by Phoenix, Arizona. The average annual growth rate is 1.7%, and forecasters predict that by 2020 the population will be 1.69 million in the city and 3.85 million in the county.

Despite a reputation for being predominantly Caucasian, San Diego's population is actually a cauldron of diversity, with more than 100 languages spoken region-wide. In fact, the area's demographic makeup is changing dramatically. While as recently as 1990 nearly three in four San Diegans identified themselves as 'white,' that figure had dropped to 60% by 1998. Meanwhile, the percentage of Latinos rose from 14.8% in 1990 to 24% in 1998. The Asian population swelled from 5.9% to 9%, while the African American population remained steady at around 6%. More than half of all San Diegans are under 35 years old.

EDUCATION

San Diegans are, overall, a well-educated bunch. The city boasts the highest percentage of college graduates and the greatest number of PhDs per capita in the US. About one in three county employees has a college degree. In 1998, residents approved bond measures to fund new schools and to improve existing facilities. Class size, from kindergarten through the third grade, is limited to 20 students.

San Diego has five universities, including the highly respected University of California San Diego and San Diego State University (see the La Jolla section in the San Diego Things to See & Do chapter for more on UCSD). There are also 10 community colleges and several private learning institutions.

ARTS
Theater

Theater has a long and lively tradition in San Diego and is one of the city's greatest cultural assets. It all began rather modestly in 1858 when a group of US soldiers founded the American Dramatic Club, recruited their wives and other local women and began producing such crowd pleasers as *The*

Smiths and the Browns of San Diego and *The Idiot Witness*. Performances took place in the old mission buildings and in private homes in Old Town. It would be another decade before San Diego got its first actual theater.

In 1868, one Thomas Tanner rented a couple of rooms at the Whaley House (still standing today at San Diego Ave and Harney St in Old Town). He built a stage in one of the bedrooms, then squeezed in enough benches to seat 150 people who came to see his song and dance revue, the Tanner Troupe. Alas, Tanner dropped dead after just two performances, and the group dissolved.

The city got its first professional performance space courtesy of Alonzo Horton whose Horton Hall, a two-story brick building that stood at 6th and F Sts, opened on Christmas day in 1869. Talent, however, was scarce, and shows hard to come by, and it took more than a year before the first professional group – the California Minstrels – inaugurated the space. If Horton's vision had set the stage, so to speak, it was the enthusiasm and determination of former railroad worker Jack Dodge (who came to town in 1880) that finally lit it up.

Dodge is the seminal figure in early San Diego cultural history. By the end of the century, he was not only manager of practically all of the city's theaters, he had also founded the City Guard Band, a hugely popular brass band for which he played the cornet. Dodge's presence provided the spark for a series of theater openings, starting with Leach's Opera House in 1884; other major stages were Louis' Opera House (1887) and the Fisher Opera House (1892; later called Isis Theater). In the absence of local talent, the theaters hosted mostly professional touring companies, which performed Gilbert & Sullivan's musical comedies and other entertaining fare.

From here it was only one small step to vaudeville, those circus-like variety shows during which the stage was often shared by jugglers, singers, magicians, actors, contortionists and the like. But more high-brow fare flourished as well and, in 1911, the great actress Sarah Bernhardt herself graced the Isis Theater. One year later, the Spreckels Theater, one of the few of the grand old theaters still standing today, opened on Broadway at 2nd Ave.

As elsewhere, the emergence of movies in the 1920s brought about the decline of live theater. Most venues put a screen in place of the curtain and called themselves 'movie palaces.' Visiting theater troupes were relegated to the Russ Auditorium at San Diego High School, a cavernous space with uncomfortable seats.

San Diego's theatrical landscape finally improved after WWII with the founding of three companies that still dominate the scene today: the Old Globe Theatre, the San Diego Civic Light Opera and the La Jolla Playhouse.

The Globe was constructed for the 1935 California-Pacific Exposition and was then saved from demolition by a group of local citizens. Its first season opened with John van Druten's *The Distaff Side* in 1937; among the cast was Craig Noel, who is still the Globe's executive director today. On hiatus during WWII, the theater reopened in 1947 thanks to the initiative of Delza Brasher Martin, who is sometimes called the 'Mother of the Globe.' In the 1950s, the Globe truly hit its stride, with actors such as Dennis Hopper and Ed Flanders honing their skills and the National Shakespeare Festival making national headlines.

The same year the Globe was revived, a trio of big-time Hollywood actors – Gregory Peck, Dorothy McGuire and Mel Ferrer – started the La Jolla Playhouse, still one of the most prominent regional theaters today. The three managed to pull in many of their movie star friends who welcomed the opportunity to act in front of a live audience instead of a camera. Over the years, the founders gradually withdrew as their own film careers demanded their full attention. Quality declined, and with it community support, and after the 1964 season, the curtain closed on the Playhouse. It was kick-started again in 1973, and 10 years later garnered a Tony Award for 'Outstanding Regional Theater.'

In the last decades of the 20th century, the San Diego theatrical landscape diversified, allowing smaller and less traditional groups to surface. Today, avant-garde companies such as Sledgehammer and Fritz Theater and the gay and lesbian Diversionary Theater provide an edgy counterpoint to mainstream troupes.

Music

European Classical Highbrow art has always enjoyed a strong following in San Diego. A philharmonic society existed as early as 1872, and 1893 saw the founding of the Amphion Club to promote classical music. On Point Loma, Katherine Tingley, leader of the Theosophical Society headquartered here, managed to assemble a quality orchestra from her students, faculty and locals.

The San Diego Symphony, founded in 1910, first performed at the US Grant Hotel, embarking on what can only be described as a roller coaster of a history. Despite enjoying great success during the 1915 Panama-California Exposition, the ensemble died a sudden death in 1920, only to be reincarnated in 1927. In the 1930s the arts thrived in San Diego, in part because of the Depression-era Federal Music Program, which brought together out-of-work musicians and welfare recipients in a joint effort to cheer up the masses. The 1935 Pacific-California Exposition proved a big success for the symphony but then WWII forced another break. By 1949 it was back in business, and everything went smoothly until bad management sent it into sudden bankruptcy in the mid-1990s. Faced with such an embarrassment, politicians and financiers came together and put the orchestra back on its feet by 1998 – hopefully for good.

The second major component of San Diego's classical music scene is the San Diego Opera, founded in 1965. The city actually dabbled in opera back in 1919 under the leadership of San Diego Symphony director Roscoe Schryock. His initial attempts were disastrous, although he did manage to set up at least one memorable performance in 1924, a production of *Rigoletto* with then-superstar Giuseppe DeLuca in the title role. Nevertheless, the company folded the following year.

In 1965, coinciding with the construction of the huge new Civic Theater, San Diego got its opera back, and it has enjoyed a loyal following ever since. Its current director is Ian Campbell, a tight-fisted Australian with a singing background.

Popular San Diego has a lively local music scene, from which home-grown talent has on occasion been propelled into the big time. The late 1970s produced Stephen Bishop, who made a name for himself with 'Save it for a Rainy Day' and also wrote the title song for the Oscar-winning 1983 movie *Tootsie*. In the 1980s, bands such as Beat Drummer and Mojo Nixon entered the scene, but it wasn't until the 1990s that San Diego's local music scene hit full stride.

The brightest star on the horizon has been singer/songwriter Jewel, who started crooning at Java Joe's coffeehouse in Ocean Beach before landing a contract with Atlantic Records. Her debut album, *Pieces of You* (1995), sold 11 million copies, and her first book of poems – while not enjoying critical acclaim – made it onto the bookshelves of millions of fans. Her second album, *Spirit*, released in November 1998, was not as successful, but Jewel continues to stay in the headlines, most recently with a second book of poems, published in summer 2000.

Pop punksters blink-182 have also had great success. Their 1997 album *Dude Ranch* catapulted the Poway-based band onto the national stage, and their 1999 release of *Enema of the State* didn't disappoint either. Riding the same musical wave, albeit with little national exposure, are bands with names like Buck-O-Nine and Sprung Monkey.

Alternative rock has also come of age in the last decade, headed by bands like the Shambles and the Rugburns. Rugburns' lead singer Steve Poltz, incidentally, cowrote Jewel's 'You Were Meant for Me,' which helped launch him on a successful solo career. Another big name is Rocket from the Crypt, which in 1996 was chosen Best

New Band by the influential British music magazine *New Musical Express* (NME).

Other San Diegans made a name of themselves only *after* leaving their home town. Eddie Vedder of Pearl Jam and Matt Cameron, drummer for Soundgarden, come to mind. And then there's enfant terrible Tom Waits, who was born in Los Angeles but grew up in National City. His stint flipping pizzas at Napoleone's later inspired one of his songs, 'The Ghosts of Saturday Night/After Hours at Napoleone's Pizza.' The same album, *Heart of Saturday Night,* also features the ballad 'San Diego Serenade.' Waits was discovered while working as a doorman for The Heritage, a local club, where he himself hit the stage between scheduled acts.

The city's local music scene celebrates itself during the annual San Diego Music Awards, held since 1982 (the event was called Entertainer Music Awards until 1990). The list of winners, determined by popular balloting, provides a good overview of what's hot in San Diego music. Based on the 2000 results, names to look out for include Eve Selis (best pop album), Convoy (best rock album), Hot Snakes (best alternative album), Steve Poltz (multiple awards), Berkley Hart (best new artist), Sprung Monkey (best rock band), Buck-O-Nine (best ska, reggae or world beat).

Visual Arts

Painting In the early days of San Diego, art was pretty much an accidental by-product, and very little of it has survived. The oldest painting known to have been created locally is an 1850 portrait of Rosario Estudilio Aguirre by San Francisco artist Leonardo Barbieri. A few years later, Henry Cheever Pratt, a Boston painter, in town to help chart the official US-Mexico boundary, staged a small exhibition of portraits of Native Americans.

The roots of a serious artistic movement in San Diego were laid in the late 19th century. In 1888, New York-born and Europe-trained Ammi Merchant Farnham (1846–1922), moved to San Diego. He is known for portraits, figures and landscapes in oil and watercolor. A few years later, in 1897, another luminary settled in the city: Charles A Fries (1854–1940), an illustrator, painter and teacher who had trained at the then-prestigious Cincinnati Art Academy and later made a name for himself with his desert and mountain landscapes.

Katherine Tingley's headquarters of the Theosophical Society on Point Loma drew East Coast painter Maurice Braun (1877–1941), a member of the society, to San Diego in 1910. Back in New York, Braun was mostly a portrait and figure painter, but he gained fame for his ethereal landscapes painted in his studio on Point Loma. Braun also founded the San Diego Academy of Art, where his students included Alfred Richard Mitchell (1888–1972), whose landscapes had bolder colors, harsher outlines and stronger brush work than Braun's.

Braun, Fries and Mitchell became the seminal figures in the city's early 20th century art world. All three won gold and silver medals for works exhibited at the 1915 Panama-California Exposition. Later that year, the trio was instrumental in founding the San Diego Art Guild to provide a showcase for budding local talent. In 1920, Fries also co-founded the Friends of Art, a group dedicated to bringing high-caliber traveling exhibits to San Diego. It was a precursor to the Fine Arts Society, which was incorporated in 1925 and charged with managing the Fine Arts Gallery, San Diego's first permanent art gallery, which opened in 1926. Over the decades, the gallery's collection grew enormously, thanks to many generous donations as well as a few acquisitions; in 1978 it was renamed to San Diego Museum of Art. Braun, Fries and Mitchell were also founding members of the La Jolla Art Association (1918) as well as the Contemporary Artists of San Diego (1929). The goal of both organizations was to bring the work of local artists to a national stage. The former is still in existence today.

Sculpture The big name in San Diego sculpture is Donal Hord (1902–66). Born in Wisconsin, Hord came to San Diego in 1916, where he studied sculpture with Anna

Valentien, herself a student of French master sculptor Auguste Rodin. Hord was influenced by both Mexican and Chinese aesthetics, and succeeded at imbuing his sculptures with an almost sensual softness and flowing naturalness. His work can be seen all over San Diego, including *Woman of Tehuántepec* at Balboa Park's House of Hospitality and *Guardian of Waters* outside the County Administration Building on the Embarcadero.

A recent arrival on the San Diego scene is French artist Niki de Saint Phalle (born in 1930), a self-taught sculptor of fantastical, colorful, oversized figures inspired by Catalan artist Antonio Gaudí. Saint Phalle, who is now based in Escondido, moved to Southern California after the death of her husband, sculptor Jean Tinguely. Her first San Diego project was *Sun God* (1983), a 14-foot-tall abstract bird sitting atop an arch, for UCSD's Stuart Collection. Other Saint Phalle sculptures are in Balboa Park – specifically, in front of the Hall of Champions Sports Museum and in the Omnimax Theater lobby. There are also several in the garden of John Cole's Bookshop in La Jolla.

The aforementioned Stuart Collection is an excellent showcase of sculpture, though not necessarily of San Diego-based or born artists.

Film

Lots of sunshine and blue skies, a diverse geography and 13 of 17 climate zones on earth in one spot are among the assets that have made San Diego a popular filming location since the invention of the camera. While the major studios are based in Los Angeles, film crews regularly descend upon this city to shoot a few scenes or, less often, an entire movie or TV show. Perhaps the most famous movie ever made here was *Some Like it Hot* (1959), filmed at the Hotel Del Coronado and starring, of course, Marilyn Monroe, Jack Lemmon and Tony Curtis. Some may also remember the TV detective show *Simon & Simon,* starring Gerald McRaney and Jameson Parker, which ran from 1981–89. For other titles, check out the boxed text 'Hollywood Goes South.'

According to Welton Jones, cultural historian and critic-at-large for the *San Diego Union-Tribune*, one could even argue that the first 'movie' was in fact shot in 1898 in San Diego – and not in Hollywood. The extremely short short film with the inspired title *Street Scene, San Diego* shows a snippet of a streetcar going through downtown. It was taken by a crew of cameramen from the Thomas Edison Company. Sugar magnate John D Spreckels also used the new technology to shoot what may have been the world's first commercial to drum up interest in his Tent City 'resort' among potential East Coast visitors.

But the local film industry didn't start in earnest until 1910 when director Allan Dwan built the first sound stage in California in the eastern suburb of La Mesa. Dwan was head of the American Film Manufacturing Company, later shortened to the 'Flying A' Company. From his base in La Mesa, he cranked out about 100 short features over the next six years, most of them with a cowboy theme and such colorful titles as *Cupid in Chaps* and *The Sagebrush Phrenologist*.

Other studios came as well, including Essanay Film Manufacturing, which later produced most of Charlie Chaplin's films, for a brief stint in 1912. In 1915, Al Lubin opened a studio in Coronado and was honored as a film pioneer at the Expo that year; despite an ambitious production schedule, he closed the facilities in 1916.

One of the first San Diego-born movie writers was Anita Loos (1888–1981), whose most famous work is the novel *Gentlemen Prefer Blondes* (1925). She later adapted the tale of Lorelei Lee, the lovable gold digger from Little Rock, into a screenplay for the 1953 film version starring Marilyn Monroe and Jane Russell.

San Diego is also the birthplace of a few big-time actors: Gregory Peck (1916), Robert Duvall (1931) and Cliff Robertson (1925), who won an Oscar for his performance in *Charly* (1968). Others got their careers started in San Diego, including Regis Philbin and Whoopi Goldberg. For more on some of these celebs, see the boxed text 'San Diego Stars' earlier in this chapter.

Hollywood Goes South

Dozens of movies were either wholly or partly filmed in San Diego. What follows is our personal 'Top 10' (in chronological order). For the complete list see the San Diego Film Commission's Web site at www.sdfilm.com.

1. *Deep Blue Sea* (1999), with Samuel Jackson
2. *Apollo 13* (1997), with Tom Hanks
3. *True Lies* (1994), with Arnold Schwarzenegger
4. *Top Gun* (1986), with Tom Cruise
5. *Scarface* (1983), with Al Pacino
6. *It's a Mad Mad Mad Mad World* (1963), with Spencer Tracey
7. *Sands of Iwo Jima* (1949), with John Wayne
8. *Here Comes the Navy* (1934), with James Cagney
9. *Tell it to the Marines* (1926), with Lon Chaney
10. *Americano* (1916), with Douglas Fairbanks

Literature

One of the earliest San Diego writers on record is Lieutenant George Horatio Derby (1823–61). Derby came to town in 1853 to divert the San Diego River back into False Bay (today's Mission Bay), but he's remembered more as a humorist than an engineer. His amusing observations of early San Diego life ran in the *San Diego Herald*, the city's first newspaper, under the pseudonym of John Phoenix. His collection of stories was also published in book form called *The Squibob Papers* and *Phoenixiana*. Derby is considered one of the top American humorists of the time.

The first novel about Southern California ever was *Ramona* (1884), by Helen Hunt Jackson. Subtitled 'The Heart and Conscience of Early California,' it tells the tragic fate ostensibly suffered by a young woman of mixed ethnic heritage (Native American-American) and her Native American husband at the hands of white American settlers in northern San Diego County. The book was a big hit and inspired movies,

songs and even the annual Ramona Pageant that reenacts the story (it takes place in Hemet in Riverside County, just north of San Diego).

Much more than a romantic love story, Hunt Jackson's book is a political treatise about the mistreatment and injustice inflicted upon the local native peoples after the dissolution of the mission system in 1834. A political activist who started fighting for Indian rights after attending a lecture by Chief Standing Bear in 1879, she also wrote *Century of Dishonor* (1881), sharply criticizing the US government's Indian policies. This led to her being appointed Indian commissioner and sent to Southern California to investigate. She died in 1885, two years before Congress' enactment of the Dawes Severalty Act, which reformed the treatment of Native Americans.

In the 20th century, one of the most famous writers living in San Diego was mystery writer Raymond Chandler, who spent most of his later life in La Jolla, where he died in 1959. He's buried in Mt Hope cemetery.

A couple of contemporary San Diego writers are following Chandler's tradition. Joseph Wambaugh is among today's most successful crime fiction writers in Southern California. A former Los Angeles Police Department detective (he left in 1974), Wambaugh has sold more than 20 million copies worldwide. Drawing on his own experience, Wambaugh has set many of his books in his adopted city, including *Floaters* (1996), which is centered around the 1995 America's Cup race, which the US team lost to New Zealand.

Abigail Padgett's mysteries also enjoy a huge following. A former court investigator with San Diego County, she somehow manages to weave engaging tales involving her three main interests: Native American culture, mental illness and the California desert. Her first five novels starred Barbara 'Bo' Bradley, a child-abuse investigator with manic depression; a new series begun in 1998 features Blue McCarren, a gay psychologist who lives in an abandoned desert motel.

On Beyond Seuss: The Global Grasp of a La Jolla Legend

Long before the walrus burped 'Goo Goo G'Joob,' there was a word wizard at work who arguably shaped more young lives than even the Beatles. If there ever was an Obiwan Kenobi of children's literature, it was Theodor Seuss Geisel of La Jolla. This literary Jedi knight's brilliance infused such childish classics as Sesame Street, countless Disney films and anyone who ever tried their hand at silly doggerel.

If you're a baby boomer, you're no less a product of Dr Seuss than you are of Dr Spock. When your parents read to you from a Seuss book, they were as astonished as you were to learn about invisible worlds, emotional elephants and creatures straight from the paintings of Hieronymous Bosch. What a talent! The man wrote as brilliantly and humorously as he drew. Great good fortune, as no collaborator could ever have kept up with either field of his brilliance.

Dr Seuss was born in 1904, and before his death in 1991 had sold more than 200 million copies of his works, a record rivaled only by Mother Goose and Mao – and they didn't win three Academy Awards. The Dartmouth- and Oxford-educated illustrator created the classic *Cat in the Hat* as the result of a publisher's request to write a book using the 250 words that – it was thought – first graders could absorb. Seuss wrote the book using only 220 words and hit a proverbial publishing home run. When Bennett Cerf bet that he couldn't write an entire book using only 50 words, Seuss responded with *Green Eggs and Ham*, a text recited by the entire 1985 graduating class at Princeton when he received an honorary PhD.

Nerds? Grinches? These staples of the American lexicon are Seuss creations along with the 'bombastic aghast' and a host of venerable creatures that will forever dwell in the thoughts of this author. Read your Tolstoy, your Hemingway. But when you want to get in touch with your inner four-year-old, read your Seuss. As the maestro himself said, 'Adults are obsolete children and the hell with them.' Childish delight is still on the bookshelves: Just look for the longest section in the children's corner. Sit on the floor, open the book and begin: 'I do not like green eggs and ham. I do not like them, Sam I Am.' The Force will be with you.

- David Peevers

Also see the Books section in the San Diego Facts for the Visitor chapter.

Architecture
Irving Gill (1870–1936) Considered by many to be the most influential San Diego architect ever, Irving Gill never studied the field formally, but apprenticed in several firms, most notably with Frank Lloyd Wright in Chicago. By the time he came to San Diego in 1893, he already had sufficient experience to win several important commissions. For his early works, Gill drew inspiration from several styles, including Arts & Crafts, Victorian and California Mission. His most famous building from that era is the Arts & Crafts Marston House in the northwest corner of Balboa Park. Over time, though, a style uniquely his own emerged. Part of Gill's approach was to adapt a building to its natural environment and to create transitions between indoor and outdoor spaces. Simplified, straight lines, white walls, long arcades, courtyards and grassy areas are among the features that characterize his work. The Bishop's School, the La Jolla Recreation Center and the La Jolla Women's Club, all commissioned by Ellen Browning Scripps, are the best examples of his mature work (also see the San Diego Things to See & Do chapter).

Bertram Grosvenor Goodhue (1869– 1924) Goodhue never lived in San Diego, but it's impossible to imagine the city without the fanciful architecture of many of the buildings in Balboa Park that he designed for the 1915 Panama-California

Exposition. Goodhue trained under James Renwick, creator of St Patrick's Cathedral in New York. Much of his early work is influenced by several historical styles, from Gothic to Egyptian to Hispanic. For Balboa Park, it was a frilly Spanish Colonial style that captured his imagination; it's best exemplified by the California Building, a San Diego landmark. In later life, he developed a simpler, more contemporary approach, and he is now considered an American Modernist.

William Templeton Johnson (1877–1957) William Templeton Johnson trained as an architect at New York's Columbia University and the Ecole des Beaux-Arts in Paris. He moved to San Diego in 1912 along with his wife Clara and four children, and almost immediately started work on the Francis W Parker School, founded by his wife. Templeton Johnson built mostly in Spanish Revival, a style characterized by courtyards, arched entryways, long covered porches and fountains. His interpretations of that theme produced such visually divergent structures as the San Diego Museum of Art (1926) in Balboa Park with its frilly façade, and the starkly minimalist Serra Museum (1929) on Presidio Hill. Other Templeton Johnson buildings are the Museum of National History (1932), the Athenaeum Music & Arts Library (1921), and the San Diego Trust & Savings Bank (1928), which is now the Courtyard Marriott.

Richard Requa (1881–1941) Originally an electrical engineer, Requa first studied architecture with Irving Gill in 1907 but soon developed his own style, which he called 'Southern California architecture.' He traveled extensively in Spain and around the Mediterranean, and, for his own works, used many of the elements he had seen: white stucco walls, wrought-iron balconies and ornamentation, Moorish arches, tile fountains and red tiled roofs were among his hallmarks. Requa was the chief architect of the 1935 California-Pacific Exposition in Balboa Park, for which he remodeled existing structures

from the 1915 Expo and added all the buildings around Pan-American Plaza (see San Diego Things to See & Do for details). The Torrey Pines Lodge in Torrey Pines State Reserve is also his work.

Lilian Rice (1888–1938) Among the first graduates of UC Berkeley's School of Architecture, Lilian Rice went on to become a successful designer of residential architecture, no small feat in this male-dominated field. She is most famous for designing Rancho Santa Fe, now an exclusive suburb in San Diego's North County. Her main goal was for her buildings to blend in perfectly with their natural surroundings, and she drew upon both Spanish-Mediterranean and Old Mexican elements to accomplish this. Inner courtyards, tiled roofs, adobe walls, beamed ceilings and varied floor levels are among features characteristic of the Rice style.

RELIGION

With about 66 denominations, San Diego's religious landscape is quite diversified although, as in the rest of the US, most of the affiliations are Christian. Of these, Catholics dominate with about 413,000 members, primarily because of the city's large Hispanic population. There are also about 47,000 Mormons, whose futuristic temple on I-5 is hard to miss (see the San Diego Things to See & Do chapter), as well as 43,000 African American Baptists, 30,000 Southern Baptists and 25,000 Presbyterians. Jewish congregations have 70,000 members.

For a directory of weekend services, complete with church addresses, consult the Friday edition of the *San Diego Union-Tribune*.

LANGUAGE

English is San Diego's primary and official language, although more than 100 languages are spoken throughout the county. Of these, Spanish is the most common, especially in communities closest to the border such as San Ysidro and Chula Vista, which have high concentrations of people of Hispanic heritage.

Facts for the Visitor

WHEN TO GO

Any time of year can be a good time to visit San Diego. The weather is best from June to September, but that's also when the beaches are most crowded and hotel prices are at their peak. During shoulder seasons, visitor numbers are smaller, prices lower and most attractions are still operating. The winter months, December, January and February, while cooler and with a greater chance of rain, can still offer beautiful days. Many points of interest, though, have shorter hours.

ORIENTATION

San Diego is a pretty easy place to find your way around. The airport, train station and Greyhound terminal are all in or near the Downtown area, which is a compact grid just east of San Diego Bay. The main north-south freeway is I-5, which parallels the coast from the Camp Pendleton Marine Corps Base in the north to the Mexican border at San Ysidro. Also going from north to south, I-805 is a detour from I-5, bypassing Downtown to the east. Interstate 8 runs east from Ocean Beach up the valley of the San Diego River (called Mission Valley), past suburbs such as El Cajon and on to the Imperial Valley and Arizona.

Waterfront attractions along the Embarcadero are just west of the Downtown grid. Coronado, with its well-known 1888-vintage Hotel del Coronado, is across San Diego Bay, accessible by a long bridge or a short ferry ride. Balboa Park, with its many museums and famous zoo, is in the northeast corner of the city, and Old Town, San Diego's original site, is a couple of miles northwest of Downtown. Above Old Town, the Presidio Hill overlooks Mission Valley, now a freeway and a commercial corridor, and just to the east of Old Town is Hillcrest, the center of the city's gay and lesbian community. At the entrance to San Diego Bay, Point Loma offers great views over sea and city from the Cabrillo National Monument.

Mission Bay, northwest of Downtown, has lagoons, parks and facilities for many recreational activities. The nearby coast – with Ocean Beach, Mission Beach and Pacific Beach – epitomizes the Southern California beach scene, while La Jolla, a little farther north, is a more upscale seaside community and the home of the University of California at San Diego (UCSD).

MAPS

In most cases, the maps in this book are comprehensive enough to help you navigate within particular neighborhoods without getting lost. All tourist offices hand out a free detailed map of Downtown.

The most widely available commercial fold-out maps are published by Rand McNally ($3.95) and Rockwell Enterprises ($2.50). Other good maps are those of the American Automobile Association (AAA), available at the organization's offices and free to members (see the Useful Organizations section for details).

The driver's bible is the annually updated, fully indexed *Thomas Guide* ($21.95), with detailed maps of the entire city. Call ☎ 800-899-6277 to order, or visit any local bookstore.

TOURIST OFFICES

Downtown, the International Visitors Information Center (Map 3; ☎ 619-236-1212) is on 1st Ave at F St – it's on the west side of the Horton Plaza complex, at 11 Horton Plaza. The friendly staff will send out a complimentary *Official Visitors Planning Guide* anywhere in the world and hands out more useful information booklets and pamphlets at the center. You can also buy discounted admission tickets to major attractions and tours, as well as phone cards (see Post & Communications later this chapter). It's open 8:30 am to 5 pm daily in summer, closed Sunday the rest of the year.

Near the Gaslamp trolley stop at the corner of 6th Ave and L St, the International

Visitors Information Center (Map 3; ☎ 619-232-8583) is multimedia-based and offers free Internet access, as well as coupons, hotel reservations and custom itineraries. Its hours vary through the year, but it's usually staffed from 9 am to 2 pm Tuesday to Saturday.

The Downtown Information Center (Map 3; ☎ 619-235-2222), 225 Broadway, promotes new residential developments in Downtown, but is also a de facto tourist information office. The multilingual staff is friendly and eager to help, and can offer you a few useful brochures and pamphlets. Also of note is a large-scale model of Downtown, which clearly shows the new Ballpark District, expanded Convention Center and other features. Hours are 9 am to 5 pm Monday to Saturday.

Coronado's Visitors Bureau (Map 4; ☎ 619-437-8788, fax 619-437-6006), 1047 B Ave, focuses on places to stay, eat and be entertained. Its hours are 9 am to 5 pm Monday to Friday, 10 am to 5 pm Saturday and 11 am to 4 pm Sunday.

The Mission Bay Visitor Information Center (Map 9; ☎ 619-276-8200, fax 619-276-6041), 2688 E Mission Bay Dr, off the Clairemont Dr exit of I-15, is convenient and easy to find. The center has tons of brochures, many with discount coupons, but the staffers aren't quite as informative as those in the Downtown offices. The center's hours are 9 am to 5 pm everyday but Sunday (9:30 am to 4:30); its Web site is www.infosandiego.com.

The Balboa Park Visitors Center (☎ 619-239-0512), in the park's House of Hospitality, gives museum hours, prices and current exhibition listings. Its hours are 9 am to 4 pm daily.

The Travelers Aid Society not only doles out general city information but can also help with emergency travel assistance. It has booths at the airport in Terminal 1 (☎ 619-231-7361) and Terminal 2 (☎ 619-231-5230), both open 8 am to 11 pm daily, and another at the Amtrak station in the Santa Fe Depot (Map 3; ☎ 619-234-5191) at 1050 Kettner Blvd, open 9 am to 5 pm daily.

Old Town State Historic Park visitors center (Map 5; ☎ 619-220-5427) is in the Robinson-Rose House on the south end of the plaza and is open 10 am to 5 pm daily.

The Gaslamp Quarter Council (☎ 619-233-5227), 614 5th Ave, Suite E, has information, brochures and books about the Gaslamp Quarter.

TRAVEL AGENCIES

Council Travel and STA Travel are full-service travel agencies that specialize in discounted tickets for students and those under 26, but they can also come up with special deals for those no longer fortunate to fit into that age group.

Council Travel has offices at 953 Garnet Ave in Pacific Beach (Map 10; ☎ 858-270-6401), inside the Le Travel Store at 743 4th Ave in Downtown (Map 3; ☎ 619-544-9632) and at the Price Center on the UCSD campus in La Jolla (Map 11; ☎ 858-452-0630). STA has a branch (Map 10; ☎ 858-270-1750) at 4475 Mission Beach Blvd in Pacific Beach.

American Express Travel Services has three San Diego offices, one in Downtown at 258 Broadway (Map 3; ☎ 619-234-4455); another in La Jolla at 1020 Prospect Ave (Map 11; ☎ 858-459-4161) and a third in Mission Valley at 7610 Hazard Center Dr (☎ 619-297-8101). All are open 9 am to 5 pm Monday to Friday, and the Hazard Center branch is also open 10 am to 3 pm Saturday.

DOCUMENTS

With the exception of Canadians, all visitors to the US must have a passport and may also be required to have a US visa. Canadians, as long as they enter from anywhere in the Western Hemisphere except Cuba, need only to have proof of Canadian citizenship, such as a citizenship card with photo ID or a passport – and plan to stay 90 days or less.

Visas

A reciprocal visa-waiver program applies to citizens of certain countries who may enter the USA for stays of 90 days or less without having to obtain a visa. Currently these countries are Andorra, Argentina, Australia, Austria, Belgium, Brunei, Denmark, Finland, France, Germany, Iceland, Ireland, Italy, Japan, Liechtenstein, Luxembourg, Monaco, The Netherlands, New Zealand, Norway, San Marino, Slovenia, Spain, Sweden, Switzerland and the UK. Under this program you must have a round-trip ticket on an airline that is participating in the visa-waiver program, proof of financial solvency, and a signed form waiving the right to a hearing of deportation; you will also not be allowed to extend your stay beyond the 90-day limit. Consult with your travel agent or contact the airlines directly for more information.

All other travelers will need to obtain a visa from a US consulate or embassy, a process that can be done by mail in most countries. Your passport should be valid for at least six months longer than your intended stay in the US, and you'll need to submit a recent photo 1½ inches square (37mm x 37mm) with the application. Documents of financial stability and/or guarantees from a US resident are sometimes required, particularly for citizens of developing countries.

Visa applicants may be required to 'demonstrate binding obligations' that will ensure their return home. Because of this requirement, those planning to travel through other countries before arriving in the US are generally better off applying for a US visa before they leave home, rather than while on the road.

Visa Extensions If you want, need or hope to stay in the US longer than the date stamped on your passport, apply for an extension *before* the stamped date. Since immigration officers usually assume that you already are or intend to be working illegally, come prepared with concrete evidence that you've been traveling extensively and plan on continuing to be a model tourist, not stopping in one place and joining the 9-to-5 brigade. A wad of traveler's checks looks much better than a solid and unmoving bank account. It's also a good idea to bring a US citizen with you to vouch for your character.

Extensions are handled in person by the US Justice Department's Immigration and Naturalization Service (INS), which has an office Downtown at 880 Front St, which is open 7 am to 2 pm Monday, Tuesday, Thursday and Friday.

Travel Insurance

No matter how you're traveling, make sure you take out travel insurance. It may seem an extravagant expense at first, but it's nowhere near the cost of a medical emergency in the US.

Ideally, coverage should not only include medical expenses and luggage theft or loss, but also cancellations or delays in your travel arrangements. The best policies also extend to the worst possible scenario, such as an accident that requires hospitalization and return flight home. Check your medical policy at home, since some may already provide worldwide coverage, in which case you only need to protect yourself against other problems.

Ask both your insurer and your ticket-issuing agency to explain the finer points, especially what supporting documentation is required in case you need to file a claim. STA Travel and Council Travel offer travel insurance options at reasonable prices. Within the US, Access America (☎ 800-284-8300) and Travel Guard (☎ 800-826-1300) are quite reasonable and reliable insurers. Make sure you have a separate record of all your ticket details.

Buy travel insurance as early as possible. If you buy it the week before you leave, you might find, for instance, that you're not covered for delays to your flight caused by strikes or other industrial action that may have been in force before you took out the insurance.

Driver's License & Permits

Bring your driver's license if you intend to drive a car. If you're a foreign visitor, an International Driving Permit is useful, though not mandatory, and it is usually available from your national automobile association for a small fee and valid for one year. Make sure to also bring your valid national license, since you will need to present it along with the international one. Driver's licenses are also a useful form of identification when seeking access to bars, shows or other age-restricted facilities.

Hostel Cards

A couple of hostels in San Diego are members of Hostelling International/American Youth Hostel (HI/AYH), which is affiliated with the International Youth Hostel Federation (IYHF). You don't need an HI/AYH card in order to stay at these hostels, but having one saves you $3 a night. At both places, you can also buy one when checking in. See the San Diego Places to Stay chapter for more information.

Student & Youth Cards

If you're a student, bring along an International Student Identification Card (ISIC), a plastic ID-style card with your photograph. These are available at your university or at student-oriented travel agencies and often entitle you to discounts on transportation (including airlines and local public transport) and on admission to museums and sights as well as meals at university cafeterias. If you're a US student, carry your school or university's ID card.

Copies

Before you leave home, you should photocopy all important documents (passport data page and visa page, credit cards, travel insurance policy, air/bus/train tickets, driving license, etc). Leave one copy with someone at home and keep another with you, separate from the originals.

It's also a good idea to store details of your vital travel documents in Lonely Planet's free online Travel Vault in case you lose the photocopies or can't be bothered with them. Your password-protected Travel Vault is accessible online anywhere in the world – create it at www.ekno.lonelyplanet.com.

EMBASSIES & CONSULATES
US Embassies & Consulates

US diplomatic offices abroad include the following:

Australia (☎ 2-6270-5000) 21 Moonah Place, Yarralumla ACT 2600
(☎ 2-9373-9200) Level 59 MLC Center 19-29 Martin Place, Sydney NSW 2000
(☎ 3-9526-5900) 553 St Kilda Rd, Melbourne, Victoria

Canada (☎ 613-238-5335) 100 Wellington St, Ottawa, Ontario K1P 5T1
(☎ 604-685-1930) 1095 W Pender St, Vancouver, BC V6E 2M6
(☎ 514-398-9695) 1155 rue St-Alexandre, Montreal, Quebec

France (☎ 01 42 96 12 02) 2 rue Saint Florentin, 75001 Paris

Germany
Embassy: (☎ 030 238 51 74) Neustädtische Kirchstrasse 4-5, Berlin
Consulate: (☎ 030 832 92 33) Clayallee 170, Berlin

Ireland (☎ 1-687-122) 42 Elgin Rd, Ballsbridge, Dublin

Japan (☎ 3-224-5000) 1-10-5 Akasaka Chome, Minato-ku, Tokyo

Mexico (☎ 5-211-0042) Paseo de la Reforma 305, 06500 Mexico City

The Netherlands (☎ 70-310-9209) Lange Voorhout 102, 2514 EJ The Hague
(☎ 20-310-9209) Museumplein 19, 1071 DJ Amsterdam

New Zealand (☎ 4-722-068) 29 Fitzherbert Terrace, Thorndon, Wellington

UK (☎ 0171-499-9000) 5 Upper Grosvenor St, London W1
(☎ 31-556-8315) 3 Regent Terrace, Edinburgh EH7 5BW
(☎ 232-328-239) Queens House, Belfast BT1 6EQ

Consulates in San Diego

Only a few countries have consular representation in San Diego and changes in personnel, address and contact information are quite frequent. Most keep only small offices that are open by appointment only.

If you can't get through to any of the offices listed below or need to get in touch with a consulate not mentioned here, call directory assistance in Washington DC (☎ 202-555-1212) for that country's main consulate or embassy.

Denmark (☎ 858-613-9471, ext 116) 550 West C St, Suite 1200

Germany (☎ 760 634 3328) 162 S Rancho Santa Fe Rd, Encinitas

Italy (☎ 858-277-3395) 5222 Balboa Ave, Suite 22

Japan (☎ 858-635-1537) 10455 Pomerado Rd

Mexico (☎ 619-231-8414, ext 226) 1549 India St

Netherlands (☎ 858-587-0300) 9255 Town Centre Dr, Suite 235

New Zealand (☎ 858-677-1485) 4365 Executive Dr, Suite 1600

Spain (☎ 619-448-7282) 10922 Anja Way, Lakeside

UK (☎ 858-459-8232) 7825 Fay Ave, Suite 200

Your Own Embassy

As a tourist, it's important to realize what the embassy or consulate of the country of which you are a citizen can and can't do to help you if you get into trouble. Generally speaking, it won't be much help in emergencies if the trouble you're in is remotely your own fault. Remember that you are bound by local law and not your own country's. Your embassy may not be sympathetic if you end up in jail after committing a crime locally, even if such actions are legal in your own country.

In genuine emergencies, you might get some assistance, but only if other channels have been exhausted. If all your money and documents are stolen, for instance, your embassy can help you get a new passport. But forget about a free ticket if you need to get home urgently – after all, that's what travel insurance is for.

CUSTOMS

US Customs allows each person over the age of 21 to bring 1 liter of liquor and 200 cigarettes duty-free into the US. Citizens of the US are allowed to import, duty-free, $400 worth of gifts from abroad, and non-US citizens are allowed to bring in $100 worth.

Amounts over $10,000 in US or foreign cash, traveler's checks or money orders need to be declared. There is no legal restriction on the amount that may be imported, but undeclared sums in excess of $10,000 may be subject to confiscation. Under no circumstances should you attempt to import non-prescription narcotic drugs, including marijuana, unless you have a hankering to try out US prisons.

If you arrive in the US from overseas, you will undergo customs and immigration formalities at your first port of entry, even if your final destination is San Diego. After clearing immigration, hand the customs form you've filled out on the plane to a customs official. Even if you have nothing to declare, you may be directed to follow the red line to an inspector who will x-ray and/or hand-search your entire luggage. Occasionally, 'dog detectives' employed by the Drug Enforcement Agency may sniff you and your luggage for narcotics or illegal foodstuffs. Luckier travelers are sent along the green line and spared this procedure.

California is an important agricultural state, so, in order to prevent the spread of pests, fungi and other diseases, most food products – especially fresh, dried and canned meat, fruit, vegetables and plants – may not be brought into the state. If you suddenly remember that pineapple in your backpack, leave it on the plane or chuck it in the trash before you reach customs. There's the threat of potential fines and jail time if you break this law, though in reality the items in question are more likely simply to be confiscated. Bakery items or cured cheeses are admissible.

MONEY
Currency

The US dollar is divided into 100 cents (¢). Coins come in denominations of 1¢ (penny), 5¢ (nickel), 10¢ (dime), 25¢ (quarter) and the seldom-seen 50¢ (half dollar). Notes, commonly called bills, come in $1, $2, $5, $10, $20, $50 and $100 denominations – $2 bills are rare, but perfectly legal. There is also a $1 coin that the government has tried unsuccessfully to bring into mass circulation; you may get one as change from ticket and stamp machines. Be aware that they look similar to quarters.

Exchange Rates

Exchange rates fluctuate daily. At press time, exchange rates for some of the major currencies were:

country	unit		US dollars
Australia	$1	=	$0.55
Canada	C$1	=	$0.66
EURO	€1	=	$0.88
France	FF1	=	$0.13
Germany	DM1	=	$0.45
Hong Kong	HK$10	=	$1.30
Japan	¥100	=	$0.90
New Zealand	NZ$1	=	$0.43
UK	UK£1	=	$1.44

Exchanging Money

Most major currencies and leading brands of traveler's checks are easily exchanged in San Diego. Banks have usually the best rates and are typically open Monday to Thursday 10 am to 5 pm, Friday to 6 pm, and Saturday to 1 pm. You may be better off changing your money into dollars or traveler's checks in your home country.

There are literally hundreds of banks around San Diego, the most prevalent being Bank of America, First Federal and Union Bank. Dependable foreign-exchange brokers are American Express and Thomas Cook. For American Express locations and hours, see Travel Agencies earlier in this chapter. Thomas Cook (☎ 800-287-7362 for all branches) has offices on the 1st level of Horton Plaza (Map 3), open 10 am to 6 pm Monday to Saturday and 11 am to 4 pm Sunday; and at 4417 La Jolla Village Dr in the University Towne Centre, next to Nordstrom (Map 11), open 10 am to 6 pm Monday to Friday, 10 am to 4 pm Saturday and Sunday.

Cash Though carrying cash is risky, it's still a good idea to travel with some ($50 or so), as it's useful to pay for small purchases. However, any cash you lose is gone forever, and very few travel insurers will come to your rescue. Those that will usually limit the amount to about $300.

Traveler's Checks Traveler's checks offer greater protection from theft or loss and in many places can be used as cash. American Express and Thomas Cook are widely accepted and have efficient replacement policies. Keeping a record of the check numbers and the checks you have used is vital when it comes to replacing lost checks. Keep this record separate from the checks themselves.

Be sure to buy traveler's checks in US dollars. Many restaurants, hotels and stores accept US-dollar traveler's checks in lieu of cash, so you'll rarely have to use a bank or pay an exchange fee. Take most of the checks in large denominations. It's only toward the end of a stay that you may want to change a small check to make sure you aren't left with too much local currency.

ATMs Automatic teller machines are perhaps the best, safest and most convenient way of obtaining cash. For a nominal service charge (usually $1 or $2), you can withdraw cash from an ATM using a bank card linked to your personal checking account. Credit card withdrawals usually have a 2% fee with a $2 minimum. Practically all banks have these 24-hour machines. Plus, Cirrus and Star are the most prevalent networks in San Diego.

Foreign visitors should note that the exchange rate with an ATM is usually the best available, though high service fees may cancel out that advantage. Check the fees and availability of services with your home bank before you leave. When using an ATM, it's best to pick one in a crowded area, since the risk of being robbed is as real here as anywhere else in the world. Avoid using ATMs at night.

Many ATM cards now double as debit cards and are increasingly accepted at gas stations, supermarkets, movie theaters and other businesses. To make a purchase or withdraw cash, you just slide your card through a machine at the cash register and key in your PIN (personal identification number). Always keep handy the telephone number for reporting lost or stolen cards.

Credit Cards Major credit cards are widely accepted. In fact, you'll find certain transactions – such as purchases or reservations (tickets, rooms, cars) over the telephone or Internet – impossible to perform without that little piece of plastic.

Even if you're not in the habit of using credit cards, it's a good idea to have one for emergencies. Visa or MasterCard are the most widely accepted.

Carry copies of your credit card numbers separately from the cards. If you lose your credit cards or they get stolen, contact the company immediately at these numbers:

American Express	☎ 800-528-4800
Discover	☎ 800-347-2683
MasterCard	☎ 800-826-2181
Visa	☎ 800-336-8472

International Transfers Western Union offers ready and fast international cash transfers through its agent offices worldwide. In San Diego, centrally located agents include Sixth Ave Mail Station (☎ 619-235-9455), 1071 6th Ave in Downtown, open 9 am to 5:30 pm Monday to Friday only; and the nearby SDJ&L Financial Services (☎ 619-234-5450), 933 5th Ave, open 9 am to 6 pm daily except Sunday.

MoneyGram money orders, offered through American Express and Thomas Cook, are similar. Cash sent becomes available as soon as the order has been entered into the computer system, ie, instantly. Since commissions are costly, you should use this service in emergencies only. Commissions are paid by the person making the transfer; the amount varies from country to country.

Security

Be cautious – but not paranoid – about carrying money. Use the safe at your hotel or hostel for your valuables and excess cash.

Put your cash, credit cards and other belongings in an envelope, seal it and sign your name across the flap – that way you can tell if anybody's opened it. If there isn't a safe, decide whether it's better to carry your funds with you or try to hide them in your room. Stashing your money in several different places is generally a good idea.

Don't display large amounts of cash in public. A money belt worn under your clothes is a good place to carry excess currency when you're on the move. Avoid carrying your wallet in a back pocket of your pants. This is a prime target for pickpockets, as are handbags and the outside pockets of day packs and fanny packs (bum bags).

Costs

A trip to San Diego can be outrageously expensive or it can be pretty reasonable; most likely it won't be dirt cheap, although there are certainly ways you can economize.

If possible, don't travel during the summer peak months, when hotels hike up rates to whatever the market will bear. Even the no-frills motel room that goes for $35 from September to May could cost double from May to September. Hostels charge the same year-round, about $15 to $20.

Dining out is a great treat and does not have to put a strain on your pocketbook. The San Diego Places to Eat chapter lists lots of good restaurants where meals cost less than $10. If you're interested in experiencing the latest chi-chi restaurant, expect to pay $40 and up per person. Overall, you can cut costs by having no or few alcoholic drinks. Those on a shoestring could keep themselves going by stocking up at supermarkets.

Public transportation is fairly inexpensive but, given the sprawl that is San Diego, getting around can be time-consuming. Car rental rates are fairly reasonable, and gasoline costs considerably less than in other countries. Parking fees, however, can add up. For more information on car travel, see the San Diego Getting Around chapter.

If you're very frugal, you can expect to survive in San Diego on $50 a day per person. If you can afford to spend twice that, you start living quite comfortably.

Tipping & Bargaining

Gratuities are not really optional in the US, as most people in service industries are paid minimum wages (currently at $5.75/hour, but a $1 hike was being considered at the time of writing) and rely upon making a reasonable living through tips. However, if service is truly appalling, don't tip (and a complaint to the manager is probably warranted). Here is a guide to customary tipping amounts:

- Restaurant servers, bartenders – 15% to 20% of the total check
- Hotel room cleaning staff – $1 or $2, left on the pillow each day
- Concierges – nothing for simple information (like directions or restaurant recommendations) to $5 to $20 for special services like securing tickets to a 'sold-out' show
- Taxi drivers – 10% to 15%
- Bellhops, skycaps in airports – $1 for the first bag, 50¢ for each additional bag

Taxes

Unlike many other countries, the US has no federal value-added tax. Each state, instead, sets its own tax: Most have sales tax, many have state income taxes, some – including California – have both.

In some cases, the tax is included in the advertised price (eg, gasoline, drinks in a bar and admission tickets for museums or theaters). Restaurant meals and drinks, accommodations and most other purchases are taxed, and this is added to the advertised cost. Unless otherwise stated, prices given in this book don't include sales tax.

In San Diego, the state sales tax is 7.5% and applies to all restaurant bills as well as most shopping. It does *not* apply to edibles, except for certain items such as alcoholic beverages. A 'transient occupancy tax' of 10.5% is added to room rates at all hotels and motels, but not hostels. Services such as manicures, haircuts or taxi rides are not taxed.

POST & COMMUNICATIONS

Postal Rates

Postage rates increase every few years. Rates for 1st-class mail within the US are 34¢ for letters up to 1oz (with additional postage required for each additional ounce) and 21¢ for postcards.

International airmail rates (except to Canada and Mexico) are 60¢ for a half-ounce letter, $1 for a 1-oz letter and 40¢ for each additional half ounce. International postcards and aerogrammes cost 50¢. Letters to Canada are 46¢ for a half-ounce letter, 52¢ for a 1-oz letter and 40¢ for a postcard. Letters to Mexico are 40¢ for a half-ounce letter, 46¢ for a 1-oz letter and 35¢ for a postcard.

The cost for parcels airmailed anywhere within the US is $3.20 for 2 pounds or less, increasing by $1.10 per pound up to $6.60 for 5 pounds. This service is called Priority Mail, and delivery takes two days. For heavier items, rates differ according to the distance mailed. Books, periodicals and computer disks can be sent by a cheaper 4th-class rate.

Sending Mail

Generally, stamps are available at post offices only, though some supermarkets sell booklets of 20 stamps as well. Stamp-dispensing machines, commonly found in convenience stores and some hotels, can be a rip-off, charging you more than face value and sometimes not giving change.

There are dozens, if not hundreds, of post office branches in San Diego County. Most have restricted opening hours, usually Monday to Friday 9 am to 5 pm and to noon on Saturday. The main post office (Map 3; ☎ 800-275-8777), 815 E St in Downtown, is open 8:30 am to 5 pm Monday to Friday and 8:30 am to noon on Saturday. Check the phone book or call ☎ 800-275-8777 for post office locations.

Letters sent within San Diego usually take one day for delivery; delivery time for intrastate and interstate mail depends on the distance and remoteness of the addressee and the type of service you have selected. First-class mail is much faster than second-class mail, but not as fast as express mail. Mail sent overseas usually takes about four to seven days, though this varies from country to country. For guaranteed fast delivery, most people rely on more costly private carrier services such as FedEx or UPS.

Receiving Mail

General Delivery (*poste restante*) mail goes to the Midway postal station (zip code 92138), which, inconveniently, is between Downtown and Mission Bay at 2535 Midway Dr, just off Barnett Ave. Mail can be picked up between 9:30 am and 5 pm Monday to Friday only. It is usually held for 30 days before being returned to sender, unless a shorter and longer period is requested by the sender or the recipient. Mail should be addressed like this:

Lucy Chang
c/o General Delivery
San Diego, CA 92138

If you have an American Express Card or traveler's checks, you may have mail sent to any Amex office (for addresses, see Travel Agencies earlier in this chapter). To avoid the $2 service charge, present your card or checks upon pick-up. The sender should make sure that the words 'Client's Mail' appear somewhere on the envelope. American Express will hold mail for 30 days but won't accept registered post or parcels.

Telephone

All phone numbers within the US consist of a three-digit area code followed by a seven-digit local number. If you are calling locally, just dial the seven-digit number. If you are calling outside your area code, dial 1 plus the three-digit area code plus the seven-digit number. If you're calling from abroad, the country code for the US is 1.

For directory assistance within San Diego, dial ☎ 411. San Diego County now has three area codes. The code for Downtown, South Bay cities and most of the eastern metropolitan area is still ☎ 619. The coastal communities from northern Mission Bay to Rancho Santa Fe are are now in the ☎ 858 area. For the rest of North County, use ☎ 760.

The 800 and 888 area codes are designated for toll-free numbers within the US – and sometimes Canada and northern Baja California as well. To obtain a toll-free number, dial ☎ 800-555-1212 (no charge).

Calls within San Diego cost a minimum of 35¢, and rates go up with distance. Long-distance rates depend on the destination and which telephone company you use - call the operator (☎ 0) for rate information. Be sure to decline the operator's offer to put your call through, though, because operator-assisted calls are considerably more expensive than direct-dial calls.

Making international calls from pay phones with cash can be expensive and frustrating, because phones are only equipped to take quarters. From many phones you'll be required to deposit sufficient coins to pay for the first three minutes. Some pay phones allow the use of credits cards, but be sure to read the small print about rates before punching in your number. You can save if the person you're calling is willing to call you back. Simply place a brief call to provide the direct number listed on the pay phone itself.

If you're staying at expensive hotels, it's best to resist making calls from your room. Most add a service charge of 50¢ to $1.50 per call even for local, calling card, credit card or toll-free calls and have especially hefty surcharges for direct long-distance calls. Just as with pay phones, it may be cheaper to ask the person you want to contact for a call-back. Paradoxically, the cheaper the hotel, the lower the surcharge; sometimes local calls are free.

For a direct international call, dial ☎ 011 plus the country code plus the area code and phone number. (To find the country code, check a local phone book or call the international operator at ☎ 00.) International rates depend on the time of day, the destination and the telephone company used. The lowest international rates available are for calls made from phones in private homes. So if you're staying with someone, find out what they pay, then reimburse them.

Prepaid Calling Cards Prepaid calling cards allow purchasers to pay in advance, then make calls by dialing a toll-free 800 number, followed by the card code (both listed on the card itself); at the prompt, you then enter the number you're trying to reach. The company's computer keeps track of how much value you have left. These cards are often a good deal and more convenient than coins when you're using pay phones.

A wide range of phone cards is available, but Lonely Planet's eKno Communication Card is aimed specifically at travelers. It provides cheap international calls, a range of message services, free email and travel information. You can join online at www ekno.lonelyplanet.com or by phone from anywhere in the US by dialing ☎ 800-707-0031. To use eKno once you have joined, dial ☎ 800-706-1333. Check the eKno Web site for joining and access numbers from other countries and updates on super budget local access numbers and new features.

For local calls especially, you may be better off with a local card, usually available in amounts of $10 and $20. The International Visitor Information Center at Horton Plaza has the best-value cards (9¢ a minute for calls within California, 11¢ to the UK), but some supermarkets, convenience stores and gas stations also sometimes sell them.

Fax

Shops that specialize in office services are the best and most reasonably-priced locations from which to send and receive faxes. You'll find Mail Boxes Etc and the 24-hour Kinko's Copies franchises throughout San Diego (check the Yellow Pages for local addresses). Hotel business service centers may charge as much as $1.50 per page within the US and up to $10 per page overseas. However, some hotels don't charge for receiving faxes.

Email & Internet Access

If you set up an email account with a free internet access service such as Hotmail (www.hotmail.com) or Yahoo (www.yahoo om), you can access your email from any computer with a Web connection. Otherwise, check with your Internet service provider, such as AOL (www.aol.com) or Compuserve, for local access numbers.

If you have your own laptop computer, modem and cable, you should be able to connect to the Internet via phone lines in hotels and private homes. For the types of problems you might encounter, and how to solve them, check out www.teleadapt.com.

All hostels now provide Internet access. Other locations for getting online include public libraries and cyber cafes. Access at libraries is usually free, but computers and telephone connections may not be state-of-the-art. Cyber cafes charge from $6 to $10 per hour and usually offer fast connections. Because many people now have a home computer with Internet access, the number of Internet cafes has actually dwindled. In San Diego, choices include WebSurfCafe (Map 6; ☎ 858-296-6500), 416 University Ave in Hillcrest; Espresso Net (Map 11; ☎ 858-453-5896), 7770 Regents Rd in the Golden Triangle area of La Jolla; and Internet Coffee (Map 3; ☎ 619-702-2233), 800 Broadway at 8th St in Downtown.

INTERNET RESOURCES

The World Wide Web is a rich resource for travelers. A good place to start your explorations is Lonely Planet's own award-winning Web site at www.lonelyplanet.com. Here you'll find succinct summaries on traveling to most places on earth, postcards from other travelers and the Thorn Tree bulletin board, where you can ask questions before you go or dispense advice after you get back. You can also find travel news and updates for many of our most popular guidebooks, and the subWWWay section links you to the most useful travel resources elsewhere on the Web.

Web resources abound for San Diego. Many of them are useful in planning and researching your trip. Here's a small selection to get you started:

San Diego Insider The ultimate guide to the city, with constantly updated, comprehensive information about events, nightlife, restaurants, attractions, weather, etc; geared to locals more than visitors; www.sandiegoinsider.com

San Diego Visitor & Convention Bureau Information about dining, sports and recreation, golf, safety tips, hotels, etc; www.sandiego.org

San Diego Art + Sol Excellent site with thorough information about the city's cultural landscape, including daily updated events listings; www.sandiegoartandsol.com

San Diego Reader The electronic edition of the entertainment weekly, packed with hot topic articles, complete events listings and printable coupons for discounts at restaurants and venues; www.sdreader.com

City of San Diego Access to city government information and services, including libraries, parks, transportation; www.sannet.gov

BOOKS

Most books are published in different editions by different publishers in different countries. As a result, a book might be a hardcover rarity in one country but readily available in paperback in another. Fortunately, bookstores and libraries can search by title or author, so your local bookstore or library is the best place to advise you on the availability of the following recommendations.

Lonely Planet

Lonely Planet publishes a couple of other titles that visitors to San Diego might find useful. For detailed information on destinations beyond the scope of this book, check out the comprehensive guide *California & Nevada* (2000). LP also publishes Pisces diving & snorkeling guides, including *Southern California* by Darren Douglas. Both are available at bookstores or may be ordered from the Lonely Planet Web site at www.lonelyplanet. com.

Guidebooks

A couple of specialized guidebooks may be worth considering for visitors to San Diego.

Shutterbugs should look into Andrew Hudson's *Photo Secrets: San Diego* (1998), a beautifully produced book, informing readers which sights to photograph and how to do it.

San Diego on Foot (1994), by Caro Mendel, takes readers on about 10 walking tours through the city's various neighborhoods, providing anecdotal and historic information as well. Jerry Schad's *Afoot and Afield in San Diego County* (1998) is a fine guide to tramping through the wildlands of San Diego County, though if pedaling is your preference, the author's *Cycling San Diego* (1992) is just as wild a ride. Daniel Greenstadt's *San Diego Mountain Bike Guide* (1998) also takes up the stick for the fat-tire crowd, detailing 32 rides. *San Diego Mountains* (1999), by Sean O'Brian, describes 12 short hikes throughout the county.

William Carroll's many titles, such as *Happenings in San Diego County* (1992), *Historic Rambles in San Diego County* (1993) and *Free Things & More* (1997) pretty much tell it like it is. And as for *Street Walking in San Diego County* (1992), it's not what you think....

For excursions into the nearby desert, the Sierra Club's *Adventuring in the California Desert* (1997) by Lynne Foster is hard to beat for breadth of coverage and solid information.

Bird lovers should check into *Birds of San Diego* (1997), by Chris Fisher and Herb Clarke, which has seasonal frequency charts as well as colored drawings of San Diego's winged denizens.

History & Politics

One of the first travelers to San Diego to record his impressions was Richard Henry Dana, whose visits to San Diego and other parts of California in 1835, during the Mexican period, are recounted in *Two Years Before the Mast*. It's a good read and widely available.

Stranger Than Fiction: Vignettes of San Diego History (1995), by Richard W Crawford, is a collection of essays detailing the lives of key players from San Diego's history. *Strangers in a Stolen Land: American Indians in San Diego* (1987), by Richard

Carrizo, examines the historical and contemporary role of the area's native population.

Secret Sites of Historic Trivia in San Diego (1994) chronicles such wild, wonderful and weird historical places as the city's U-turn bridges, Dead Men's Point and the Wizard of Oz house.

Wyatt Earp: The Missing Years – San Diego in the 1880s (1998), by Kenneth Cilch, reports on what happened to Earp after Tombstone. It's spiked with facts and photographs, and makes for a worthwhile and entertaining read.

Fiction

Local crime novelist Joseph Wambaugh's works tend to present the less-than-sunny side of San Diego. Look for *Finnegan's Week* (1996), *Fugitive Nights* (1997) and *Floaters* (1996). Likewise, the detective novels of Abigail Padgett are rife with local references. See *The Dollmaker's Daughters* (1998) and *Strawgirl* (1995).

NEWSPAPERS & MAGAZINES

The daily *San Diego Union-Tribune* is not a bad daily newspaper, but the *Los Angeles Times* and the *New York Times* are conspicuously available, even from sidewalk vending machines. For information on what's happening in town, and particularly on the active music, art, and theater scene, pick up a free *San Diego Reader* from just about any convenience store or cafe. It comes out every Thursday, but copies can all be gone by the weekend.

A number of free publications have useful information and discount coupons mixed in with the advertisements. The widely available *San Diego This Week,* which actually comes out twice a month, has coupons and listings of events. The *Guide to Downtown* is a similar magazine, which emphasizes downtown eating and entertainment.

San Diego Magazine is a high-brow glossy with a safe selection of articles that matches its largely conservative readership. A February cover showing a young couple enjoying a Valentine breakfast in bed (completely covered up) prompted one reader to liken the publication to *Penthouse* and others to threaten to cancel their subscriptions. Good features are the annual guides to nightlife and restaurants.

RADIO & TV

San Diego County has eight major television stations and several dozen radio stations, including numerous Spanish-language ones. The major network affiliates are XETV Channel 6 (Fox), KFMB Channel 8 (CBS), KGTV Channel 10 (ABC) and KNSD Channel 39 (NBC). Independent stations are KPBS Channel 15 (public TV), KSWB Channel 69 (WB Network), KUSI Channel 51 (Independent) and XEWT Channel 12 (TVA-Tijuana).

For radio, check out KCEO 1000 AM and KFMB 760 AM for talk, news and traffic. For a listing of San Diego stations, see the Web site www.radioguide.com.

PHOTOGRAPHY & VIDEO
Film & Equipment

In general, buy film for the purpose you intend to use it. For general purpose shooting – for either prints or slides – 100 ASA film is just about the most useful and versatile as it gives you good color and enough speed to capture most situations on film. If you plan to shoot in dark areas or in brightly lit night scenes without a tripod, switch to 400 ASA.

Drugstores are a good place to get your film processed cheaply. If you drop it off by noon, you can usually pick it up the next day. A good place for professional processing and electronic imaging is Chromacolor (Map 3; ☎ 619-232-9900), 1953 India St in Little Italy, which has a two-hour turnaround on E-6 slides and also does digital slides and color prints. A few doors south is Nelson Photo Supplies (Map 3; ☎ 619-234-6621), 1909 India St, a Kodak and Fuji pro dealer that also sells most major-brand cameras and accessories.

Technical Tips

Both San Diego and Tijuana usually offer plenty of light for photography. When sunlight is strong, and the sun is high in the sky, photographs tend to have harsh shadows.

It's best to shoot during early morning and late afternoon, when the sun is low and the light is softer.

A polarizing filter is a most useful piece of gear, as it deepens the blue of the sky and water, eliminates many reflections and makes clouds appear quite dramatic. The effect of a polarizer is strongest when you point your camera 90 degrees away from the sun. By spinning the filter around you'll see a pretty fair approximation of what the effect will be on film.

In places where light levels are low, using fast film or your camera's fill-flash function may be helpful. Just remember: normal camera flash is only effective from 10 to 15 feet (3m to 5m), so don't waste it trying to light up an entire stadium. A monopod or lightweight tripod is an invaluable piece of gear for 'steadying up' your camera for slow exposures or when using a telephoto lens. Alternatively, jam your camera against anything at hand – a church pew, a tree, a street sign – to steady up. And remember: 'Blurry is a worry. Steady is ready.'

Airport Security

All flight passengers have to pass their luggage through X-ray machines. In general, airport X-ray technology isn't supposed to jeopardize lower-speed film (under 1600 ISO). Recently, however, new high-powered machines designed to inspect *checked* luggage have been installed at major airports around the world. These machines conduct high-energy scans that may destroy unprocessed film. Be sure to carry film and loaded cameras in your hand-luggage and ask airport security people to inspect them manually. Pack all your film into a clear plastic bag that you can quickly whip out of your luggage. It helps greatly to have a couple of rolls of 1600 ASA film right on top as this clearly shows security people that X-rays will damage your film. This not only saves time at inspection points but also helps minimize confrontations with security staff. In this age of terrorism, their job is tough, but they can also add to your preflight hell, big time.

TIME

Both San Diego and Tijuana are on Pacific Standard Time (PST), which is eight hours behind Greenwich Mean Time (GMT). Thus when it is noon in either city, it is 8 pm in London, 9 am in Honolulu, 3 pm in New York, 4 am (the next day) in Singapore, and 6 am (the next day) in Sydney or Auckland.

Daylight savings time is in effect from the last Sunday in April to the last Sunday in October. Clocks are set ahead one hour in the spring ('spring forward') and set back one hour in the fall ('fall back'), meaning that sunset is an hour later during the long days of summer.

ELECTRICITY

Electric current in the US and Mexico is 110V, 60 Hz; most plugs and sockets are the same as well. If your equipment requires a different outlet, bring an adapter or buy one in a local electronics store.

WEIGHTS & MEASURES

When it comes to measurements San Diego, like the rest of the US, stubbornly refuses to adopt the metric system. For information at a glance, see the conversion chart on the inside back cover of this book.

LAUNDRY

Most hostels and many mid-priced motels offer coin-operated guest laundry facilities. Larger hotels, however, charge exorbitant prices for one-day service. (How does $2 for a pair of underpants sound?) In such cases, you may want to do your own wash in your bathroom, or deliver your load to a commercial cleaner that will charge you as much per pound as you would have paid the hotel for those skivvies.

Self-service coin-operated Laundromats abound as well. If you haven't already spotted one, ask at your hotel or try any of the following. In Downtown, you'll find one on 4th St, next to the Golden West Hotel (Map 3) and in Ocean Beach, there's one at the corner of Santa Monica Ave and Cable St (Map 8). Pacific Beach has a coin laundry at 1057 Garnet Ave (Map 10), next to a liquor store, and there's another at 4617 Cass St (Map 10).

In Mission Beach, you'll find Cleaners & Laundry (Map 9), at 3817 Mission Beach Blvd, where you can do your own wash or drop off a load.

HEALTH

San Diego is a typical developed nation destination when it comes to health. The only foreign visitors who may be required to have immunizations are those coming from areas currently experiencing an outbreak of cholera or yellow fever.

Precautions

While San Diego's water is safe to drink, it does not taste great, and most people prefer bottled water. It's the sun that presents far greater health risks. Unless you fancy having the complexion of a lobster or are foolish enough to ignore skin cancer warnings, cover every exposed body part with high-protection-factor sunscreen whenever outdoors – and not just when lying by the pool or going to the beach. Days often start out cool and overcast only to turn gloriously sunny by lunchtime, so carry a small tube with you.

Coastal communities aside, it can get unbearably hot in the summer, making heat exhaustion a common problem. It's easily avoided by drinking lots of liquids, preferably plain water. To cut costs, you might consider carrying a water bottle with you, refilling it at water fountains or in restrooms.

Health Insurance

The quality of health care in San Diego is outstanding but it's also very expensive, and if you don't have insurance, even minor health concerns can easily bust your entire travel budget. Unless your health plan at home provides coverage, definitely take out travel health insurance. Some policies specifically exclude 'dangerous activities' like scuba diving, motorcycling and even trekking. If these activities are on your agenda, search for policies that include coverage for them.

While you may find a policy that pays doctors or hospitals directly, be aware that many private doctors and clinics will demand payment at the time of service. Unless you need acute treatment, it's best to call around and choose one willing to accept your insurance. No matter what the circumstances, be sure to keep all receipts and documentation. Some policies ask you to call back (reverse charges) to a center in your home country for an immediate assessment of your problem. Also check whether the policy covers ambulance fees or an emergency flight home.

For suggestions about where to obtain reliable policies, see the Travel Insurance earlier in this chapter.

Medical Services

If you've had an accident resulting in injuries that require immediate treatment, or have an acute illness, call the emergency number ☎ 911. This is a free call from any phone, and it will connect you to an emergency operator who will dispatch the appropriate people to assist you.

For outpatient treatment of non-life threatening ailments – such as a sprained ankle, a bladder infection or a serious flu – ask your hotel staff or someone you know to recommend a doctor, or check under Clinics in the Yellow Pages.

Many hospitals offer medical services through their emergency rooms. Fees here are even higher than at regular clinics, so you should only come here if you think you truly need instant medical attention. See the Emergencies section later in this chapter for hospital information.

Non-prescription medications, as well as condoms and contraceptive sponges, are available in all major drug stores. Prescription drugs are filled at every pharmacy. Pharmacies at some large drugstore chains, such as Sav-On and Rite Aid, stay open 24 hours.

WOMEN TRAVELERS

Women don't need to exercise special caution while visiting San Diego. The usual common sense rules – don't walk alone at night, be aware of your surroundings, avoid 'bad' neighborhoods – apply here as much as anywhere else.

Given strict US anti-sexual harassment laws, getting hassled by men is a much rarer occurrence here than in other countries. Some men may interpret a woman drinking alone in a bar as a bid for male company, but most will respect a firm but polite 'no thank you.' If someone continues to harass you, protesting loudly will often make the offender slink away with embarrassment – or will at least draw attention to your predicament. If you are assaulted, call the police (☎ 911) or the 24-hour Rape and Battering Hotline (☎ 619-233-3088).

The YWCA San Diego (☎ 619-270-4504), 2550 Garnet Ave in Pacific Beach, operates a major outreach program, especially for women who have been abused. Services include counseling offered on a sliding scale and educational and support groups. The San Diego Domestic Violence Council operates a hotline at ☎ 888-305-7233.

Planned Parenthood (☎ 800-230-7526) provides gynecological care, birth control and testing for pregnancy and sexually transmitted diseases. The San Diego Planned Parenthood clinic is in Mission Valley at 1075 Camino del Rio South.

GAY & LESBIAN TRAVELERS

Hillcrest is by far San Diego's most open neighborhood toward homosexuality, although Middletown and North Park also have their share of clubs, facilities and businesses catering primarily to gays.

Outside of these areas, gays and lesbians seem for the most part to keep a fairly low profile, and the sight of homosexual couples holding hands or showing affection in public is rather rare.

The community's main newspaper – available for free at businesses throughout the area – is the *Gay & Lesbian Times,* published Thursdays. It's a lively mix of well-researched articles concerning community news and hot button issues of national importance, book reviews, society pages and event and entertainment schedules.

Resources & Organizations

The Gay & Lesbian Center (Map 6; ☎ 619-692-2077), 3909 Centre St in Hillcrest, functions as the community's clearinghouse and is the second-oldest such nonprofit support agency in the nation (having been around since 1973). It organizes social activities and events and provides counseling and educational and health awareness programs and services. Hours are 9 am to 10 pm Monday to Friday, to 7 pm Saturday and to 5 pm Sunday.

Obelisk Bookstore (Map 6; ☎ 619-297-4171), at 1029 University Ave in Hillcrest, caters particularly to gay, lesbian, bisexual and transgender readers.

DISABLED TRAVELERS

Getting around as a mobility-impaired individual is never easy, but, as big cities go, San Diego is certainly among the more accessible. Disabled travelers planning a visit should obtain *Access in San Diego,* a booklet published and updated annually by the nonprofit organization Accessible San Diego (☎ 858-279-0704, fax 858-279-5118), 1010 2nd Ave, Suite 110A. It is packed with detailed information about hotels with roll-in showers, accessible public transportation, restaurants with Braille menus, lift-equipped shuttles and getting around at San Diego's famous attractions. It can be ordered by sending a check or money order for $5 to Accessible San Diego, PO Box 124526, San Diego, CA 92112-4526.

The Access Center (☎ 619-293-3500, TDD 619-293-7757), 1295 University Ave in Hillcrest, can refer you to wheelchair-accessible accommodations and wheelchair sale and repair facilities.

The Metro Transit System has dozens of routes with wheelchair-accessible buses and trolleys. Specific information is available at (☎ 619-233-3004, TTY/TDD 619-234-5005). Both the Coaster Express Rail and the San Diego Trolley are wheelchair accessible.

SENIOR TRAVELERS

Although the qualifying age for discounts varies, people 50 years old and up can expect to receive cut rates and benefits. Be sure to ask for senior discounts at hotels, restaurants, museums and attractions. Unless you're lucky enough to look 20 years younger than your actual age, it's highly unlikely that you'll ever be asked for ID.

If it makes you more comfortable, a good card is issued to those over 50 by the American Association of Retired Person (AARP; ☎ 202-434-2277), 601 E St NW, Washington, DC 20049. Membership is available to US residents and costs just $9 a year.

SAN DIEGO FOR CHILDREN

Successful travel with young children requires planning and effort. Don't try to overdo things; even for adults, packing too much into the time available can cause problems. And make sure the activities include the kids as well – balance that day in Balboa Park with a visit to the zoo or the beach the next day. Include the kids in the trip planning; if they've helped to work out where you are going, they will be much more interested when they get there. Lonely Planet's *Travel with Children* by Maureen Wheeler is a good source of information for this kind of thing.

Most car-rental firms have children's safety seats for hire at a nominal cost, but be sure to book them in advance. The same goes for highchairs and cots (cribs); they're common in many restaurants and hotels, but numbers are limited. The choice of baby food, infant formulas, soy and cow's milk, disposable nappies (diapers) and the like is great in supermarkets. Diaper-changing stations can be found in many public toilets in malls, department stores and family-oriented restaurants.

It's perfectly fine to bring your kids, even toddlers, along to casual restaurants (though not to many upscale ones), cafes and daytime events.

Most of the larger hotels offer a baby-sitting service, and others may be able to help you make arrangements or get you in touch with an agency. Be sure to ask whether your sitter is licensed and bonded, what the charge is per hour, whether there's a

minimum and whether meals and transportation cost extra.

It's easy to keep kids entertained in San Diego, given the myriad choices for outdoor explorations along the beaches, in the mountains and even in the urban core. See the Activities section in the San Diego Things to See & Do chapter.

San Diego has several companies and venues offering theater for children. See Children & Youth Theater in the San Diego Entertainment chapter for details.

USEFUL ORGANIZATIONS

The Automobile Association of America has several offices throughout San Diego. It provides its members and those of affiliated foreign clubs with motoring information, maps, tour books, Mexican car insurance (see the Tijuana Getting There & Away chapter) and travel planning in general. Most importantly, perhaps, it provides free emergency road services and towing (☎ 800-400-4222).

In San Diego, the downtown AAA office (Map 3; ☎ 619-233-1000) is at 815 Date St; there's another (☎ 619-483-4960) at 4973 Clairemont Dr, about 9 miles north of Downtown.

LIBRARIES

San Diego's main public library (Map 3; ☎ 619-236-5870) is at 820 E St in Downtown, about two blocks east of the Gaslamp. It's open 10 am to 9 pm Monday to Thursday, 9:30 am to 5:30 pm Friday and Saturday and 1 am to 5 pm Sunday. In addition, there are smaller branch libraries throughout San Diego (check the Yellow Pages). La Jolla also has the private Athenaeum Music & Arts Library (see the San Diego Things to See & Do chapter), and there are also, of course, libraries at the universities.

DANGERS & ANNOYANCES

Compared to other large metropolitan areas, the crime rate for San Diego is one of the lowest in the country and has declined by more than 50% in the last decade. There were 106 murders in 1999 and 810 reported rapes, as well as 83,426 property-related crimes. Statistically, the most crimes were committed in National City (54.7 per 1000 people) and Chula Vista (42.0 per 1000). Property crimes (burglary, theft) are highest in well-off neighborhoods such as La Jolla.

If you take ordinary precautions, chances are you won't be victimized. Areas to avoid include the streets east of 8th Ave in Downtown, and Balboa Park after dark.

When driving, always lock your car and put valuables out of sight. Leaving guidebooks and maps on display alerts potential thieves that you are a visitor and may make you more susceptible to break-ins. Don't leave money or cameras in view in restaurants or bars. Beware of pickpockets and petty thieves in crowds.

EMERGENCIES

In case of emergency, phone ☎ 911 and request assistance from police, fire department, ambulance or paramedics.

For emergency medical care, one option is Scripps Hospital (Map 11; ☎ 858-457-4123), 9888 Genesee Dr in La Jolla, which is widely regarded as San Diego's finest hospital. Urgent medical attention is also available 24 hours a day at Scripps Mercy Hospital (Map 6; ☎ 619-294-8111), 4077 5th Ave in Hillcrest, and Mission Bay Memorial Hospital (☎ 619-274-7721), 3030 Bunker Hill St.

If you have something stolen, report it to the police – you may need a police report to make a claim if you have a travel insurance policy, especially for big-ticket items like cameras or computers. If your credit cards, cash cards, or traveler's checks have been stolen, notify your bank or the relevant company as soon as possible. For refunds for lost or stolen traveler's checks (not credit cards) call American Express (☎ 800-221-7282), MasterCard (☎ 800-223-9920), Thomas Cook (☎ 800-223-7373) or Visa (☎ 800-227-6811).

Foreign visitors who lose their passport should contact the nearest consulate (see the Consulates in San Diego section, earlier in this chapter). Consulates usually issue a temporary 'get you home' passport, leaving you to apply for a permanent replacement after you get back. Having a photocopy of the important pages of your passport will make replacement much easier.

LEGAL MATTERS

If you are stopped by the police for a traffic offense, you'll usually be given a ticket stating the amount of the fine, which you have 30 days to pay. Nude sunbathing in public, or going topless in the case of women, is against the law, and you may be fined for indecent exposure. An exception is Black's Beach in Torrey Pines State Park, which is a clothing-optional beach popular with gay men.

If you are arrested for more serious offenses, you are allowed to remain silent. There is no legal obligation to speak to a police officer if you don't wish, but never walk away from one until given permission. Anyone arrested is legally allowed (and given) the right to make one phone call. If you don't have a lawyer or family member to help you, call your consulate.

It's generally forbidden to have an open container of an alcoholic beverage in public, whether you're in your car, in a park or on the sidewalk, although drinking is permitted on some beaches during certain hours.

The drinking age is 21 and strictly enforced. If you are, or look, under 21, you may be asked to show a photo ID to prove your age when attempting to purchases alcohol. If you are driving under the influence of drugs or alcohol – no matter what your age – you could incur stiff fines, license suspension, penalties, even jail time, especially if you're involved in an accident, whether you're at fault or not.

BUSINESS HOURS

Regular office hours are from 9 am to 5 pm, but there are certainly no hard and fast rules. Most retail shops stay open until 7 or 8 pm Monday to Friday and to 6 pm on Saturday, but mall shops don't usually close until 8 or 9 pm Monday to Friday and 6 or 7 pm Saturday and Sunday. Finding 24-hour supermarkets, convenience stores or gas stations is generally no problem anywhere.

Post offices are open from 9 am to 5 pm Monday to Friday, and some branches are also open from 8:30 or 9 am to noon on Saturday. Banks are usually open from either 9 or 10 am to 4 or 5 pm Monday to Friday; a few are open also to 1 or 2 pm on Saturday. Check with the individual branch for precise hours.

PUBLIC HOLIDAYS & SPECIAL EVENTS

California observes most US national holidays. On these days, all government offices (including post offices) and banks are closed; some individual businesses, museums and restaurants may close as well, particularly on Thanksgiving, Christmas, and New Year's Day. Many holidays are observed on the nearest Monday.

New Year's Day January 1

Martin Luther King Jr Day – 3rd Monday in January

Presidents' Day – 3rd Monday in February

Easter – 3rd Monday in February

Memorial Day – Last Monday in May

Independence Day (also called the Fourth of July) July 4

Labor Day – 1st Monday in September

Columbus Day – 2nd Monday in October

Veterans' Day November 11

Thanksgiving Day – 4th Thursday in November

Christmas Day December 25

San Diego has a packed calendar of special events, including many community, cultural and sporting events. The list below is just a small sampling. Dates for most events shift slightly from year to year, so for specifics call the number listed with each entry, or contact the International Visitor Information Center at ☎ 619-236-1212.

January

Penguin Day Ski Fest People water-skiing without wet suits, trying to earn the Penguin Patch (☎ 858-270-0840); January 1

February

Chinese New Year Chinese food, culture and martial arts at 3rd and J Sts, Downtown (☎ 619-234-4447); early in the month

Kuumba Fest African American art, tradition and cultural heritage festival, at the Lyceum Theater, Horton Plaza (☎ 619-544-1000); mid-month

Mardi Gras Fat Tuesday celebration, with a parade and a giant street party with food and drink from local restaurants, in the Gaslamp Quarter (☎ 619-233-5227); dates vary

March

Ocean Beach Kite Festival Kite making, decorating, flying and competitions, at Ocean Beach Recreation Center (☎ 619-531-1527); early in the month

Saint Patrick's Day Parade Parade starting at 6th Ave and Juniper St at 11 am, followed by Irish Festival with music, food, entertainment and a beer garden (☎ 858-268-9111); mid-month

April

Del Mar National Horse Show Prestigious national event featuring national and international championship riders, draft horse, dressage and western hunter-jumper competitions (☎ 858-792-4252); mid-April to early May

Sony Art Walk Free two-day festival with participants meeting visual and performing artists in their studios, galleries and in staged areas during self-guided tours, starting in Little Italy (☎ 619-615-1090); late in the month

May

Cinco de Mayo Mexican national day, celebrated with gusto, Old Town and elsewhere in the county (☎ 619-296-3161); May 5–7

American Indian Cultural Days Native American dancing, music and arts displays, in Balboa Park (☎ 619-281-5964); mid-month

Ethnic Food Fair Dancing, music and foods of 30 nations, at the House of Pacific Relations cottages in Balboa Park (☎ 619-234-0739); late in the month

June

Rock 'n' Roll Marathon Fast and entertaining marathon with 26 bands playing live music along the route from Balboa Park to the Naval Training Center (☎ 858-450-6510); early in the month

Indian Fair Native American cultural exhibition with tribal dances, arts, crafts and ethnic food for sale, at the Museum of Man in Balboa Park (☎ 619-293-2001); early in the month

La Jolla Festival of the Arts & Food Faire Top US artists and food, at La Jolla Country Day School (☎ 858-456-1268); early in the month

Del Mar Fair Huge county fair with headline acts and hundreds of carnival rides and shows, flower and garden shows and more, at the Del Mar Fairgrounds (☎ 858-755-1161 or 858-793-5555); June 15 to July 4

La Jolla Concerts by the Sea Free outdoor concerts every Sunday from 2 to 4 pm, in Scripps Park at La Jolla Cove (☎ 619-645-8115); June to September

July

Fourth of July Celebrating throughout the city, with special festivities in La Jolla, Chula Vista, Old Town and – one of the most popular – Coronado; July 4

US Open Sandcastle Competition Amazing sandcastle-building competition, at Imperial Beach Pier (☎ 619-424-6663); late in the month

Over-the-Line Tournament Lots of over-the-top teams in this very local variant of beach softball, on Fiesta Island (☎ 619-688-0817); two weekends in July

San Diego Lesbian & Gay Parade, Rally & Festival Varied weekend activities, throughout Hillcrest and at Marston Point in Balboa Park (☎ 619-297-7683); late in the month

August

Latin American Festival Crafts, demonstrations, food and entertainment from around Latin America, at Bazaar del Mundo, Balboa Park (☎ 619-296-3266); early in the month

Summerfest La Jolla Chamber Music Festival Two-week series showcasing international performers (☎ 858-459-3728); early in mid-month

America's Finest City Half Marathon Race starting at 7 am at Cabrillo National Monument, going around San Diego Bay and into Downtown, ending in Balboa Park (☎ 858-792-2900); mid-month

World Body Surfing Championships Body surfers, equipped only with swim fins, competing and performing on the ocean waves, in Oceanside (☎ 760-966-4535); mid-month

September

San Diego Street Scene Street festival featuring music on outdoor stages, in the Gaslamp Quarter (☎ 619-557-8490); early in the month

La Jolla Rough Water Swim Largest rough-water swimming competition in the US, at La Jolla Cove (☎ 858-456-2100); early in the month

Old Town Fall Fiesta Celebrating Mexican Independence Day with 1800s Mexican-period games, townspeople in historic garb and a 'fan-dango' (major Mexican-style party) in the evening (☎ 619-220-5422); September 16

October

Fleet Week City tribute to the navy and the coast guard stationed in San Diego, featuring ship parades, ship and submarine tours and the Miramar Air Show (☎ 619-236-1212); mid-month or later

Columbus Day Parade & Festival Celebration honoring Christopher Columbus with parade, street fair and street painting, at Amici Park in Little Italy (☎ 619-698-0545); mid-month

Underwater Pumpkin Carving Contest Scuba divers carving pumpkins under water, at La Jolla Shores (☎ 858-565-6054); late in the month

Dia de los Muertos Celebrating the Day of the Dead (actually November 2), traditional Mexican folk holiday, with processions and elaborate altars, sugar-skull crafting demonstrations, in Bazaar del Mundo (☎ 619-491-0110); late October to early November

November

Thanksgiving Dixieland Jazz Festival Dixieland bands converging on the Town & Country Hotel (☎ 619-297-5277); late in the month

Del Mar Fairground Holiday of Lights Racetrack infield filled with 250 lighted holiday displays, seen by driving past them (☎ 858-793-5555); late November to January 1

December

Christmas on El Prado Crafts, carols and candlelight parade, throughout Balboa Park (☎ 619-239-0512); December 1 and 2

Port of San Diego Bay Parade of Lights Dozens of decorated, illuminated boats, afloat in procession, on the harbor (no phone, www. sdparade-oflights.org); two weekends in December

Old Town Posadas Traditional Latin candlelight procession, re-creating the Holy Family's search for shelter, Old Town (☎ 619-220-5422); mid-month

First Night San Diego Alcohol-free street party with food, dancing and fireworks at midnight, in Downtown's Embarcadero Marina Park North (☎ 619-296-8731); December 31

WORK

If you're not a US citizen or legal resident (with a Green Card), there's a lot of red tape involved in getting work in the US, and rather severe penalties (a heavy fine for your employer, deportation for yourself) if you're caught working illegally. If you have particular skills, as well as a sponsoring employer or close relative living in the US, you have a reasonable chance of getting a special working visa from an American embassy before you leave your own country.

The type of visa varies, depending on how long you're staying and the kind of work you plan to do. Generally you need either a J-1 visa, which you can obtain by joining a visitor-exchange program, or an H-2B visa, which you get when being sponsored by a US employer. The latter is not easy to obtain, since the employer has to prove that no US citizen or permanent resident is available to do the job; the former is issued mostly to students for work in summer camps. If you lack connections, it's unlikely you'll be granted a working visa.

Information on legal student employment opportunities is best obtained from a university, either in your own country or in the US.

Getting There & Away

AIR

Most flights into San Diego International Airport–Lindbergh Field (☎ 619-231-2100), about 3 miles west of Downtown, are domestic. Coming in from overseas, you'll most likely change flights – and clear US Customs – at one of the major US gateway airports, such as Los Angeles, Chicago or Miami. Only British Airways operates a nonstop flight to San Diego from London Gatwick.

Lindbergh Field has three terminals, including the Commuter Terminal where you can take short hops aboard Alaska Commuter, American Eagle, Skywest, Northwest Link, Delta Connection, United Express and US Airways Express. All other airlines land at either Terminal 1 or Terminal 2. For a complete list of airlines serving San Diego, see the boxed text.

Hotel and car rental information, as well as Traveler's Aid desks, are in all terminals

Warning

The information in this chapter is particularly vulnerable to change: Prices for international travel are volatile, routes are introduced and canceled, schedules change, special deals come and go, and rules and visa requirements are amended. Airlines and governments seem to take a perverse pleasure in making price structures and regulations as complicated as possible. You should check directly with the airline or a travel agent to make sure you understand how a fare (and ticket you may buy) works. In addition, the travel industry is highly competitive and there are many lurks and perks.

The upshot of this is that you should get opinions, quotes and advice from as many airlines and travel agents as possible before you part with your hard-earned cash. The details given in this chapter should be regarded as pointers and are not a substitute for your own careful, up-to-date research.

near the baggage claim area. The Lost & Found office (☎ 619-686-8002) is on the 1st floor of the baggage claim area in Terminal 2. Both main terminals have food courts and shops, and there's a snack bar in the Commuter Terminal.

Departure Tax

Airport departure taxes are normally included in the cost of tickets bought in the US, though they may not be included in the price of tickets purchased abroad.

Buying Tickets

If you're flying to San Diego from overseas, the airfare is likely to be the biggest expense in your budget. Fortunately, stiff competition has resulted in widespread discounting. Get your ticket as early as possible, because some of the cheapest fares must be bought weeks or months in advance, and popular flights sell out early. Lower fares are generally available by traveling midweek, staying over a Saturday night and taking advantage of short-lived promotional offers. To ensure that you get the best deal, set aside a few hours to research the market. The Internet is a useful resource, and most travel agencies and airlines have their own Web sites.

The days when some travel agents routinely fleeced travelers by running off with their money are, happily, almost over. Paying by credit card generally offers protection, as most card issuers provide refunds if you can prove you didn't get what you paid for. You may decide to pay slightly more than the rock-bottom fare by opting for the safety of an established travel agent. Firms such as STA Travel and Council Travel (both with offices worldwide), Travel CUTS in Canada, Usit Campus (formerly Campus Travel) in the UK and Flight Centre in Australia are not going to disappear overnight, and they do offer good prices to most destinations. These companies also sell discounted tickets for people under 26 and students.

Travelers with Special Needs

Most international airlines can cater to people with special needs – travelers with disabilities, people with young children and even children traveling alone.

Travelers with special dietary preferences (vegetarian, kosher, etc) can request appropriate meals in advance. If you are traveling in a wheelchair, most international airports can provide an escort from check-in desk to plane when needed, and ramps, lifts, toilets and phones are generally available.

Airlines usually allow babies up to two years of age to fly for 10% of the adult fare, although a few may allow them free of charge. Reputable international airlines usually provide diapers (nappies), tissues, talcum and all the other paraphernalia needed to keep babies clean, dry and half-happy. For children between the ages of two and 12, the fare on international flights is usually 50% of the regular fare, or 67% of a discounted fare.

Other Parts of the US

Discount travel agents in the US are known as consolidators (although you won't see a sign on the door saying 'Consolidator'). San Francisco is the country's consolidator capital, although good deals can also be found in Los Angeles, New York and other big cities. Consolidators are listed in the Yellow Pages (under Travel Agents) or in the major daily newspapers. *The New York Times,* the *Los Angeles Times,* the *Chicago Tribune* and the *San Francisco Chronicle* all produce weekly travel sections with travel agency ads.

Council Travel, the largest student travel organization in the US, has around 60 offices in the country; its head office (☎ 800-226-8624) is at 205 E 42nd St, New York, NY 10017. Call for the office nearest you, or visit the Web site at www.ciee.org.

STA Travel also has offices throughout the US. Call ☎ 800-777-0112 for locations, or visit the Web site at www.statravel.com.

Canada

Canadian discount air ticket sellers are also known as consolidators. The *Globe & Mail,* the *Toronto Star,* the *Montreal Gazette* and the *Vancouver Sun* carry travel agents' ads and are good places to look for cheap fares. Travel CUTS (☎ 800-667-2887) is Canada's

---

Airlines Serving San Diego

All of the following airlines have offices at the airport:

Airline	Phone Number	Web Site
Terminal 1		
Aeroméxico	☎ 800-237-6639	www.aeromexico.com
Air Canada	☎ 800-776-3000	www.aircanada.ca
Alaska	☎ 800-426-0333	www.alaskaair.com
Southwest	☎ 800-435-9792	www.iflyswa.com
United	☎ 800-241-6522	www.ual.com
TWA	☎ 800-221-2000	www.twa.com
US Airways	☎ 800-428-4322	www.usairways.com
Terminal 2		
American Airlines	☎ 800-433-7300	www.americanair.com
America West	☎ 800-235-9292	www.americawest.com
British Airways	☎ 800-247-9297	www.british-airways.com
Continental Airlines	☎ 800-231-0856	www.flycontinental.com
Delta Airlines	☎ 800-221-1212	www.delta-air.com
Northwestern	☎ 800-225-2525	www.nwa.com

national student travel agency, with offices in all major cities. Its Web address is www.travelcuts.com.

Australia & New Zealand

If you're traveling to San Diego across the Pacific, you'll most likely land in San Francisco or Los Angeles and catch a connecting flight from there. The main carriers are Qantas, Air New Zealand and United. Prices are higher if you wish to stop over in Hawaii or plan to stay abroad for more than two months.

The travel sections of weekend newspapers, such as the *Age* in Melbourne, the *Sydney Morning Herald* and the *New Zealand Herald* are good sources for discounted airfares. Two respected agents for cheap fares are STA Travel and Flight Centre. STA Travel (☎ 03-9349 2411) is headquartered at 224 Faraday St, Carlton, VIC 3053 and has branches in other major cities and on university campuses. Call ☎ 131 776 Australiawide for your nearest branch, or visit the STA Web site at www .statravel.com.au. Flight Centre (☎ 131 600 Australiawide) has a central office at 82 Elizabeth St in Sydney and dozens more throughout Australia. Its Web address is www.flightcentre.com.au.

In New Zealand, Flight Centre (☎ 09-309 6171) has a big office in Auckland at National Bank Towers (corner of Queen and Darby Sts) and many branches throughout the country. STA Travel (☎ 09-309 0458) has its main office at 10 High St, Auckland, plus other branches in Auckland, as well as in Hamilton, Palmerston North, Wellington, Christchurch and Dunedin. The Web address is www.sta.travel.com.au.

The UK

In the UK, airline ticket discounters are known as bucket shops. Travel agent ads appear in the travel pages of the Saturday edition of the *Independent* and the Sunday *Times*. Also look for free magazines, such as *TNT,* widely available in London outside the main railway and underground stations.

STA Travel (☎ 020-7361 6161) is at 86 Old Brompton Rd, London SW7 3LQ, and has other offices in London and Manchester (www.statravel.co.uk). Usit Campus (☎ 020-7730 3402), 52 Grosvenor Gardens, London SW1 WOAG, has branches throughout the UK (www.usitcampus.com). Both agencies sell tickets to all travelers but cater especially to young people and students.

Other recommended London travel agencies include Bridge the World (☎ 020-7734 7447), 4 Regent Place, London W1R 5FB; Flightbookers (☎ 020-7757 2000), 177-178 Tottenham Court Rd, London W1P 9LF; and Trailfinders (☎ 020-7938 3939), 194 Kensington High St, London W8 7RG.

Continental Europe

Though London is the travel discount capital of Europe, a range of good deals is also available for traveling from other major cities.

France has a network of student travel agencies that sells discount tickets to travelers of all ages. OTU Voyages (☎ 01 44 41 38 50) has a central Paris office at 39 ave Georges Bernanos (5e) and 42 offices around the country. The Web address is www.otu.fr. Acceuil des Jeunes en France (☎ 01 42 77 87 80), 119 rue Saint Martin (4e), is another popular discount travel agency. Other service- and bargain-oriented Paris agencies are Nouvelles Frontières (☎ 08 03 33 33 33), 5 ave de l'Opéra (1er), and Voyageurs du Monde (☎ 01 42 86 16 00), 55 rue Sainte Anne (2e).

In Belgium, Acotra Student Travel Agency (☎ 02-512 86 07), at rue de la Madeline in Brussels, and WATS Reizen (☎ 03-226 16 26), at de Keyserlei 44 in Antwerp, are both well-known agencies. In Switzerland, SSR Voyages (☎ 01-297 11 11), which specializes in student, youth and budget fares, has branches in major Swiss cities, including Zurich at Leonhardstrasse 10. The Web address is www.ssr.ch. In the Netherlands, NBBS Reizen is the official student travel agency, with offices around the country; the one in Amsterdam (☎ 020-624 09 89) is at Rokin 66.

BUS
Other Parts of the US

Greyhound (☎ 800-231-2222), the only nationwide bus company, serves San Diego

Air Travel Glossary

Cancellation Penalties If you have to cancel or change a discounted ticket, there are often heavy penalties involved; insurance can sometimes be taken out against these penalties. Some airlines impose penalties on regular tickets as well, particularly against 'no-show' passengers.

Courier Fares Businesses often need to send urgent documents or freight securely and quickly. Courier companies hire people to accompany the package through customs and, in return, offer a discount ticket which is sometimes a phenomenal bargain. However, you may have to surrender all your baggage allowance and take only carry-on luggage.

Full Fares Airlines traditionally offer 1st class (coded F), business class (coded J) and economy class (coded Y) tickets. These days there are so many promotional and discounted fares available that few passengers pay full economy fare.

Lost Tickets If you lose your airline ticket an airline will usually treat it like a travellers cheque and, after inquiries, issue you with another one. Legally, however, an airline is entitled to treat it like cash and if you lose it then it's gone forever. Take good care of your tickets.

Onward Tickets An entry requirement for many countries is that you have a ticket out of the country. If you're unsure of your next move, the easiest solution is to buy the cheapest onward ticket to a neighbouring country or a ticket from a reliable airline which can later be refunded if you do not use it.

Open-Jaw Tickets These are return tickets where you fly out to one place but return from another. If available, this can save you backtracking to your arrival point.

Overbooking Since every flight has some passengers who fail to show up, airlines often book more passengers than they have seats. Usually excess passengers make up for the no-shows, but occasionally somebody gets 'bumped' onto the next available flight. Guess who it is most likely to be? The passengers who check in late.

Promotional Fares These are officially discounted fares, available from travel agencies or direct from the airline.

Reconfirmation If you don't reconfirm your flight at least 72 hours prior to departure, the airline may delete your name from the passenger list. Ring to find out if your airline requires reconfirmation.

Restrictions Discounted tickets often have various restrictions on them – such as needing to be paid for in advance and incurring a penalty to be altered. Others are restrictions on the minimum and maximum period you must be away.

Round-the-World Tickets RTW tickets give you a limited period (usually a year) in which to circumnavigate the globe. You can go anywhere the carrying airlines go, as long as you don't backtrack. The number of stopovers or total number of separate flights is decided before you set off and they usually cost a bit more than a basic return flight.

Transferred Tickets Airline tickets cannot be transferred from one person to another. Travelers sometimes try to sell the return half of their ticket, but officials can ask you to prove that you are the person named on the ticket. On an international flight tickets are compared with passports.

Travel Periods Ticket prices vary with the time of year. There is a low (off-peak) season and a high (peak) season, and often a low-shoulder season and a high-shoulder season as well. Usually the fare depends on your outward flight – if you depart in the high season and return in the low season, you pay the high-season fare.

from cities all over North America. The station (Map 3; ☎ 619-239-3266) is at 120 W Broadway and has luggage lockers ($2 for six hours) and telephones. Buses are clean and comfortable and equipped with air-conditioning, toilets and reclining seats. Smoking is not permitted.

Greyhound's prices are reasonable, though bargain airfares can occasionally match or undercut its fares (for example, to San Francisco). On shorter routes, it may be cheaper and more convenient to rent a car than to ride the bus, especially if there's more than one of you traveling.

The standard one-way/roundtrip fare to and from Los Angeles is $13/23; buses depart almost every half hour and the journey takes from 2¼ to 3¾ hours, depending on the number of stops en route. There is a bus to Anaheim, the home of Disneyland, which runs nine times a day for the same price (and about the same trip duration).

Service between San Francisco and San Diego requires a transfer in Los Angeles and costs $50/95. The journey takes 11 hours, and there are nine departures daily. There are two direct buses to Las Vegas and seven more that require you to change in either Los Angeles or San Bernardino. The trip takes from 7½ to 13½ hours and costs $41/78.

Phoenix is served by 10 buses, four of them direct; trip duration is from eight to 11½ hours and the cost is $41/77. For other destinations, call Greyhound or check the Greyhound Web site at www.greyhound.com.

All fares listed above are for midweek travel. Fares for Saturday and Sunday travel are slightly higher; children, students and seniors qualify for discounted fares. Tickets are also cheaper if purchased seven or 14 days in advance. If there are two of you, you may qualify for the 'companion fare,' which allows two people to travel for the price of one.

You can buy tickets in person at the terminal or through a ticket agent, over the phone (☎ 800-229-9424) or on the Internet with a major credit card. Tickets can be mailed to a US address or be picked up at the terminal with proper identification.

Mexico

Greyhound is the only company with direct service from San Diego to Tijuana, where you can connect to other buses serving destinations throughout Mexico. See the boxed text 'Crossing the US-Mexican Border' in the San Diego Getting Around chapter for details.

Greyhound also operates seven daily buses from San Diego to Calexico, on the US side of the border, across from Mexicali. The trip takes three hours and costs $20.50/32. Service from Calexico is limited to two buses a day.

TRAIN

America's national rail system, Amtrak (☎ 800-872-7245) operates up and down the California coast and all across the US. In San Diego, trains arrive and depart from the Santa Fe depot at 1050 Kettner Blvd at the west end of C St.

Amtrak's only direct services to and from San Diego are along the coast. Starting in June 2000, the old *San Diegan* trains were phased out to be replaced by the sleek new *Pacific Surfliner,* a fleet of state-of-the-art double-deck cars chugging along the coast as far north as San Luis Obispo. Seating is available in coach and business class. All seats have laptop computer outlets, and there's a cafe car as well. From San Diego, the *Surfliner* makes nine roundtrips to Los Angeles; four continue on to Santa Barbara and one of these heads farther north to San Luis Obispo. There's some nice coastal scenery along the way.

Travel to San Francisco is a bit more complicated. From San Diego, you can catch a motor coach to Bakersfield and board the *San Joaquin* to Emeryville (near Oakland), then change to a motor coach to downtown San Francisco. Or, you can take the slightly faster but more expensive *Pacific Surfliner* to Los Angeles and then switch to the *Coast Starlight* to Oakland, from where a motor coach will take you to

San Francisco. Service to other parts of the US also requires a change in Los Angeles. Amtrak's Web site at www.amtrak.com has more information. Reservations can be made online, by phone or in person at the station.

Standard coach fares between San Diego and Los Angeles are $25 each way and the trip takes 2¾ hours. Fares to San Francisco cost $56 via Bakersfield (14 hours) or $93 via Los Angeles (12 hours). Trips to and from Santa Barbara cost $30 each way (5½ hours). Children, students and seniors qualify for discounted fares. Advance bookings are suggested during summer and around major holidays.

If you're planning on doing a lot of traveling, you should look into a rail pass. Different passes become available all the time and all offer substantial savings over individual tickets. At the time of writing, offers included the California Pass, which allows for seven days of travel within a 21-day period throughout the entire state and costs $159. The Southern California Pass is good for five days of travel within a 7-day period in Southern California only and costs $99. You may not use long-distance trains (such as the *Coast Starlight, Southwest Chief* and *Sunset Limited*).

CAR & MOTORCYCLE

If you're driving a car or riding a motorcycle into San Diego, there are several routes by which you might enter the metropolitan area.

From Los Angeles and points farther north, I-5 travels due south right into downtown San Diego and all the way to the border at San Ysidro. Just north of La Jolla, I-805 splits off from I-5, leading south through the eastern metropolitan area, rejoining I-5 just before the San Ysidro border crossing.

Interstate 15 also enters San Diego from the north, coming all the way from Las Vegas and traveling through Riverside County before hitting San Diego County just south of Temecula. It too culminates in central San Diego.

The main access road from the east is I-8, which originates south of Phoenix, Arizona and winds its way along the Mexican border, passing the southern edge of Anza-Borrego Desert State Park before finally ending in Ocean Beach.

San Diego County's mostly rural east is crisscrossed by numerous smaller highways and country roads, most notably Hwy 78 from Escondido to Julian and the Anza-Borrego Desert State Park.

The normal freeway speed limit is 65mph (104km/h) but may occasionally be raised to 70mph (112km/h) or 75mph (120km/h) on open road.

Mexico

For details on traveling to Mexico with your own vehicle, see the boxed text 'Crossing the US-Mexican Border' in the San Diego Getting Around chapter and the Tijuana Getting There & Away chapter.

HITCHHIKING

Hitching is never entirely safe anywhere in the world and we flat don't recommend it. Travelers undeterred by the potential risk should be aware that on the whole, hitchhiking is uncommon in modern-day America and hitchers are generally viewed with suspicion: few motorists are willing to let a thumb stop them. Use extreme caution, both when hitchhiking and picking up hitchhikers.

For obvious reasons, women are especially vulnerable and should never hitchhike alone or even with another woman. Drivers are often reluctant to pick up men, so most likely a man and a woman together have the best chance of getting a ride and of being safe hitching. You can hitchhike on roads and highways; on freeways you must stand at the on-ramp. The best method for hitching a ride may be to ask someone pulling into a gas station; this also allows you to check out the person (and vice versa), though be prepared for more refusals than offers.

ORGANIZED TOURS

Grayline (☎ 619-491-0011, 800-331-5077) and the local San Diego Scenic Tours

(☎ 858-273-8687) operate narrated bus tours to major Southern California attractions, including Universal Studios in Los Angeles ($74) and Disneyland in Anaheim, Orange County ($72). Both also offer half- or full-day trips to Tijuana for $28 to $50 and day trips to Ensenada for $58.

Baja California Tours (☎ 858-454-7166, 800-336-5454, fax 858-454-2703) in La Jolla

also specializes in short-term guided tours to Tijuana, Playas de Rosarito, Puerto Nuevo and Ensenada. A three-day/two-night package to Ensenada, for instance, starts at US$99 per person, including accommodations and transportation. This company also offers themed specialty tours, often set around local events such as wine festivals or bicycle races.

Getting Around

TO/FROM THE AIRPORT

Bus No 992 – nicknamed The Flyer – operates at 10- to 15-minute intervals between the airport and Downtown. Buses leave from 4:52 am to 1:21 pm and make several stops along Broadway before heading north on Harbor Dr to the airport, where they serve Terminals 1 and 2. The trip takes about 15 minutes and costs $2.

Several companies operate door-to-door shuttles from all three airport terminals. Buses leave from the Transportation Plaza across from Terminals 1 and 2 (take the skybridge), and curbside from just outside the Commuter Terminal. The shuttle will drop you off right at your destination, but you may have to wait your turn along the route, because half a dozen other passengers need to be accommodated as well.

Per-person fares depend on the distance traveled; figure about $9.50 to Mission Valley's Hotel Circle, $6.50 to Old Town or Downtown and $12.50 to La Jolla. For some of the shorter trips, taxis charge only slightly more and may therefore be preferable, especially if there's more than one of you traveling.

If you're going *to* the airport, call the shuttle company a day or so ahead to make arrangements for a pick-up time and location. Cloud 9 Shuttle (☎ 619-505-4950, 800-974-8885) is the most established company; others include Xpress Shuttle (☎ 619-295-1900), Airport Shuttle (☎ 619-234-4403) and Seaside Shuttle (☎ 619-281-6451).

Many hotels, motels and hostels offer free shuttle service to and from the airport for registered guests. You can summon one from the courtesy phones located at the reservation boards in the baggage claim areas.

Car & Taxi

If you don't already have a rental car reservation, you'll find desks for all major agencies near the baggage claim areas in Terminal 1 and 2. The actual rental facilities – where you can pick up your car – are outside of the airport; a free shuttle bus will take you there. For details on renting a car, see Car Rental later in this chapter.

Curbside taxi service is available from all three terminals. The five to 10-minute trip downtown costs $8 to $11.

PUBLIC TRANSPORTATION

The central clearinghouse for public transportation is the Transit Store (Map 3) at 102 Broadway at 1st Ave in Downtown, open 8:30 am to 5:30 pm Monday to Friday and noon to 4 pm Saturday and Sunday. This is where you can pick up a free *Regional Transit Map* as well as tickets, bicycle permits and monthly passes.

For route and fare information by telephone, call ☎ 619-233-3004 or 800-266-6883 where operators are available 5:30 am to 8:30 pm Monday to Friday, 8 to 5 pm Saturday and Sunday. For 24-hour taped information, call ☎ 619-685-4900. For route planning via the Internet, go to www.sdcommute.com.

San Diego Trolley

The San Diego Trolley is a fast and efficient light-rail system. Two trolley lines run to and from the downtown terminal in America Plaza, next to the Santa Fe Depot. The Blue Line goes south to the San Ysidro border and north to Old Town, then continues east through Mission Valley as far as the Mission San Diego de Alcalá. The Orange Line goes east, past the Convention Center to El Cajon and Santee.

Trolleys run between 4:20 am to 2:20 am at 15-minute intervals during the day, and every 30 minutes in the evening. The Blue Line continues running all night on Saturday.

Bus

MTS is the umbrella organization of three bus operators: the San Diego Transit Corporation (SDTC), the North County Transit District (NCTD) and the County Transit System (CTS). Together, they cover the entire metropolitan area – North County, La Jolla, the beaches, the South Bay and other communities. Getting around by bus is possible but, for all but short, direct trips, quite time-consuming. If you're staying out late, getting back by bus might be difficult, as some buses stop running as early as 6 pm, others at 9 pm, midnight or even 2 am. Call the information line or ask the bus driver during your outbound journey for details.

There are literally dozens of routes serving most neighborhoods and practically all attractions. Useful routes to/from Downtown include the following:

No 3 – Balboa Park, UCSD

No 4 – National City

No 5 – Old Town, Little Italy

No 7 – Seaport Village, Balboa Park

No 25 – Mission Valley, Fashion Valley, Hillcrest

No 30 – Pacific Beach, University Towne Centre

No 34 – Sports Arena, Mission Beach, Belmont Park, Pacific Beach, Stephen Birch Aquarium, UCSD, University Towne Centre

No 35 – Ocean Beach

No 901 – Coronado

Tickets & Passes On buses, most trips cost $1.75, although some short ones are only $1.25; express buses cost $2, and superfast commuter express buses cost $2.75 to $3.25. Drivers do not make change.

A single journey fare for the San Diego Trolley is $1 within the Downtown area, then rise in increments of 25¢ to a maximum of $2.25. Tickets are dispensed from vending machines on the station platforms and are valid for three hours from the time of purchase. Machines give change.

Transfers are free as along as you continue your trip on a bus or trolley that has the same or lower fare as the beginning leg of your

Navigating San Diego

The following list details how to get to some of the most important neighborhoods and sights by public transportation. In addition, route maps can be found on the Internet at www.sdcommute.com.

Balboa Park
bus Nos 1, 3, 7, 7a, 7b, 25

Cabrillo National Monument
bus No 26 (from Old Town Transit Center)

Coronado
bus Nos 19, 901, 902/3/4

Embarcadero
bus Nos 2, 4, 15, 20, 22, 23, 29, 40, 70, 115, 210, 901/2/3, 932, 992

Gaslamp Quarter/Downtown
most downtown bus routes, trolley Blue line and Orange line

Hillcrest
bus No 25

Legoland
bus No 344, *Coaster*

Mission Beach/Belmont Park
bus No 34

Mission Valley/Fashion Valley Mall
bus No 25, trolley Blue Line

Ocean Beach
bus No 35

Old Town
trolley Blue Line, *Coaster*

Pacific Beach
bus No 30, 34

**Qualcomm Stadium/
Mission San Diego de Alcalá**
bus No 13, trolley Blue Line

San Diego Zoo
bus Nos 7, 7a, 7b

Seaport Village
bus Nos 7, 7a, 7b, trolley Orange Line

SeaWorld
bus Nos 9, 27 (from Old Town Transit Center)

Stephen Birch Aquarium
bus No 34, 34b

UCSD
bus Nos 3, 34

University Towne Centre
bus Nos 30, 34

Wild Animal Park
bus Nos 307, 878, 879

trip; otherwise you must pay the difference. Transfers are good for up to two hours.

If you ride a lot, there are a couple of ways to cut costs. Saver Packs give you 13 tickets (good for trolley or bus travel) for the price of 10. The cost is $16.90 to $37.70, depending on the price of the regular one-way ticket. Tickets must be handed to the bus driver or validated in a trolley station ticket machine before boarding. More useful and less complicated is the Day Tripper ticket, which gives you unlimited travel for one, two, three or four days for $5/8/10/12. If you're in town for an extended stay, consider a monthly pass, which allows for unlimited travel for $50 during one calendar month. All tickets and passes are sold at the Transit Store.

Coaster

A commuter rail service, the *Coaster,* leaves the Santa Fe Depot and runs up the coast to North County, with stops in Solana Beach, Encinitas, Carlsbad and Oceanside. In the metropolitan area, it stops at the Sorrento Valley station (where there's a connecting shuttle to UCSD) and Old Town. Tickets are available from vending machines at stations and must be validated prior to boarding. Machines give change. Fares range from $3 to $3.75 and depend on the distance traveled; 10-trip ticket packs cost $27 to $33.

There are nine daily trains in each direction Monday to Friday; the first trains leave Oceanside at 5:23 am and the Santa Fe Depot at 6:33 am; the last ones depart at 5:28 pm and 6:42 pm, respectively. On Saturday, there are four trains only.

For information call Regional Transit at ☎ 619-233-3004 from San Diego or ☎ 800-266-6883 from North County, or check the Web site at www.sdcommute.com.

CAR & MOTORCYCLE

Driving is the most convenient and fastest way to get around San Diego. The city sprawls over such a huge geographical area that you'll likely want to spend some time behind the wheel – unless of course time is no factor, you're focusing your explorations on one particular neighborhood, or money is extremely tight.

All in all, San Diego has a well-developed and fairly uncongested highway system that's relatively easy to navigate. Four interstate freeways (I-5, I-8, I-15 and I-805) and six major state highways crisscross the city. Traffic jams can occur at any time of day but are most likely during the rush-hour commutes.

Driving Rules

Speed limits, unless posted otherwise, are 35mph (56Km/h) on city streets and 65mph (104Km/h) on freeways and some major highways. Watch for school zones, were the speed limit can be as low as 15mph during school hours – these limits are strictly enforced. *Never* pass a schoolbus when its rear red lights are flashing: Children are getting off the bus at these times. When you encounter an ambulance with its sirens wailing, steer over to the right curb and halt, allowing it to pass.

Seatbelts – and motorcycle helmets – must be worn at all times. It's illegal for anybody in the car (not just the driver) to consume alcohol while driving. Any open containers of booze must be stashed in the trunk. Keep your driver's license, registration papers and insurance information with you, in case you get stopped by the police.

Parking

Parking is one of the San Diego area's biggest transportation bugaboos. Metered parking often costs 25¢ per 15 minutes and may be limited to one hour. Beware of colored curbs. Red means no parking, yellow and white both indicate loading zones, green is for a 20-minute limit, blue is reserved for disabled drivers. Parking patrols issue tickets relentlessly; you may pay as much as $40 for simply being 30 seconds late returning to your vehicle. Always study signposts for restrictions.

Parking at motels and cheaper hotels is usually free, while fancier ones charge anywhere from $5 to $20 a day on top of the room rate. Valet parking is ubiquitous and can be both a convenience and a scam. In areas where public parking is at a premium (the Gaslamp Quarter, for example), valets are a welcome sight. But in others, where you watch the attendant drive your car a few feet to the restaurant's own parking lot and then charge you $3.50 for the 'favor,' it can be infuriating.

Street parking – sometimes free, sometimes metered – can be found in most neighborhoods, but parking in Downtown can get very expensive. Most lots and garages charge a flat fee upon entry, at least $7, sometimes even $10. The Horton Plaza mall offers three hours of free parking with validation; after that it's $2 per hour. Getting in and out of this garage, however, can be time-consuming and an exercise in frustration. Pay lots southwest of the mall charge about $5 per entry; you can stay up to 24 hours. If you don't mind walking a few blocks, you can drop off your vehicle in the big lot at the western end of Broadway at Harbor Dr, right by the Broadway Pier, for $3.

Car Rental

Most of the big-name rental companies have desks at the airport. It's definitely worth shopping around – prices vary widely, even from day to day within the same company. If you happen to fly into Los Angeles, rent a car there; greater competition in that city usually translates into lower rates.

In order to rent a car, you will need a credit card and a driver's license. Rental rates for mid-size cars range from $35 to $45 per day, $180 to $220 per week, more in peak season; larger or luxury cars are considerably more expensive. Most rental agencies require that drivers be at least 21 years old; drivers under 25 must normally pay a surcharge of $5 to $15 per day. Rates do not include the 7.5% sales tax or insurance, which adds $9 to $11 a day for a loss-damage waiver (covering damage to the rented car) and again for a liability insurance supplement (covering personal injury as well as damage to the other car) to your rental cost. These are usually optional, but highly advisable, considering your liability in case of an accident.

Only some agencies permit their rental cars to be taken into Mexico and, they do only if you buy supplemental Mexican car insurance from them (see the Tijuana Getting There & Away chapter for why this is important). Avis and Dollar allow their vehicles to be driven anywhere in Baja California if cars are rented from certain locations, including the airports in San Diego and Los Angeles. Supplemental insurance from Avis is $18 per day and $25 from Dollar. Budget allows you to take a car 200 miles down the peninsula and charges $20 a day for insurance. Cars may be rented from any Budget office. Hertz and Enterprise also sometimes allow their cars to travel across the border.

In Little Italy you'll find California Rent a Car (Map 3; ☎ 619-238-9999), 904 W Grape St, and West Coast Rent a Car (Map 3; ☎ 619-544-0606), practically next door at 834 W Grape St, which both rent to drivers as young as 18, although you must purchase extra insurance from them (about $17 a day). They also allow you to take the car into Mexico but you must purchase your own insurance before crossing the border.

The chart below shows which major international agencies are represented in San Diego and how to contact them. Some independent ones may have lower rates and more relaxed conditions.

Avis (☎ 800-331-1084, 619-231-7171)
www.avis.com

Alamo (☎ 800-462-5266, 619-297-0311)
www.goalamo.com

Budget (☎ 800-472-3325, 619-279-2900)
www.drivebudget.com

Dollar (☎ 800-800-4000, 619-234-3388)
www.dollar.com

Enterprise (☎ 800-736-8227, 858-457-4909)
www.enterprise.com

Hertz (☎ 800-654-3131, N/A)
www.hertz.com

National (☎ 800-227-7368, 619-231-7100)
www.nationalcar.com

Thrifty (☎ 800-847-4389, 619-239-2281)
www.thrifty.com

Motorcycle Rental

The Southern California climate is biker-friendly, but city traffic is not. Still, if you've always wanted to experience that *Easy Rider* feeling, you could head out of town on a rented bike. Eagle Rider San Diego (☎ 619-222-8822, 800-437-4337), 3445 Midway Dr No A, in Point Loma, rents Harley Davidsons by the hour, day or week, as does Rebel (☎ 858-292-6200, 888-737-3255), 5600 Kearny Mesa Rd in Kearny Mesa. Both have a range of models to choose from, including the Bad Boy and the Heritage Softtail Classic. Most rentals go for $75 to $150 a day. Helmets are required by law in California for drivers and passengers, and the law is strictly enforced.

TAXI

Unlike in New York, Chicago and other US cities, you can't just thrust your arm out and expect to hail a taxi in San Diego. Except for those lined up outside airports, train and bus stations, and major hotels, cabbies respond to phone calls rather than hand waves. Established companies include American Cab (☎ 619-234-1111), Orange Cab (☎ 619-291-3333), San Diego Cab (☎ 619-226-7294) and Yellow Cab (☎ 619-234-6161). In Coronado, you'll find the Coronado Cab Company (☎ 619-435-6211), while in La Jolla, you'll find the La Jolla Cab (☎ 858-453-4222). Fares are around $1.80 to start, plus about $1.90 per mile.

BICYCLE

Some areas in San Diego are great for cycling, particularly Pacific Beach, Mission Beach, Mission Bay and Coronado. For suggestions, see the Activities section in the San Diego Things to See & Do chapter.

All public buses are equipped with bike racks and will transport two-wheelers for free. Inform the driver before boarding, then stow your bike on the rack on the tail end of the bus. Useful routes include bus No 34 between Downtown and La Jolla (via Ocean Beach, Mission Bay, Mission Beach and Pacific Beach), No 41 between Fashion Valley Center and UCSD, No 150 between Downtown and University Towne Centre, No 301 between University Towne Centre and Oceanside, and No 902 between Down-

town and Coronado. For more information call ☎ 619-233-3004.

Any bike with a permit rides free on the trolley; you can pick one up for $4 from the Transit Store (see Public Transportation earlier in this chapter). The bike-storage area is in the back of the trolley. The *Coaster* trains also accommodate bicycles for free. Enter through doors marked with a bicycle logo, then secure your bike in one of the racks on the lower level. Taking a bike on the Coronado Ferry costs 50¢.

The following outfits all rent various types of bicycles, from mountain and road bikes to kids' bikes and cruisers. Rates vary by company, the type of bike you're renting and the rental period. In general, expect to pay about $5 per hour, $10 to $14 per half-day (four hours) and $15 to $25 per day. Most places listed here also rent in-line skates, skateboards, boogie boards and other fun equipment.

Bike Cab Co (Map 3; ☎ 619-232-4700), 523 Island Ave, Downtown

Bike Rentals (Map 3), on 5th St at the corner of Island Ave, Downtown

Holland's Bike (Map 4; ☎ 619-435-3153), 977 Orange Ave, Coronado

Hamel's Beach Rentals (Map 9; ☎ 858-488-5050), 704 Ventura Place, Mission Beach

Blazing Saddles (Map 9; ☎ 858-488-9595), 3221 Mission Blvd, Mission Beach

Cheap Rentals (Map 9; ☎ 858-488-9070), 3685 Mission Blvd, Mission Beach

Bike Rentals (Map 10), near the beach at Thomas Ave, Pacific Beach

BOAT

The Coronado Ferry (☎ 619-234-4111) leaves hourly on the hour between 9 am and 9 pm (10 pm on Friday and Saturday) from the Broadway Pier on the Embarcadero. It returns from the Ferry Landing Marketplace on Coronado on the half hour from 9:30 am to 9:30 pm (10:30 pm Saturday and Sunday). The one-way fare is $2; bicycles are $0.50.

For more individualized transportation, you can also call a Water Taxi (☎ 619-235-8294) daily from 10 am to 10 pm. The per-person fare is $5 between any two points in the northern bay; trips to the southern bay cost significantly more. Pick-ups can be arranged from any landing.

WALKING

You may need to use your own vehicle or public transportation to get from A to B within San Diego, but once you're in a particular neighborhood, your own two feet are the best means of transportation. See the San Diego Things to See & Do chapter for some neighborhood walking tours.

ORGANIZED TOURS

Both Hornblower/Invader Cruises (☎ 619-234-8687) and Harbor Excursions (☎ 619-234-4111) depart from the Broadway Pier for one-hour sightseeing tours, six times daily (four times from October to April) and for two-hour tours, three times daily (one from October to April). Prices are $13 for adults, $11 for military personnel and seniors and $6.50 for children; two-hour tours are $18/16/9. Hornblower also has nightly dinner-dance cruises for $49 per person ($54 on Saturday).

Crossing the US-Mexican Border

Every day an average of 226,000 people and 82,000 cars cross the US-Mexican border at San Ysidro, making it the world's busiest border crossing. Open 24 hours a day, the border is about 20 miles south of downtown San Diego and about a 10-minute walk from downtown Tijuana. The alternative crossing at Mesa de Otay, 5 miles east of San Ysidro, is open 6 am to 10 pm daily. Since  there is no public transport to Mesa de Otay, it's really only convenient for drivers.

You can cross the San Ysidro border on foot, by car or by bus from either side (see map on page 60). The various options are outlined here, but for additional details you should also consult the San Diego Getting There & Away and Tijuana Getting There & Away chapters.

San Diego Trolley The San Diego Trolley Blue Line is the cheapest, easiest and most efficient way to travel to the border from central San Diego. Trains leave on the 45-minute journey every 15 or 30 minutes from early morning to late at night and around the clock on Saturday. The fare is $2. If you're arriving at the airport and headed straight to the border, take bus No 992 and transfer to the trolley at America Plaza (request a transfer). The trolley terminus is on the US side of the border, from where you'll continue on foot (see Walking, below).

Bus Greyhound has almost hourly departures from its San Diego downtown terminal at 120 W Broadway to the border and into Tijuana proper. The trip to San Ysidro takes 30 minutes and costs $7.50/14.50 one-way/roundtrip. You could get off there and walk across the border (see Walking, below) but, oddly, it's cheaper to stay aboard and continue into Tijuana, which adds 20 minutes to the trip but brings the fare down to $5/8. Buses first stop at the Antigua Central Camionera, which is a couple of minutes' walk away from Avenida Revolución in downtown Tijuana (see Map 13). From there, they continue for another 30 minutes to the Central Camionera in Mesa de Otay – but the only reason you'd want to go there is to catch another bus to other parts of Mexico.

The first Greyhound leaves downtown San Diego at 5:30 am and the last one leaves at 11:30 pm. From Tijuana's Antigua Central Camionera, the first San Diego bus leaves at 3:25 am and the last at 9:15 pm. From San Ysidro the first bus leaves at 4:10 am, the last at 10:50 pm.

A cheaper but more time-consuming alternative is public bus No 932, which goes from various stops along Broadway in downtown San Diego (eg, 4th and Broadway) to San Ysidro in about 90

Several companies run narrated bus tours of the city and surrounding attractions. Grayline (☎ 619-491-0011, 800-331-5077) has four-hour city tours, twice daily in summer (once daily October to April) for $25/11 for adults/children, and trips to the Wild Animal Park, Sea World and the San Diego Zoo. San Diego Scenic Tours (☎ 858-273-8687) covers the city for similar prices. Both companies offer four-hour trips to Tijuana for $26, and San Diego Scenic offers an eight-hour shopping trip to Tijuana for the same price.

Not to be confused with the San Diego Trolley, which run on rails, the Old Town Trolley is a green and orange bus done up to resemble an old-fashioned streetcar. Old Town Trolley Tours (☎ 619-298-8687) do a loop around the main attractions around Downtown, including Balboa Park and Old Town, and in Coronado. You can get on or off at any number of stops, staying to look around as long as you wish. Trolleys start operating at 9 am and run every 30 minutes or so until 4:45 pm October to April and 6 pm in summer. You can start at any trolley

Crossing the US-Mexican Border

minutes for $1.75. Unless you enjoy long bus rides, you'd be better off taking the San Diego Trolley.

Car & Motorcycle Unless you're planning an extended stay or thorough exploration of Tijuana, taking a car across the border is probably more hassle than it's worth. If you do decide to take one, though, the most important thing you must do is get Mexican car insurance either beforehand or at the border crossing (see the Insurance section in the Tijuana Getting There & Away chapter). There's usually no delay coming into Mexico, where immigration and customs checks are conducted on a random basis only. Entering the US, however, can take up to three hours, especially after holiday weekends. Lanes 9 to 12 are reserved for carpools of at least three passengers, but only from 5 am to 10 pm Monday to Friday. The alternative crossing at Mesa de Otay is much less congested. Remember, though, that it takes time to drive there and return to I-5 after crossing the border.

Many visitors coming from San Diego choose to leave their car on the US side of the border and either walk or take a shuttle across. Several parking lots are located just off the Camino de la Plaza exit (the last US exit) off I-5. A popular lot is Border Station Parking at 4570 Camino de la Plaza, which charges US$7 per day. Also here is a small tourist information kiosk with maps and pamphlets.

This parking lot also doubles as the northern terminus of Mexicoach (☎ 685-14-70, 619-428-9517 in the US), a bright red shuttle bus operating between the border and the Terminal Turístico Tijuana on Avenida Revolución. Buses depart at 15- to 30-minute intervals from 9 am to 9 pm daily. The one-way fare is US$1. This is a convenient and cheap way to get to downtown Tijuana if you don't want to walk.

Walking To cross the border on foot from San Ysidro, simply take the pedestrian bridge, then pass through the turnstiles, and you're on Mexican soil. There's a tourist office about 150 feet along the walkway and another by the yellow taxi stand. To reach Avenida Revolución, turn right just before the taxi stand, then continue west past souvenir hawkers and taco stands to a large outdoor mall called Plaza Viva Tijuana. From its far end another pedestrian bridge leads across the Río Tijuana. From here continue west along Calle 1a (Calle Comercio), past countless more souvenir shops, to the foot of Avenida Revolución. The entire walk takes 10 to 15 minutes.

Walking from Tijuana to San Ysidro also involves a pedestrian bridge and turnstiles, but you'll also have to deal with US Customs & Immigration.

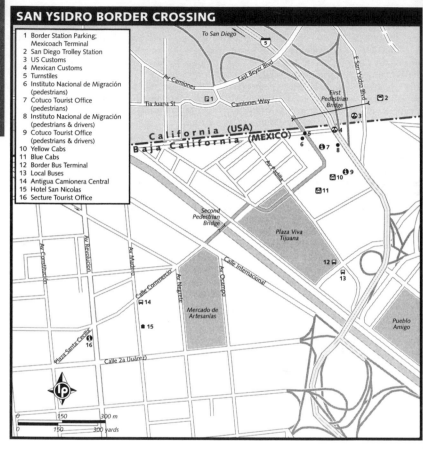

SAN YSIDRO BORDER CROSSING

1 Border Station Parking;
  Mexicoach Terminal
2 San Diego Trolley Station
3 US Customs
4 Mexican Customs
5 Turnstiles
6 Instituto Nacional de Migración
  (pedestrians)
7 Cotuco Tourist Office
  (pedestrians)
8 Instituto Nacional de Migración
  (pedestrians & drivers)
9 Cotuco Tourist Office
  (pedestrians & drivers)
10 Yellow Cabs
11 Blue Cabs
12 Border Bus Terminal
13 Local Buses
14 Antigua Camionera Central
15 Hotel San Nicolas
16 Secture Tourist Office

stop (they are well marked with orange and are usually next to a regular San Diego Transit bus stop), though the official trolley stand is on Twiggs St in Old Town (which is convenient for parking). The tours make quite a good introduction to the city, and the commentary is entertaining. The cost is $24, or $12 for children 4 to 12.

On Friday morning the Old Town Trolley also runs a tour of some of the military bases, including ships in port, the San Diego Naval Station, the North Island Naval Air Station and other military facilities ($22/8 for adults/children).

San Diego's version of a rickshaw is the pedicab – a carriage pulled behind a bicycle – that takes up to four people. If you don't mind the idea of being propelled by human muscle and sweat, these could be a good way to see Downtown. The drivers (pedalers?) often have tips on what's happening around town. You can flag an empty pedicab, or call Bikecabs (☎ 888-245-3222) and they'll pick you up. They operate 10 am to midnight daily, until 3 am on Friday and Saturday. Rates are negotiable and depend on distance covered and time spent; they should not exceed $50 per hour.

Things to See & Do

DOWNTOWN (MAP 3)

San Diego's Downtown is adjacent to the waterfront in the area first acquired, subdivided and promoted by Alonzo Horton in 1867. Most of the land on the water side of the trolley line is landfill: Until the mid-1920s, the south end of 5th Ave was the main unloading dock for cargo boats. Fishing boats used to toe up where the Convention Center now stands.

In the 1960s, Downtown was a depressing combination of uninteresting office complexes and creeping inner-urban dereliction. Since then, redevelopment (begun in the late '70s) has turned the tide. Today, a number of pre-1900 'skyscrapers' survive, albeit dwarfed by their towering, mirrored modern counterparts.

The heart and soul of Downtown is the Gaslamp Quarter, which covers about eight blocks along 4th and 5th Aves from Broadway south to Harbor Dr and the Convention Center. It is bordered on its northern end by Broadway, the main drag, which travels east from the waterfront – the Embarcadero – right through the middle of town, skirting the popular Horton Plaza shopping mall. East of the Gaslamp, the East Village is a major construction site and possible home of a new Padres baseball park. Finally, in the northwest corner of Downtown, Little Italy is a vibrant Italian-American neighborhood.

Gaslamp Quarter

When Horton first established New Town San Diego in 1867, 5th Ave was its main street and home to its main industries – saloons, gambling joints, bordellos and opium dens. As more respectable businesses grew up along Broadway, the 5th Ave area became known as the Stingaree, a red-light district. By the 1960s it was a skid row of flophouses and bars, its seedy atmosphere making it so unattractive to developers that many of its older buildings survived as others around town were being razed. In the early 1980s, when developers started thinking about demolition and rebuilding, local protests and the Gaslamp Quarter Council saved the area.

Wrought-iron streetlamps in the style of 19th-century gas lamps were installed, along with trees and brick sidewalks. Restored buildings dating from the 1870s to the 1920s now house restaurants, bars, galleries and theaters. The 16-block area south of Broadway between 4th and 6th Aves is designated a National Historic District, and development is strictly controlled.

An enjoyable time to visit is on a warm evening when people throng the streets and crowd the outdoor tables (see the San Diego Places to Eat and Entertainment chapters). To get a feel for the Gaslamp Quarter architecture and history, it's better to come and walk around during the day.

To get a full historical picture, take a guided walking tour offered by the Gaslamp

---

Highlights

- Finding your favorite(s) among Balboa Park's 15 museums

- Snorkeling or diving alongside sea urchins and Garibaldi fish at La Jolla Cove

- Lunching alfresco at Prado (Balboa Park), Casa de Bandini (Old Town) or Brockton Villa (La Jolla) – see San Diego Places to Eat

- Rambling around Torrey Pines State Preserve, with superb ocean views, unique plant life and relative solitude

- Soaking up the SoCal vibe along Ocean Front Walk between Pacific Beach and Mission Beach

- Catching cool jazz at Croce's or Dizzy's in the Gaslamp Quarter – see San Diego Entertainment

- Meeting exotic creatures at the Wild Animal Park, San Diego Zoo or SeaWorld

Quarter Historical Foundation (☎ 619-233-4692) from its headquarters in the William Heath Davis House at 410 Island Ave. The one-hour tour starts at 11 am Saturday and costs $8, or $5 students and seniors, including admission to the museum. You can also rent an audiotape with a self-paced tour, narrated by the character 'Wyatt Earp,' for $5/3.

If you'd like to take your own tour, here is a walk that hits the historic and architectural highlights.

Gaslamp Quarter Walking Tour Start at the **William Heath Davis House** (1850) at the corner of Island and 4th Ave, the oldest surviving structure of Alonzo Horton's New Town. It is one of 14 prefabricated houses that Davis had shipped around Cape Horn from Maine in 1850. He never actually lived here, but Horton did for a year, from 1868–69. The building is plain, the type called a 'saltbox.' Originally at State and Market Sts, it was moved here in 1984. Inside is a **museum**, with 19th-century furnishings and a working kitchen, maintained by the Gaslamp Quarter Historical Foundation. It's open 11 am to 4 pm, closed Monday; admission is $3.

Walk north on 4th Ave. The building at No 558, currently home to the fancy Chive restaurant, housed the **Royal Pie Bakery** for more than 125 years, the last 75 or so under the ownership of the Kuhnel family. When the Kuhnels bought the property in 1920, the Anchor Hotel, a place of questionable repute, occupied the 2nd floor. An indignant Martha Kuhnel had little tolerance for 'rampant immorality,' and quickly put an end to the operation.

Continue north for a couple of blocks to F St. On the northeast corner stands the **Ingle Building** (1906), now the Hard Rock Café, which was nearly wiped out in a 1980 fire, but has been restored to its original glory. In the process, the brilliant stained-glass windows, once plastered over, were uncovered, although the visual stunner – a kaleidoscopic stained-glass dome – was moved here from an Elks Lodge building.

Turn right onto E St, one block farther north, and walk over to 5th Ave, turn right

again. The Baroque Revival–style edifice at No 835 across the street is the magnificent **Louis Bank of Commerce** (1888), San Diego's first granite building. It is one of the architectural gems of the Gaslamp, with a detailed façade and a pair of small, frilly towers. Despite the name, it only housed a bank until 1893, then re-opened as an oyster bar that was a regular haunt of Wyatt Earp. Later, the enterprising Madam Coara ran her popular bordello, called the Golden Poppy Hotel, in the upper floors. To prevent confusion, the dresses worn by her gaggle of girls matched the color of the doors to their rooms. The building currently houses a restaurant and bar.

Across the street, at No 840, is the **San Diego Hardware Building** (1910), which houses one of San Diego's oldest private businesses, a hardware store established in 1892. The building started life as a dance hall, and then contained a Woolworth store until 1923, when the current tenant moved in. Note the original wooden floors, storefront windows and metal ceilings.

Another jewel of a building is at the intersection of 5th Ave and F St. The Romanesque-style **Keating Building** (1890) was built in George's honor by his widow Fannie (look for his name in the top cornice). Boasting all the modern conveniences of the day, including a wire-cage elevator and a steam-heating system, only the city's top dogs could afford renting office space here. In 1985, another widow, Ingrid Croce, opened her restaurant and bar on the ground floor – in honor of her husband, Jim.

Across the street, at No 809, the **Marston Building** (1881), now housing Fio's restaurant, is also of note. The proud Italianate Victorian structure began life as George Marston's first department store; it later became a chain and was sold to the Broadway company in 1970 (which in turn was gobbled up by Macy's in the 1990s). Much of the building actually dates to 1903, rebuilt then after a fire damaged the original.

On the southwest corner of this intersection stands the **Spencer-Ogden Building** (1874), the oldest structure continuously owned by the same families. It was bought by two men, Spencer and Ogden, in 1881, and has been held by several business-people, including a turn-of-the-20th-century dentist known as 'Painless Parker,' several drugists and an importer. It is now a night-club called the Bitter End.

One block farther south, at the intersection with G St, looms the majestic **Old City Hall** (1874), a Florentine Italianate confection with 16-foot ceilings and 12-foot windows. Note the brick arches and antique-style columns. Around 1900, the city's entire government, including the police department and city council chambers, fit inside this structure. Inside is a wrought-iron cage elevator. It currently houses the Jimmy Love's nightclub.

The last building on the tour, less than two blocks south at No 536, is the **Lincoln Hotel** (1913), a four-story steel-frame with Oriental style elements, including a flat red clay tile roof and a façade festooned with decorative hollow clay tile. It originally housed a wine store on the ground floor and a hotel above.

Turning right on Island Ave will take you right back to the William Heath Davis House.

Broadway & Around

Downtown's major thoroughfare is a mix of historic brick office buildings on its eastern end and sleek glass and steel towers built by modern mavens of industry farther west. It's a functional street, home also to the Santa Fe train depot, the San Diego Trolley American Plaza terminal and the Greyhound bus station.

First Interstate Building This magnificent tan structure on the northwest corner of 6th St and Broadway has the elegance and architectural integrity of a fine Old World cathedral. Built in Romanesque Revival style by William Templeton Johnson, the former bank building is now the Courtyard by Marriott hotel (see the San Diego Places to Stay chapter). An arched entrance framed by carved sandstone garlands leads into the breathtaking lobby. Look up at the gorgeous coffered Spanish ceiling sup-

ported by an arched gallery with wrought-iron railings. Reception still uses some of the old-fashioned brass teller windows.

Samuel I Fox Building The building across the street, at 531 Broadway, is another magnificent creation of Templeton Johnson. Look for details such as cast-iron decorative grills, sculpted terra-cotta, a bas-relief of heraldic lions and walnut window frames. Built in 1929, it housed the Lion Clothing company until 1984.

Copley Symphony Hall Two blocks north of Broadway, at 750 B St, this acoustically wonderful, plush venue – originally known as Fox Theater – with 2400 seats was California's third largest at its opening as a vaudeville and movie house in 1929. In the 1980s its block, bounded by A and B Sts and 7th and 8th Aves, was razed and redeveloped, but the theater was spared. In 1984 the San Diego Symphony (SDS) purchased the exuberant Spanish Rococo–style structure and restored it, employing the same company that had designed the original interior. The effort paid off, but when the orchestra went bankrupt a few years later, the hall felt into disuse. In 1998, the SDS was revived and so was the theater. See the San Diego Entertainment chapter for concert details.

Horton Plaza Park Just south of Broadway between 3rd and 4th Aves, Horton Plaza Park is overshadowed (quite literally) by Horton Plaza mall and the garish neon façades of Sam Goody's and Planet Hollywood, this 'park' on the south side of Broadway is about as conducive to lingering as an ant hill. Devoid of grass or benches, its only redeeming element is the 1909 **Irving Gill fountain**. Modeled after the 334 BC monument to Lysicrates in Athens, it is a tribute to happiness and music. Lighting illuminates the cascading water, creating an effect that was a technological breakthrough at the time. Six Corinthian columns support a frieze and dome.

The fountain anchors an area set aside by Horton in 1870 for the entertainment of his guests at the Horton House hotel across the street. In 1894, after falling on bad times, at age 81, Horton deeded the plaza to the city for $100 per month for the rest of his life, up to $10,000. He lived to draw the final payment in April 1903.

Horton Plaza This giant mall behind Horton Plaza Park was the sparkplug of San Diego's downtown redevelopment. Conceived and promoted by mall developer Ernie Hahn, this huge project involved the leveling of seven city blocks and the construction of a five-level complex with 2300 parking spaces. It has a multi-screen cinema, two live theaters, restaurants, cafes and 140 shops in what has been described as a 'postmodern interpretation of an Italian hillside town' with an abstract version of the Cathedral of Siena as its focal point. That may be a stretch. The festival marketplace created here by architect Jon Jerde rather calls to mind the seductive excesses of both Las Vegas and of Disneyland (Jerde also gave the world Universal City Walk in Los Angeles).

From the outside, the plaza is uninviting (critics say it 'turns its back on Downtown,' which, at the time of construction, was really run-down). Inside, a 1907 Jessop Clock (big and four-sided) provides a touch of nostalgia, and the color scheme is anything but dull. What with disorienting curved spaces and changes in levels, it can feel as if you're walking through an MC Escher drawing. The top-floor food court is not cheap, but is a great place for people-watching.

On the mall's northern flank are two obelisks, one covered with a colorful mosaic extending down into the foyer of the Lyceum Theater, and another in front of the Westin Hotel, which sports an ocean motif. For more on Horton Plaza see the San Diego Shopping chapter.

Spreckels Theater Commissioned by John D Spreckels, this beautiful theater at 1st Ave and Broadway was one of the most modern in the American West at its 1912 opening. The flamboyant interior features a marble lobby, delicate carvings and orna-

mentation, ceiling paintings and even statues showing the Muses frolicking with dolphins. Among the more unusual productions staged in its long history was *Ben Hur,* which required actors and horses to charge off stage and onto 2nd Ave, then back onstage through the 1st Ave entrance. The theater is still a popular venue (see the San Diego Entertainment chapter).

Santa Fe Depot This winsome historic railroad station – used by Amtrak today – transports you back to the Golden Age of train travel. It was constructed for the 1915 Panama-California Expo in Spanish Colonial style. Shiny domes capping the duet of white towers are made of blue and yellow tile, similar to the ones atop the California Building in Balboa Park. The cheerful tile is continued in the waiting room. Also here is an excellent model of the aircraft carrier the USS *Midway,* which is scheduled to house the new Aircraft Carrier Museum at Navy Pier on the Embarcadero (see the boxed text 'San Diego & the Military'). The depot is at 1050 Kettner Blvd.

The Santa Fe Depot also contains the offices of the **San Diego Railroad Museum**, which has 90 major pieces of rolling stock – freight cars, locomotives, passenger cars – on display in locations throughout San Diego County.

Some of the museum's collection is at the La Mesa Depot (see La Mesa in the Eastern Metro section later in this chapter), but most of the operation is based at the depot in Campo, about 45 miles southeast of Downtown across the border from the Mexican town of Tecate. From here, members run trips aboard restored trains on weekends at 11 am and 2:30 pm. A standard train consists of a diesel-electric locomotive pulling several vintage coaches and special cars. The journey lasts 90 minutes and costs $12, or $3 children. Most Saturdays you can also take a half-day trip to Tecate for $40, or $20 children ($100 in first class), with trains chugging downhill from 2500 feet, passing three tunnels on the way. Call ☎ 619-595-3030 for reservations

San Diego Harbor

DAVID PEEVERS

Casa del Prado, Balboa Park, San Diego

RICK GERHARTER

Louis Bank of Commerce, Gaslamp Quarter

DAVID PEEVERS

Shopping at Horton Plaza, San Diego

ANTHONY PIDGEON

View of Cabrillo National Monument

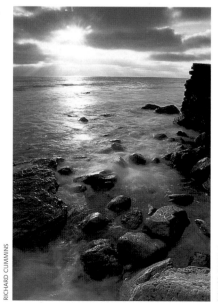

Sunset from Cabrillo National Monument

Shutterbugging, Sunset Cliffs, Point Loma

and information. To get to Campo, head east on I-8 about 45 miles to Buckman Springs Rd, go south on that road for about 10 miles, then west on Hwy 94 for about 1½ miles.

Museum of Contemporary Art Opposite the train station, on American Plaza, the MCA is the Downtown branch of this La Jolla–based institution, which has presented innovative artwork since the 1960s. The ever-changing exhibits of painting and sculpture are publicized widely (see the *San Diego Reader* or call the museum). Outside the entrance is the huge *Hammering Man* sculpture by Jonathan Borofsky.

For more about the permanent collection, see the La Jolla section later in this chapter. The museum (☎ 619-234-1001), at 1001 Kettner Blvd, is open 11 am to 5 pm, closed Wednesday. Admission is free except for special exhibits; docent tours are Saturday and Sunday at 2 and 3 pm.

Embarcadero

San Diego's waterfront, built mostly on landfill, is 500 yards wider than it was in the late 1800s. It's a clean, attractive and well-manicured area west of Downtown. Since most of the shipyards and naval facilities are farther southeast (near the Coronado Bay Bridge) and at National City, this area is geared toward pedestrians. You can take a pleasant walk along the Embarcadero from the Maritime Museum, past ships and seafood restaurants, to Seaport Village and the San Diego Convention Center. A few more attractions and museums lie within a couple of blocks inland.

Maritime Museum The Maritime Museum consists of three restored vessels moored at 1306 N Harbor Dr just north of Ash St – look for the 100-foot-high masts of the square-rigger *Star of India*. Built on the Isle of Man (England) and launched in 1863, the tall ship plied the England-India trade route, carried immigrants to New Zealand, became a trading ship based in Hawaii and, finally, worked the Alaskan salmon fisheries. All in all, she circumnavigated the

globe 21 times, and still sails today as a rented vessel for corporate, private or official functions.

Moored right next to her is the ferryboat *Berkeley* (1898), which once operated between San Francisco and Oakland. Exhibits on the main deck chronicle the rise and fall of the local fishing industry. See also models of early explorer ships, including Cabrillo's *San Salvador,* and displays related to the US Navy. A steep flight of stairs descends to the engine room where, if you're lucky, you can watch museum staff demonstrate the ship's rare triple-expansion steam engine. On the upper deck is the former passenger lounge with polished wooden benches and beautiful stained glass windows.

The third vessel is the *Medea* (1904), one in only three remaining steam yachts. Built in Scotland, it's a compact but luxurious boat that served in both world wars and has since been beautifully restored to its civilian heyday style.

The museum (☎ 619-234-9153) is open 9 am to 8 pm daily (to 9 pm in summer), admission to all three vessels is $6, or $4 seniors and teens, $2 children.

In summer the museum organizes a popular **Movies Before the Mast** series of film classics with a nautical theme. During intermission, patrons warm up with a bowl of New England clam chowder. Call the museum for details.

County Administration Center This imposing streamline moderne edifice opposite the Maritime Museum was built in 1936 with money from the Works Progress Administration (WPA). President Franklin D Roosevelt himself came out West in 1938 to dedicate the structure, which is considered one of the finest public buildings in the country. Outside the main entrance is *Guardian of Waters,* a giant sculpture by San Diego artist Donal Hord of a pioneer woman shouldering a water jug. The building is open 8 am to 5 pm weekdays only; the inexpensive cafeteria on the 4th floor, which has a nice view of the waterfront, is open to the public.

Embarcadero Piers South of the Maritime Museum you'll walk past several piers. First up is the B Street Pier, which serves as San Diego's cruise ship terminal. On Tuesday, Royal Caribbean's 1500-passenger *Viking Serenade* is usually in port, and other major liners also stop by en route to Mexico. Harbor cruises and the Coronado Ferry depart from the north side of the Broadway Pier (see the San Diego Getting Around chapter). The next pier is the Navy Pier, which is closed to the public. On the south side of the G Street Pier is Tuna Harbor, where commercial fisherman congregate; there are also a couple of fine fish restaurants here (see the San Diego Places to Eat chapter).

Seaport Village Neither a port nor a village, this collection of novelty shops, restaurants and snack outlets has an unconvincing maritime theme with ersatz turn-of-the-20th-century seafront architecture. It's touristy and twee, but not a bad place to look for souvenirs and have a bite to eat. At its northern end is the nostalgic **Broadway Flying Horses Carousel**, designed by Carl Louff and brought here from Coney Island. Closer to the Hyatt Hotel is a 45-foot-tall replica of the **Mukilteo Lighthouse**; the original is in Everett, Washington. Seaport Village (☎ 619-235-4014) is open 10 am to 9 pm daily (to 10 pm in summer); two hours of parking are free with purchase.

San Diego Convention Center Built in a successful attempt to promote the city as a site for major conventions, this unusual-looking complex opened in 1989 and is booked solid more than 5 years into the

San Diego & the Military

San Diego County has the questionable distinction of being the largest military complex in the world. From Camp Pendleton Marine Base on its northern border to the 32nd Street Naval Station close to the Mexican border, the military is omnipresent. Between those two are seven more installations, including the Marine Corps Air Station Miramar (where much of the movie *Top Gun* was filmed), the Naval Amphibious Base in Coronado and the Naval Submarine Base on Point Loma.

In fact, San Diego is the only city where the military presence has actually increased, despite budget cuts in the 1990s. And it is set to grow even more: In 2003 the aircraft carrier USS *Ronald Reagan* will be home-based in San Diego Bay, and in 2005 the USS *Nimitz* will arrive. They will join the USS *Constellation* and the USS *John C Stennis*, already in port – four of six aircraft carriers in the Pacific Fleet will be stationed in San Diego.

Other figures are staggering too: The military employs 150,000 active duty and civil service personnel in San Diego, a figure which includes 35% of the entire US Marine Corps and 30% of the US Navy. The military is also the second most important economic factor, generating 20% ($16.3 billion) of the city's gross regional product, only topped by manufacturing.

The military also plays a factor in tourism, drawing many visitors to the city. As you stroll alongside the bay, you look out at warships. Fighter planes and helicopters roar above your head. And you're likely to run into uniformed personnel in the streets, at restaurants and just about anywhere else. Besides such chance encounters, there are also several opportunities to get a closer look at all this military might.

San Diego Aircraft Carrier Museum

Scheduled to open in mid to late 2001, this one-of-a-kind museum aboard the decommissioned USS *Midway* should be a major attraction in the port of San Diego. The first angled deck carrier in the US fleet, it was in service from 1947 until 1991 and was in Vietnam and Desert Storm. If all goes according to plan, its home will be the Navy Pier on the Embarcadero in Downtown. Planned

21st century. In 2000 a vast $10 million expansion doubled its size, creating more and larger meeting rooms, exhibit space and pre-function, lobby and registration areas.

The design, by Canadian avant-garde architect Arthur Erickson, is said to have been inspired by an ocean liner. It features large cylindrical windows (portholes?) and a dramatic roof space sheltered by white Teflon 'sails.' The Convention Center (☎ 619-525-5000) is on Harbor Dr between 3rd and 5th Ave; free tours are sometimes offered, and it's open to the public most days if you just want to have a look inside. Also look past the masts in the nearby Marriott's marina for Embarcadero Marina Park, where there's a public fishing pier and an open-air amphitheater, which presents free concerts on summer evenings.

San Diego Children's Museum For young children, a visit to this interactive museum will be a special treat. Many of its play stations are creative and educational. One of the most popular is the Big Hat, a giant Dr Seuss–inspired striped hat that contains materials and patterns for making hats. Cora's Rain House is a small shed inside which youngsters can draw, color or paint while hearing 'rain' fall on the roof. The Paper Factory explains how paper, is made and invites tots to participate in the process. There are giant construction toys, a clay workshop, a stage with costumes for impromptu theater, as well as storytelling, music, activities and changing exhibits.

The museum (☎ 619-233-8792), 200 Island Ave, is open 10 am to 3 pm Tuesday to Friday and 10 am to 4 pm weekends; admission is $6 for ages two and up.

San Diego & the Military

highlights are an extensive collection of naval aviation aircraft, displays on the history of naval aviation, flight simulators and virtual reality rides, and a below-deck theater. Check with the tourist offices or call ☎ 619-702-7700 for an update.

Marine Corps Recruit Depot Command Museum

Housed in a building designed by Bertram Goodhue (main architect of the 1915 Exposition), this museum tells the history of the recruit depot and honors those who have been stationed here. Exhibits, which include weapons, uniforms, training films, paintings and memorabilia, tell the story of the various wars that saw US engagement in the 20th century, from WWI to Desert Storm.

The museum (☎ 619-524-6038) is in Building 26 of the Marine Corps Recruit Depot on Pacific Hwy at Barnett Ave – look for the signs and enter at Gate 4. Hours are 8 am to 4 pm (Thursday to 5 pm), Saturday noon to 4 pm; admission is free.

Tours

Free public tours of aircraft carriers and surface force ships (destroyers, cruisers, helicopter carriers, frigates) were suspended in October 2000 due to a heightened security alert following the bombing of the USS *Cole* in Yemen. Normally, tours are conducted on weekends and no reservations are required. To find out whether tours have resumed, call ☎ 619-437-2735.

An excellent way to get close to some Navy ships, including submarines and aircraft carriers, is on a two-hour Harbor Cruise. Old Town Trolley Tours also runs a weekly tour that goes onto the bases. For more information on either, see Organized Tours in the Getting Around chapter.

Fleet Week

San Diego's biggest tribute to the Navy is Fleet Week which, despite the name, lasts nine days, starting sometime in mid-October. Flagship events are ship parades, ship and submarine tours and the Miramar Air Show. Call ☎ 619-236-1212 for details.

Asian/Pacific Historic Thematic District On the southwestern edge of Downtown, and overlapping the Gaslamp Quarter, this recently created district recognizes the contributions made to San Diego by immigrants from Japan, Vietnam and other Asian countries, but most of all from China.

Never as large or as influential as its counterparts in San Francisco or even Los Angeles, San Diego's historic Chinatown once occupied an area between Market and K Sts and 2nd and 5th Aves. The first Chinese arrived in San Diego in the 1850s, after having tried their luck during the 1849 Gold Rush in northern California. They dominated the fishing industry until 1890 and also were construction workers and merchants. With Chinatown located next to the Stingaree, San Diego's infamous red-light district, Chinese-operated opium dens and gambling halls flourished.

The most prominent of the early Chinese settlers was the merchant Ah Quin. A community leader, who later became known as the 'mayor of Chinatown,' Ah Quin also was a labor broker in the construction of the California Southern Railroad. Fluent in English, he helped his fellow immigrants as an interpreter and raised a family of 12 kids.

The Chinese population grew slowly, in part because of the Chinese Exclusions Act of 1882, which prevented immigrants from becoming US citizens and imposed many other restrictions. Immigration picked up when the laws were repealed in 1943, and today about 50,000 Chinese-Americans live in San Diego – although no longer in historic Chinatown.

Among the few buildings remaining from the area's heyday are the Chinese Consolidated Benevolent Association (1911) at 428 3rd Ave; the Ying-On Merchants & Labor Benevolent Association (1925) at 500 3rd Ave; the Plants & Fireproofing Building (1928) at 540 3rd Ave; Ah Quin's residence (1888) located at 429 3rd Ave; the Lincoln Hotel (1913) at 536 5th Ave and the Chinese Mission.

San Diego's modern Chinatown is in the Kearny Mesa/Clairemont Mesa area, about 8 miles north of Downtown. For details on points of interest there, see the Mid-City section later in this chapter.

Chinese Mission The anchor of historic Chinatown, this small stucco structure served as the mission of San Diego's Chinese community from 1927 to 1960. It originally stood at 645 1st Ave, but was moved to 404 3rd Ave to make room for Horton Plaza mall. Designed by Louis J Gill (Irving Gill's nephew) and renovated by Joseph Wong, it features a roofline accented by red tiles and a central bell tower. The mission was mainly a social gathering place but later was also used as a language school for Chinese, as well as Japanese, immigrants

Today it houses the **San Diego Chinese Historical Museum** (☎ 619-338-9888), which traces the story of the local Chinese from their homeland origins to their arrival in the US and their challenges encountered after settling here. Objects excavated from the old Chinatown, including ceramics and bone toothbrushes, are on display. Perhaps more interesting are the opium pipes, ivory dice and an ancient Chinese lottery machine from the Stingaree's prime.

A surprising highlight is the building's Asian garden. A gate dedicated to Dr Sun Yat-Sen, and created by one of his descendants, leads into a lush environment guarded by a bronze statue of Confucius. A waterfall, fishpond, bridge and stone path create the meditative quality commonly found in Eastern gardens.

The museum is open Tuesday to Sunday 10:30 am to 4 pm (Sunday from noon); free

Chicano Park Unlike any other community parks where picnic areas and children's playgrounds are the norm, Chicano Park is an edgy, urban place underneath the eastern ramps of the Coronado Bridge, on National Ave at Crosby St, in the largely Mexican American community of Logan Heights.

Since 1973, dozens of artists have covered the support pylons of the bridge with murals creating an amazing outdoor museum of contemporary Chicano art. Themes reflect the heroes and hopes of Chicanos but also their struggles and history. There are more

The Difficult Birth of Chicano Park

To the people of Logan Heights, Chicano Park is more than a neighborhood gathering place – it is a symbol of pride in their heritage and in the spirit of self-determination that fueled its creation. A predominantly Mexican American neighborhood since the 1940s, the integrity of Logan Heights had been gradually dismantled since WWII when the Navy moved into the area fronting the bay, cutting off community access to the waterfront. A change in city zoning laws in the 1950s allowed junkyards (still there today) to move into the residential area. In 1963, the arrival of I-5 bisected the neighborhood, displacing many locals. And finally, in 1969, it was Logan Heights that was chosen as the place for the eastern anchor of the Coronado Bridge.

Ironically, it was the construction of the bridge that gave the barrio Chicano Park, albeit not without a struggle. Residents had begun asking for a community park in 1967, and in 1969 city officials offered to set aside a 1.8-acre plot of land beneath the Coronado Bridge for this purpose. Then, on April 22, 1970, city tractors and bulldozers arrived – not to build a park but to erect the headquarters of the California Highway Patrol! It was the final in a long series of insults. Residents had had enough and, led by Chicano activists, quickly mobilized and occupied the site, preventing construction. People from all over the state flocked to San Diego to join the protesters in a show of solidarity. After 12 days, the city council agreed to talk, and by June the development of the park was officially authorized and funds set aside.

Then nothing happened for three more years.

It was a dozen local artists, led by Salvador Torres, who finally took things into their own hands by obtaining permission to decorate the support pylons of the bridge with murals in the tradition of the great Mexican muralists Diego Rivera, José Luis Orozco and Alfonso Sisqueiros. In 1980, Chicano Park was designated a San Diego Historic Site. To this day, a festive celebration on April 22 recalls the day when local residents banded together to fight for their park and, perhaps more importantly, for an ounce of respect.

---

than 40 murals now by such artists as Victor Orozco Ochoa, Mario Torero, Salvador Torres, Yolanda Lopez and José Montoya. For an account of the creation of the park, see the boxed text 'The Difficult Birth of Chicano Park.'

Little Italy

In the northwest corner of Downtown, Little Italy is a vibrant Italian-American neighborhood and one of the most pleasant places to stay – handy to the freeway, walking distance to the harbor and close to good eats. It is bounded by Hawthorn and Ash Sts on the north and south, and Front St and the waterfront on the east and west.

The area was settled in the mid-19th century by Italian immigrants, mostly fishermen and their families, who created a cohesive community. They enjoyed a booming fish industry and whiskey trade (which some

claim was backed by local Mafia). When I-5 was completed in 1962, the heart (and, many say, soul) of the area was destroyed. Buildings were condemned and entire blocks were demolished for the freeway's construction. After its completion, increased traffic turned pedestrian streets and harbor access routes into busy thoroughfares. Still, the area (especially along India St) is a good place to find imported foods, Italian newspapers and people who speak with their hands as much as with their mouths. See the San Diego Places to Eat chapter, for restaurant recommendations.

There are also furniture and art stores that cater to the architects who have recently found the neighborhood interesting. Check out the newish live-work lofts on Kettner Blvd between Fir and Grape Sts, designed collectively by four architecture firms that won a competition to build on the space after it was abandoned by a major supermarket chain.

Our Lady of the Rosary Catholic Church The spiritual hub of Little Italy, this attractive white-washed structure, at the corner of State and Date Sts, contains a treasure trove of some impressive art. It is the brainchild of Father Sylvester Rabagliati, a traveling missionary who spent two years raising money – much of it donated by immigrant fishing families from the Italian port of Genoa – before construction could begin in 1923. Just two years later, the barrel-vaulted, single-nave church, built in Romantic Genovese style and awash in religious imagery, was consecrated.

Its ceiling and wall paintings are the work of Fausto Tasca, a Venetian artist living in Los Angeles. They depict the apostles and evangelists, as well as Biblical scenes, including the crucifixion and the Last Judgment. The iconography includes statues of religious figures by Carlos Romanelli and some nice stained-glass windows showing the 15 mysteries of the rosary. Two marble sculptures incorporated into the main façade represent St Peter and Christopher Columbus, who hailed from Genoa.

The church (☎ 619-234-4820) is open 7 am to 4 pm daily (Sunday to 1 pm); mass is held at least twice daily. Across the street in Amici Park, cultural and community events often take place.

Firehouse Museum This small museum has exhibits depicting some of San Diego's 'hottest' moments. It is in a converted fire station-cum-fire-department repair shop that was in operation in the 1940s and '50s. There's a collection of historical fire-fighting memorabilia, mostly from San Diego but also from other countries (eg, England, Germany, Canada). Highlights include restored fire engines, the oldest being an 1841 Lancaster, as well as fire alarm boxes and fire extinguishers. The museum (☎ 619-232-3473) is at 1572 Columbia St and open 10 am to 2 pm Wednesday to Friday, to 4 pm weekends; admission is $2, or $1 seniors and teens, free if under 12.

East Village

The area east of the Gaslamp Quarter is the site of one of the most ambitious redevelopment projects in the city's history. A new neighborhood, built entirely from scratch, is

---

Field of Dreams or Nightmares?

The anchor of the East Village redevelopment was to be a state-of-the art baseball park, the new home of the San Diego Padres. But at the time of writing, it had become highly questionable whether the $411 million project would ever get off the ground. Construction kicked off in May 2000, and for a while it looked as if everything was proceeding smoothly. But then, in October that same year, Padres owner John Moores and president and CEO Larry Lucchino called an indefinite 'time out' because the money that had been advanced by both the city and the Padres had been exhausted and no secure financial plan was in place. What had happened?

Financing of the project, which was approved by 60% of voters in November 1998, was to come through a public-private partnership between the city of San Diego and the Padres. In order to meet its financial commitment, the city was supposed to issue bonds in the amount of $225 million. It failed to do that in time for the project to stay on schedule, in large part because of a legal cloud created by a federal investigation of city council member Valerie Stallings. The investigation was prompted by Stallings' stock dealings at the time of the ballpark vote, involving a company controlled by Moores that had netted her $14,000 in profit.

Meanwhile, the construction site was abandoned, concrete columns, steel bars and all, at least until the end of the federal probe.

At the time of writing, everyone was holding their breath about whether the city would eventually be able to sell those bonds, allowing construction to resume, or whether San Diego's ambitious ballpark project would simply become an embarrassing boondoggle. Stay tuned.

being superimposed on a 26-block area bordered by 6th Ave, Market St, I-5 and Harbor Dr. It replaces a dusty enclave of abandoned warehouses, downtrodden shops, homeless shelters and soup kitchens, but also artists' studios and lofts.

At the heart of the redevelopment is the new San Diego Padres Ballpark, but a luxury hotel with about 850 rooms, as well as 150,000 sq feet of stores and 600,000 sq feet of office space are also part of the vision, as is a much-needed new main public library. Almost 60% of voters approved the project in the November 1998 ballot despite its $1 billion price tag. Much of the construction was supposed to be completed by 2002, but this deadline now seems unlikely, given the legal troubles and financial woes surrounding the mega-project (see boxed text 'Field of Dreams or Nightmares?')

Villa Montezuma This frilly Victorian villa once belonged to Jesse Shepard, a British pianist and opera singer who had made a name for himself in the salons of Europe in the early 1880s. On a trip to America, Shepard was talked into staying in San Diego by developers William and John High, who thought his presence would attract upscale buyers for their land. As an incentive, they promised him a new house.

Clearly, Shepard's architectural tastes tended toward the frivolous. His house, completed in 1887, is an exuberant hodge-podge of architectural elements borrowed from various periods, including neoclassical gables, Renaissance reliefs and a baroque onion-dome tower. (A butler, who hanged himself in the tower, is said to haunt the place.) Of note are the stained-glass windows depicting Beethoven, Shakespeare and other artistic idols of the quirky owner. Shepard and his life-partner, Lawrence Tonner, lived here for a year, then returned to Europe, where Shepard pursued a literary career. He died in Los Angeles in 1927.

The villa is at 1925 K St at 20th Ave, just east of I-5. Guided tours are given 10 am to 4:30 pm Friday to Sunday and cost $5, or $4 seniors, $2 ages 6 to 17. For details call ☎ 619-239-2211.

CORONADO (MAP 4)

The laid-back community of Coronado, population 28,500, is right across the bay from downtown San Diego and is a combination of suburbia, retirement village and upscale resort. Administratively, it is a separate city from San Diego. It's known for closely guarding its ambience and environmental quality.

Coronado is joined to the mainland by a spectacular bridge and by a long, narrow sand spit, the Silver Strand, which runs south to Imperial Beach. Nevertheless, it's often referred to as Coronado Island. The locals like to call it 'the Village.' The North Island Naval Air Station occupies the northern end; a big chunk of land that was once an actual island.

In 1888 Elisha Babcock and Hampton Story opened the Hotel del Coronado, the showy centerpiece of a new resort, and by 1900 they were broke. John D Spreckels, the millionaire who, among many other things, bankrolled the first rail line to San Diego, took over Coronado and turned the whole place into a fashionable West Coast gateway.

Information The Coronado Visitors Bureau (☎ 619-437-8788), 1047 B Ave, is open 9 am to 5 pm weekdays, 10 am to 5 pm Saturday and 11 am to 4 pm Sunday. For Coronado background, take a guided 90-minute **Historical Walking Tour** ($8), starting at the Glorietta Bay Inn at 1630 Glorietta Blvd across from the Hotel Del at 11 am Tuesday, Thursday and Saturday. For information call Nancy Cobb at ☎ 619-435-5993.

Coronado Bridge The graceful Coronado Bridge is to San Diego what the Golden Gate is to San Francisco. Inaugurated in August 1969, it created a permanent link between downtown San Diego and Coronado, which had been served by ferries only. The bridge's dramatic 90-degree curve has not only aesthetic value, but also allowed engineers to make it long enough – 2.12 miles – to achieve a 4.67% grade, bringing it to a sufficient height (200 feet at its maximum) to clear all ships except aircraft carriers. Some 68,000 cars drive across it daily; a $1 toll is collected for inbound traffic but carpools are free.

Hotel del Coronado Commonly known as the Hotel Del (☎ 619-435-6611), this place is a much-loved San Diego institution. It's architecturally quirky, with its conical towers, cupolas, turrets, balconies and dormer windows. It's an all-timber building, and the cavernous public spaces reflect the background of railroad depot-designing architects James and Merritt Reed. The acres of polished wood give the interior a warm, old-fashioned feel.

The Del was where Edward (then Prince of Wales) first met Mrs Simpson (then Mrs Spenser) in 1920, though the two did not become an item until some years later. Other hotel guests have included US presidents and other dignitaries – pictures and mementos are displayed in the hotel's History Gallery. Hotel Del starred in the 1959 movie *Some Like It Hot,* which earned it a lasting association with Marilyn Monroe.

In 2000 the hotel underwent a thorough restoration. Historic tours for guests and visitors, normally given daily except Sunday, were suspended but are expected to resume post-renovation. Call, or ask the concierge. See also the San Diego Places to Stay chapter.

Coronado Museum of History and Art Stop by this brand-new, state-of-the-art museum to find out what has made Coronado tick since the day in 1885 when Elisha Babcock and HL Story bought the peninsula for what was then a small fortune, $110,000. Housed in the 1910 Bank of Commerce and Trust Building, the museum has three themed galleries: general city history, the Army and Navy on Coronado, and the Hotel Del. A fourth gallery is used for traveling art exhibits. Period costumes, photographs, letters, maps, menus and other artifacts, many associated with such celebrities as Marilyn Monroe and Frank Baum, creator of the Wizard of Oz, are on display. The museum (☎ 619-435-7242), 1100 Orange Ave, is open 10 am to 4 pm, Sunday from noon, closed Wednesday; admission is $4, or $3 seniors, $2 ages 10 to 18.

Bicycling The best way to spend a day in Coronado is to come by ferry and cruise around by bike. You can rent one at Bike and Surrey Rentals at the Ferry Landing Marketplace for about $5/hour, or bring one on the ferry for 50¢. The main drag across Coronado is Orange Ave, which passes through the well-clipped Spreckels Park and then swings south toward the Hotel del Coronado. There are some designated bicycle routes that avoid Orange Ave (get a map when you rent your bike).

BALBOA PARK

Balboa Park is a beautiful, sprawling expanse of 1200 acres, courtesy of both nature and human ingenuity. The park's gardens, floral beds, shaded groves and generous grassy areas invite strolling, picnicking and relaxing. These are complemented by a cultural cocktail of 15 museums, intriguing architecture, several performance venues and, of course, the world-famous San Diego Zoo.

History

Maps dating from 1868 that show Alonzo Horton's planned additions to San Diego included a 1400-acre park at the northeast corner of what was to become the Downtown area. The decision to provide for a large park is usually attributed to far-sighted civic leaders, but it was also consistent with the short-term interests of the shrewd Mr Horton. By restricting the areas available for future development, the value of the land in his subdivision would be enhanced. Though the expansive park looked good on the map, it was still bare hilltops, chaparral and steep-sided *arroyos* until 1892, when Kate Sessions started her nursery on the site, paying rent to the city in trees (see boxed text 'The Legacy of Kate Sessions').

By the turn of the 20th century, what was originally called City Park had become a well-loved part of San Diego, and a contest was held to find a suitable name. The

BALBOA PARK

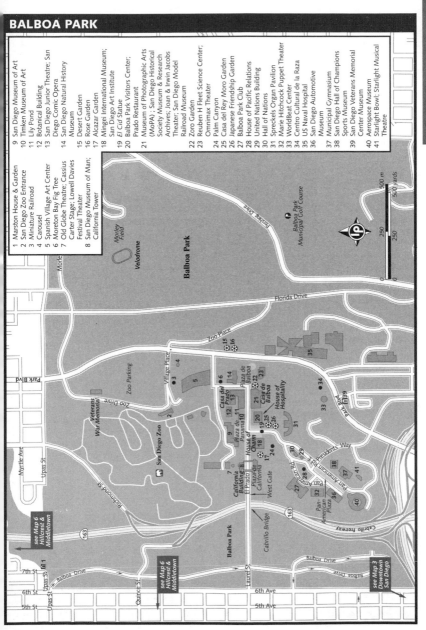

1 Marston House & Garden
2 San Diego Zoo Entrance
3 Miniature Railroad
4 Carousel
5 Spanish Village Art Center
6 Moreton Bay Fig Tree
7 Old Globe Theatre; Cassius
   Carter Stage; Lowell Davies
   Festival Theater
8 San Diego Museum of Man;
   California Tower

9   San Diego Museum of Art
10 Timken Museum of Art
11 Lily Pond
12 Botanical Building
13 San Diego Junior Theatre; San
    Diego Comic Opera
14 San Diego Natural History
    Museum
15 Desert Garden
16 Rose Garden
17 Alcazar Garden
18 Mingei International Museum;
    San Diego Art Institute
19 El Cid Statue
20 Balboa Park Visitors Center;
    Prado Restaurant
21 Museum of Photographic Arts
    (MoPA) ; San Diego Historical
    Society Museum & Research
    Archives; Joan & Irwin Jacobs
    Theater; San Diego Model
    Railroad Museum
22 Zoro Garden
23 Reuben H Fleet Science Center;
    Omnimax Theater
24 Palm Canyon
25 Casa del Rey Moro Garden
26 Japanese Friendship Garden
27 Balboa Park Club
28 House of Pacific Relations
29 United Nations Building
30 Hall of Nations
31 Spreckels Organ Pavilion
32 Marie Hitchcock Puppet Theater
33 WorldBeat Center
34 Centro Cultural de la Raza
35 US Naval Hospital
36 San Diego Automotive
    Museum
37 Municipal Gymnasium
38 San Diego Hall of Champions
    Sports Museum
39 San Diego Veterans Memorial
    Center Museum
40 Aerospace Museum
41 Starlight Bowl; Starlight Musical
    Theatre

winning entry honored Vasco Núñez de Balboa, a Spanish conquistador and the first European to sight the Pacific Ocean.

The 1915–16 Panama-California Exposition, which celebrated the completion of the Panama Canal, went beyond its Spanish Revival theme. Irving Gill's modern, minimalist architecture was rejected in favor of the beaux arts style and baroque decoration of New Yorkers Bertram Goodhue and Carlton Winslow. The exposition buildings were meant to be temporary and were constructed largely of stucco, chicken wire, plaster, hemp and horsehair. They were so popular, however, that many continued to be used. As the originals deteriorated, they were replaced with durable concrete structures. These buildings now house the museums along El Prado, the park's main pedestrian thoroughfare.

The Pacific-California Exposition was staged in Balboa Park in 1935, with new buildings erected southwest of El Prado around the Pan American Plaza. The architectural theme was expanded to include the whole New World, from indigenous styles (some of the buildings have Pueblo Indian and even Mayan and Aztec influences) through to the 20th century. Most of these have been preserved too and now house other exhibits, museums and theaters.

Orientation & Information

The park's main attractions are found in the area bordered by Hwy 163 (Cabrillo Freeway) to the west and Park Blvd to the east. The main east-west thoroughfare is El Prado, anchored by the Plaza de Panama; most of the museums and theaters are along here. More can be found around Pan-American Plaza, southwest of Plaza de Panama. The most stunning architecture is found around Plaza de California, on the western edge. The zoo occupies 200 acres in the northern third of the park. East of Park Blvd are the sports facilities of Morley Field, with tennis courts, a swimming pool, a velodrome, nine- and 18-hole golf courses and 4½ miles of hiking trails through Florida Canyon. About 350 acres have been given over to the Cabrillo Freeway, the US Naval Hospital and other non-park uses.

Balboa Park's Visitors Center (☎ 619-239-0512), in the House of Hospitality at 1549 El Prado, is open daily from 9 am to 4 pm. This is a good place to pick up maps ($1) and free pamphlets and ask the friendly staff questions.

The Legacy of Kate Sessions

Kate O Sessions graduated in botany from the University of California at Berkeley in 1881, a time when few women attended a university and even fewer studied the natural sciences. She came to San Diego as a schoolteacher but soon began working as a horticulturist, establishing gardens for the fashionable homes of the city's emerging elite. In 1892, in need of space for a nursery, she proposed an unusual deal to city officials: She would have the use of 30 acres of city-owned Balboa Park for her nursery in return for planting 100 trees a year and donating 300 others for placement throughout San Diego. The city agreed, and Kate Sessions more than fulfilled her side of the bargain. Within 10 years, Balboa Park had shade trees, lawns, paths and flower beds. Over a 35-year period she planted some 10,000 trees and shrubs, and became known as 'The Mother of Balboa Park.'

In 1910 she moved her nursery to the newly developing suburb of Mission Hills, where she persuaded developers to leave some of the canyons in their natural state. She later moved to Pacific Beach, where her memory has been honored by the creation of Kate Sessions Park. She was an active horticulturist up to the 1930s, working on gardens from Coronado to La Jolla. Her work surrounds the houses of some of San Diego's best-known architects. The trademarks of her style – shady arbors hung with bougainvillea and informal plantings softening steep hillsides – define much of what is lovely today in San Diego landscaping.

- James Lyon

Also for sale here is the Balboa Passport ($25), which is good for one-time entry to each of the park's 13 museums within one week from the day of purchase.

Getting There & Around

Balboa Park is easily reached from Downtown on buses Nos 7, 7A or 7B along Park Blvd. By car, Park Blvd provides access to free parking areas near most of the exhibits, but the most scenic approach is over the Cabrillo Bridge. From the west, El Prado is an extension of Laurel St, which crosses Cabrillo Bridge with the Cabrillo Freeway 120 feet below. Make a point of driving this stretch of freeway (Hwy 163) – the steep roadsides, lush with hanging greenery, look like a rain-forest gorge.

Walking is definitely the best way to get around the park. The footsore can hop on the Balboa Park Tram, which stops at various points on a continuous loop through the main areas of the park. (It's actually a bus not a tram, and is not to be confused with the Old Town Trolley tour bus.)

Plaza de California

If you enter Balboa Park from Cabrillo Bridge – the most scenic approach – this is the first plaza you'll reach and it's also the most visually arresting and architecturally accomplished. En route, you'll pass through the West Gate, the main entrance to the 1915 Panama-California Exposition. Note the figures above the archway, which represent the Atlantic and Pacific Oceans, while the decoration on the arch itself symbolizes the Panama Canal linking the two.

To your left looms the **California Building**, one of Bertram Goodhue's most ornate Spanish Colonial–style creations. It's lorded over by the 200-foot-high California Tower, a San Diego landmark sheathed in blue and yellow ceramic tiles. Its 100-bell carillon chimes every 15 minutes.

The splendid dome behind the tower was inspired by the Hagia Sofia mosque in Istanbul, while the star-shaped design is modeled on the Church of Santa Prisca and San Sebastián in Taxco, Mexico. The pièce de résistance, though, is the building's facade, a veritable tapestry in stone said to be inspired by the churrigueresque church of Tepotzotlán near Mexico City.

Integrated into the dizzying floral ornamentation is a who's who of early San Diego historical figures. The central sculpture at the top is Father Junípero Serra. Shown on the left of the building (top to bottom) are King Philip III of Spain, who sponsored the explorations of Sebastián Vizcaíno, depicted below him; George Vancouver, the first English navigator to reach San Diego Bay in 1783; and Father Luis Jayme, the first missionary to be martyred during a native people's revolt. On the opposite side are (again top to bottom): King Charles I of Spain, the patron of explorer Juan Rodríguez Cabrillo shown below him; Gaspar de Portolá, California's first Spanish governor; and Father Antonio de la Ascención, Vizcaíno's cartographer.

San Diego Museum of Man In the California Building is one of the park's most fascinating museums. Its world-class collection of artifacts – pottery, jewelry, baskets, physical remains – represents a journey through the history of humankind. In the early 20th century, several anthropologists and archeologists led expeditions to the American Southwest, Guatemala, Alaska, Siberia, Africa and the Philippines to amass about 5000 objects. Many of these were displayed in the exhibit 'The Story of Man through the Ages' mounted for the 1915 exposition, and later formed the foundation of the museum. Today, the holdings number more than 70,000.

Permanent exhibits include displays illustrating the customs and traditions of the Kumeyaay, the area's Native American tribe. The museum also has an excellent collection of baskets and pottery from tribes throughout the American Southwest, highlighting their artistic heritage through both current and traditional works.

The museum also tells the story of evolution through fossils, stone tools and dioramas. A primate exhibit compares the skeletons of humans, apes and monkeys. Another exhibit, Life Cycles & Ceremonies,

Balboa Park on a Shoestring

For those with a slim wallet, Balboa Park is a godsend. Spending a few hours strolling around and admiring the gardens and architectural flights of fancy is free and rewarding. But, for culture lovers, there's plenty more to do without spending a penny.

Museums The excellent Timken Museum of Art, the Centro Cultural de la Raza and the Veterans Memorial Center Museum never charge admission. But come to the park on Tuesday for free entry to some of the park's other headliners. Note that admission still applies for special, temporary exhibits. Below is a guide to the museums' free admission days.

First Tuesday of the Month
Reuben H Fleet Science Center
San Diego Model Railroad Museum
San Diego Natural History Museum

Second Tuesday of the Month
Museum of Photographic Arts
San Diego Hall of Champions
Sports Museum
San Diego Historical Society
Museum & Research Archives

Third Tuesday of the Month
Japanese Friendship Garden
Mingei International Museum
San Diego Art Institute
San Diego Museum of Art
San Diego Museum of Man

Fourth Tuesday of the Month
Aerospace Museum
San Diego Automotive Museum

DAVID PEEVERS

San Diego Museum of Man

Walking Tours On Tuesday and Sunday at 1 pm, you can learn more about the park's history or botanical treasures by joining a ranger-led tour. There are also-called Offshoot Tours at 10 am Saturday, with rotating topics: park history (first Saturday), palm trees (second Saturday), introduction to park trees (third Saturday), desert vegetation (fourth Saturday) and the Palisades area where the 1935 exhibition was held (fifth Saturday). Rain or groups smaller than four people cancel the tours, which are also suspended from Thanksgiving to mid-January.

For architecture buffs, the Committee of 100, a preservation group, offers free tours on the first Wednesday of the month at 9:30 am, while birders could join volunteers from the Natural History Museum on monthly tours on the first Thursday of the month, 7:30 to 9:30 am (call ☎ 619-232-3821, ext 7). All tours depart from the visitors center and, except for the birding tour, last one hour.

Concerts On Sunday at 2 pm, the sounds of the mighty Spreckels Organ ring through the park during free hour-long concerts by San Diego civic organist Robert Plimpton and various guest artists. As an encore, the International Organ Festival makes its splash on Monday at 7:30 pm in July and August. Call ☎ 619-702-8138 for details.

Also on Sunday at 2 pm, music and dance performances by international groups take place at the House of Pacific Relations (see that section for details).

looks at how different cultures celebrate such milestones as birth, marriage and death. Life & Death on the Nile, about the ancient Egyptians, provides insight into their everyday rituals as well as preparations for the afterlife.

A recent addition to the museum is the Children's Discovery Center, a playful environment intended to help kids better understand the various exhibits. The inaugural experience had them exploring an Egyptian noble's home and decoding a secret message.

The museum (☎ 619-239-2001) is open 10 am to 4:30 pm daily; admission is $6, or $5 seniors, $3 ages 6 to 17.

Old Globe Theatre Behind the Museum of Man, the Old Globe Theatre complex, which incorporates the Cassius Carter Stage and the outdoor Lowell Davies Festival Theater, is one of San Diego's most beloved thespian venues.

The namesake theater is a replica of Shakespeare's original Old Globe – the 'Wooden O' – which stood on the southern bank of the Thames River from 1599 to 1642. The San Diego version was built for the 1935 Pacific-California Exposition and originally delighted audiences with 40-minute renditions of Shakespeare's greatest hits. Post-exposition it was remodeled into a permanent facility by the nonprofit San Diego Community Theatre. Its first regular season in 1937 opened with John Van Druten's *The Distaff Side*. The cast included Craig Noel who – in true Shakespearean fashion – would guide the theater through the decades as actor, director and artistic director; he continues to serve as executive director to this day.

In 1969, in order too complement its bill of classic plays, the Old Globe converted a former restaurant into the **Cassius Carter Centre Stage** dedicated to experimental theater. Calamity struck in 1978, when much of the complex burned in an arson fire, but the plays went on at the newly built outdoor Festival Stage. It too was later destroyed by arson fire, but rose from the ashes as the **Lowell Davies Festival Theatre**,

which now forms the third part of the Old Globe complex.

The 581-seat Old Globe itself reopened in 1982 with *As You Like It*, then went on to receive a Tony award in 1984 for its ongoing contribution to the theater arts. The company currently does a dozen main productions a year and is the city's biggest arts institution and employer. See the San Diego Entertainment chapter for performance and ticket details.

Plaza de Panama

From Plaza de California a short walk east leads to Plaza de Panama, the park's central square. The equestrian statue on the south side depicts El Cid, who led the Spanish revolt against the Moors in the 11th century.

House of Charm In the plaza's southwest corner stands a Spanish Colonial–style structure known as the **House of Charm**. It dates back to the 1915 Panama-California Exposition but got its name during the 1935 fair, when it was a souvenir market. Badly worn, it was torn down in 1994 and replaced with an exact replica. Today it houses the following two museums.

The **Mingei International Museum**, one of Balboa Park's most intriguing museums, is a world folk art collection of handmade objects from toys to utensils, jewelry to domestic pottery. The museum's unusual name was first coined by a Japanese scholar, Dr Soetsu Yanagi, in the early 20th century; it combines the Japanese words *min* (all people) and *gei* (art), and loosely translates as 'art of the people.' The museum (☎ 619-239-0003) is open 10 am to 4 pm, closed Monday; admission is $5, or $2 ages 6 to 17 and students.

The **San Diego Art Institute** focuses on works by emerging and established San Diego artists. Exhibits change every six weeks and represent many media, including oil, acrylic, watercolor, pen and ink, collage, mixed media, photography and sculpture. The David Fleet Young Artists Gallery presents work produced at area schools. The gallery (☎ 619-236-0011) is open 10 am to 4 pm Tuesday to Saturday, from noon

Sunday; admission is $3, or $2 seniors, free for children under the age of 12.

San Diego Museum of Art Dominating the northern flank of Plaza de Panama, the San Diego Art Museum is considered one of the preeminent of its kind on the West Coast. Its main claims to fame are its extensive collections of Italian Renaissance and Spanish Baroque paintings, but over the years it has branched out to include American, Asian and modern art.

The museum started as the Fine Arts Gallery of San Diego. After the 1915 expo, local leaders felt the fledgling city needed to have its own permanent art collection. Mr and Mrs Appleton Bridges funded the building, and San Diego architect William Templeton Johnson got the design job. Johnson was inspired by the Plateresque, a style in vogue in 16th-century Spain, so called because its elaborate ornamentation resembles filigree silverwork. The façade is particularly ornate, with sculptures of Spanish artists – Ribera, Murillo, El Greco among them – most of whom have pieces in the museum.

Traveling exhibitions of international stature draw the biggest crowds these days, but the permanent collection is also remarkable. Goya's *Marqués de Sofraga* and El Greco's *St Peter Penitent* are among the works by Spanish masters, but there are other great European works, including Gustave Courbet's *Silent Pool* and Rubens' *Allegory of Eternity*. There are also some worthwhile American landscape paintings. Highlights of the modern collection include Dalís *Spectre du Soir* and Matisse's *Bouquet,* as well as works by such favorites as René Magritte, Alexej Jawlensky, Max Beckmann, Georgia O'Keefe and Robert Delaunay.

The museum also owns an impressive amount of Asian art, from millennia-old Chinese jade ornaments and funerary effigies to Japanese armor and lacquerware. The jewels of the Asian collection, though, are the East Indian paintings donated by Edwin Binney in 1991. This collection provides a thorough overview of Indian art through the centuries and is considered the best and most comprehensive assemblage of such work outside of the Indian subcontinent. The museum's Sculpture Garden has pieces by Alexander Calder and Henry Moore.

The museum (☎ 619-232-7931) is open 10 am to 4:30 pm Tuesday to Sunday. Admission is $8, or $6 seniors and ages 18 to 24, $3 ages 6 to 17; ticket prices increase during special exhibits. Free docent tours are offered Tuesday, Wednesday, Thursday and Saturday at 11 am and 1 pm.

Timken Museum of Art Distinctive for *not* being in Spanish Revival style, this 1965 building on the eastern edge of the square houses the Putnam collection. Nicknamed San Diego's 'jewel box for the arts,' it features a small but refined collection of five centuries of European and American master paintings from the early Renaissance through the 19th century. Dutch and Flemish artists such as Rembrandt and Rubens, Frans Hals and Pieter Bruegel the Elder are represented, as are Frenchman Jean Baptiste-Camille Corot, Jacques Louis David and Jean-Honoré Fragonard.

The name dropping continues with American artists such as Albert Bierstadt, John Singleton Copley and Eastman Johnson. There's also a sampling of Italian artists and a wonderful selection of Russian icons. Don't miss the Timken (☎ 619-239-5548), which is free. Hours are 10 am to 4:30 pm Tuesday to Saturday, from 1:30 pm Sunday; closed Monday and the month of September.

House of Hospitality The southeastern corner of the Plaza de Panama is occupied by the House of Hospitality, home to the park's visitors center (see Orientation & Information earlier in this chapter) and the popular Prado restaurant (see the San Diego Places to Eat chapter). It was torn down in 1995 and completely rebuilt by 1997. Of note is the sculpture of a seated Aztec woman *Woman of Tehuántepec* by Donal Hord in the central courtyard; it dates back to the 1935 exhibit.

Spreckels Organ Pavilion It's a short walk from the southern end of Plaza de Panama to the white metal benches that provide seating for concerts played on what is purported to be the world's largest outdoor pipe organ. Housed in an ornate pavilion flanked by a semicircular colonnade, it features 4518 pipes ranging in size from 32 feet to a thumbnail. Donated by John D Spreckels for the 1915 exposition, the organ came with the stipulation that San Diego must have an official organist, a position currently held by Robert Plimpton. See the boxed text 'Balboa Park on a Shoestring' for concert information.

Japanese Friendship Garden Behind the organ, this lovely garden was revamped in 2000 and is again a tranquil place for meditation and contemplation. It is a harmonious fusion of Japanese garden concepts and Zen symbolism with San Diego's climate and the park's topography. A koi pond and waterfall are integrated into a carefully designed environment of azaleas, bamboo, maple, magnolias, pine and other plants and trees. There's a sand and stone garden, a performance area and an exhibit space. Tea ceremonies take place in the new tea house. The garden (☎ 619-232-2721) is open 10 am to 4 pm, closed Monday; admission is $3, or $2.50 seniors, $2 ages 7 to 17.

Pan-American Plaza

This plaza is now a large parking lot southwest of the Spreckels Organ, but during the 1935 Pacific-California Exposition it was anchored by a spectacular fountain nicknamed Singing Fountain for the colorful light and water shows staged here nightly to complement the concerts held at what today is the Starlight Bowl on the plaza's southeastern edge.

As you approach the plaza, the **United Nations Building** is on your right. It houses a Unicef International Gift Shop, open daily, with a good selection of stationery, jewelry and candy; most of its proceeds go back to the artists.

House of Pacific Relations Just south of the United Nations Building, on the plaza's

northeastern edge. the House of Pacific Relations (☎ 619-234-0739) is really a collection of 17 one-story stucco cottages. Left over from the 1915 exposition when each headquartered a participating country, today they showcase the cultural heritage and customs of about 20 different nations. Each country – Argentina to Ukraine – has furnished and decorated its house in traditional ways.

All are open to the public for free from noon to 5 pm every Sunday and on the fourth Tuesday of the month. During those same hours, but only from March to October, an international festival of crafts, foods, arts and traditional costumes takes place in the complex. Each week a different country presents its music and dances during a free performance at 2 pm. On the last Sunday in May there's an ethnic food festival.

Just west of the houses are the **Balboa Park Club** and the **Palisades Building**, home of the Marie Hitchcock Puppet Theatre (see the San Diego Entertainment chapter).

San Diego Automotive Museum Car buffs will delight in the fleet of vintage vehicles – restored to perfection – on view at this museum, which takes visitors on a journey from the classic to the rare, the elegant to the outrageous. Exhibits rotate, but at any given time you might see classics like a wooden 1941 Packard or a shiny 1955 Porsche 550 ('Spyder') sharing space with Lonie Mattar's 'Fabulous $75,000 Cadillac' or a stainless-steel-finish 1981 DeLorean. Motorcycles star in one corner, and there's a comprehensive research library with rare publications, photos and vintage films.

The museum (☎ 619-231-2886) is open 10 am to 4:30 pm (5:30 pm in summer) daily; admission is $7, or $6 seniors, $3 ages 6 to 17.

Aerospace Museum A Balboa Park highlight, this museum on the south end of the plaza captures the mystique of flight in an entertaining and enlightening way. It's worth the admission, but some of the most interesting exhibits are actually on display before you reach the turnstiles.

Outside the circular museum, you'll be greeted by a spy plane Blackbird SR-71, one of the fastest jets ever built, in use from 1966 to 1990. Made almost entirely from titanium (93%), it could fly above 85,000 feet and cover the distance from New York to London in well under two hours. The US military denied its existence until it was partly declassified in the early 1990s.

Inside the entrance rotunda are two more highlights: a replica of the *Spirit of St Louis,* the plane flown by Charles Lindbergh in his 1927 solo crossing of the Atlantic; and a replica of the US Navy's first airplane, the hydroplane Curtiss A-1 Triad, which could operate both on land and sea.

The main exhibit begins with the International Aerospace Hall of Fame, a gallery of oil paintings depicting heroes of air and space flight, including Neil Armstrong, Amelia Earhart, Chuck Yeager and the Wright Brothers. This segues into an engaging chronology of flight, starting with the earliest attempts at overcoming gravity, including Leonardo da Vinci's 'helicopter,' the Montgolfier brothers' balloon and Otto Lilienthal's glider. A replica Wright Flyer, the one the Wright brothers used for the world's first successful powered flight at Kitty Hawk in December 1903, symbolizes the dawn of airplanes.

The beginnings of aerial combat in WWI are depicted with reconstructed fighter planes such as the Spad and the Fokker Triplane, while WWII is represented by a British Spitfire, a Japanese Zero-Sen A6M and a US Hellcat F6F, all of them original. Don't miss the courtyard, where a Phantom jet pursues a Russian MiG-17 between art deco lamp posts. The exhibit concludes with a space-age exhibit, including replicas of Mercury, Gemini and Apollo spacecraft as well as space suits and moon rocks.

The museum also makes a special effort to highlight the accomplishments of airborne women. A separate gallery honors pioneers like Harriet Quimby, the first licensed pilot in the US (1911), and Sally Ride, the first American woman in space (1983).

The Aerospace Museum (☎ 619-234-8291) is open 10 am to 4:30 pm (to 5:30 pm from late May to early September) daily; admission is $8, or $6 seniors, $3 ages 6 to 17.

Just east of here is the **Starlight Bowl**, where the Starlight Musical Theatre presents its annual summer season. It was built for the 1935 exposition and has been remodeled three times. The San Diego Entertainment chapter has details. The next building is the **Municipal Gymnasium**, which was closed at the time of research.

San Diego Hall of Champions Sports Museum This fairly recent addition (mid-1999) to Balboa Park is in the former Federal Building, which easily has the most pleasing architecture on Pan-American Plaza. Its entrance is based on the governor's palace in the ancient Mayan city of Uxmal in the Yucatán, Mexico. Before renovation, it was a single-story gymnasium with badminton and volleyball courts.

The museum is still a work in progress. The ground floor houses the Sportability Challenge, a series of interactive machines for testing various aspects of your fitness, like reaction, strength, flexibility and speed. While this sounds good, many machines were out of order during a recent visit. Upstairs is the Breitbard Hall of Champions, a wall of plaques honoring San Diego sports figures such as baseball player Ted Williams,

football player Marcus Allen, tennis star Maureen Connolly and boater Dennis Conner. In the basement, uniforms, trophies, baseball bats and balls, swimsuits and other sports memorabilia from San Diego sports heroes are enshrined in glass vitrines.

The museum (☎ 619-234-2544) is open from 10 am to 4:30 pm daily and costs $4 adults, $3 seniors and $2 those under 17.

El Prado

This central west-east promenade connects Plaza de California with Plaza de Panama and, finally, with the Plaza de Balboa on the eastern edge.

Botanical Building This building, northeast of the Timken Museum, looks lovely from El Prado, reflected in a large lily pond that was used for hydrotherapy in WWII, when the US Navy took over most of the park. Looking like a giant birdcage, the building's central dome and two wings are covered with redwood lathes, allowing sunlight to filter down on the collection of tropical plants and ferns. It's free, and the planting changes every season (there's a great poinsettia display in December). It's closed Thursday.

Casa del Prado This is one of the handsomest buildings along El Prado, but there is little to draw the visitor inside. It was built for the 1915 exposition, and an earthquake in 1968 caused so much damage that it was condemned. It was rebuilt with the support of community arts groups, who now use it for theater and dance performances (see the San Diego Entertainment chapter).

Casa de Balboa On the south side of El Prado stands the House of Commerce & Industry, now known as Casa de Balboa, which was designed by Goodhue in Spanish Colonial style for the 1915 exposition and later used for a variety of purposes until it burned down in 1978. As were many other park buildings, it was faithfully reconstructed, including concrete decorations cast from pieces of the original. It now

houses three museums, each with a museum shop and small cafe.

The recently doubled gallery space of the **Museum of Photographic Arts** (MoPA), the centerpiece of Casa de Balboa, is characterized by stark white walls, ceilings of cathedral proportions and wooden floors. Together these elements form an ideal backdrop for showing off the masterful 'paintings in light' displayed here during regularly changing exhibitions. Contemporary photographers of international standing are given as much exposure as time-honored artists like Ansel Adams and Bret Weston.

Lectures, workshops and a film series also bring in the crowds, and the bookstore has a huge selection of photo-related books. MoPA (☎ 619-238-7559) is open 10 am to 5 pm daily; admission is $6, or $4 for seniors, students and military. See the San Diego Entertainment chapter for film series information.

Pioneer outpost to high-tech city, the **San Diego Historical Society Museum & Research Archives** leaves no stone unturned when it comes to telling the story of San Diego's rich and sometimes wacky past. Exhibits focus on particular themes, such as the recent 'Weird San Diego,' which introduced visitors to Moro the Human Iceberg and the Human Fly, among others. Other shows are more traditional, like an overview of 20th-century costume history.

For a personal plunge into the city's past, the museum's research archives are a must. Thousands of manuscripts, maps, drawings, books and biographies are waiting to be perused. There's also a historic photo collection with 2 million images from 1867 to the present, a 100-seat theater and a museum store with a good section of San Diego-related books.

The museum (☎ 619-232-6203) is open 10 am to 4:30 pm Tuesday to Sunday; admission is $5, or $4 seniors and students, $2 ages 5 to 12. The archives are open 10 am to 4 pm Thursday to Saturday.

The railroads were instrumental in opening up the western US, a fact paid tribute to in the **San Diego Model Railroad Museum**, the country's largest permanent model and toy train exhibit. Spread over 24,000 sq feet are four giant scale models of actual railroads in the Southwest, including the legendary San Diego & Arizona Eastern route, part of which is used by the San Diego Trolley today. It was known as the 'Impossible Railroad' because of the rough terrain traversed, including the treacherous Carrizo Gorge, with one of the largest timber trestles in the nation. Another model shows the Tehachapi Pass route, characterized by its endless sharp curves. At one point, the engine of a 100-car train crosses directly over its caboose 90 feet below. Kids will like the Toy Train Gallery, where they can play with a Lionel train set.

The museum (☎ 619-696-0199) is open 11 am to 4 pm Tuesday to Friday, to 5 pm on weekends; admission is $4, or $3 seniors, $2.50 students, free if under 15.

Plaza de Balboa

The easternmost plaza in the park is anchored by a magnificent gushing fountain that delights young and old on those hot summer days.

Reuben H Fleet Science Center On the south side of Plaza de Balboa is this popular hands-on science museum-cum-Omnimax theater. It's named for its main benefactor, Reuben H Fleet, an army major who, in 1918, commanded the first unit to fly US mail from New York to Washington DC.

The Science Center is divided into several interactive areas. Things kick off with **Explorazone**, where kids push buttons, twist knobs and slide levers in a series of displays and 'experiments' intended to teach basic scientific principles. From here it's off to 'virtual reality.' In **Meteor Storm**, you become part of a video story where you blast through space on 'hover sleds' while trying to avoid a swarm of meteorites. The meteorite theme continues in **Suitors**, a motion-simulator ride where passengers become scientists working on preventing a meteor's collision with Earth. From out of this world, it's back to **TechnoVation**, which showcases recent accomplishments in

science and technology by San Diego's high-tech companies.

Perhaps even more popular than the exhibits is the **Omnimax Theater** (see Cinemas in the San Diego Entertainment chapter).

Science Center (☎ 619-238-1233) hours vary by season, but doors are usually open from 9:30 am to 6 pm Monday and Tuesday and to 9 pm the rest of the week. Admission to the exhibits only is $6.50 for anyone over 13, or $5 for seniors and ages 3 to 12.

San Diego Natural History Museum On the north side of Plaza de Balboa, this museum in a 1933 William Templeton Johnson building was enlarged and renovated in 2000. It houses exhibits focused on the evolution and diversity of Southern California and Baja California, boasting plenty of rocks, fossils and stuffed animals, as well as an impressive collection of dinosaur skeletons and a California fault-line exhibit to liven things up a bit. In the Desert Discovery Lab you can study plants, insects and other animals, while the Hall of Desert Ecology features rock wall grottoes with live scorpions and tarantulas.

The museum also displays the largest rattlesnake collection in the country, a fin whale skull that is 20 feet long, and other whale skeletal parts displayed in Whale Hall. There are special children's programs almost every Saturday and Sunday. The museum (☎ 619-232-3821) is open 9:30 am to 4:30 pm daily (to 5:30 pm from June to September). Admission varies by exhibit but is usually about $7 with discounts for seniors, students and children. The museum also arranges field trips and nature hikes in Balboa Park and farther afield.

Spanish Village Art Center Behind the Natural History Museum is a grassy square with a magnificent **Moreton Bay fig tree** (sorry, no climbing). Opposite is a group of small tiled cottages, billed by park authorities as 'an authentic reproduction of an ancient village in Spain,' which are rented out as artists' studios. You can watch potters, jewelers, glass blowers, painters and sculptors churn out pricey decorative items,

11 am to 4 pm daily. North of the Spanish Village Art Center is a 1924 **carousel** and a **miniature railroad**; both operate from 11 am to 4:30 pm on weekends and holidays (daily in summer) and charge $1 per ride.

Along Park Boulevard

Park Blvd is the main thoroughfare through the park; it separates the cultural section in the west from the more utilitarian eastern side. On the southern end of this side is the huge US Naval Hospital. Vast areas north and farther east are set aside for recreational sports at Morley Field, where you'll find a tennis club, a municipal pool, baseball diamonds, an 18-hole golf course and even a Frisbee golf course.

WorldBeat Center Dedicated to African and African American arts and culture, this center (☎ 619-210-1190) hosts art exhibits and film series, as well as dance and other performances to raise cultural awareness and pride among blacks. A series of workshops, including African dance and drum making, are offered; also on site is KWBC 89.1, a 24-hour reggae radio station.

Centro Cultural de la Raza What World-Beat Center is for African Americans, the Centro is for Latinos. The two even share an outdoor amphitheater, where ceremonial dances and rituals are held. The Centro (☎ 619-235-6135) is in a circular steel building that's actually a converted water tank decorated with impressive and bright murals. Of note is the art gallery, open noon to 5 pm Thursday to Sunday; free ($3 suggested donation).

San Diego Veterans Memorial Center Museum Across the street, this museum honors those who served their country in all branches of the military, through displays of documents, memorabilia and historical objects going back to the Civil War. It is in the former chapel of the US Naval Hospital (☎ 619-239-2300) and is open 10 am to 4 pm daily with free admission (donations welcome). Tours run by docents, who are veterans, run throughout the day.

Gardens of Balboa Park

Balboa Park includes a number of garden areas, embodying distinct horticultural styles and geographical zones. To learn more about the gardens, take a free weekly Offshoot Tours (see the boxed text 'Balboa Park on a Shoestring'). If you're exploring on your own, visit (from west to east):

Alcazar Garden, just east of Plaza de California, is a formal, Spanish-style garden with trimmed hedges, flowerbeds, colorful tiles and fountains; it was modeled on the gardens of the Alcazar palace in Seville, Spain.

Palm Canyon, south of the House of Charm, has more than 50 species of palms, as well as magnolia trees.

Casa del Rey Moro Garden, south of the House of Hospitality, recreates the Moorish gardens of Ronda, southern Spain, birthplace of the bullfight.

Zoro Garden is a sunken rock garden adjacent to the Casa de Balboa on the south side of El Prado. A nudist colony during the 1935 exhibition, it now contains a butterfly garden.

Rose Garden has 2400 roses representing some 180 varieties; peak blooming season is April and May, although many go strong until December.

Desert Garden, north of the footbridge that enters Plaza de Balboa, has plenty of cacti, aloes and agaves and is most interesting in winter.

Florida Canyon, east of Park Blvd, provides an idea of the San Diego landscape before the Spanish settlement. The Natural History Museum (☎ 619-232-3821) conducts guided walks in the canyon.

San Diego Zoo

The zoo is one of San Diego's biggest attractions, and anyone interested in the natural world should allow a full day to see it. More than 3800 animals, representing more than 800 species, are exhibited in a beautifully landscaped setting, typically in enclosures that replicate their natural habitats.

History The San Diego Zoo began with the 1915 Panama-California Exposition and the enthusiasm of one local man, Dr Harry Wegeforth. The exposition featured an assortment of animals in cages along Park Blvd. It's now San Diego folklore that

Wegeforth, hearing the roar of one of the caged lions, exclaimed, 'Wouldn't it be wonderful to have a zoo in San Diego? I believe I'll build one.' He started his campaign in 1916 in the newspaper and soon formed the Zoological Society of San Diego. By pulling a few strings, Dr Wegeforth then ensured that quarantine requirements made it almost impossible to remove exotic animals from the county, so the society was able to acquire much of the menagerie left over from the exposition.

As a private organization, the Zoological Society could not be given a site on public land, but in 1921 a nice compromise was reached. The society donated all the animals and facilities to the city, and the city provided 200 acres of Balboa Park to use as a zoo to then be administered by the society. Though the site was bisected by canyons and largely barren, these problems were turned to advantage: canyons provided a means of separating different groups of animals to prevent the spread of disease, and could be landscaped to simulate appropriate natural settings.

Wegeforth had a talent for extracting money from wealthy benefactors – sugar king John D Spreckels warned that the wily surgeon would 'cut you off at the pockets.' One of the first big donations was from newspaper heiress Ellen Browning Scripps, who paid for a perimeter fence, which was to enforce the payment of admission fees as much as to keep the animals in.

Local support for the zoo meant that unorthodox ways were often found to add to its collection. San Diegans brought in various finds, such as seals and snakes, which were never refused. Rattlesnakes caught in Balboa Park were often profitably traded for animals from other zoos. In one exchange, the zoo provided fleas for a New York flea circus.

The US Navy unofficially contributed an assortment of animals that had been adopted as mascots but could no longer be kept on ships. US Marines landing in Nicaragua were offered prizes if they captured beasts for Dr Wegeforth. During the 1930s Wegeforth himself traveled the world, collecting jaguars from Venezuela, orangutans from Borneo and marsupials from Australia. On a trip to India, Wegeforth contracted pneumonia and malaria; he died in 1941. His final contributions to the zoo were

---

Panda-Mania at the San Diego Zoo

When Bai Yun and her mate Shi Shi arrived in San Diego in 1996 it was to begin a 12-year study to help the Chinese government and conservationists understand and protect the endangered giant panda species. Bai Yun's life had been rather cushy in panda terms: She was born in the Wolong Giant Panda Conservation Center in central China. Shi Shi's road to San Diego was a little rockier. He was found ripped to pieces and near death in China's Sichuan Province, the presumed victim of an assault by another male panda. Fortunately, Chinese and World Wildlife Fund veterinarians were able to restore him enough to survive – though no longer in the wild. But Bai Yun and Shi Shi took to each other and the result – Hua Mei – was born on August 21, 1999, the first giant panda born in the Western Hemisphere since 1990.

Bai Yun quickly proved that her maternal instincts hadn't been dulled by captivity, and the 5-ounce cub soon began to flourish. Though no longer dwelling in the Chinese mountains at heights between 4000 and 12,000 feet, the panda family seems destined to draw throngs of adoring visitors for years to come. Most likely, they'll be able to observe them doing what they do best: eating. Panda's spend about 12 hours a day feeding, and that's a lot of bamboo – and entertainment. For a sneak preview, check out the Panda Cam at the zoo web Site at www.sandiegozoo.com.

- David Peevers

three elephants, which arrived in San Diego two months after his death.

By the end of WWII, the San Diego Zoo had a worldwide reputation, and it helped to rebuild the collections of European zoos that had been devastated by the war. The Zoological Society continued at the forefront of zoo management with the introduction of 'bioclimatic' habitats, which allowed different types of animals to share a simulated natural environment. In the 1960s the society started work on an 1800-acre Wild Animal Park, 32 miles north of Downtown (see the Escondido section in the San Diego Excursions chapter), which now provides free-range areas for many large animals.

Information The zoo (☎ 619-234-3153) is in the northern part of Balboa Park and has a free parking lot off Park Blvd. Bus No 7 will get you there from Downtown. The information booth is just to the left of the entrance as you come in – if you want to leave the zoo and return, get your hand stamped here.

Opening hours vary by season, so call before you visit. In summer, hours are often extended until 10 pm. The regular daily admission price is $18, or $8 ages 3 to 11. The deluxe admission package costs $26/14 and includes a 40-minute guided bus tour as well as a round-trip 'Skyfari' aerial tram ride. Discount zoo coupons are widely available. A combined ticket will enable you to visit both the San Diego Zoo and the Wild Animal Park within a five-day period costs $38.35/23.15.

It's wise to arrive early, as many animals are most active in the morning. You might start with a tour in a double-decker bus, which gives you a good overview and includes an informative commentary. Animal shows are held in the two amphitheaters (no extra charge), and they're usually entertaining, especially for kids who might need a rest anyway. The Skyfari cable car crosses the park and can save you some walking time, though you might have to wait in line for it. Facilities are provided for disabled visitors – call the zoo (☎ 619-231-1515 ext 4526) for specific information.

For more thorough commentary on the various exhibits, rent a Zoophone, an audio guide available in English, Spanish, French, Japanese and German, for $4.

Highlights The zoo and the Wild Animal Park share an active program of breeding endangered species in captivity for reintroduction into their natural habitats. This has been done with a number of species, including the Arabian oryx, the Bali starling and the California condor.

The zoo gardens are well-known. They now include some plants that are used for the specialized food requirements of particular animals.

The zoo has expanded its entertainment and educational role in the community with the opening of a children's zoo exhibit (where youngsters can pet small critters) and of outdoor theaters for animal shows. Both children and adults will enjoy the animal nursery, home to the zoo's newest arrivals.

Most visitors will have their own favorites. The koalas are so popular here that

RICHARD CUMMINS

Butterfly, San Diego Wild Animal Park

Australians may be surprised to find them an unofficial symbol of San Diego. The Komodo dragon, an Indonesian lizard that grows up to 10 feet long, not only looks fearsome but strides around the reptile house in a menacing manner.

Tiger River, a realistic, re-created Asian rain forest, is one of the newer bioclimatic exhibits. Gorilla Tropics is an African rain forest. A third bioclimatic environment is the Sun Bear Forest, where Asian bears are famously playful.

The large Scripps Aviary and Rainforest Aviary are both impressive structures, where carefully placed feeders allow some close-up viewing. Finally, don't miss the African Rock Kopje (outcrop), where klipspringers (small antelopes) demonstrate their rock-climbing agility.

OLD TOWN (MAP 5)

Old Town is the birthplace of San Diego and, by extension, of California. It was here Padre Junípero Serra established the Mission de San Diego de Alcalá, the first of his chain of 21 missions. It was protected by a presidio (fort), from which sprang the first Spanish civilian settlement in California – the Pueblo de San Diego in 1835.

This square mile of land (10 times what is there today) remained the center of American San Diego until the fire of 1872, after which the city's focus moved to Horton's 'New Town' subdivision in what is today's Downtown.

Old Town experienced decades of decay and decline until John D Spreckels built a trolley line from New Town in the 1920s and, to attract passengers, began tinkering with the old district. It would be another four decades before the old settlement's historic significance was recognized. In 1968 the historic core of the area was declared the Old Town State Historic Park, archaeological work began and several surviving buildings were restored. Other structures were rebuilt, and the area is now a six-block pedestrian district (there are parking lots around the edges) with shade trees, a large open plaza and a cluster of shops and restaurants.

The Old Town Transit Center, on the trolley line at Taylor St at the northwest edge of Old Town, is a stop for the *Coaster* commuter train, the San Diego Trolley (red line) and buses Nos 4 and 5 from Downtown; Old Town Trolley tours stop southeast of the plaza on Twiggs St.

Information

The Old Town State Historic Park Visitor's Center (☎ 619-220-5427) is in the Robinson-Rose House on the northwest end of the plaza and is open 10 am to 5 pm daily. If you're interested in historical background, pick up a copy of the *Old Town San Diego State Historic Park Tour Guide & Brief History* ($2). A highlight here is a model of Old Town in 1872. There are free ranger-led tours at 11 am and 2 pm daily.

Walking Tour

For those who want to explore on their own, here is a spin around Old Town that highlights the most important sites within the state historic park and the surrounding areas, including Heritage Park and Presidio Hill. Unless noted, exhibits are open 10 am to 5 pm and are free.

The tour starts at the visitors center in the **Robinson-Rose House**. Built by Texan lawyer James Robinson in 1853 as his family home, it also housed the offices of the railroad and of the short-lived *San Diego Herald,* the fledgling pueblo's first newspaper. James' widow sold the building to one Louis Rose in 1857, who all but abandoned it after a fire destroyed the roof in 1874.

The Robinson-Rose House opens onto the large and shady **Old Town Plaza**. The center of social life under Mexican rule, this was where retired soldiers took their ladies for a spin and where bullfights and bearbaiting entertained the crowds. On July 28, 1846, the American flag flapped in the California breeze for the first time from the pole in the center of the plaza. Renamed Washington Square, it remained the heart of the young community under the Americans. Walk along the right (southwestern) side of the plaza. The reconstructed buildings here, now overpriced kitsch shops, once housed general stores, a bank, gaming halls and boarding houses, as well as saloons where settlers celebrated or drowned their sorrows; arguments would often end in gunfights.

Along here you'll find the **Casa de Machado y Silvas** (1830), where the Mexican flag was hidden during the Mexican-American War. In 1854 it became the Commercial Restaurant, which has been re-created, complete with set tables. Two doors southeast is the **Colorado House** (1851), which began life as a hotel and is now the Wells Fargo History Museum (☎ 619-238-3929). Established after the great California gold rush of the late 1840s, the Wells Fargo Co, through its banking and stagecoach operations, became synonymous with the establishment of the American West. This one-room museum relives that era with an 1867 stagecoach, maps, photos and early coins and scales.

The building next door was San Diego's first **courthouse** (1848). Built by Mormon soldiers, it was also the office of the mayor, city clerk and other officials after San Diego became the first incorporated city in California in 1850.

Turn right onto a dirt walkway, over to the one-room **Mason Street School** (1865), the city's first public school and now a museum (☎ 619-297-1183); it is open daily from 10 am to 4 pm. (See the boxed text 'Ahead of Her Time.') Behind the school is the **Casa Machado Stewart** (1838), an original adobe with old-timey furnishings and vegetable garden.

Backtrack along Mason St, northeast of the schoolhouse, and head for the magnificent **Casa de Estudillo**, on the far side of San Diego Ave. The largest and most famous of the original adobe mansions, it was built in 1829 by Presidio commandant Jose María de Estudillo as his private residence, and remained in the family until 1887. Restored by John D Spreckels in 1910, the large home has period rooms with beamed ceilings, brick floors and whitewashed walls. There's also an outdoor kitchen and garden courtyard. Get a self-guided tour map at the house.

Back on San Diego Ave, just southeast of Mason St, is the **Dental Museum**, which sheds lights on 19th century dentistry techniques. Torture instruments such as the Morrison dental engine, drill and extraction forceps are on display, as is a dental chair and ancient dentures.

Across the street is the **San Diego Union Museum** (1854), where the *Union*'s first edition was published in October 1868. A four-page weekly, it contained a few ads, short stories and anecdotes – but very little news! Inside you can see the actual printing press and the editor's office. The structure, incidentally, was the area's first prefab wood frame, shipped around Cape Horn from Maine in 1851.

Next up, at the corner of San Diego Ave and Twiggs St, is the **Chapel of the Immaculate Conception**, the oldest church in San Diego aside from the Mission. It was built in the 1850s as a private home and converted by a wealthy local rancher who had pledged to give San Diego its first parish church if the lawsuit in which he was embroiled ended successfully for him. He's buried in

Ahead of Her Time

San Diego's first teacher was Mary Chase Walker, a determined and headstrong woman who had come to California in 1865 from Massachusetts. At the Old Town Mason Street School, she taught about 35 children in all eight grades in a single room with no plumbing, and with heating solely by an iron stove. According to her memoirs, tardiness among the kids was common because clocks were not, and attendance was sporadic, largely because of the many fiestas and bullfights. Mary lasted 11 months, forced to resign when enrollment dropped after she had lunch with a black woman. She married one of the few people who supported her, school board president Edward Morse, and spent the rest of her life working for the suffragette movement and supporting causes of the poor.

one of the side chapels. Unfortunately, church doors are often locked.

Twiggs St marks the southeastern border of the state historic park. One of the most intriguing sites in the rest of Old Town is the **Whaley House** (1856), a nondescript structure at the corner of San Diego Ave and Harney St. It is the city's oldest brick building, conceived and constructed by the ingenious Thomas Whaley, San Diego's first brickmaker, who used seashells as the main ingredient for the plaster and mortar. Aside from being home to five generations of Whaleys, the building has been a granary, courthouse, theater, saloon, dairy, Sunday school, hall of records, general store and funeral parlor. What's more, in the early 1960s it was *officially* certified as haunted by the US Department of Commerce (see boxed text 'The Horror! The Horror!').

If you dare go inside, you'll see a moderately interesting collection of period furniture, including a piano from the movie *Gone with the Wind*, plus a life mask of Abraham Lincoln and various other odds and ends. The home (☎ 619-298-2482) is open 10 am to 4:30 pm daily (closed Tuesday from October to May); admission is $4, or $3 seniors, $2 ages 5 to 17.

From here you could make a little detour three blocks farther southeast to **El Campo Santo**, San Diego's first cemetery, or just turn right (northeast) on Harney St and walk a block to Juan St. On your right, on a gentle hillside, is **Heritage Park**, a 7.8-acre park with six magnificent Victorian homes moved here, to Heritage Park Row, after WWII when Downtown expansion threatened their demolition. The county now leases them to private or corporate entities, which must guarantee their preservation. You'll find shops, a lawyer's office, nonprofits, a tea parlor and even a B&B (see the San Diego Places to Stay chapter).

The first large building at the end of the lawn is the **Temple Beth Israel**, San Diego's first synagogue built in Classic Revival style in 1889 and now used for weddings, receptions and bar mitzvahs. The first house up Heritage Park Row is the rather plain **Senlis Cottage** (1896), a pale pink structure once inhabited by Eugene Senlis, an employee of Balboa Park 'mother' Kate Sessions. It is almost dwarfed by its next-door neighbor, the exuberant **Sherman Gilbert House**, a splendid confection built in 1887 in the so-called 'Stick Eastlake' style. Its later owners, the sisters Bess and Gertrude Gilbert, both art patrons, brought glamour to the place by hosting receptions featuring performers such as dancer Anna Pavlova and pianist Artur Rubinstein.

Next up is the Italianate **Bushyhead House** (1887), first inhabited by the *San Diego Union*'s owner, who doubled as the town's police chief. Atop the hill you will find the elegant **Christian House** (1879), now a B&B. Built in quintessential Queen Anne–style, it features a romantic veranda and fairytale turrets topped by slate 'witch's hats.'

On the west side of the walkway are the **McConaughy House** (1887), once a hospital and now a gift shop, and the less frilly **Burton House** (1893), where you can relive the period over a cuppa English tea.

Across from Heritage Park, at the corner of Juan and Harney Sts, is the **Mormon Battalion Memorial Visitor's Center**, which commemorates the tribulations endured by 500 Mormons during their 2000-mile march from the mustering station in Fort Leavenworth, Iowa, to San Diego to aid American troops during the Mexican-American War (32 of them died). It is considered the longest infantry march in history.

Inside there isn't much to see, but a member of the Church of Latter-Day Saints, which runs the center, will swoop on you the moment you step through the door and happily flesh out the story. Afterward, you will be asked to view a 20-minute movie – unless you're keen on learning more about the Mormon Church, decline the offer with a polite smile and leave. The center (☎ 619-298-3317) is open daily from 9 am to 9 pm and admission is free.

Continue on Juan St, where, at the corner of Mason St, the **Casa de Carillo** (1820) was the first private house in San Diego; it's now the pro shop for the Presidio Hills Golf Course. Turning left (southwest) on Mason

St takes you back to the plaza. On your left is the magnificent **Casa de Bandini**, the private home of Juan Bandini and his family. It was bought by stagecoach baron

---

The Horror! The Horror!

'Is that your final answer?' It's possible that these were the words spoken by game show host Regis Philbin – then a local San Diego media celebrity – when ghosts accosted him in the bewitched Whaley House. This particular 'bump in the night' rocketed San Diego's most famous haunt into the airways and saw it designated by the US Department of Commerce as an officially haunted house in the early '60s. A government-certified spook house? Go figure. But since that time the Whaley House has become a destination, not only for the undead but for tourists as well. Heed ye the 'facts.'

Thomas Whaley from New York came to California in the Gold Rush year of 1849 and eventually settled in San Diego in 1855. And, by various accounts, he and his wife Anna have 'lived' here ever since, part of a gaggle of dissatisfied souls not willing to shuffle off this mortal coil peacefully. Family pets, a child whose throat was slashed by a clothesline and who died in one of the Whaleys' arms, and the Whaleys themselves. Even good old 'Yankee Jim Robinson,' a thief who apparently tried to steal a local schooner, still hangs around the property, where he was hung: on the very spot where Whaley witnessed the execution shortly before buying the house.

Crying children, odd scents from a nonexistent kitchen and the occasional floating by of the various denizens may raise the hair on the back of your neck. But what's really a pleasure in this city of military might and material obsession is this palpable connection with the 'great beyond,' manifest in its storied house of the undead. Why so many have been seduced to the site of so much death, and afterlife, you'll have to divine for yourself. If you dare! Ha-Ha-Haaaar!

– David Peevers

Albert Seeley and turned into the Cosmopolitan Hotel, which, for many years, served as the social heart of Old Town. It is now an excellent Mexican restaurant (see the San Diego Places to Eat chapter) and has a beautiful courtyard and rooms decorated with antiques and curios.

Seeley and the stagecoach era are recalled next door in the **Seeley Stables**, an intriguing museum that on the ground floor chronicles the history of stagecoach travel, then, upstairs, examines Native American history. It's open daily from 10 am to 9 pm; there's also a small visitors center.

Stroll over to the plaza's northwest corner to the **Bazaar del Mundo**, a colorful labyrinth of shops and restaurants, the most touristy part of Old Town, but fun nevertheless. It is the brainchild of design artist Diane Powers, whose vision turned an abandoned motel court into this bright oasis three decades ago. Ponder the day's events over a cappuccino or margarita, or browse through the Mexican and South American folk art for sale. Depending on that day's schedule, you may also be showered with the sonorous sounds of strolling mariachis or be treated to a tribal dance. If you need to replenish energies, there are five restaurants, some of them quite good (see the San Diego Places to Eat chapter).

Depending on your constitution, you could conclude your tour right here, or head over the hill to the site of the original mission and fort.

Presidio Hill

In 1769 Father Junípero Serra and Gaspar de Portolá established the first Spanish settlement in California on Presidio Hill. Sometimes referred to as 'Plymouth Rock of the West,' it overlooks the valley of the San Diego River. Before the Spaniards arrived, the native Tipai-Kumeyaay people used this hill for sacred ceremonies. In 1774 the mission was moved to a site in today's Mission Valley, about 5 miles east, but the presidio remained and grew into a bustling colony. Its decline began when Mexico gained independence from Spain in 1821 and the soldiers began moving down the hill into today's Old Town.

Nothing remains of the original buildings, although with some imagination their outline may still be divined underneath the neatly kept lawns.

Walk up from Old Town along Mason St and get excellent views of San Diego Bay and Mission Valley. Atop the hill, Presidio Park has a few walking trails and shaded benches. A large cross, constructed with tiles from the original mission, commemorates Padre Serra; it stands on the site of the Presidio commandant's house.

Junípero Serra Museum The beautiful building that houses this museum is a Spanish Colonial style structure conceived by the prolific William Templeton Johnson in 1929. The views from the 70-foot tower are tremendous. Inside is an interesting collection of artifacts and pictures from the Mission and rancho periods. Clothing, furniture, tools, ceramics, even a cannon and cannonball provide an introduction to the earliest days of European settlement, through the presidio's abandonment in 1837. Many of the items were unearthed during the museum's excavations (still ongoing) throughout the original settlement. The museum (☎ 619-297-3258) is open 10 am to 4:30 pm Friday to Sunday; admission is $5, under 13 free.

Fort Stockton Up the hill from the museum, a flagpole, cannon, some plaques and earth walls comprise the Fort Stockton Memorial, named for commander Robert Stockton, who took over the prior fort for the Americans in 1847. Its origin goes back to 1838, still the Mexican period, when San Diegans defended themselves against attacks from northern forces. In 1846, when marines of the USS *Cyane* seized San Diego, it was renamed Fort Dupont after the sloop's commander. After he and his men left, Mexicans retook the pueblo but were eventually subdued by Stockton. The nearby El Charro Statue, a bicentennial gift to the city from Mexico, depicts a Mexican cowboy on horseback.

MID-CITY

This section covers the neighborhoods of Hillcrest, Middletown and Mission Valley, which lie north of Downtown but east of I-5, along I-8 and west of I-805.

Hillcrest (Map 6)

Hillcrest, the first suburban real estate development in San Diego, is north and west of Balboa Park. Its main artery is University Ave. Here you'll see the work of many of San Diego's best-known architects from the early 20th century, including Irving Gill and William Templeton Johnson. The Mediterranean and Spanish Colonial styles, as well as the influence of the Arts and Crafts movement, make an interesting contrast with the Victorian houses from an earlier era.

Hillcrest is one of San Diego's liveliest and most eclectic areas, and the center of its gay and lesbian community. To look around, start at the **Hillcrest Gateway**, a neon arch across University Ave at 5th Ave, the commercial hub of the neighborhood. North on 5th Ave, between University Ave and Washington St, is the colorfully postmodern **Village Hillcrest Center**. There you will find the **Hillcrest Cinemas** multiplex, restaurants and shops, as well as News Etc, a newsstand with a great selection. South on 5th Ave is an interesting block of stores selling vintage clothing, music and books (see the San Diego Shopping chapter). Go east on University Ave to No 535, the 1928 **Kahn Building** – an original Hillcrest commercial building with architectural elements that border on kitsch.

A few blocks farther east, accessible from the northeastern corner of the parking lot behind the Ralph's supermarket at 1020 University Ave, is an unusual piece of award-winning public art: the **Vermont Street Pedestrian Bridge**. Thanks to John D Spreckels, a bridge had connected the hip 'hood of Hillcrest with tony University Heights immediately to the north since 1923. By the late 1970s, however, termites has feasted their way through most of the wooden trestles, so the unsafe bridge was torn down. Its replacement, inaugurated in 1994, is a 416-foot cobalt-blue creation courtesy of the local all-woman design team of Stone Paper Scissors. Quotes from Dr Seuss, Kate Sessions, Irving Gill and even a fortune cookie have been etched into the 32 stainless steel panels that serve as the railings. The walkway features a Zen-inspired geometric design sandblasted into the rock and concrete. To reflect the different characters of the adjacent neighborhoods, the pattern becomes softer and more organic as it moves toward University Heights, a residential neighborhood of Craftsman-style bungalows.

Bankers Hill In the late 19th and early 20th centuries, it became fashionable to live in the area north of Downtown and west of Balboa Park. Many San Diego professionals built stately homes here, earning the neighborhood the moniker Bankers Hill, or Pill Hill. Until I-5 was built, these upscale heights had unobstructed views of the bay and of Point Loma. The area plunged into decline in the 1960s when modernism ruled, but recovered in the 1980s when preservation concerns moved to the forefront.

A few ornate Victorian mansions survive, notably the 1889 **Long-Waterman House**, 2408 1st Ave. Easily recognized by its towers, gables, bay windows and veranda, it was the home of former California governor Robert Waterman. Also notable is the **Timkin House**, one block to the north.

A quirky neighborhood landmark is the 375-foot long **Spruce St Footbridge** that spans a deep arroyo (canyon) between Front and Brant Sts. This miniature 'Golden Gate' suspension bridge dates from 1912, when it served as a shortcut for crossing over to the streetcar stop on 4th Ave. You can walk along its rustic planks, come nose to leaf with eucalyptus trees or sway – gently or not so gently – above the ravine.

A bit farther east on Spruce St is the **Spruce Street Forum**, a small but elegant venue with top-notch performers (see the San Diego Entertainment chapter). While here, also pop in at the **Porter Troupe Gallery** (☎ 619-292-9096), which focuses on introducing art by under-represented groups (mostly ethnic minorities and African Americans). It's open Tuesday to Saturday 1 to 6 pm.

South of here is the **Quince Street Bridge**, a more solid canyon crossing, whose wooden trestles have been anchored in the soil since 1905. It was refurbished in 1988 after its slated demolition was vigorously protested by community activists.

DAVID PEEVERS

Quince Street Bridge

Marston House & Garden On the northwestern edge of Balboa Park, at 3525 7th Ave, is the former home of George Marston, department store magnate, philanthropist and founder of the San Diego Historical Society. The house was designed in 1904 by William Hebbard and Irving Gill and is a fine example of the American Craftsman style. The interior is a showcase of period furnishings and decorative objects by top manufacturers like Stickley, Ellis and Roycroft; Tiffany lamps provide atmospheric lighting. Incongruously, there's also an exhibit of pottery and Native American baskets. The house (☎ 619-298-3142) has a romantic English garden and is open 10 am to 4:30 pm Friday to Sunday; admission is $5, or $4 seniors and students.

Middletown (Map 6)

Middletown lies north and east of I-5. Part of it overlaps Little Italy, which is covered in the Downtown section earlier in this chapter. Largely residential, Middletown doesn't have much in the way of sightseeing, but is full of interesting places to stay, eat, dance and listen to music (see the San Diego Places to Eat, Places to Stay and Entertainment chapters for details).

The two most happening streets are India St, which parallels I-5, and Washington`St. There's a shingled complex where the two intersect, once known as the **India Street Art Colony**. Opened in the 1970s by architect and artist Raoul Marquis, the space's art studios, import shops and theaters have been replaced by an excellent cafe and some first-rate inexpensive eateries. Across I-5 on Washington St, the **Mission Brewery Plaza** brewed Bavarian beer from 1913 to 1918 before Prohibition closed it down. It switched to processing seaweed (used as a food thickener and coloring agent) for American Agar until 1987. In 1989 the original chimney, tile roof and cupola, which were exempted from coastal height limitations, were restored, and the plaza was put on the National Register of Historic Places. It's now a business complex and is mostly just interesting from afar.

Noteworthy **private homes** around here include 4346 Valle Vista, the former home of architect Richard Requa, who designed many of the 1935 Pacific-California Exposition buildings. Also look for William Templeton Johnson's former residence, at 4520 Trias St.

Mission Valley (Map 7)

Mission Valley, bordered on the south by I-8, has a handful of interesting and historic sights. The freeway parallels the San Diego River, once the most reliable source of freshwater for the crops and the livestock of the early missions. The river valley was frequently flooded until, in the mid-1950s, dams were completed upstream. In the 1950s and '60s there was disagreement over the valley's development, but I-8 now runs its length and is dotted with hotels and shopping centers. Some green, open space remains, but much of that is golf courses and country clubs. The restored Mission San

Diego de Alcalá is definitely worth a visit, but Mission Valley's most touted feature now is its triad of shopping centers: Fashion Valley, the Hazard Center and Mission Valley Center.

The San Diego Trolley runs the length of the valley, from Downtown to the mission, with stops at Qualcomm Stadium and all the shopping centers (see the San Diego Shopping chapter for details).

Mission San Diego de Alcalá The first in the chain of 21 California missions, San Diego de Alcalá is a long rectangle in typically modest Spanish Mission style, with a flat, beamed ceiling, a brick floor and whitewashed, sparsely ornamented walls. A side door opens to the nicest part of the complex, the little garden, a peaceful oasis with a lush profusion of botanical wonders. A gleaming white statue of St Francis (with the dove) and a bronze sculpture of Serra peek out from a backdrop of palm trees, cacti and bougainvillea; it's all lorded over by a 46-feet *campanario* (bell tower). On the other side of the church, near the entrance, you can still see some adobe ruins.

The church and the buildings are about 95% rebuilt, although some of the original buttresses and walls were integrated into the restoration. Abandoned since secularization in 1834, the crumbling buildings proved sufficient shelter for the US military, which used it as army barracks from 1846, the outbreak of the Mexican-American War, until 1862.

Despite minor efforts, serious restoration did not begin until 1931, spurred by financing from locals and the Hearst Foundation, a philanthropic organization funded by one of California's most influential families. The mission was rededicated as a parish church in 1941 and made into a basilica minor, an honorable distinction, by Pope Paul VI in 1976. The little emblem above the main entrance denotes the papal insignia.

The mission is on Friars Rd two blocks north of I-8, between I-15 and Mission Gorge Rd; from the Mission trolley stop, walk two blocks north and turn right onto Friars Rd. The mission's visitors center

(☎ 619-281-8449) has a friendly staff, some good books and some tacky souvenirs. The mission is open 9 am to 5 pm daily; self-guided taped tours cost $3, or $2 students and seniors, $1 children under 12.

Qualcomm Stadium Home of the professional San Diego Chargers football team, the San Diego Padres baseball team (at least until completion of their new downtown ballpark, whenever that may be) and the SDSU's Aztec football team, this modern sports palace looks like a giant concrete UFO that's landed right next to I-8, the Mission Valley Freeway. It was built at the urging of influential sportswriter Jack Murphy, who had convinced Chargers owner Barron Hilton to move his team from Los Angeles to San Diego. Problem was that the city didn't have a major league stadium – so Murphy twisted some arms and convinced the city fathers and mothers to build one. They did, and San Diego Stadium opened in 1967.

After Murphy's death in 1980, the voters approved naming the stadium for him, and it came to be known affectionately as 'The Murph.'

It was by the power of mammon – not the power of the people – that the stadium got its current name. When the city needed money to complete a controversial $78 million stadium expansion in 1997, local telecomm giant Qualcomm rode to the rescue to the tune of $18 million – in exchange for naming rights until 2017. 'The Murph' is dead, long live the 'Q.'

The expansion, which increased seating capacity to 75,500 for football and 65,900 for baseball, paved the way for San Diego's hosting Superbowl XXXII in 1998, which pitched the winning Denver Broncos against the Green Bay Packers. A huge financial and publicity success, it silenced many expansion detractors. With the Padres getting their own ballpark, the Chargers will remain at Qualcomm, which also hosts large-scale events like rock concerts.

One-hour tours are offered 9 am to 3 pm Monday to Friday by prior arrangement (☎ 619-641-3150), although only for groups. The cost is $2 per person with a $50 minimum. If you're lucky, you might be able to join a scheduled tour.

Kearny Mesa North of Mission Valley proper, Kearny Mesa is San Diego's Asian community. Its main thoroughfare is Convoy St, which heads north from the intersection of Hwy 163 and I-805. Along here you'll find a wild cacophony of shops catering to Asian Americans and recent immigrants from several countries, including China, Vietnam and Korea.

Browse in shops offering everything from cheap kitsch to exquisite silk clothing and art. at family-run establishments, marvel at culinary oddities such as dried sea cucumber, elk antlers and picked ginseng – or browse the aisles of the large Ranch 99 Market (☎ 619-565-7799), 7730 Clairemont Mesa Dr, where tonight's dinner can still be heard clucking or seen swimming. Elsewhere, herbalists, following ancient recipes passed down through generations, mix mysterious ingredients to cure ailments from impotence to bad breath. Chinese dim sum and dumplings, Korean barbecue and fragrant Japanese noodle soups are some of the delicious, authentic foods served in the area's restaurants (see the San Diego Places to Eat chapter for specific suggestions).

POINT LOMA & OCEAN BEACH (MAP 8)

Point Loma is the peninsula that to hangs down across the entrance to San Diego Bay, protecting it from the Pacific Ocean. Access to much of it is limited because of US military installations – the Naval Submarine Base, the US Naval Training Center and the Naval Research Station are all based here; the huge North Island Naval Air Station is just on the other side of the channel on the northern end of Coronado. San Diego's international airport, Lindbergh Field, forms the easternmost part of the peninsula on the bay side. On the Pacific side is the community of Ocean Beach, one of the most laid-back, eccentric and distinctly bohemian parts of town. Its northern border is marked by the San Diego River.

Point Loma

San Diego's first fishing boats were based at Point Loma, and, in the 19th century, whalers dragged carcasses onto its shores to extract the oil. Chinese fishermen settled on the harbor side of the point in the 1860s, but were forced off in 1888 when the US Congress passed the Scott Act prohibiting anyone without citizenship papers from entering the area. Coming home from a normal day's run outside the international boundary (30 miles offshore), the Chinese were met by officials who prohibited them from re-entering the harbor. Portuguese fishing families came 50 years later – around the same time that Italian immigrants settled on the other side of the harbor – and established a permanent community. The Portuguese Hall is still a hub of activity, and many people living on Point Loma are of Portuguese descent.

The tidal flats of Loma Portal, where Point Loma joins the mainland, were used as an airstrip in 1927 by Charles Lindbergh for flight testing the *Spirit of St Louis*. The following year a functioning airport was established, and named Lindbergh Field. It has expanded considerably and is now known as San Diego International Airport.

Cabrillo National Monument On the southern tip of the peninsula, this monument is among the best places in San Diego to visit. It was established in 1913 to commemorate Portuguese explorer Juan Rodríguez Cabrillo, who led the first Spanish exploration of the West Coast. The visitors center (☎ 619-557-5450) has an excellent presentation on Cabrillo's trip and also information about native inhabitants and the natural history of the area. The nearby lookout area has a landmark **statue of Cabrillo** and a great view over Coronado, the Naval Air Station, the bay and the city.

The **Bayside Trail** zigzags around the monument for about 2 miles, passing through native coastal sage shrub and near remnants of a WWII-era defense system, which includes gun batteries, fire-control stations and searchlight bunkers. A small **military exhibit** tells the story of the 19th Coast Artillery at Fort Rosecrans, which defended San Diego, a prime military target, during WWII. The largest guns were at Battery Ashburn, northwest of the park entrance. A short video explains how the geometric principle of triangulation was used to aim 16-inch guns at targets up to 28 miles away.

The monument and visitors center are open 9 am to 5:15 pm daily. Admission, payable at the gate and good for unlimited entries for a week, is $5 per car, $2 if you're on a bike or a bus (No 26 from Downtown).

A short walk from the visitors center brings you to the 1854 **Old Point Loma Lighthouse**. It sits atop the point, from where its oil lamp could be seen from 39 miles away – but it lasted only until 1891 because the point was so often shrouded in mist. It was declared a national monument in 1913 and is now a museum. You'll see typical lighthouse furniture from the late 19th century, including lamps and picture frames hand-covered with hundreds of shells, testimony to the long, lonely nights endured by lighthouse keepers.

Nearby is the **Whale Overlook** (see Whale Watching in the Activities section later in this chapter) and, on the ocean side of the point, you can drive or walk down to the **tide pools**, which are really only interesting at low tide. Look for anemones, starfish, crabs, limpets and dead man's fingers (thin, tubular seaweed), but don't damage or remove anything – it's all protected by law.

Old Point Loma Lighthouse

Fort Rosecrans National Cemetery En route to the monument, you'll pass the sea of white headstones that form this military cemetery, a burial ground since the 1870s. Some 50,000 US veterans and victims of war are buried here, including casualties of the Battle at San Pasqual during the Mexican-American War in 1846 (they were transferred here). Also buried here are victims of a boiler explosion on the gunboat USS *Bennington* in July 1905 in San Diego Harbor.

Point Loma Nazarene University Occupying a choice spot of land above the Pacific Ocean, this private liberal arts school is affiliated with the Church of the Nazarene, an evangelical protestant denomination founded in Los Angeles at the turn-of-the-20th-century.

A school has stood on these grounds since 1900 when Katherine A Tingley, the leader of the Theosophical Society, bought 132 acres of prime real estate and moved the organization's international headquarters here. She established the School for the Revival of the Lost Mysteries of Antiquity – also called Raja Yoga School – and supplemented her students' academic curriculum with music, drama and even military skills. She formed youth and adult symphony orchestras with her staff and students.

Several of the original buildings still stand. The **Greek Amphitheater** was the first such open-air theater of its kind in the US at its 1901 opening; it is dramatically positioned with tall trees and the ocean for a backdrop. Tingley's private home, now called **Cabrillo Hall**, is a two-story flat-roofed wooden building in the center of campus. Near the entrance gate, **Mieras Hall**, financed by the Spaulding family (of sporting goods fame), is a rounded white structure topped by an onion-shaped purple glass dome that makes the whole thing look like a sugar bowl. Purple, incidentally, was Tingley's favorite color, and why she was called the 'Purple Mother of Lomaland.'

After her death in 1929, the school lasted until 1942 before being taken over by a couple of other schools; it became Point Loma Nazarene University in 1973.

Sunset Cliffs Point Loma Nazarene University sits above a lovely park with a small beach and tidal pools called Sunset Cliffs Park. Jutting out from its northern end is Sunset Cliffs Blvd, which parallels the shore up to the southern edge of Ocean Beach and is one of the most scenic stretches of road in all of San Diego. Lined by expensive homes on its eastern side, the pavement gives way to mud-colored cliffs on the ocean side.

Wind and water have had their way with the sandstone, which has been shaped into otherworldly formations. The waves, naturally, attract a fair number of surfers; watching their antics and the sunset are among the main reasons people come here. With unobstructed ocean views, Sunset Cliffs is also great for walking, jogging, biking or in-line skating.

Harbor Island & Shelter Island Soil dredged from the bottom of the harbor was used to build Shelter Island (1950) and Harbor Island (1969), which are not really islands, but T-shaped peninsulas joined to the mainland by causeways. They now provide moorings for a huge flotilla of pleasure boats and are covered with hotels, restaurants, boatyards and parking lots.

There's a classic view of San Diego from here, across the bay through a forest of masts. On the right as you head for Shelter Island, the pointy building, which resembles the tower of the Hotel del Coronado, is the clubhouse of the San Diego Yacht Club, which held the America's Cup yachting trophy from 1987 to 1995.

Shelter Island has a couple of interesting pieces of public art. At its far western end is the **Friendship Bell**, designed by Masahiko Katori as a gift from Yokohama, San Diego's Japanese sister city. In the center of the island is the **Tunaman's Memorial**, which commemorates the members of San Diego's tuna fleet, once the largest in the world. The bronze sculpture was designed by Franco Vianello, himself a commercial fisherman.

Ocean Beach

San Diego's most bohemian seaside community once had a sleazy reputation, but more recently OB (as it's commonly called) has moved up the scale. Still a long way from pretentious, it's more compact than San Diego's other beach towns, making it enjoyable for strolling. Newport Ave, the main drag, is well stocked with surf shops, music stores, used-clothing places and, in the 4800 and 4900 blocks, antique consignment stores. Street performers and food vendors who frequent the **OB Farmers' Market**, from 4 to 7 pm Wednesday (until 8 pm from June to September), make it one of San Diego's most enjoyable.

The half-mile-long **Ocean Beach Municipal Pier** is good for fishing and a breath of fresh air. Just north of the pier, near the end of Newport Ave, is 'beach scene' headquarters, with volleyball courts and sunset barbecues. It can get crowded all the way up to Voltaire St. North of here is **Dog Beach**, one of only a few beaches in town where dogs can run unleashed and chase birds around the marshy area where the San Diego River meets the sea.

MISSION BAY & BEACHES

In the 18th century, the mouth of the San Diego River formed a shallow bay when the river flowed, and a marshy swamp when it didn't – the Spanish called it False Bay. After WWII, a combination of civic vision and coastal engineering turned the swamp into a 7-sq-mile playground, with 27 miles of

shoreline and 90 acres of park. With financing from public bonds and expertise from the US Army Corps of Engineers, the river was channeled to the sea, the bay was dredged and millions of tons of sludge were used to build islands, coves and peninsulas. A quarter of the new land has been leased to hotels, boatyards and other businesses, repaying the bonds and providing ongoing revenue for the city.

The attractions of Mission Bay run from luxurious resort hotels to free outdoor activities. Kite flying is popular in Mission Bay Park, and there's cycling and in-line skating on the miles of smooth paths. You can rent equipment just off East Mission Bay Dr, opposite the Hilton, or at the Catamaran Resort Hotel in Mission Beach. Beach volleyball is big on Fiesta Island.

The waters around Fiesta Island are used by power boats and water-skiers; the Hilton Beach Resort (☎ 619-276-4010) rents the necessary equipment. Sailing, windsurfing and kayaking dominate the waters in northwest Mission Bay.

The *Bahia Belle* (☎ 619-488-0551) is a floating bar and a stern-wheeler paddleboat. It cruises between two resort hotels, the Catamaran and the Bahia. Call for times, which vary depending on the season. It's a beautiful way to see the bay and costs $6, plus drinks, but is free for guests of either resort.

For details on water sports and equipment rental, see the Activities section later in this chapter.

SeaWorld (Map 9)

One of San Diego's best known and most popular attractions, SeaWorld opened in 1964, the brainchild of four fraternity brothers from the University of California, Los Angeles. What began with a few small shows and saltwater aquariums has evolved into a four-star attraction that appeals to people of all ages. Shamu, one of SeaWorld's killer whales, has become an unofficial symbol of the city.

The park is commercial, but nonetheless entertaining and slightly educational. Even if some of the animal shows are disturbingly reminiscent of old-fashioned circus acts, Sea-

Waxing surfboards, La Jolla Shores

Seal siesta near downtown La Jolla

Surf scenes, Mission Beach

Belmont Park thrills – the Giant Dipper

San Diego holiday parade – Santa working on his tan

RICK GERHARTER

Lattes in San Diego's Little Italy

RICK GERHARTER

Sea World? Shamu World!

DAVID PEEVERS

Lily-trimmer, Balboa Park's Botanical Building

ANTHONY PIDGEON

World has a serious side in its efforts at animal conservation, rescue, rehabilitation, breeding and research. Beautiful landscaping – accomplished with more than 4500 plant species – throughout the park is in relaxing counterpoint to the sensory assault of the shows and attractions.

A few words of advice up front: set aside a full day for SeaWorld and get here early in the morning to beat the crowds. The summer months are not just the hottest but also the busiest, so be prepared for long waits in stifling heat. Bring a hat, suntan lotion, patience and – if cutting costs is your aim – bottled water and something to eat (there are picnic tables by the entrance). Some attractions, including the popular Wild Arctic exhibit, have a minimum height requirement of 42 inches.

Information SeaWorld (☎ 619-226-3901) opens its gates at 9 am daily from Memorial to Labor Day, and at 10 am daily the rest of the year. Tickets sales end 1½ hours before closing time, which is around sunset most of the year, but as late as 11 pm in summer.

Admission is $40 for anyone over 11 and $30 for ages three to 11. Discount coupons are available, but the extras really add up – parking costs $8, the food is expensive and it's hard to escape spending something on the ubiquitous SeaWorld souvenirs.

Ways to get the best value for your ticket include a re-entry stamp, which lets you go out for a break and return later the same day (this works well in summer when the park is open late); a combination ticket that's also good for Universal Studios (in Los Angeles) within two weeks from date of purchase for $75/55; and a two-day pass that gives you admission on two consecutive days for $44/34. Twelve-month passes cost $75/60 and include free parking and a host of other discounts and benefits.

If you're interested in a behind-the-scenes look at the work and research areas, there are 90-minute guided tours, which include reserved seating at the Shamu show. Tours cost $8/7.

The park is easy to find by car – take SeaWorld Dr off I-5 less than a mile north of where it intersects with I-8. By bus, take No 9 from Downtown.

Shows The shows starring trained animals distinguish SeaWorld from a regular zoo. Expect lots of special effects, high-tech gadgetry, animal trainers that wouldn't look out of place in *Bay Watch* and programs that entertain and amaze.

Shamu Adventure is the most visually spectacular and entertaining show, and the one you won't want to miss. Throughout the 30-minute program, the three star performers – Shamu, Baby Shamu and Namu – glide, leap, dive and flip through the water while interacting with each other, the audience and their trainers. The shiny black and white creatures are an awesome sight. If you want to stay dry, avoid the first 14 rows. After the show, you can observe the animals more closely from observation decks and an underwater glass tunnel.

Those who grew up with the TV series *Flipper* will probably have childhood flashbacks during **Dolphin Discovery**, an entertaining and high-energy show that is similar in form and content to the Shamu Adventure. Besides dolphins, it features pilot whales. To meet the creatures, you can plunk down $125 per person, walk into their tank and feed and touch them. Reservations are required (☎ 877-436-5746).

In **Fools with Tools**, two sea lions with 'tude – Clyde and Seamore – perform in their own version of the TV sit-com *Home Improvement* along with their trainer, Ace. The Sea Lion & Sea Otter Stadium has been transformed into the TV studio 'Cable Channel 99.' It's all goofy and funny and kids love it, but one can't help but feel sorry for these creatures engaged in this circus-like silliness.

The newest show, **Pirates 4-D**, isn't really a show but a 17-minute 3-D comedy movie that follows the adventures of a hapless pirate crew stranded on a Caribbean island. It was written by Eric Idle of *Monty Python* fame and stars him and actor Leslie Nielsen (of *The Naked Gun,* etc). The fourth dimension is provided by the audience, which is treated to a host of special effects (buzzing seats, water cannons, simulated bat attacks and other such fun nonsense).

In **Wings of the World**, some 50 birds perform neat tricks on cue and interact with the audience. The biggest moment is when three hawks nose-dive like reverse rockets from a balloon 300 feet in the air right onto their trainers outstretched arms.

Exhibits The shows are the park's flashy headliners, but for close-up views of the animals you'll need to visit the exhibits. Here are some of the best:

In **Penguin Encounter**, Adélie, king, macaroni and lots of other penguin species share this habitat that faithfully simulates Antarctic living conditions. The temperature behind the glass-enclosed space is a constant 25°F, but light conditions change with the seasons just as nature dictates. So, if you're visiting in July (winter in Antarctica), you'll see them waddle and swim in near-darkness at all times.

The **Wild Arctic** takes you on a simulated-motion ride aboard a helicopter to Base Station Wild Arctic, a recreated research station where you encounter polar bears, beluga whales, walruses and seals. Kids love roaming through the polar bear dens (complete with growling sounds) and touching a 25-foot ice wall, but watching the giant walrus in its crammed quarters can be a tad depressing.

Time seems to slow down at **Manatee Rescue**, one of the most enchanting exhibits in the park. Housed in a giant aquarium, these gentle vegetarian giants swim around in slow motion, munching on lettuce leaves or resting on the recreated ocean floor. All of them were rescued and rehabilitated, their wounds and scars still visible. Alligator gars – unusual fish with 'gator-like snouts – prehistoric looking arapaima and redtail catfish share space with the manatee, which is an endangered species.

You'll have a close-up – if not personal – encounter with dozens of sharks as you walk through a 57-foot long acrylic tube called **Shark Encounter**. Species include blacktip and whitetip, reef, bonnethead and sand tiger sharks, some of them impressively large, although not big enough to trigger *Jaws*-style nightmares.

Mission Beach & Pacific Beach (Maps 9 & 10)

From the South Mission Jetty at the southern tip of Mission Beach to Pacific Beach Point at the north end of Pacific Beach are ? miles of solid So-Cal beach scene. **Ocean Front Walk**, the beachfront boardwalk, can get crowded with joggers, in-line skaters and bicyclists any time of the year and is one of the best people-watching venues in San Diego. On a warm summer weekend parking becomes impossible and suntanned bodies cover the beach from end to end. Belmont Park, full of family-oriented attractions, is another major draw. Mission Blvd gets so crowded that police often just close it down.

Down at the Mission Beach end, many small houses and apartments are rented for the summer, and the hedonism is concentrated in a narrow strip between the ocean and Mission Bay. Up in Pacific Beach (or PB), activity spreads inland, especially along Garnet Ave, which is well supplied with bars, restaurants and used clothing stores. At the ocean end of Garnet, the Crystal Pier is a popular place to fish or watch surfers.

For details on renting bikes or surfing gear, see the Activities section later in this chapter.

Belmont Park This miniature Coney Island–style amusement park has been a Mission Beach fixture since 1925. The star attraction here is the restored **Giant Dipper**, a classic wooden roller coaster that was declared a National Historic Landmark in 1987. For more history, check out the small exhibit in the ticket kiosk.

The creaky ride ($3.50) clocks in at just under two minutes and covers 2600 feet; the highest drop is 70 feet and the top speed about 50 mph. It's open 11 am to 10 pm (to 11 pm on Friday and Saturday) June to September, less the rest of the year.

Other big draws are **The Plunge**, an historic Olympic-sized indoor pool with a giant whale mural by prolific artist Wyland. More modern attractions include the Pirates Cove children's play zone, and Venturer II, which features combination video game–virtual reality machines. There are also beachwear boutiques, a bar and some places to eat. Belmont Park entry is free; pay separately for the attractions. Parking is $5.

LA JOLLA (MAP 11)

La Jolla is the wealthy suburban northern neighbor of Pacific Beach. Its name is often translated from Spanish as 'the jewel,' though indigenous peoples called the place 'mut la Hoya, la Hoya' – the place of many caves. In any case, it's pronounced 'la HOY-ya.'

The area was subdivided in the 1880s but started developing with purpose when Ellen Browning Scripps (see the boxed text) moved here in 1897. The newspaperwoman and heiress acquired much of the land along Prospect St, which she then donated to various community uses. Not only did she support local institutions such as the Bishop's School and the La Jolla Woman's Club, she had them designed by Irving Gill. His work set the architectural tone of the community – an unadorned Mediterranean style characterized by arches, colonnades, palm trees, red-tile roofs and pale stucco.

North of downtown La Jolla, the scientific community makes its home, anchored by University of California, San Diego, Scripps Institution of Oceanography and the Salk Institute. There are numerous minor research facilities as well.

To the east is the 'Golden Triangle,' bounded by I-5, I-805 and Hwy 52, a new-money residential area and the University Towne Centre, a giant outdoor mall with its own Olympic-size iceskating rink (see the San Diego Shopping chapter for details).

Downtown La Jolla

The compact town sits atop cliffs, surrounded on three sides by the ocean. Distant views of Pacific blue are glimpsed through windows and from between buildings, but there is little interaction between the heart of downtown and the sea. The main thoroughfares, Prospect St and Girard Ave, are known for having the 'three Rs' –

Ellen Browning Scripps

Newspaper owner and philanthropist Ellen Browning Scripps was a woman ahead of her time. Born in London, England in 1836, she came to the US in 1844 when her father moved the family following the death of her mother. They settled in Rushville, Illinois, where she got her education at private schools and a seminary before taking up teaching. In 1856 she enrolled in Knox College, from where she graduated in 1859, only to return to the schoolhouse for another eight years. Her newspaper experience began in 1870 but didn't really get too serious until 1873, when she invested a considerable portion of her savings in her brother James' newspaper, the Detroit *Evening*. Despite its small size, it became a successful publication, and in 1878 the Scripps siblings founded another daily, the Cleveland *Press*.

In 1896 Scripps retired to La Jolla. By that time she had grown wealthy in her own right, and she turned to philanthropy more or less full-time after inheriting a huge fortune from her brother George in 1900. No one knows how much she gave away up to the time of her death in 1932, but it was millions and millions of dollars. Schools, zoos, hospitals, churches, museums, scientific institutions – her generosity extended into many areas. And nowhere did it leave a greater mark than in La Jolla, where Scripps spent the last 35 years of her long life.

restaurants, rugs and real estate – making La Jolla San Diego's best place for high-class shopping. Galleries sell paintings, sculpture and home accessories, and small boutiques fill in the needs not met by retail chains like Ralph Lauren and Banana Republic. Alternative health guru Deepak Chopra's Center for Well Being (☎ 858-551-7788), 7630 Fay Ave, attracts wellness-conscious people from around the globe.

Walking Tour This tour takes in some of La Jolla's main cultural, natural, historical and architectural sights. It covers about 2 miles and should take one to two hours.

Start out at the venerable **La Valencia Hotel**, 1132 Prospect St, easily recognized by its pink façade, blue and yellow domed tower and Mediterranean landscaping. Designed by William Templeton Johnson, it opened in 1926 and, through the decades, has hosted the rich, the moneyed, the titled, the famous, the military and the just plain normal. Greta Garbo, Mary Pickford, Lilian Gish, Charlie Chaplin and even Groucho Marx were regular guests. Its clubby Whaling Bar was a favorite hangout of Gregory Peck and, later, Dr Seuss.

Leaving 'La V' – as it is sometimes known – head southwest on Prospect St, then left on Girard Ave where, at the corner of Wall St, is the **Athenaeum Music & Arts Library** (☎ 858-454-5872). This small, sophisticated century-old library is an impressive storehouse of records, tapes and videos as well as thousands of books on music and the arts. If you want to research the history of jazz or listen to an out-of-print recording of Beethoven's Fifth, this diminutive den of culture is your place. It also has an intimate auditorium for classical, chamber and jazz recitals. A gallery shows works by local and national artists. Hours are 10 am to 5:30 pm Tuesday to Saturday (to 8:30 pm on Wednesday).

La Jolla – Where Dr Seuss meets Gregory Peck

Return to Prospect, turn left and go fo about 200 yards to get to the most histori part of La Jolla. On your right at No 780 i the vine- and flower-covered entrance c **John Cole's Bookshop**, in a cottage bough by Ellen Browning Scripps in 1905 and rem ovated to Irving Gill's design. Around th corner on Eads Ave, the **La Jolla Historica Society** (☎ 858-459-5335) has vintage photo and beach memorabilia – think old bathin costumes and lifeguard buoys. It's ope noon to 4:30 pm Tuesday and Thursday Back on Prospect St looms the square towe of the **St James' By-the-Sea Episcopa Church**, at the corner of Silverado St, whic has a massive wooden beamed ceiling an brilliant stained-glass windows.

Also here are several excellent example of Gill's architecture, all commissioned b Scripps: the **La Jolla Woman's Club** (1916 at the corner of Silverado St and Drape Ave, and, just south of here, in a little park the **La Jolla Recreation Center**. One bloc farther south, the **Bishop's School** (1910) i among Gill's most accomplished structure The modern building across from the recre ation center is the **Museum of Contempo rary Art** (see later in this section).

From the school, go north on La Joll Blvd, then right on Coast Blvd, which turn into a wonderful walking path that skir the shoreline for a half-mile. Along here i the **Children's Pool**, where a jetty (funde by – you guessed it – Ellen Brownin Scripps) protects the beach. Originally in tended to give La Jolla kiddies a safe plac to frolic, the beach has been taken over b sea lions, and the elementary set is kept ou by a fence. If you like sea lions, this is great place to view them up close as the lounge on the shore. But the creatures hav also become a subject of controversy. Pro tecting them enables them to multiply at greater rate, but the fear is that a large se lion population will attract their natura predator – the great white shark – an un welcome visitor to surfers and swimmers.

East of the Children's Pool, La Jolla only 'skyscraper' – the infamous mid-]'6 **939 Coast Building** – created the impetu for current building codes, which limit ne structures west of I-5 to a height of 30 feet. Atop Point La Jolla at the path's northeastern end, **Ellen Browning Scripps Park** is a tidy expanse of green lawns and palm trees overlooking La Jolla Cove on the north. The cove's lovely little beach offers great snorkeling and is popular with rough-water swimmers.

The offshore area from Point La Jolla north to Scripps Pier, marked by white buoys, is **San Diego–La Jolla Underwater Park**, a protected zone with a variety of marine life, some kelp forest and interesting reefs and canyons (see Scuba Diving in the Activities section).

Waves have carved a series of caves in the sandstone cliffs east of the cove. The largest is **Sunny Jim Cave**, which can be reached via an underground staircase from a little kiosk at 1325 Coast Blvd ($2).

From here work your way uphill back to Prospect St. You'll see the La Valencia will be about 300 yards on your right, completing the loop.

Museum of Contemporary Art

The 'mother' of the MCA in Downtown, this museum has been a center of La Jolla culture since 1941. It's building was designed by Gill in 1916 as the home of Ellen Browning Scripps. The latest renovation in 1996, by Philadelphia-born postmodern architect Robert Venturi, added a dramatic lobby. Several exhibits are staged throughout the year, some of them traveling shows, others come from the permanent collection of 3000 post-1950 works in all media. The museum's strengths are its collections of 1960s and 1970s minimalist and pop art, of contemporary conceptual art, and of 'border art' from both San Diego and Tijuana.

The museum (☎ 858-454-3541), at 700 Prospect St, is open 11 am to 5 pm (Thursday to 8 pm) daily except Wednesday between Labor Day and Memorial Day, and from 11 am to 8 pm (to 5 pm weekends) the rest of the year. Admission is $4, or $2 students and seniors, free the first Sunday and third Tuesday of the month. Free guided tours run at 2 and 3 pm Tuesday, Saturday and Sunday, 6 and 7 pm Thursday.

Soledad Mountain

For a 360° view of La Jolla, take Nautilus St east from La Jolla Blvd, turn left on La Jolla Scenic Dr and follow it to Soledad Mountain Park. The large cross on top was the subject of an unsuccessful lawsuit in the late 1960s – residents objected to the sectarian religious symbol on publicly owned land.

La Jolla Shores

Called 'the Shores,' this area northeast of La Jolla Cove is where the cliffs meet the wide, sandy beaches that stretch north to Del Mar (see the North County Coast section in the San Diego Excursions chapter). Primarily residential, the tony Shores is home to the members-only La Jolla Beach and Tennis Club (its orange tile roof is visible from La Jolla Cove) and **Kellogg City Park**, whose beachside playground is good for families with children. To reach the beach, take La Jolla Shores Dr north from Torrey Pines Rd, then west at the first stoplight. The waves here are gentle enough for beginning surfers, and kayakers can usually launch from the shore.

Scripps Institution of Oceanography

Marine scientists worked here as early as 1910 and, helped by donations from the Scripps family, SIO has become one of the world's largest marine research institutions. It is now part of UCSD, and its pier is a landmark. The SIO, north of La Jolla Shores off La Jolla Shores Dr, is not to be confused with the Scripps Research Institute (10550 Torrey Pines Rd), a private, nonprofit biomedical research organization.

Stephen Birch Aquarium at Scripps This aquarium is a public education project of SIO, with brilliant displays on the marine sciences and of marine life. The **Hall of Fishes** has more than 30 tanks divided into four geographical areas: the Northwest Coast, Southern California, Mexico and Tropical Seas. Popular exhibits include ethereal jellyfish, mystical sea horses, graceful octopi, fierce wolf eels, carnivorous cuttlefish and the sneaky stone fish. Entire environments, including coral reefs and lagoons, have been re-created to house these underwater creatures. On the outside terrace, with great views of the bay and the Scripps Pier, are tide pool touch tanks and friendly docents to answer questions.

Another museum wing houses **Exploring Blue Planet**, an exhibit on the science of oceanography and how it helps researchers understand the goings-on of Earth. Thematically divided into water, land, air and life, it features display panels and interactive exhibits explaining the correlation of these natural forces. Big crowds gather in front of the 'ocean supermarket' – a wall of products including lipstick, toothpaste and Cheese Whiz, which can be 'scanned' to show which ocean ingredients (such as kelp, algae, oil) they contain.

The aquarium (☎ 858-534-3474), at 2300 Exhibition Way off N Torrey Pines Rd, is open 9 am to 5 pm daily; admission is $8.50, or $7.50 seniors, $6 students, $5 ages 3 to 17.

Salk Institute

This private institution for biomedical research was founded in 1960 by Jonas Salk, the polio prevention pioneer. Study areas include the organization and operation of the brain, the control of gene activity, and the molecular origins of cancer, AIDS and other diseases.

San Diego County donated 27 acres of land, the March of Dimes provided financing, and Louis Kahn designed the building. Completed in 1965, it is regarded as a modern masterpiece, with its classically proportioned travertine-marble plaza, and cubist, mirror-glass laboratory blocks

framing a perfect view of the Pacific. The Salk Institute attracts the best scientists to work in a research-only environment. The facilities were recently expanded, with new laboratories designed by Jack McAllister, a follower of Kahn's work.

The Salk Institute (☎ 858-453-4100 ext 1200) is at 10010 N Torrey Pines Rd; tour the building with a volunteer guide at 11 am and noon Monday to Friday. Buses Nos 41 and 301 go along N Torrey Pines Rd.

Torrey Pines State Beach

Some of the best beaches in the county are north of the Salk Institute up to Torrey Pines State Reserve. At extreme low tides (about twice a year), you can walk from the Shores north to Del Mar along the beach. The Torrey Pines Glider Port, at the end of Torrey Pines Scenic Dr, is the place for hang-gliders and paragliders to launch themselves into the sea breezes that rise over the cliffs. It's a beautiful sight – tandem flights are available if you can't resist. Down below is Blacks Beach, where bathing suits are technically required but practically absent. This particular beach is a popular hangout for gay men.

Torrey Pines State Reserve

This urban oasis is a highlight of a La Jolla visit, and well worth exploring. It is home to the rarest species of pine trees in North America, the Torrey pine *(Pinus torreyana)*. Having adapted to sparse rainfall and sandy, stony soils, this gnarled and wind sculpted tree occurs naturally in two spots only: this state reserve along the coast between La Jolla and Del Mar, and on Santa Rosa Island, which is part of the Channel Islands National Park off the coast of Santa Barbara. Both have an estimated population of between 4000 and 5000 trees.

In the 16th century Spanish explorers first recorded the large bluff-top grove which they could spot from the sea, on their maps as Punta de los Arboles (Point of the Trees). The species itself was named in 1850 by visiting botanist Charles Christopher Parry after his friend and colleague John Torrey of New York.

The 2000-acre park is a delight to explore; there are several hiking trails to guide you along. Steep sandstone gullies have eroded into wonderfully textured surfaces, and the views over the ocean and north to Oceanside are superb, especially at sunset. There are viewing platforms right at the edge of the bluff, also good for spotting gray whales during their winter migration. In spring, wildflowers cloak much of the reserve in a colorful blanket, while in the early morning during fall and winter you can see flocks of California quail. Torrey Pines State Beach can be accessed by trail from the reserve, as well.

The main access road, off N Torrey Pines Rd at the reserve's north end, leads to the Torrey Pines Lodge, built in 1923 by (drum roll, please) Ellen Browning Scripps. Originally a restaurant, it is now the park's visitors center. The simple adobe structure was modeled after Hopi Indian dwellings in Arizona and, according to a newspaper article published at the time, constructed with their help to ensure authenticity. Scripps also spearheaded the effort to protect the unusual trees, although California didn't officially create the reserve until 1959.

The visitors center (☎ 858-755-2063) is open daily from 9 am to sunset and has good displays on local flora and fauna, as well as maps. Hook up with a ranger on a guided nature walk, offered on weekends and holidays at 11:30 am and 1:30 pm. Entry and parking is $4 per car; there's no charge to walk in. If you want to hike, park near the driving range on N Torrey Pines Rd and take the paved path northwest until you reach the box of trail maps at the beginning of the Broken Arrow Trail. Camping, smoking and picnicking are allowed only on the beach. The reserve is open from 8 am till sunset daily.

University of California, San Diego

A campus of the University of California, UCSD was established in 1960 and now has more than 18,000 students and an excellent academic reputation, particularly for its math and science programs. It lies on rolling coastal hills in a park-like setting, with many fragrant eucalyptus trees. Its most distinctive structure is the **Geisel Library**, an upside-down pyramid of glass and concrete named after children's author and La Jolla resident Theodor Geisel, better known as Dr Seuss (see boxed text 'On Beyond Seuss: The Global Grasp of a La Jolla Legend' in the Facts about San Diego chapter). He and his wife Audrey contributed substantially to the library, which was named in his honor in 1995, following his death. All of Geisel's manuscripts, notes and sketches are part of the collection, and there a selection of his drawings and books on the ground level.

From the east side of the library's second level, an allegorical snake created by artist Alexis Smith winds down a native California plant garden past an enormous marble copy of John Milton's *Paradise Lost*. The piece is part of the **Stuart Collection** of outdoor sculptures spread around campus. Other works are Niki de Saint Phalle's *Sun God,* Bruce Nauman's *Vices & Virtues* (which spells out seven of each in huge neon letters), Robert Irwin's very blue *Fence,* and a forest of talking trees. Most installations are near the Geisel Library, and details are available from the Visual Arts Building or the Price Center. The campus is home to the prestigious **La Jolla Playhouse**, based at the Mandell Weiss Center for the Performing Arts (also see the San Diego Entertainment chapter).

Free 90-minute campus tours are offered every Sunday at 2 pm (by minivan on the first and third and on foot the second and fourth Sunday). Tours leave from the

Torrey pine

Gilman Visitor Information Booth on Gilman Dr on the southern edge of campus. Parking is free on weekends. Call ☎ 858-534-4414 for reservations and information.

Mormon Temple

Anyone driving through La Jolla on I-5 for the first time will rub their eyes in disbelief when passing by the San Diego temple of the Church of Latter-Day Saints. Dedicated in 1993, this gleaming white confection seems partly inspired by the NASA space shuttle and partly by Disney's Sleeping Beauty's castle. Clad in marble chips with plaster, it consists of two spiky towers, orbited by a foursome of smaller ones, that together seem to literally pierce the sky. It's at once bombastic and awe-inspiring, an effect that is not diluted by a closer inspection. Nonmembers are not allowed inside, but no one will stop you from wandering the immaculately landscaped grounds. The entrance is at 7474 Charmant Dr.

EASTERN METRO AREA

These towns started out as lower and middle class bedroom communities, but real estate prices elsewhere have brought in many younger families, who still find affordable housing here. Places like El Cajon and La Mesa, while far from fashionable, are evolving into cities with their own infrastructure and identity. For a visitor, there isn't too much to see and do, although Mission Trails Regional Park is a wonderful outdoor recreation area, and there are a couple of special-interest museums, as well.

Mission Trails Regional Park (Map 2)

Spreading across 5800 acres of rugged mountainous area about 8 miles northeast of Downtown, Mission Trails is one of the nation's largest urban parks. It is an accessible and popular recreational getaway for locals, who come for a wide range of outdoor pursuits, including hiking, biking, fishing and picnicking. The park's most historical site is the **Old Mission Dam**, built by indigenous peoples to store water for the Mission San Diego de Alcalá. Many of the most popular trails start from here, including the one through Oak Canyon, Father Juníperro Serra Trail and the trail to **Cowles Mountain** (1591 feet), the city's highest point, with great unrestricted views. **Lake Murray** is good for fishing (open Wednesday and weekends, November to Labor Day).

Stop by the excellent visitors center (☎ 619-668-3275), 1 Father Junípero Serra Trail, to pick up a map and information; hours are 9 am to 5 pm daily. Rangers also lead guided hikes several times weekly. The gift store sells baskets and pottery made by local Kumeyaay, as well as books and various trinkets.

El Cajon (Map 1)

East of Mission Trails Regional Park, El Cajon with 98,000 residents is one of the largest incorporated cities within San Diego County. It ranks among the nations top 20 for high-tech jobs in the defense, transportation and energy industries. Originally part of the land that belonged to the Mission San Diego de Alcalá, the city became a stagecoach stop in the 1870s but didn't really grow much until the 1950s.

The main reason to visit is to catch a show at the **East County Performing Arts Center** (see the San Diego Entertainment chapter) or to drop in at the **Heritage of the Americas Museum** (☎ 619-670-5194), which focuses on the tribal cultures of North and South America. It displays jewelry, moccasins, pipes, pottery and even a baby carriage. Highlights include a buffalo-hide robe once worn by Cheyenne Chief Thunderbird and a couple of duckbill dinosaur eggs. The museum is on the Cuyamaca College campus at 12110 Cuyamaca College Dr W and open 10 am to 4 pm Tuesday to Friday, from noon Saturday; admission is $3, or $2 seniors. Take the Cuyamaca College Dr W exit off Jamacha Rd (Hwy 54).

La Mesa (Map 2)

South of El Cajon, La Mesa, which was incorporated in 1912 with just 700 people, has grown into a sprawling suburb of 60,000. In the 19th century, grazing cattle and sheep uled the land, but the arrival of water with the completion of the San Diego Flume in 1887 brought in lemon and orange growers. The railroad, which came to La Mesa a year later, also spurred growth.

The La Mesa Historical Society is headquartered in the restored 1908 **McKinney House** (☎ 619-466-0197), 8369 University Ave at Pine St, which is open noon to 3 pm Saturday or by appointment. La Mesa is served by the San Diego Trolley and bisected by I-8. The main commercial site is Grossmont Shopping Center, with more than 100 stores, although locals also shop along La Mesa Blvd, the lively main drag.

Faithfully restored to its 1915 condition, the **La Mesa Depot** is a reminder of railroading's infancy. Now an annex of the San Diego Railroad Museum, it lets visitors get close to a steam locomotive, as well as a handful of historic freight cars. The building, at the corner of Spring St and La Mesa Blvd, once housed an antique store run by the eccentric Flossie Beadle, and was also at times a worm farm and chicken coop. Volunteers keep the museum (☎ 619-595-3030) open 9 am to 4 pm on Saturday only; admission is free.

Opened in 1997, the small **Computer Museum** is a journey through more than a century of communication technology. On display are major milestones, from the 1906 Brunsviga Midget calculator to a 1930s Hollerith manual punch card system (actually invented in the 1880s for the US Census), to the typewriter-shaped Apple II (late 1970s). Some of the exhibits are interactive, and a wall of fame highlights the accomplishments of seminal figures in the computer world, including Seymour Cray and Bill Gates. The museum is on the Coleman College campus at 7380 Parkway Dr and is open 10 am to 4 pm Tuesday to Saturday. Take the Lake Murray exit off I-8, then head east on Parkway Dr.

SOUTH BAY

Between Downtown and the Mexican border, the South Bay area is the least affluent part of San Diego; it is interesting to see that San Diego does have a gritty side.

Most people pass through aboard the San Diego Trolley en route to the border. But those who choose to delve into the neighborhoods will discover a number of places far less bleak than what they might see from the train.

National City (Map 2)

A city of 60,000 within San Diego County, National City starts more or less south of the Coronado Bridge. It was first developed in the 1870s and still has several Victorian homes, including the interesting **Granger Music Hall** at 1615 E 4th St.

Despite such gems, National City retains an industrial flair, in part because of the dominating presence of the 32nd St Naval Station, which has occupied all the land fronting San Diego Bay since WWII.

In August 2000 a new **Trolley and Railroad Museum** (☎ 619-474-4400) opened at the National City Depot at Bay Marina Dr and Harrison Ave, two blocks west of I-5. Inside the restored 1886 depot are historical photos and displays, as well as several electric streetcars that rattled through San Diego between 1886 and 1949. The museum is open noon to 4 pm weekends only; admission is free.

Chula Vista (Map 2)

The city of Chula Vista extends from the bay to the hills, and, despite being a sprawling suburb, it still has some of the citrus orchards for which it was once renowned. City administrators have worked hard to polish up the city's image by attracting several high-profile facilities, with mixed success.

ARCO US Olympic Training Center Blood, sweat and tears, along with shrieks of joy and triumph, have filled this state-of-the-art training facility since its opening in 1995. Olympic hopefuls come to hone their skills at this 150-acre camp on the western shore of the Lower Otay Reservoir. It is one in a trio of such facilities in the country – the others being in Lake Placid and Colorado Springs – and the only one with a climate conducive to year-round training.

The Chula Vista site boasts a 50-lane archery range, the largest permanent facility in North America; tennis courts and soccer fields (four of each); an all-weather field hockey surface; a 400m track; a 15,000-sq-foot boathouse for canoes; a 2000m course for canoeing/kayaking and rowing; and an 0.9-mile cycling course.

You can sneak a peek at the facilities – and maybe catch some athletes in action – during free tours (☎ 619-482-6103) offered daily 9 am to 4 pm (Sunday from 11 am) from the Copley Visitor Center. After watching a short video on the Olympic movement, you'll stroll the Olympic Path, then look at training fields, tracks and athlete dorms. The tour ends in the store, where you can buy souvenirs with the Olympic logo. The training center is at 1750 Wueste Rd at the intersection with Orange Rd.

Sweetwater Marsh National Wildlife Refuge At the northern end of Chula Vista's waterfront, this 316-acre area is one of the few salt marshes left on the Pacific Coast and an important shorebird and waterfowl habitat. Some 200 bird species inhabit the refuge, including the California least tern, the light-footed clapper rail and Palmer's frankenia, all endangered species.

For more on the refuge, visit the **Chula Vista Nature Center**. Bring your binoculars or rent some at the bookstore, then climb to the observation deck to look for winged creatures. You can also take a self-guided tour along interpretative trails or join a ranger-led tour. Kids enjoy petting the center's resident bat rays and leopard sharks; other activities are offered as well.

The center (☎ 619-409-5900), 1000 Gunpowder Point Dr, is open 10 am to 5 pm daily in summer but closed on Monday and public holidays the rest of the year. Admission is $3.50, or $2.50 seniors, $1 ages 6 to 17.

To drive, take the E St exit from I-5 and go west to the parking lot; free shuttles run to the nature center every 25 minutes until 4 pm. The shuttle also picks up from the E St Trolley station.

Knott's Soak City USA This 32-acre water park is a cool place to be from early May until late September, its scheduled months of operation. Previously White Water Canyon, the financially troubled park was taken over and renamed in 2000 by the Knott's theme park conglomerate.

Designed to resemble the Southern California coast in the 1950s, it offers 22 water rides from the mild to the wild, including four high-speed slides and six body slides. **Palisades Plunge** and **Solana Storm Watch Tower** are riotous tube rides.

There's a height requirement of 48 inches for all but the body slides. Also open to all is **Balboa Bay**, a 500,000-gallon wave pool and the **Coronado Express**, a family raft ride that plunges 688 feet. There are several food stands (bringing in your own food is discouraged) and a couple of stores.

Knott's Soak City is at 2052 Entertainment Circle and open daily during the season. Because hours vary and often change, it's best to call ☎ 619-661-7373 for times on the day of your visit. In fine weather, the season may run to the end of October. Admission is $20 ages 12 and over, or $14 ages 3 to 11; after 3 pm admission is $12 for all ages.

To get there, take Main St off I-5 in Chula Vista, head east for 5 miles and turn right on Entertainment Circle. The entrance is next to the Coors Amphitheater. From I-805 take the Main St–Auto Park Dr exit and go east 2 miles.

Coors Amphitheater Opened in July 1998 at a cost of $20 million, this outdoor amphitheater (☎ 619-671-3600) is at 2050 Entertainment Circle. It provides San Diego with a state-of-the-art concert space and is regularly booked with major headliners such as Pearl Jam, the Spice Girls and James Taylor. Also see the San Diego Entertainment chapter.

Imperial Beach (Map 2)

The southernmost of San Diego's coastal communities, Imperial Beach began life as a getaway for visitors from the hot inland areas, especially Imperial Valley, which is what gave the town its name. These days IB s is it called, is best known as the site of the annual US Open Sandcastle contest, which takes place every July and pitches pros and amateur in an amazing battle against each other and nature.

The contest takes place on either side of the **Imperial Beach Pier**, which juts 1500 feet into the ocean. Unlicensed fishing is legal from the pier, but you might not want to eat your catch, as the waters are often heavily polluted. The main culprit is runoff from the Tijuana River, which just south of town discharges millions of gallons of raw sewage into the Pacific each day. The contamination obviously also puts a damper on swimming and surfing, despite nice beaches and good waves. The Border Environment Cooperation Commission is trying to get a handle on the problem.

Surfhenge In the history of California surfing, Imperial Beach occupies a special spot. As early as the 1940s surfers from near and far would come here to surf what were then the biggest known waves off the US coast. To honor this heritage, the newly spruced-up Pier Plaza, at the foot of the Imperial Beach pier (off Seacoast Dr), has been turned into an outdoor museum honoring the sport and its pioneers. The centerpiece is La Jolla artist Malcolm Jones' *Surfhenge,* four 16 to 20-foot tall acrylic surfboard-shaped arches. Around the plaza are 10 Technicolored benches made from various styles and shapes of surfboards that have been in vogue through the decades. In the ground next to each are plaques commemorating important surfing pioneers.

Tijuana River Estuary Reserve The Tijuana River enters the Pacific Ocean just south of IB. Its final stretch becomes an intertidal coastal estuary that is home to some 370 species of native and migratory birds. This 2530-acre reserve encompasses the largest remaining salt marsh in Southern California. Birds such as the light-footed clapper rail, the least Bell's vireo and the snow plover come here to nest, breed and feed. Unusual plants include the salt marsh bird's beak.

The visitors center (☎ 619-575-3613), 301 Caspian Way, is on the northern edge of the reserve, which is also called the **Tijuana Slough National Wildlife Refuge**. It's open 10 am to 5 pm daily and contains exhibits and a library. The reserve is crisscrossed by 8 miles of walking and horseback trails that give access to prime bird watching territory. You can explore on your own or join free guided nature and birding tours offered most weekends through the visitors center (call for schedule). To get there, take Coronado Ave off I-5, head west to Imperial Beach and turn left on 3rd St, then left again onto Caspian Way.

Border Field State Park Not the most scenic of the California state parks, Border Field marks the southernmost portion of the Tijuana River Estuary and literally rubs against the Mexican border. The park has 2 miles of sandy beach as well as horseback and walking trails. In spring colorful bursts of wildflowers enliven the stark chaparral.

Unfortunately, it's not all as lovely as it may sound. Green border patrol trucks perch on the hillsides aided by helicopters to deter would-be illegal immigrants. Tall poles with floodlighting provide further aesthetic distraction and, if you're really unlucky, raw sewage spilling over from the Tijuana River will have you hopscotching around with your nose clamped. Don't even think about swimming here.

So why visit at all? There's something surreal about standing right next to a border fence, ugly as it may be, extending all the way into the ocean. And while there's no civilization on the US side for several miles northward, the Mexican community of Playas de Tijuana is practically built against the border itself. For details on the border from the Mexican side, see the Playas de Tijuana section in the Tijuana Things to See & Do chapter.

The park is usually open 9:30 am to around sunset daily. Call ☎ 619-575-3613 for updated information. To get there, take the Dairy Rd exit off I-5, then continue west along Monument Rd until you can go no farther.

San Ysidro (Map 2)

You can take the San Diego trolley to one of the busiest international border crossings in the world, San Ysidro – 'Gateway to Mexico.' It is largely populated by Mexican Americans and well supplied with Mexican restaurants, money changers and sellers of Mexican auto insurance, particularly along San Ysidro Blvd. See the boxed text 'Crossing the US-Mexican Border' and the map in the San Diego Getting Around chapter.

Life's a Beach in San Diego

Beaches beckon all along the San Diego County coastline. Plenty of sunshine, warm air and lots of activities draw people to the shorefront year-round. Surfing, sailing, swimming, sunbathing, volleyball, beachcombing – or simply strolling along the sand – are all enjoyed by locals and visitors alike.

Water temperatures become tolerable by late spring and are highest (about 70°F) in August and September. In winter the Pacific becomes chilly, which doesn't stop surfers from hitting the swells in wetsuits. Many beaches have showers and restrooms, lifeguards, snack stands and regular clean-ups. With miles and miles of wide sandy shores to enjoy, the beaches rarely get packed with people. The most popular and populated beaches are those in Mission and Pacific Beach, although La Jolla and Ocean Beach can get busy too.

Hazards are few but shouldn't be ignored. Swimming is usually prohibited for three days after major storms because of dangerously high pollution levels from untreated runoff sweeping into the ocean through storm drains.

Another danger is riptides, strong currents that can occur when cross-currents collide and can drag swimmers away from the shore. Look for white, frothy water and flat waves. According to the US Lifesaving Association, people caught in riptides account for 80% of lifeguard rescues.

The following beaches (north to south), though by no means a complete list, are some highlights:

Oceanside Beaches This northern county town's beaches are a long and wide ribbon of sand, great for sunbathing, swimming and water sports. Infrastructure includes RV camping, lifeguards, restrooms and equipment concessions.

Moonlight Beach Picnic tables, barbecue pits, restrooms and lots of fine sand make Moonlight a popular family destination. Come here for swimming, tanning or watching beach volleyball. The nearest eateries are about a half-mile away in central Encinitas. Take the Encinitas Blvd exit off I-5 and head west, or walk five blocks from the *Coaster* station.

Swami's This narrow, pebbly beach in Encinitas is the preferred playground of dedicated surfers. Reached via a set of stairs, it's not really suitable for sunbathing or swimming, though at low tide beachcombers will find plenty. The little park above the beach has phones, tables and restrooms and is also a favorite sunset or whale-watching spot.

Torrey Pines State Beach This 2-mile-long sandy beach stretches south from Del Mar almost to La Jolla. Much of it snuggles against a 300-feet high phalanx of cliffs. Access via the unstable cliffs is difficult, and it may be easier to approach from beaches to the north or south. Lifeguards are not always on duty. Surfing is good at the beach's southern end. To get here, take the Carmel Valley Rd exit off I-5 and turn left at Torrey Pines State Beach.

Black's Beach Between Torrey Pines State Beach and La Jolla Shores is Black's Beach, the only one in the county where bathing suits are technically required but practically absent. This is a popular hangout for gay men. It's also a popular surfing beach and boasts the best sandy-bottom surfing breaks because of its location above the La Jolla Submarine Canyon.

ACTIVITIES

You can pretty much be outdoors year-round in San Diego, the city that puts the 'sun' in sunny California. Below you'll find suggestions for some of the many activities offered here.

Surfing

Surfing is big in San Diego, and the waves can get crowded. Fall offers the best chance for strong swells and offshore Santa Ana winds. In summer, swells come from the south and southwest, and in winter from the

Life's a Beach in San Diego

La Jolla Shores This is your quintessential Southern California beach, big and wide with white sand and lots of people who seem to have just stepped off the cover of Cosmo or GQ. The San Diego–La Jolla Underwater Ecological Reserve is just offshore, and kayakers can launch off the beach with ease. There's a separate area for surfers, and the waves here are gentle enough for beginners. Kellogg Park, behind the lifeguard tower, has a grassy playground.

La Jolla Cove This lovely little beach wedged between the sandstone cliffs is part of the San Diego–La Jolla Underwater Park Ecological Reserve and offers some of the best snorkeling and diving around (with visibility of 30 feet and more). It's crowded most of the time, so come early to claim your space. Ellen Browning Scripps Park, atop the bluff, is popular with picnickers and also has a restroom with showers. A lifeguard is on duty year-round.

Windansea Beach This rocky beach is a favorite with surfers and often gets crowded. There's also a separate area for swimmers, but it's not really suitable for families because of shorebreak, which means that rough waves break right on the shoreline. Lifeguards are usually on duty daily in summer, and on weekends in spring and fall. There are no restrooms or showers, and parking is scarce.

Pacific Beach & Mission Beach Starting south of Crystal Pier, this is the northernmost of a 2-mile stretch of beach also known as The Strand; it follows the coast from south of La Jolla to the Mission Bay Channel entrance. The Strand is the most popular beach in the county and gets jammed on summer weekends. It is paralleled by a paved boardwalk perfect for cycling, walking and in-line skating. Lifeguards are on duty year-round.

Mission Bay Beaches The 4600-acre Mission Bay Park has 27 miles of shore, including 19 miles of sandy beaches in pretty coves and inlets. It is ground central for water sports and teems with rowers, water-skiers, kayakers and boaters. Swimming is allowed only on beaches with lifeguards, including Bonita Cove, Crown Point Shores, De Anza Cove, Tecolote Shores, Leisure Lagoon and Ventura Cove. The Northern Wildlife Preserve, on the bay's northern edge, near Crown Point, is home to many bird species. Lifeguards are usually around from spring to fall, and parking is plentiful, as are restrooms.

Ocean Beach Starting just south of the Mission Bay channel entrance, this wide beach is about a mile long and has a real neighborhoody feel. At its northern end is Dog Beach, one of only two beaches in San Diego where dogs are allowed to roam without a leash, though owners must clean up after them (the other beach is Fiesta Island in Mission Bay). Surfers gather in the waters beneath and just north of the pier. There are separate areas for swimmers and surfers, as well as volleyball courts near the northern end.

Coronado Beach This is a genteel beach, wide, clean, with white sand, especially around the Hotel del Coronado. It gets crowded with families, especially on weekends, when parking can be nightmarish. Parents with kids in tow will like this beach because of the gentle slope going down into the water.

west and northwest. Spring brings more onshore winds, but the surfing can still be good. In winter, you'll need a wet suit. For the latest beach, weather and surf reports, call City Lifeguard at ☎ 619-221-8824.

Beginners looking to rent equipment should head to Mission Beach or Pacific Beach, where the waves are gentle. Places such as Bob's Mission Surf (Map 10; ☎ 858-483-8837), 4320 Mission Blvd near Grand Ave, and the Pacific Beach Surf Shop (Map 10; ☎ 858-488-9575), 747 Pacific Beach Dr, rent boards ($10/15 half-day/day) and wet suits ($6/10).

The best surf breaks, from south to north, are at Imperial Beach (especially in winter); Coronado (good in summer, with south swell and north wind); Point Loma (reef breaks that are less accessible, but therefore less crowded; best in winter); Sunset Cliffs in Ocean Beach; Mission Beach (beach break, good for beginners); Crystal Pier in Pacific Beach (steep and fast waves); Tourmaline Surfing Park (popular with longboarders); Big Rock (California's version of Hawaii's Pipeline with steep, hollow, gnarly tubes), Windansea (hot reef break, best at medium to low tide; crowded, not for beginners); La Jolla Shores (beach break, best in winter) and Blacks Beach (fast, powerful waves). Farther up the coast, in North County, there are breaks at Cardiff State Beach, San Elijo State Beach, Swami's, Carlsbad State Beach and Oceanside.

Body surfing is good at Coronado, Mission Beach, Pacific Beach, Boomer Beach near La Jolla Cove (for the experienced only; best with a big swell) and La Jolla Shores. To get into the 'whomp' (the forceful tubes that break directly on shore), know what you're doing and head to Windansea or the beach at the end of Sea Lane (both in La Jolla).

If the only place you've ever surfed is the Internet, you can learn the real thing at the San Diego Surf Academy (☎ 858-565-6892, 800-447-7873, fax 858-279-5778, ✉ info@surfSDSA.com), which offers instruction by appointment at Tourmaline Park and also holds surf camps at San Elijo State Beach in Cardiff-by-the-Sea (see the San Diego Ex-

cursions chapter). Group lessons are $25 per person per hour (two-hour minimum), one-on-one sessions are $45 per hour, and the six-day/five-night camps cost $750. Check their Web site (www.surfSDSA.com) for details.

Scuba Diving & Snorkeling

The waters off San Diego County are wonderful playgrounds for divers and snorkelers. Rock reefs, shipwrecks and kelp beds all invite exploration and attract a variety of fish. There are sites suited for all levels of skill and experience; wet suits are advisable year-round. For current dive conditions call ☎ 619-221-8824.

Some of California's best diving is in the San Diego-La Jolla Underwater Park Ecological Reserve. The 6000 acres of look-but-don't-touch underwater real estate is accessible from La Jolla Cove. Depths average 10 to 30 feet, which, on good-visibility days, make for snorkeling as well. Ever-present are the spectacular, bright orange Garibaldi fish – California's official state fish and a protected species (there's a $500 fine for hooking one of these).

Near the Marine Room restaurant, you'll swim in the company of reef sharks and rays. Other La Jolla sites include North and South Bird Rock, Casa Cove, and the 100-foot deep La Jolla Canyon for more experienced divers. Beginners should stick to Kellogg Park (in La Jolla Shores) and La Jolla Cove. Sunset Cliffs, which also has great reefs, is another popular spot.

Farther out are forests of giant Californian kelp, which grows up to 3 feet per day, making it one of the world's fastest growing plants. These rich waters are a habitat for numerous species, including octopus and eels, small sharks, halibut, spiny lobster and, of course, the Garibaldi. Kelp forests can also be found off Point Loma.

Another popular dive site is Wreck Alley off Mission Beach, where several submerged structures and boats have formed an artificial reef. These include a 165-foot Coast Guard cutter snuggled against the ocean floor at 85 feet deep and the recently sunk *Yukon*, a 366-foot Canadian destroyer.

Established dive shops, which rent and sell equipment and offer instruction and certification, include San Diego Divers Supply (Map 9; ☎ 619-224-3439, fax 224-0596), 4004 Sports Arena Blvd just south of Mission Bay; Diving Locker (Map 10; ☎ 858-272-1120), 1020 Grand Ave in Pacific Beach; OE Express (Map 11; ☎ 858-454-6195), 2158 Avenida de la Playa in La Jolla; Sports Chalet (Map 11; ☎ 858-453-5656), 4525 La Jolla Village Dr in University Towne Centre. Divers Discount Supply (Map 7; ☎ 619-285-1000) is just what it says and is at 4560 Alvarado Canyon Rd in Mission Valley.

A popular thrill is to swim with the big sharks – well almost. You descend inside a steel cage and watch – and photograph – as an instructor in a steel mesh suit outside the cage feeds blue and mako sharks. Several companies offer this for about $260, including San Diego Shark Diving (Map 7; ☎ 619-299-8560, 888-737-4275) at 6747 Friars Rd in Mission Valley.

Kayaking

Ocean kayaking is a good way to see sea life and explore cliffs and caves inaccessible from land. For beginners, the flat waters of La Jolla Cove and Mission Bay are best, while Tourmaline Surfing Beach (near the border of La Jolla and Pacific Beach) presents challenges to more experienced kayakers. The two basic kayak types are decked (sit-inside) and open-top (sit-on-top).

Southwest Kayaks (Map 9; ☎ 619-222-3616, fax 619-222-3671, ✉ kayaked@aol.com), 2590 Ingraham St at the Dana Landing Marina, is co-owned by kayaking legend Ed Gillet. The company offers guided trips and classes for beginners to experts, starting at $45, including equipment. Kayaks rent for $25/35 per half-day/day; hourly rentals are from $10 to $15. Mission Bay Sportcenter (Map 9; ☎ 858-488-1004), 1010 Santa Clara Place in Mission Bay, charges $13 to $18 for hourly rentals, $39 to $54 for four hours and $44 to $60 per day.

In La Jolla, the best place for kayaking gear and information is OE Express (see Diving & Snorkeling earlier for contact information). They rent kayaks for $25/35

single/double for two hours, $35/45 for four hours or $50/65 all day. Nearby La Jolla Kayak & Company (Map 11; ☎ 858-459-1114), 2199 Avenida de la Playa, charges the same. Their guided 'Kayak Tour of the 7 Caves' is a popular 90-minute excursion available for $35.

Fishing

The most popular public fishing piers are in Imperial Beach, the Embarcadero, Shelter Island, Ocean Beach and Pacific Beach's Crystal Pier. The best time of year for pier fishing is April to October. Offshore catches can include barracuda, bass and yellowtail. In summer, albacore is a special attraction. There's also great fishing in the county's many lakes. A recorded service (☎ 619-465-3474) provides information.

Most fish and shellfish may be taken year-round, but there are limits, minimum sizes, methods of taking and other regulations. These are outlined in a Department of Fish and Game booklet, which is also on the Internet at www.dfg.ca.gov.

Several companies offer half-day and overnight ocean fishing trips for open parties, meaning anyone can join in until the boat is full. All companies also offer private charters. Be sure to make reservations, especially on summer weekends.

Competition is fierce and prices among companies are similar. Half-day trips (6 to 11:30 am or 12:30 to 5:30 pm) cost $29; twilight trips from 6 to 10:30 pm are $22; and overnight trips to Mexico range from $85 to

$150, including bunk and Mexican fishing permit, depending on the destination and season. Tackle costs from $7 to $12. The following are all established companies.

H&M Landing (Map 8; ☎ 619-222-1144, fax 619-222-0784, ✉ hmmail@hmlanding.com), 2803 Emerson St on Shelter Island

Seaforth Sportfishing (Map 9; ☎ 619-224-3383, ✉ webmaster@seaforthlanding.com), 1717 Quivira Rd in Quivira Basin, Mission Bay

Islandia Sportfishing (Map 9; ☎ 619-222-1164, fax 619-224-0348, ✉ fishin@islandiasport.com), 1551 W Mission Bay Dr in Mission Bay

Licenses A California state fishing license is required for people over 16 years, except if fishing from a public ocean pier. One-day licenses (ocean only) are $6.05; two or 10-day licenses (ocean or freshwater) are $10.25/28.10. Annual licenses are $28.10 for California residents and $75.85 for nonresidents. Boat companies, bait and tackle shops, chain sporting goods stores like Big 5 or Sports Chalet all issue these licenses, as does the Department of Fish and Game (☎ 858-467-4201), 4949 Viewridge Ave.

Boating
Power and sailboats, rowboats, kayaks and canoes can be rented in Mission Bay from the following companies:

Mission Bay Sportcenter (Map 9; ☎ 619-488-1004), 1010 Santa Clara Place

CP Watersports (Map 9; ☎ 619-275-8945), at the Hilton Beach Resort, 1775 E Mission Bay Dr

Adventure Sports (Map 9; ☎ 619-226-8611), at the Dana Inn & Marina, 1710 W Mission Dr and at Campland on the Bay (Map 9; ☎ 858-581-9300); see Camping under San Diego Places to Stay

Seaforth Boat Rentals (☎ 888-834-2628), with three locations: Mission Bay at 1641 Quivira Rd (Map 9; ☎ 619-223-1681), Downtown at 333 West Harbor Dr, Gate 1 (Map 3; ☎ 619-239-2628) and Coronado at 1715 Strand Way (Map 4; ☎ 619-437-1514)

Experienced sailors can charter yachts for trips on San Diego Bay and out into the Pacific. Quite a few charter companies are around Shelter Island and Harbor Island,

including San Diego Yacht Charters (Map 8; ☎ 619-297-4555), 1880 Harbor Island Dr, and Harbor Sailboats (Map 8; ☎ 619-291-9568), 2040 Harbor Island Dr, Suite 104.

Whale Watching
Majestic gray whales pass San Diego from mid-December to late February on their way south and again in mid-March on their way back. The Whale Overlook in Cabrillo National Monument, on the southern tip of the Point Loma peninsula, is the best place to spot whales from land (bring binoculars). The ranger station here also has exhibits and related programs. Views are also good from Torrey Pines State Reserve and La Jolla Cove.

To get up close and personal, take one of the whale watching cruises that operate daily during the migration. The cost is around $15 to $20 for adults and $10 for children for a three-hour trip. Some outfits guarantee a sighting, and many have discount coupons in the *San Diego Reader*. Contact H&M Landing (☎ 619-222-1144), Seaforth

Sportfishing (☎ 619-224-3383), Hornblower/Invader Cruises (☎ 619-234-8687) or San Diego Harbor Excursions (☎ 619-234-4111).

Bicycling
Although many of San Diego's roads are not particularly bicyclist-friendly, you'll find many designated bike trails throughout the county. San Diego Ridelink publishes the excellent *San Diego Region Bike Map*, which details numerous bike paths, lanes and routes. It is available at tourist offices or by calling ☎ 619-231-2453.

Among the most popular cycling areas is the boardwalk in Pacific and Mission Beach, but it can get crowded, especially on weekends. Enjoy the same great ocean views without the crowds by biking through Coronado and south on Silver Strand to Imperial

Beach. Another good route is the bike lane paralleling Hwy 209 to the Cabrillo National Monument on Point Loma. Sunset Cliffs Rd between Point Loma and Ocean Beach is spectacular at – you guessed it – sunset. Mountain bikers will find trails in Mission Trails Regional Park, Torrey Pines State Park and elsewhere; for detailed route descriptions, pick up a copy of Daniel Greenstadt's *San Diego Mountain Bike Guide*.

For a thrilling experience, you could join Gravity Activated Sports (☎ 760-742-2294, 800-985-4427) for the Palomar Plunge. You'll be transported up Palomar Mountain (see the San Diego Excursions chapter), where you'll check out the famous telescope, have lunch and then cruise 16 miles downhill (a 5000-foot drop) on a paved two-lane highway. See their Web site at www.gasports.com.

Also see the San Diego Getting Around chapter for information about renting bicycles and taking them on public transport.

Horseback Riding

Sandy's Rental Stable (☎ 619-424-3124), 2060 Hollister St in Imperial Beach, next to the Tijuana Slough Estuary and Border Field State Park, leads horseback tours. The one-hour natural trail ride is $30, and the three-hour combined beach and nature trail ride is $60. The minimum age is seven.

Hang Gliding

Glider riders hang at Torrey Pines Glider Port (☎ 858-452-9858), 2800 Torrey Pines Scenic Dr, La Jolla, which is famous as a gliding location. Tandem flights in a hang glider are $125 for 20 to 30 minutes, including ground instruction.

Experienced pilots can join in if they have a USHGA Hang 4 rating and take out an associate membership in the Torrey Pines Hang Glider Association.

Golf

San Diegans are a golf-crazed bunch, as supported by the number of courses – 90 – throughout the county and the fact that at least 20 major golf manufacturers are based here. Besides dozens of public courses, there are also private clubs and semiprivate courses, meaning members are allowed to bring guests. All courses mentioned here are public. The San Diego Convention & Visitors Bureau publishes an annual Golf Guide, which details the most important courses. It is available for free at tourist offices.

Getting tee times is tough at some courses, and you should call as early as possible. Otherwise, you could use a broker who might get you on the fairway even if everything's officially booked. Try The Golfer at ☎ 877-486-4653 and M&M Tee Times (☎ 858-456-8300, 800-867-7397) and Select Tee Times (☎ 858-638-4555).

One central course is the **Riverwalk Golf Club** (Map 7; ☎ 619-698-4653), 1150 Fashion Valley Rd, right along the San Diego River in Mission Valley. In the 1950s and '60s it was the Stardust Country Club and the site of the San Diego Open. There are three nine-hole courses, with 13 of the 27 holes built around water. Green fees run $48 to $98, depending on the day and time.

In El Cajon, in the eastern metropolitan area, is by far the best value for the money, **Singing Hills Resort** (☎ 619-442-3425, 800-457-5568), 3007 Dehesa Rd. Spread over 425 acres, it is in a spectacular valley ringed by mountains and natural rock outcroppings. There are two 18-hole championship and one 18-hole executive courses. PGA and other championships have been held here, and the Women's School of Golf enjoys national stature. If you love golf, you should consider staying at the resort. Various reasonably priced packages are available. Otherwise, green fees range from $15 to $37 midweek and $15 to $45 weekends, plus $16 to $22 for a golf cart.

From the mountains to the sea – **Torrey Pines Golf Course** (☎ 858-452-3226), 11480 N Torrey Pines Rd in La Jolla, is home of the PGA's Buick Invitational every February and one of the most famous courses in the nation. On the bluffs above the ocean are two courses, the South Course (par 72, 6705 yards) being a bit harder than the North Course (par 72, 6326 yards); the 7th and the 12th holes are considered among the toughest in town. Green fees are $47 midweek, $52 weekends, carts are $28.

Places to Stay

Tourism is a major industry in San Diego, where more than 45,000 hotel rooms vie for guests. Clearly, where you want to stay will dictate to a great extent how much you'll end up paying. Budget lodgings are scarce in La Jolla or around Mission Bay but abundant in Downtown and around Hotel Circle in Mission Valley. Seasonal price fluctuations also affect room rates. In summer (between Memorial Day and Labor Day), rates, especially in the beach communities, may increase 50% or more, reflecting the greater demand for rooms. The same is true around major holidays such as July 4, Labor Day, Thanksgiving, Christmas and New Year's. During those times, budget beds are as rare as a baby panda.

Hotels that cater to business travelers often charge considerably lower rates Friday and Saturday nights than during the week, when corporate expense accounts rule. A fancy suite that might run $190 Sunday through Thursday night could be a bargain $100 on the weekend. The opposite is true of hotels catering to leisure travelers.

While differences between single and double occupancy are usually minor, the number of beds does make a difference: Rooms with two queen-size beds cost more than those with one king-size bed. Hotels with only a few rooms may charge more than places with many. Room location may also affect price, and recently renovated or larger rooms are likely to cost a bit more. Hotels facing a noisy street may charge more for quieter rooms.

The cheapest lodging option – about $15 to $20 – is a bunk in a hostel. Hostels are communal affairs with four- to eight-bed dorms (sometimes gender-segregated), shared washrooms and showers, kitchens, laundry rooms and TV rooms. Some hostels also have private rooms for about $35 to $60 per night, double occupancy, which is about the same rate as the rooms at cheap motels. Expect the latter to be low-frill

places with basic amenities (including TV and phone), adequate to rest your head but not to hang out. You'll find them listed under 'Budget' in this book.

The closer you are to the coast, Old Town, or to upscale neighborhoods like La Jolla, the more likely you'll be paying $80 to $120 per night, per room. Spending just a little extra, from $120 to $150, generally buys more comfort and such amenities as refrigerators, microwaves, spas and voice mail. This spectrum of accommodations is listed as 'Mid-Range.'

San Diego has many luxurious properties with rooms costing $150 and up (these fall under 'Top End'). Often these are lavish, full-service resorts with extravagant landscaping and facilities; rooms and public areas are modern and nicely furnished, perhaps adorned with art and fresh flowers; many have special touches like a rooftop swimming pool, tennis courts or in-house massages. The sky's the limit in terms of price, and some suites and penthouses may cost $1000 or more a night. Upscale lodgings like these tend to cluster in Downtown, La Jolla and around Mission Bay.

Whenever possible, this book provides the range of rates a hotel may charge, though changes occur frequently and unpredictably. Rooms get renovated, managers change, and independent hotels are taken over by chains. Thus, prices quoted in this book are merely intended as guidelines.

Discounts

Members of the American Automobile Association (AAA) or AARP (see the Senior Travelers section in the San Diego Facts for the Visitors chapter) often qualify for discounts of 10% or more off the published rates, as do university students, military personnel and travel-industry members. Some hotels give small discounts if you make reservations via the Internet. Also look out at gas stations and tourist offices for freebie ad rags packed with hotel discount coupons. In general, make it a habit to ask about discounts when booking a room.

Taxes & Extra Charges

Your final hotel bill will swell with taxes, tips, parking and phone connection charges that will increase in proportion to the cost of your accommodations. The 'transient occupancy tax' on all hotel and motel rooms is 10.5%.

Other charges will be less of a concern, unless you're staying in a top-end hotel where you'll be expected to tip bellhops and concierges in addition to cleaning staff, restaurant servers and bartenders. While parking is generally free at budget and mid-range properties, it will run $7 to $20 daily at upscale hotels, plus tips for valets. And while motels rarely charge more than 25¢ for local phone calls (often these are free), big hotels may stick you with up to $1 per call. If you're calling long distance, you'll pay through the nose unless you use a credit or calling card, and then you'll still have that pesky connection fee.

Reservations

This chapter lists toll-free 800 telephone numbers whenever they are available. Note that these numbers are meant to be used only to ask for information or to make a reservation; for private calls to a guest's room, use the direct hotel number and ask to be transferred. If you're having trouble finding accommodations, consider using one of the following free hotel-reservation services:

Alliance Reservations Network (☎ 800-434-7894); www.sandiegohotel.org

California Reservations (☎ 415-252-1107, 800-576-0003); www.californiares.com

Central Reservation Service (☎ 800-548-3311); www.reservations-services.com

Hotel Reservations Network (☎ 800-964-6835); www.hotelreservations.com

Sights of San Diego (☎ 800-434-7894); www.sightsofsandiego.com

PLACES TO STAY – BUDGET
Camping

San Diego County has plenty of private, county and state campgrounds, but most are not very central and/or cater exclusively to RVs. Generally open year-round, they quickly fill to capacity in summer; early reservations are a good idea here, especially for weekend travel.

In addition to the central campgrounds mentioned below, the parks and recreation departments of San Diego County and the State of California maintain dozens of camping facilities throughout the area, often in scenic, backcountry locales. Some of these are mentioned in the San Diego Excursions chapter, but for complete information and reservations, contact Parknet at ☎ 800-444-7275, daily from 8 am to 5 pm. For on-line reservations, log on to the Web site www.reserveamerica.com. There's a $7.50 fee per reservation. For county-administered campgrounds, call ☎ 858-694-3049.

The following campgrounds are all fairly close to the beaches and attractions, but only the first two allow tent camping. ***Campland on the Bay*** (*Map 9;* ☎ *858-581-4260, 800-422-9386, fax 858-581-4206, 2211 Pacific Beach Dr*) has more than 40 acres fronting Mission Bay and can hold up to 650 tents and RVs. Facilities include a restaurant, pool and boating facilities and full RV hookups. Sites range from $27 to $67.50 in winter, $25 to $97.50 in summer. The priciest ones are the private 'Supersites' with Jacuzzi, gas grill, cable TV and other luxuries. The location is great, but the tent area is not very attractive (too many RVs, not enough trees) and can be crowded. Reservations are a must in summer.

Less central but considerably nicer, with attractive landscaping and grassy and shaded sites, is the ***San Diego Metro KOA*** (☎ *619-427-3601, 800-762-5267, fax 619-427-3622, 111 N 2nd Ave),* in Chula Vista, about 5 miles southeast of Downtown. It charges $29 for tent sites, $37.50 for RVs with full hookups, and $41/49 for one/two bedroom cabins. Prices are for two people, extra adults are $4 each. Amenities include a swimming pool, hot tub and sauna.

The closest RV park to the border crossing is ***International Motor Inn RV Park*** (☎ *619-428-4486, 190 E Calle Primero)* in San Ysidro (take the Via de San Ysidro exit off I-5). It's smallish but has a pool and full hookups and charges $23 for two people, $2 for each additional person.

If you want to be closer to Downtown, consider **De Anza Harbor Resort** *(Map 9; ☎ 858-273-3214, 800-924-7529, fax 858-274-0362, 2727 De Anza Rd)*, an all RV resort adjacent to the Mission Bay golf course. Sites are paved, and a wide range of sports and social activities are offered. Rates are $27 to $33 in winter, $39 to $45 in summer.

Hostels

San Diego has several hostels, including two affiliated with Hostelling International/ American Youth Hostels (HI/AYH). All take credit cards and none have a curfew. Reservations are essential in summer and a good idea the rest of the year. Our listings include Web addresses that you can check for additional details, including directions on how to get to each hostel by public transport. Prices include taxes.

HI/AYH Hostels At HI hostels, dormitories are gender-segregated, and alcohol and smoking are prohibited. Both hostels take reservations by phone, fax and email with a credit card. If you're using snail mail, you'll need to include a check, US bank draft or money order and a self-addressed and stamped envelope. The various options are explained in greater detail at the HI Web site at www.hiayh.org, which also provides access to 'E-beds,' an online reservation system.

The **HI San Diego Downtown Hostel** *(Map 3; ☎ 619-525-1531, 800-909-4776/hostel code 43, fax 619-338-0129, @ hisddwntwn@ aol.com, 521 Market St)* is smack dab in the Gaslamp Quarter, handy to public transportation and nightlife. Clean and quiet, it has skylights throughout and a safe and pleasant ambience. The communal kitchen is well-equipped, and the long list of amenities includes laundry, Internet access, a game and TV room, free coffee and tea, free airport pick-ups, plus daily activities. Check-in is from 7 am to midnight. Beds are $18 ($21 for non-members), including linen; private rooms are $44/54 single/double. The Web address is www.hostelweb.com/sandiego/ downtown.htm.

The **HI San Diego Point Loma Hostel** *(Map 8; ☎ 619-223-4778, 800-909-4776/hostel code 44, fax 619-223-1883, @ hisdptloma@ aol.com, 3790 Udall St)*, in Loma Portal, is about 1 mile east of the beach and close to Ocean Beach's lively nightlife and restaurants. It's tricky to find and a bit complicated to reach with public transport, but has a nice, laid-back atmosphere. Guests hang out in the central courtyard or engage in international cook-offs in the large kitchen (a supermarket is just across the street). The hostel also has a laundry and rents out bikes. Dorm beds are $15 ($18 non-members), and doubles and triples go for $36/54 ($42/63 non-members). Check-in is from 8 am to 10 pm. The hostel's Web address is www .hostelweb.com/sandiego/pointloma.htm.

Independent Hostels San Diego's private hostels have comparable rates to HI/AYH hostels but no alcohol or smoking restrictions. In addition to dorms, a few singles/ doubles, sometimes with private bathrooms, are usually available. Communal facilities include a kitchen, laundry, notice board and TV room. Most of these hostels are geared toward non-US travelers, although US residents are allowed if they have a passport and international plane ticket.

In the Gaslamp Quarter, **USA Hostel San Diego** *(Map 3; ☎ 619-232-3100, 800-438-8622, fax 619-232-3106, @ sandiego@ usahostels.com, 726 5th Ave)*, formerly the Grand Pacific Hostel, is a Victorian-era hotel refitted with six-bed dorms ($18/$115 per day/week) and private rooms ($25 to $55 per day, or $157 to $351 per week), including sheets and breakfast. Free shuttles to the beach or area attractions are offered sporadically, as are day tours, in-house parties and beach barbecues. The lounge and kitchen areas are quite nice. Besides international travelers, US citizens with passports showing overseas travel within the last year are welcome. See the Web site at www.usahostels.com.

Also known as The Baltic Inn, and really more a large hotel than a traditional hostel, the ***Downtown Youth Hostel*** *(Map 3; ☎ 619-237-0687, 521 6th Ave)* has 206 private rooms with sink and WC (showers are shared), TV, microwave and refrigerator. Drawing an international crowd from ages 18 to 80, the Baltic is clean and quiet. The cost for single occupancy is $20 a day or $73 to $140 weekly, depending on room size and location. Two people in the room pay $25 per day and $90 to $140 per week.

Only a couple of blocks from a nice beach, ***Ocean Beach International Hostel*** *(Map 8; ☎ 619-223-7873, 800-339-7263, fax 619-223-7881, ◙ obihostel@aol.com, 4961 Newport Ave)* is ensconced in a 95-year-old historic former hotel turned into a friendly, fun hostel hugely popular with European travelers. Matching the relaxed and funky vibe of Ocean Beach, it's clean and in good shape. Free all-you-can-eat barbecues take place twice weekly, and there's a large kitchen and dining room. The cost is $15 to $17 per bed in a four-person dorm and $34 to $38 for the few doubles; rates include breakfast. See the Web site at http://members.aol.com/OBIhostel/hostel.

Don't come to the ***Banana Bungalow San Diego*** *(Map 10; ☎ 858-273-3060, 800-546-7835, fax 858-273-1440, ◙ sdres@bananabungalow.com, 707 Reed Ave)* in Pacific Beach to catch up on your sleep. As raucous as Animal House, as full of intrigue as Big Brother and as global as the United Nations, this place is party central. The beachfront location and jungle-theme decor provide the backdrop for keg parties, barbecues and volleyball tournaments. To tell mom all about it, there are pay phones, Internet access and a fax machine. Bunks in renovated, reasonably clean dorms cost from $16 to $20, including sheets, blankets and breakfast. Phone ahead for free pickups from the airport, Amtrak or Greyhound stations. Stays require a passport and an overseas plane ticket. The hostel's Web site is at www.bananabungalow.com.

Hotels
Downtown (Map 3) Note that some of the cheapest Downtown hotels provide what is sometimes called SRO (single room occupancy), which means that they rent no-frills rooms, by the day, week or month, to people who might otherwise be homeless. Low-budget travelers often stay in these places and find them quite tolerable, though some regular guests can be, well, quite colorful. Developers would like to get rid of SROs, but they actually serve an important social function. Weekly rates are cheaper, but there is typically a key deposit. In the cheapest rooms, you share a hall bathroom.

The ***Golden West Hotel*** *(☎ 619-233-7594, fax 619-233-4009, 720 4th Ave)* allows the cash-strapped to stay in a historical landmark, but it's often full with long-term residents. An art deco marquee gives way to a spacious lobby with stained-glass skylights and oak paneling. Single rooms are comfortable if basic and cost $22 without private bath and $29 with. A few double rooms rent out on a weekly basis only, starting at $150.

In much the same vein, but slightly pricier, is the related ***Maryland Hotel*** *(☎ 619-239-9243, fax 619-235-8968, 630 F St)* with rather large, clean but no-frills singles going for $37 to $67. The better value is the weekly rate, starting at $130/190 single/double for rooms with shower and WC.

Another old-timey downtown place is the ***Pickwick Hotel*** *(☎ 619-234-9200, fax 619-544-9879, 132 Broadway)*, in a 1926 building where rooms have received a recent update. Drivers will find the secured underground parking an asset, while families will appreciate that children under 16 stay free. On-site amenities include a coin-op laundry, and fax and copy service. Rates are $55/60.

The ***Pacifica Hotel*** *(☎ 619-235-9240, 1546 2nd Ave)* is clean and nicely designed and only five blocks from the town center. Rooms have basic cooking facilities, and the hotel has a laundry, market and deli on the premises. Single/double, all with shared bath, from $30/40 and also rent by the week.

The ***Rodeway Inn*** *(☎ 619-239-2285, 800-522-1528, fax 619-235-6951, 833 Ash St)* is an impeccably run budget motel with friendly and helpful staff and clean rooms. Larger ones come with a balcony, refrigerator and separate sitting area. A well-kept small sauna and whirlpool are on the premises as well. Rates range from $59 to $129, and include a generous continental breakfast.

Next door, the 67-room *Comfort Inn Downtown* (☎ 619-232-2525, fax 619-687-3024, 719 Ash St) is another nicer-than-average contender with a free 24-hour shuttle to the airport, Greyhound and Amtrak stations as its distinctive asset. Rates are $49 to $89 single, $51 to $99 double.

Corinthian Suites (☎ 619-236-1600, fax 619-231-4734, 1840 4th Ave) is modern, friendly and within walking distance of Balboa Park, which is just north of Downtown. A lovely courtyard anchored by a tiled fountain gives way to rooms decked out in fresh and appealing color schemes. For those too tired to head out, there's a microwave to pop some corn, a fridge to chill your drink and cable TV to keep you entertained. Rates are a very reasonable $45 to $60 single, $55 to $65 double.

La Pensione (☎ 619-236-8000, 800-232-4683, fax 619-236-8088, 🖂 la-pensione@travelbase.com, 1700 India St), in the heart of Little Italy, is one of the top bargains in town. Built around a tiled courtyard, it exudes a European flair, with its black marble lobby and light-flooded, modern rooms, which are smallish but adequately equipped and great value at $49 to $79. There's also free subterranean parking.

A step up from most chain hotels, the *Super 8 Bayview* (☎ 619-544-0164, 800-537-9902, fax 619-237-9940, 1835 Columbia St), in Little Italy, gives you comfortable rooms and a central location without robbing your bank account. The 102 rooms are good-sized, and there's a spanking new swimming pool and Jacuzzi. Rates include continental breakfast and range from $38 to $79.

The *Inn at the YMCA* (☎ 619-234-5252, fax 619-234-5272, 500 W Broadway) is in a 1924 landmark building. Rates of $40/50 include access to the Y's fitness facilities, including aerobics classes, heated indoor pool and saunas.

For weekly stays, consider the postmodern, rather hip *J Street Inn* (☎ 619-696-6922, fax 619-696-1295, 222 J St); rooms have microwave and refrigerator and cost $179 single, and $199 to $230 double.

Coronado (Map 4) The cheapest lodging on Coronado is at the *El Rancho Motel* (☎ 619-435-2251, 370 Orange Ave), but with only eight units, snagging a room here requires some luck – or advance reservations. If you get to stay, you'll get exceptional value in rooms with beamed ceilings, air-con, microwave and refrigerator for $45 to $90.

A bit dearer, but still fairly affordable, is the *Coronado Inn* (☎ 619-435-4121, 800-598-6624, fax 619-435-6296, 266 Orange Ave). The low structure with neoclassical touches flanks a sundeck with pool and has air-conditioned rooms with microwaves and refrigerators. The cost is $85 to $140, and includes continental breakfast.

Old Town (Map 5) True budget options in Old Town proper are scarce. You might try *Old Town Plaza Hotel* (☎ 619-291-9100, 888-478-7829, fax 619-291-4717, 2380 Moore St), recently spruced up and now glowing in subtle California Mission decor. Comfortable, if nothing special, the hotel charges $64/74 single/double, including continental breakfast.

Hillcrest (Map 6) A solid budget option in Hillcrest is the *Friendship Hotel* (☎ 619-298-9898, 3942 8th Ave), with basic rooms costing just $25 to $40 ($125 to $150 weekly). It's in a quiet side street within walking distance of restaurants and nightlife.

Mission Valley (Map 7) Lined north and south of I-8, along a road that's has been appropriately dubbed Hotel Circle, are a series of hotels and motels, most of them national chains. While the location among car dealerships and golf courses may not be scenic, many people like to stay here because of low prices and easy access to Old Town, shopping centers and the San Diego Trolley.

The *Hotel Circle Inn & Suites* (☎ 619-881-6800, 800-772-7711, fax 619-542-1227, 2201 Hotel Circle S) has a restaurant that makes famous apple pancakes. The hotel has a range of rooms, as well as large suites for up to six people. The suites all feature full kitchens. Rates range from $59 to $139.

East of the Hotel Circle Inn & Suites is the ***Ramada Plaza Hotel*** (☎ 619-291-6500, 800-405-9102, fax 619-294-7531, 2151 Hotel Circle S), which exudes considerable charm in its stylish peaches-and-cream-colored public areas, as well as in its rooms and suites, which are pleasantly appointed with floral curtains and bedspreads, leafy plants and a sitting area. Business travelers will like the large work desks and data ports, and there's a pool to work out the kinks. Rates start at $69 in winter and $99 in summer.

There are also plenty of budget chain motels around here, including ***Econolodge*** (☎ 619-692-1288, fax 619-298-0668, 445 Hotel Circle S), ***Howard Johnson Hotel Circle*** (☎ 619-293-7792, fax 619-298-5321, 1631 Hotel Circle S) and the ***Vagabond Inn*** (☎ 619-297-1691, fax 619-692-9009, 625 Hotel Circle S). ***Best Inn & Suites*** (☎ 619-287-8730, 5399 Adobe Falls Rd) and ***Super 8 Motel*** (☎ 619-281-2222, fax 619-280-3462, 4380 Alvarado Canyon Rd) are both a few miles farther inland, near Qualcomm Stadium.

Point Loma & Ocean Beach (Map 8) A

family place ('no pets, no parties'), ***Ocean Villa Motel*** (☎ 619-224-3481, 800-759-0012, 5142 W Point Loma Blvd) is in Ocean Beach. It's clean and well-run and has a heated pool and good-sized rooms, some with kitchenette and private balcony; from $60.

Right by the beach and within spitting distance of funky bars and restaurants, the ***Ocean Beach Motel*** (☎ 619-223-7191, 5080 Newport Ave) has seen better days, but the location is hard to beat and the rates are quite reasonable. Rooms, some with ocean views, range from $59 to $79 per night or $250 to $441 per week.

Several 'plain Jane' budget motels cluster along Rosecrans St, the main thoroughfare going to Point Loma, about 1/2 to 1 mile southwest of Old Town. Closest and cheapest is the ***El Rio Motel*** (☎ 619-298-9852, fax 619-296-7312), at No 3880, which is downtrodden and has zero frills but is clean, and priced around $45/55. Another independent along here, ***Loma***

Lodge (☎ 619-222-0511, 800-266-0511, fax 619-222-1084, 3202 Rosecrans St) is an adequate budget choice and even has a pool. Rates are $39 to $59 single, $49 to $65 double, with a few family rooms for $52 to $69, including basic breakfast. At the ***Super 8 Motel*** (☎ 619-224-2311, fax 619-224-2608), at No 3275, rates come in at around $50. Larger suites with microwave and refrigerator are $90.

A step up is the ***Howard Johnson Inn*** (☎ 619-224-8266, 800-742-4627, fax 619-225-8715, 3330 Rosecrans St), which puts coffeemakers in each room and runs free shuttles to the airport and area attractions. Rates start at $59/69, including small breakfast, but may rise to a less budget-friendly $109/129.

Mission Bay & Beaches (Maps 9 & 10) Room rates along the beaches change

with the seasons, and even budget places charge considerably higher prices in summer, when demand often exceeds supply.

North of Mission Bay, if you want little more than a roof over your head, the ***Sleepy Time Motel*** (☎ 858-483-4222, 4545 Mission Bay Dr) or the nearby ***Trade Winds Motel*** (☎ 858-273-4616, 4305 Mission Bay Dr) may do in a pinch. Both charge about $30/40 single/double and also rent rooms by the

Staying in town is fine; but near the beach, sublime.

week in winter. If you've got a little more to spend, you'll get greater comforts at the *Comfort Inn* (☎ 858-483-9800, fax 858-483-4010, 4610 DeSoto St), which charges $49 to $89 for rooms with mini-fridge, microwave and coffeemaker.

An ordinary motel with a great location – in Mission Beach just steps away from both ocean and bay beaches – the small *Santa Clara Motel* (☎ 858-488-1193, 839 Santa Clara Place) is a good value in the off-season, with prices from $45/50; but these surge to $95 and up in summer. Each of the 17 units has its own parking spot, a real bonus in this part of town.

The Chains

National hotel chains dominate San Diego's lodging scene. Several individual properties are described throughout this chapter, but space limitations make it impossible to include them all. Call the following toll-free reservation numbers of the various chains to find out about additional hotels and motels in the San Diego area.

Budget

Days Inn	☎ 800-325-2525
Econo Lodge	☎ 800-446-6900
Motel 6	☎ 800-466-8356
Super 8 Motels	☎ 800-800-8000
Travelodge	☎ 800-255-3050
Vagabond Inns	☎ 800-522-1555

Mid-Range

Best Western	☎ 800-528-1234
Comfort Inns	☎ 800-228-5150
Howard Johnson	☎ 800-654-2000
Quality Inn	☎ 800-228-5151
Radisson Hotels	☎ 800-333-3333
Ramada Inns	☎ 800-272-6232

Top-End

Doubletree Hotels	☎ 800-222-8733
Hilton Hotels	☎ 800-445-8667
Holiday Inns	☎ 800-465-4329
Hyatt	☎ 800-228-9000
Marriott Hotels	☎ 800-228-9290
Sheraton Hotels	☎ 800-325-3535

Pacific Beach offers several options. The *Sea Coast Palms Inn* (☎ 858-483-6780, 800-554-6555, fax 858-270-9472, 4760 Mission Blvd) is a pleasant if nondescript motel a block from the beach. Rooms wrap around a pleasant courtyard and feature microwaves and refrigerators. Rates are $70 to $100, or $20 more in summer.

You'll enjoy front-row views of the sunset if you snare one of the ocean-facing rooms at the *Diamond Head Inn* (☎ 858-273-1900, 800-498-8449, fax 858-274-3341, 605 Diamond St); some have kitchenettes. Rates range from $59 to $141, including continental breakfast; children stay free in their parents' room.

If easy access to nightlife is a priority, consider staying at the *Pacific Shores Inn* (☎ 858-483-6300, 800-826-0715, fax 858-483-9276, 4802 Mission Blvd), steps from the beach and from Garnet Ave, the main drag. There's a heated pool as well. Rates include basic breakfast and range from $63 to $88 single, $68 to $93 double; larger units cost $73 to $103.

The *Surfer Motor Lodge* (☎ 858-483-7070, 711 Pacific Beach Dr) is a relaxed hangout with pool. Rooms would benefit from an overhaul, but all feature refrigerator, phone and TV, and some have kitchenettes and ocean-view balconies. Rates range from $73 to $92.

At the *Beach Haven Inn* (☎ 858-272-3812, 800-831-6323, fax 858-272-3532, 4740 Mission Blvd), a block from the beach, you can kick off the day with a free continental breakfast and newspaper. The 23 air-conditioned rooms offer a good value for the area, starting at $69/75, although summer rates can surge to $120/155.

If everything else is full, consider the *Mission Bay Motel* (☎ 858-483-6440, fax 858-270-1685, 4221 Mission Blvd). It overlooks a parking lot and a busy street, but rooms cost $55 in the off-season ($100 in summer) and are close to the beach and Garnet Ave.

La Jolla (Map 11) The only wallet-friendly option in central La Jolla is the *La Jolla Cove Travelodge* (☎ 858-454-0791, fax 858-459-8534, 1141 Silverado St), where rooms (with air-con) start at $50/60 and up to double that in summer. Amenities and room rates are similar at the *La Jolla Beach Travelodge* (☎ 858-454-1075, fax 858-454-1075, 6750 La Jolla Blvd), a short drive south and a block from Windansea Beach. If the ocean's too cold, you could swim in the heated pool or take to the bubbles in the Jacuzzi. Across the street, at No 6705, *Holiday Inn Express* (☎ 858-454-7101, fax 858-454-6957) has similar amenities, plus free continental breakfast, for $79 to $149.

Additional reasonably priced lodgings cluster south on La Jolla Blvd in the area close to the rocky surfers' beach known as Bird Rock (near restaurants and the water but not a swimming beach). The *Inn at La Jolla* (☎ 858-454-6121, 800-367-6467, fax 858-459-1377, 5440 La Jolla Blvd) is a perfectly adequate choice and even has a spa and a nine-hole putting green. Rates range from $60 to $95.

An oldie but goodie is the *La Jolla Biltmore Motel* (☎ 858-459-6446, 5385 La Jolla Blvd), where amenities are few but prices are quite good: $52 Sunday to Thursday and $68 Friday and Saturday; rooms with two queen-size beds are $10 more.

On the beach side of the boulevard is the friendly *La Jolla Shores* (☎ 858-454-0175, fax 858-459-1377, 5390 La Jolla Blvd), another reliable standby which charges $59 to $125 for largish regular rooms, $10 more for those with kitchenette and another $10 for suites, all including continental breakfast.

PLACES TO STAY – MID-RANGE
Downtown (Map 3)

A recent thorough renovation has cloaked the venerable *Bristol San Diego* (☎ 619-232-6141, 800-662-4477, fax 619-232-1948, 1055 1st Ave) in a youthful, spunky new look and outfitted it with all modern amenities and communication devices (including wireless data port, voicemail, Web TV) that are de rigueur in the Internet age. Managed by a descendant of the legendary Wyatt Earp, its 102 light-flooded guest rooms – where bold primary colors compare with gleaming white walls and stylish furnishings – blend the contemporary cool of European boutique hotels with traditional American charm. A generous continental breakfast, included in the rate, is served in the restaurant, which is popular with the lunch crowd from nearby City Hall. With rates starting at $99/109 single/double, this is one of the best Downtown values.

At the *Villager Lodge-Gaslamp* (☎ 619-238-4100, 800-598-1810, fax 619-238-5310, 660 G St), the emphasis is on convenience not style. Newly renovated rooms are functionally furnished with refrigerators, microwaves, coffeemakers, irons and wet bars, and there's a guest laundry on the premises. Rates range from $70 to $120, and there's a 30% discount for international visitors who stay seven days or more.

The *Gaslamp Plaza Suites* (☎ 619-232-9500, 800-874-8770, fax 619-238-9945, 520 E St) occupies the 1913 Watts-Robinson Building. This 11-story former office building was San Diego's first 'skyscraper.' Enter through a lovely lobby with marble floors, then pass through brass elevator doors to head up to your nicely furnished room or suite, where microwave, refrigerator and VCR are considered standard equipment. The main downside is the street and traffic noise. Rates range from $93 to $139 for rooms, $139 to $179 for suites.

The *Ramada Inn & Suites* (☎ 619-234-0155, 800-664-4400, fax 619-231-807, 830 6th Ave), in the 1913 Hotel St James, is a charming choice in the Gaslamp Quarter. Amenities are decidedly modern and include coffeemakers, a fitness center and massage therapy room, and valet parking. The Joan Crawford Bar in the lobby was once the personal property of the movie star herself. Rates range from $89 to $129 single or double occupancy.

Best Western Bayside Inn (☎ 619-233-7500, 800-341-1818, fax 619-239-8060, 555 W Ash St) is a modern high-rise that appeals to both business and leisure travelers. It offers some amenities more typical of a larger and more expensive hotel, including bay views, heated outdoor pool and spa, and central location. Rooms with small balconies cost $99 to $139 single, $119 to $149 double. Parking is free.

Aesthetically challenged on the outside, the ***Clarion Hotel Bay View*** *(☎ 619-696-0234, 800-766-0234, fax 619-231-8199, ✉ info@ clarionbayview.com, 660 K St)* has decent rooms equipped with all the major accouterments and most have views. The coolest spot, though, is the rooftop spa where you can work up a sweat in the sauna, on the sun deck or using the exercise machines. At night you can soak up the view beneath a canopy of stars. Rates start at $99/109 and top out at $159/179.

The ***Quality Inn & Suites Downtown Harborview*** *(☎ 619-696-0911, 800-404-6835, fax 619-234-9416, 1430 7th Ave)* is a rare Downtown hotel with a pool. It also offers free round-the-clock shuttles to airport and Amtrak, local phone calls and continental breakfast. Rooms have data port phones and coffeemakers, and there's secured parking. Rates range from $60 to $100 single and $70 to $120 double.

Coronado (Map 4)

The ***Crown City Inn*** *(☎ 619-435-3116, 800-422-1173, fax 619-435-6750, 520 Orange Ave)* has 33 rooms with microwave, refrigerator and iron included; decor is contemporary. A guest laundry, heated pool and an all-day restaurant are also on the premises. Rooms start at $89/99 single/double, rising as high as $125/145 in summer. ***La Avenida Inn*** *(☎ 619-435-3191, 800-437-0162, fax 619-435-5024, 1315 Orange Ave)* is modern and

---

Gay & Lesbian Lodging

By law, no hotel may turn away gay or lesbian couples, though some may frown upon homosexual guests or pretend to be full. Any hotel located in Hillcrest and surrounds is likely to be tolerant, but the ones listed here cater specifically to a gay and lesbian clientele.

• ***Dimitri's Guesthouse*** *(Map 3; ☎ 619-238-5547, 931 21st Ave)*, south of Balboa Park, rents five comfortable rooms in a turn-of-the-20th-century house to men only. There's a sundeck, hot tub and swimming pool for frolicking.

• ***Balboa Park Inn*** *(Map 6; ☎ 619-298-0823, 800-938-8181, fax 619-294-8070, ✉ info@ balboaparkinn.com, 3402 Park Blvd)* is a handsome foursome of Spanish Colonial–style cottages. Each of the 26 suites has its own name and theme, from 'Greystoke' to 'Casa de Oro' to 'Tara's Suite' (think *Gone with the Wind)* and accompanying appropriate decor. Suites vary by size and price ($89 to $189), but all include refrigerators, coffeemakers, free local phone calls and – as a special touch – continental breakfast and newspaper brought right to your bedside.

• ***Hillcrest Inn Hotel*** *(Map 6; ☎ 619-293-7078, 800-258-2280, fax 619-298-3861, ✉ hillcrestinn@ juno.com, 3754 5th Ave)* has 45 rooms, half of them for nonsmokers and all outfitted with private bath, microwave and refrigerator. Guests can also relax in the hot tub and on the sunning terrace. Rates are $55 to $59. Both straights and gays are welcome (but no children).

• ***Kasa Korbett*** *(Map 6; ☎ 619-291-3962, 800-757-5272, ✉ kasakorbett@hotmail.com, 4050 Front St)*, an intimate inn in a remodeled American Craftsman home in Hillcrest, caters to both lesbians and gay men. The four rooms have geographic names and decor (Atlantic, Gulf Coast, Pacific, Baja) and feature in-room baths, private deck and double vanities. Continental breakfast, served on the brick patio, is included in the rates of $79 to $99.

• ***Beach Place*** *(Map 8; ☎ 619-225-0746, 2158 Sunset Cliffs Blvd)*, in Ocean Beach, is primarily geared toward men, though women are welcome as well. Small apartments with kitchen, deck and a little garden cost just $50 to $60. There's a large hot tub in the courtyard. Nudity and smoking are permitted.

nondescript, but rooms are perfectly adequate, although perhaps a tad overpriced at $115 to $195.

Old Town (Map 5)

Handy to the San Diego Trolley and to Old Town shopping and dining, the ***Best Western Hacienda Hotel*** (*☎ 619-298-4707, 800-528-1234, fax 619-298-4771, 4041 Harney St)* is a pleasant suites-only facility with high ceilings and basic kitchens; rates run from $135 to $165. The terraced property also has a pool, workout room, Jacuzzi, in-room VCRs and, in the lobby, a lending library.

A recent multimillion dollar renovation has propelled the ***Holiday Inn Hotel & Suites Old Town*** (*☎ 619-260-8500, 800-255-3544, fax 619-297-2078, 2435 Jefferson St)* into a new league, one where creature comforts are taken more seriously than in the past. Rates range from $89 to $139 for rooms and $149 to $195 for suites.

Padre Trail Inn (*☎ 619-297-3291, 800-255-9988, fax 619-692-2080, 4200 Taylor St),* vaguely reminiscent of a Spanish hacienda, has a nice pool, bar and restaurant, and air-conditioned rooms, with coffeemaker and cable TV, for $80 to $100.

Hillcrest (Map 6)

Self-caterers could cook entire gourmet meals in the fully equipped kitchens at the ***Sommerset Suites Hotel*** (*☎ 619-692-5200, 800-962-9665, fax 619-692-5299, 606 Washington St)*. Those with more limited culinary know-how may like the big, free breakfast buffet. Nicely furnished suites come with a full set of communication devices, and the pool and spa are good places to wrap up a busy day. Rates start at $89 for studio suites, $109 for one-bedroom suites and $139 for executive suites.

Mission Valley (Map 7)

With its on-site convention center, the ***Town & Country Hotel*** (*☎ 619-291-7131, 800-772-8527, fax 619-294-4681, 500 Hotel Circle N)* is a popular base of operations for mid-size business gatherings. But, thanks to a resort-style layout and its proximity to the Fashion Valley Mall and a golf course, this place also gets its share of the leisure crowd. Rates start at $125/145, although specials often keep rooms filled off-peak.

Comfort Inn Suites (*☎ 619-294-3444, 800-222-2929, fax 619-260-0746, 631 Camino del Rio S)* is geared toward families and has roomy quarters with microwaves, small refrigerators and coffeemakers. Rates, including continental breakfast, range from $90 to $140; additional adults are $8 but children are free.

At the ***Regency Plaza*** (*☎ 619-291-8790, 800-619-1549, fax 619-260-0147, 1515 Hotel Circle S),* the lobby and rooms sport a sophisticated aesthetic vaguely reminiscent of European boutique hotels. All 217 rooms have balconies and a sitting area with a sofa bed. Pool, spa and fitness room are on the premises, and a newspaper is delivered to your door every morning. Prices start at $99 per room.

If you have a taste for the exotic, try the ***Hanalei Hotel*** (*☎ 619-297-1101, 800-882-0858, fax 619-297-6049, 2270 Hotel Circle N),* with an endearingly over-the-top Polynesian theme. Sip your mai tai while lounging poolside, or do the hula at the hotel's luaus. Rooms have balconies overlooking the courtyard or a golf course. Many consider the Hanalei one of San Diego's best bargains: rooms range from $79 to $129, and suites go for $150 to $250.

Mid-priced chain hotels in Mission Valley include the ***Doubletree Hotel*** (*☎ 619-297-5466, fax 619-297-5499, 7450 Hazard Center Dr),* the ***Holiday Inn Select*** (*☎ 619-291-5720, fax 619-297-7362, 595 Hotel Circle S),* the ***Quality Resort*** (*☎ 619-298-8282, fax 619-295-5610, 875 Hotel Circle S),* the ***Radisson Hotel*** (*☎ 619-260-0111, fax 619-497-0813, 1433 Camino del Rio S)* and the ***Ramada Limited*** (*☎ 619-295-6886, fax 619-296-9661, 641 Camino del Rio S).*

Point Loma & Ocean Beach (Map 8)

If your tots are tagging along, you could save a bundle by camping out at the ***Best Western Island Palms Hotel*** (*☎ 619-222-0561, 877-484-3725, fax 619-222-9760, 2051 Shelter Island Dr),* where kids under 18 stay free in their parents' room. Other assets include a bay-view pool and spa, and a private marina. There's a free shuttle to the airport, Amtrak and Greyhound stations. Rooms are sheathed in fresh, aquatic colors and equipped with all modern comforts. Rates are $129/179 single/double, suites $199 to $279.

One of the area's nicest properties is the *Shelter Pointe Hotel & Marina* (☎ 619-221-8000, 800-566-2524, 619-221-5953, 1551 Shelter Island Dr). It has appealing Spanish Mediterranean architecture and two pools; it's close to a sandy beach with volleyball courts. Rooms are comfortable and contemporary with warm decor; most have patios and bay views. Prices run $109 to $139 single, $119 to $149 double and $199 to $229 suite.

Mission Bay & Beaches (Map 9)

Close to SeaWorld, the *Dana Inn & Marina* (☎ 619-222-6440, fax 619-222-5916, 1710 W Mission Bay Dr) caters to the active traveler and to families. It counts two tennis courts, rental boats, bicycles and canoes among its offerings. Rooms cost from $109 to $175.

In Pacific Beach, front-row sea views are guaranteed at the *Best Western Blue Sea Lodge* (☎ 858-488-4700, 800-258-3732, fax 858-488-7276, 707 Pacific Beach Dr). Most rooms have a private patio for tanking up on ocean breezes, and there's also an ocean-front pool and spa area. Rooms, furnished in contemporary style, are smallish, but feature plenty of amenities; rates range from $99 to $149 single and $129 to $179 double.

One of the most interesting places to stay in all of San Diego is the *Crystal Pier Hotel* (☎ 858-483-6983, 800-748-5894, fax 858-483-6811) – the address is 4500 Ocean Blvd but your quarters are actually clapboard cottages right on the 1927 landmark pier itself. Trimmed with blue awnings and flower boxes, all have small kitchens and patios. Winter rates range from $135 for the original cottages (one to four people), up to $270 for newer and larger cottages (some sleep up to six people), with a two-night minimum stay. Summer rates go for $195 to $305, with a three-night minimum. Rates were expected to increase for 2001.

Despite the highfalutin name, the *Surf & Sand Inn by the Beach* (☎ 858-483-7420, fax 858-483-8143, 4666 Mission Blvd) is really just a basic motel and no great shakes when it comes to amenities. Most rooms face noisy Mission Blvd and are a bit long in the tooth. Still, most have air-con and small refrigerators, and there's a coin laundry on the premises. Rates of $100 to $120 are steep for what you get, though off-season deals may be available.

La Jolla (Map 11)

The *Andrea Villa Inn* (☎ 858-459-3311, 800-411-2141, fax 858-459-1320, ✆ info@ andreavilla.com, 2402 Torrey Pines Rd) has 49 rooms, including 20 with small kitchenettes, and a heated pool and spa. Rates, which include a large continental breakfast and admission to the Club La Jolla fitness center, range from $85 to $135, or $20 more in summer. There's a two-night minimum stay in August and on summer Friday and Saturday nights.

Downtown, the nonsmoking *Prospect Park Inn* (☎ 858-454-0133, 800-433-1609, fax 858-454-2056, 1110 Prospect St) is an outstanding property with European touches. Rates, starting at $120, include breakfast served on the sun deck with ocean views; complimentary drinks are served in the library in the afternoon.

Tucked behind the San Diego Museum of Contemporary Art, the 13-room *Scripps Inn* (☎ 858-454-3391, fax 858-456-0389, 555 Coast Blvd) is a relaxed gem with recently remodeled well-lit Mediterranean-style rooms. All overlook the sea and have a fold-out sofa in addition to a king-size bed, as well as small refrigerators. Breakfasts of fresh coffee and French pastries are best enjoyed on the 2nd-floor deck. Rates start at $145. This place often sells out – book early.

Best Western Inn by the Sea (☎ 858-459-4461, 800-462-9732, 800-526-4545 within CA, 7830 Fay Ave) is a comfortable option within walking distance of shopping, dining and the beach. Prices range from $109 to $175 single and $155 to $209 double, including free continental breakfast, parking, newspaper and local phone calls.

To 'B' or not to 'B': Bed & Breakfasts in San Diego

Those who like their lodgings with a personal, historic or eccentric touch should check out the following selection of B&Bs:

- **Katy's Herbs & Things** (Map 2; ☎ 619-544-0375, 800-544-0568, fax 619-696-6877, 2818 Juniper St) is run by an enthusiastic herb lover and features two one-bedroom suites with kitchenette and private patio near the herb garden. It's in a peaceful cul-de-sac in Florida Canyon, on the eastern edge of Balboa Park, overlooking the municipal golf course. Rates are $80 to $100.

- **Heritage Park Inn** (Map 5; ☎ 619-299-6832, 800-995-2470, fax 619-299-9465, @ innkeeper@ heritageparkinn.com, 2470 Heritage Park Row), part of the collection of Victorian houses in Old Town's Heritage Park, time-warps you to a pre-industrial age. The dozen rooms in this 1889 Queen Anne–style mansion look right out of a Laura Ashley catalog and feature polished antiques, claw foot tubs and featherbeds. Candlelight breakfasts and afternoon tea on the veranda are cherished indulgences, while vintage movies flicker through the parlor nightly. Rates range from $100 to $235, depending on room size, amenities and decor.

- **Keating House** (Map 6 ; ☎ 619-239-8585, 800-995-8644, fax 619-239-5774, 2331 2nd Ave), west of Balboa Park, is a romantic hideaway without excessive frills. Flanked by other elegant homes, this turreted and gabled confection has six rooms in the main house – where fireplaces in the foyer, parlor and dining area invite quiet conversation – and two more in the guest cottage. Only the latter have private baths. Rates range from $65 to $85.

- **Blom House** (Map 7; ☎ 858-467-0890, 800-797-2566, fax 858-467-0890, 1372 Minden Dr) sits near the end of a cul-de-sac above I-8, just a short drive from Fashion Valley Mall and Qualcomm Stadium. Its three snug suites all have private bath (with terry robes), 14-foot ceilings and amenities such as TV and VCRs, irons and coffeemakers. A popular feature is the large deck with a steaming hot tub. Rates are $79 to $100 single and $95 to $135 double, and include homemade cookies, afternoon tea and after-dinner drinks.

- **San Diego Yacht & Breakfast** (Map 8; ☎ 619-297-9484, 800-922-4836, fax 619-295-9182, 1880 Harbor Island Dr, G-Dock) is a floating B&B in Harbor Island where you can be rocked to sleep aboard a motor yacht, sailboat or dockside villa. Catered candlelight dinners are optional. Rates for rooms, most with private bath, range from $105 to $595.

- **Bed & Breakfast Inn at La Jolla** (Map 11; ☎ 858-456-2066, fax 858-456-1510, 7753 Draper Ave) is in a 1913 Irving Gill house with a Kate Sessions garden – surely a San Diego classic. Fifteen rooms range in price from $110 to $250 and include little extras such as fresh flowers. The location is also unbeatable – walking distance to most La Jolla sights.

PLACES TO STAY – TOP END
Downtown (Map 3)

The nicest new Downtown hotel is the *Hilton San Diego Gaslamp Quarter* (☎ 619-231-4040, fax 619-231-6439, 401 K St), with a prime location across from the Convention Center. Intimate for a Hilton, it has light-flooded public areas. The rooms have a distinctive personality – stylish and peppy. With original art and designer furniture throughout, and a color scheme of soothing ochre and olive tones, it feels more like you're staying at a rich friend's house than at a chain hotel. Business travelers will appreciate the large desks and fully wired rooms which have two phone lines, high-speed

Internet access, fax machine and, of course, TV. Rates range from $129 to $299.

Standing sentinel above San Diego Bay, the **Hyatt Regency San Diego** (☎ 619-232-1234, 800-233-1234, fax 619-233-6464, 1 Market Place) is certainly Downtown's most prominent hotel, and not just because of its white rocket-shaped outline. The striking lobby has the loftiness of a Gothic cathedral, and there's an air of efficiency everywhere, from the moment the valet first takes your key until check-out time. Every room has grand views of Coronado Island, the flotilla of war ships lying in port, or the city. The top floor cocktail lounge is a good place to wrap up a day. Rates range from $189 to $345.

A relative newcomer, the **Courtyard by Marriott** (☎ 619-446-3000, 800-321-2211, fax 619-446-3010, 530 Broadway) occupies one of Downtown's historic landmarks: the First Interstate Building (see the San Diego Things to See & Do chapter). This place goes after the business crowd, which can choose from five meeting rooms, including the old bank vault. The 246 rooms, including 17 suites, are comfortable and feature large desks, two-line phones, voice mail and data ports. The usual rate is $169; prices often drop on weekends.

The landmark **US Grant Hotel** (☎ 619-232-3121, 800-334-6957, fax 619-232-3626, 326 Broadway) has been *the* place to hobnob since 1910. The brainchild of the son of president Ulysses S Grant, it has hosted a galaxy of presidents, pop stars and dignitaries (Charles Lindbergh, Albert Einstein and John F Kennedy, to drop just a few names). Rich mahogany furniture in the rooms and marble tubs in the baths are typical. Rates start at $185/205, or $295 for suites.

The **Horton Grand Hotel** (☎ 619-544-1886, 800-542-1886, fax 619-239-3823, 311 Island Ave), reconstructed on this site from two 19th-century hotels, is more nostalgic than historic, but lots of people seem happy to pay $140 to $170 for a frilly room with lace curtains and a gas-fueled fireplace. Ladies may rent period hats to take their English High Tea – offered Friday and Saturday afternoon – in style.

With enough rooms (1354) to house a small village, the **Marriott Hotel & Marina** (☎ 619-234-1500, 800-228-9290, fax 619-234-8678, 333 W Harbor Dr) is usually invaded by the expense-account crowd. Most never find the time to enjoy the hotel's leisure facilities: two lagoon-sized pools with waterfalls, Jacuzzis, sauna, fitness center, tennis courts, bicycles and boats. Staying here will set you back $170 to $300.

You'd never know it from the outside, but the **Westgate Hotel** (☎ 619-238-1818, 800-221-3802, fax 619-557-3737, 1055 Second Ave) has a lobby that mimics a room in Versailles and drips with antiques, Baccarat crystal chandeliers, French tapestries and Persian carpets. Rooms are oversized and brim with top-notch amenities. All this splendor comes with a price tag starting at $209/269 single/double.

Coronado (Map 4)

It's possible that you could check in at **Loews Coronado Bay Resort** (☎ 619-424-4000, 800-815-6397, fax 619-424-4400, 4000 Coronado Bay Rd) and never want to leave. A long menu of tempting facilities, activities and indulgences awaits at this superb property ensconced on Crown Isle, a private peninsula 4 miles south of downtown Coronado. Perhaps you'd expect a swimming pool (they have three), fitness center and spa, bike and boat rentals and tennis courts. But how about a romantic gondola ride, poolside 'dive-in' movies viewed while floating in inner tubes or a Feng Shui lesson? There are also special services for kids and pets. All rooms have ocean-view terraces, fresh colors and the full range of amenities. Rates are $235/285 single/double, suites are $425; children under 18 stay free in their parents' room.

A $55 million mega-renovation at the **Hotel del Coronado** (☎ 619-435-6611, 800-468-3533-5, fax 619-522-8238, 1500 Orange Ave) has updated rooms, public areas and restaurants. Facilities include tennis courts, swimming pool, spa, shops and restaurants, all fronting the Pacific Ocean. Nearly half the 691 rooms are not in the historic main hotel, but in an adjacent seven-story modern building with no historical feel at all. Prices run from $205 to $595.

Point Loma & Ocean Beach (Map 8)

On Shelter Island, *Humphrey's Half Moon Inn* (☎ 619-224-3411, 800-542-7400, fax 619-224-3478, ✉ res@halfmooninn.com, 2303 Shelter Island Dr) has a tropical island atmosphere, with palm trees and ponds. A nice outdoor pool and spa invite a dip. Most of the 182 rooms and suites have balconies with views of the city skyline or the bay. Parking and airport transfers are free. Rates start at $149/159. The hotel is next to Humphrey's Concerts by the Bay, home to a popular summer outdoor concert series (see the San Diego Entertainment chapter).

The humongous *Sheraton Harbor Island* (☎ 619-291-2900, fax 619-293-0689, 1380 Harbor Island Dr), since undergoing an $11 million renovation, offers the full luxury treatment. The 'standard' rooms are anything but, and there's nice landscaping, with lagoon-like pools, a Jacuzzi and sauna and tennis courts. Rates are $180 to $270.

Mission Bay (Map 9)

Water rats will be right in their element at the *Catamaran Resort* (☎ 858-488-1081, 800-422-8386, fax 858-488-1387, 3999 Mission Blvd), on a prime piece of bay real estate since 1950. It's a Polynesian fantasy world with koi ponds, a waterfall and tiki-torch lined walkways. Toys (including boogie boards) are for rent; landlubbers can go for the bicycles or in-line skates. Guests can also enjoy free bay cruises aboard the *Bahia Belle*, a historic Mississippi-style sternwheeler. Rooms have balconies or patios and start at $159 single or double.

About 2 miles south, the affiliated *Bahia Resort Hotel* (☎ 858-488-0551, 800-576-4229, fax 858-488-7055, 998 W Mission Bay Dr) offers much the same, but is a bit dated, which is reflected in the rates starting at $140.

San Diego Paradise Point Resort (☎ 858-274-4630, fax 858-581-5929, 1404 Vacation Rd) is set amidst several acres of lush landscaping highlighted by water-lily ponds, lagoons, waterfalls and fountains. Guests can enjoy massages on their private lanai (patio) or discover their inner Pete Sampras on the six lighted tennis courts. The place is

an indulgence not suited for the cash-strapped: rates range from $155 to $210 single and $165 to $235 double.

La Jolla (Map 11)

Luxury is taken very seriously at the new *Hotel Parisi* (☎ 858-454-1511, 877-472-7474, fax 858-454-1531, 1111 Prospect St) in downtown La Jolla. With fresh flowers and original art throughout, and only 20 over-sized suites, this splendid boutique hotel has the feel, sophistication and look of a private Mediterranean retreat. Rates from $210 to $375 include breakfast and parking.

Across the street and down in the next block is the historic *La Valencia* (☎ 858-454-0771, 800-451-0772, fax 858-456-3921, 1132 Prospect St). Year-round rates in this old-fashioned jewel range from $250 on the low end to $2500 for the top suite. See also the San Diego Things to See & Do chapter.

Even older by seven years, the much smaller – and recently renovated – *La Grande Colonial* (☎ 858-454-2181, fax 858-454-5679, 910 Prospect St) is another quiet retreat. This is the place where elegant, mature couples gather in front of the lounge fireplace for afternoon tea. Luxurious rooms (but without air-con) start at $170, those with ocean view are about $20 more.

The seaside *Sea Lodge Hotel* (☎ 858-459-8271, 800-237-5211, fax 858-456-9346, 8110 Camino del Oro) is a sprawling 128-unit property vaguely reminiscent of a Mexican hacienda. Rooms feature beamed ceilings, ocean-view balconies and the full range of amenities. A heated pool, sauna and two tennis courts are also part of the grounds. Rates range from $165 to $379, depending on room size and location.

LONG-TERM RENTALS

In addition to what's listed in this chapter, there is a wealth of summer rentals in the beach areas. If you have a group of friends or family, and you want to stay for a week or more, renting a place can be an excellent value. Try agents such as Mission Bay Vacations (☎ 858-488-6773, 800-882-8626) or Penny Realty (☎ 858-272-3900, 800-748-6704) – but call early.

Places to Eat

With some 6400 restaurants, San Diego's dining scene is as diverse as its population. You can enjoy Mexican *huevos rancheros* for breakfast, a Thai curry for lunch, and fish and chips for dinner – all in one neighborhood. Standard American fare is served at diners, coffee shops and fast-food chains; pizza is ubiquitous too.

In this book, restaurants are divided into three price categories: 'Budget' covers those places with $8 and under main dishes; 'Mid-Range,' between $10 and $15; and 'Top End,' $20 and up.

Unless noted otherwise, restaurants here are open daily for lunch and dinner. Hours, however, change frequently, so we advise calling ahead.

Dining out in San Diego tends toward the casual, although you should still dress appropriately. That definitely means shoes and shirt; a jacket is appropriate for men at some upscale restaurants. If you're heading for a popular eatery – especially on Friday or Saturday night – make a reservation. It's customary to wait by the entrance until the host or hostess seats you; only in very casual places and self-service restaurants may you pick a table yourself.

Most restaurants figure on several seatings per night, so the expectation is that you'll leave soon after you've finished your meal. In most cases, your server will bring you the bill; in some top restaurants it may be presented only after you've requested it (though to hustle you along, someone might come by your table every two minutes asking if you'd like to order anything else). Smoking in restaurants and bars is prohibited by state law, although outdoor areas are usually exempt.

FOOD
Breakfast

Big breakfasts are an affordable way to fill up, provided you can stomach large quantities of food before noon. A breakfast of pancakes, eggs and sausage or a hearty omelet costs around $5 to $8. It often includes home fries (diced potatoes fried with onions, bell peppers or spices) or hash browns (shredded or sliced potatoes fried to a golden brown), toast and 'bottomless cups' (unlimited refills) of coffee. You get a choice of how your eggs are cooked – scrambled, sunny-side up (cooked yolk-side up), over easy (flipped, but with a runny yolk), or over hard (flipped with a hard yolk). Many eateries offer budget breakfast specials until 10 or 11 am.

Lunch

Usually served from 11:30 am to 2 pm, lunch is another inexpensive meal. Prices for the same dishes are often a third or more cheaper than at dinnertime. For a bustling lunch scene head to the Gaslamp Quarter. Many ethnic eateries – Indian, Thai, Chinese – usually have three-course set lunches for around $7.

Dinner

Many restaurants offer 'early-bird specials,' which feature a complete meal (usually the menu is limited) for under $10, between 4 and 6 pm. San Diego also has several restaurant-bars with great happy hours (usually between 4 and 7 pm Monday to Friday only) when spending a few dollars on drinks gets you free or heavily discounted appetizers – anything from a bowl of peanuts to a full hot buffet. People tend to eat early, and outside the tourist areas, many restaurants are deserted by 10 pm.

Cuisines

Eating healthy is very much part of the California lifestyle that gave birth to 'California cuisine' in the mid-1980s. Pioneers like Berkeley-based Alice Waters and Wolfgang Puck of Los Angeles created gourmet concoctions revolving around fresh, seasonal ingredients, unusual flavor fusions and artistic presentation. A typical dish would be a serving of grilled mahi mahi with sides of sautéed spinach greens and wild-rice pilaf.

An offshoot of California cuisine is Pacific Rim food, a term coined in the 1990s. Its focus is on the blending of local ingredients and seasonings with Chinese or Japanese cooking methods. Meat and fish are seasoned with adventurous combinations of turmeric, cilantro (fresh coriander), ginger, garlic, chili paste and fresh fruit juices (usually citrus), and served with Asian staples such as rice, sweet potatoes or buckwheat (udon) noodles.

Fish and shellfish figure big on menus in San Diego from the lowly – but delicious – fish taco to oysters on the half-shell and seared ahi tuna. What's on the menu often depends on the day's catch, which has the obvious advantage of complete freshness. Some of the best seafood restaurants predictably cluster along the waterfront.

Ethnic foods are widely available, with Mexican, Chinese, Italian and Thai being the most prevalent. For details about Mexican dishes, see the Tijuana Places to Eat chapter.

Predictable, unexciting and certainly not healthy, fast food chains are cheap, reliable standbys any time of day. For hamburgers, there's McDonald's, Burger King and Carl's Jr. Unique to California is the venerable In-N-Out Burger, which has a brief menu and a die-hard clientele. Taco Bell and Del Taco serve Mexican fast food; Domino's Pizza and Pizza Hut deliver.

DRINKS
Nonalcoholic
Most restaurants provide customers with free ice water, which is safe to drink. All the usual soft drinks are available. 'Lemonade' is a lemon-sugar-ice water mix: if you want the clear, fizzy stuff that the British call lemonade, ask for Sprite or 7-Up. Bottled fizzy mineral water like Perrier or Pellegrino is popular too. Another refreshing drinks is iced tea, which can be sweetened to taste.

Many restaurants offer milk, including low-fat varieties. You can often get fresh-squeezed orange juice at better restaurants, but packaged juices are more common.

Coffee is served much more often than tea, usually with a choice of regular or 'decaf.' Drinkers of English-style tea will be disappointed: tea is usually a cup or pot of hot water with a tea bag next to it. It's usually served with a slice of lemon, but you can ask for milk as well. Specify whether you want black or herbal tea.

Alcoholic
Persons under the age of 21 (minors) are prohibited from consuming alcohol in California. If you look under 21 (even if you're not), be sure to carry a picture ID (eg, a driver's license or passport) as proof of age to enter a bar, order alcohol at a restaurant or buy alcohol at a supermarket. Servers have the right to ask to see your ID and may refuse service without it. Minors are not allowed in bars and pubs, even to order nonalcoholic beverages. This means that most dance clubs are also off-limits to minors, although a few have solved the under-age problem with a segregated drinking area. Minors are, however, welcome in the dining areas of restaurants where alcohol may be served. Many California restaurants are only licensed to serve wine and beer and not 'hard liquor' such as cognac and whisky.

Beer The big name brands of domestic beer are available everywhere, though you may find them lacking in taste. Beer sold in the US has a lower alcohol content than that in most other countries, which may be why many visitors find it bland. Microbreweries, or 'brewpubs,' have become popular. These brew various beers on the premises, and you can get up to a dozen different types on tap.

Note that 'lite' beer means lower in calories (90 instead of 180), but not necessarily lower in alcohol. But it brings up the question: is there such a thing as 'light' beer?

Wine California produces excellent vintage wines and some very affordable generic varieties. The wines produced in the Napa and Sonoma valleys, north of San Francisco, are widely considered the best, but those from the Temecula Valley, just north of San Diego County, are gaining in

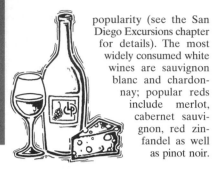

popularity (see the San Diego Excursions chapter for details). The most widely consumed white wines are sauvignon blanc and chardonnay; popular reds include merlot, cabernet sauvignon, red zinfandel as well as pinot noir.

Spirits All bars have a big range of 'hard' liquor – gin, brandy, rum, vodka, whiskey – invariably served with lots of ice ('on the rocks'), unless you ask for 'straight up.'

Tequila, from Mexico, is popular in such drinks as a margarita or tequila sunrise (see the Tijuana Places to Eat chapter for more on tequila). The American taste for cocktails originated during Prohibition, when lots of flavorful mixers were used to disguise the taste of bathtub gin. These days there are thousands of named cocktail recipes, and many bars will have their own special concoction with a fancy or a bawdy name, like the Screaming Orgasm or the Slow-Easy-Screw-up-Against-the-Wall.

PLACES TO EAT – BUDGET
Downtown (Map 3)
Gaslamp Quarter For quick, cheap and healthy grub, the Baja-style Mexican food at *Rubio's* (☎ 619-231-7731, 901 4th Ave), a popular chain founded by a San Diego State University student, will do in a pinch. Be sure to try the fish tacos. Other branches around town include the one in Pacific Beach on Grand Ave between Bayard and Cass Sts (Map 10).

At least as popular, but serving more traditional Mexican dishes is the nearby *El Indio* (☎ 619-239-8151, 409 F St). In business since 1940, this self-service place has fed generations of locals and visitors. The burritos are killer, but it's famous for the fluffy tamales. A special menu accommodates vegetarians. The original branch is in Middletown (☎ 619-299-0333, 3695 India St).

Whimsical decor, a lively flair and mountains of pasta are all assets of the *Old Spaghetti Factory* (☎ 619-233-4323, 275 5th Ave). You're guaranteed to fill up on big portions served along with salad, piping hot sourdough bread, ice cream for dessert and as much coffee or tea as you can handle. Great for families and the budget-minded.

Catering mostly to office workers, the *Downtown Fish Joint* (☎ 619-235-8840, 407 C St) makes giant sandwiches stuffed with succulent shrimp, calamari, North Atlantic cod or other fishy fare for less than $7. Combo platters are only slightly more. It is open from 11 am to 5 pm Monday to Friday only.

The Cheese Shop (☎ 619-232-2303, 627 4th Ave) is a daytime deli much loved by locals for its generously stuffed gourmet sandwiches and coffee.

For a more casual atmosphere, try the legendary *Dick's Last Resort* (☎ 619-231-9100 345 4th Ave), which has buckets of beer and barbecue, plus heaping helpings of fried food, ribs and burgers all served with a dollop of irreverence on its large patio.

Embarcadero & Seaport Village The *Anthony's Fishette*, a self-service counter that's part of Anthony's Fish Grotto (see Places to Eat – Mid-Range, later in this chapter) has lots of deep-fried everything, including excellent fish and chips with coleslaw for around $5. Grab your food and find a table on the plank terrace with harbor views.

Gyros, souvlaki, spanikopita (spinach-and-cheese pie in filo pastry) – these exotic dishes are the building blocks of Greek cuisine. They're also the perennial crowd pleasers at the *Greek Islands Cafe* (☎ 619-239-5216) in Seaport Village, in business for more than 20 years. The most expensive item is $9 and you can eat inside or out with a view of the bay.

Little Italy Buzzing *Filippi's Pizza Grotto* (☎ 619-232-5094, 1747 India St) is the kind of restaurant that's as comfortable as a hug from an old friend. A heady mélange of arlic and onion, spices and tomato hangs in the air, as do hundreds of Chianti bottles uspended from the ceiling. Pizza (around 10, feeds two to three) takes center stage ut the no-nonsense pasta dishes are good oo. Sharing is OK. There's another branch Map 10; ☎ 619-483-6222, 962 Garnet Ave) n Pacific Beach.

A few doors north of Filippi's, **Mona Lisa** ☎ 619-234-4893, 2061 India St) has hearty neals for $6 to $11, and **Mimmo's Italian** **Village** (☎ 619-239-3710, 1743 India St) has errific hot and cold sandwiches and pasta alads from $3; both double as markets and arry a variety of imported and fresh food ems.

Coronado (Map 4)

Café 1134 (☎ 619-437-1134, 1134 Orange Ave) is an artsy café-cum-wine-bar-cum allery, which serves full breakfasts as well s gourmet sandwiches, like brie cheese vith pesto, for less than $7. **Danny's Palm** **Bar & Grill** (☎ 619-435-3171, 965 Orange Ave) is a tunnel-shaped dive with character, vhere you sidle up to the bar or wedge ourself into a naughahyde booth in back. The thing to get is the slam burger, which vill keep you fed for the rest of the day for mere $4.75. A neat mural opposite the bar dds to the low-key ambience.

With breakfast served around the clock, ou won't know what time it is at the **Nite** k **Day Café** (☎ 619-435-9776, 847 Orange Ave), but it's a step *back* in time, for sure. Enjoy your patty melts, BLTs, burgers and ther hash-house fare at the counter while eing serenaded with '50s music from a ikebox.

Old Town (Map 5)

A local favorite is the **Old Town Mexican** **Café** (☎ 619-297-4330, 2489 San Diego Ave). t has a big bar, dining room and patio and xcellent food; the *carnitas* (roasted and hredded pork with onions and peppers) re famous, and served with lots of condi-nents – from cilantro to avocado – and varm tortillas that you can watch being nade. The café is open for breakfast, lunch nd dinner. Most dishes are under $8.

One of the least expensive but most au-thentic places around here is **Carne Estrada** (☎ 619-296-1112), a take-out *taquería* at the corner of San Diego Ave and Harney St, where items cost less than $5.

Hillcrest & Middletown (Map 6)

Downtown Hillcrest offers up a number of good-value eating choices. **Taste of Thai** (☎ 619-291-7525, 527 University Ave) is a long-standing local favorite, with modern, pleasant, minimalist decor. Standards like pad-thai are tangy and delicious, but house specialties like the Thai Boat – a bonanza of seafood steamed in foil with wine and special herbs – are tempting too. Vegetari-ans have plenty to choose from, and most dishes can be made to suit any level of spice tolerance. The only down-side: crammed-together tables allow for zero privacy.

Taste of Thai gets serious competition from relative newcomer **Kitima Thai** (☎ 619-298-2929, 406 University Ave). En-sconced in a loft-like space with framed original Thai artwork gracing the walls, this place is definitely a winner in the looks de-partment. But the food – fragrant, light and complex – leaves little to be desired either. All dishes – most of them under $8 – can be toned down in spiciness, and most can be adapted to suit vegetarians.

Hamburger Mary's (☎ 619-491-0400, 308 University Ave) is a self-consciously gay eatery, but everybody is welcome to try their 'special tease,' a daily special such as top sirloin steak with soup or salad and fries, and other fun fare like the 'Hunka Hunka Burnin' Love' burger. Mary's has good mar-garitas, and is famous for its Sunday cham-pagne brunch buffet ($12.95). The nicest tables are outdoors amid the flower plots and plants. The affiliated **Kickers,** next door, is a gay bar with a country & western theme.

Happy days are here again at the **Corvette Diner** (☎ 619-542-1001, 3946 5th Ave), which takes its '50s theme to the max. A sunshine-colored namesake car anchors the restaurant, waitresses prance about in poodle skirts, and hip patrons join kids at the soda fountain. Despite the decor, the food is unmistakably 21st century all-American, with an emphasis on lean and healthy.

Bread & Cie (☎ 619-683-9322, 350 University Ave) is a café where delicious Euro-style breads spiked with wholesome ingredients put the 'wonder' into Wonder Bread. All are handcrafted in the bakery in back and can be turned into yummy sandwiches costing around $5. It is open to 7 pm, weekends to 6 pm.

South of Hillcrest, on the western edge of Balboa Park, are a couple of favorites. At **Vegetarian Zone** (☎ 619-298-7302, 2949 5th Ave), considered to be the best all-veggie restaurant in town, even die-hard meat freaks are likely to find something enticing on the menu. The Greek spinach and feta pie gets rave reviews, but hardly any of the salads, sandwiches and casseroles sacrifice flavor or substance. The Zone also does weekend brunch and has a deli for take-outs.

A visit to **Extraordinary Desserts** (☎ 619-294-7001, 2929 5th Ave), next door, is a serious indulgence. A peaceful retreat where the decor is infused with both Middle Eastern and French touches, it has indoor and outdoor seating and lots of flowers. Ah, yes – and desserts! Fruit, creme, custard, pastry – health food it ain't, but what a worthwhile guilty pleasure this is.

In western Middletown, where India St meets Washington St, there is a well-known block of casual eateries. The **Shakespeare Pub & Grille** (☎ 619-299-0230, 3701 India St) is one of the most authentic English ale houses in town, with darts, a large selection of lagers and ales on tap and pub grub such as fish and chips, beef stew, and bangers and mash for around $6 a plate. Its Sunday roast beef special for $10, served all day, is popular too. Soccer fans flock here for the weekly live broadcasts.

For some of the best value in town, make a beeline to Saffron, which has two separate sections. **Saffron Thai Grilled Chicken** (☎ 619-574-0177, 3731 India St) specializes in charcoal-grilled chicken that's been marinated in fragrant spices. It's served with a choice of half a dozen homemade sauces, including peanut, chutney and sweet pepper, as well as a salad and jasmine rice. Half a

chicken with two sauces costs $6.48, bu smaller portions are available too. Nex door, **Saffron Noodles & Saté** (☎ 619-574-7737, 3737 India St) is where you can dig into big bowls of steaming noodle soup or order a plate of stir-fried noodles paired with various ingredients. Most dishes cost around $6. Both Saffrons close at 9 pm, Sunday a 8 pm. There's a terrace for outdoor eating.

Also around here is **Gelato Vero Caff** (☎ 619-295-9269), right at Washington and India Sts, which has San Diego's best Italian style ice cream. It's open late and display local artists' work.

Mission Valley & Normal Heights (Map 7)

San Diego does not have a centralized Chi natown, but Convoy St in Kearny Mesa, jus north of Mission Valley near the Mont gomery Field airport, is a veritable Asia restaurant row. One of the best is th **Dumpling Inn** (☎ 858-268-9638, 461 Convoy St), where the uninspired surround ings belie the quality of the food. The bes thing on the menu is the steaming broth teeming with plump noodles, marinate meats and vegetables.

On the same street at No 3906, the **Orig inal Pancake House** (☎ 858-565-1740, open 7 am to 3 pm, gets rave reviews for it huge breakfasts. The baked apple pancake are the size of small UFOs and the omelet are not much smaller.

In Normal Heights, on Book Row, **Jyoti Bihanga** (☎ 619-282-4116, 3351 Adams Ave is a vegetarian restaurant operated by stu dents of Indian guru Sri Chinmoy. Th menu includes animal-product-free version of traditional favorites such as nachos and burgers; the 'neat loaf' is made entirely from grains and vegetables. Everything's mod estly priced, but the Sunday all-you-can-ea buffet brunch for $7 is a steal.

Point Loma & Ocean Beach (Map 8)

One of the liveliest places for seafood is th market-cum-deli at **Point Loma Seafood** (☎ 619-223-1109, 2805 Emerson St), in th Shelter Island Marina. Sushi, sandwiche and seafood platters ($4 to $8) are made with the freshest fish available, and they sell fresh bread, beer and wine to go with it.

In Ocean Beach, Newport Ave has several good budget eateries. The **Old Townhouse** (☎ 619-222-1880), at No 4941, is an old-fashioned greasy spoon where you can nurse a hangover with breakfast (served all day). Or you can dig into generously filled sandwiches served with a mountain of fries, or other artery-clogging feasts.

For burgers, the place to be is **Hodad's** (☎ 619-224-4623), across the street at No 5010. The name is surfer-speak for 'wannabe surfers,' and the place does indeed crawl with dudes and dudettes sinking their sparkling teeth into juicy patties, which start at $2.50. Veggie burgers are served too.

Saying 'lively' to describe **Livingstone's** (☎ 619-224-8088, 5026 Newport Ave) is an understatement. Especially at sunset, the place brims with young folks downing beers by the pitcher and tucking into Mexican food that won't take a bite out of their wallets (almost nothing is over $5). Breakfast is served till 3 pm.

For healthy Mexican fare, wander over to **Rancho's Cocina** (☎ 619-226-7619, 1830 Sunset Cliffs Blvd), a New Age hole-in-the-wall two blocks south of Newport Ave. Popular items include shitake burritos and tempeh fajitas, both priced around $5 and best consumed on the tiny patio deck, which is concealed by a flower-bedecked hedge. The only down side is the slow and attitudinous staff.

On the beach at the end of Saratoga Ave, **Dempsey's** (☎ 619-222-7740) looks like a shack but serves excellent breakfasts and lunches.

Mission Beach (Map 9)
The **Mission Café** (☎ 858-488-9060, 3795 Mission Blvd), open 7 am to 3 pm, offers conscientious cuisine (their words) and has a fascinating Chino-Latino menu. For breakfast, the egg dishes paired with rosemary-scented potatoes are popular, but lunches can bring concoctions like ginger-sesame chicken rolled up in tortillas. It's a comfortable hangout, also famous for its coffee.

Pacific Beach (Map 10)
In the beach and party towns, breakfast seems to be the most important meal of the day, judging by the number of excellent places.

In Pacific Beach, a long-time favorite is **Kono's** (☎ 858-483-1669, 704 Garnet Ave), across from the Crystal Pier, where, on a Saturday or Sunday morning, lines start wrapping around the block (well, almost) shortly after sunrise. The $5 breakfast burritos and blueberry pancakes are excellent, but anything served with the homemade potatoes is a winner.

Another good place to replenish energies after a night of partying is the **Broken Yolk** (☎ 858-270-9655), on the eastern end of Garnet at No 1851. For the hair of the dog, greet the new day with a glass of champagne, for only 75¢. The menu features – count 'em – 24 omelet specials, including the ironman/ironwoman version made with 12 eggs; if that isn't a heart attack on a plate, what is? If you finish it, you get a free T-shirt. It is open from 6 am to 3 pm daily.

Another popular breakfast place is **The Eggery** (☎ 858-274-3122, 4150 Mission Blvd), open 7 am to 2 pm. Ensconced in a shopping mall, it has cheerful, country-style decor and a patio with ocean views. Some say you'll find the best French toast in town here.

EZ-Jay's Sandwiches (☎ 858-483-0123, 1088 Garnet Ave) makes delicious hot and cold sandwiches to eat in or take out. Most come in 6-, 8- or 12-inch sizes, and cost from $3 to $5.50. The perennial bestseller is the Biter's Deluxe: charbroiled chicken teamed up with honey mustard and melted Swiss cheese. Salads are available as well.

Avoid **Fred's Mexican Cafe** (☎ 858-483-8226, 1165-B Garnet Ave) if you're on a diet. Their burritos, each weighing more than 1lb, are fit for royalty at prices even paupers can afford (most under $3!). The fajitas, sizzling and served with black beans, rice and flour tortillas, are delicious too. House margaritas are pretty honest, and cost just $2.

At **World Curry** (☎ 858-270-4455, 1433 Garnet Ave), you can sample the many flavors and ingredients that different countries put into what is essentially a fragrant

Great Breakfast Spots

Nutrition experts have said for years that breakfast is the most important meal of the day; but for many, this daily meal doesn't agree with the daily grind. But now that you're on vacation, you might as well get the day started with one of life's greatest pleasures: a leisurely breakfast. Buy a newspaper and head on over to any of the following places, which all do a bit more than brew hot coffee and scramble a few eggs. Most are – perhaps predictably – in the more laid-back beach towns, and all are described in greater detail under their respective area headings:

- Coronado – Nite & Day Café

- Hillcrest & Middletown – Crest Cafe, The Gathering, Hamburger Mary's

- Mission Valley – Original Pancake House

- Ocean Beach – Old Townhouse, Livingstone's, Dempsey's

- Mission Beach – Mission Café, Firehouse Beach Cafe (see Map 10)

- Pacific Beach – Kono's, Broken Yolk, The Eggery

- La Jolla – Harry's Coffee Shop, The Pannikin, Brockton Villa

stew. Thai curries are creamy and coconut milk-based. Japanese curries are mixed with potatoes and carrots. And Caribbean curry is distinguished by black beans and pineapple. All are served in regular ($5.50) or large ($7) portions with jasmine rice and a side salad. Several selections are suitable for vegetarians.

Prefer something less exotic? Nearby, the ***Down Under*** (☎ 858-581-1103, 1341 Garnet Ave) makes yummy burgers and meat pies for $4 to $7.

La Jolla (Map 11)

An excellent budget choice is ***Don Carlos Taco Shop*** (☎ 858-456-0462, 737 Pearl St), where $4 buys anything on the menu – the rolled beef tacos and the fish and potato burrito are recommended.

For breakfast or lunch, pop in at ***Harry's Coffee Shop*** (☎ 858-454-7381, 7545 Girard Ave), open daily 5:30 am to 3 pm, a local institution that's a favorite with professional athletes and has been reviewed in the *New York Times*. The crispy waffles, topped with fresh fruit or pecans, are mouthwatering and the omelets are good too. In fine weather, the best seats are on the patio.

The tunnel-shaped ***Girard Gourmet*** (☎ 858-454-3321, 7837 Girard Ave) is a quality deli with heaped-up sandwiches, salads, ready-to-eat Italian dishes such as lasagna and delicious pastries. It's take-out only, with most items priced from $4 to $8.

The Living Room (1010 Prospect St) gets an international student crowd from the adjacent language school. It has a nice selection of salads ($6, half-size $4), as well as sandwiches and deli dishes, such as quiche Lorraine and turkey lasagna, for under $8. It's open late. Another La Jolla standby, especially for breakfast, is ***The Pannikin*** (☎ 858-454-5453, 7467 Girard Ave), which has been 'wakin' up San Diego since 1964.

Self-Catering

San Diego's climate is conducive to picnicking, and you'll find many delis, markets and cafés which stock all the necessary items from premade salads to single-serving bottles of wine. Supermarkets such as ***Ralphs*** or ***Vons*** are ubiquitous and have competitive prices; some even have salad bars, delis and bakeries. Ralphs has a central Downtown branch (*Map 3;* ☎ 619-595-1581 101 G St), just south of Horton Plaza.

Each supermarket has different specials every week. To benefit from the biggest discounts, you may have to become a 'club' member, a free formality that's instantly accomplished by filling out a short form. In return, you'll be given a 'club card' that has to be presented at the cash register. The Sunday edition of the *San Diego Union Tribune* has coupons that that can be clipped to help you cut costs further. Another option is going to '99 cent' stores, where everything costs just that, though food items are usually limited to cans and candy.

Hands-down the best food market in San Diego (and elsewhere in California for that matter) is *Trader Joe's*, which packs its bare-bones, warehouse-like stores with gourmet foods at discount prices. The international cheese counter is legendary, as are its wine and beer selections. San Diego has branches in Hillcrest (☎ 619-296-3122, 1090 University Ave) and in Pacific Beach (Map 10; ☎ 858-272-7235, 1211 Garnet Ave).

Whole Foods is a chain of supermarkets catering to health-conscious shoppers. It is a bonanza of everything organic, natural and fresh for everyone from carnivores to vegans at premium prices. Its San Diego branch (Map 6; ☎ 619-294-2800, 711 University Ave), in Hillcrest, also has a café. Another contender in this category is *OB People's Market* (Map 8; ☎ 619-224-1387, 4765 Voltaire St), at Sunset Cliffs Blvd in Ocean Beach, an organic co-op with bulk foods and an excellent take-out vegan deli.

PLACES TO EAT – MID-RANGE
Downtown (Map 3)
Gaslamp Quarter *Sammy's Woodfired Pizza* (☎ 619-230-8888, 770 4th St) is a casual place where the creativity has gone into the food, not the decor. You might like the goat cheese pizza with wild mushrooms, garlic and spinach, but even old standbys like the pepperoni are exceptional. The inventive pasta and salads are convincing too. If you've got room left, go for a sugar high with the 'messy sundae.' Other branches include one in La Jolla (☎ 858-456-5222, 702 Pearl St) and another in Mission Valley (☎ 619-298-8222, 1620 Camino de la Reina).

The building at the corner of 5th Ave and Island St has been an Asian restaurant since it opened its doors as Nanking Cafe in 1912; it's now the excellent, elegant *Royal Thai Cuisine* (☎ 619-230-8424). Menu headliners include honey duck and Siamese catfish, although more conventional dishes are delectable too. There is also a trio of multicourse dinners (banquets) for $17 per person, and lunch specials for $6. There's a second location in La Jolla (☎ 858-551-8424, 757 Pearl St).

Rock Bottom Brewery (☎ 619-231-7000, 401 G St) is a lively microbrewery and restaurant. Five handcrafted brews are on tap, including three ales and a smooth stout. The menu features standards like salad, pizza and pasta; if you're not overly hungry, the appetizers are big enough to make a meal (especially the nachos). There's an upstairs lounge and the semi-outdoor Starlight Loft for smoking; it all turns into a pop-music dance club on weekends nights.

Bandar (☎ 619-238-0101, 825 4th Ave) is an exotic hole-in-the-wall that has been showered with awards and accolades. It has sidewalk seating, and food that is low-fat, healthy and flavorful. Dishes mostly consist of huge portions of magically marinated meat served with fragrant rice.

Nearby, *Dakota Grill & Spirits* (☎ 619-234-5554, 901 5th Ave) has exceptional California/Western cuisine, complemented by several microbrews and a long wine list. In true California style, there's an open kitchen where you can watch the staff prepare grilled meats (around $20), wood-fired pizzas ($11.50) and salads ($6). Upstairs, a pianist plays Wednesday to Saturday nights; in the basement, the Club 66 disco (admission free with dinner) keeps the young set on its feet. The dress code here, unlike elsewhere in the Gaslamp, is relaxed.

For a change from nouveau Italian, we recommend *Buca di Beppo* (☎ 619-233-7272, 705 6th Ave). Here the down-home food is garlicky, powerfully flavored and doled out in megaportions. The tangy sauces are made fresh daily, as are the outsized bread loaves. Bring some friends and dig in – leftovers are guaranteed.

The *Star of India* (☎ 619-544-9891, 423 F St) is a first-class restaurant with enchanting decor and north Indian food, including curries, tandoori-style lamb and chicken and vegetarian choices. The lunch buffet is $8. There's another branch in La Jolla (☎ 858-459-3355) at 1000 Prospect St.

Embarcadero & Seaport Village Tucked away in a beautiful ivy-covered brick building, *Karl Strauss Brewery* (☎ 619-234-2739, 1157 Columbia St) is a comfortable eatery where the pan-American food is infused with Germanic touches and goes down especially well with a mug of the house brew. The sandwiches, pizzas and salads are big enough for a meal and inexpensive enough for the budget-conscious, with more substantial meals costing from $12 to $15. There's another branch in La Jolla (see the San Diego Entertainment chapter).

Nearby, *Kansas City Barbeque* (☎ 619-231-9680, 610 W Market St) wows diners with its finger-lickin' barbecued beef, chicken, sausages and chicken, all served with two side dishes. It's even had a brush with Hollywood, serving as the backdrop for the sleazy bar scene in *Top Gun*. Most nights this is a happening place.

If you can't afford the Star of the Sea (see Places to Eat – Top End, later in this chapter), but still have tastes that lean toward the gourmet, try *Anthony's Fish Grotto* (☎ 619-232-5103, 1360 N Harbor Dr), the Star of the Sea's simpler and cheaper culinary cousin. Around for more than half a century, this place is often packed at lunchtime and also does brisk business at night. The 'family favorites' selection is huge and costs mostly under $10; a la carte dishes average $15.

Coronado (Map 4)

The *Coronado Brewing Co* (☎ 619-437-4452, 170 Orange Ave) has a patio, delicious home brew and lots of foods that are good for the soul if not for the waistline (read: sandwiches with fries, pizza, pasta), mostly under $10.

Mc P's Irish Pub & Grill (☎ 619-435-5280, 1107 Orange Ave) is owned by an ex-Navy Seal and consequently is popular with the military set. Typical pub fare, including corned beef and cabbage and mulligan stew, go down well with a pint of Guinness, especially on their lovely 'paddy-o' (their pun). There's nightly entertainment as well.

Old Town (Map 5)

Casa de Bandini (☎ 619-297-8211, 2660 Calhoun St), right in the state historic park, is a visual and culinary treat. Housed in a grand 1829 adobe – once a private home,

then a hotel – it has rustically elegant dining rooms dripping with history. In summer, the flower-festooned courtyard anchored by a tiled fountain is the preferred place to sit. The food is traditional Mexican, ranging from $8 to $16, and the servers, dressed in folkloric garb, are quick with a smile.

Bazaar del Mundo, at the northwestern corner of the Old Town Plaza, has three restaurants with lively atmosphere and adequate food. The most popular is *Casa de Pico* (☎ 619-296-3267), a riotously colorful eatery where the tables of choice are in the outdoor patio; there's almost always a line. The Mexican fare is adapted to gringo tastes but still good, and the margaritas are super-sized. *Lino's* (☎ 619-299-7124) makes Italian standards, while *Rancho El Nopal* (☎ 619-295-0585) has Mexican and Southwestern food.

Rockin' Baja Lobster (☎ 619-260-0305, 3890 Twiggs St) is a lively eatery where an informal atmosphere appeals to a young party crowd. Seafood is served by the bucket, along with Caesar's salad and all-you-can-eat rice, beans, salsa and tortillas. A bucket for one ($17) is enough for two, though they do charge $4 extra for sharing. Good margaritas, too.

Hillcrest & Middletown (Map 6)

Some food critics consider *Bombay* (☎ 619-298-3155, 3975 5th Ave) to be the best Indian restaurant in San Diego. Judging by the steady stream of clients pouring into this exotically appointed eatery, they may well be right. Lunch specials are $9 and a la carte curries go for $13 to $16; vegetarian dishes start at $10.

Crest Cafe (☎ 619-295-2510, 425 Robinson Ave) has nice art deco decor and is open all day. Breakfast, served till noon, is especially popular and yields such culinary treats as macadamia nut pancakes. Otherwise, it's pretty much updated and slimmed down diner fare, with an emphasis on homemade.

Montana's American Grill (☎ 619-297-0722, 1421 University Ave) is a classy lunch or dinner destination. It has an extensive wine list, full bar, pastas ($8 to $13), grilled fish and meat ($9 to $22) and live jazz most weekend nights.

For American cuisine without any pretense, try **The Gathering** (☎ 619-260-0400, 902 W Washington St), a traditional neighborhood eatery where you can eat breakfast till 2 pm. If the light's too bright on the sidewalk terrace, move indoors to the comfy dining room where, from 6:30 pm onward Thursday to Sunday, magic tricks are performed at your table. Dinners start at $12.50, but breakfasts are $5 to $8 and most lunches come in under $10.

A few blocks south, **Fifth & Hawthorn** (☎ 619-544-0940, 515 Hawthorn St) is popular with the pre-theater dinner crowd. The restaurant has come up with a unique concept for gourmets on a budget: for $44 two people get to share an appetizer, dessert and bottle of wine, and each gets their own soup or salad and main course. This is an incredible value considering that a la carte main courses – seafood is the specialty – average $17. Reservations are recommended.

Also nearby is **Hob Nob Hill** (☎ 619-239-8176, 2271 1st Ave), a no-nonsense coffee shop that has served stick-to-the-ribs American home-cooking since the Eisenhower era (and still has the decor to prove it). Tables start filling in the morning, when patrons chow down on omelets, pancakes or waffles (served all day); then demand shifts over to salads and sandwiches for lunch. Meaty main courses (lamb shank, roast prime rib) cost under $10 and come with a bewildering choice of soup or salad. It closes at 9 pm.

In Balboa Park itself, the nicest restaurant is **Prado** (☎ 619-557-9441, 1549 El Prado), which is inside the House of Hospitality along Plaza de Panama. In summer, the flower-bedecked terrace is perfect for sampling the restaurant's eclectic California-Mediterranean cuisine. The banquettes and painted beam ceiling in the main dining room also provide a suitably festive setting. Most dishes cost less than $14; there's a good happy hour, with half-price appetizer-and-drink specials.

Mission Valley & Kearny Heights (Maps 7 & 2)

A pleasant surprise awaits in the Hazard Center shopping mall, where trendy diners eat their way up and down the 'boot' at **Prego Ristorante** (☎ 619-294-4700, 1370 Frazee Rd). It takes major self-control not to fill up on delicious, warm bread baked on site before digging into classic Italian fare prepared in an open kitchen. If you stick to pizza and pasta, most mains cost under $14.

In Kearny Mesa, on San Diego's Chinese restaurant row, is **Jasmine** (☎ 858-268-0888, 4609 Convoy St), where you can look dinner in the eye as it swims in one of eight tanks inside the restaurant. The other specialty is dim sum. Literally meaning 'touching your heart a little at a time' in Cantonese, dim sum involves selecting bite-sized portions of various dishes from carts maneuvered around the dining room by servers. Very Hong Kong, very authentic. **Emerald Chinese Seafood** (☎ 858-565-6888, 3707 Convoy St) has a stellar reputation for super-fresh fish and seafood.

Carnivores will have a field day at **Korea House** (☎ 858-560-0080, 4620 Convoy St), which has special tables with grill units where diners prepare their own barbecue. The noodle dishes and beef dumplings are good as well.

Point Loma & Ocean Beach (Map 8)

Dirndl-clad waitresses, beer hall music and oil paintings of romantic castles – you'll find all the German clichés at the **Kaiserhof** (☎ 619-224-0606, 2253 Sunset Cliffs). But you'll also be treated to some of the best that comes out of the kitchen in the land of Bach and Beethoven. Sausages, pork chops, marinated beef rouladen, sauerkraut and red cabbage are just some of the favorites. In summer, the beer garden is great for winding down with a cold one. Closed Sunday nights and Monday.

Mission Beach (Map 9)

At **Saska's** (☎ 858-488-7311, 3768 Mission Blvd), the cooking is with an accent on steak and seafood, although pasta, salads and even sushi add variety to the menu. After 11 pm, the night owl crowd invades the rustic venue for the late-night breakfast served until 3 am. There's also a nice rooftop terrace to lounge on.

The *Firehouse Beach Cafe* (☎ 858-272-1999, 722 Grand Ave), in business for more than three decades, has a cool sun deck overlooking the beach. It's popular for breakfast and lunch ($3.50 to $8), as well as dinners built around seafood and steak, which top out at $15. All day Friday, beer costs just $1 per bottle, and there's a daily happy hour from 3 to 7 pm.

Pacific Beach (Map 10)

Sushi is the star of the show at *Zen 5* (☎ 858-490-0121, 1130 Garnet Ave), a young, energetic restaurant with fast, friendly servers. Zen's fishy morsels are some of the best – fresh, plump and nicely presented. Don't leave without trying the albacore tuna and the yellowtail. The best bargain is at dinnertime: If you order at least five selections per table (priced from $3.50 to $8.95), the food bill is 50% off.

The floor-to-ceiling windows at *Karinya's Thai* (☎ 858-270-5050, 825 Garnet Ave) may make you feel like you're sitting in a fish bowl, but that's easy to put up with once you're digging into the creatively prepared dishes. The appetizers especially are a departure from mainstream Thai fare. Order the sampler ($10) for an introduction. Seating is either western-style or on floor cushions at low tables. Mains start at $8.

Ingrid's Restaurant & Deli (☎ 858-270-4250, 1520 Garnet Ave), inside a cute little cottage, offers a full menu of traditional German favorites, from table-bending platters of sausages to rouladen (stuffed beef rolls) and sauerkraut with smoked ribs. Most dishes are under $10, and there are nightly specials. The attached deli is the place to pick up meats, cheeses and cookies for a picnic on the beach.

Right on the boardwalk, *World Famous* (☎ 858-272-3100, 711 Pacific Beach Dr) is the kind of place where surfers and seniors, business folks and tourists gather for superior seafood and fish dishes. Most mains are $15 to $20, but for those counting their pennies, the Bitchin' Burger for $6 or the $1.50 lobster tacos on Wednesday are definitely options.

Similar in appearance, location and menu, *The Green Flash* (☎ 858-270-7715, 701 Thomas Ave) is a bit pricier. Steak and seafood combinations start at $22 at dinnertime, although prime rib can be had for $14. Lunches are more casual, and top off at $12, complete with free views of passing babes and dudes. Happy hour runs Monday to Friday from 3 to 7 pm.

La Jolla (Map 11)

Alfonso's (☎ 858-454-2232, 1251 Prospect St) is definitely not your standard Mexican eatery, which is reflected both in the quality of the food *and* the prices. Crowd favorites are anything featuring *carne asada*, which is grilled steak marinated in a secret sauce based on an ancient family recipe. The margaritas are wicked; on most nights Alfonso himself can be seen wandering among the tables.

Spice & Rice (☎ 858-456-0466, 7734 Girard Ave) is a lovely Thai restaurant where interesting black metal-wicker chairs sit around tables cloaked in stiff linen. The menu features all the usual favorites, but is at its most creative when it comes to appetizers, separated into 'spicy' and 'sweet.' Regular dishes start at $9, but lunches can be had for $6.50.

The Spot (☎ 858-459-0800, 1005 Prospect St) may be across from the La Valencia Hotel, but it couldn't have a more different ambience. With a menu catering to all tastes and budgets – burgers, pizza, steak and lobster – and a kitchen that stays busy till 1 am, this is one of the few La Jolla late-night hangouts. There's a lively bar scene and a mixed crowd, from tourists to students to surfers.

Brockton Villa (☎ 858-454-7393, 1235 Coast Blvd) is in a charming 19th-century beach cottage overlooking La Jolla Cove. Popular at any time of day, its California cuisine menu is loaded with unconventionally prepared items (like seafood paella tossed with warm caper vinaigrette). For breakfast – perhaps the nicest time – try the eggs steam-scrambled in an espresso machine. Prices here are reasonable at breakfast and lunch, but average $20 at dinner (closed Monday night).

Restaurante Piatti (☎ 858-454-1589, 2182 Avenida de la Playa) is a popular Italian place, where lunch in the beautiful bougainvillea-festooned courtyard is a favorite pastime of the leisure set. Dishes feature fresh ingredients in inspired creations with a healthful, low-fat bent. Pastas start at $10; most main courses cost a few dollars more.

Across the street, *Barbarella* (☎ 858-454-7373, 2171 Avenida de la Playa) is a more casual Italian bistro, with a younger, hipper crowd and an amazing pizza oven designed by Niki de Saint Phalle. Pasta, salads, pizza range from $9 to $17.

PLACES TO EAT – TOP END
Downtown (Map 3)

Gaslamp Quarter *Chive* (☎ 619-232-4483, 558 4th Ave) is among the city's most cutting-edge restaurants, in both cuisine and decor. All white and brushed-steel postmodern minimalism, it has a slightly clinical feel, but thankfully the food is perky enough to keep you off Prozac. Tender duck or beef, as well as superb fresh seafood, paired with complex sauces and inventive side dishes, are indicative of the chef's talent.

There's no shortage of Italian trattorias in the Gaslamp. Among the consistently good ones is *Fio's Cucina Italiana* (☎ 619-234-3467, 801 5th Ave), a modern dining hall in a Victorian Italianate building that was once a department store. The chef works wonders with fish and seafood, but the pasta and pizza are good too, and the wine list is extensive. Another perennial favorite is *Trattoria La Strada* (☎ 619-239-3400, 702 5th Ave), which has won accolades for its magnificent Northern Italian cuisine.

Olé Madrid (☎ 619-557-0146, 751 5th Ave) has benches evoking the work of artist Friedensreich Hundertwasser, and serves Spanish tapas, paella and other typical fare. The same is true of *Café Sevilla* (☎ 619-233-

5979, 555 4th Ave), where the signature dish is paella ($18). On Friday and Saturday you can get dinner and a flamenco show for $35 (make reservations). There's also an attached nightclub (see the San Diego Entertainment chapter).

Ingrid Croce, widow of singer Jim Croce, is owner and executive chef at *Croce's Restaurant & Jazz Bar* (☎ 619-233-4355, 802 5th Ave) and *Croce's Top Hat Bar & Grill* (☎ 619-232-4338). Both have live music (see the San Diego Entertainment chapter) and serve good but pretty pricey salads, pastas and contemporary American fare. It is open for breakfast, lunch and dinner.

Spacious and mercifully kitsch-free, *Athens Market* (☎ 619-234-1955, 109 W F St) makes the most of standard Greek fare such as moussaka and dolmades (stuffed grape leaves). The menu is meat-heavy, but there are salads and a tasty (*avgolémono*) soup to provide variety. If you can't decide, order the Athens Market Special, a sampler of four dishes for $20.

La Provence (☎ 619-544-0661, 714 4th Ave) may take its Provençal theme a bit to extremes, but with its cheerful patterned table cloths and woodsy ambience, it's still a fine place to tuck into some country-style French food. If there's a wait, you could pass time by studying the menu written on the large windows. Next door is a wine bar with live music (mostly jazz) from 10 pm to 1 am Thursday to Saturday.

No gimmicks, just solid Southern French food is what's on the table at *Vignola* (☎ 619-231-1111, 828 6th Ave), in the historic Hotel St James (now Ramada Inn & Suites). Charming owner-chef Fabrice Poigin comes straight from the land of Edith Piaf and Claude Monet, and often emerges from the kitchen to greet guests. His wicked way with seafood, quality meats and vegetables ensure a memorable dining experience.

In the US Grant Hotel, the *Grant Grill* (☎ 619-239-6806, 619-232-3121), with masculine leather booths and subdued lighting, serves pricey continental cuisine prepared in a rotisserie kitchen imported from Europe. It's popular with power lunchers

Getting with the Times

Betty Friedan had penned the *Feminine Mystique*, Janis Joplin had revolutionized rock 'n roll, Jane Goodall had hung out with apes, but the wave of female emancipation had apparently not yet reached that bastion of masculinity, the Grant Grill of the US Grant Hotel. At lunchtime at least, the clubby quarters were open only to the Y-chromosome crowd, the juicy steaks and potatoes kept out of reach of female would-be power lunchers. In 1971, three women attorneys, refused admission after the maitre d' pointed at a sign saying 'Men Only until 3 pm,' finally got mad. And then they got even. They sued, they won, and the Grant Grill has been co-ed ever since.

from nearby City Hall and the courts. Lunch is served Monday to Friday only, breakfast and dinner daily. Also see boxed text 'Getting with the Times.'

Embarcadero & Seaport Village For dock-fresh fishy fare, you could do worse than booking a table at *Star of the Sea* (☎ 619-232-7408, *1360 N Harbor Dr*), where you dine above the water with a view of the historic tall ship *Star of India* moored next door. This is the classiest, and costliest, venue of the Anthony's restaurants, but the quality is first-rate – a good place to impress or celebrate. Jackets are required.

A little farther north, in Tuna Harbor, are two more fine seafood restaurants. *The Fish Market* (☎ 619-232-3474) is an oyster and sushi bar where a meal costs $6 to $15. Upstairs, the *Top of the Market* (☎ 619-234-4867) is more elegant and expensive.

Coronado (Map 4)

Dining takes place in a restored 1899 landmark cottage, but the bistro food at *Chez Loma* (☎ 619-435-0661, *1132 Loma Ave*) has definitely been updated for the 21st century. The emphasis is on fresh fish, but meats and pastas show up on the menu as well. It's pricey, but you can save by coming

before 6 pm and ordering the three-course prix fixe dinner for $18; later the same will cost $28. It is open for dinner only, plus Sunday brunch.

Hotel restaurants usually deserve to go unmentioned, but the *Azzura Point* (☎ 619-424-4000) at the Loews Coronado Bay Resort (see the San Diego Places to Stay chapter) is an exception. Come here for a special treat or if the occasion calls for a romantic setting. Chef James Boyce comes up with magical creations inspired by both Mediterranean and Californian cuisine. Main courses average $30. It's all complemented by a superb wine list and even better views. Dress nicely (jacket recommended).

Old Town (Map 5)

In more than 20 years in business, *Café Pacífica* (☎ 619-291-6666, *2414 San Diego Ave*) has built a loyal clientele that enjoys its sophisticated ambience in a New England cabin-style setting. With a focus on California cuisine, the menu changes seasonally and is strongest in the grilled fish department. Mains range from $16 to $25.

Nearby, *El Agave Tequilería* (☎ 619-220-0692, *2304 San Diego Ave*) is the kind of place where ordinary dishes become exceptional under the guidance of a skilled chef. Sure, the menu features the familiar quesadillas and tacos but here they come with intricate, unusual fillings. One particular standout is the chicken with mole (a sauce made from dozens of 'secret' ingredients, including chocolate). Tequila fans will delight in the huge array of the potent agave-based spirit.

Hillcrest & Middletown (Map 6)

Chef Deborah Scott's *Kemo Sabe* (☎ 619-220-6802, *3958 5th Ave*) is the bright new star in the galaxy of Hillcrest eateries. Effortlessly blending Southwestern and Far Eastern flavors, she seduces diners with such inspired concoctions as coconut calamari or charbroiled ginger ahi with chile black beans. Main courses go for $12 to $24, and a stellar wine list complements the menu.

What do India, Morocco, Lebanon, Japan, China and San Diego all have in common?

Answer: They are all located 33° north of the equator. This geographic connection inspired the concept behind San Diego's most adventurous restaurant, ***Parallel 33*** *(☎ 619-260-0033, 741 W Washington St)*. The extensive menu presents gourmet versions of dishes from all those countries – *samosas* from India, *b'stilla* from Morocco and seared ahi from Japan. Main courses average $20.

La Jolla (Map 11)

A stomping ground for the rich, lissome and famous, ***Tapenade*** *(☎ 858-551-7500, 7612 Fay Ave)* has it all: gorgeous 1930s supper club decor, unobtrusive but attentive service and, of course, chef Jean-Michel Diot, who digs deep into his rich repertory of French cuisine to produce one culinary feast after another. A la carte mains start at $22, making the three-course 'sunset menu' (served from 5:30 to 6:30 pm) a veritable steal at $25. Two-course lunches are $15.

Roppongi *(☎ 858-551-5252, 875 Prospect St)* is one of those rare concept restaurants that convinces with substance, not flash. The name is Japanese for 'six trees,' and the menu blends that many Asian cuisines: Chinese, Vietnamese, Korean, Thai, Indian and Japanese. This works especially well for appetizers (here called 'Asian tapas'); it's easy to make a meal of two or three. Less of a success is the dining room itself, which has hotel-like 'charm' despite being based on Feng Shui principles.

Trattoria Acqua *(☎ 858-454-0709, 1298 Prospect St)* has first-rate Northern Italian cuisine, ocean views and perhaps the most romantic courtyard dining in town. Pick from gourmet pizza ($11), pasta ($15) or seafood ($19), all prepared with more than a soupçon of flair. It has a spectacular wine list and also serve weekend brunch.

Next door, in the same woodsy Coast Walk complex, the ***Crab Catcher*** *(☎ 858-454-9587, 1298 Prospect St)* is well-renowned for its seafood. Sunday champagne brunch, starting at $12, is a great value, as is the happy hour from 4 to 7 pm Monday to Friday with $2 margaritas, beer or champagne and half-price appetizers. The crab nachos for $5 will feed two.

Top o' the Cove *(☎ 858-454-7779, 1216 Prospect St)* is regarded by many as the Rolls Royce of the La Jolla dining world. A refined emporium of Franco-California cuisine, the main dining room caters to the well-heeled, with fish and meat mains costing $30 to $35. The monetarily disadvantaged could nibble on a $10 sandwich in the café, where the terrace offers the same spectacular coastal views as the main restaurant.

At the ***Marine Room*** *(☎ 858-459-7222, 2000 Spindrift Dr)*, only a wall of plate glass comes between you and the crashing waves. Views of the sun setting over the ocean are free; the French cuisine – given the serious treatment here – is not. This is *the* place to see 'old La Jolla money' chowing down.

Entertainment

There's a lot going on in San Diego, and for what's hot, your best source of information is the free weekly *San Diego Reader,* available at many restaurants, shops and bars throughout the city. Also good is the *San Diego Union Tribune*'s Night & Day section, a supplement to the Thursday edition. Both are packed with comprehensive listings and reviews of movies, plays, galleries and gigs. The San Diego Performing Arts League publishes a free bimonthly *What's Playing* booklet, available at the International Visitor Information Center in Horton Plaza as well as in coffeehouses, restaurants and theaters around town. Or check the Web site at www.sandiegoperforms.com. Another good source is www.sandiegoartandsol.com.

Buying Tickets

The central ticket source for concerts, sporting events, theater, musicals, etc is Ticketmaster (☎ 619-220-8497). Most likely you'll have to deal with an annoying wait and an overworked staff before being asked to pay a per-ticket 'convenience' charge *plus* a per-order 'handling charge' in addition to your ticket price. You must have a credit card to charge tickets, which will be either mailed to you or held for pick-up at the will-call counter of your event's venue. Tickets may also be ordered online at www.ticketmaster.com.

Times Arts Tix, in Horton Plaza Park on Broadway, sells half-price tickets for same-day evening or next-day matinee performances in theater, music and dance. Call ☎ 619-497-5000 for a recorded message listing which tickets are available. The kiosk is open 10 am to 7 pm Tuesday to Saturday, although this varies slightly throughout the year. Sales are first-come, first-served (cash only). Times Arts Tix is also a Ticketmaster outlet.

MAJOR VENUES

San Diego has several large, multipurpose venues with year-round schedules of rock, pop and classical concerts, Broadway shows, ballet troupes, magic shows, and lots more.

The 3000-seat *Civic Theatre (Map 3; ☎ 619-570-1100, 401 B Street),* is the largest and most modern performance space in San Diego. Blockbuster stars such as Luciano Pavarotti, David Copperfield and the Bolshoi Ballet come to perform in this plush venue, which is also home to the San Diego Opera, the California Ballet, the La Jolla Chamber Music Society and the San Diego Playgoers.

A smaller venue and one with an intriguing schedule, is *4th & B Street (Map 3; ☎ 619-231-4343, 345 B St)* where one recent weekly lineup included a comedy show, a salsa band and a zydeco group from New Orleans. It may be eclectic but the bookings are almost always top-caliber.

The indoor *San Diego Sports Arena (Map 8; ☎ 619-224-4176, 35 Sports Arena Blvd)* has been around since the 1970s hosting everything from Pearl Jam to the World Wrestling Federation to Disney on Ice. It is the regular home of the San Diego Gulls ice hockey team. A recent renovation has seriously improved the acoustics of the hall, which seats 16,000.

The *SDSU Open Air Amphitheatre (☎ 619-594-6947, 5500 Campanile Dr),* on the San Diego State University campus, is the oldest outdoor amphitheater in the city, built in 1934 as a WPA project. It holds up to 4600 people and has welcomed major artists like Joe Cocker, Savage Garden and the Gypsy Kings (whose music is more suited to smaller stages). Eavesdropping on concerts from the outside used to be easier, but some say it's still possible.

Near the border, in Chula Vista (Map 2), is the spanking new *Coors Amphitheater (☎ 619-671-3600, 2050 Entertainment Circle),* a state-of-the-art facility with excellent acoustics, which brings in major artists – who used to bypass San Diego. There's seating for 10,000, with a lawn area for 10,000 more. The lineup often includes Santana, Christina Aguilera and other Latin stars, drawing well-heeled Tijuanenses across the border. The concert season runs March to October.

Outside of central San Diego awaits a trio of major venues. In North County's Escondido (Map 1), the home of Wild Animal Park, is the *California Center for the Arts* (☎ *760-839-4140, 340 N Escondido Rd*), which has a 1524-seat concert hall and a 408-seat theater, as well as a museum, gallery and conference center. This is where you'll see touring shows like *Riverdance* or *Annie*, but also Jackson Browne and the Buena Vista Social Club. The 800-seat *Poway Center for the Performing Arts* (☎ *858-748-0505, 1598 Espola Rd*) in Poway (Map 1), just off I-15, is similar.

In El Cajon (Map 1) is the *East County Performing Arts Center* (☎ *619-440-2277, 210 E Main St)*, which caters more to the gray-haired set. A typical lineup might include Paul Anka, Bob Newhart or the Everly Brothers.

THEATER
Theater thrives in San Diego. Tickets are available at the theater box office in person, by phone and sometimes online, as well as through Ticketmaster and Times Arts Tix.

Major Theaters
The much-acclaimed *La Jolla Playhouse* (Map 11; ☎ *858-550-1010, 2910 La Jolla Village Dr*) was founded in 1947 by Gregory Peck, Dorothy McGuire and Mel Ferrer. Innovative productions of musicals, comedies, world premieres and classics, many of which move on to other venues – including Broadway – are staged here. Performances take place at the Mandell Weiss Center for the Performing Arts on the UCSD campus. Student and senior discounts are available except for Friday and Saturday shows; public rush tickets ($10) go on sale 10 minutes before curtain.

Shakespeare and the classics are the meat and potatoes of the *Old Globe Theatre* (☎ *619-239-2255*), a popular theater complex in Balboa Park. The occasional new play livens up the menu, including Neil Simon and Stephen Sondheim premieres. The season consists of 12 or 13 productions performed on three stages: the 581-seat Old Globe itself, a replica of Shakespeare's

London theater; the 225-seat Cassius Carter Centre Stage and the 612-seat outdoor Lowell Davies Festival Theatre. Tickets range from $35 to $42, or $31 for students and seniors.

The *San Diego Repertory Theatre (Map 3; ☎ 619-544-1000, Horton Plaza)* is San Diego's most multicultural troupe, producing sometimes adventurous plays by artists of all backgrounds for audiences that are just as diverse. Recurrent events include Kuumba Fest, an African-American festival; the San Diego Jewish Arts Festival and a production of *A Christmas Carol*. It has also garnered a reputation for lesser-known classics, such as Shakespeare's *Cymbeline*. Performances take place on the two stages of the Lyceum Theater, underneath Horton Plaza.

The Coronado-based *Lamb's Players Theatre (Map 4; ☎ 619-437-0600, 1142 Orange Ave)* is an ensemble cast and San Diego's only year-round repertory theater. Besides musicals, drama and comedies, it also takes on new work by emerging writers, especially those who explore various aspects of life from a Judeo-Christian perspective. Performances are in the Spreckels Building, an intimate space with 350 seats wrapping around the stage, providing unencumbered sightlines. Tickets range from $14 to $34, with a $4 discount for seniors and online ticket purchases. Rush tickets ($10) are sold 10 minutes before curtain.

The *San Diego Playgoers* (☎ *619-570-1100),* produces big, splashy Broadway and international shows at the Civic Theatre (see Major Venues, earlier). This is where you're most likely to see *Phantom of the Opera*, *Riverdance* and *Cabaret*. Ticket prices vary by performance.

Smaller Theaters
For theater that's adventurous, provocative and cutting-edge, check out *Sledgehammer (Map 3; ☎ 619-544-1484, 1620 6th Ave)*, based in St Cecilia's, a converted funeral chapel. The group makes creative use of space, comes up with weird stage designs and experiments with theatrical forms. In a similar vein, the Downtown *Fritz Theater (Map 3; ☎ 619-233-7505, 420 3rd Ave)*

presents innovative contemporary plays, including works by emerging San Diego artists and fresh takes on classics.

In the Gaslamp Quarter, the *Horton Grand Theater* (Map 3; ☎ 619-234-9583, 444 4th Ave) has been the long-term home of the off-beat comedy *Triple Espresso*. The exuberantly decorated *Spreckels Theater* (Map 3; ☎ 619-235-9500, 121 Broadway) presents a varied schedule of theater, dance and music events.

The 256-seat *Theatre in Old Town* (Map 5; ☎ 619-688-2494, 4040 Twiggs St) is home to an open-ended run of *Forever Plaid*, a musical comedy featuring hit songs from the '50s and '60s (think 'Three Coins in a Fountain' and other corny stuff). Tickets are $25 to $35. Plays with gay, lesbian and bisexual themes are the focus of the *Diversionary Theater* (Map 7; ☎ 619-220-0097, 4545 Park Blvd) in Hillcrest. Founded in 1985, its productions explore homosexuality in both historical and contemporary contexts.

In La Jolla, the *UCSD Department of Theater and Dance* (☎ 858-534-3791) is a professional training program that ranks third in the country. Performances range from classical to pushing the envelope and mostly take place at the Mandell Weiss Center for the Performing Arts on the southern edge of campus.

Dinner Theater

Dinner theater is a popular form of entertainment in San Diego, and several companies operate throughout the county. Performance venues vary, as does quality – read current reviews in the *Reader* and don't expect Lawrence Olivier-caliber here! Ticket prices often include a three-course meal and also tax, gratuities and a drink. Check with each company to avoid surprises.

Perennial favorites include *Joey's & Maria's Comedy Italian Wedding* (☎ 800-944-5639); *Mystery Cafe Dinner Theater* ☎ 619-544-1600), which has a regular gig at the Imperial House restaurant at 505 Kalmia St on the western edge of Balboa Park and *HIT Productions*, which stands for Hilarious Interactive Theater (☎ 619-561-8673).

Comedy Clubs

San Diego's only major comedy venue is the well-established *Comedy Store* (Map 11; ☎ 858-454-9176, 916 Pearl St) in La Jolla. It is open nightly, serving meals, drinks and chuckles. A cover charge applies ($6 to $12 on weekends with a two-drink minimum).

Comedy Sportz (☎ 619-295-4999, 3717 India St) at the Marquis Theater is an improv show put on by the National Comedy Theater. It literally pitches 'teams' wearing uniforms and standing on Astroturf against each other. Depending on who's up, this can be funny as hell, or just plain hell. Show times are Friday at 8 pm and Saturday at 7:30 and 9:45 pm; tickets are $11, or $9 students, seniors and children.

4th & B Street (Map 3; ☎ 619-231-4343, 345 B St) is another venue where comedy frequently makes it onto the lineup.

Children's & Youth Theater

Marie Hitchcock Puppet Theater (☎ 619-685-5045) is a lovely little theater in the Palisades Building in Balboa Park with year-round performances by resident puppeteers and guest artists. Show times are Wednesday to Friday at 10 am to 11:30 am and weekends at 11 am, 1 and 2:30 pm. Tickets are $2 children, $3 adults; $1 more for guest performers. *Icarus Puppet Company* (☎ 619-563-5252, 800-449-4479) is another professional company that performs throughout San Diego, usually in libraries and often for free.

What do Dennis Hopper and Raquel Welch have in common? Both honed their thespian skills in classes offered through the *San Diego Junior Theatre* (☎ 619-239-8355, Casa del Prado, Balboa Park), the country's oldest children's theater (since 1948). Kids ages eight to 18 who have completed at least one of the classes perform in the six annual productions; international classics such as *Pippi Longstocking* and *The Music Man* are typical. Ticket prices vary, but are reasonable.

OPERA & MUSICAL THEATER

Highbrow arts enjoy a loyal following in San Diego, which is why several companies have managed to survive here for decades.

The **San Diego Opera** (Map 3; ☎ 619-570-1100) presents high-quality, eclectic programming, including such operatic warhorses as Mozart's *Magic Flute,* and more eccentric stuff, such as Beethoven's *Fidelio,* set in a revolutionary banana republic. Stars such as Placido Domingo, José Carreras and Cecilia Bartoli have appeared on its stage at the Civic Theatre (see Major Venues, above). Operas are usually sung in the original language with super-titles in English. The season runs from January to May. Tickets cost from $35 to $115, but a limited number of standing-room tickets ($18) are available just before curtain (arrive an hour early to get in line). With a standing-room ticket you can take any empty seat once the lights go down.

The **Starlight Musical Theatre** (☎ 619-544-7827) is a summer series at the 4000-seat outdoor Starlight Bowl in Balboa Park featuring three popular musicals produced by the San Diego Civic Light Opera. Founded in 1945, it is one of the oldest continuous musical theater companies in the nation. Performances here are rather bizarre: Since the Bowl is in the airport flight path, shows are abruptly suspended every time an airplane flies over. Red and green lights behind the stage, not visible to the audience, signal to the actors when to stop and when to resume. Tickets range from $21.50 to $39.50.

Since 1979 the **San Diego Comic Opera** (☎ 619-239-8836, *Casa del Prado*) in Balboa Park has delighted audiences with lively productions of light-hearted opera, musical theater and operetta. Works by Gilbert and Sullivan and Giacomo Rossini are as much part of the menu as Leonard Bernstein and Cole Porter. Performances feature a live orchestra and cost $17 to $25, with discounts for seniors and students; children under 12 pay $10. With only 19 rows, there's not a bad seat in the house. The season runs from mid-June to mid-November.

BALLET & DANCE

The San Diego Dance Alliance is a central clearinghouse for all things dance-related, and is a good source for upcoming events.

Call ☎ 619-239-9255 or check the Web site at www.artemedia.com/organizations/sdada.

San Diego has several professional ballet companies. The **California Ballet Company** (☎ 858-560-6741) offers several productions annually, most of them crowd-pleasers such as *The Nutcracker* and *Sleeping Beauty*. Founded in 1968 by John and Maxine Mahon, it is still directed by the latter. Performances take place throughout the county, including the Downtown Civic Theater, the Poway Center for the Arts in Poway and the California Center for the Arts in Escondido.

For more innovative programming, look to the **San Diego Ballet** (☎ 619-294-7378). Since 1991 it has been presenting a repertory of high-quality contemporary ballet, including experimental new works like *Luna Lunera,* based on the poetry of García Lorca.

Another company is **City Ballet** (☎ 858-274-6058), which presents both classical and contemporary works at various venues (check local listings). Its December *Nutcracker* at the Spreckels Theater and its eccentric *Ballet on the Edge* in spring at the La Jolla Museum of Contemporary Art are both popular.

Modern dance, too, has its place in San Diego. The much-acclaimed **John Malashock & Dance** (☎ 619-260-1622), led by a former lead dancer with Twyla Tharp, is in residence at the Old Globe in Balboa Park. Another renowned company is the **San Diego Dance Theater** (☎ 858-484-7791), directed by the well-respected Jean Isaacs, who sometimes collaborates with Tijuana-based Grupo de Danza de Minerva Tapia. Other companies to watch for include the **Patricia Rincon Dance Collective**, **McCaleb Dancers** and **Eveoke Dance Theatre**. Many shows take place at Sushi (see the boxed text 'Sights & Sounds at Sushi').

International folk dance is the focus at **Nations of San Diego**, a festival co-produced by the San Diego Repertory Theater and the San Diego Dance Alliance. It features more than 100 dancers and musicians from different ethnic backgrounds on stage at the Lyceum Theater in Horton Plaza. Call ☎ 619-239-9255 or 619-544-1000 for details.

SAN DIEGO

Sights & Sounds at Sushi

Sushi Performance & Visual Art Space (Map 3; ☎ 619-235-8466, 320 11th Ave) – 'Sushi' for short – has nothing to do with rice and raw fish. 'Raw' is, however, the operative word for many of the performances taking place at this cutting-edge urban venue in the East Village. Part of the Rein-Carnation Project, a rehabilitated Carnation Dairy factory that also contains living and work lofts, Sushi is a well-known launching pad for offbeat, up-and-coming artists. Whoopi Goldberg, controversial performance artist Karen Finley, Latino comedy troupe Culture Clash and Eric Bogosian all got their careers fired up here. Dance, readings, theater, performance art – no matter what is on Sushi's eclectic menu, you're in for a weirdly wonderful experience.

CLASSICAL MUSIC

For serious music lovers, there's no finer place than the Copley Symphony Hall, home to the *San Diego Symphony (Map 3; ☎ 619-235-0804, 750 B St)*. This accomplished orchestra presents classical and family concerts, as well as the innovative Light Bulb Series, an interactive program intended to demystify classical music. In summer the symphony moves outdoors to the Navy Pier at 960 N Harbor Drive (Map 3) for its more light-hearted Summer Pops season. For more on the Copley Symphony Hall, see the Things to See & Do chapter.

The *Spruce Street Forum (Map 6; ☎ 619-295-0301, 301 Spruce St)* in Middletown is one of the city's most refined small performance spaces. The entertainment roster is heavy on highbrow musicians – both local and from afar – and eclectic art exhibits also make use of this bright, light-filled environment. Tickets are usually a budget-friendly $10; exhibits are free. Doors are open from 1 pm Thursday to Saturday only.

The motto of the *La Jolla Symphony & Chorus (☎ 858-534-4637)* is 'Classics & Beyond' of which the 'beyond' make up almost half of the repertory. Besides traditional favorites, you'll be treated to sitar concerts, concerts for mariachi and orchestra, or an oratorio based on the poems of Pablo Neruda. Performances take place at UCSD's Mandeville Auditorium (Map 11), 9500 Gilman Drive, from November to May.

High-caliber performances of small orchestral works are the hallmarks of the *San Diego Chamber Orchestra (☎ 888-848-7326, 760-753-6402)* whose season runs from September to April. Under long-time artistic director Donald Barra, the orchestra has built up an impressive resume of recordings and performed with big-name soloists. Venues range from Copley Symphony Hall in Downtown to the Sherwood Auditorium at the Museum of Contemporary Art at 700 Prospect St in Jolla, and even the 4th & B Street nightclub at 345 B St.

The *San Diego Master Chorale (☎ 619-262-6683)* is a critically acclaimed volunteer 120-voice chorus. Founded in 1961, it presents stand-alone recitals and is also the chorus for the San Diego Opera and the San Diego Chamber Orchestra.

Also look for concerts presented by the *La Jolla Chamber Music Society*, which brings world-renowned soloists and orchestras to San Diego. Its two-week SummerFest delights audiences with multiple concerts all day long, some of them free. Call ☎ 858-459-3728 for details.

CINEMAS

Movie theaters in San Diego are mostly huge multiplexes with up to 20 screens showing first-release Hollywood blockbusters. The newest releases often sell out quickly on Friday and Saturday nights. The first shows start around 11 am or so, and the last around 10 pm. Tickets range from $7 to $8.50, with discounts of up to 50% available to children, students, seniors and for shows starting before 4 or 6 pm. Check the *Reader* or call ☎ 619-444-3456 for schedules.

The most glamorous Downtown mega-movie theater is Pacific Theater's *Gaslamp 15 (Map 3; ☎ 619-232-0400, 701 5th Ave)*, ensconced in a stately mock-Victorian with art deco decor, plush carpets and a sweeping staircase. Only drop in at the Gaslamp's more contemporary cousin, the **UA Horton Plaza 14** *(Map 3;* ☎ *619-234-4661, 457 Horton Plaza)* if you've got no other choice. The sound quality is behind the times, seats are uncomfortable and most of the theaters are pretty small. If you're driving, the cheapest parking for either Downtown theater is in Horton Plaza itself; three hours are free with purchase *(any* purchase will do).

Parking is free at the trio of Mission Valley multiplexes attached to each of the area's big malls: **AMC Fashion Valley 18** *(Map 7;* ☎ *858-558-2262, 7057 Friars Rd)*; **AMC Mission Valley 20** *(Map 7;* ☎ *858-558-2262, 1640 Camino del Rio N)* and the **Mann Hazard Center 7** *(Map 7;* ☎ *619-291-7777, 7510 Hazard Center Dr)*.

La Jolla has the **AMC La Jolla 12** *(*☎ *858-558-2234, 8657 Villa La Jolla Dr)* at Nobel Dr by the La Jolla Village Square mall (Map 11).

Smaller Theaters & Art Houses

Cozy, independent neighborhood theaters are more or less extinct in San Diego. The few that remain are your only chance to see a foreign, off-beat, non-commercial, cult, documentary or classic film. The sound may not be THX, the seats may be hard, but hopefully the filmic fare flickering before you makes more than up for these inconveniences.

The 'biggest' of these dinosaurs is the **Hillcrest Cinemas** *(Map 6;* ☎ *619-299-2100, 3965 5th Ave)*, in Hillcrest, with five screens, and **La Jolla Village Theatres** *(Map 11;* ☎ *858-453-7831, 8879 Villa La Jolla Dr)* with four. Truly vintage theaters are the **Ken Cinema** *(Map 7;* ☎ *619-283-5909, 4061 Adams Ave)* in Kensington, and **The Cove** *(Map 11;* ☎ *858-459-5404, 7730 Girard Ave)* in La Jolla, both with just one screen each.

Other Film Venues

An excellent new venue is the **Joan & Irwin Jacobs Theater** *(*☎ *619-238-7559)* (named for the Qualcomm founders who helped finance the space) at the Museum of Photographic Arts in Balboa Park. It presents highbrow film series on a particular theme (eg, Great

Female Performers), a particular director (eg, Robert Frank) or a filmic genre (eg, film noir). Screenings are Wednesday to Saturday (sometimes also Tuesday) evenings and Sunday afternoons and are usually double features. The admission of $7.50, or $5 for students and seniors, is good for all movies shown during that session.

Also in Balboa Park is the world's first **Omnimax Theater** *(*☎ *619-238-1233)*, part of the Reuben H Fleet Science Center, in operation since 1973. Movies usually have a nature theme and are shown on a dome – a tilted, wraparound screen 10 times regular size. The 152-speakers create sensations that range from fantastic to OK, depending on what's showing. Show times vary, but there's usually at least one per hour. Tickets for one film are $11 for anyone over 13, $8 for those under 13 and $9 for seniors; for two films

Garden Cabaret

Modeled after Italian outdoor cinemas but updated with heat lamps, table seating and whimsical decor, San Diego's Garden Cabaret is an extremely enjoyable place to see a movie. The program is usually heavy on Hollywood classics – think *Some Like It Hot, Rear Window, Roman Holiday* – and films with contemporary historical significance (a slew of Kubrick films were shown after he died).

For the 2000 season, the summer series moved from its original site in Hillcrest to the University Towne Centre mall in La Jolla (Map 11), where, every Sunday night from late June to October, the square fronting the fast-food court and iceskating rink is converted into an outdoor theater with a 20-foot screen.

Shows are preceded by a few cartoons, just like in the early years of Hollywood cinema. Seating starts at 7:30 pm for the 8:30 pm show and costs $9, or $8 for students and seniors. There's coffee, tea, designer sodas, decadent desserts and (of course) popcorn. Call the box office (☎ 619-295-4221) for show information.

prices are $15/12/13; admission to the Science Center exhibits is included in the price.

BARS & BREWERIES
Downtown

San Diego's first liquor license was granted in the 1930s and is still held by the original owner of the *Waterfront (Map 3; ☎ 619-232-9656, 2044 Kettner Blvd)* – which actually was *on* the waterfront until the harbor was filled and the airport built. Recently the little watering hole's future was thought to be under threat from a developer but, surprise! This was one developer with vision and heart, who, rather than leveling the landmark, ended up incorporating it into his new apartment building.

One of the most popular places in the Gaslamp Quarter is the *Bitter End (Map 3; ☎ 619-338-9300, 770 5th Ave)*, which is really three places in one: the downstairs dance club where 20-somethings dress to impress the attitudinous bouncers, then get all sweaty on the wee dance floor; the center bar, which is a meat market for the middle-aged; and the clubby upstairs lounge, which brings in the sedate set intent on martinis and clever conversation. Energy levels perk up during Martini Madness Thursdays, when prices drop to $3.25 (the Black Martini is the bar's signature drink).

As you walk up 5th Street, look for the staircase leading down into the sidewalk to the *Onyx Room (Map 3; ☎ 619-235-6699, 852 5th Ave)*, a classy, candlelit joint where it's easy to numb out over beer or cocktails after a hard day's work or turf-pounding. Live jazz is offered several times weekly, and on Friday and Saturday night the place teems with young professionals kicking up their heels to Top 40 tunes.

Dick's Last Resort (Map 3; ☎ 619-231-9100, 345 4th Ave) is one of the Gaslamp's more notorious hangouts and comes complete with pool tables, darts and a big patio. Nearby, the newish *Hang Ten Brewing Co (Map 3; ☎ 619-437-4452, 310 5th Ave)*, at K St, brews nearly a dozen beers, which it serves up along with good food and sports TV.

Hillcrest & Middletown

The *Aero Club (Map 6; ☎ 619-297-7211, 3365 India St)* has been on solid ground in the local bar scene since the 1940s. Originally the kind of place where aerospace workers capped off the day's shift, it now attracts a mixed crowd of friendly hipsters and still-happening boomers. While concentrating on which of the 20 beers on tap to order, check out the nifty mural behind the bar.

The Alibi (Map 6; ☎ 619-295-0881, 1403 University Ave) in Hillcrest is a quintessential dive bar – and one of the area's few straight places – with a lively pool scene. Put your name on the list, a quarter in the well-stocked juke box and order a Big Dipper (a 23-ounce glass of Bud for $2) – and you'll fit right in.

Another legendary watering hole is *The Lamplighter (Map 6; ☎ 619-298-3624, 817 W Washington St)*. 'The Lamp' to locals, it is a truly mixed bar where, on any given night, truck drivers and accountants share the karaoke stage with neighborhood old farts and coeds. A real scene.

Mission Bay & Beaches

Margarita fans should make the *Coaster Saloon (Map 9; ☎ 858-488-4438, 744 Ventura Place)*, in Mission Beach, a destination on Thursday when a respectable version of Jimmy Buffet's favorite drink costs just $1.25. The all-u-can-eat barbecue dinners for a mere $5 are legendary, and the view of the Giant Dipper roller coaster from the small sidewalk terrace is free.

One of the most frenetic party zones is in Pacific Beach: *The Open Bar (Map 10; ☎ 858-270-3221, 4302 Mission Blvd)*, where you may have to shoehorn your way onto the large wooden patio facing the busy boulevard.

Margarita Rocks (Map 10; ☎ 858-272-2780, 959 Hornblend Ave), in Pacific Beach, really 'rocks' on weekends when the cavernous bar-cum-dance club fills with hard bodies showing off tummies and tattoos. Those not on a fitness program can fill up at the free 40-foot-long happy hour buffet or order the $5 steak served nightly, except Monday, from 5 pm to midnight.

La Jolla

Bar hopping in La Jolla means mostly sipping martinis and Chivas at sophisticated establishments. A nostalgic favorite is the clubby, wood-paneled **Whaling Bar** *(Map 11; ☎ 858-454-0771, 1132 Prospect St)* at the La Valencia Hotel, the preferred watering hole of Gregory Peck and Dr Seuss.

On the microbrewery scene, try the **Karl Strauss Brewery** *(Map 11; ☎ 858-551-2739)*, at the corner of Wall St and Herschel Ave, where pints are $2 from 4 to 7 pm weekdays. *La Jolla Brewing Company (Map 11; ☎ 619-456-2739, 7536 Fay Ave)* is another good choice.

LIVE MUSIC
Downtown

If you're over 25, you'll probably feel past the expiration date at **Buffalo Joe's** *(Map 3; ☎ 619-236-1616, 600 5th Ave)*, where weekend partying to disco and Top 40 is taken seriously. Other nights, it's live music from blues to swing to zydeco. Best thing: the wacky bartenders. Best time to come: happy hour.

Club Sevilla *(Map 3; ☎ 619-233-5979, 555 4th Ave)*, the dance club beneath Café Sevilla (see the San Diego Places to Eat chapter), sizzles with 10-piece salsa/merengue and Latin rock bands Sunday to Thursday, and DJ-served Latin-Euro dance tunes on Friday and Saturday. The crowd is dressy and young and has little of the stuck-up factor common in the Gaslamp.

Hillcrest & Middletown

Just north of Little Italy, **Casbah** *(Map 6; ☎ 619-232-4355, 2501 Kettner Blvd)* is a fun place with an underground vibe; it's a breeding ground for alternative rock bands. Nirvana and Smashing Pumpkins both cut their teeth here long before hitting the big time. It's smallish and seating is at a premium.

A fairly new entry in San Diego's underground club scene is the nearby **Pirate's Den** *(Map 6; ☎ 619-260-1200, 2812 Kettner Blvd)*, a largish space where candlelight and artworks temper an edgy industrial look. The focus is on Latin music – as in salsa, cumbia and jazz – played by DJs and live

bands; the popular B-Side Players are regular guests. This place doesn't really get jumping until 11 pm or midnight. Closed Sunday. Cover (usually $5) for bands.

One of the coolest spots, just north of Balboa Park, is the **Turquoise Room** *(Map 7; ☎ 619-283-3135, 4356 30th St)*, a retro lounge inside the 1959 Aztec bowling alley. Scenesters regularly swarm this place for the strong, inexpensive drinks and inspired band choices, and sometimes even go for the ninepins.

Point Loma & Ocean Beach

Humphrey's Concerts by the Bay (Map 8; ☎ 619-523-1010, 2241 Shelter Island Dr), next to Humphrey's Half Moon Inn, is a 1300-seat outdoor venue romantically located right on the Shelter Island waterfront. Since 1982 its popular summer concert series – which runs May through October – has brought entertainers like Dana Carvey, Harry Belafonte and Vonda Shepard (of Ally McBeal fame); shows often sell out early.

Counterculture rules at **Dream Street** *(Map 8; ☎ 619-222-8131, 2228 Bacon St)*, where the decor is positively post-atomic and the mostly alternative rock bands have colorful names such as Clusterfunk and Bedroom Heroes. Three or four per night draw in the crowd, mostly young, tattooed and pierced, Wednesday to Saturday (cover $5 or $6). Other nights are tamer, with features like Brazilian Night or even karaoke.

Zero snob factor, a good lineup of local and touring bands and a low cover are the winning attributes of **Winston's** *(Map 8; ☎ 858-222-6822, 1921 Bacon St)*, up the street. The young crowd grooves mostly on reggae, with the occasional alternative rock and acid jazz outfit thrown in.

Mission Bay & Beaches

The time to be at the **Barefoot Bar & Grill** *(Map 9; ☎ 858-274-4630, 1404 Vacation Rd)*, right on the water at the San Diego Paradise Point Resort, is Sunday, for the all-day weekend wrapup party. Live bands, tanned and tight flesh, raging hormones – it takes the personality of a zombie *not* to make new friends here. Prices are high, drinks are watery and the staff is overworked, but that's stopping no one from 'hanging loose.' Friday karaoke nights are big too.

If the scene at the beachside *Canes (Map 9; ☎ 858-488-1780, 3105 Ocean Front Walk)* in Mission Beach seems a bit loopy at times, it's because the place is right behind the Giant Dipper. Cool rock bands keep the two dance floors hopping through the night. For a break, watch the sunset from the rooftop deck. By day, this place reverts to being a restaurant with cheap burgers and salads.

Slightly older folks (30s and up) may feel more comfortable at the laid-back *Cannibal Bar (Map 9; ☎ 858-488-1081, 3999 Mission Blvd)*, in the Catamaran Hotel. It's often packed with tourists, but locals also find their way here. Bands cover the musical spectrum – reggae to rock to swing to '80s tunes.

In Pacific Beach, near the waterfront, *Blind Melons (Map 10; ☎ 858-483-7844, 710 Garnet Ave)* is a no-frills, no-nonsense kind of place with little to distract you from the music. It's mostly R&B, but the occasional jazz and rock concerts draw relaxed patrons of all ages. Cover is around $10.

JAZZ & BLUES

Most of the live jazz and blues places are in and around the Gaslamp Quarter. The best known is *Croce's Restaurant & Jazz Bar (Map 3; ☎ 619-233-4355, 802 5th Ave)* where Latin, Afro-Cuban, classic and just about every other jazz genre finds its way onto the stage nightly. R&B rules upstairs at *Croce's Top Hat Bar & Grill*. The entire emporium is run by Ingrid Croce, widow of Jim (think 'Bad, Bad Leroy Brown') and also features a popular, if pricey, restaurant. Cover is usually $3 to $5 during the week and slightly more on weekends. Expect mostly conventioneers and tourists; locals have 'been here, done that' long ago.

Jazz purists won't want to miss *Dizzy's (Map 3; ☎ 858-270-7467, 344 7th Ave)*, a no-nonsense parlor whose functional look is warmed by candlelight and top-rated musicians. No alcohol or food are served and all ages are welcome. Open Wednesday to Saturday; cover is around $8.

Patrick's II (Map 3; ☎ 619-233-3077, 428 F St) is as comfortable as an old shoe and often packed to the gills with no-nonsense hard-boozing regulars here to enjoy high-caliber blues. Cover is usually free during the week and $5 or less on weekends.

One of the hottest Gaslamp places is the *Juke Joint Café (Map 3; ☎ 619-232-7684, 327 4th Ave)*, which packs them in most nights with jazz talent from near and far. Trumpet player Gilbert Castellanos' regular Thursday gig often draws a full house, and reservations are recommended for the weekend performances. Various dance clubs take over after the show Thursday to Saturday.

Humphrey's Backstage Lounge (Map 8; ☎ 619-224-3577, 2241 Shelter Island Dr) on Shelter Island offers jazz, blues and funk with a view of the ocean Sunday through Thursday and disco/Top 40 dancing on weekend nights. Cover is none or low and the Happy Hour (daily except Sunday) is a winner. For big-name summer concerts, check out the schedule of Humphrey's Concerts by the Bay (see Clubs & Live Music earlier in this chapter).

Jazz is the sound of choice in tony La Jolla, and there's plenty of it. *Galoka (Map11; ☎ 858-551-8610, 5662 La Jolla Blvd)* offers up a varied menu that includes local and regional jazz talent. There's almost never a cover.

Crescent Shores Grill (Map 11; ☎ 858-459-0541, 7955 La Jolla Shores Dr), the 11th-floor restaurant of the Hotel La Jolla, is also fast becoming a popular jazz boîte showcasing local talent Tuesday to Saturday nights. Come for the sunset views and Happy Hour specials (weekdays 5 to 7 pm), then stay for the free concerts.

Torreyana Grille (☎ 619-450-4571, 10950 Torrey Pines Rd) in the Hilton Torrey Pines often has jazz.

FOLK MUSIC

As in other cities, San Diego's folk scene is concentrated in its Irish pubs. One of the best is *The Field (Map 3; ☎ 619-232-9840, 544 5th Ave)* in Downtown. This place feels as if someone had taken down a Dublin pub, piece by piece, and reassembled it in the Gaslamp Quarter. Fact is, someone did. All the decor was transplanted from the Emerald Isle, as were many of the bartenders. Come for a pint and potatoes (there's a full menu) and stay for excellent Irish folk music.

Irish bands also belt out the brogue most nights at the *The Ould Sod (Map 7; ☎ 619-284-6594, 3373 Adams Ave)* in Normal Heights, which is as cozy and comfortable as you'd expect an Irish pub to be. Happy hour is daily except Sunday.

Twiggs Tea & Coffee (Map 7; ☎ 619-296-0616, 4590 Park Blvd), in University Heights, is a great place to while away an afternoon over a game of chess, deep conversation or a serious caffeine jolt from an oversized cup. At night, the folk and acoustic artists at this unpretentious joint are likely to bring you right back down to Earth.

On Coronado, *Mc P's Irish Pub & Grill* (see the San Diego Places to Eat chapter) also has live folk music daily.

DANCE CLUBS
San Diego has no shortage of places to shake your booty. Establishments are typically open Thursday to Saturday, have a cover from free to $10 and run different 'theme parties' nightly – '80s hits to Latin, Top 40 to techno.

E Street Alley (Map 3; ☎ 619-231-9200), literally in an alley off E Street between 4th and 5th Ave, is a perennial player in any 'best club of the Gaslamp' survey. From Thursday to Saturday DJs spin mostly house and techno for a trendy clientele that likes to dance – inspired by the, for once, spacious dance floor. Plush velvet sofas and armchairs in the lounge invite relaxing, and if you need a dose of protein, refuel at the upstairs sushi restaurant. If you eat here first, you save the $10 cover.

Tsunami Beach Club (Map 3; ☎ 619-231-9283, 802 6th Ave), Downtown, makes waves among the navy guys and college kids, so don't come here if you're in a committed relationship and/or were listening to '80s music back in the '80s. Servers in beachwear prance about and the dance floor is heavy with hard bodies writhing to pop and

hip hop. The action gets rolling Wednesday to Saturday after 9 pm.

Club Montage (Map 8; ☎ 619-294-9590, 2028 Hancock St), just southwest of Old Town, is one of San Diego's hippest cathedrals of dance with a crowd that's young, trendy and good-looking. Survey the crammed dance floor – throbbing with high-intensity techno – from the upstairs balcony, or head to the rooftop bar for a breather and a great view of the skyline. Wednesday is college night, gays rule Thursday and Saturday; Friday is mixed.

At *Club Tremors (Map 10; ☎ 858-272-7278, 860 Garnet Ave)*, in Pacific Beach, the weekend lineup with DJ-spun dance music starts on Thursday and winds down Sunday with reggae bands and happy hour till midnight. It's in the back of the *Pacific Beach Bar & Grill*, a high-voltage place that draws a mixed crowd of college kids, military types and yuppies. There's no cover but lines are long.

Moondoggies (Map 10; ☎ 858-483-6550, 832 Garnet Ave) – or 'the Dog' as it's called – is usually jumping with energy-laden 20-somethings on a fun night out. The action starts warming up during happy hour, best enjoyed while basking in the setting sun on the vast glass-enclosed patio. Inside's a battery of big-screen TVs, pool tables and the stage where local bands thrash it out most nights. On Thursday all drinks are $2, including cocktails with names like K-9 Colada and Doggarita.

COFFEEHOUSES
Coffeehouses in San Diego are popular hangouts for chatting, reading and doing homework, as well as for being nighttime venues, often with live music.

With what might best be described as 'baroque industrial' decor (think: velvet banquettes and metal chairs) and an outside terrace (smoking is OK), *Cafe Lulu (Map 3; ☎ 619-238-0114, 419 F St)* in the Gaslamp Quarter is a cool spot for cappuccino, light meals and talk. At *New World Coffee (Map 3; ☎ 619-702-5436, 1602 Front St)*, in Little Italy you can either relax or get wired with their espresso or other strong coffee drinks.

An Ocean Beach favorite in a former church, mellow *Java Joe's (Map 8; ☎ 619-523-0356, 1956 Bacon St)* is as funky and worn at the edges as a beloved teddy bear. It's also a favorite stop-over for bands playing the San Diego circuit. Mondays are open-mic nights.

Despite the exotic name, *Café Zanzibar (Map 10; ☎ 858-272-4762, 976 Garnet Ave)* in Pacific Beach feels more like a European coffeehouse, the kind of cultured place conducive to quiet conversation, glossy magazine reading or letter writing. Besides coffee-based drinks, there's an extensive menu of gourmet sandwiches, pizza or salads with prices hovering around $7. Breakfast is served all day.

Café 976 (Map 10; ☎ 858-272-0976, 976 Felspar St) is in a yellow clapboard house surrounded by an enchanting garden of roses, old trees and leafy plants that's great for chat and java. This is also one of the few cafés catering to tea lovers, with more than 30 black, herbal and flavored varieties on hand. Their list of coffee specialty drinks is long and creative but at nearly $4 each they're a bit costly. Soup and sandwiches are available, if you get the munchies.

Top-notch folk, world music and R&B performers vamp it up nightly at gargoyle-festooned *Lestat's Coffeehouse (Map 7; ☎ 619-282-0437, 3343 Adams Ave)* in Normal Heights, named for the main character in Anne Rice's best-selling vampire novels. Eternal life? Doubtful. Great coffee? Definitely.

Claire de Lune Coffeehouse (Map 7; ☎ 619-688-9845, 2906 University Ave) in North Park is a comfortable hangout with a no-attitude, artsy flair. Plop into one of the brightly colored armchairs or try the not-quite-so-comfy wrought-iron patio chairs. There's free jazz and acoustic guitar on weekend nights and poetry readings on Tuesday.

GAY & LESBIAN VENUES

San Diego's nightlife scene for gay men and lesbians is small but lively, and, predictably, concentrated in Hillcrest. *The Brass Rail (Map 6; ☎ 619-298-2233, 3796 5th Ave)*,

perhaps the city's oldest gay bar, has a different music theme nightly, from Latin to African to Top 40. The Brass Rail also gets its share of straights and has lots of 'toys' to play with, like a pinball machine, pool table and dart board. *Number One Fifth Ave (Map 6; ☎ 619-299-1911, 3845 5th Ave)*, across the street in the next block, is a tiny neighborhood joint with a patio.

A few blocks east, at *Rich's (Map 6; ☎ 619-497-4588, 1051 University Ave)*, DJs shower a mixed crowd with Latin, techno, pop and House from Wednesday to Sunday. Thursday attracts straights and bisexuals, and there's a patio for smoking. A few doors down, *Flicks (Map 6; ☎ 619-297-2056, 1017 University Ave)* is a conventional video bar dominated by big screens and is mostly a place to hang and nurse a drink. Sort of like Starbucks with alcohol.

Retro *The Flame (Map 6; ☎ 619-295-4163, 3780 Park Blvd)* is the city's oldest and most popular lesbian lounge. Recently remodeled, the plush decor now features pink padded walls, drapery and red lighting. There's a large dance floor and an indoor cigar bar. On Tuesday, the 'boyz' take over after finishing up across the street at *Numbers (Map 6; ☎ 619-294-9005, 3811 Park Blvd)*. This comfortable neighborhood bar also comes with big-screen videos, a pool table and smoking patio.

About three-fourths mile north of here, in University Heights, *Bourbon Street (Map 7; ☎ 619-291-0173, 4612 Park Blvd)* has a mixed male/female crowd and a New Orleans theme. Bands here are mostly of

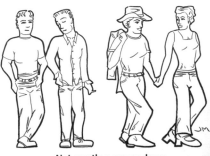

Not exactly a square dance

the pop persuasion, and Thursday night is the most happening.

Another cluster of bars is in North Park, about 1 mile east of Hillcrest. As the name suggests, *Shooterz (Map 2; ☎ 619-574-0744, 3815 30th St)* is a popular place for pool and also has theme nights; Goth night is legendary. *Wolfs (☎ 619-291-3730, 3004 30th St)* and *Pecs (Map 7; ☎ 619-296-0889, 2046 University Ave)* are the main leather and Levi's bars around town. Pecs is especially popular as a meeting venue for gay clubs, including the Harley crowd. The tech-styled *Zone (☎ 619-295-8072, 3040 North Park Way)*, formerly the Arena Club, is decorated with black & white photos of beauteous bods and also popular with the leather and Levi's crowd.

Middletown has a couple of scene favorites. The biggest dance club is *Club Montage*, which is taken over by gay gym bunnies every Thursday and Saturday (see Dance Clubs earlier in this chapter). In the same neighborhood is *Club Bombay (Map 6; ☎ 619-296-6789, 3175 India St)*, which is lesbian-owned but also draws its share of gay men. It's famous for Sunday barbecues with cheap burgers and beer. From Thursday to Saturday, local lesbian bands hold the small stage.

SPECTATOR SPORTS
Baseball
The San Diego Padres came to San Diego in 1968. Since that time they have had their struggles, but have won three National

---

Through Cups Won & Cups Lost, San Diego Stays Afloat

Oh, the horror of it all! For an unbroken 132 years it was called the 'Americas Cup' for one good reason: no team other than the American had ever won this race series, the world's supreme sailing event. Loss of the Cup – to the Australians, no less finally befell the hapless San Diego Yacht Club skipper, Dennis Connor, arguably the finest sailor since Sir Francis Drake, in 1983. Connor still sails, but the Cup itself seems destined – every few years – to shuttle between those two 'islands' Australia and New Zealand which, we're told, lie somewhere south of Hawaii.

But, as with Seattle and San Francisco, San Diego's soul is still defined by the sea. Quite apart from hosting one of the mightiest fighting fleets in the world, the city promotes constant maritime events and world-class competitions. The following is a partial listing of nautical events and festivals that will help you to take part in San Diego's seaside delights.

The San Diego Union-Tribune's **New Year's Day Race**, held at Shelter Island, kicks off the year with a traditional regatta for single- and multi-hulled vessels.

March witnesses the annual **America's Schooner Cup Charity Regatta**, over the course of two days, in San Diego Harbor. Awards ceremonies are held at the Kona Kai International Yacht Club. No need for wind when, in April at Crown Point Shores in Mission Bay, the annual **San Diego Crew Classic** plays host to more than 3000 rowers in a festive atmosphere featuring parachute teams and entertainment.

Early May brings about 80 of the world's most beautiful powerboats to race along the San Diego waterfront in the **Port of San Diego Offshore Grand Prix**. Viewing sites run from Embarcadero Marina Park to Harbor Island.

In mid-June the city hosts the **Catalina 22 National Championship Regatta** at the Mission Bay Yacht Club, with boats coming from all over the country. Also around then is the **Wooden Boat Festival**, when more than 50 classic boats gather.

In mid-September the city vibrates as the **Thunderboats** – the world's fastest – throttle up for the 'World Series' of powerboat racing on Mission Bay. Come October, it's time for the festival and entertainment surrounding the **Oceanside Offshore Grand Prix** for powerboats at Oceanside harbor.

Barring the return of a certain Cup, these events will just have to do.

-David Peevers

League Western Division championships and two pennants. They've been to the World Series twice, losing four out of five to the heavily favored Detroit Tigers in 1984, and getting swept in four in 1998 by the dynasty-building New York Yankees. Their marquee player over the years has been eight-time NL batting champion Tony Gwynn, who has turned down big-money offers from other teams to stay with the Padres. Hall-of-Fame Padres alums include Rollie Fingers and Dave Winfield.

Until their new ballpark in the East Village is completed (see the San Diego Things to See & Do chapter), San Diego's National League baseball team will continue to play at **Qualcomm Stadium** (*Map 7;* ☎ *619-280-4636, 9449 Friars Rd*) in Mission Valley. The season goes from April to October. Tickets, which range from $5 to $24, are usually available at the gate unless it's a game crucial to the standings or the LA Dodgers are in town on a Friday or Saturday night. Get tickets through Ticketmaster by phone or online or – with no service charges – in person at the stadium, Gate C, from 9 am to 6 pm weekdays, 10 am to 4 pm Saturday.

Football

The San Diego Chargers pro football team, which is also based at Qualcomm Stadium, has never brought home the bacon – the Super Bowl trophy, that is – although they did have a shot at winning in 1996, only to be beaten by the San Francisco 49ers. The team, which is nicknamed 'Bolts' for the strike of lightning on its uniforms, nevertheless manages to get the fans 'charged up' and regularly draws sellout crowds, especially when its fiercest rivals, the Oakland Raiders or the Denver Broncos, are in town. The season lasts from August to January, and tickets start at $24, topping off at $232.

The San Diego State University Aztecs played as part of the Western Athletic Conference until 1999 when they moved to the newly formed Mountain West Conference. The Aztecs, too, play at Qualcomm, and tickets range from $8 to $30. Both Chargers and Aztec tickets are sold at Gate E in the stadium; Aztec tickets are also available through the campus ticket office (☎ 619-283-7378, 888-737-8039) and online through www.ticketmaster.com.

The week after Christmas, San Diego hosts the Holiday Bowl, which pitches top-ranked college teams from different conferences against one another. Tickets, which range from $30 to $50, are sold through Ticketmaster or the bowl's ticket office at ☎ 619-283-5808.

Parking at Qualcomm Stadium is $6. If you drive, arrive as early as possible (two hours before the game starts) to avoid serious congestion. Better yet, use public transport – the San Diego Trolley Blue Line stops right at the stadium.

Horse Racing

See the Del Mar section in the San Diego Excursions chapter for details about races at the Del Mar Fairgrounds.

Ice Hockey

San Diego does not have a National Hockey League team, but the San Diego Gulls, who play in the West Coast Hockey League, have gone to the championship finals several times. The season runs from October to March, with games at the **San Diego Sports Arena** (*Map 2;* ☎ *619-224-4176, 3500 Sports Arena Blvd*). Tickets are $5 to $15, available through Ticketmaster, or at the arena box office 10 am to 5 pm weekdays, to 3 pm Saturday. Parking is $5. The neighborhood has a tendency to be a little rough after dark.

Shopping

WHAT TO BUY
Books

Every shopping mall has a bookshop, usually of the large, chain-owned kind. UCSD has an excellent bookstore on campus at the Price Center (Map 11; ☎ 858-534-7323) and a branch Downtown in the American Plaza opposite the Santa Fe Depot (Map 3).

Also Downtown, Wahrenbrooks Book House (Map 3; ☎ 619-232-0132), 726 Broadway, and William Burgett (Map 3; ☎ 619-238-7323), at the corner of 7th Ave and C St, are the most established stores. On Coronado, Bay Books (Map 4; ☎ 619-435-0070), 1029 Orange Ave, has attractive displays and a pleasant ambience that invites browsing and lingering. In La Jolla, family-run Warwick's (Map 11; ☎ 858-454-0347), 7812 Girard Ave, is a good general bookstore with attentive and knowledgeable staff and frequent celebrity author book signings. Notable as much for its history as for its collection is John Cole's Bookshop (Map 11; ☎ 858-454-4766), 780 Prospect St, in the former home of Ellen Browning Scripps.

At 413 Market St is Gaslamp Books, Prints & Antiques (Map 3; ☎ 619-237-1492), which doubles as a museum, since the owner displays all sorts of memorabilia that he's collected during his 50-plus years in San Diego.

The heaviest concentration of used, rare and out-of-print books is along Book Row on Adams Avenue in Normal Heights. Choices include Book Brokers (Map 7; ☎ 619-280-2665), at No 3287, which specializes in first editions, art and military titles. Adams Avenue Bookstore (Map 7; ☎ 619-281-3330), at No 3502, emphasizes Western Americana, mystery and theology.

The block of 5th Avenue just south of University Avenue in Hillcrest is also fertile used book territory. Try the huge 5th Avenue Books (Map 6; ☎ 619-291-4660) at No 3838 or Bountiful Books (Map 6; ☎ 619-491-0660) at No 3834.

In Old Town's Bazaar del Mundo, Libros (Map 5; ☎ 619-299-1139) has a good selection of San Diego history books and books in Spanish. Another good source for this kind of material is Casa del Libro (Map 6; ☎ 619-299-9331), 1735 University Ave in Hillcrest.

Among shops specialized in travel are Le Travel Store (Map 3; ☎ 619-544-0005), 745 4th Ave in the Gaslamp, which has a helpful staff and an excellent selection of maps, travel guides and accessories. In Horton Plaza is a branch of Rand McNally Map & Travel (Map 3; ☎ 619-234-3341), which stocks books, atlases, globes, travel accessories and, of course, maps. Traveler's Depot (Map 10; ☎ 858-483-1421), 1655 Garnet Ave, Pacific Beach, also has a good inventory.

The Map Centre (Map 2; ☎ 619-291-3830), 2611 University Ave, has got the whole world under its tiny roof. This is the place to go when you need a street map of Paris, an atlas of the United States, or trekking maps of the Himalayas.

New Age devotees enjoy browsing the shelves of Inner Truth Bookstore (Map 7; ☎ 619-584-4693), a self-proclaimed 'bookstore of the spirit' at 3506 Adams Ave. Prince & the Pauper (Map 7; ☎ 619-283-4380), at 3201 Adams Ave, focuses on children's book, especially collectibles.

Sports & Outdoor Equipment

One of the best shops for outdoor needs is REI (Recreational Equipment Incorporated; ☎ 858-279-4400), with a large inventory and knowledgeable staff at 5556 Copley Drive in Clairemont Mesa, just south of Marine Corps Air Station Miramar (Map 2). Its main competition is the smaller Adventure 16 Outdoor & Travel Outfitters, with branches at Horton Plaza (Map 3; ☎ 619-234-1751) Downtown and in Mission Valley at 4620 Alvarado Canyon Rd (Map 7; ☎ 619-283-2374).

For swimwear, women should head to Pilar's Beachwear (Map 9; ☎ 858-488-3056), 3745 Mission Blvd in Mission Beach, which has all the latest styles in all sizes. Nearby, Gone Bananas (Map 9; ☎ 858-488-4900, 3785 Mission Blvd) also has a large selection of mix-and-match bikinis and one-pieces, including Body Glove, Mossimo, Sauvage and three dozen other brands.

South Coast Surf Shops (Map 8; ☎ 619-223-7017), at 5023 Newport Ave in Ocean Beach, has beach apparel and surf gear from Quiksilver, Hurley, Billabong and O'Neill. South Coast Wahines (Map 10; ☎ 858-273-7600), 4500 Ocean Front Blvd, at the foot of the Crystal Pier in Pacific Beach, is similar but caters just to women.

Play it Again Sports (Map 10; ☎ 858-490-0222), 1401 Garnet Ave, also in Pacific Beach, sells and rents used and new sports equipment and accessories like surfboards, inline skates, skateboards and other tools of the trade.

Music
Tower Records, the Wherehouse and Sam Goody's are among the mainstream music stores with branches in most malls and throughout the city. For used CDs, Music Trader outlets have great selections; central branches are Downtown at 931 4th Ave (Map 3; ☎ 619-232-2565), in Pacific Beach at 1084 Garnet Ave (Map 10; ☎ 858-272-2274) and in Hillcrest at 630 University Ave (Map 6; ☎ 619-543-0007). Also good for used stuff is Off the Record (Map 6; ☎ 619-298-4755), at 3849 5th Ave, in Hillcrest, a treasure trove if you like alternative, punk and Goth music.

For rare vinyl, Nickelodeon Records (Map 7; ☎ 619-284-6083), 3335 Adams Ave on Antique Row in Normal Heights, has a stunning collection. Be it rock, pop, jazz, or whatever you fancy, you'll find that long-lost record here. If not, try nearby Folk Arts Rare Records (Map 7; ☎ 619-282-7833), 3611 Adams Ave, which also does custom taping from a library of 90,000 hours of music.

Attire
Mainstream Look for mainstream clothing at the malls (see Where to Shop later in this chapter). Besides department stores like Robinson's-May, Macy's, Nordstrom and Mervyn's, you'll find the ubiquitous Gap, Banana Republic, Ann Taylor, Ralph Lauren, Structure, Express and other chains. La Jolla and upscale department stores like Neiman Marcus and Saks Fifth Ave are good sources for designer wear. For less run-of-the-mill clothing, you'll have to delve into the city's hipper and more youthful neighborhoods, including Pacific Beach, Ocean Beach and Hillcrest.

Dream Girls (Map 8; ☎ 619-223-4836), 5054 Newport Ave in Ocean Beach, has cool clothes for young women, inexpensive costume jewelry and a small selection of shoes. For the right accessory, stop in at Blondstone (Map 8; ☎ 619-223-2563) at No 4925, a stylish jewelry studio where artists turn silver and sea objects (mermaid stone, shells, moonstone) into unique, affordable creations.

In Pacific Beach, The River (Map 10; ☎ 858-270-3022), 1020 Garnet Ave, has edgy, urban clothing for both sexes at decent prices. It's a high-energy environment with friendly staff. LA Rack (Map 10; ☎ 858-483-1365), across the street at 1031 Garnet Ave, is similar. Mileage Clubwear (Map 10; ☎ 858-581-1085), 959 Garnet Ave, has one-of-a-kind outfits and accessories that will fit the bill for anything from a trance party to a '30s swing night. The $5 Store (Map 10; 1461 Garnet Ave) is just what it says, with racks of new women's fashions at $5 per item. The quality leaves much to be desired, but at this price, you've little to lose.

Hillcrest's International Male (Map 6; ☎ 619-294-8600), at 3964 5th Ave, appeals primarily to the gay populace, but its stylish, high-quality clothes look good on anybody with a Y chromosome. Nearby, Apparel Zone (Map 6; ☎ 619-682-4062), 500 University Ave, has heavily discounted designer clothes (think: Armani, Jil Sander, etc) for men and women.

Vintage Thrift-loving hipsters regularly scour the racks at the city's vintage clothing stores for that unique look. Most stores buy, sell and trade. One of the largest and oldest is Aardvark's Odd Ark (Map 10; ☎ 858-274-3597) at 979 Garnet Ave in Pacific Beach, which has Hawaiian shirts, suede vests, zoot suits, glamour gowns and other fun stuff. The Buff (Map 10; ☎ 858-581-2833), at No1059, has a range of outrageous clothes, many suitable for Halloween costumes, plus hot accessories.

Buffalo Exchange (Map 10; ☎ 858-273-6227), 1007 Garnet Ave, has a more conservative bent, and stocks both vintage and contemporary fashions, including name brands. Quality is high, but prices are mercifully low. A Hillcrest branch (Map 6; ☎ 619-298-4411) is at 3862 5th Ave. Across the street at No 3847, Flashbacks (Map 6; ☎ 619-291-4200) is a bit pricier but recycles top-notch retro outfits and has some exuberant current styles. Classier still is Wear it Again Sam (Map 6; ☎ 619-299-0185), 3922 Park Blvd, which has vintage clothing from the 1900s through the '60s for both genders.

In the Gaslamp, in the basement of Croce's at 440 F St, is Shake Rag (Map 3; ☎ 619-237-4955), which advertises 'an entire century's worth of fashion' presented on 6000 sq feet. It's not super-cheap (shirts from $12, jackets from $18), but the selection is unbeatable.

Antiques

Downtown, Normal Heights and Ocean Beach have the greatest concentration of antiques stores in San Diego.

Just east of the Gaslamp, at 850 Island Ave, is Merchants Passage (Map 3; ☎ 619-696-1146), a cooperative of dozens of vendors filling a 20,000 square foot warehouse with collectibles, art and accessories. Available here is a listing of several other Downtown antique stores.

Adams Avenue is San Diego's main 'antique row,' cutting across University Heights in the west, Normal Heights and Kensington in the east. The greatest concentration of shops is in Normal Heights between I-805 and I-15. There are dozens of shops, including Retreads (Map 7; ☎ 619-284-3999), 3220 Adams Ave, specializing in furniture, and Back from Tomboctou (Map 7; ☎ 619-282-8708) at No 3564, with art and antiques from around the world. For a store directory, check the Adams Ave business

association Web site at www.gothere.com/AdamsAve.

A good place for antiquing is the 4800 block of Newport Ave in Ocean Beach. Ocean Beach Antique Mall (Map 8; ☎ 619-223-6170), 4878 Newport Ave, and the Newport Avenue Antique Center (Map 8; ☎ 619-222-8686) at No 4864 are just two of the half dozen or so large stores along here.

WHERE TO SHOP

'Mall-ification' – the proliferation of the suburban mall – has hit San Diego with a vengeance, and most locals shop at huge, multistory complexes. For visitors, too, these giant vessels of commerce have great appeal for their convenience and variety. For a more individual flavor, though, it's fun to seek out specialty shops and boutiques in the neighborhoods.

Shopping Districts

San Diego has many shopping districts, the most important of which are outlined below. The What to Buy section has descriptions of some of the neighborhood stores.

Downtown (Map 3) shopping is concentrated in Horton Plaza, although a few stores selling clothing, home furnishings, jewelry and other items still brave high rents in the **Gaslamp Quarter**. On the waterfront, **Seaport Village** has tourist-oriented stores, including one for kites and one for hot sauces. Browsing can be fun, even if bargains are rare here or in the **Ferry Landing Marketplace**, a similar complex across the bay in Coronado (Map 4).

Museums in **Balboa Park** have interesting shops selling books, toys and other items related to their exhibits. The park's Spanish Village sells paintings (mostly watercolors) of the San Diego area.

Old Town (Map 5) is anchored by the **Bazaar del Mundo**, a colorful cluster of stores selling nice but tourist-oriented items from throughout Latin America such as folk crafts, woven textiles, ceramics and carved animals.

Hillcrest (Map 6) is known for its hip fashions, vintage clothing and design stores, especially along **University Avenue**. To the north, malls dominate along I-8 in **Mission Valley** (Map 7). Southeast from here is **Adams Avenue**, San Diego's 'antique row,' which winds through of University Heights, Normal Heights and Kensington.

Ocean Beach's **Newport Avenue**, west of Sunset Cliffs, has a dual personality. The first few blocks bulge with antiques and used furniture stores, while the stretch closer to the beach is spiked with head shops (The Black at No 5017 is famous), psychedelic supply stores, and funky, clothing, jewelry and accessory boutiques (Map 8).

To blend into the Southern California beach scene, you'll need a hat, sunglasses and the right swimsuit. What better place to get all of these de rigueur accoutrements than San Diego's beach communities? Stores with beach paraphernalia naturally congregate near the ocean, but there's a particularly heavy concentration along **Mission Blvd**, as it snakes through Mission Beach (Map 9) and Pacific Beach (Map 10). Also in Pacific Beach is **Garnet Avenue**, which is chock-full of hip club wear and vintage clothing stores.

La Jolla's **Prospect Ave** is known for its up-up-upscale fashion designer, carpet and jewelry stores, as well as art galleries (Map 11). **Girard Avenue** has retail chain stores like Gap, Banana Republic, Armani Xchange and Ralph Lauren.

Shopping Malls

Nothing defines shopping in San Diego more than the mall, a Southern California invention springing from the growth of suburbia and peoples' reliance on cars. More than a place to shop, malls define and reflect the commercialism so prevalent here. A mall is a home away from home, a safe haven where meeting friends and having cappuccino is as much part of the day as browsing the sales at Nordstrom. Movies have even been made about this phenomenon (eg *Scenes from a Mall* and *Mall Rats)*, and Frank and Moon-Unit Zappa's song *Valley Girl* was inspired by a Los Angeles mall.

Parking is free at the following shopping centers, and all have casual eateries to sustain you through the day. If you need a break, multiplex movie theaters await. Shopping hours are generally 10 am to 8 pm weekdays, to 7 pm Saturday, and 11 am to 6 pm Sunday.

Horton Plaza (Map 3; ☎ 619-238-1596), Downtown, is the most central of San Diego's malls and the most visually appealing. For the shopper in a hurry, however, this multilevel maze of narrow walkways, elevators, escalators and stairs is a nightmare. Bring time, patience and curiosity, and you'll have fun browsing eclectic boutiques and specialty stores, like the Warner Bros Store, Disney Store, FAO Schwartz or Discovery Channel. Nordstrom, Macy's and Mervyn's are the department store anchors. Horton Plaza occupies several blocks between Broadway and G St and 1st and 4th Aves.

Fashion Valley (Map 7; ☎ 619-688-9113), 7007 Friars Rd in Mission Valley, is the epitome of the Southern California shopping mall, a mecca of merchandise and a trendy showcase of consumer goods. It's convenient to all the hotels along Hotel Circle. Shopping here is taken very seriously, with six anchors to choose from: the upscale Nordstrom, Saks Fifth Avenue and Neiman Marcus, all known for their couture, apparel and jewelry departments; and the more mainstream Macy's, Robinson's-May and JC Penney.

If you can't get enough, head a mile or so east to Mission Valley Center (Map 7, ☎ 619-296-6375), 1640 Camino del Rio N, which has been given a new lease on life thanks to a new 20-screen multiplex movie theater. More down-market than Fashion Valley, it has Montgomery Ward as a main store, as well as discount designer clothing at Loehman's and Nordstrom Rack.

Mirror, mirror on the wall, the University Towne Centre (UTC, Map 11; ☎ 858-546-8858), 4545 La Jolla Village Drive in La Jolla, is the largest of the 'm-all.' Some 160 stores, sprawling in an outdoor environment, vie for your attention – and wallet. Wear comfortable shoes and expect to spend a day to see it all, from megastores like Macy's, Nordstrom, Robinson-May and Sears to a full complement of retail chains like Pottery Barn, Sports Chalet and Crate

& Barrel. To top it off, UTC has its own Olympic-size ice rink.

Outlet Malls

At outlet malls, upscale and mainstream retail stores purportedly sell off their stock at reduced prices, sometimes as much as 50% to 70% off. While bargains are possible, prices are not always lower than at regular store sales. Beware of damaged or irregular items or those left over from the previous season. The lime-green shirt that was so fashionable last year may get you ticketed by the fashion police this summer. Service in these stores is minimal; there are fewer employees, dressing rooms and mirrors.

The closest outlet mall to central San Diego is the San Diego Factory Outlet Center (Map 2; ☎ 619-690-2999) at Camino de la Plaza in San Ysidro, right on the border. Choose from 35 stores, including Calvin Klein, Dockers, Levi's, Nike and Vitamin World.

In North County, the Carlsbad Company Stores mall (North County map, San Diego Excursions chapter; ☎ 888-790-7467), 5620 Paseo del Norte, is a major attraction. Shoppers are drawn to the 75 outlets by major brands, including The Gap, Kenneth Cole, Ralph Lauren and Brooks Brothers. It's near the Flower Fields and Legoland.

Farmers Markets

California is well-known for its super-fresh produce, and vendors at weekly farmers markets in the city's neighborhoods offer the best in quality and freshness. In San Diego alone, some 6000 farmers work in the agricultural 'industry,' which accounts for an annual $1 billion revenue. All produce is state-certified, meaning it's sold by the grower, is grown in California and meets state quality standards. Some stands also sport the label 'certified organic,' meaning that produce has been grown without pesticides.

Farmers markets are great for stocking up on groceries or for putting together a picnic. Many also sell flowers and homemade specialty food items like flavored tzaziki cream, handcrafted breads and olives.

Elsewhere, markets provide a glimpse into local life and are fun to browse, even without buying. Here's a selection:

Coronado – corner of 1st and B Sts at the Ferry Landing Marketplace (Tuesday 2:30 to 6 pm)

Hillcrest – corner of Normal and Cleveland Sts located in the parking lot of the Department of Motor Vehicles (Sunday 9 am to noon)

Ocean Beach – 4900 block of Newport Ave (Wednesday 4 to 8 pm, to 7 pm in winter)

Pacific Beach – Mission Blvd between Reed Ave and Pacific Beach Blvd at the Promenade Mall (Saturday 8 am to noon)

La Jolla – Girard Ave at Genter St at the La Jolla Elementary School (Sunday 9 am to 1 pm)

Thrift Shops

These shops are usually operated by charities such as Goodwill, Boys & Girls Club or the Salvation Army, and sell donated used clothing, housewares, books, furniture and other items, often at ridiculously low prices (shirts for $2, skirts for $3, dresses for $5, jackets for $8, etc). Most of the proceeds go back to the charity.

If you've spilled red wine on the only pair of shorts you brought, or weren't prepared for that sudden dinner invitation, you're bound to find amazing bargains for just a fraction of what you'd pay in regular stores, including brand-name and designer items.

You'll find thrift stores around town, but not in the most fashionable neighborhoods. An exception is the small cluster on the eastern end of Garnet Ave in Pacific Beach, between Haines and Gresham Aves. Here you'll find an excellent Goodwill Thrift Store (Map 10; ☎ 858-274-4969) at 1430 Garnet Ave, which has clean, color-sorted clothing for men and women and – a special plus – two tidy dressing rooms. Practically across the street at No 1454, Children Hospital Thrift Stores (Map 10; ☎ 858-490-6400) is almost as good.

Thrift stores also abound in Downtown's East Village, but here they cater primarily to the city's low-income and homeless population. Places worth a browse include the Disabled American Veterans Thrift Store

(Map 3; ☎ 619-232-0141), at 1488 Market St, and Baras Foundation (Map 3; ☎ 619-232-2255), across the street at No 1455. Check the Yellow Pages (under Thrift Shops) for more listings of area stores.

Flea Markets

For really cheap stuff, try Kobey's Swap Meet (☎ 619-226-0650), a massive flea market in the parking lot of the Sports Arena at 3500 Sports Arena Blvd (Map 2), from 7 am to 3 pm Friday to Sunday. On sale are new and used items, including sunglasses, clothing, jewelry, produce, flowers and plants, tools and furniture. Admission is 50¢ on Friday, $1 on weekends; parking is free.

Garage Sales

As you're driving through San Diego neighborhoods on Friday and Saturday, you're likely to notice signs attached to traffic signals, street signs and telephone poles announcing a 'moving sale,' 'estate sale,' 'multi-family sale,' 'garage sale' and so on, along with an address and the date. Whatever they're called, these homemade sales are a godsend for the serious bargain hunter. For sellers it's a way to clean out closets and make a buck on the side. For treasure hunters, garage sales can yield everything from vintage earrings to furniture, usually at rock-bottom prices. Haggling, of course, is just part of the fun. Hit the road early for the best finds.

Excursions

The previous chapters have all focused on metropolitan San Diego, but there are numerous points of interest just a short hop away. This chapter covers towns and attractions in the remainder of San Diego County, then dips north to Disneyland and the wine country of Temecula. For more escapes throughout Southern California and the rest of the state, check out Lonely Planet's guide to *California & Nevada*.

San Diego County

Outside of metropolitan San Diego, the true diversity of the county reveals itself. You'll find sophisticated coastal communities, agricultural inland valleys, old-timey mountain towns, harsh desert areas and plenty of territory that so far has been touched little by civilization. This section first explores North County's coastal communities, then heads inland for a swing through the rural areas and finishes off with the mountains and deserts in the backcountry.

The San Diego North County Convention & Visitors Bureau (☎ 760-745-4741, 800-848-3336, fax 760-745-4796, ✆ info@sandiegonorth.com), based in Escondido at 360 N Escondido Blvd, is an excellent source for further information. They will mail out a free visitors guide and also have a thorough Web site at www.sandiegonorth.com.

NORTH COUNTY COAST

San Diego's coastal suburbs extend up the coast from Del Mar to the US Marine Corps base at Camp Pendleton. Although only a few miles from metropolitan San Diego, these towns are far removed from the urban bustle and have a more laid-back, slow-moving character. Many resemble the San Diego of 30 years ago, even if increasing development (especially east of I-5) is turning the area into a giant bedroom community for San Diego and Orange County.

Del Mar

This is the ritziest and most pretentious of North County's seaside suburbs, the kind of place that makes a virtue of ostentation. It has excellent, if pricey, restaurants, unique galleries, high-end boutiques and a horse-racing track, which is also the site of the annual county fair. Several golf courses, horse ranches and polo clubs in the vicinity are enjoyed by the mostly well-educated, well-moneyed and noticeably homogenous local population.

Downtown Del Mar (also called 'the village') extends for about a mile along Camino del Mar. At its hub, where 15th St crosses Camino del Mar, the very tasteful Del Mar Plaza – designed by Jon Jerde of Horton Plaza fame – overlooks the water with terraces, restaurants and quality boutiques. Esmeralda's Books & Coffee (☎ 858-755-2707), at the top of the plaza near Il Fornaio, has colorful artwork and often gets well-known authors for its weekly readings. At the beach end of 15th St, Seagrove Park overlooks the ocean.

Information At the Greater Del Mar Chamber of Commerce (☎ 858-755-4844), 1104 Camino del Mar, you'll find racks of pamphlets and can provide basic information about area attractions. It's open 9 am to 5 pm Monday to Friday.

Del Mar Racetrack & Fairgrounds The Del Mar Racetrack (☎ 858-793-5533), Via de la Valle, just off I-5, was started in 1937 by a group including Bing Crosby and Jimmy Durante, and its lush gardens and pink, Mediterranean-style architecture are delightful. Crosby's 'Where the Surf meets the Turf' has become the theme song of Del Mar.

The thoroughbred racing season runs from mid-July to mid-September; gates open at noon Monday to Friday and 11:30 am weekends. Track admission is $5. Races take place daily except Tuesday. Satellite wagering is offered the rest of the year.

SAN DIEGO

SAN DIEGO EXCURSIONS

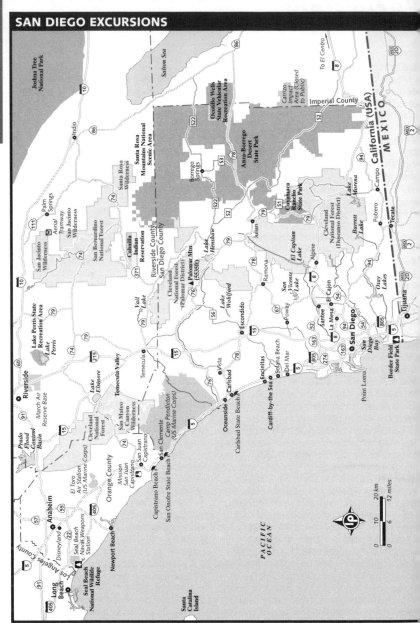

From mid-June to July 4, the Del Mar Fair (☎ 858-793-5555) is a major event, with livestock exhibits, carnival shows, rides and big-name performers every night. Admission is $10 for adults.

Hot-Air Ballooning Brightly colored hot-air balloons are a trademark of the skies above Del Mar. For pleasure flights, contact Skysurfer Balloon Company (☎ 858-481-5800, 800-660-6809, fax 858-481-7500) at 1221 Camino del Mar. The *San Diego Reader* carries other balloon company listings and frequently contains hot-air excursion discount coupons. Flights are usually at sunrise or sunset, last an hour (though up to three hours may be required for instruction and transportation) and cost around $130 Monday to Friday, $150 weekends.

Places to Stay Staying near the beach in Del Mar is nice, and there are plenty of hotels, although be prepared for sticker shock. One of the cheapest options is the *Del Mar Motel* (☎ 858-755-1534, 800-223-8449, 1702 Coast Blvd), where singles/doubles cost $80/120 in winter and $120/170 in summer.

If you're going to splurge, there are few places better to do it than at the *L'Auberge Del Mar Resort and Spa* (☎ 858-259-1515, 800-553-1336, fax 858-755-4940, 1540 Camino Del Mar), right across from Del Mar Plaza. Built on the grounds of the historic Hotel Del Mar – where Charlie Chaplin and Lucille Ball once frolicked (though not with each other) – its reincarnation continues to draw celebrities, including Bonnie Raitt and Mel Brooks. A perfect blend of European-style elegance and American sophistication, this romantic boutique hotel dazzles with its harmonious design, impeccable service and a varied menu of activities.

Take a class from the tennis pro at the resort's academy or indulge in facials and massage at the classy day spa. The beach is within view and the pool, Jacuzzi and sun deck are generously sized. So are the rooms, which feature balconies, gas fireplaces and a host of upscale amenities. Rates start at $225.

Places to Eat The patio and restaurants atop Del Mar Plaza have one of San Diego's best vantage points. *Pacifica Del Mar* (☎ 858-792-0476) has excellent California cuisine and fresh fish main courses ($17 to $22), while *Epazote* (☎ 858-259-9966) offers an interesting Southwest-style menu ($15 to $24). If you stick to pizza and pasta, *Il Fornaio* (☎ 858-755-8876) is somewhat more affordable ($10 to $15). The restaurant at the L'Auberge, called *The Dining Room*, also offers gourmet cuisine.

For cheaper fare, you can head to *Cafe 222* (☎ 858-794-6838), diagonally across from the plaza, which does breakfasts, burgers, sandwiches and salads from $6 to $8; many items are half-price during Happy Hour from 3 to 6 pm.

Two blocks south, at 13th Street, *Garden Taste* (☎ 858-793-1500) serves 'kosher/organic/vegan' food for $7.50 to $12.50; it's open from 10 am to 8 pm, closed Friday after 3 pm and all day Saturday.

Solana Beach

Solana Beach, the next town north, is considerably more down to earth, with good beaches and the recently dubbed Design District along Cedros Ave, which runs parallel to S21. The small visitor kiosk (☎ 858-350-6006) at 103 N Cedros, near the intersection with Lomas Santa Fe Drive, is open 10 am to 4 or 5 pm daily.

Cedros Design District A row of warehouses has been converted into a unique shopping environment of stores selling art, home furnishings, antiques or handmade clothing. Also here is a branch of Adventure 16 (☎ 858-755-7662), an outdoor clothing and equipment outfitter. Other stores of note include the Cedros Trading Company (☎ 858-794-9016) with imported furniture and accessories and the Antique Warehouse (☎ 858-755-5156), an indoor mall with about 100 dealers.

One of the first businesses in this complex was the *Belly Up Tavern* (☎ 858-481-8140), a hugely popular music venue that regularly gets great bands. Cover charge is $4 to $7, or even $10 for top acts.

SAN DIEGO

Places to Eat The *Wild Note Cafe (☎ 858-259-7310, 143 S Cedros Ave)*, adjacent to the Belly Up, is a cool and jazzy spot whose dishes have Asian or Middle Eastern touches; main courses start at $6 for lunch and $13 for dinner. Two long-standing Mexican restaurants are worth looking up – *Fidel's (☎ 858-755-5292, 607 Valley Ave)* and *Tony's Jacal (☎ 858-755-2274, 621 Valley Ave)*. Valley Ave goes north of Via de la Valle, just west of I-5. Both places offer meals for less than $10.

Cardiff-by-the-Sea

Shortened to 'Cardiff' by most, this noncentralized stretch of restaurants, surf shops and other businesses along the Pacific Hwy is good for surfing and popular with the laid-back crowd. At Cardiff State Beach, just south of the town 'center,' the surf break on the reef is mostly popular with longboarders, but it gets very good at low tide with a big north swell. A little farther north, San Elijo State Beach has good winter waves. Along here, stretched out for nearly a mile is the newly overhauled and extremely popular campground at *San Elijo State Beach (☎ 760-753-5091)*, which overlooks the surf at the end of Birmingham Dr, and has 171 tent and RV sites from $15 to $28; early reservations are essential in summer – book with Parknet (☎ 800-444-7275) or online at www.reserveamerica.com.

The nearby **San Elijo Lagoon** is a 1000-acre ecological preserve popular with bird watchers for its abundance of herons, coots, terns, ducks, egrets and about 250 more species. A 7-mile network of trails leads through the area.

There are plenty of eateries in town, but for breakfast or lunch be sure to visit the energetic and youthful *Pipe's Cafe (☎ 760-632-0056, 121 Liverpool Dr)*, where you can gobble up enough carbos to sustain you through the day. Back at Cardiff State Beach is another cluster of interesting restaurants. *Ki's Restaurant (☎ 760-436-5236, 2591 Coast Hwy 1010)* has a nice ocean-view terrace and great smoothies ($3.50), and health-burgers and salads for around $8. Nearby *Las Olas (☎ 760-942-1860, 2655 Coast Hwy 101)* is a

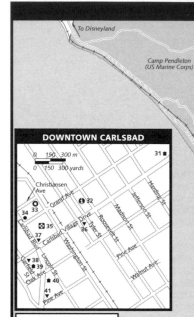

DOWNTOWN CARLSBAD

SAN DIEGO NORTH COUNTY

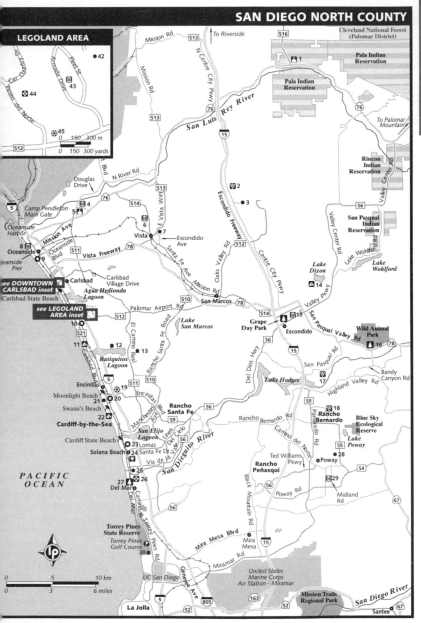

LEGOLAND AREA

42

43

44

45

0   150   300 m
0   150   300 yards

To Riverside

Mission Rd

S13

S16

Cleveland National Forest
(Palomar District)

Pala Indian
Reservation

1

Pala Indian
Reservation

N Centre City Pkwy

76

San Luis Rey River

To Palomar
Mountain

76

Rincon
Indian
Reservation

15

Valley Center Rd

Escondido Freeway

2

3

San Pasqual
Indian
Reservation

Douglas
Drive

N River Rd

S13

S14

Camp Pendleton
Main Gate

5

5   4

Oceanside
Harbor

8

Oceanside

9

S11

Oceanside
Blvd

Vista Freeway

Vista

6

7

Escondido
Ave

78

Santa Fe Ave

Mission Rd

Oaks Valley Rd

Escondido Rd

Valley Pkwy

Centre City Pkwy

S6

S6

Lake
Dixon

14

Valley Center Rd

Lake Wohlford Rd

Lake
Wohlford

eanside
Pier

Mission Ave

see DOWNTOWN
CARLSBAD inset

Carlsbad

Carlsbad State Beach

Carlsbad
Village Drive

Agua Hedionda
Lagoon

Palomar Airport Rd

S10

San Marcos

78

Lake
San Marcos

15

Grape
Day Park

Escondido

S14

15

San Pasqual Valley Rd

Wild Animal
Park

16

78

see LEGOLAND
AREA inset

S12

10

S21

11

El Camino Real

12

13

Rancho Santa Fe Road

Del Dios Hwy

San Pasqual Rd

Lake Hodges

Highland Valley Rd

17

Bandy
Canyon Rd

Batiquitos
Lagoon

5

Encinitas

19

S11

S10

Moonlight Beach
21

Swami's Beach

22

Cardiff-by-the-Sea

Cardiff State Beach

Encinitas Blvd

Manchester Ave

20

San Elijo
Lagoon

Rancho
Santa Fe

S9

S6

San Dieguito River

56

Rancho Bernardo Rd

Rancho
Santa Fe

Camino del Norte

S5

Rancho
Bernardo

18

Blue Sky
Ecological
Reserve

Lake
Poway

S5

28

PACIFIC
OCEAN

23

24

25

26

27

Del Mar

Lomas
Santa Fe Dr

Solana Beach

Via de la Valle

Camino Del Mar

El Camino Real

Del Mar Heights

Ted Williams
Pkwy

Rancho
Peñasqui

Poway

29

Midland
Rd

S4

67

Poway Rd

56

Torrey Pines
State Reserve

Torrey Pines
Golf Course

30

N Torrey Pines Rd

Genesee Ave

Mira Mesa Blvd

Black Mountain Rd

Mira
Mesa

15

Miramar Rd

United States
Marine Corps
Air Station - Miramar

Mission Trails
Regional Park

San Diego River

67

UC San Diego

La Jolla

5

52

805

163

52

Santee

0   5   10 km
0   3   6 miles

brightly decorated Mexican eatery with friendly staff, daily Happy Hour (all day Monday) and a mixed crowd of surfers, suits, bikers and travelers. The restaurants on the beach side of the road serve mostly seafood and are considerably more expensive.

Encinitas

Cardiff is in fact a district of the larger community of Encinitas, which, in turn, once belonged to the former Spanish Rancho San Dieguito, along with Solana Beach and the unincorporated area of Rancho Santa Fe. The inland hills are used for commercial flower farming, most notably by the **Paul Ecke Poinsettia Ranch**, established in 1928. In December there's an enormous poinsettia display at the ranch, and in spring the flowers grow in bands of brilliant color, which look spectacular from I-5.

Encinitas' business district follows Highway 101 (S21) from about I St in the south to Encinitas Blvd in the north. The Lumberyard is a nicely designed shopping center with several casual eateries, while the 1928 *La Paloma Theater (☎ 760-436-7469, 471 S Coast Hwy 101)* shows current movies nightly.

Self-Realization Fellowship Entering Encinitas from the south along Hwy 101 (S21), you are greeted by the gold lotus domes of this spiritual retreat and hermitage. Founded in 1920 by Yogi Paramahansa Yoganada, a widely admired guru born and educated in India, the fellowship is dedicated to helping people of all races, creeds and cultures on their spiritual search. Sri Yogananda spent 30 years of his life in the US, opening this site in 1937 and thus making Encinitas a magnet for holistic healers and natural lifestyle seekers. The lotus domes are the only things that remain of the original temple, which once stood on the edge of the bluff before succumbing to erosion many years ago.

You can still wander to the site through the Eden-esque **Meditation Garden**, which exudes tranquility and peacefulness. Feel stress and anxiety evaporate while strolling along the narrow paths flanked by ferns,

orchids, palms and other lush vegetation observe the sunlight as it filters through the canopy illuminating a sprightly waterfall and koi pond. Admission to the grounds, open 9 am to 5 pm daily (Sunday from 11 am), is free. The entrance is west of Hwy 101 at 215 K St. Also here is the turn-out for Swami's, a powerful reef break surfed by territorial locals. There's a parking lot just south of the hermitage, on the west side of Old Hwy 101 that gives a good view of the surf.

Quail Botanical Gardens The 30-acre Quail Botanical Gardens has a large collection of California native plants, palms, ferns and sections planted with flora of various regions, including the Himalayas, Australia and Central America. It also boasts the largest collection of bamboo in the United States. You'll see it all while wandering a network of trails that leads through canyons and up hillsides. The gardens (☎ 760-436-3036) are open 9 am to 5 pm daily; $5/4/2 adults/seniors/children ages 5 to 12. Take the Encinitas Blvd exit from I-5.

Rancho Santa Fe In the 1920s, Rancho Santa Fe, inland from Encinitas on County Road S9, was subdivided as a residential community that attracted Hollywood types such as Bing Crosby, Douglas Fairbanks and Mary Pickford. National City-born architect Lilian Rice, who graduated from UC Berkeley and studied with a disciple of Irving Gill planned the community and designed many of the original homes in the elegant Spanish mission style.

Places to Stay & Eat The *Moonlight Beach Motel (☎ 760-753-0623, 800-323-1259, fax 760-944-9827, 233 2nd St)* is close to beach and shopping and has decent rooms costing $56 to $82. Larger and newer is the *Days Inn (☎ 760-944-0260, 800-795-6044, fax 760-944-2803, 133 Encinitas Rd)*, where 12 rooms cost $49 to $99, including continental breakfast. It's three blocks from the beach.

For eats, *Tomiko (☎ 760-633-3587, 8? Encinitas Blvd)* is one of the best Japanese restaurants in the county; there's a sushi bar, but the real creativity goes into the updated Asian fare prepared by chef Kazuo. For good pizza, steaks and salads, try the casual *Chesapeake Bar & Grill (☎ 760-943-0177, 1068 N El Camino Real)*.

Carlsbad

In many ways the hub of coastal North County, Carlsbad – home of Legoland – is a particularly good base for families to explore area attractions while staying close to shopping, restaurants and the beach. Rather than being stretched out along the highway like most North County communities, it has a solid downtown of four square blocks between I-5 and Carlsbad Blvd which run north-south and are connected by Carlsbad Village Dr running east-west.

The town came into being when the railroad came through in the 1880s. John Frazier, an early homesteader, former sailor and ship's captain, sank a well and found water that had a high mineral content, supposedly the identical mineral content of spa water in Karlsbad, Bohemia (hence the town's name), now called Karlovy Vary in the Czech Republic. He capitalized on the aquatic similarities of the two places and built a grand spa hotel, which prospered until the 1930s. In 1993, Ludvik Grigoras, a native of Karlovy Vary, restored the old well, dug another, bottled the water and reopened a mineral spa in the Alt Karlsbad Hanse House, a nouveau half-timbered edifice that stands on the site of the original hotel. Massages, facials and wraps are applied in Egyptian and Roman themed treatment rooms that look like they belong in Las Vegas. The site of Frazier's original mineral well is right outside the Hanse House, as is a statue of the man.

The long, sandy beaches of Carlsbad are great for walking and seashell hunting. Good access is from Carlsbad Blvd, two blocks south of Carlsbad Village Dr, where there's a boardwalk, rest rooms and free parking.

Orientation & Information Carlsbad's center, also known as 'the village,' is around the intersection of Hwy 101, here called Carlsbad Blvd, and Carlsbad Village Dr. Many restaurants and hotels can be found here, but most of the big attractions, including Legoland and the Carlsbad Company Stores outlet mall (see the San Diego Shopping chapter), are on the eastern side of I-5, about 3 miles south of downtown.

The Visitor Information Center (☎ 760-434-6093, 800-227-5722, fax 760-434-6056) is housed in the original 1887 Santa Fe railroad depot at 400 Carlsbad Village Drive. Hours are 9 am to 5 pm Monday to Friday, 10 am to 4 pm Saturday and 10 am to 3 pm Sunday.

Legoland California Local citizens, fearing traffic congestion and the other effects of rampant tourism, nearly quashed the opening of Legoland California (the original is in Denmark), but traffic now slips smoothly off I-5, directed by large freeway signs that mark the way to the attraction. And the overall appearance of the place is far less touristy than, say, SeaWorld. In fact, locals now seem quite proud of the town's newest point of interest, which is exceeded in size and popularity only by the beach.

Legoland is an enchanting fantasy environment built entirely of those little colored plastic building blocks that many of us grew up with. There are bicycles to ride around the grounds, a boat tour of some exhibits, and many opportunities to build (and buy) your own Lego structures. It's all rather low-key compared with bigger, flashier parks like Disneyland and therefore especially suited for younger children (10 and under).

Visually the most stunning area is Miniland, which recreates American landmarks at 1/20th their actual size. More than 20 million Lego bricks were used to build such places as the White House and the Capitol building; the New York skyline complete with Chrysler Building, Rockefeller Center and Grand Central Station; San Francisco with the Golden Gate Bridge and the Transamerica Building, and many more. Some, like a Mardi Gras celebration in New Orleans' French Quarter, even feature animated Lego figurines.

Youngsters love the rides, which are gentle by today's standards. There's a Driving School where kids get their Lego license after completing a driving course in an electric car; the Sky Cycle where guests pedal – ET-like – above the park; and Fairy Tale Brook, a boat ride through landscapes recreating scenes from favorite legends. Older kids will prefer the Dragon, a small roller coaster ride, or Mindstorms, where they have 45 minutes to build a robot.

Legoland California (☎ 760-918-5346) is open 9 am to 9 pm daily mid-June to Labor Day and 10 am to 5 pm otherwise. Admission is $34/29 adults/children ages 3 to 16; two-day tickets are $42/37 and annual passes $79/59. Parking is $7.

To get to Legoland, take the Legoland/Cannon Rd exit off I-5 and follow the signs. From downtown Carlsbad or downtown San Diego, take the *Coaster* to the Poinsettia Station, from where bus No 344 goes straight to the park.

The Flower Fields From March to May, the 50-acre flower fields of Carlsbad Ranch are ablaze in a sea of carmine, saffron and the snow-white blossom of ranunculus flowers. Bring a picnic, a canvas or just your curiosity – this is a spectacular sight to behold. The fields are two blocks east of I-5; take the Palomar Airport Rd exit, go east, then left on Paseo del Norte Road – look for the windmill. Call ☎ 760-431-0352 for hours, prices or an events schedule.

Museum of Making Music This new museum takes a journey through more than 100 years of the music industry in America. Guided along by some 450 instruments, listening stations and explanatory panels, you'll learn about the early beginnings in the 1890s to the Jazz Age of the 1920s, the Big Band '40s, the Rock 'n' Roll '50s all the way to the MTV era. The museum (☎ 877-551-9976), at 5760 Armada Dr near the Flower Fields and Legoland, is open 10 am to 5 pm (closed Monday) and costs $5/3 adults/seniors, students and children.

Children's Discovery Museum Small kids are delighted by the various exhibits and interactive play stations of this educational and fun museum. It's in downtown Carlsbad in Suite 103 of the Village Faire

Shopping Centre behind Neiman's Restaurant at 300 Carlsbad Village Dr. Hours are noon to 5 pm (from 10 am on Friday and Saturday), closed Monday; admission is $4

Batiquitos Lagoon On the southern edge of Carlsbad, separating it from Encinitas, is this lagoon, one of the last remaining tidal wetlands in California. A self-guided tour lets you explore area plants, including the prickly pear cactus, coastal sage scrub and eucalyptus trees, as well as lagoon birds like the great heron and the snowy egret. One of the artificial islands in the lagoon is a nesting site for the California least tern and the western snowy plover, both endangered species. The ultra-deluxe Four Seasons Aviara resort and golf course hugs the lagoon's northern edge while its eastern side is bordered by the equally luxurious La Costa Resort & Spa.

Places to Stay You can camp at *South Carlsbad State Beach* (☎ 760-438-3143), miles south of the town center on Carlsbad Blvd. There are 222 tent and RV sites costing from $15 to $24, which can be booked through Parknet (☎ 800-444-7275) or online at www.reserveamerica.com.

Other accommodations are plentiful but they tend to be expensive, especially in summer. Best value is probably *Motel* (☎ 760-434-7135, 1006 Carlsbad Village Dr, for $45/49 single/double, or one of the other chain-operated motels in the area. An adequate independent is the beachside *Surf Motel* (☎ 760-729-7961, 800-523-9170, fax 760-434-6642, 3136 Carlsbad Blvd), which charges $59 to $99.

More upscale options include the *Carlsbad Inn* (☎ 760-434-7020, 800-235-3939, fax 760-729-4853, 3075 Carlsbad Blvd), also near the beach, with rooms from $169 to $238. Top of the line is the *La Costa Resort & Spa* (☎ 760-438-9111, 800-854-5000, fax 760-438-3758, 2100 Costa Del Mar Rd), just off El Camino Real 2 miles east of I-5, with acres of grounds, all sorts of recreational facilities and rooms from $300 to $470.

Places to Eat Locals often choose *The Armenian Cafe* (☎ 760-720-2233), on Carlsbad

Blvd two blocks south of Carlsbad Village Dr, which does stuffed pita sandwiches from $6 and is known for its rack of lamb ($19). Seating on the outdoor terrace is especially pleasant. For good Mexican food, head past Oak Ave to *Fidel's* (☎ 760-729-0903), where everything is big: the bar, the portions and the outdoor patio. Next door, the *Daily News Cafe* is popular for breakfast.

For some of the freshest, honest-to-goodness seafood, go to the *Fishhouse Vera Cruz* (☎ 760-434-6777, 417 Carlsbad Village Dr). The best bargains are at lunchtime when a big serving of Atlantic cod or Cajun fish kebabs, with two side dishes, costs just $6.

Neiman's Restaurant (☎ 760-729-4131), in the Queen Anne-style building at 2978 Carlsbad Blvd, has great drinks and food specials during Happy Hour, which here runs from 11 am to 6 pm; there's also nightly entertainment from salsa to big band swing to house, reggae and hip hop.

Vista

About 7 miles inland from Carlsbad, this agricultural community has a couple of worthwhile attractions warranting a quick stop. The **Antique Gas & Steam Engine Museum** (☎ 760-941-1791, 800-587-2867), 2040 N Santa Fe Ave, highlights old-timey and modern farming techniques. Exhibits are supplemented with demonstrations in planting, threshing, harvesting and other activities. Museum hours are 10 am to 4 pm daily; admission is $3.

For a glimpse at life in Vista in the mid-19th century, visit the **Rancho Buena Vista Adobe** (☎ 760-639-6154), 651 E Vista Way, the lone remnant from the original 1845 land grant. It's in excellent shape and contains period furniture and artifacts that can be seen on guided tours offered 10 am to 3 pm Wednesday to Saturday, from 12:30 pm Sunday. The adobe is closed on holidays, rainy days and when rented for a private function.

Oceanside

Oceanside is the northernmost of San Diego County's coastal communities and has 3½ miles of beach. Early settlers were mostly English gentry who introduced agri-

culture to the fertile San Luis Rey Valley in the 19th century. Today it is the home base for many of the employees who work on, or for, the big Camp Pendleton Marine Base on the town's northern border. The world's largest amphibious training base thoroughly influences the character of Oceanside where shops sell military-style clothing and most men sport crew cuts. For a taste of old Oceanside, you'll have to travel 4 miles inland where the 'King of the Missions' holds court and historic buildings and memorabilia are preserved in Heritage Park.

Orientation & Information The heart of Oceanside's downtown is where Coast Hwy meets Mission Ave. Just west of here is the pier, while Oceanside Harbor is a short drive farther north. This part of town is also where you'll find most of the accommodations. Also here is the Oceanside Chamber of Commerce (☎ 760-722-1534), 928 Coast Hwy, which hands out city-related information and is open Monday to Friday 10 am to 4:30 pm. Right next door is a branch of the California Welcome Center (☎ 760-721-1101), which has friendly staff and the same local information, in addition to oodles of brochures about the rest of the state. It's open daily 9 am to 5 pm.

Oceanside Municipal Pier This massive wooden pier, extending 1942 feet out to sea, is so long that there's a little golf buggy to transport people to the end (50¢ each way). There are bait and tackle shops, with poles to rent and lights for night fishing (no license required), as well as snack bars, a McDonald's and a '50s-style diner (see Places to Stay & Eat, later this chapter).

California Surf Museum Surfing is huge in Oceanside, which hosts several major competitions throughout the year. A history of these contests, plus photos, old boards and other equipment, trophies and memorabilia make up the backbone of the exhibits in this museum-cum-surf shop (☎ 760-721-6876), 223 N Coast Hwy at Pier View Way. In addition to permanent displays, organizers put up a new brand exhibit every six months, showcasing pioneering legends from the world of surfing, like Duke Kahanamoku (the Olympic gold medal swimmer and surfing pioneer who died in 1968). Admission is free and hours are 10 am to 4 pm, closed Tuesday and Wednesday.

Oceanside Harbor At the northern end of the waterfront, the extensive Oceanside Harbor provides slips for 900 permanent and 50 visiting boats. At the south end of the harbor, Cape Cod-style Harbor Village, a group of shops, picnic tables and restaurants, has a distinctly nautical flavor.

Helgren's (☎ 760-722-2133), 315 Harbor Dr S, offers a variety of sport fishing trips. Open party boats go out daily; half day trips (10 am to 3 pm) cost $25; 3/4-day trips (7 am to 4 pm) cost $35; fishing licenses and various discounts are available. From December to April, Helgren's also operates whale-watching trips for $15 and one-hour coastal cruises for $10.

If you want to explore the ocean under your own steam, turn to Oceanside Boat Rentals of America (☎ 760-722-0028), 256 Harbor Dr S, which rents power, sail, electric and pedal boats, as well as kayaks and waverunners.

Mission San Luis Rey Francia The 18th of the 21 California missions, the 'King of the Missions' was named for French king Saint Louis IX and dedicated in 1798. Architecturally, it was the largest and most refined in the chain and also the most successful in recruiting Indian converts; at its peak almost 3000 neophytes lived and worked here. A ruin after secularization, San Luis was rescued by a Franciscan missionary in 1892 and it is still administered today by Franciscans who hold mass and operate a retreat center.

Inside the Hispano-Moorish structure are displays on work and life in the mission, with some original religious art and artifacts. Note the wooden cupola made from pine grown on nearby Palomar Mountain and the partly original Moorish-style pulpit. Also on view are 18th- and 19th- century vestments (religious robes) and the original

baptismal font hand-hammered from copper by Mission Indians. The altars are a blend of neoclassical and baroque styles. The mission (☎ 760-757-3651) is 4 miles inland at 4050 Mission Ave (Hwy 76); admission is $4/3 adults/students. It's open 10 am to 4:30 pm daily.

Behind the mission, tranquil **Heritage Park Village & Museum** preserves historic structures from the early 20th century, including a doctor's office, a jail and a blacksmith shop. The grounds open 9 am to 4 pm daily, but access to the buildings is only on Sunday from 1 to 4 pm. Call ☎ 760-966-454. for details.

Places to Stay & Eat Budget motels abound but may fill up on weekends and in summer. Cheapest of the bunch is the nice-looking **Motel 9** (☎ 760-722-1887, fax 760-757-1861, 822 N Coast Hwy), which has large rooms and suites from $40 to $90. A step up is the **Guesthouse Inn & Suites** (☎ 760-722-1904, 800-914-2230, fax 760-722-1168, 1103 N Coast Hwy), which has comfy rooms with air-con and data ports, as well as a pool. Prices range from $50 to $120.

Oceanside has an astonishing number of eateries, most of them of the easy-going, informal kind. The mid-priced, '50s-style **Ruby's** (☎ 760-433-7829), at the far end of the pier, has a full bar, good burgers and milk shakes. For a more genuine flashback to the days of yore, visit **101 Cafe** (☎ 760-722-5220, 631 S Coast Hwy), in business since 1928 and still going strong. Expect big portions of inexpensive food, a well-used juke box and old-timey photographs.

Camp Pendleton

Driving through on I-5, you can often see Marines making amphibious 'attacks' on the beaches. For a closer look, you can do a free self-guided driving tour of Camp Pendleton (☎ 760-725-5569) daily during daylight hours. You'll be given a brochure highlighting historic and Marine Corps related sights when checking in at the main gate, which is just off I-5 north of Oceanside. Bring your driver's license and vehicle registration. The base is sometimes closed to outside visitors due to training or combat-preparation procedures.

Getting There & Around

San Diego's North County Coast is, for the most part, an easy trip from the city. From metropolitan San Diego, N Torrey Pines Rd is the most scenic approach to Del Mar, and you can continue along the coast on S21 (which changes its name from Camino del Mar to Pacific Coast Hwy to Old Hwy 101, going north). A quicker route is I-5, which continues to Los Angeles and beyond.

Local buses, operated by the North County Transit District (NCTD), connect the various communities. A useful line is bus No 301, which follows the coast road from University Towne Centre in La Jolla to Oceanside every 30 minutes from about 5:30 am to 10 pm daily; tickets are $1.50 (exact fare required).

Greyhound buses stop at Del Mar, Carlsbad, Solana Beach, Encinitas and Oceanside, although the *Coaster* commuter train is faster and more convenient. For more on either, see the San Diego Getting Around chapter.

To get to Vista from either Carlsbad or Oceanside, take bus No 301 to the Cassidy Street stop on Coast Hwy, then switch to bus No 302, direction Escondido ($1.50).

NORTH COUNTY INLAND

Interstate Hwy 15 heads north from San Diego, through Poway, Rancho Bernardo and Escondido to the Riverside County line. The number one attraction is the Wild Animal Park near Escondido, but there are also some interesting historical sites, and the area provides access to the scenic backcountry around Palomar (see the San Diego Backcountry section later in this chapter).

Poway

These days, this rural community of 50,000 is best known for its state-of-the-art **Poway Center for the Performing Arts** (see the San Diego Entertainment chapter). For visitors, perhaps the greatest appeal lies in its slow-moving country atmosphere. **Old Poway**

Park (☎ 858-679-4313), 14134 Midland Rd, is an assemblage of historic buildings, including a church, Templars Hall and Nelson House. Kids love the Train Barn, which houses a 1907 steam engine and an 1894 Los Angeles trolley. Rides are offered 10 am to 4 pm Saturday, 11 am to 2 pm Sunday. Also here is the **Heritage Museum**, open 9 am to 4 pm weekends only.

Tract homes give way to wilderness the farther east you go. **Lake Poway**, at the eastern terminus of Lake Poway Rd, is a major getaway for locals and offers fishing (it is stocked with trout), boating, camping, hiking etc but, ironically, no swimming. A concession stand sells fishing licenses and rents boats (no fishing or boating on Monday and Tuesday and all of October). The lake is surrounded by a wilderness area with access to numerous trails, including the 3-mile lake loop and the 2½-mile hike to Mt Woodson. The **Blue Sky Ecological Reserve** is a 700-acre protected area that is especially rewarding for birders.

Rancho Bernardo

This placid, affluent community, characterized by mission-style houses, golf courses and parks, was master-planned, which gives it an air of artificiality. The main reason to stop is the friendly **Bernardo Winery** (☎ 858-487-1866), the area's oldest operating

winery. There are 12 gift shops (closed Monday), a restaurant and, of course, a tasting room, where you can sample the latest crops free of charge. The winery is at 13330 Paseo del Verano Norte and is open 9 am to 5 pm daily.

Places to Stay & Eat Accommodations in Rancho Bernardo are mostly upscale. One of the choicest places to stay is **Rancho Bernardo Inn** (☎ 858-675-8500, 800-542-6096, fax 858-487-1611, 17660 Bernardo Oaks Dr), which has won awards for beautiful landscaping, great amenities and a full range of fitness pursuits, from a championship golf course to lighted tennis courts. Rates range from $125 to $230 single/double. Cheaper options include several chain hotels, including a pleasant **Holiday Inn** (☎ 858-485-6530, 800-777-6055, fax 858-485-7819, 17065 W Bernardo Dr), which charges $109 to $129.

Anthony's Fish Grotto (☎ 858-451-2070, 11666 Avena Place) serves up dependable fish and seafood in a casual ambiance, with main courses mostly in the $10 to $20 range. If you're in the mood for dressing up (jackets for men are required), try **El Bizcocho** (☎ 858-675-8500) at the Rancho Bernardo Inn, mentioned above. It is sure to be a memorable – and pricey – dining experience. Reservations are essential.

Escondido

This quiet satellite town of 128,000 is the commercial hub of inland North County. Besides the numerous antique shops and two wineries, the main draw is the **California Center for the Arts**, a mixed-use facility anchored by a concert hall, a smaller theater and conference center (see the San Diego Entertainment chapter). The complex includes an **art museum** (☎ 760-839-4120), featuring changing exhibits of 20th-century paintings, sculpture, photography and installations. Hours are 10 am to 5 pm (Sunday from noon), closed Monday; admission is $5/4/3 adults/seniors/students and children ages 12 to 18.

Escondido's history is given center stage at the **Heritage Walk** (☎ 760-743-8207), a collection of retired Victorian buildings, including a library, barn, windmill and railroad depot. It's in Grape Day Park at 321 N Broadway and the buildings are open 1 to 4 pm Thursday to Saturday; admission is free.

Places to Stay & Eat There's no shortage of places to stay, with all budgets covered.

The **Escondido RV Resort** (☎ 760-740-5000, 800-331-3556, 1740 Seven Oaks Rd) has 67 sites, a TV lounge, heated pool and spa and store for $35 to $40 per site, but prices vary widely by season. Tent campers can try **Lake Dixon** (☎ 760-741-3328, 839-4680, 1700 La Hondra Dr), which has a pleasant setting and 45 sites costing $16 with full hookups and $12 for tents.

Among the cheapest motels is **Palms Inn** (☎ 760-743-9733, 800-727-8932, 2650 S Escondido Blvd), which includes continental breakfast in its rates of $50/60 single/double. Chain motels include **Super 8** and **Best Western Escondido**.

For casual eats, try the **Centre City Cafe** (☎ 760-489-6011, 2680 Escondido Blvd), a local hangout known for its down-home style food. Somewhat more upscale is **Sirino's** (☎ 760-745-3835, 113 W Grand Ave), which has an inspired Mediterranean menu at mid- to upper range prices.

Wild Animal Park

Since the early 1960s, the San Diego Zoological Society has been developing this 1800-acre, free-range animal park, which is far from an ordinary zoo. Entire herds of animals roam through large enclosures that recreate their natural habitat, be it the Asian plains, the Mongolian steppe or East Africa. Come early in the day, since the animals are more active in the morning and many of them – especially crowd pleasers like the lions and elephants – are no-shows during the midday heat.

The park (☎ 760-747-8702) opens 9 am to 6 pm daily in summer, to 4 pm the rest of the year; you can stay another hour after the gates close. Admission is $22/15 adults/children ages 3 to 11, including the Bush Line ride and all animal shows. Discount coupons are widely available. A combined ticket to visit both the San Diego Zoo and the Wild Animal Park within a five-day period costs $38.35/23.15. Parking is $5.

For a real safari experience, photo caravan tours go right in among the animals, but they're quite expensive ($85 to $105, depending on the length of the tour), and reservations are required – call the main number and ask for guest relations. Facilities and services for disabled visitors are available, as are baby strollers. There are also plenty of souvenir shops and suitable places to eat.

A good way to start off a visit is to get an overview of the park during a 55-minute narrated ride aboard the **Wgasa Bush Line Railway**. The elephants, zebras, rhinos, giraffes, antelope and other animals look wonderful in the wide open spaces, though

California Condors

The California condor (Gymnogyps californianus) is one of the largest flying birds in the world. It weighs up to 20lb and has a life span of 40 years. Even more impressive is its wing span, which averages 9 feet and allows it to soar and glide for hours without beating its wings. In the wild, carrion is the main diet of these giant vultures.

Until a few years ago, however, not a single condor remained in the wild; they were a species brought to the brink of extinction by human intrusion. Although it's been illegal to kill condors for about a century, their numbers declined steadily as a result of contamination and pollution, as well as collisions with power lines and other accidents. In 1967 the depleted condors limped onto the federal endangered species list.

To turn things around, a team of scientists launched extensive conservation efforts, but it was too little, too late. In the mid-'80s, the world's last surviving 27 condors were captured and taken to breeding programs in the San Diego and LA zoos. It was a risky gamble, but the consensus was that there was nothing to lose.

Fortunately, this tale has a happy ending – at least for now. The first condor chick was hatched in captivity in 1988, and in 1992 the first captive-bred birds soared back into the wild. By 2000, their population had climbed back up to 150. So far, they're doing well, but only the future will tell whether the condor is back in full swing.

you won't be as close to them as you would be in a zoo (bring binoculars).

From there, it's off by foot to explore the various exhibit areas at your own pace. A highlight not far from the entrance is the **lowland gorilla enclosure** where a family of apes inadvertently provides hilarious entertainment by just going about life naturally.

From here it's not far to **Heart of Africa**, an exotic journey along a winding dirt path. Pick up a free field guide at the trailhead to help you identify the animals, since there are no cages and no labels. You'll encounter warthogs, okapi, oryx, giraffes, cheetahs, impalas, wattled cranes, flamingoes and many other birds and mammals. At a feeding area you can buy 'cookies' for the giraffes, which occasionally amble over from their watering hole; this is a great opportunity for close-up photographs of these gangly giants.

From here you could continue on the **Kilimanjaro Safari Walk**, a 1¾-mile trail skirting the huge East Africa enclosure that will give you a chance to observe large animals like elephants, rhinos, tigers and lions.

One of the newest exhibits is **Condor Ridge**, which showcases animals, some endangered, from North America. A short trail leads from a pine forest, where thick-billed parrots roam, to a grassland habitat that's home to porcupines and falcons. The path culminates in a viewing platform from which you can observe the elusive bighorn sheep and California condors (see boxed text 'California Condors: Giants of the Skies'). Interpretive displays provide background on the birds.

There are plenty of other areas of interest. At the **Petting Kraal** you can often touch some of the youngest animals in the park. Several **animal shows** are held on stages throughout the park, starting between 11 am and 4:30 pm. Get a map and a schedule as you enter.

San Pasqual Battlefield State Park

About a quarter mile east of the Wild Animal Park is the setting of one of the bloodiest battles in the Mexican-American War. It pitted American troops (Dragoons), led by

General Stephen Kearny, against a cavalry group under Andrés Pico (Californios), which was camped out at the nearby Indian pueblo of San Pasqual. Twenty-one Americans died during the fierce fighting and another 16 were wounded; Kearny was forced to retreat, a major victory by the Californios (who won the battle but lost the war).

At the visitors center (☎ 760-489-0076), a short video puts the battle in the context of the Mexican-American War. Displays explain life at the pueblo of San Pasqual and there are historic weapons as well. The battle itself is reenacted every December. Park hours are 10 am to 5 pm Friday to Sunday; admission is free.

Wineries

Spanish missionaries planted some of California's first grapevines around Escondido.

Welk Resort Center

Lawrence Welk, also known as 'Mr Bubbles,' was the man responsible for 'champagne music' and the 'wunnerful, wunnerful' Lawrence Welk Show in the 1940s and '50s, which was one of the longest-running music programs in US TV history. The sprawling resort is part retirement community, part hotel and time-share facility and includes golf courses, pools, tennis courts and shops.

The Lawrence Welk Theater (☎ 760-749-3448, 888-802-7469) runs a year-round season, mostly of crowd-pleasing musicals and variety shows. Tickets run $29 to $32. In the lobby the Lawrence Welk Museum has memorabilia of legendary Larry's life and work. It opens at 9 am daily and usually closes just after the final curtain drops. Also on the grounds is the Lawrence Welk Restaurant, which has all-you-can-eat buffet lunches and dinners ($11.95/16.95). Show and dinner packages are $38 to $40.

The Welk Resort Center (☎ 760-749-3000, 800-932-9355) is at 8860 Lawrence Welk Dr, about 7 miles north of Escondido.

Orfila Vineyards (☎ 760-738-6500), 13455 San Pasqual Rd, is in a lovely setting overlooking the San Pasqual Valley and has a large rose garden. It is open 10 am to 6 pm daily (until 5 pm in winter), with guided tours at 2 pm. Two tastes of wine are free, four more cost $3.

Deer Park Winery & Auto Museum (☎ 760-749-1666), 29013 Champagne Blvd just north of the Welk Resort Center, is touted as the world's only combination winery and car museum – it specializes in convertibles, and has more than 100 on display. Vintage radios, Barbie dolls, historic wine-making equipment and Americana of all sorts are also part of this eclectic collection. It is open daily 10 am to 5 pm. Admission is $6/4 adults/seniors, children under 12 are free. In the tasting room, you get two sips free or all six for $5, including a souvenir glass.

Mission San Antonio De Pala

This nicely restored, remote mission started existence in 1816 as an *asistencia* to Mission San Luis Rey. Originally it was to have been one of a chain of inland missions; conditions seemed favorable and good soil and plenty of water resulted in its quick expansion. The plan, however, faltered eventually, as did the whole mission system a few years later.

Located on the Pala Indian Reservation, this is the sole surviving California mission still ministering to a Native American population. It is currently run by a group of Barnabite friars who took over from the Franciscans in 1996. The largely reconstructed, simple structure consists of a long chapel decorated with paintings by local Native Americans; the floor is original. Of note is the bell tower, modeled after one in Juarez, Mexico, which stands apart from the main church, a unique design element. The mission cemetery is one of the oldest in California and preserves numerous wooden crosses.

The mission (☎ 760-742-3317) is open 7:30 am to 5 pm daily except Monday; a small museum keeps hours of 9:30 am to 4 pm. Admission to the church is free, to the museum $2. It is just off Hwy 76 in Pala, about 6 miles east of I-15 (look for signs).

Bus No 388 makes the trip out here from the Escondido Transit Center three times daily except Sunday.

Getting There & Around

The inland valley is served by bus No 20, which runs daily between downtown San Diego and the Escondido Transit Center at 700 W Valley Parkway; departures are every 15 to 30 minutes, $2. Bus No 810 is an express service along the same route; every 15 minutes Monday to Friday between 5:30 am and 6:30 pm, $3.25. From the transit center, bus No 308 travels southwest to Solana Beach every 40 to 60 minutes (no weekend evening service), $1.50.

Communities north of Escondido are served by bus No 302, which runs every 20 to 30 minutes ($1.50) all the way to Oceanside. Express bus No 320 along Hwy 78 also serves Oceanside every half hour ($1.50). Greyhound (☎ 760-722-1587) buses also stop at the Transit Center.

Getting to Poway by bus can be a bit time consuming, as it is east of the main route and requires a change from bus No 20 to bus No 844 at the Paseo Montril stop in Rancho Peñasqui ($2).

Wild Animal Park is just north of Hwy 78, 5 miles east of I-15 from the Via Rancho Parkway exit. Using public transport is not really practical unless you're staying in Escondido from where bus No 307 makes the 15-minute trip out several times daily except Sunday. But if you're staying in metropolitan San Diego, you're in for a 3½- to four-hour journey involving multiple transfers. If you don't have your own car, you may be better off joining an organized tour (see the San Diego Getting Around chapter).

SAN DIEGO BACKCOUNTRY

Going inland from San Diego, you quickly get into sparsely populated rural areas a world away from the highly developed coast. Much of San Diego County's backcountry is covered by the Cleveland National Forest, which offers camping, hiking and mountain biking.

If you're exploring the Cleveland National Forest by car, you must obtain a National Forest Adventure Pass in order to use forest facilities, including hiking trails. Passes cost $5 a day or $30 a year and are available from any ranger station or visitor center. You don't need a pass if you're just driving through the forest or for stopping at a ranger station or visitor center. Otherwise, those caught without one are subject to a $100 fine.

Highway 79 is a scenic route through the backcountry, from the wine-producing area near Temecula (in Riverside County), south via the old gold-mining area of Julian, to Cuyamaca Rancho State Park and I-8. To explore the backcountry, it's best to have a car, though you can get to most places on buses. Call Northeast Rural Bus System (☎ 760-767-4287).

Palomar Mountain

At 6140 feet, Palomar Mountain is the centerpiece of three promontories that make up the 25-mile-long Palomar Range. It is densely forested with pine, oak, fir and cedar and receives several feet of snow each year. Although there are two self-register, first-come, first-served United States Forest Service (USFS) campgrounds near the top of the mountain (*Fry Creek* and *Observatory*; call ☎ 760-788-0250 for details), people come for the day to see the 200-inch Hale telescope at the **Palomar Observatory** (☎ 760-742-2119) near Palomar Mountain State Park, in use since 1948. Visitors may tour the gift shop (open daily July 1 to August 31, weekends otherwise) and look at the telescope from a viewing gallery from 9 am to 4 pm daily. Since this is primarily a research facility, there are no tours or telescope viewing on night visits. Admission is free.

Since the California Institute of Technology owns most of the land surrounding the observatory, hiking is limited. There is the 2.2-mile Observatory National Recreation Trail, which goes from Observatory Campground up to the observatory itself; this is a good one-way trail if you arrange transportation to get yourself back, or it can be done as an out-and-back starting at either end. To reach the observatory from Hwy 76, take the East Grade Rd (County Hwy S7) or steep and windy South Grade Rd

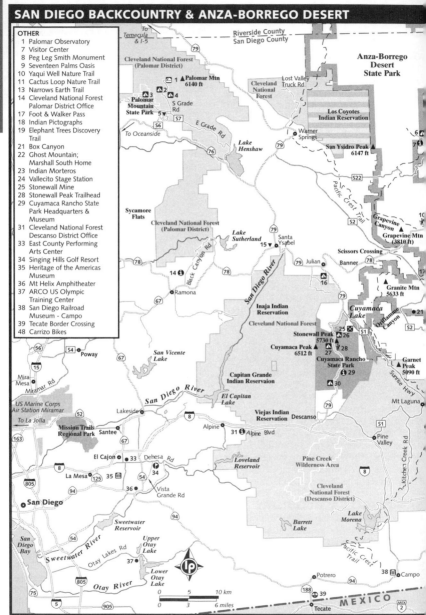

SAN DIEGO BACKCOUNTRY & ANZA-BORREGO DESERT

OTHER
1 Palomar Observatory
7 Visitor Center
8 Peg Leg Smith Monument
9 Seventeen Palms Oasis
10 Yaqui Well Nature Trail
11 Cactus Loop Nature Trail
13 Narrows Earth Trail
14 Cleveland National Forest Palomar District Office
17 Foot & Walker Pass
18 Indian Pictographs
19 Elephant Trees Discovery Trail
21 Box Canyon
22 Ghost Mountain; Marshall South Home
23 Indian Morteros
24 Vallecito Stage Station
25 Stonewall Mine
28 Stonewall Peak Trailhead
29 Cuyamaca Rancho State Park Headquarters & Museum
31 Cleveland National Forest Descanso District Office
33 East County Performing Arts Center
34 Singing Hills Golf Resort
35 Heritage of the Americas Museum
36 Mt Helix Amphitheater
37 ARCO US Olympic Training Center
38 San Diego Railroad Museum - Campo
39 Tecate Border Crossing
48 Carrizo Bikes

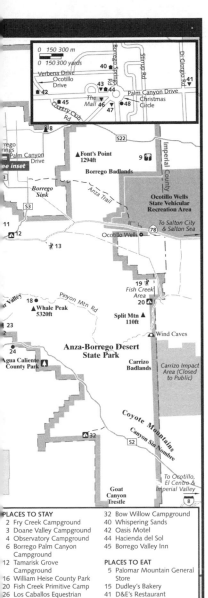

(County Hwy S6) to the junction, where the Palomar Mountain General Store, open daily, has food and supplies. The observatory is 5 miles north, well marked by road signs.

West of the junction, S7 goes to **Palomar Mountain State Park** (☎ 760-742-3462), a thickly forested area teeming with incense cedar, pine, oak, white fir, spruce, as well as azalea and lilac. Look out for deer, squirrels and raccoons. There's a map posted at the entrance station, where you pay the $5 day-use fee. The fee is waived if you camp at Doane Valley Campground ($15). Booking through Parknet (☎ 800-444-7275 or www.reserveamerica.com) is recommended.

At the northern tip of the Palomar Range, the **Agua Tibia Wilderness** area is specially protected and requires a wilderness permit for entry. Originally set aside to protect the night skies around the observatory from the lights of encroaching suburbia, the wilderness is filled with wildlife, including wild pigs, prairie falcons and golden eagles. Maps and permits can be obtained from the Cleveland National Forest Palomar District Ranger headquarters (☎ 760-788-0250) at 1634 Black Canyon Rd in Ramona, which is about 15 miles southeast of Escondido on Hwy 78.

Julian

The gold rush came to San Diego in 1869, after a cattleman named Fred Coleman found specks of placer deposits in a creek near present-day Julian. When quartz gold was discovered, hard-rock mines were started and the town was established in 1870. These days Julian, population 3500, is in orchard country and has a reasonably well-preserved 19th-century main street and an economy built upon B&Bs and apple pies. The local chamber of commerce (☎ 760-765-1857) is at 2129 Main St.

The **Eagle Mining Company** (☎ 760-765-0036) maintains two of the original mines, the Eagle and the High Peak, up C St a few blocks east of Main St. Displays like minerals and machinery provide an introduction to the mysteries of mining, but to truly appreciate the art, you should join a guided tour through the tunnels in the hard rock mine.

These last little over one hour and run on a spontaneous basis, more or less determined by demand, between 10 am and 2 pm ($8/4/1 adults/seniors and students/children).

The **Julian Pioneer Museum** (☎ 760-765-0227), 2811 Washington St, has an unexceptional collection of old clothing, tools and photos, but is more interesting for its Indian artifacts and lace. It's worth a short browse and a small donation and is open 10 am to 4 pm daily, except Monday, from April to November and weekends only in winter.

Places to Stay & Eat For camping, you have to go out of town about 3 miles to *William Heise County Park* (☎ 760-565-3600), which has 61 RV and 41 tent sites for $12 to $14 in a pretty setting; cabins are $35. For reservations, call ☎ 877-565-3600 from within San Diego or ☎ 858-565-3600 from outside. To get there, go west of Julian on Hwy 78, left at Pine Hills Rd and left again at Deer Lake Park Rd. There are also a few private campground/RV parks south of town on Hwy 79. Alternatively, go down to Cuyamaca Rancho State Park (☎ 760-765-0755).

Accommodations in Julian are mostly pricey B&Bs. Places fill up on weekends and holidays, and many have a two-night minimum stay. Among the more affordable is the *Julian Lodge* (☎ 760-765-1420, 2720 C St), where 23 units cost from $62/72 single/double.

Many of the restaurants and cafes on Main St sell lunches and apple pies. *Miner's Diner* (☎ 760-765-3753, 2134 Main St) is an old-fashioned soda fountain in an 1886 brick building and sells burgers, sandwiches and baked goods. Also good for burgers is unpretentious *Buffalo Bill's* (☎ 760-765-1560) on 3rd St at B St, although it's only open for breakfast and lunch.

Near the town of Santa Ysabel, northwest of Julian at the intersection of Hwys 78 and 79, *Dudley's Bakery* (☎ 760-765-0488) is enormously popular for homemade bread, cakes and pastries. They're closed Monday and Tuesday.

Cuyamaca Rancho State Park

Delightful for the variety of its landscapes, Cuyamaca Rancho is a lush, cool contrast to

the coastal areas and deserts. Situated 6 miles north of I-8 on Hwy 79, its 33 sq miles embrace meadows with spring wildflowers, forests of oak, willow, sycamore and pine, and wild animals such as deer, raccoons, bobcats and squirrels; there's also rich bird life.

The genesis of the park was in 1870 when gold was discovered just south of Lake Cuyamaca. By 1872 the town of Cuyamaca had grown up around the Stonewall Mine, and from 1887 to 1891 California governor Robert Waterman developed the area with gusto. When the ore – and Waterman's interest in the mine – petered out, homesteaders tried to make the area into a resort. A Mr Dyars, who was a descendant of a gold rush '49er, bought the rancho in 1923 and 10 years later helped create the state park. The Dyars' former home is now the park headquarters (☎ 760-765-0755), open 8 am to 4:30 pm Monday to Friday, and a museum with a good display on local Native American culture (open daily; free).

The park is popular with hikers, mountain bikers and equestrians and has miles of well-defined trails that start from trailhead parking lots along Hwy 79; maps are posted at each trailhead. Two recommended hikes are the 5½-mile (round-trip) climb to Cuyamaca Peak (6512 feet), offering a panoramic view, and the 4½-mile hike up Stonewall Peak (5730 feet) to look over the old mine site. You can also drive to the mine site: turn east off Hwy 79 at the 'Los Caballos Campground' sign, 1 mile north of Paso Picacho Campground.

There are two drive-in campgrounds in the park, *Green Valley* and *Paso Picacho*, both charging $12 per site ($15 from April to October); Paso Picacho also has cabins for $30. Also here is *Los Caballos*, an equestrian campground equipped with corrals (also $12/15). For reservations call Parknet (☎ 800-444-7275) or go online at reserveamerica.com.

Highway 79, which can be approached from the north, via Julian, or the south, off I-8, goes right through the park. Coming from the south, there's a shop, pay phone and a place to eat (closed Tuesday) at Descanso. There's also a shop, bar and restaurant at Lake Cuyamaca on the north side of the park. For maps and information, stop at one of the campground entrance kiosks or (in winter) at the office upstairs in the park headquarters. There's a $5 day-use fee, which you put in an envelope when you park.

Anza-Borrego Desert State Park

The desert that contains the 600,000-acre Anza-Borrego Desert State Park has some of the most spectacular and accessible desert scenery you'll find anywhere. The human history here goes back 10,000 years, recorded in ancient Native American pictographs. Spanish explorer Juan Bautista de Anza passed through in 1774, pioneering an immigrant trail from Mexico. The Mormon Battalion came this way to fight the Californios, and the Southern Emigrant Trail and the Butterfield Stageline followed a route along the Vallecito Valley in the southern part of the park.

There are three different sections to the park, each near a major travel artery; you really need a car to get around and to access the many points of interest.

The area around Borrego Springs is the most visited and can get crowded on weekends, especially during the wildflower bloom in February and March (call ☎ 760-767-4684 for updated blooming information). It's a good destination for first timers and day-trippers, since it's home to the excellent visitor center. From here, easy-to-reach sights include Font's Point to the east and Borrego Palm Canyon to the west. The Fish Creek area is popular with off-road vehicles, but also contains interesting geology and spectacular wind caves. The desert's southernmost region, near Ocotillo (not to be confused with Ocotillo Wells farther north), is the least visited and has few developed trails and facilities. Attractions here, besides the solitude, include Goat Canyon Trestle and the Carrizo Badlands.

The Anza-Borrego Desert State Park Visitors Center (☎ 760-767-5311), on the western end of Palm Canyon Dr, some 2 miles west of Borrego Springs (see below), is open 9 am to 5 pm daily October to May, otherwise weekends and holidays only. It has a small theater with a short slide show on the natural history of the park as well as exhibits on desert flora and fauna and plenty of publications. The staff is helpful and well informed.

Borrego Springs Centered around Christmas Circle, this little town is completely surrounded by the Anza-Borrego Desert State Park and is its commercial hub. The town provides lodging, shops, restaurants and gas to park visitors. There are several golf courses, expensive resorts and several mobile home and RV parks catering to hundreds of 'snowbirds' escaping northern winters.

Peg Leg Smith Monument & Liars Contest Northeast of Borrego Springs, where S22 takes a 90° turn to the east, there's a pile of rocks just north of the road. This is a monument to Thomas Long 'Peg Leg' Smith – mountain man, fur trapper, Indian fighter, horse thief, liar and Wild West legend. Around 1829, Peg Leg passed through Borrego Springs on his way to Los Angeles and supposedly picked up some rocks that were later found to be pure gold. Strangely, he didn't return to the area until the 1850s, when he was unable to find the lode. Nevertheless, he told lots of people about it, and many came to search for the gold and add to the myths.

On the first Saturday of April, the Peg Leg Liars Contest is a hilarious event in which amateur liars compete in the western tradition of telling tall tales. Anyone can enter, so long as the story is about gold and mining in the Southwest, is less than five minutes long and is anything but the truth.

Font's Point A 4-mile dirt road, usually passable without 4WD goes south of S22 to Font's Point, which offers a spectacular panorama over the Borrego Valley to the west and the Borrego Badlands to the south. Walking the 4 miles to the point is a good way to *really* be amazed when the desert seemingly drops from beneath your feet.

Split Mountain Going south from Hwy 78 at Ocotillo Wells, paved Split Mountain Rd leads to a dirt-road turnoff for Fish Creek

Primitive Camp and Split Mountain. The road goes right through the mountain flanked by 600-foot-high walls created by earthquakes and erosion. The gorge is about 2 miles long. At its south end, steep trails lead up to delicate caves carved into the sandstone outcroppings by wind. On Split Mountain Rd you pass the Elephant Trees Discovery Trail, one of the few places to see a herd of the unusual elephant trees, and a small ranger station. The road is very popular with off-road vehicle drivers, but is usually navigable by passenger car, although vehicles with high clearance are preferable.

Blair Valley This area, near S2 some 8 miles southeast of Scissors Crossing, has pleasant campsites and some attractive walks, but is also of particular archaeological interest. Short trails lead to sites with pictographs by indigenous people and *morteros* (hollows in rocks used for grinding seeds).

A monument at Foot and Walker Pass marks a difficult spot on the Butterfield Overland Stage Route, and in Box Canyon you can still see the marks of wagons on the Emigrant Trail. A steep 1-mile climb leads to Ghost Mountain and the remains of a house occupied by the family of desert recluse Marshall South.

Vallecito Stage Station Going west on S2, both the Southern Emigrant Trail and the Butterfield Overland Stage Route crossed the fiercely hot and dry Imperial Valley, then followed the Vallecito Creek up into the mountains for the final part of the journey to the coast. The supposedly haunted Vallecito station was built in 1852 as a major stop on the route, though the present building is a 1934 reconstruction.

Hiking The Borrego Palm Canyon Nature Trail is a popular self-guiding loop trail that goes northeast from the Borrego Palm Canyon Campground, climbing 350 feet in 3 miles past a palm grove and waterfall, which make a delightful oasis in the dry rocky countryside.

A variety of other short trails have been laid out, many of them with informative little signs or self-guiding brochures – different trails highlight different features. The 1-mile Cactus Loop Nature Trail is a good place to see a variety of cacti. Nearby, the 2-mile Yaqui Well Nature Trail has many labeled desert plants and passes a natural water hole that attracts a rich variety of bird life as well as the occasional bighorn sheep in winter. The Narrows Earth Trail, 2 miles east of Tamarisk Grove, is a short trail that highlights the local geology but also has some unusual chuparosa shrubs, which attract hummingbirds.

A dirt road, which may require 4WD, goes 3 miles off S22 to within a few hundred yards of Seventeen Palms Oasis, which is a permanent water source and a great place to spot wildlife.

Mountain Biking Both primitive roads and paved roads are open to bikes. Popular routes are Grapevine Canyon, Oriflamme Canyon and Canyon Sin Nombre. The visitors center has a free mountain bike guide. Carrizo Bikes (☎ 760-767-3872), 648 Palm Canyon Dr in Borrego Springs, rents bikes for $7 per hour or $29 for 24 hours, and also leads guided rides.

Places to Stay & Eat The park has two developed campgrounds, reservations for which can be made through Parknet at 800-444-7275 or www.reserveamerica.com. *Borrego Palm Canyon*, 2 miles west of Borrego Springs, has basic tent sites for $10 to $16 and others with hookups for $16 to $22, but don't expect a shady haven. *Tamarisk Grove Campground*, on S3, 12 miles south of Borrego Springs near Hwy 78, is smaller but has more shelter and 27 non-hookup sites for $10 to $16.

Bow Willow Campground, off S2 in the southern part of the park, has only 16 first-come, first-served sites, with water, toilets, tables and fire pits, for $7 to $9.

There are several other campsites in the park – Culp Valley, Arroyo Seco, Yaqui Well, Yaqui Pass, Fish Creek and Mountain Palm Springs – that are free but have no water and only minimal facilities. Camping is permitted just about everywhere, though not within 200 yards of any water source; a required backcountry camping permit ($5) can be purchased at the visitor center. You can't light a fire on the ground, and gathering vegetation (dead or alive) is prohibited.

The only hotels in the park are in Borrego Springs. *The Oasis Motel* (☎ 760-767-5409, 366 Palm Canyon Dr) is OK and about the cheapest place in town, from around $40 in summer, $55 in winter ($10 more on weekends); some rooms with kitchenettes cost an extra $10. *Hacienda del Sol* (☎ 760-767-5442, 610 Palm Canyon Dr) is the most central lodging option with a whole range of accommodations. Regular rooms are $55, larger duplexes and cottages range from $85 to $125 and have full kitchens and patios.

Whispering Sands (☎ 760-767-3322, 2376 Borrego Springs Rd) has friendly hosts, some of the cute amenities of a B&B (hammocks, breakfast, guest kitchen) as well as digital TV and barbecues. Rates are $65 to $85 midweek and $95 to $105 weekends with a two-night minimum stay.

Borrego Valley Inn (☎ 760-767-0311, 800-333-5810, fax 760-767-0900, 405 Palm Canyon Rd) has 14 beautifully decorated rooms with a Southwestern theme, great views and a patio; some have fireplaces and kitchenettes. There are two outdoor spas and two pools and mountain bike rentals ($7/half-day). Rates of $95 to $130 midweek and $105 to $150 weekends include a continental breakfast buffet.

In Borrego Springs, the *Borrego Springs Market* on the southwest edge of Christmas Circle is well stocked and has a deli. Several undistinguished restaurants congregate along Palm Canyon Dr, with a few in The Mall, a small shopping center on the south side of the road. Most places close around 8 pm. An exception is *Bernard's* (☎ 760-767-5666), in the Mall (on the south side), which has food service – mostly continental – until 9 pm. Prices are reasonable, if not cheap, and the Wednesday $2.50 hamburger nights are hard to beat. Closed Sunday.

Pablito's (☎ 760-767-5753, 590 Palm Canyon Dr) serves big portions of authentic Mexican food all day long. Locals recommend *D&E's Restaurant* (☎ 760-767-4954, 818 Palm Canyon Dr) for Italian food (main courses are around $8).

Getting There & Around Coming from San Diego, the longest route is via I-8 to S2, but it's freeway most of the way. Many people come through Julian, though Hwy 78 through Escondido can be quite busy with traffic. An extremely pleasant, if curvy, route is Hwy 79 through Cuyamaca State Park. Plan on 2½ hours of driving, whichever route you take.

A park-use permit ($5) is required for any car leaving the highway to access the park and is good for overnight camping in the backcountry; a three-day permit costs $10. Some of the roads in the park are unpaved and not always passable by passenger car. Always check at the visitors center about current conditions before setting out.

Beyond San Diego County

DISNEYLAND

For first-time visitors to Southern California, a trip to Disneyland (☎ 714-781-4565, 213-626-8605; www.disneyland.com) is as *de rigeur* as visiting the Eiffel Tower in Paris. When Walt Disney first trotted out his famous mouse in 1928, it was the beginning of a commercial bonanza that's been relentlessly refined since then. Disney has become a legend of corporate success – and excess – in virtually every field it has entered: movies, TV, publishing, music and merchandise.

Opened in 1955 by Walt Disney himself, Disneyland is 'imagineered' to be the 'happiest place on earth,' from the impeccably clean, pastel-colored sidewalks to the personal hygiene of park employees, all of whom are referred to as 'cast members.' Buildings, rides and costumes are brightly colored and employees grin to the point of rictus, fully aware that if they treat just one person rudely, they may well lose their jobs.

You can see the entire park in a day, but it requires two or three days if you want to go on all the rides. The summer months are not just the hottest but also the busiest, so be prepared for long waits in stifling heat. In general, visiting midweek is better and, naturally, arriving early in the day is best. Bring a hat, suntan lotion, patience and – if cutting costs is your aim – bottled water. Many rides have minimum age and height requirements, so prepare the kids to avoid tantrums.

Information

Opening hours for Disneyland are highly arbitrary and depend on the marketing department's projected attendance numbers. In the off-season, you might expect the park to be open 10 am to 8 pm Monday to Thursday, to 10 pm Friday, to midnight Saturday and to 9 pm Sunday. During summer, weekday hours are often 8 am to 10 pm, extending to midnight on weekends.

One-, two- and three-day passes cost $41/76/99 for adults and $31/57/75 for children. Better value for multiple visits are the new Flex Passports, which cost $76/57 for three and $99/75 for five days of admission within a 14-day period. Parking is $7. There's a baby care center, currency exchange office and banks and a kennel.

Rides & Attractions

You enter Disneyland on **Main Street USA**, a cheery re-creation of small-town America circa 1900 with myriad shops, including the Candy Emporium. Stop to have your picture taken with Mickey and Minnie or any of the other Disney characters that usually hang around here. Plunge on into the seven Disney 'lands' centered around Sleeping Beauty's Castle.

Main Street ends in the Central Plaza. Immediately on your right is **Tomorrowland**, the high-tech showpiece of the park. On the Star Tours ride you're clamped into a 'Star-Speeder' vehicle piloted by a dysfunctional android for a wild and bumpy ride through deep space. Space Mountain will take your head off as you hurtle into complete darkness at frightening speed, and you *will* scream long and loud. On Rocket Rods, you'll blast off on a four-minute breakneck journey. 'Honey, I Shrunk the Audience' lets

you experience what it's like to become sub-miniature and be threatened by insects.

In **Adventureland**, to the left of Central Plaza, the highlight is the Indiana Jones Adventure. Enormous Humvee-type vehicles lurch off for frightening encounters in re-creations of themes and stunts from the famous movie trilogy. Also here is the Jungle Cruise, a mellow expedition through tropical rainforests, featuring encounters with roaring hippopotami and other jungle denizens.

Just beyond is **New Orleans Square**, where offerings include the Haunted Mansion, beguiling you with hokey frights and sights. Also here is the subterranean float through the tawdry land of Pirates of the Caribbean, where buccaneers' skeletons perch atop their mounds of booty. You'll see comical piratical figures loot, plunder and pillage while the villages burn.

Frontierland harks back to the rip-roaring days of the Old West, when cowboys made their own kind of law and order. This is a low-key area of the park, and even small children will emerge unshaken from a ride on the Big Thunder Mountain Railroad roller coaster. Another family favorite is a churning trip aboard the sternwheeler Mark Twain Riverboat.

Fantasyland, in the park center, is approached via Sleeping Beauty's Castle and is filled with the characters and experiences of classic children's stories. Here you'll find Dumbo the Elephant, Peter Pan and rides straight out of Alice in Wonderland. The amazing It's a Small World ride is a float past hundreds of animatronic children from all of the world's cultures joined in singing the theme song of the place. Youngsters are enthralled by this musical voyage, but a warning: days after you've finished picking Disney popcorn out of your teeth, this earworm of a song will still be batting around in your head. (The only sure antidote is listening to the entire collection of Led Zeppelin.) A classic ride is the Matterhorn Bobsled, a roller coaster that's certainly gentle by today's standard but fun nonetheless.

At the northern edge of the park is **Mickey's Toon Town**, another favorite with he elementary school set. This is where Mickey and Minnie make their home (separate ones, of course, this *is* Disney), where Donald keeps his boat, Goofy has a Bounce House, Chip 'n Dale a Treehouse and Roger Rabbit invites you to a Car Toon Spin.

Places to Stay & Eat

The clean and friendly HI *Fullerton Hacienda Hostel* (☎ 714-738-3721, fax 714-738-9925, 1700 N Harbor Blvd) has 20 beds in three dorms costing $11 to $13 each. Bus No 47 runs to the hostel from the Greyhound station; from the Anaheim Amtrak station, take bus No 41. Bus No 43A, which goes straight to Disneyland, stops out front.

The area immediately surrounding Disneyland teems with reasonably-priced motels with all the major chains (Motel 6, Travelodge, Econo Lodge etc) represented. Prices are around $60, sometimes including small breakfast. Most offer shuttle service to Disneyland. Prices may be slightly higher between May and October.

Within Disneyland, the nicest restaurants are the *Blue Bayou* for Southern fried chicken and the like, and *Bengal Barbecue* for more healthful salads and chicken. Otherwise it's mostly burgers, fries, ice cream, and buckets of popcorn.

Outside the park, pickings are slim when it comes to anything other than hotel or chain restaurants. Among the choices are *Tony Roma* (☎ 714-520-0200, 1640 S Harbor Blvd) for ribs, *IHOP (International House of Pancakes;* ☎ 714-635-0933, 1560 S Harbor Blvd) for 24-hour hash house staples and the *PCH Grill* (☎ 714-999-0990, 1717 S West St), inside the Disneyland Pacific Hotel, for California cuisine.

Getting There & Away

Disneyland is at 1313 Harbor Blvd in Anaheim, about 95 miles north of downtown San Diego. Take the Disneyland exit off I-5, then follow the numerous signs.

Amtrak's *Pacific Surfliner* goes through Anaheim from San Diego 10 times daily. The trip takes about two hours, and the first trains leaves the Santa Fe Depot at 6:12 am; the last

train back to San Diego leaves Anaheim at 10:30 pm. The fare is $16 each way.

Greyhound runs nine direct buses to Anaheim in 2½ hours. The first one leaves downtown San Diego at 6:05 am and the last one from Anaheim is at 9:30 pm; the fare is $13, or $22 roundtrip.

Grayline runs organized bus tours that include admission and transportation; see the San Diego Getting There & Away chapter for details.

MISSION SAN JUAN CAPISTRANO

This is one of California's most visited and most beautiful missions (☎ 949-234-1300), with a lush garden and graceful arches, at 31882 Camino Capistrano in San Juan Capistrano, about 65 miles north of downtown San Diego. The charming Father Serra Chapel – whitewashed and decorated with colorful symbols – is the only building still standing where Father Junípero Serra said Mass. Serra founded this mission on November 1, 1776 and tended it personally for many years. With access to San Clemente harbor, and as the only development between San Diego and Los Angeles, this was one of the most important missions in the chain. Like most, it acted as a gathering point for travelers and local land owners, and sustained its own activity with mills, granaries, livestock, crops and other small industry.

Plan on spending at least an hour looking at the grounds and exhibits in the mission museum. The bookstore and gift shop both have mission and early California- related materials. The mission is open 8:30 am to 5 pm daily; admission is $6/5 adults/seniors and children under 12.

The town of San Capistrano is also where the legendary swallows return each year – on March 19, the feast of Saint Joseph – after wintering in South America, just like the song says.

Surrounding the mission are converted adobes that now house Mexican restaurants, art galleries and gift shops. Two blocks south, across Via Capistrano, is a historic district with several adobes dating back to the mission's founding. They once housed businesspeople who thrived on mission activity.

If you're driving, take I-5 due north and get off in San Juan Capistrano. Amtrak's *Pacific Surfliner* makes nine stops daily; the first train leaves the Santa Fe Depot at 6:12 am and the last one from Capistrano is at 11.05 pm. The trip takes about 1½ hours and costs $12 each way. The station is one block from the mission.

TEMECULA VALLEY

The Temecula Valley in Riverside County is the southernmost wine-growing region in California. Wine production started here in the mid-1960s, and the quality has improved steadily over the decades. Developers and tourists have discovered the area with a vengeance, and construction on both sides of I-5 is threatening to turn an idyllic enclave of rolling hills into another tract-home travesty.

The wineries are found along Rancho California Rd, east of I-5. The other area attraction is **Old Town Temecula** itself, which lies about 4 miles west of the freeway. Front St, the main drag, is lined by historic houses, most of which contain overpriced antique stores. Those interested in a bit of history should stop by the **Temecula Valley Museum** (☎ 909-694-6480), 28315 Mercedes St, where they will learn about the town's famous son, Erle Stanley Gardner, the creator of the Perry Mason novels. Other items on display include Native American artifacts, ancient household and farming equipment and an interesting diorama of Temecula of yore. It's open 10 am to 5 pm (Sunday from 1 pm), closed Monday; $2 donation requested.

Look for the bronze plaques attached to many of the buildings that explain a bit about their history. Places to look out for include the Welty Building, which used to be a saloon and is now an antique store; the First National Bank of Temecula, now housing a Mexican restaurant; and the Temecula Mercantile building on Main St.

Wineries

Touring the wineries is a popular pastime, and on most weekends Rancho California Rd is chock-a-block with day-trippers from

Los Angeles, Orange County and San Diego. A microclimate mixing hot inland temperatures in the daytime with cool ocean breezes is what makes this area so suitable for wine-growing. All wineries have tasting rooms where you can sample their product, though usually for a fee of up to $7 including a souvenir glass. Some also give tours, and all have shops where you can buy their wines. The larger outfits have restaurants. Most are open 10 am to 5 pm daily, but this may vary; it's best to call ahead.

The largest of the wineries is **Callaway Vineyard & Winery** (☎ 909-676-4001, 800-472-2377), which makes good chardonnay and merlot (tasting $5). Across the street **Thornton Winery** (☎ 909-699-0099), in a sturdy stone building, is another big one and makes decent sparkling wine in addition to its varietals ($7). **Mount Palomar Winery** (☎ 909-676-5047, 800-854-5177), at No 33820, experiments – often successfully – with several varietals common to Italy but rare in California, including Cortese and Sangiovese ($3, or $5 with souvenir glass). **Cilurzo Vineyard & Winery** (☎ 909-676-5250), at Calle Contento 41220, is a smaller outfit that makes an exceptional petite sirah and charges just $1 for six wines.

Other wineries either on or just off Rancho California Rd are

Hart Winery (☎ 909-676-6300) 41300 Avenida Biona ($2)

Temecula Crest Winery (☎ 909-676-8231) 40620 Calle Contento ($4)

Maurice Car'rie Winery (☎ 909-676-1711) 34225 Rancho California Rd (free)

Keyways Vineyard & Winery (☎ 909-302-7888) 37338 De Portola Rd ($2)

Van Roekel Vineyards & Winery (☎ 909-699-6961) 34567 Rancho California Rd ($4)

Santa Margarita Winery (☎ 909-676-4431) 33490 Madera de Playa (free)

Baily Vineyard & Winery (☎ 909-676-9463) 33440 La Serena ($5)

Stuart Cellars (☎ 909-676-6414) 33515 Rancho California Rd ($4)

Filsinger Vineyards & Winery (☎ 909-302-6650) 39050 De Portola Rd ($1)

MAP 1 SAN DIEGO COUNTY

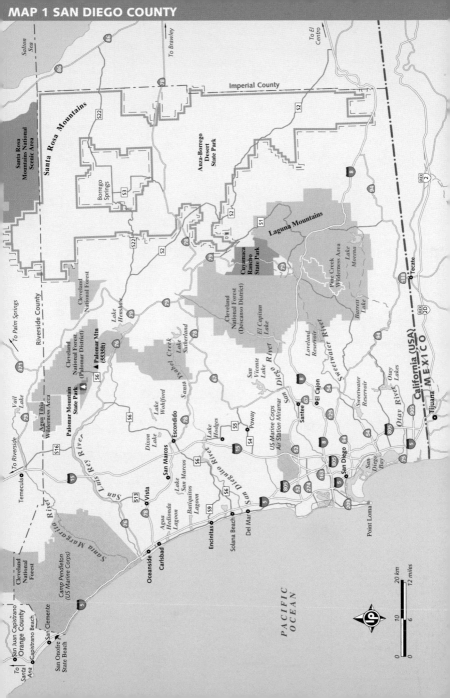

MAP 2 METROPOLITAN SAN DIEGO

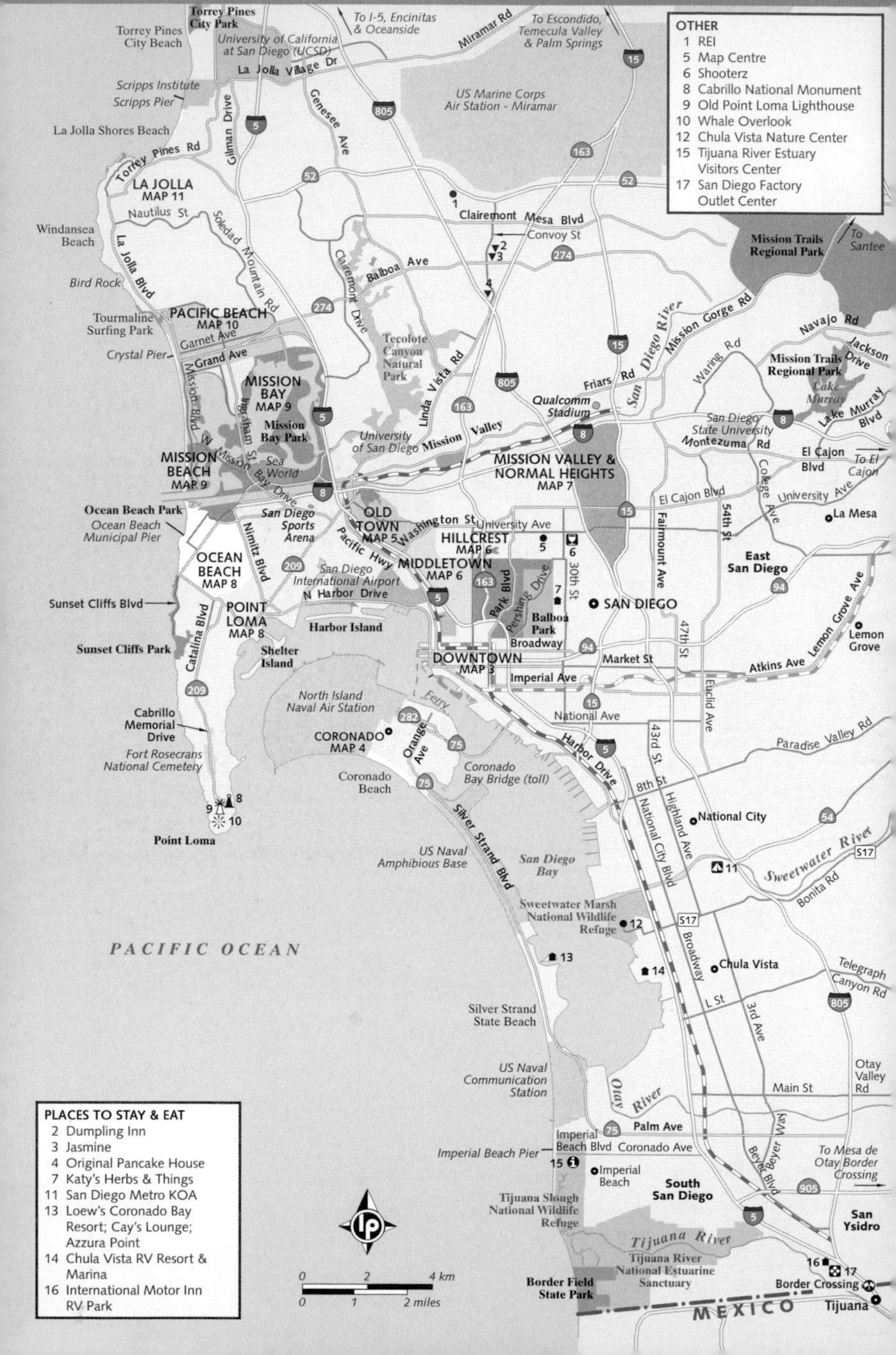

To I-5, Encinitas & Oceanside
To Escondido, Temecula Valley & Palm Springs
To Santee
To El Cajon
To Mesa de Otay Border Crossing

OTHER
1 REI
5 Map Centre
6 Shooterz
8 Cabrillo National Monument
9 Old Point Loma Lighthouse
10 Whale Overlook
12 Chula Vista Nature Center
15 Tijuana River Estuary Visitors Center
17 San Diego Factory Outlet Center

PLACES TO STAY & EAT
2 Dumpling Inn
3 Jasmine
4 Original Pancake House
7 Katy's Herbs & Things
11 San Diego Metro KOA
13 Loew's Coronado Bay Resort; Cay's Lounge; Azzura Point
14 Chula Vista RV Resort & Marina
16 International Motor Inn RV Park

Torrey Pines City Park
Torrey Pines City Beach
Scripps Institute
Scripps Pier
La Jolla Shores Beach
Windansea Beach
Bird Rock
Tourmaline Surfing Park
Crystal Pier
Ocean Beach Park
Ocean Beach Municipal Pier
Sunset Cliffs Blvd
Sunset Cliffs Park
Cabrillo Memorial Drive
Fort Rosecrans National Cemetery
Point Loma

University of California at San Diego (UCSD)
La Jolla Village Dr
US Marine Corps Air Station - Miramar
Miramar Rd

LA JOLLA MAP 11
Nautilus St
La Jolla Blvd
Torrey Pines Rd
Genesee Ave
Gilman Drive
Soledad Mountain Rd
Garnet Ave
Grand Ave
Balboa Ave
Clairemont Mesa Blvd
Convoy St
Claremont Drive
Linda Vista Rd
Tecolote Canyon Natural Park

PACIFIC BEACH MAP 10
MISSION BAY MAP 9
Mission Bay Park
MISSION BEACH MAP 9
Sea World
University of San Diego
Mission Valley
Qualcomm Stadium
San Diego River
Mission Gorge Rd
Friars Rd
Waring Rd

Mission Trails Regional Park
Navajo Rd
Jackson Drive
Lake Murray
Lake Murray Blvd
Montezuma Rd
El Cajon Blvd
College Ave
San Diego State University
University Ave
La Mesa
East San Diego
Lemon Grove Ave
Lemon Grove

OCEAN BEACH MAP 8
POINT LOMA MAP 8
Nimitz Blvd
Catalina Blvd
San Diego Sports Arena
San Diego International Airport
Harbor Drive
Harbor Island
Shelter Island
North Island Naval Air Station

OLD TOWN MAP 5
Washington St
MIDDLETOWN MAP 6
HILLCREST MAP 6
Balboa Park
Park Blvd
Pershing Drive
University Ave
30th St
Fairmount Ave
54th St
47th St

DOWNTOWN MAP 3
Broadway
Market St
Imperial Ave
National Ave
Atkins Ave
43rd St
8th St
Highland Ave
National City Blvd
Harbor Drive
Euclid Ave
Paradise Valley Rd

CORONADO MAP 4
Orange Ave
Coronado Beach
Coronado Bay Bridge (toll)
Silver Strand Blvd
San Diego Bay
US Naval Amphibious Base

National City
Sweetwater River
Bonita Rd
Sweetwater Marsh National Wildlife Refuge
Chula Vista
Telegraph Canyon Rd
3rd Ave
L St
Otay Valley Rd
Main St
Beyer Way

Silver Strand State Beach
US Naval Communication Station
Otay River
Palm Ave
Imperial Beach Blvd
Coronado Ave
Imperial Beach Pier
Imperial Beach
South San Diego
San Ysidro
Tijuana Slough National Wildlife Refuge
Tijuana River
Tijuana River National Estuarine Sanctuary
Border Field State Park
Border Crossing
Tijuana

PACIFIC OCEAN

MEXICO

Mission Trails Regional Park

US Marine Corps Air Station - Miramar

0   2   4 km
0   1   2 miles

olorful apartments, downtown San Diego

rch Aquarium fountain, La Jolla

Surfer dudes, Ocean Beach

MAP 3 DOWNTOWN SAN DIEGO

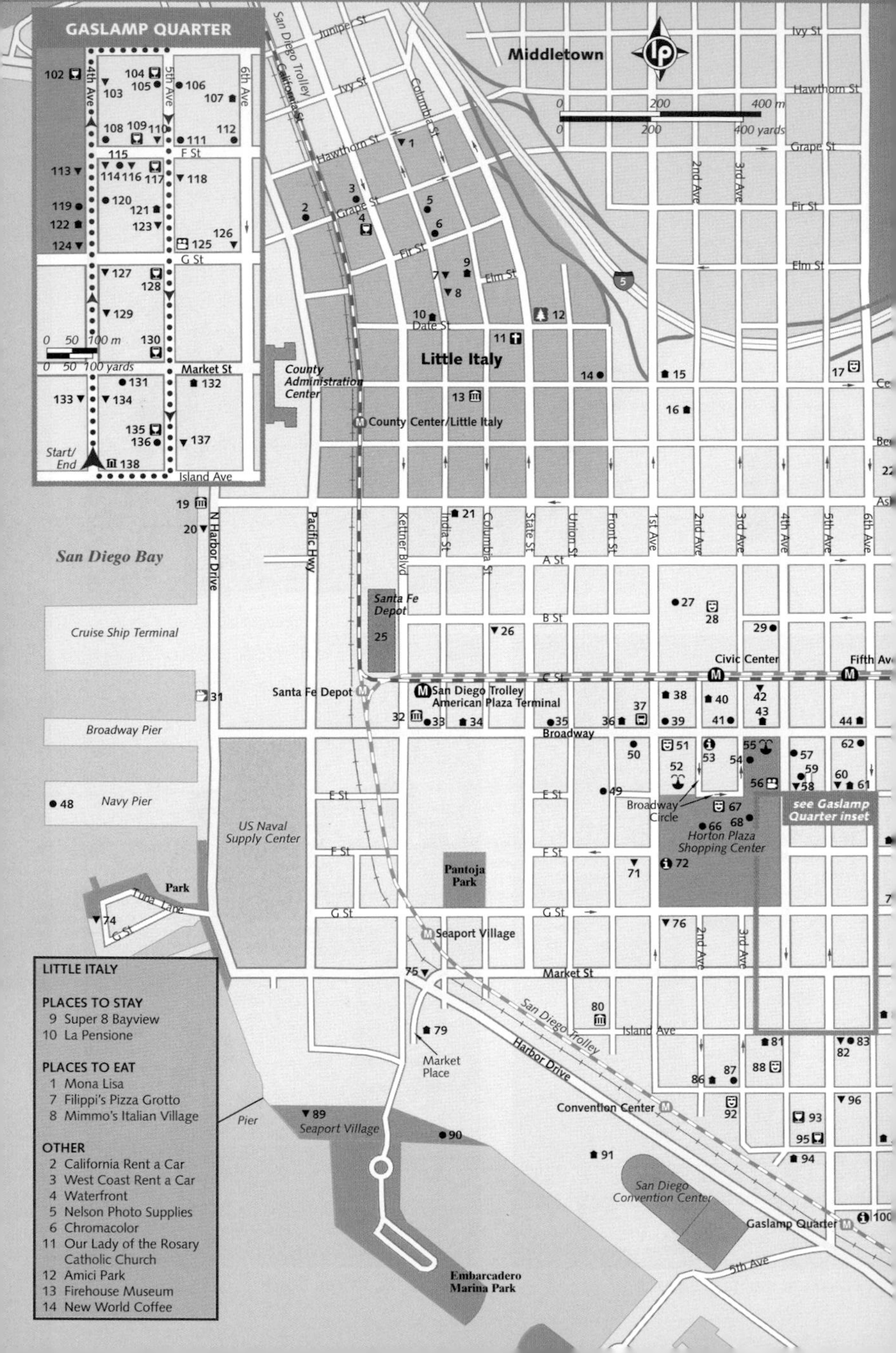

GASLAMP QUARTER

102 ▼

104 ▼ 105 ●   106 ▼
103 ●   107 ▼

108 ● 109 ● 110 ▼
▼ 111   112 ▼

115 ●
113 ▼   114 116 117
118 ▼

119 ●   120 ●
121 ●
122 ▮   123 ▼
124 ▼   125 ▮   126 ▮

G St

127 ▼
128 ●

▼ 129

130 ▮

0 50 100 m
0 50 100 yards

Market St

133 ▼   131 ▮
134 ▼   132 ▮

135 ●
136 ●   137 ▼

Start/
End ▮ 138

Island Ave

4th Ave · 5th Ave · 6th Ave
California St

Middletown

Ivy St
Hawthorn St
Grape St
Fir St
Elm St

San Diego Trolley
Juniper St
Ivy St
Columbia St
Hawthorn St

▼ 1
3 ▮
2 ●   4 ▮
5 ●
6 ●
9 ●
7 ▼   8 ▼
10 ▮
Date St
11 ▮
▲ 12

Little Italy

14 ●   ▮ 15

13 ▮   16 ▮

17 ▮

Ⓜ County Center/Little Italy

County
Administration
Center

2nd Ave · 3rd Ave · 4th Ave · 5th Ave · 6th Ave
5

San Diego Bay

19 ▮
20 ▼

Cruise Ship Terminal

Broadway Pier

● 48   *Navy Pier*

▮ 31

*Santa Fe
Depot*
25

Santa Fe Depot Ⓜ

32 ▮ 33 ▮ 34 ▮

Park
▼ 74

*US Naval
Supply Center*

*Pantoja
Park*

Ⓜ Seaport Village

75 ▼

● 79

Pier

▼ 89

● 90

*Market
Place*

Seaport Village

N Harbor Drive · Pacific Hwy · Kettner Blvd · India St · Columbia St · State St · Union St · Front St · 1st Ave · 2nd Ave · 3rd Ave · 4th Ave · 5th Ave · 6th Ave

▮ 21
A St
B St
▼ 26
● 27
▮ 28
29 ●

Ⓜ San Diego Trolley
American Plaza Terminal

Broadway

35 ●
36 ●   ▮ 38   ▮ 40
39 ●   41 ●
37 ▼
50 ●

Civic Center   Fifth Av

42 ▮
43 ▮
44 ▮

▮ 51
52 ● 53 ▮   54 ●   55 ▮   57 ●
62 ▮
59 ●
56 ▮   58 ▼   60 ▼
61 ▮

*Broadway
Circle*

66 ● 68 ●
67 ●

ⓘ 72

71 ▼

*Horton Plaza
Shopping Center*

*see Gaslamp
Quarter inset*

▼ 76

80 ●

Island Ave

▮ 81
82
▼ ● 83

86 ● 87 ▮   88 ▮

▼ 96

Convention Center Ⓜ

92 ▮
▮ 93
95 ▮
▮ 94

● 91

*San Diego
Convention Center*

Gaslamp Quarter Ⓜ   ▮ 100

*Embarcadero
Marina Park*

LITTLE ITALY

PLACES TO STAY
9 Super 8 Bayview
10 La Pensione

PLACES TO EAT
1 Mona Lisa
7 Filippi's Pizza Grotto
8 Mimmo's Italian Village

OTHER
2 California Rent a Car
3 West Coast Rent a Car
4 Waterfront
5 Nelson Photo Supplies
6 Chromacolor
11 Our Lady of the Rosary
   Catholic Church
12 Amici Park
13 Firehouse Museum
14 New World Coffee

DOWNTOWN

PLACES TO STAY
Holiday Inn Harbor View
Pacifica Hotel
Best Western Bayside Inn
Quality Inn & Suites
Downtown Harborview
Comfort Inn Downtown
Rodeway Inn
Inn at the YMCA
Pickwick Hotel

38 Bristol San Diego
40 Westgate Hotel
43 US Grant Hotel; Grant Grill
44 Courtyard by Marriott; First Interstate Building
61 Gaslamp Plaza Suites
65 Dimitri's Guesthouse
73 Villager Lodge - Gaslamp
79 Hyatt Regency San Diego
81 Horton Grand Hotel
84 Downtown Youth Hostel (The Baltic Inn)
86 J Street Inn
91 Marriott Hotel & Marina
94 Hilton San Diego - Gaslamp Quarter
97 Clarion Hotel Bay View
107 Ramada Inn & Suites; Vignola
121 USA Hostel San Diego
122 Golden West Hotel
132 HI San Diego Downtown Hostel

PLACES TO EAT
20 Anthony's Fishette; Anthony's Fish Grotto; Star of the Sea
26 Karl Strauss Brewery
42 Downtown Fish Joint
58 Rubio's
60 Dakota Grill & Spirits; Club 66
71 Athens Market
74 The Fish Market; Top of the Market

75 Kansas City Barbeque
76 Ralphs
82 Royal Thai Cuisine
89 Seaport Deli; Greek Islands Café
96 Old Spaghetti Factory
103 Bandar
110 Croce's Top Hat Bar & Grill; Keating Building; Croce's Restaurant & Jazz Bar; Shake Rag
113 Sammy's Woodfired Pizza
114 El Indio
116 Star of India
118 Olé Madrid
123 Trattoria La Strada
124 La Provence
126 Buca di Beppo
127 Rock Bottom Brewery
129 The Cheese Shop
133 Chive; former Royal Pie Bakery
134 Café/Club Sevilla
137 Fred's Mexican Café

OTHER
17 Sledgehammer; St Cecilia's
18 AAA
19 Maritime Museum
25 Travelers Aid; Amtrak Station
27 San Diego Concourse; City Administration
28 San Diego Opera; Civic Theatre; San Diego Playgoers
29 4th & B Street

30 Copley Symphony Hall; San Diego Symphony
31 San Diego Harbor Excursions; Ferry to Coronado Island
32 Museum of Contemporary Art
33 UCSD Bookstore
35 Hall of Justice
39 Greyhound Bus Station
39 Transit Store
45 American Express
45 William Burgett
46 Wahrenbrooks Book House
47 Internet Coffee
48 Future Site of San Diego Aircraft Carrier Museum
49 *Excalibur* Sculpture
50 *Light, Water, Rock* Sculpture
51 Spreckels Theater
52 Obelisk Fountain
53 Downtown Information Center
54 Times Arts Tix
55 Irving Gill Fountain; Horton Plaza Park
56 UA Horton Plaza 14
57 Music Trader
59 E Street Alley
62 Samuel I Fox Building
63 Main Public Library
64 San Diego Police Headquarters
66 Rand McNally's Map & Travel
67 San Diego Repertory Theater (Lyceum Theater)
68 Thomas Cook
70 Main Post Office
72 International Visitors Information Center - Horton Plaza
77 Baras Foundation
78 Disabled American Veterans Thrift Store
80 San Diego Children's Museum
83 Bicycle & Pedicabs
85 Merchants Passage
87 Chinese Mission
88 Horton Grand Theater
90 Seaforth Boat Rentals
92 Fritz Theater
93 Dick's Last Resort
95 Hang Ten Brewing Company
98 Dizzy's
99 Sushi Performance & Visual Art Space
100 International Information Center
101 Villa Montezuma
102 Juke Joint Café
104 Onyx Room
105 San Diego Hardware Building
106 Louis Bank of Commerce
108 Ingle Building; Hard Rock Café
109 Patrick's II
111 Marston Building; Fio's
112 Tsunami Beach Club
115 Cafe Lulu
117 Bitter End; Spencer-Ogden Building
119 Coin Laundry
120 Le Travel Store; Council Travel
125 Gaslamp 15
128 Old City Hall
130 Buffalo Joe's
131 Gaslamp Books & Antiques
135 The Field
136 Lincoln Hotel
138 William Heath Davis House; Gaslamp Quarter Historical Foundation

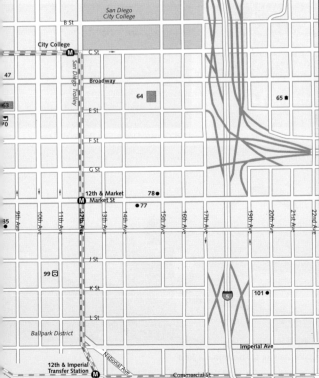

DAVID PEEVERS

Nightlife fever, San Diego style

EDDIE BRADY

San Diego Trolley

RICHARD CUMMINS

USS *Constellation*, San Diego skyline

EDDIE BRADY

Torrey Pines Glider Port pilot waiting for his turn, La Jolla

e ever-fashionable Hotel del Coronado

ed skies over tuna boats, Seaport Village

MAP 4 CORONADO

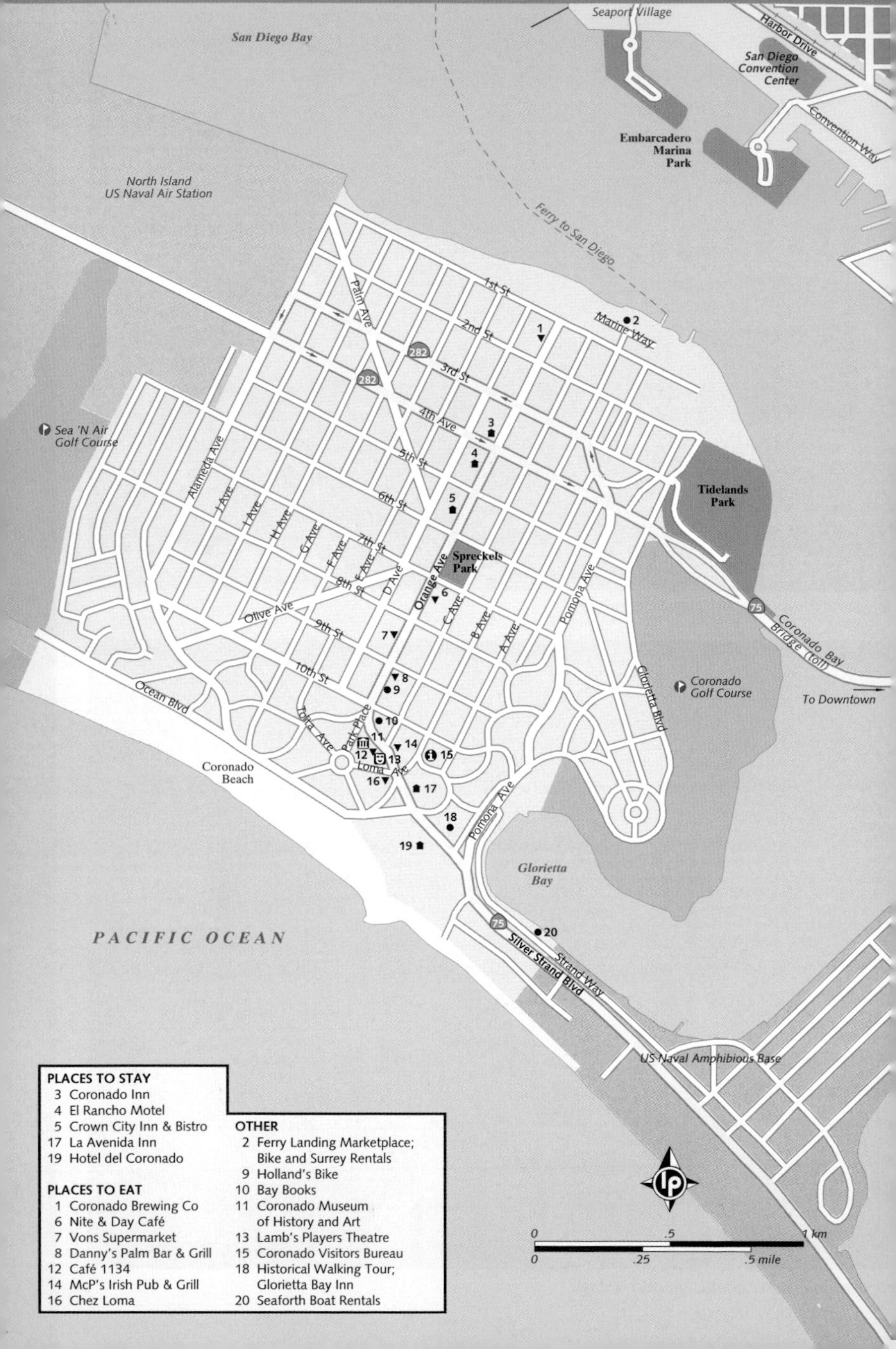

San Diego Bay

Seaport Village

Harbor Drive

North Island
US Naval Air Station

San Diego
Convention
Center

Embarcadero
Marina
Park

Convention Way

Ferry to San Diego

Palm Ave

1st St

2nd St

Marine Way

282

3rd St

282

4th Ave

5th St

Sea 'N Air
Golf Course

Tidelands
Park

6th St

Alameda Ave

I Ave

H Ave

G Ave

F Ave

D Ave

7th St

Spreckels
Park

Orange Ave

C Ave

B Ave

A Ave

Pomona Ave

Olive Ave

9th St

Glorietta Blvd

Coronado
Golf Course

10th St

Ocean Blvd

Loma Ave

Park Place

To Downtown

75

Coronado Bay
Bridge (Toll)

Coronado
Beach

Flora Ave

Pomona Ave

PACIFIC OCEAN

Glorietta
Bay

75

Silver Strand Blvd

Strand Way

US Naval Amphibious Base

PLACES TO STAY
3 Coronado Inn
4 El Rancho Motel
5 Crown City Inn & Bistro
17 La Avenida Inn
19 Hotel del Coronado

PLACES TO EAT
1 Coronado Brewing Co
6 Nite & Day Café
7 Vons Supermarket
8 Danny's Palm Bar & Grill
12 Café 1134
14 McP's Irish Pub & Grill
16 Chez Loma

OTHER
2 Ferry Landing Marketplace;
   Bike and Surrey Rentals
9 Holland's Bike
10 Bay Books
11 Coronado Museum
   of History and Art
13 Lamb's Players Theatre
15 Coronado Visitors Bureau
18 Historical Walking Tour;
   Glorietta Bay Inn
20 Seaforth Boat Rentals

0   .5   1 km
0   .25   .5 mile

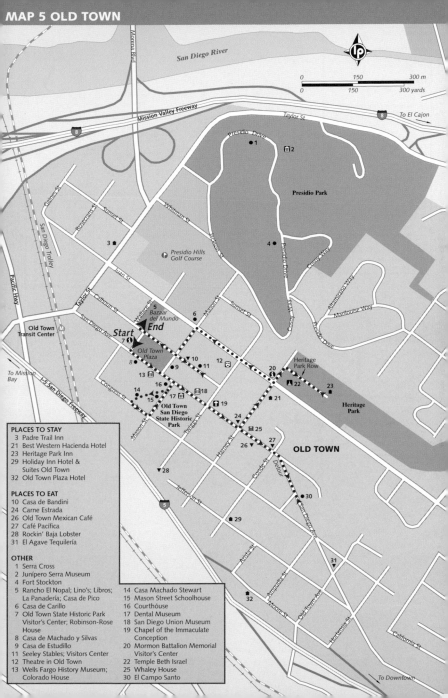

MAP 5 OLD TOWN

San Diego River

To El Cajon

Presidio Park

Presidio Hills
Golf Course

Bazaar
del Mundo

Start

End

Old Town
Transit Center

To Mission
Bay

Old Town
Plaza

Old Town
San Diego
State Historic
Park

Heritage
Park Row

Heritage
Park

OLD TOWN

To Downtown

PLACES TO STAY
3 Padre Trail Inn
21 Best Western Hacienda Hotel
23 Heritage Park Inn
29 Holiday Inn Hotel &
   Suites Old Town
32 Old Town Plaza Hotel

PLACES TO EAT
10 Casa de Bandini
24 Carne Estrada
26 Old Town Mexican Café
27 Café Pacifica
28 Rockin' Baja Lobster
31 El Agave Tequilería

OTHER
1 Serra Cross
2 Junípero Serra Museum
4 Fort Stockton
5 Rancho El Nopal; Lino's; Libros;
   La Panadería; Casa de Pico
6 Casa de Carillo
7 Old Town State Historic Park
   Visitor's Center; Robinson-Rose
   House
8 Casa de Machado y Silvas
9 Casa de Estudillo
11 Seeley Stables; Visitors Center
12 Theatre in Old Town
13 Wells Fargo History Museum;
   Colorado House

14 Casa Machado Stewart
15 Mason Street Schoolhouse
16 Courthouse
17 Dental Museum
18 San Diego Union Museum
19 Chapel of the Immaculate
   Conception
20 Mormon Battalion Memorial
   Visitor's Center
22 Temple Beth Israel
25 Whaley House
30 El Campo Santo

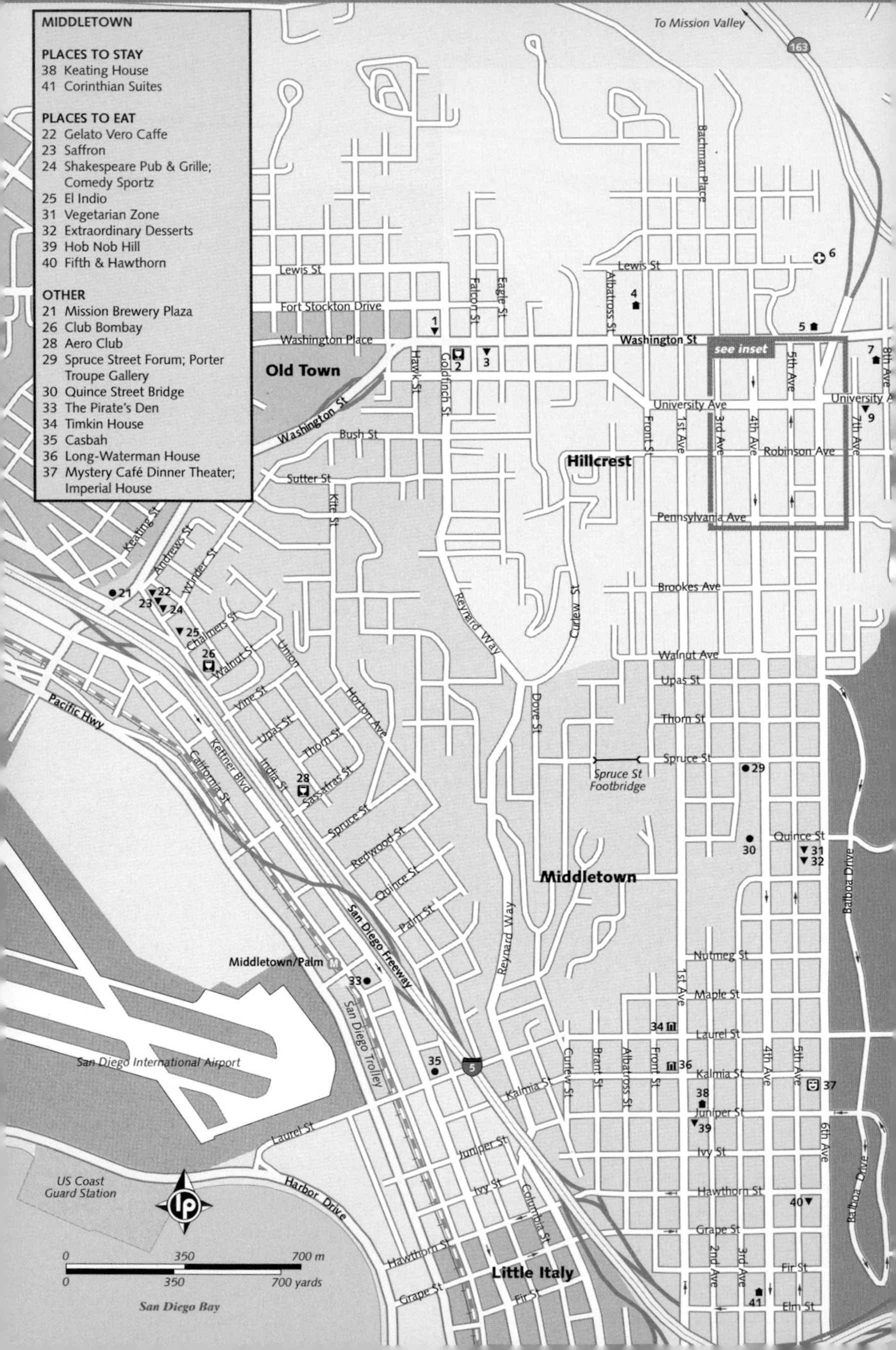

MAP 6 HILLCREST & MIDDLETOWN

MIDDLETOWN

PLACES TO STAY
38 Keating House
41 Corinthian Suites

PLACES TO EAT
22 Gelato Vero Caffe
23 Saffron
24 Shakespeare Pub & Grille;
    Comedy Sportz
25 El Indio
31 Vegetarian Zone
32 Extraordinary Desserts
39 Hob Nob Hill
40 Fifth & Hawthorn

OTHER
21 Mission Brewery Plaza
26 Club Bombay
28 Aero Club
29 Spruce Street Forum; Porter
    Troupe Gallery
30 Quince Street Bridge
33 The Pirate's Den
34 Timkin House
35 Casbah
36 Long-Waterman House
37 Mystery Café Dinner Theater;
    Imperial House

To Mission Valley
163

Lewis St
Fort Stockton Drive
Washington Place

Lewis St
Washington St
see inset

6

5

7
8th Ave

University Ave
University A
Robinson Ave

Old Town

Hillcrest

Bush St

Sutter St

Brookes Ave

Pennsylvania Ave

Walnut Ave
Upas St

21
22
23   24
25
26

Thorn St
Spruce St

29

Spruce St
Footbridge

Quince St
30   31
32

Middletown

Pacific Hwy

Aero Club 28

Middletown/Palm

33

San Diego International Airport

35

5

34
36
Kalmia St
38
Juniper St
39

Nutmeg St
Maple St
Laurel St

37

40

US Coast
Guard Station

Laurel St

Harbor Drive

Juniper St
Ivy St

Ivy St
Hawthorn St

Grape St
Fir St

41
Elm St

0   350   700 m
0   350   700 yards

San Diego Bay

Little Italy

HILLCREST

PLACES TO STAY
4 Kasa Korbett
5 Sommerset Suites Hotel
7 Friendship Hotel
27 Balboa Park Inn
64 Hillcrest Inn Hotel

PLACES TO EAT
1 The Gathering
3 Parallel 33
9 Whole Foods
15 Montana's American Grill
43 Bombay
44 Kemo Sabe
46 Corvette Diner
48 Hamburger Mary's
49 Bread & Cie
50 Kitima Thai
53 Taste of Thai
62 Crest Café

OTHER
2 The Lamplighter
6 Scripps Mercy Hospital

8 Hillcrest Farmers Market
10 Flicks
11 Obelisk Bookstore
12 Rich's
13 Access Center
14 The Alibi
16 Gay & Lesbian Center
17 Casa del Libro
18 Wear it Again Sam
19 The Flame
20 Numbers
42 International Male
45 Hillcrest Cinemas; Village
    Hillcrest Center; News Etc
47 Music Trader
51 WebSurfCafe
52 Apparel Zone
54 Buffalo Exchange
55 Off the Record
56 Kalin Building
57 5th Avenue Books
58 Flashbacks
59 Number One Fifth Ave
60 Bountiful Books
61 Blue Door Literary Bookstore
63 Brass Rail

Street scene in Hillcrest

The Hillcrest Gateway

Doorway in Hillcrest

Hillcrest Farmers Market

ANTHONY PIDGEON

nny day in Old Town

DAVID PEEVERS

n Diego de Alcalá, the first of California's 21 Spanish missions

MAP 7 MISSION VALLEY & NORMAL HEIGHTS

LP

0   .5   1 km
0   .25   .5 mile

To North Coast

Genesee Ave

Linda Vista Rd

Murray Ridge Rd

Tecolote
Canyon
Natural
Park

163

805

Qualcomm Way

Friars Rd

Ulric St

Mission Center Rd

Camino del Rio E

Linda Vista Rd

Mission Valley

Rio Vista

6

11

10

9

Hazard Center Drive

Hazard Center

Mission Valley
Center

Mission Valley
Center

12

13

8

7

Fashion Valley Shopping Center

Fashion Valley
Transit Center

Camino de la Reina

Camino del Rio N

Camino del Rio N

Camino del Rio S

Camino del Rio S

Friars Rd

Fashion Valley Rd

Riverwalk Golf Course

26

27

28

29

30

31

Adams Ave

Madison Ave

Monroe Ave

Meade Ave

El Cajon Blvd

Hotel Circle N

Hotel Circle S

To Ocean
Beach

8

19

20

21

22

23

24

25

Bachman Place

Cleveland Ave

Campus Ave

North Ave

Mississippi St

Park Blvd

Lewis St
Fort Stockton Drive

HILLCREST

OLD TOWN

Washington St

Washington St

University Ave

6th Ave

5th Ave

4th Ave

1st Ave

Columbia St

Georgia St

Florida St

Alabama St

Louisiana St

Texas St

Arizona St

Hamilton St

Oregon St

Lincoln Ave

Lincoln Ave

Richmond St

Normal St

Park Blvd

163

33

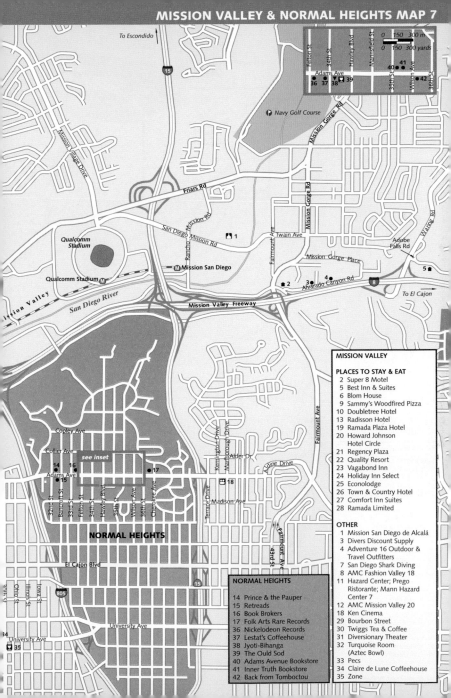

MISSION VALLEY & NORMAL HEIGHTS MAP 7

MISSION VALLEY

PLACES TO STAY & EAT
- 2 Super 8 Motel
- 5 Best Inn & Suites
- 6 Blom House
- 9 Sammy's Woodfired Pizza
- 10 Doubletree Hotel
- 13 Radisson Hotel
- 19 Ramada Plaza Hotel
- 20 Howard Johnson Hotel Circle
- 21 Regency Plaza
- 22 Quality Resort
- 23 Vagabond Inn
- 24 Holiday Inn Select
- 25 Econolodge
- 26 Town & Country Hotel
- 27 Comfort Inn Suites
- 28 Ramada Limited

OTHER
- 1 Mission San Diego de Alcalá
- 3 Divers Discount Supply
- 4 Adventure 16 Outdoor & Travel Outfitters
- 7 San Diego Shark Diving
- 8 AMC Fashion Valley 18
- 11 Hazard Center; Prego Ristorante; Mann Hazard Center 7
- 12 AMC Mission Valley 20
- 18 Ken Cinema
- 29 Bourbon Street
- 30 Twiggs Tea & Coffee
- 31 Diversionary Theater
- 32 Turquoise Room (Aztec Bowl)
- 33 Pecs
- 34 Claire de Lune Coffeehouse
- 35 Zone

NORMAL HEIGHTS
- 14 Prince & the Pauper
- 15 Retreads
- 16 Book Brokers
- 17 Folk Arts Rare Records
- 36 Nickelodeon Records
- 37 Lestat's Coffeehouse
- 38 Jyoti-Bihanga
- 39 The Ould Sod
- 40 Adams Avenue Bookstore
- 41 Inner Truth Bookstore
- 42 Back from Tomboctou

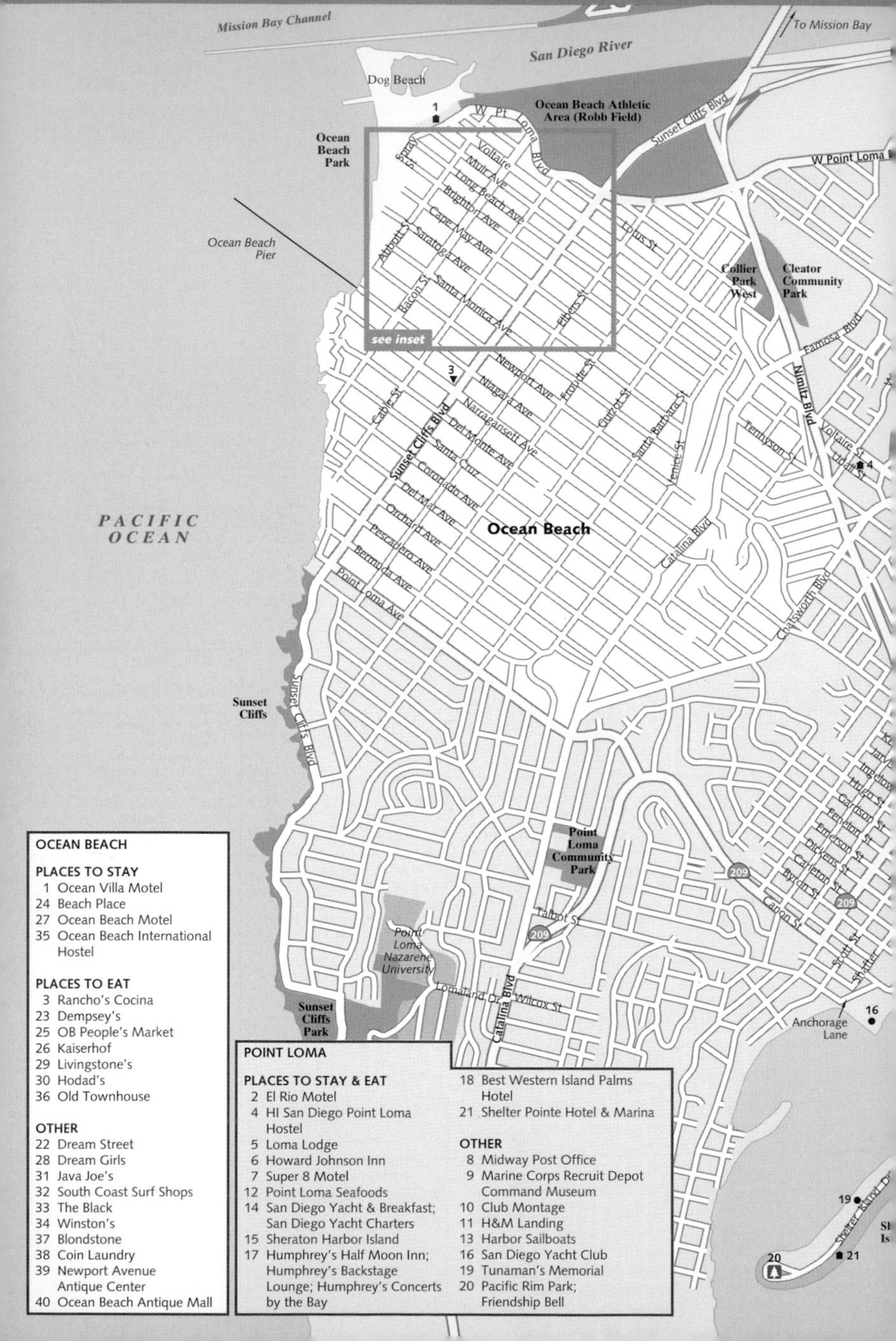

MAP 8 POINT LOMA & OCEAN BEACH

Mission Bay Channel

San Diego River

To Mission Bay

Dog Beach

Ocean Beach Athletic Area (Robb Field)

Ocean Beach Park

W Pt Loma Blvd

W Point Loma

Sunset Cliffs Blvd

Spray St
Voltaire St
Muir Ave
Long Beach Ave
Bright Ave
Cape May Ave
Saratoga Ave
Santa Monica Ave

Abbott St
Bacon St

Collier Park West

Cleator Community Park

Ocean Beach Pier

see inset

Newport Ave
Niagara Ave
Narragansett Ave
Del Monte Ave
Santa Cruz
Del Mar Ave
Orchard Ave
Pescadero Ave
Bermuda Ave
Point Loma Ave

Froude St
Guizot St
Ebers St
Etiwanda St

Santa Barbara St
Catalina Blvd

Famosa Blvd
Nimitz Blvd
Voltaire St
Tennyson St
Chatsworth Blvd

PACIFIC OCEAN

Ocean Beach

Sunset Cliffs Blvd

Sunset Cliffs

Point Loma Community Park

Point Loma Nazarene University

Talbot St

209

Sunset Cliffs Park

Catalina Blvd
Lomaland Dr
Wilcox St

209

Kellogg St
Keats St
Ingelow St
Hugo St
Garrison St
Emerson St
Dickens St
Carleton St
Byron St

Anchorage Lane

16

19

20

21

Shelter Island Dr

OCEAN BEACH

PLACES TO STAY
1 Ocean Villa Motel
24 Beach Place
27 Ocean Beach Motel
35 Ocean Beach International Hostel

PLACES TO EAT
3 Rancho's Cocina
23 Dempsey's
25 OB People's Market
26 Kaiserhof
29 Livingstone's
30 Hodad's
36 Old Townhouse

OTHER
22 Dream Street
28 Dream Girls
31 Java Joe's
32 South Coast Surf Shops
33 The Black
34 Winston's
37 Blondstone
38 Coin Laundry
39 Newport Avenue Antique Center
40 Ocean Beach Antique Mall

POINT LOMA

PLACES TO STAY & EAT
2 El Rio Motel
4 HI San Diego Point Loma Hostel
5 Loma Lodge
6 Howard Johnson Inn
7 Super 8 Motel
12 Point Loma Seafoods
14 San Diego Yacht & Breakfast; San Diego Yacht Charters
15 Sheraton Harbor Island
17 Humphrey's Half Moon Inn; Humphrey's Backstage Lounge; Humphrey's Concerts by the Bay

18 Best Western Island Palms Hotel
21 Shelter Pointe Hotel & Marina

OTHER
8 Midway Post Office
9 Marine Corps Recruit Depot Command Museum
10 Club Montage
11 H&M Landing
13 Harbor Sailboats
16 San Diego Yacht Club
19 Tunaman's Memorial
20 Pacific Rim Park; Friendship Bell

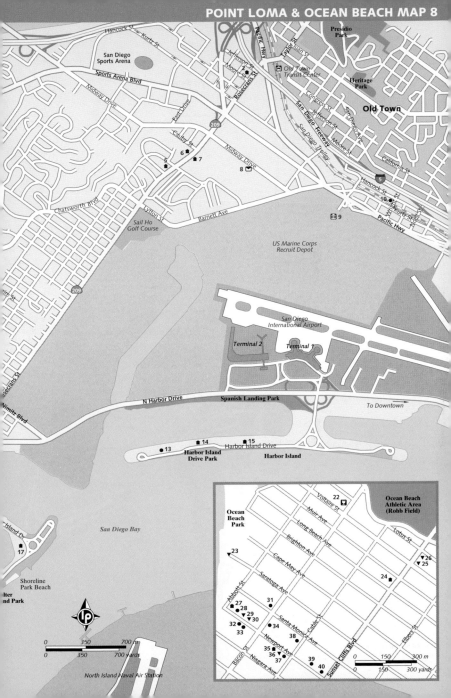

Presidio Park

San Diego Sports Arena

Hancock St

Kurtz St

Jefferson St

Moore St

Sports Arena Blvd

Pacific Hwy

Taylor

Juan St

Old Town Transit Center

Heritage Park

Congress St

Jefferson St

Old Town

Rosecrans St

San Diego Ave

San Diego Freeway

Midway Drive

Barnett Dr

San Diego Trolley

Moore St

San Diego Ave

California St

209

Cauby St

6 ■ 7

5

Midway Drive

8 ✉

Hancock St

5

10 ■ Kurtz St

Chatsworth Blvd

Lytton St

Barnett Ave

9

Pacific Hwy

Sail Ho Golf Course

209

US Marine Corps Recruit Depot

Nimitz Blvd

San Diego International Airport

Terminal 2

Terminal 1

N Harbor Drive

Spanish Landing Park

To Downtown

14

15

13

Harbor Island Drive Park

Harbor Island Drive

Harbor Island

Island Dr

17

San Diego Bay

Shoreline Park Beach

nd Park

Voltaire St

22

Ocean Beach Athletic Area (Robb Field)

Ocean Beach Park

Muir Ave

Long Beach Ave

Brighton Ave

Lotus St

23

Cape May Ave

Saratoga Ave

26

25

24

Abbott St

27

28

31

Santa Monica Ave

29

30

34

Cable St

Froude St

32

33

38

Newport Ave

35

36

37

Niagara Ave

39

40

Sunset Cliffs Blvd

Bacon St

0   350   700 m

0   350   700 yards

0   150   300 m

0   150   300 yards

North Island Naval Air Station

MAP 9 MISSION BAY & MISSION BEACH

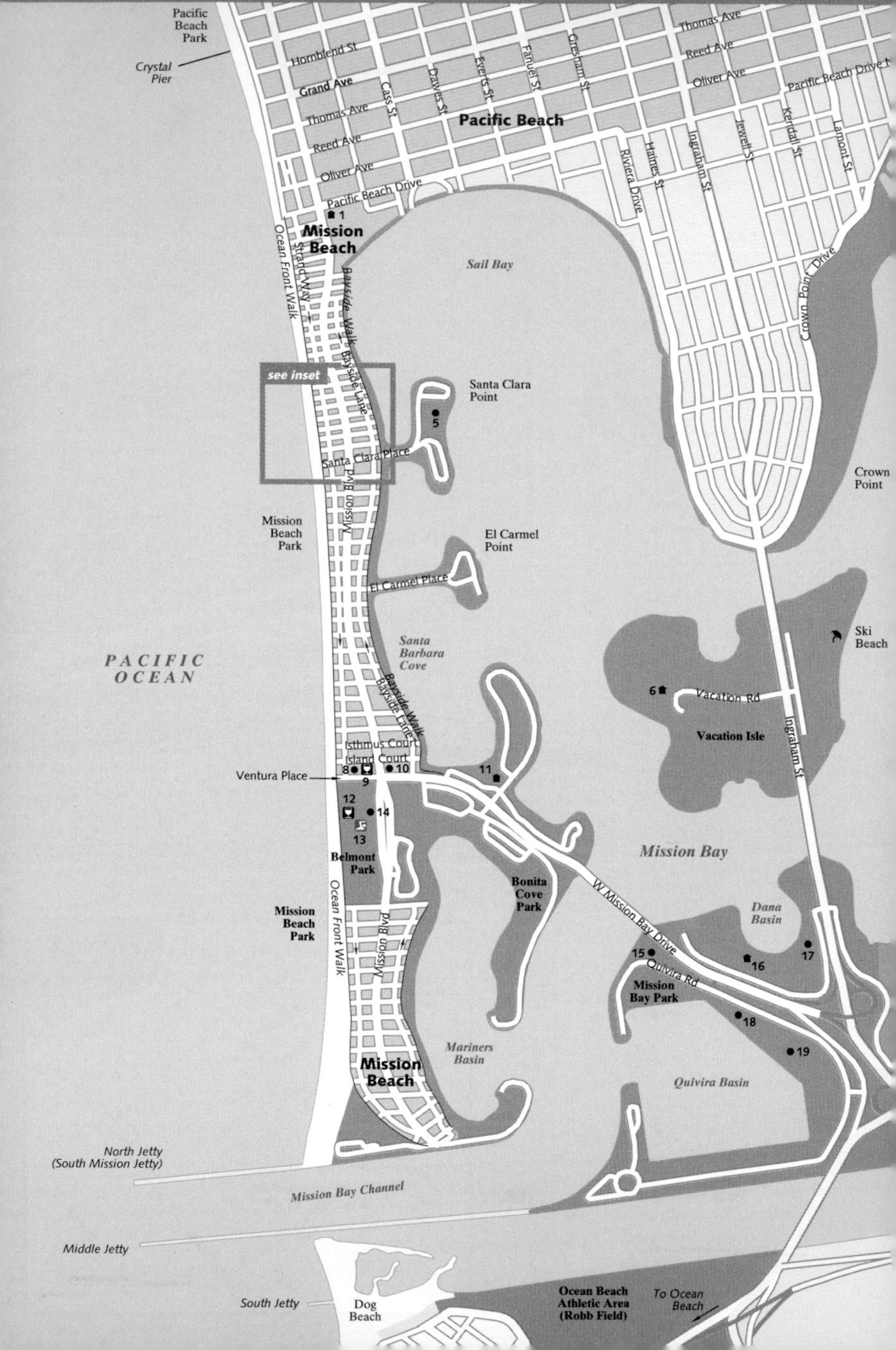

Pacific Beach Park

Crystal Pier

Pacific Beach

Hornblend St
Grand Ave
Thomas Ave
Reed Ave
Oliver Ave
Pacific Beach Drive

Thomas Ave
Reed Ave
Oliver Ave
Pacific Beach Drive

Cass St
Dawes St
Everts St
Fanuel St
Gresham St
Haines St
Riviera Drive
Jewell St
Ingraham St
Kendall St
Lamont St

Crown Point Drive

Mission Beach

Ocean Front Walk
Mission Blvd

Bayside Walk

Bayside Lane

Sail Bay

see inset

Santa Clara Point

Santa Clara Place

El Carmel Point

Mission Beach Park

El Carmel Place

Bayside Walk

Bayside Lane

Santa Barbara Cove

Isthmus Court
Island Court

Ventura Place

Belmont Park

Mission Beach Park

Ocean Front Walk

Mission Blvd

PACIFIC OCEAN

Crown Point

Ski Beach

Vacation Rd
Vacation Isle

Ingraham St

Mission Bay

W Mission Bay Drive

Bonita Cove Park

Dana Basin

Quivira Rd
Mission Bay Park

Mission Beach

Mariners Basin

Quivira Basin

North Jetty
(South Mission Jetty)

Mission Bay Channel

Middle Jetty

South Jetty   Dog Beach

Ocean Beach Athletic Area (Robb Field)

To Ocean Beach

1
5
6
8
9
10
11
12
13
14
15
16
17
18
19

Mission Bay Park

2

De Anza Cove

De Anza Harbor Route

Rose Creek Shore Drive

3

Claremont Drive

4

Mission Bay Park

Mission Bay

Fiesta Island

Fiesta Island Rd

7

E Mission Bay Drive

Pacific Passage

Sea World

Mission Bay Park

Sea World Drive

San Diego River

Mission Bay Drive

Hancock St

Kurtz St

20

21

San Diego Sports Arena

Sports Arena Blvd

Gesner St

Denver St

Ingulf St

Milton St

Morena Blvd

Morena Blvd

W Moreno Blvd

Friars Rd

University of San Diego

Southern Wildlife Reserve

400   800 m
400   800 yards

Inset: Mission Beach

Seagirt Court
22
Salem Court
23 24
San Jose Place
25
Rockaway Court
Redondo Court
Queenstown Court
26
Pismo Court
Portsmouth Court
27
Santa Clara Place
28

Ocean Front Walk
Bayside Walk
Bayside Lane
Strand Way

Pacific Ocean

0   100   200 m
0   100   200 yards

MAP 10 PACIFIC BEACH

Inset (Garnet Ave / Restaurant Row)

0   150   300 m
0   150   300 yards

Felspar St
Ocean Blvd
Mission Blvd
Bayard St
La Jolla-Mirest Drive
Cass St
Dawes St

43 ▽ 44 ▽
47 ▼ 48 ●
50 ●
53 ● 55 ▼
Garnet Ave (Restaurant Row)
45 ● 46 ●
49 ●
51 ● 52 ● 54 ●
56 ●
38 ▼ 39 ●
40 ● 41 ▼ 42 ▼
37 ■
Hornblend St
57 ☐
58 ●

Main Map

To La Jolla

Colima St
Taft Ave
Linda Rosa Ave
La Jolla-Mirest Drive
Cardano Drive
Soledad Rd

Bird Rock Park

Van Nuys St
Archer St
Agate St

La Jolla Blvd

Turquoise St
Sapphire St
Tourmaline St
Opal St
Loring St
Wilbur St
Beryl St

Pacific Beach

Palisades Park

Law St
Chalcedony St
6 ■
Mission Blvd
Bayard St
Ingraham St
Fanuel St

Missouri St
7 ■
8 ●
Diamond St

Pacific Beach Recreation Center

9 ●
10 ●
Emerald St
11 ● 12 ●
13 ●
18 ● 20 ● 22 ●
16 ▼ 17 ● 19 ● 21 ●

Ocean Blvd
Pacific Beach Park
Felspar St
14 ● 15 ▼
Garnet Ave (Restaurant Row)
Hornblend St

Fanuel St
Crown St
Thomas Ave
Reed Ave
Oliver Ave

see inset

Crystal Pier

26 ▼ 25 ▼
Grand Ave
27 ▼
28 ☐
Thomas Ave
29 ▼
Reed Ave
30 ▼
31 ● 32 ▼ 33 ■
Oliver Ave
Cass St
Dawes St
Pacific Beach Drive
Riviera Drive
Hames St

PACIFIC OCEAN

35 ● 34 ▼
36 ▼

Ocean Front Walk
Strand Way

Mission Beach
Mission Bay Park
Sail Bay

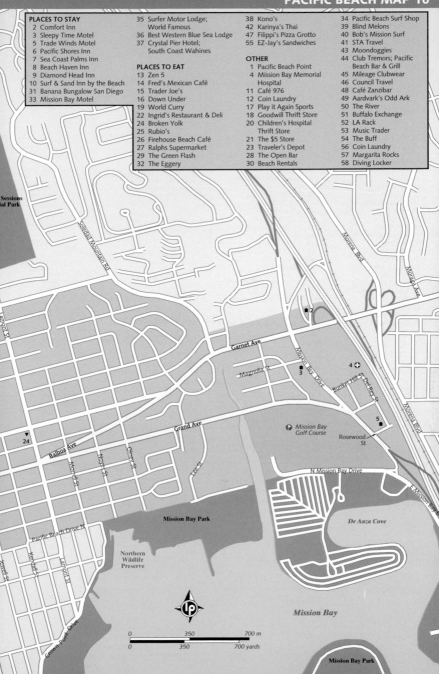

PLACES TO STAY
2 Comfort Inn
3 Sleepy Time Motel
5 Trade Winds Motel
6 Pacific Shores Inn
7 Sea Coast Palms Inn
8 Beach Haven Inn
9 Diamond Head Inn
10 Surf & Sand Inn by the Beach
31 Banana Bungalow San Diego
33 Mission Bay Motel

35 Surfer Motor Lodge;
   World Famous
36 Best Western Blue Sea Lodge
37 Crystal Pier Hotel;
   South Coast Wahines

PLACES TO EAT
13 Zen 5
14 Fred's Mexican Café
15 Trader Joe's
16 Down Under
19 World Curry
22 Ingrid's Restaurant & Deli
24 Broken Yolk
25 Rubio's
26 Firehouse Beach Café
27 Ralphs Supermarket
29 The Green Flash
32 The Eggery

38 Kono's
42 Karinya's Thai
47 Filippi's Pizza Grotto
55 EZ-Jay's Sandwiches

OTHER
1 Pacific Beach Point
4 Mission Bay Memorial
   Hospital
11 Café 976
12 Coin Laundry
17 Play it Again Sports
18 Goodwill Thrift Store
20 Children's Hospital
   Thrift Store
21 The $5 Store
23 Traveler's Depot
28 The Open Bar
30 Beach Rentals

34 Pacific Beach Surf Shop
39 Blind Melons
40 Bob's Mission Surf
41 STA Travel
43 Moondoggies
44 Club Tremors; Pacific
   Beach Bar & Grill
45 Mileage Clubwear
46 Council Travel
48 Café Zanzibar
49 Aardvark's Odd Ark
50 The River
51 Buffalo Exchange
52 LA Rack
53 Music Trader
54 The Buff
56 Coin Laundry
57 Margarita Rocks
58 Diving Locker

MAP 11 LA JOLLA

LA JOLLA SHORES

La Jolla
Shores
Beach

Torrey Pines
City Beach

Torrey Pines
City Beach

Spindrift
Golf Course

0   150 300 m

0 150 300 yards

25
26 27
28
29
30
31

PACIFIC OCEAN

Scripps Pier

●12

Scripps Shores Drive

Kellogg
City Park
La Jolla
Shores Beach

see LA JOLLA
SHORES inset

Point
La Jolla

La Jolla
Cove

La Jolla Bay

La Jolla
Caves

●17

Hidden
Valley Rd

La Jolla
Community
Park

Girard Ave

Torrey Pines Rd

La Jolla
Natural Park

Whispering
Sands Beach

Pearl St

see DOWNTOWN inset

La Jolla
Country Club

Windansea
Beach

Nautilus St

Nautilus St

Bonair St
Playa Del Norte
Playa Del Sur
Gravilla St
Kolmar St

19 20

Bonair Wy
Bonair St
Bonair
Place

Vickers St

La Jolla Blvd

La Jolla Mesa Drive

Bird Rock

Bird Rock Ave

Forward St

21

Midway St

Chelsea Ave
Calumet Ave

22
23 24

Colima St

Bird
Rock
Park

Van Nuys St

Archer St

Taft Ave

0   .5   1 km
0   .25   .5 mile

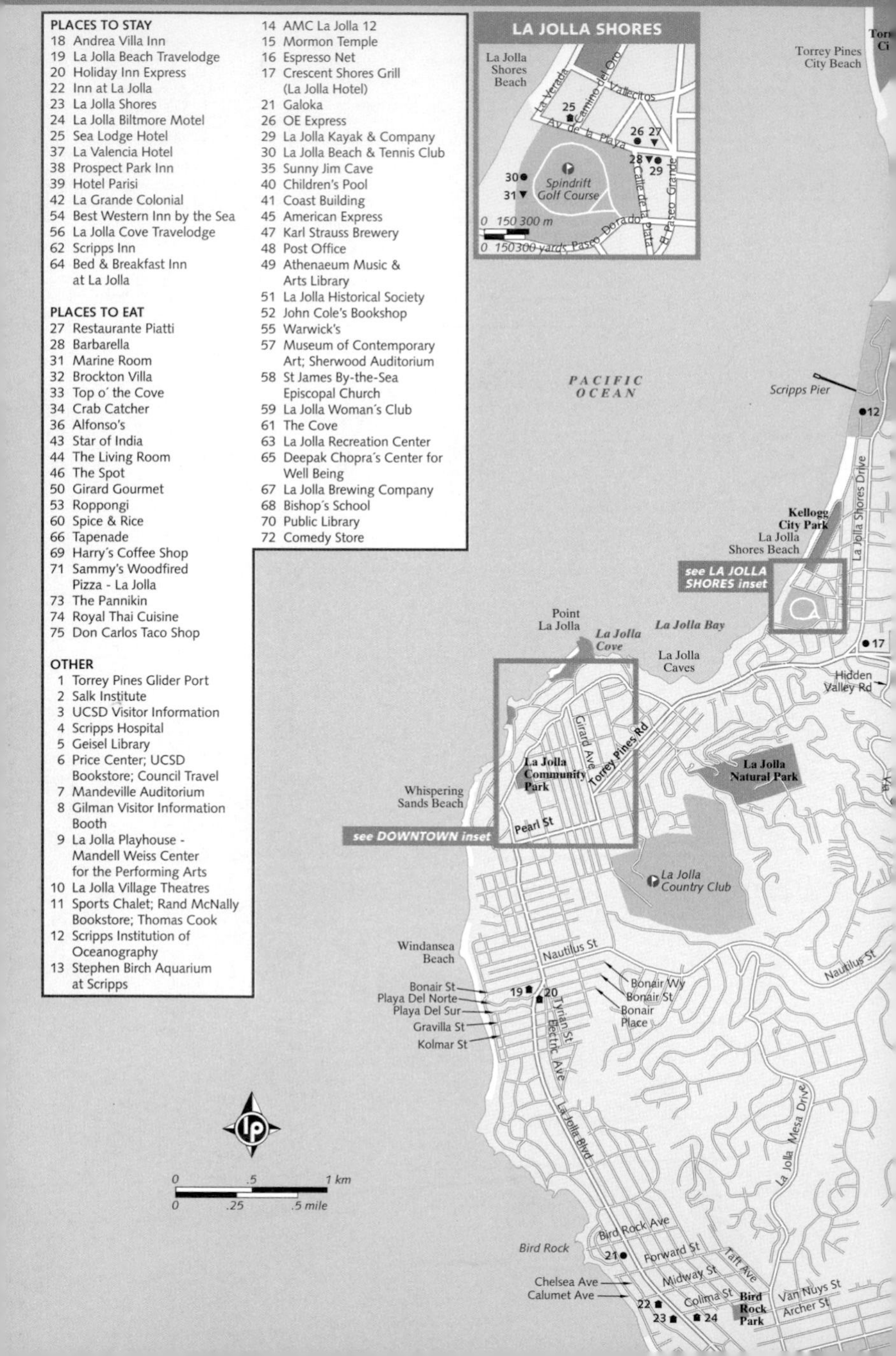

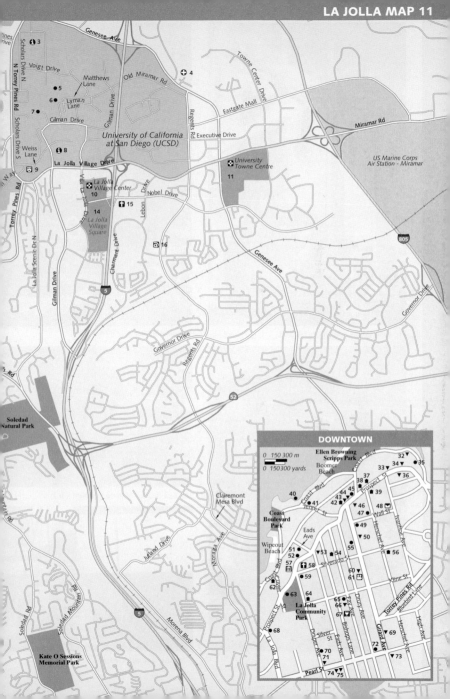

Genesee Ave
Towne Center Drive
Old Miramar Rd
Scholars Drive N
Voigt Drive
N Torrey Pines Rd
Matthews Lane
Lyman Lane
Gilman Drive
Scholars Drive S
Weiss Lane
Gilman Drive
La Jolla Village Drive
Gilman Drive
Regents Rd
Eastgate Mall
Miramar Rd
Executive Drive

3
4
5
6
7
8
9

University of California at San Diego (UCSD)

US Marine Corps
Air Station - Miramar

University Towne Centre
11

La Jolla Village Center
10
La Jolla Village Square
14
15
16

Nobel Drive
Lebon Drive
Charmant Drive
Towne Center Drive
Governor Drive

5
805

Genesee Ave

Governor Drive
Regents Rd

52

Soledad Natural Park

Clairemont Mesa Blvd

Jutland Drive
Morena Ave

5
Morena Blvd

Kate O Sessions Memorial Park

Soledad Mountain Rd
Balboa Ave

0 150 300 m
0 150 300 yards

Ellen Browning Scripps Park
Boomer Beach

Coast Blvd
Prospect St
Jenner St
Eads Ave

Coast Boulevard Park

Wipeout Beach

Coast Blvd
Prospect St

La Jolla Community Park

Silverado St
Wall St
Girard Ave
Drury Ave
Ivanhoe Ave
Herschel Ave
Fay Ave
Cave St
Kline St
Torrey Pines Rd
Bishops Lane
Pearl St
High Ave

32
33
34
35
36
37
38
39
40
41
42
43
44
45
46
47
48
49
50
51
52
53
54
55
56
57
58
59
60
61
62
63
64
65
66
67
68
70
71
72
73
74
75

DAVID PEEVERS

Frontón Palacio Jai Alai, Tijuana

DAVID PEEVERS

Magical Mexican crafts

DAVID PEEVERS

Tijuana arts and crafts

ANDREA SCHULTE-PEEVERS

Jail cell mural, Museo Foreign Club

DAVID PEEVERS

Keeping Tijuana clean

Facts about Tijuana

HISTORY
Prehistory & Mission Period
Until Europeans reached Baja California in the 16th century, upward of 48,000 nomadic hunter-gatherers lived on the peninsula. The area of today's Tijuana was inhabited by the Kumeyaay, who belong to the linguistic group of the Yumanos. They lived in small communities called rancherías, ranging in size from a few families to 200 people or more. They slept in the open, in caves or in simple dwellings made of local materials near a dependable water source such as a spring or stream. Some of the artifacts found in the area, such as arrowheads and kitchen utensils, are displayed at the Museo de las Californias. A few Kumeyaay still live in the rancho of San Jose de la Zorra, about 20 miles (32km) inland from La Misión.

Spanish explorers, who had tried to establish a permanent settlement in southern Baja California starting in 1552, never set foot near the area of Tijuana – but the missionaries did. In 1773 the Dominicans picked up where the Jesuits and the Franciscans, who had founded a string of missions in the southern and central peninsula, had left off, and established several more missions in northern Baja – Tijuana fell under the jurisdiction of the Mission San Diego de Alcalá. When, in 1832, the governor of the Baja territory put an end to the mission system, only the Dominican missions remained intact, as they were considered the only outposts of civilization that connected barren Baja with flourishing Alta California.

Rancho Tía Juana
The Kumeyaay called the area 'tijuan' or 'tiuan,' which means 'close to the water' in their language. The first mention of a Ranchería Tía Juana' – a corruption of the Indian name – dates back to 1809. To formalize settlement of its far-flung territories, the federal government in 1828 decreed that land concessions would be granted to anybody willing to inhabit and cultivate a particular area. Thus it was that, in 1829, territorial governor José María Echendía granted 24,700 acres (10,000 hectares) of land to Santiago Argüello Moraga, who gave his 'realm' the name Rancho Tía Juana.

After the Mexican-American War in 1848, under the Treaty de Guadalupe Hidalgo, Mexico lost New Mexico, Arizona and Alta California to the US. The border between Baja and Alta California, which had been about 20 miles (32km) farther south, near Misión del Descanso, now became the US-Mexican border and was relocated north to Rancho Tía Juana. For the next several decades, though, it was an imaginary line, and the settlement remained a dusty backwater even after the Mexican government opened a formal customs depot there in 1874.

Foreign Investment & City Founding
In the 1880s, the Mexican government, under autocratic President Porfirio Díaz, began encouraging US and European investment in Baja California. As a result, parts of northern Baja, which had been a complete outback without infrastructure, were transformed. The main investor was the International Company of Mexico (ICM), based in the US state of Connecticut.

The ICM made a down payment of US$5 million toward a total price of US$16 million for the right to develop large areas of northern Baja, mostly in Ensenada and as far south as San Quintín. The venture eventually failed, as the company managed to attract only a few settlers, most of whom gave up after several rainless years.

Rancho Tía Juana had not been part of all this activity, but its residents also recognized the need to improve the infrastructure and attract some sort of development. On July 11, 1889, an Ensenada judge granted the descendants of Santiago Argüello the official title to the land and the right to develop the rancho. The founding of Tijuana is now celebrated on this date.

The Fledgling Town

From the beginning, Tijuana's growth was tied to tourism. One of the first steps taken by the Argüello family was to capitalize on the area's mineral hot springs, which had long been enjoyed by the indigenous people. Shortly after the city's founding, they rented the springs to David Hoffman, a San Diegan doctor, who built Tijuana's first 'spa.' Calling his establishment Agua Caliente Sulphur Hot Springs, Hoffman's homemade pump filled six individual tubs housed in a wooden shack. He kept it going for a while, then handed over the operation to the Mizony family, before it eventually fell back to the Argüellos in 1896.

The Argüellos added a small hotel and, over time, the little spa began making a name for itself among San Diegans. This was in no small part due to the marketing efforts of wily William Ruben, owner of a horse-drawn carriage service between San Diego and the dusty pueblo. Despite such efforts, the population grew very slowly, to only 242 in 1900 and less than 1000 by the end of WWI.

Revolution & Its Aftermath

The Mexican Revolution of 1910 lasted a decade and temporarily interrupted growth. War had little impact on most of Baja California, but in 1911 a ragtag army of the Liberal Party, an anarchist force under the influence of exiled Mexican intellectual Ricardo Flores Magón, swept through northern Baja's border towns from Mexicali to Tijuana in an attempt to establish a regional power base. Militant labor organizations like the Industrial Workers of the World (IWW, or 'Wobblies') from the US assisted the revolutionaries – many of whom had been imprisoned or exiled in mainland California – with money and weapons.

The Magonistas, as Flores Magón's forces were known, took Tijuana in a single morning as curious onlookers watched from across the border. However, attempts to establish a government failed because many of the Magonistas were foreign mercenaries

with no interest in structured governmen[t] When the Mexican army approache[d] Tijuana, the rebel 'government' crumble[d] and the Magonistas fled across the border

Prohibition & the 'Golden Age'

Ironically, it was the passage of legislation [in] the US that eventually pump-prime[d] Tijuana's economy. In 1919 the 18th Amen[d]ment to the Constitution – better known [as] Prohibition – outlawed the production, tran[s]portation and sale of alcoholic beverage[s] north of the border. Mainland Californian[s] now came in droves to Tijuana for drinkin[g,] gambling and sex. Hollywood's top name[s] frolicked at the Agua Caliente Spa & Casin[o] (see the boxed text 'America's Deauvill[e:] Tijuana's Days of Glam' in the Tijuana Thing[s] to See & Do chapter). During these years, th[e] city paved streets, improved the water system built schools and attracted industries such [as] breweries, distilleries and even an aircra[ft] factory (headed by later Mexican presiden[t] Abelardo Rodríguez, for whom Tijuana's in[ternational airport is named).

The Agua Caliente closed in 1935 (an[d] later became a high school), after Presiden[t] Lázaro Cárdenas outlawed casinos. But th[e] Great Depression of the 1930s probabl[y] had a greater impact than executive inte[rvention. As bankrupt US-owned businesse[s] reverted to Mexican control and norther[n] Baja became a customs-free zone, joble[ss] Mexican returnees from the US remaine[d] in Tijuana rather than going back to the[ir] hometowns, doubling the city's populatio[n] (to about 16,500) by 1940.

World War II

During WWII, with the US Army absorbin[g] nearly all able-bodied American men, the U[S] and Mexican governments established [a] *bracero* (guest worker) program, allowin[g] Mexicans north of the border to alleviat[e] serious labor shortages. This program, lastin[g] until 1964, led to major growth in border-are[a] commerce, and by 1960 Tijuana's populatio[n] had grown tenfold to more than 180,000.

Immediately after WWII, the city exper[i]enced probably its seamiest era as the inf[a]mous Avenida Revolución attracted U[S]

Lovely Rita

From the fleshpots of Tijuana to the hearts of a nation, the beauty and myth of Rita Hayworth blazed like a comet. Temperamental, vulnerable, gifted, carnal, elegant, drop-dead beautiful and tragic – Rita Hayworth was *woman* to an entire generation of filmgoers. Rita – *not* Ginger – was Fred Astaire's favorite dance partner. And, years before Grace Kelly traded up from Hollywood to royalty, it was Rita who married Prince Aly Khan, the future Aga Khan.

Rita Hayworth was born Margarita Carmen Cansino in 1918 in New York to a Spanish-Jewish father and an Irish-British mother. Her father, an accomplished dancer, enrolled her in dance classes at age three, then teamed up with her as the Dancing Cansinos. The act was soon pulling in $1500 a week, but the lure of bigger money and the glitter of nearby Hollywood brought the family to Tijuana. Here, a prematurely ripe teenager – now calling herself Rita – became her domineering father's dance partner in raging south-of-the-border clubs. Legend has it that Mexico's most famed drink – the margarita – was named after none other than Miss Cansino.

At the age of 15, Rita was spotted by Hollywood studio exec Harry Cohn and signed to a contract with Twentieth Century Pictures. Once in Hollywood, she adopted her mother's maiden name – Hayworth – got a nose job and went to work.

Hayworth's success on the silver screen did not translate into her private life, which was marked by a string of failed marriages. Her film career crumbled in the '50s, but soon a shadow loomed that was much larger than the loss of fame: Rita Hayworth was in the early stages of Alzheimer's, though it wasn't diagnosed until the 1980s. She was cared for by her daughter – the Princess Aga Khan – until she died on May 14, 1987.

- David Peevers

ervicemen from nearby San Diego. In recent ears, Tijuana has cleaned up its act considerbly, though the Zona Norte at the northern nd of Avenida Revolución retains some of ne style (and substance) of the postwar era.

oom to the Present

n every decade since the end of WWII 'ijuana's population has more or less oubled. The current population growth ate is 5.7% per year, twice the national verage and some 85,000 people in real umbers. Foreign and domestic investment f US$1.5 billion annually – much of it in ne burgeoning maquiladora industry (see ne boxed text 'Maquiladoras: Solution or roblem?') – fuel job creation, which stands t about 45,000 per annum.

All this has turned Tijuana into one of the nost dynamic cities in Mexico. But its unontrolled growth has also brought serious social and environmental problems. Demand seriously outpaces the government's ability to provide adequate housing, water and sewage service, as well as paved roads, treatment plants and public health services for many parts of the city. Contamination of the Río Tijuana, which enters the US northwest of the San Ysidro border crossing, is a major binational environmental issue.

Over the last two decades, Tijuana has also become a major gateway into the US for the drug trade. Mexican cartels, especially Tijuana-based Arellano Félix clan, dominate the cocaine, heroin, methamphetamine and marijuana trades. Despite increased cooperation between US and Mexican authorities, officials estimate that 90% of production still makes it to market. Drug-related crime is rampant. When Tijuana's police chief died in a hail of bullets in March 2000, he became the 70th murder victim in the city that year.

Part of the problem is lack of training among police officers. Many have only basic training, and cities like Tijuana find it difficult to replace the large number of officers who are constantly being fired for corruption. The state government is only now building a police academy to train a professional force Growing pains are inevitable, but in the end Tijuana is likely to emerge triumphantly. Young in comparison with the rest of Mexico and even the US, it is still a kind of frontier town, imbued with the energy, creativity and pioneer spirit that goes along with this.

CLIMATE

The climate and weather in Tijuana is very similar to San Diego. For details see the Climate section in the Facts about San Diego chapter.

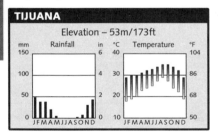

ECOLOGY & ENVIRONMENT

To come to the point: Tijuana is an ecological disaster. This is partly the result of exponential population growth, which has far outpaced the city's ability to provide adequate infrastructure. The other major reason is low compliance with and lax enforcement of existing environmental regulations. Finally, a sad lack of environmental education has resulted in widespread ignorance and indifference among the general populace.

Air Pollution

Air pollution is a major border-region environmental problem. In 1995, nearly 170,000 cars were registered in Tijuana. While this is a small number compared to San Diego's 1.9 million vehicles, the Mexican fleet contributes disproportionately to the problem because of poor vehicle maintenance, ineffi-

cient older cars and the continued use o leaded fuel. The air is most toxic at the Sa Ysidro border, crossed by 82,000 vehicle (1999 figure) on an average day, with man of them forced to idle for long periods o time before crossing.

Tijuana's dusty, unpaved streets, espe cially in the outer residential areas, exacer bate the problem by releasing small particle (PM10), including fecal dust, into the air. Fo years, another major culprit has been th Rosarito power plant, which still uses fue oil – not cleaner-burning natural gas – t generate electricity for northern Baja' households; it is currently being overhaule

Water Pollution

The supply of fresh water and the treatmen of sewage are constant problems in Tijuana The growing population is putting an in creasing strain on the supply of potabl water in the city, which, like San Dieg imports a significant portion of its suppl from the Colorado River (although mos comes from wells). Some 100,000 people i several of Tijuana's makeshift *colonia* (neighborhoods) do not have running wate let alone sewage disposal.

For decades, up to 15 million gallons (6 million liters) daily of raw sewage have le the city via the Río Tijuana channel, whic discharges straight into the Pacific Ocea near Imperial Beach in San Diego. Thi threatens not just marine life but also th sensitive ecosystem of the Tijuana Rive Estuary. A new binational treatment plan just north of the border now intercep much of this junk, but it cannot completel prevent continuing ocean contaminatio Tijuana's own treatment plant, built in 198 is hopelessly inadequate. Built to treat 2 million gallons of water per day, it no treats at least 25 million, meaning tha sewage that is only partially treated ente the ocean just north of Playas de Rosarito

Further strain is caused by maquiladora releasing hazardous solvents and heav metals into the water system instead of di posing of them properly. Outright dumping also common, in large part to avoid the hig cost of adequate disposal or storage. C ourse all of this is illegal even under Mexican law. Enforcement, however, is next to nil. Eventually these chemical pollutants work their way into the groundwater, gravely threatening Tijuana's drinking water supply.

GOVERNMENT & POLITICS
Mexico is a federal republic of 31 states and one federal district. Each state is subdivided into *municipios*, roughly equivalent to US counties. Tijuana is by far the most populous municipio in the state of Baja California, which extends from the border to the 28th parallel, the northern border of the state of Baja California Sur. The capital of Baja California is Mexicali.

Tijuana was an early hotbed for the Partido de Acción Nacional (PAN), the party of current president Vicente Fox, whose 2000 election victory ended the Partido Institucional Revolucionario's (PRI) 71-year stranglehold on federal government. Eleven years earlier Tijuana, along with the rest of Baja California, had become the first state in the nation to elect a non-PRI governor, PAN's Ernesto Ruffo Appel. The subsequent two governors were also PAN members, as is Tijuana's mayor, Francisco Vega de la Madrid. Mayoral elections take place every three years.

ECONOMY
Tijuana is one of the most economically dynamic cities in Mexico, in large part due to its proximity to markets in San Diego and California in general. Almost all products manufactured in Tijuana are exported to the US, with San Diego buying about 36% and other California cities the remainder.

TIJUANA

Maquiladoras: Solution or Problem?

Maquiladoras are factories (wholly or partly foreign owned) that import raw materials, parts and equipment for duty-free processing or assembly by inexpensive Mexican labor. This industry is Mexico's second largest source of hard currency, after oil sales.

The maquiladora program was born in 1964 to create jobs for returning *braceros* (Mexicans who were temporarily allowed to work in the US to alleviate labor shortages). Investment really took off in 1994, after the peso devaluation and the implementation of the North American Free Trade Agreement (NAFTA).

In May 2000 the state of Baja California had 1199 maquiladoras, with 267,000 employees. About 800 are in Tijuana, where nearly one person in three is a maquiladora worker. Most factories are in the industrial eastern district of Mesa de Otay and do assembly of electronics, textiles, furniture and household appliances. More than 13 million TV sets are put together here annually, more than anywhere else in the world; Tijuana has been nicknamed the 'TV-City.'

While the industry does provide jobs and keep down the prices of consumer goods in the US and other countries, it takes a human toll. It looks good on the surface: Maquiladora wages are nearly double the average in Mexico (about US$1 per hour), and jobs provide training and other benefits such as transportation or food coupons. Fact is, though, that most workers cannot make ends meet. Many work two jobs just to afford food and rent. Children as young as 14 quit school to work on the assembly lines to help their families survive.

There are other problems, too. Few maquiladoras provide adequate health and safety training, and poor ventilation and exposure to chemicals have led to an increase in birth defects. Dumping of hazardous waste has polluted the soil in residential areas near factories, causing environmental and health problems. Sexual harassment goes unchecked, and workers trying to unionize are fired or blacklisted.

With these conditions, it is no surprise that illegal exodus to the US has abated little. Many youngsters follow in the footsteps of their uncles, cousins and friends, knowing that in the US they can make more money in an hour as an undocumented worker than in a day at a Tijuana maquiladora.

The main engines powering the local economy are the maquiladoras (see the boxed text 'Maquiladoras: Solution or Problem?' earlier in this chapter), followed by the general service sector, which includes tourism. In 1999, Tijuana's gross regional product was US$8 billion, or nearly one-twelfth that of San Diego's ($91.6 billion). At 0.5%, the city's unemployment rate is significantly lower than the national average of 2.5%. But Tijuana is a long way from the promised land many migrants hope to find.

Wages here are higher by about 11% over the rest of Baja California and by 17% over Mexico. But they're still frighteningly low. In 1999, the minimum wage was 34.45 pesos per day, or about US$3.60 (a 240% increase since 1990). To supplement the family income, some kids as young as eight bag groceries in supermarkets. As a study by the Universidad Iberoamericana in Tijuana shows, making ends meet is a daily struggle

Current president Vicente Fox

for nearly half of the city's families, who live at or below the poverty level.

One problem people face is being stuck earning factory-level wages, in part because the Mexican system does not encourage the formation of small and midsize businesses. Getting loans is impossible for those with subsistence-level incomes, and even the cities have next to no control over how their tax revenue is spent: Most of it goes to the federal government, which distributes it around the country according to its perceived priorities.

One significant factor in Tijuana's economy is the roughly 35,000 workers who legally commute to jobs in San Diego. Although most have low-paying service positions (house cleaners, gardeners, construction workers), their monthly wages far exceed what workers south of the border make. An average maquiladora worker earns about US$1 per hour or about US$160 a month. By contrast, even an unskilled laborer easily earns at least US$250 a week – or about US$1000 a month – in San Diego.

With wages so low, it is easier to understand the desperation that prompts many Mexicans unable to obtain US visas to cross the border illegally (see the boxed text 'The Porous Border').

POPULATION & PEOPLE

Officially, Tijuana's population was placed at 1.2 million in the year 2000, but actual figures are likely to be much higher, perhaps approaching 2 million. Historically the city's growth rate has been three times as high as San Diego's, averaging 5.5% in the 1990s compared to 1.7% for its northern neighbor.

Most of the 85,000 annual newcomers are migrants from other parts of the country, in particular *mestizos* (people of mixed Indian and European heritage) from north-central and western Mexico. Since the 1990s, Tijuana has also experienced an influx of about 15,000 Mixtec Indians from the southern states. About 10,000 non-Mexicans also call the city home, most of them Americans and Chinese. Tijuana is a very young city: One in four inhabitants is under 18, and 60% are between 18 and 65.

EDUCATION

Primary and secondary education are provided by a system of state, federal, municipal and private schools. A burgeoning school-age population, however, has put severe strains on the system, as increased demand has not been met with increased budgets. Classes are taught in two shifts, with many teachers working both in order to bolster meager salaries, sacrificing class preparation in the process.

Salaries may be low, but they do account for about 95% of the education budget, leaving only 5% for operating expenses – 70% of which goes for water and electricity. This leaves almost nothing for maintenance, books and infrastructure.

Still, Tijuana children stay in school longer than youngsters in the rest of Mexico, although certainly not as long as students in the US. School attendance is compulsory from age six to 14, but in 1990 only 88% of Tijuana children actually went to school. Average attendance was only 6.6 years (4.7 nationwide), and the secondary-school dropout rate was about 40%. Not surprisingly, many wealthy Tijuana families opt to send their children to schools in San Diego.

Tijuana is also home to 10 public and private universities, with nearly 14,000 students. The most popular major is business administration, but electronics, computer studies and vocational fields such as mechanics and carpentry are offered as well. The Universidad Autónoma de Baja California, the Centro de Enseñanza Técnica y Superior (CETYS) and El Colegio de la Frontera Norte are the most respected. Also see Universities in the Tijuana Facts for the Visitor chapter.

ARTS
Music

Tijuana has a strong musical tradition that goes back at least to the late 1950s when bona fide blues man Javier Batiz (then mentor to a teenage Carlos Santana) and his group, The TJs, drew crowds to outdoor performances at the Parque Teniente Guerero and at dance halls throughout downtown Tijuana (also see the boxed text 'Carlos Santana: From Tijuana's Mean Streets to Solid Gold' in the Tijuana Entertainment chapter). Batiz inspired scores of other groups, like the Thunderkings, the Rockin' Devils and Los Strangers, and also played with Gene Ross, a blues legend from the US South. In the 1970s, though, as elsewhere in the world, live music took a downturn with the arrival of disco and pop.

Batiz still plays on occasion, but most popular music coming out of Tijuana is rock

The Porous Border

In recent years, the exploding job market in Tijuana and other border towns has been a magnet for hundreds of thousands of migrants from poorer parts of Mexico and Central America. Most find work in maquiladoras or elsewhere and settle down, but many use the region as a jumping off point to the US.

In 1994, the Clinton administration initiated Operation Gatekeeper, a costly attempt to curb illegal immigration. Stepped-up measures include a metal fence, a huge contingent of border patrol agents and sophisticated equipment – floodlights, infrared scopes and motion-detecting ground sensors. But these efforts have done little to stem the flow of border crossers, even if they've made their lives a little harder. It's estimated for every undocumented worker arrested, at least two manage to slip into the US. In San Diego alone, almost half a million people are caught every year.

Illegal immigration is big business. Many would-be illegal aliens (called *pollos*, or chickens) hire a *coyote* or *pollero*, a smuggler who charges as much as US$2000 per person for merely crossing the border, and more for transportation to Los Angeles or beyond. Part of this money is allegedly often used to pay off US immigration officials. Some coyotes operate as individuals, but most are part of highly organized gangs with members on both sides of the border.

and pop. Popular bands playing the circuit include the rock en español bands Genero Humano, Specimen, Los Gatos de la Azotea, La Otra Mitad and El Resto. Other groups to look out for include El Rosario (soft rock and pop); Ohtli (alternative rock); Nona Delichas, with a female lead singer (pop); Los Hijos de Sancho (fusion jazz); and Almalafa (ska).

Tijuana's most recent musical movement is called 'Nortec,' an improbable fusion of techno and norteña. Watch for bands with names like Fussible and Bostich.

Traditional Music These days the guy in the car next to you is less likely to listen to good ol' rock 'n roll than to *banda, norteña* or *ranchera* music, traditional styles introduced to Tijuana by the many migrants from other, mostly rural and poor, parts of Mexico.

Norteña has roots in *corridos,* folk ballads dealing with Latino/Anglo strife in the borderlands in the 19th century, and themes from the Mexican Revolution. Today's songs, some officially banned by the Mexican government, focus more on the trials and tribulations of small-time smugglers or drug runners trying to survive big-time corruption and crime. The accordion is the characteristic instrument, although backing for the singer is also guitar-based, with bass and drums. Local heroes are Los Tucanes de Tijuana, but the superstars of the genre are Los Tigres del Norte, from Mexicali, who added saxophone and absorbed popular cumbia rhythms from Colombia. Other major norteña bands are Los Martinez and Los Huaracanes del Norte.

Banda is a 1990s derivative of norteña, substituting large brass sections for guitars and accordion, and playing a combination of Latin and more traditional Mexican rhythms. Banda Machos, Banda Cuisillos and Banda Aguacaliente are big names.

Ranchera is Mexico's urban 'country music.' Developed in the expanding cities of the 20th century, it's mostly melodramatic, sentimental stuff with a nostalgia for rural roots: vocalist-and-combo music, maybe with a mariachi backing. Eugenia León, Juan Gabriel and Alejandro Fernández are among the leading ranchera artists.

Classical Music Well-known and respected beyond Tijuana is the Orquesta de Baja California, with 13 members – more of a large chamber group than a full orchestra. Founded in 1992, it includes Americans and Mexicans but has at its core several accomplished Russian musicians who came to Tijuana after the 1990 breakup of the Soviet Union. Its founder and artistic director is Eduardo García Barrios, who studied at Moscow's Tchaikovsky Conservatory. Barrios also founded Mexico's first orchestra-led music academy, which has since evolved into the Conservatorio Estatal de Música (State Music Conservatory), based at Cecut.

Affiliated with the conservatory is the Centro Hispanoamericano de Guitarra, directed by internationally renowned classical guitarist Roberto Limón. The center's main purpose is the preservation and dissemination of classical guitar music by composers with Hispanic and Latin American roots. Its Escuela de Guitarra Clásica has more than 100 students, who frequently stage concerts and recitals. Every October, Limón organizes the Festival Hispanoamericano de Guitarra, which brings together top talent from around the world.

Young performers also show off their skill with the Sinfonía Juvenil de Tijuana, founded in 1996 by Sergio Ramirez Cárdenas and based at the Casa de Cultura in Playas de Tijuana. In 2000, the group produced Mozart's one-act opera *Bastián y Bastiana* in collaboration with several high schools in Southern California and with binational sponsorship.

Visual Arts

Tijuana and the borderlands have long been a fertile environment for the visual arts, although forms of expression have changed over the years. Until roughly the 1980s, local art had a populist and unselfconscious character rooted in folk traditions. It reflected the background of the majority of city residents, poorly educated country folk lured to Tijuana by the promise of jobs.

As Tijuana began to grow into a metropolis, a better-educated middle class emerged, bringing a whole new generation of artists, many with formal arts training. They used their skills like a voice, in many cases a voice of protest, as they moved away from art for aesthetics' sake to art for expressing their intellectual – and usually critical – thought processes. Art became politicized; the daily struggles and the search for identity of the people of the border region became overarching themes. Canvases were eschewed in favor of conceptual, performance and installation art, which had grown out of the Euro-American artistic underground of the 1960s

Some groups, like the Taller de Arte Fronterizo (Border Art Workshop), founded in 1984 by a group of artists from both San Diego and Tijuana, even regarded art as means to effect political change.

Some of the most remarkable – and ambitious – artistic collaborations between San Diego and Tijuana have been the inSITE exhibitions, held triennially since 1991. The project brings artists from around the world to the border zone to create provocative site-specific installations for public spaces in both cities. In 2000, performance art was included in the presentations.

Of the hundreds of visual artists working in Tijuana today, two stand out. Marcos Ramirez is the only local artist with a work on permanent display at San Diego's Museum of Contemporary Art. He was also selected to participate in New York's Whitney Museum Biennial, considered the most prestigious showcase of contemporary American art. One of the most prolific artists is muralist Oscar Ortega Corral, who has won numerous awards and participated in countless exhibits. His work is in such diverse places as the Mi Barra bar and the Cinque Café-Bar in Plaza Fiesta, the Auditorio Municipal and bridges near the border.

Other Tijuana artists of note include Tania Candiani, Roberto Rosique, Javier Galaviz, Silvia Galindo, Franco Méndez Calvillo and Jose Luís Pastor.

Dance

Dance is one of the most popular art forms in Tijuana. One of its most prominent figures is Ricardo Peralta, a modern and ballet dancer as well as an actor, teacher and choreographer. Peralta, whose career began in

TIJUANA

The 'Tijuana Bibles'

Oh, there's been a long and lusty tradition in the erotic arts throughout the ages. Witness the carvings of the temple at Karnak. Thumb the 'pillow books' created for uninformed brides and grooms by gifted – though lunatic – Japanese woodcut artists. Erotic visions have found their rightful place in all but the most Calvinist societies. But perhaps nowhere was more graphic, accomplished and downright goofy porn produced than in the thousands of cheap little booklets that became collectively known as the 'Tijuana Bibles.' Millions of these wacky wham-bam-boom! books sold from the early 1920s through the '50s throughout the US.

Oddly, the connection between these masterful manuals of smut and Tijuana is rather tenuous. Most likely it was the city's reputation for rampant sexual activity that lent these tawdry tomes a title that clicked with potential buyers. Also known as 'Bluesies' or 'Tilly and Mac books' (among a host of less-printable names) the 'Bibles' just seemed to sell better when coupled with Tijuana titillation.

Titles such as 'She Saw the World's Fair – And How!' were churned out by cartoonists with names such as 'O Whattacan' and featured the couplings of Rita Hayworth and Prince Aly Khan, Mae West and half of Disney's animated characters, Joseph Stalin ('The biggest prick in Russia!'), Mussolini and Hitler. Interracial – even inter-species – hijinx were the norm in the 'Bibles,' which were as inaccurate for their stereotypes as they were for their stupendous anatomical exaggerations.

Even today you can find somewhat tamed versions of the bibles for sale in countless pushcarts in the Tijuana streets. (It's hilarious to find Mexican cartoonists accompanying various sexual improprieties by 'sound-balloons' containing word creations such as 'Fnorkk!' and the ever-popular 'Schlupppp!'.)

But it was those hard-working visionaries of the '20s and '30s who truly put the comedy of human sexuality – and, by extension, so to speak, Tijuana – on the libidinal map. As Henry Miller once quipped of those times, 'I think there was just as much f***in' goin' on back then. We just didn't talk about it as much.'

- David Peevers

1980 in Mexico, teaches at Tijuana's Centro de Artes Escénicar del Noroeste (CAEN; North-western Center for Stage Arts), based at the Centro Cultural (Cecut), and at the Centro Contemporáneo del Arte y Movimiento (Contemporary Center for Art & Movement). He is artistic director of the troupe Danza Performa, which frequently performs around Tijuana and other cities, including San Diego.

Another name to look for is Grupo de Danza Minerva Tapia. In 1995, Tapia founded her own ensemble with six professional dancers from both sides of the border who had trained in ballet and modern dance. The group, noted for its contemporary style paired with meticulous classical techniques, has also collaborated with Jean Isaac's San Diego Dance Theater.

In April, Tijuana hosts local, national and international professional talent at the Festival Internacional de Danza Contemporánea held at Cecut. Later that month, on the 29th, the Día Internacional de la Danza dancers take over downtown; up to 30 groups perform jazz, folklore, ballet and modern dance all along Avenida Revolución.

The umbrella organization for many of Tijuana's smaller and amateur dance groups is the Compañía de Danza de Baja California, which brings together Tijuana's best dancers for special performances, including productions of *The Nutcracker,* shown at Cecut in December, and *Swan Lake,* performed in July at the Parque de la Amistad in Mesa de Otay.

Theater

Like dance and painting, Tijuana theater grew with the universities and the Casas de la Cultura, and numerous theater companies have offered aspiring actors an opportunity to develop their talents. The Compañia del Sótano, directed by Herbert Axel, is based at the Casa de Cultura in Playas de Tijuana and presents a merry menu of theatrical fare ranging from the cutting edge to the classical; new works by local writers are given as much exposure as those by established national figures.

The highly recognized La Divina Fauna is the resident company of CAEN. Since

1990 it has been guided by Edward Coward, a director, actor and dramatis considered one of Mexican theater' shining lights. Born in Tijuana in 1967, he published his first book in 1984. He mos recently won acclaim for *Guía Nocturne* (Night Guide), a work about three adoles cents who dream of becoming artists; it' based on the first letter of Rainer Mari Rilke's *Letters to a Young Poet.*

Other ensembles to look for include the Compañia Andrés Soler and the Teatro de UABC. Every October, the Cecut-sponsored Festival Internacional del Teatro (International Theater Festival) presents high-calibe local, national and international groups.

Literature

Tijuana's literary scene has produce several outstanding writers and poets. Lui Humberto Crosthwaite is a Tijuana-born journalist who writes for *Enlace,* the Spanish-language supplement to the *San Diego Union-Tribune,* and has publishe several novels and short stories, mostly or border culture and issues.

Alfonso García Cortéz teaches at the Universidad Iberoamericana Noroeste and is a widely published poet and early member of the binational Taco Shop Poets self-titled 'guerilla poets' who started out in 1994 by giving impromptu readings at taco shops in California and Tijuana.

Another promising poet is Noé Carrillo Martínez, born in the city in 1970, whose minimalist, introspective works have been published in two volumes, *El Tiempo cade día* (1996) and *Aquí debería estar tu nombre* (1998). Tijuanense Elizabeth Cazessus is a feminist poet and performance artist. Julio Rodríguez Barajas, a dramatist, historian and retired professor, has written about many aspects of Baja California and Tijuana. From the pen of Tijuana-born but now Mexico City-based journalist Federico Campbell come a couple of books of short stories dealing with life in this border boomtown. Another well-established journalist is Rubén Vizcaíno, who produces a cultural supplement to the *El Mexicano* newspaper.

SOCIETY & CONDUCT
Most Mexicans are fiercely proud of their country. Their strong sense of nationalism has at least in part been fueled by the foreign economic domination to which the country has been subjected through much of its recent history – first by the British and the US during the Porfiriato in the 19th century and, today, many feel, by the US again. The classic Mexican attitude toward the US is a combination of envy and resentment that a poor neighbor feels for a rich one. The word gringo, incidentally, isn't exactly a compliment, but it's not necessarily an insult either. Much depends on context, and it can be purely descriptive or even friendly.

RELIGION
Like other Mexicans, Tijuanenses are almost exclusively Roman Catholic. The Mexican Catholic Church is one of Latin America's most conservative and rarely gets involved with political issues such as human rights or poverty.

By all accounts, Tijuanenses are fairly devout. Churches abound, and mass, held several times daily, is well attended. Even outside of services, pews and chapels in churches like the Catedral de Nuestra Señora de Guadalupe in downtown are filled with worshippers throughout the day. The Virgin of Guadalupe is, in fact, the church's most binding symbol. She's a dark-skinned manifestation of the Virgin Mary who appeared to an indigenous Mexican in 1531 on a hill near Mexico City. The Virgin became a crucial link between Catholic and indigenous spirituality. As Mexico grew into a mestizo society, the Virgin became the most potent symbol of Mexican Catholicism. She is the country's patron, her blue-cloaked image is ubiquitous, and her name is invoked in religious ceremonies, political speeches and literature.

LANGUAGE
Spanish is Mexico's official language, but English is fairly wide-spoken in Tijuana –

TIJUANA

Spanglish: Cross-Border Communication

Spanish speakers on both sides of the US-Mexico border have unselfconsciously adopted many English words. The best marker of the cultural border, as opposed to the political border, might be the geographical point where bathrooms taps start to be marked 'C' and 'F' for *caliente* and *frío* rather than 'H' and 'C' for 'hot' and 'cold.'

Following are a few common border terms with their English and standard Spanish equivalents. For purposes of differentiation, some of the border-Spanish spellings are phoneticized, but this can be misleading because the words themselves are rarely written down. Spanglish is essentially an oral language, though occasionally English words are adopted as written and given a Spanish tone.

English	Spanglish	Standard Spanish
brake	el breque	el freno
clutch	el clutch	el embrague
junk	el yonke	las chacharas
lunch	el lonche	el almuerzo
pickup truck	la pickup	la camioneta
rug/carpet	la carpeta*	la alfombra
six-pack	el six pack	n/a
truck	la troca	el camión
vacuum cleaner	la vaquium	la aspiradora
yard (distance)	la yarda	vara
yard (lawn)	la yarda	el jardín

*In standard Spanish, *carpeta* means 'notebook.'

certainly along Avenida Revolución and other tourist areas. Intrepid travelers venturing beyond these places, though, will find that a few words of Spanish will go a long way toward easing communication. Throughout the border zone, you'll find that many words have evolved Spanish-English (Spanglish) hybrids; see the boxed text for examples of this linguistic phenomenon. Also see the Menu Translator appendix for a quick plunge into the primary local language.

Facts for the Visitor

WHEN TO GO

Any time of year can be a good time to visit Tijuana, although summers can be stifling hot and winters can bring rain and chilly nights. Hotel prices hold pretty steady year-round, and it's usually no problem to find a room.

ORIENTATION

Tijuana parallels the US border for about 12 miles (19km). Downtown Tijuana (sometimes called Zona Centro in this book) is a 10- to 15-minute walk southwest of the San Ysidro border crossing and consists of a grid pattern of north-south *avenidas* (avenues) and east-west *calles* (streets). Most streets have numbers that are more frequently used than their names, which is why this book usually includes both when providing addresses. Avenida Revolución (also called 'La Revo'), five blocks to the west, is the city's main tourist artery; businesses along streets just west of here such as Avenida Constitución and Avenida Niños Héroes cater more to locals.

East of the Zona Centro, the Zona Río, Tijuana's new commercial center, flanks the Río Tijuana. Paseo de los Héroes, Via Poniente and Blvd Sánchez Taboada all parallel the river. Northeast of here is the hilltop district of Mesa de Otay, home to another border crossing, the airport, the main university, residential neighborhoods and large shopping malls. The main thoroughfares are Calzada Tecnológico and Carretera al Aeropuerto. West of downtown lie both hillside shantytowns, known as *asentamientos irregulares* (literally, irregular settlements), and spiffy suburbs. Playas de Tijuana, on the coast, is a middle class to upscale neighborhood.

Formally, Tijuana is subdivided into hundreds of neighborhoods or districts called either *fraccionamientos* (abbreviated Fracc) or *colonias* (abbreviated (Col), and addresses are much easier to locate if one knows the district name. For a visitor the four most important are: Colonia Cacho, a pleasant residential neighborhood south of Zona Centro; Colonia América, just east of here, where the El Toreo bullring is; Fraccionamiento Chapultepec (the city's ritziest neighborhood), about 1 mile (1.6km) east of here and home to the Club Campestre golf course; and Fraccionamiento Hipódromo, immediately east and anchored by the Agua Caliente racetrack. All four are connected by Boulevard Agua Caliente, one of the major east-west thoroughfares, and have numerous hotels and restaurants.

Matador

Beyond the racetrack, where Blvd Agua Caliente turns into Blvd Gustavo Díaz Ordaz, are several large shopping malls and the residential suburbs of La Mesa and La Presa.

A new numbering system for street addresses has created some confusion because some businesses still use the old system – you'll often see two numbers displayed at a single site. Also confusing is that some streets have more than one name, such as Paseo de Tijuana, also known as Paseo or Avenida Centenario.

MAPS

Maps and Tijuana are not a happy marriage, as most reliable mapmakers seem unable – or unwilling – to keep up with the constantly growing city. The maps in this book should be sufficient for general navigating around town. The free one handed out by the tourist offices pinpoints the locations of some restaurants and hotels but leaves out many minor streets and is not always accurate.

TIJUANA

Professionally produced maps are available in the convenience stores of top-end hotels, and better bookstores and department stores like Dorian's and Sanborn's (see the Tijuana Shopping chapter) may stock them too. The most common is the locally produced Guía T *Plano de la Ciudad de Tijuana*. This is the most current and complete map to be found, but it is cluttered with annoying advertisements and, even worse, has no street index and only a marginally helpful index of the colonias. Another choice is the Guía Roji map, which lacks many newer streets but does have a useful index and is easier to read than the Guía T map. Unfortunately, it is not widely available.

TOURIST OFFICES
Local Tourist Offices

Tourist information is disseminated by two main agencies: the Tijuana-based Cotuco (Comité de Turismo y Convenciones, ie, Committee on Tourism & Conventions – sometimes also confusingly known as Fondo Mixto Tijuana or Tijuana Tourism Board) and the state-run Secture (Secretaría de Turismo del Estado). Neither has much printed material but most staff members speak English and can answer questions.

Cotuco has two information offices at the San Ysidro border. One caters to visitors crossing on foot and is located about 150 feet (50m) past the turnstiles at the foot of the first pedestrian bridge (see the border crossing map in the San Diego Getting Around Chapter). It is open 9 am to 7 pm daily.

The other office (see the border crossing map in the San Diego Getting Around chapter; ☎ 683-14-05) is more convenient for car travelers, but it's easily missed amid the tangle of lanes and signs. As you drive toward Mexican customs, stay in one of the right lanes (but make sure it's labeled 'Nothing to Declare'), then start looking for a small ochre building on your right immediately after you've gone under a walking bridge; Cotuco is located next to the yellow cabs, and there's even a small parking space. This office also sells auto insurance; if you haven't obtained any before

entering Mexico, we strongly urge you to do so here. Hours are 9 am to 7 pm (10 am to 2 pm Sunday).

Cotuco's head office (Map 14; ☎ 684-05-37, fax 684-77-82; @ info@seetijuana.com) is not set up to handle foot traffic, but if you're in the Zona Río and need help, the staff will happily oblige. It's located at Paseo de los Héroes 9365, Suite 201, and open 9 am to 6 pm Monday to Friday. This office also operates a toll-free information line at ☎ 888-775-2417 (accessible from the US only).

Secture's office is on Avenida Revolución at Calle 1a (Map 13). It's open from 8 am to 5 pm (from 10 am Saturday and Sunday). The Tourist Assistance Office (☎ 688-05-05), which helps if you encounter a legal problem, is also here (also see Legal Matters later this chapter).

Tourist Offices Abroad

At the time of writing, Secture, Mexico's national tourism ministry, had closed all of its 13 international offices. A reorganization is allegedly afoot, but it remains unclear if and when offices will reopen. Check with the Mexican consulate in your country about Secture's current status.

DOCUMENTS

Although all information outlined below was accurate at the time of writing, Mexico has occasionally – and without warning – changed existing regulations. It's always best to check with the Mexican consulate or embassy in your country before leaving home.

Passports

Though it's not recommended, visitors from the US can enter Tijuana without a passport if they have official photo identification such as a driver's license. Officially, they also need some proof of citizenship, such as a notarized birth certificate or their original certificate of naturalization (not a copy). In reality, though, these documents are rarely checked upon re-entering the US.

Citizens of other countries who are permanent residents in the US have to present their Permanent Resident Alien Card

('Green Card') and should also bring their passport.

Canadian tourists may enter Mexico with official photo identification plus proof of citizenship, such as a birth certificate or notarized affidavit of it. Naturalized Canadian citizens, however, require a valid passport.

Citizens from all other countries must have a valid passport and, in some cases, a tourist visa.

Visas

Citizens of the US, Canada, EU countries, Australia, New Zealand, Norway, Switzerland, Iceland, Israel, Japan, Argentina and Chile are among those who do not need visas to enter Mexico as tourists. Visas are required for most African, Asian and Eastern European citizens. Some nationals also need to produce a round-trip ticket to enter Mexico. Check well before your trip with your local Mexican embassy or consulate.

Non-US citizens passing through the US on the way to or from Mexico – or visiting Mexico from the US – should check their US visa requirements.

If you're a US or Canadian citizen visiting Mexico on business for 30 days or less, you must complete form FMN (Forma Migratoria NAFTA). It is available from Mexican consulates or at the border and requires a passport or original birth certificate, plus a company letter stating the purpose of your trip and the source of your income.

If your stay exceeds 30 days, you will need to apply for an FM3 visa at a Mexican consulate before you arrive in Mexico. Bring your passport, company letter, two passport-sized photographs and US$70. This visa is good for multiple entries within one year.

Travel Insurance

Mexican medical treatment is generally inexpensive for common diseases and minor treatments, but most doctors and hospitals require payment at the time of service. If you're in serious medical trouble, you may feel more comfortable obtaining treatment from your doctor at home. Travel insurance

can cover the costs of getting you back. Some US health policies may stay in effect (at least for a limited time) if you travel abroad, but it's worth checking exactly what you'll be covered for in Mexico. Everyone not covered in Mexico under their private or national health plan should obtain travel insurance.

Plane ticket loss is also covered by most travel insurance policies. Make sure you have a separate record or photocopy of all your ticket details. Also make a copy of your policy. Other possible coverage includes theft and flight delays or cancellations.

If possible, take out a policy that covers an ambulance or an emergency flight home; otherwise, consider medical evacuation insurance. It can cost as little as US$50 for a 30-day trip, as opposed to thousands of dollars for an actual evacuation. Reputable companies include San Diego–based American Care (☎ 800-941-2582, 619-486-8844) and Critical Air Medicine (☎ 800-247-8326, 619-571-0482).

So you can get reimbursement from your insurance, get receipts from all doctors, hospitals and pharmacies and keep all documentation. Some policies may require you to make a collect call to a center in your home country before you see a physician.

Driver's License & Permits

US or Canadian citizens and permanent residents in either country need a valid national driver's license *or* an International Driving Permit (IDP) to drive in Mexico. Other nationals should have both their national license and an IDP. Everyone should have their car's registration papers.

Renting a vehicle in Mexico requires a driver's license and major credit card. A vehicle permit is only required for travel in mainland Mexico. For more information on car rental see the Tijuana Getting There & Away chapter.

Tourist Card (FMT)

If you're only visiting Tijuana or the immediate border area (including all the destinations described in the Tijuana Excursions chapter) and are staying 72 hours or less, you do *not* need a Mexican tourist card.

If, however, you're staying longer or are traveling to the Mexican mainland or south of Ensenada or San Felipe on the Baja peninsula, you will need the 'Forma Migratoria para Turista' (FMT). It's highly likely that you will be asked to show this document at roadside military checkpoints. If you don't have the right papers, you may be sent back north to obtain them before being allowed to proceed – clearly a major hassle.

Travelers arriving by air automatically receive the card, but those arriving by land must obtain it from the Instituto Nacional de Migración (INM, National Immigration Institute) at border crossings. In San Ysidro, pedestrians will find one to the right of the turnstiles; drivers should make their way over to Mexican Customs on the right immediately after crossing the border (past the automatic signal). The office is in the row of low buildings. Be sure to have the form stamped by an immigration official, and keep it with you until you leave Mexico. Many people don't bother obtaining a tourist card even if they're staying in Tijuana for more than 72 hours. This is probably OK, but could work against you if you get into trouble with the law in an unrelated matter. The card is free and quickly obtained with minimum bureaucracy – so why risk it?

One section of the card – to be filled in by the immigration officer – deals with the length of your stay in Mexico. You may be asked a couple of questions about how long you want to stay and what you'll be doing, but normally you will be given the maximum 180 days if you ask for it. It's always advisable to put down more days than you think you'll need, in case you are delayed or change your plans. The card is good for multiple entries.

Tourist Fee

Since July 1, 1999, foreign tourists of any age and business travelers have been charged a fee, which, at the time of writing, was 170 pesos (about US$18). If you enter Mexico by air, this is included in your airfare.

You do *not* have to pay the tourist fee if you're entering Baja California by land for a visit of less than 72 hours and don't go south of Ensenada or San Felipe.

Everyone else must pay the fee at a Mexican bank (see the list on the back of your tourist card). It's best to do so right at the border. Bank hours in San Ysidro are 8 am to 10 pm Monday to Friday, to 6 pm Saturday and noon to 4 pm Sunday; the bank in Otay Mesa is open 10 am to 6 pm daily. Present your tourist card or business visitor card, which will be stamped to prove that you have paid.

This fee is payable only once in any 180-day period and entitles you to multiple entries. If you are going to return within the stipulated period, retain your stamped tourist/business visitor's card when leaving Mexico.

Minors' Forms

Every year numerous parents try to run away from the US or Canada to Mexico with their children to escape the legal machinations of the children's other parent. To prevent this, minors (people under 18) entering Mexico without one or both of their parents are required to show a notarized consent form signed by the absent parent or parents, giving permission for the young traveler to enter Mexico. This form is available from Mexican consulates. In the case of divorced parents, a custody document may be acceptable. If one or both parents are dead or the traveler has only one legal parent, a notarized statement to that effect may be required.

These rules are aimed primarily at visitors from the US and Canada, but in fact apply to all nationalities. Enforcement, however, is fairly lax.

Copies

Before leaving home, photocopy all important documents (passport data and visa pages, credit cards, travel insurance policy, air/bus/train tickets, driver's license, etc). See the Copies section in the San Diego Facts for the Visitor chapter for more details.

EMBASSIES & CONSULATES

Mexico has extensive diplomatic representation around the world, especially in the US.

In general, consulates deal with tourist inquiries, embassies with diplomatic matters, which is why our list includes consulates only.

Mexican Consulates Abroad

Australia
(☎ 02-9326-1311, fax 9327-1110; ✉ comexsyd@ bigpond.com.au) 135-153 New South Head Rd Level 1, Edgecliff, Sydney NSW 2027

Canada
Montréal: (☎ 514-288-2502, fax 288-8287; ✉ comexmt@mmic.net) 2055 rue Peel, Bureau 1000, Montréal, Québec H3A 1V4
Toronto: (☎ 416-368-2875, fax 368-8342; ✉ consulad@interlog.com) 199 Bay St W, Suite 4440, Toronto, Ontario M5L 1E9
Vancouver: (☎ 604-684-3547, fax 684-2485; ✉ mexico@direct.ca) 1130 W Pender St, Vancouver, British Columbia V6E 4A4

France
(☎ 01 42 86 56 20, fax 49 26 02 78, 42 86 05 80; ✉ consulmex.paris@wanadoo.fr) 4 rue Notre Dame des Victoires, 75002 Paris

Germany
Berlin: (☎ 030-327 65 04/5/6, fax 32 77 11 21; ✉ rfaemb@edina.com) Kurfürstendamm 72, 10709 Berlin
Frankfurt/Main: (☎ 069-299 87 50, fax 069-29 98 75 75; ✉ consulmex_@compuserve.com) Taunusanlage 21, 60325 Frankfurt/Main

UK
(☎ 020-7235-6393) 8 Halkin St, London SW1X 7DW

Mexican Consulates in the US

Mexico keeps consular representation in most US states, including in the following cities. Check www.embassyofmexico.org for a complete list.

Arizona
Phoenix: (☎ 602-242-7398, fax 242-2957) 1990 W Camelback Rd, Suite 110, Phoenix, AZ 85015
Tucson: (☎ 520-882-559, fax 882-8959) 553 S Stone Ave, Tucson, AZ 85701

California
Calexico: (☎ 760-357-3863, fax 357-6284) 331 W 2nd St, Calexico, CA 92231
Los Angeles: (☎ 213-351-6800, fax 351-6844) 2401 W 6th St, Los Angeles, CA 90057
Sacramento: (☎ 916-441-3287, fax 363-0625) 1010 8th St, Sacramento, CA 95827
San Diego: (☎ 619-231-8414, fax 231-48-02) 1549 India St, San Diego, CA 92101

San Francisco: (☎ 415-392-5554, fax 392-3233) 870 Market St, Suite 528, San Francisco, CA 94102
San Jose: (☎ 408-298-5581, fax 294-4506) 380 N 1st St, Suite 102, San Jose, CA 95112

Colorado
(☎ 303-331-1867, fax 830-2655) 48 Steele St, Denver, CO 80206

Florida
(☎ 305-716-4977, fax 593-2758) 1200 NW 78th Ave, Suite 200, Miami, FL 33126

Georgia
(☎ 404-266-2233, fax 266-2309) 2600 Apple Valley Rd, Atlanta, GA 30319

Illinois
(☎ 312-855-0066, fax 855-9257) 300 N Michigan Ave 2nd Floor, Chicago, IL 60601

Massachusetts
(☎ 617-426-4942, fax 695-1957) 20 Park Plaza, Suite 506, Boston, MA 02116

Michigan
(☎ 313-567-7713, fax 567-7543) 600 Renaissance St, Suite 1510, Detroit, MI 48243

New Mexico
(☎ 505-247-2147, fax 842-9490) 401 5th St NW, Albuquerque, NM 87102

New York
(☎ 212-217-6400, fax 217-6493) 27 E 39th St, New York, NY 10016

Oregon
(☎ 503-274-1442, fax 274-1540) 1234 SW Morrison, Portland, OR 97205

Puerto Rico
(☎ 787-764-0258, fax 250-0042) Avenida Muñoz Rivera 654, Suite 1837, San Juan, Puerto Rico 00918

Texas
Austin: (☎ 512-478-2300, fax 478-8008) 200 E 6th St, Suite 200, Austin, TX 78701
Dallas: (☎ 214-630-7341, fax 630-3511) 8855 Stemmons Freeway, Dallas, TX 75247
El Paso: (☎ 915-533-3644, fax 532-7163) 910 E San Antonio St, El Paso, TX 79901
Houston: (☎ 713-339-4701, fax 789-4060) 10440 W Office St, Houston, TX 77042
San Antonio: (☎ 210-227-1085, fax 227-1817) 127 Navarro St, San Antonio, TX 78205

Utah
(☎ 801-521-8502, fax 521-0534) 458 East 200 S, Suite 110, Salt Lake City, UT 84111

Washington
(☎ 206-448-8419, fax 448-4771) 2132 3rd Ave, Seattle, WA 98121

Washington, DC
(☎ 202-736-1000, fax 797-8458; ✉ consulwas@ aol.com) 2827 16th St NW, Washington, DC 20009

Foreign Consulates in Tijuana

In addition to consulates listed below, China, Finland, Japan, Gambia, Honduras, Korea and Norway are also represented in Tijuana. The Canadian consulate will also assist citizens of Australia and Belize.

Austria (☎ 686-53-80/81) Blvd Agua Caliente 10535, Suite 803, Edificio Gallegos, Fracc Chapultepec

Canada (Map 14; ☎ 684-04-61, fax 684-03-01) Germán Gedovius 10411, Zona Río

France (Map 13; ☎ 685-71-77, fax 684-20-94) Avenida Revolución 1651, 3rd Floor, Zona Centro

Germany (☎ 680-18-30, 680-25-12) Calle Cantera 400-304, Edificio Ole, Playas de Tijuana

Italy (☎ 686-23-78) Santa María 155, Col Gavilondo, Zona Centro

Spain (☎ 686-57-80) Avenida Los Olivos 3401, Fracc Cubillas

UK (☎ 681-73-23, fax 681-84-02) Blvd Salinas 1500, Fracc Aviación

USA (Map 15; ☎ 681-74-00, fax 681-80-16; ☎ 619-692-2154 answering service in San Diego) Tapachula 96, Col Hipódromo

Your Own Consulate or Embassy

Please see the San Diego Facts for the Visitor chapter for information on the role of your country's consulate or embassy in your travels.

CUSTOMS

For limits on duty-free merchandise allowed into the US from Mexico, see Customs in the San Diego Facts for the Visitor chapter. For more details, read the online booklet *Know Before You Go* at www.customs.gov/travel/travel.htm.

The value of goods visitors may bring into Mexico duty-free is limited to US$50 if arriving by land and US$300 if arriving by sea or air. Travel-related items for personal use may also be brought in duty-free. These include clothing and toiletries; medicine for personal use, with a prescription in the case of psychotropic drugs; one still, video or movie camera; up to 12 rolls of film or videocassettes; one portable computer; and, if you're 18 or older, 3L of wine, beer or liquor and 400 cigarettes. Amounts exceeding the duty-free limit may be taxed at 32.8%. In general, Mexican customs conducts spot-checks only. It's illegal to bring in firearms or ammunition unless you have a permit issued by a Mexican consulate or embassy.

MONEY
Currency

The Mexican peso is divided into 100 centavos. Coins come in denominations of five, 10, 20 and 50 centavos and one, two, five, 10, 20 and 50 pesos; and there are notes of 10, 20, 50, 100, 200 and 500 pesos. Pesos and US dollars are accepted interchangeably in Tijuana and much of northern Baja California. The $ sign confusingly also refers to Mexican pesos, and many Tijuana merchants don't make it fully clear which currency they mean when they price items. Always confirm whether you're paying dollars or pesos before buying. Note that all prices in the Tijuana chapters are given in US dollars.

Exchange Rates

The peso has been relatively stable since the currency crisis of 1994-95 when it lost 60% of its value in three months. Exchange rates at press time were:

country	unit		pesos
Australia	A$1	=	5.45
Belize	BZ$1	=	4.97
Canada	C$1	=	6.48
Euro	€1	=	9.16
France	FF1	=	1.40
Germany	DM1	=	4.68
Guatemala	Q1	=	1.26
Japan	¥100	=	8.36
New Zealand	NZ$1	=	4.38
UK	UK£1	=	14.33
USA	US$1	=	9.8

Exchanging Money

Money can be exchanged at banks, hotels and *casas de cambio* (exchange houses). Rates may vary a bit from one bank or cambio to another. Different rates are often posted for *efectivo* (cash) and *documento* (traveler's checks). Cambios are usually quicker and less bureaucratic than banks and have longer hours. But banks rarely charge commission, and cambios do. Hotels generally offer poor rates and may charge commission to boot.

Carrying cash is risky, but you will need it for bus and taxi drivers, small purchases at convenience stores, casual restaurants, tips and so on.

Most banks will cash traveler's checks, but the paperwork involved can be tiresome, and some may limit the amount to US$200. Major-brand checks in standard US dollar denominations are best. American Express is widely accepted and has an efficient replacement policy. In Tijuana, AmEx is represented by Viajes Carrousel (Map 14; ☎ 684-05-56, 684-36-61) on Blvd Sánchez Taboada at Avenida José Orozco. In case of loss, you can also call the 24-hour hotline in Mexico City collect at ☎ 5-326-27-00.

Automated teller machines (ATMs) are common and the easiest way to get cash pesos from a credit card or a home bank account. Many are accessible around the clock and link with several networks such as Cirrus, Star and Plus. Exchange rates tend to be better, but often a fee will be charged to your account. Use ATMs during banking hours to guard against robbery or in case the machine 'swallows' your card or doesn't spit out the correct amount of cash.

Airlines, car rental companies, travel agents and many hotels, restaurants and shops in Tijuana accept credit cards; Pemex gas stations, bars and nightclubs generally do not. Smaller merchants also prefer cash and may charge a 3% to 6% *recargo* (surcharge) for credit cards. Fraud, such as double charging or tinkering with the total, is not uncommon in Tijuana (see Dangers & Annoyances later in this chapter).

MasterCard and Visa are widely accepted, and American Express is coming along. If you use a credit card to withdraw cash from ATMs, be aware that often you'll start paying interest immediately and pay a fee as well; check with your credit card company.

If you need money wired to you, a quick method is Western Union's 'Dinero en

Minutos' (Money in Minutes). In Tijuana, this is offered by the Telecomm office next to the main post office at Avenida Negrete 2050, open 8 am to 7 pm Monday to Friday and to 1 pm Saturdays. Some stores are also Western Union agents; look for black-and-yellow signs reading 'Western Union' and 'Dinero en Minutos.'

The sender pays the money – along with a fee – at their Western Union branch and gives the details on who is to receive it and where. When you pick it up, take photo identification. Western Union has offices worldwide; information is available at ☎ 5-721-30-80 or 5-546-73-61 in Mexico, 800-325-6000 in the US, or at www.westernunion.com.

Security
See the Security section of the San Diego Facts for the Visitor chapter for tips on keeping your cash, credit cards and valuables safe during your travels.

Costs
Prices in Tijuana are high by Mexican standards and often not much lower than in San Diego or other US cities. The secret to traveling economically is to cut costs when possible, as on accommodations and food.

For solo travelers, lodging is likely to be the largest travel budget item. In most hotels, double occupancy costs little more than single occupancy, and triples or quadruples are available in many places for only a few dollars more than doubles.

Buying your food in supermarkets is the cheapest way to stay nourished, but it may be inconvenient, and you'll be missing out on some interesting culinary experiences. Sidewalk stands that sell a few tacos for US$1 are generally the cheapest places to fill up at, but hygienic standards are not always adequate and many visitors develop intestinal problems from food prepared in such places.

Spending a little more (between US$3 and US$5) will let you enjoy good, if not fancy, food in casual but established sit-down restaurants. At lunchtime you can save by ordering the *comida corrida,* a set menu that usually includes two courses and a soft drink for around US$3.50. Dinners are generally more expensive but, except at the swankiest places, you should be able to get away for about US$20 for an appetizer, main course and one alcoholic drink.

Exploring Tijuana's nightlife can take a serious toll on your wallet. Unless you stick to beer, alcohol is surprisingly expensive. A small glass of wine averages US$4, and margaritas are rarely served for less than US$4.50. Nightclub admission can be up to US$10.

Walking will be your main method of transport if your Tijuana explorations are in the immediate border area (Zona Centro and Zona Río). Otherwise, buses and route taxis cost only US 50¢; most cab rides are less than US$6.

Museum admission won't impact your budget either, as most places are either free or max out at US$1.50.

Tipping & Bargaining

In restaurants, it is customary to tip 10% to 15% of the bill, and poorly paid cleaning maids are grateful for even a small tip. A porter in a mid-range hotel would be happy with US$1 for carrying two bags. Taxi drivers generally don't expect tips unless they provide some special service, but gas station attendants do (three or four pesos will do).

Even though you may bargain down the price of some hotel rooms, especially in budget and mid-range places and in the off-season, the rates are normally fairly firm. In street markets and many souvenir shops, however, bargaining is the rule. Cab fares (for individual taxis only, not for route taxis; see the Tijuana Getting Around chapter), should be negotiated before getting into the car.

Taxes

In Baja California, the *Impuesto de Valor Agregado* (Value-Added Tax), abbreviated IVA ('EE-bah'), is 10%. By law the tax must be included in virtually any price; exceptions are hotels, especially top-end ones, where the IVA is usually added to the quoted room rate, as is a 2% lodging tax.

POST & COMMUNICATIONS

Tijuana's main post office *(oficina de correos)* is at Avenida Negrete 2050, at the corner of Calle 11a (PE Calles) and is open 8 am to 5 pm weekdays and 9 am to 1 pm Saturday. Here you can buy postage stamps and receive and send mail.

Post

A domestic letter or postcard weighing 20g or less costs US 32¢, while airmail rates are US 45¢ to the US or Canada, US 55¢ to Europe and US 60¢ to Australia, New Zealand or Asia. Items weighing between 20g and 50g cost US 75¢, US 85¢ and US$1, respectively.

The Mexican postal service is slow and unreliable; packages in particular sometimes go missing. Write *'Vía Aérea'* (air mail) on all correspondence and send important mail registered *(certificado* or *registrado)* to ensure delivery (there's a US 80¢ extra charge for international mail). Airmail letters to the US and Canada take about four to 14 days; to Europe, one to three weeks; to Australia, New Zealand or Asia, a month or more.

Inbound mail usually takes as long as outbound mail, and international packages entering Mexico may go missing just like outbound ones. To prevent theft, register shipments or use a courier service such as DHL, UPS or FedEx. In order to receive letters and packages care of a post office, have the sender write the address as follows (for example):

Jane SMITH (last name capitalized)
Lista de Correos
Correos Central
Tijuana
Baja California
MEXICO

When the letter reaches the post office, the name of the addressee is placed on a daily updated list *(Lista)* usually displayed in the post office lobby. Bring a passport or ID when picking up your mail. While 'Lista' mail is returned to the sender after only 10 days, 'poste restante' mail will be held for up to one month. If you're going to pick up your mail more than 10 days after it has arrived, have senders put 'Poste Restante' in place of 'Lista de Correos' in the address. As no list is posted, you'll have to check with a postal worker to see if it's arrived. Both services are free.

Telephone

As of 2000, all phone numbers within Mexico consist of a seven-digit local number plus an area code. The area code for Tijuana and all of northern Baja (including Rosarito, Ensenada, Tecate, Mexicali and San Felipe) is 6. For calls within Tijuana, simply dial the seven-digit number. If you're calling a Mexican number in another town, dial 01+area code+local number (this applies even when calling another town in the same area code). If you're calling an international number, you must dial 00+country code+area code+local number. The country code for the US and Canada is 1. See the boxed text 'International Country Codes' for others or call the international operator at ☎ 090. Domestic operators are at ☎ 020. For directory information, dial ☎ 040.

Mexican toll-free numbers – ☎ 800 followed by seven digits – always require the ☎ 01 prefix. Some US and Canada toll-free numbers can also be reached from Mexico (dial ☎ 001 before the 800), but you may have to pay for the call. Some businesses in northern Baja have 800 numbers that work from the United States, though connections are pretty unreliable.

Pay Phones Pay phones, the cheapest way to make calls, abound in Tijuana. The most established phone company, and the most reliable for costs, is Telnor. Most Telnor pay phones accept coins and or *tarjetas Ladatel*, prepaid phone cards sold in denominations of 30, 50 or 100 pesos (about US$3, US$5 and US$10) at pharmacies, liquor stores and shops – look for the blue-and-yellow sign reading *De Venta Aquí Ladatel*. Telnor phones work for local, national and international calls. Toll-free, collect and emergency numbers don't require a coin deposit or phone card.

Costs Local calls are cheap (usually 1 peso). A three-minute call to the US costs around US$2 and to other countries (the UK, for instance) around US$7. For specific national and international rates, call the (usually English-speaking) international operator at ☎ 090.

Budget hotel rates often include free local calls, while top-end hotels tend to charge exorbitantly for all calls. Always check rates with the hotel operator before making anything but a local call.

Scams Beware of non-Telnor phones claiming that they accept credit cards or that you can make easy collect calls to the US. A three-minute call on these phones can cost you US$30 to US$50. The operator may quote you cheap rates, but you won't know your final tally until it's posted on your next credit card bill – by then, it'll be impossible to prove that you were told a different rate.

Casetas de Teléfono There are plenty of long-distance phone stations in the Zona Centro and at the bus stations. An on-the-spot operator connects the call for you, and you take it in a booth. This is usually more expensive than Telnor pay phones, but not always. You don't need a phone card, and they eliminate street noise. Confirm the exact per-minute rate for the call you intend to make and ask about connection fees or other surcharges. Many of these places offer off-peak discounts.

North American Calling Cards If you have an AT&T, MCI or Sprint card, or a

International Country Codes	
Australia	☎ 61
Canada	☎ 1
France	☎ 33
Germany	☎ 49
Italy	☎ 39
New Zealand	☎ 64
Spain	☎ 34
UK	☎ 44
USA	☎ 1

TIJUANA

Canadian calling card, you can use it for calls from Mexico to the US or Canada by dialing the access numbers below. These calls can be quite expensive, so check rates before going to Mexico.

AT&T	☎ 001-800-462-4240
MCI	☎ 001-800-674-7000
Sprint	☎ 001-800-877-8000
AT&T Canada	☎ 001-800-123-0201
Bell Canada	☎ 001-800-010-1990

Collect Calls A *llamada por cobrar* (collect call) can cost the receiving party much more than if *they* call *you,* so you may prefer to find a phone where you can receive an incoming call, then pay for a quick call to the other party to ask them to call you back.

If you do need to make a collect call, you can do so from pay phones without a coin deposit or phone card. Call an operator at ☎ 020 for domestic calls, or ☎ 090 for international calls. Some telephone casetas and hotels will make collect calls for you, but rates can be outrageous.

Calling Mexico To call a number in Mexico from another country, dial your country's international access code+52+area code+local number; 52 is Mexico's country code.

Fax

Public fax service is offered by some midrange and practically all top-end hotels. Internet cafes can usually send a fax as well, as can the Telecomm office at Avenida Negrete 2050. Also look for *'Fax Público'* signs on shops, businesses and telephone casetas, and in bus stations and airports. Typically you pay around US$1.50 to US$2 a page to the US or Canada, US$2.50 to Europe or Australasia.

Email & Internet Access

The Internet Age has definitely arrived in Tijuana and, since most residents cannot afford a home PC, cybercafes have proliferated at satellite speed.

The full-service cafe @qui.net (Map 13; mobile ☎ 044-6-641-67-23, 044-6-702-40-19), Calle Brasil 9030 in Colonia Cacho, has the best rates around, fast computers and connections, and friendly faces. It's open from 9 am to midnight daily. Prices are US$2 per hour till noon, including with free coffee and cookies, and US$2.50 thereafter.

In Plaza Río, The Net (Map 14; ☎ 634-67-14), upstairs from Copy Pronto, is open 8 am to 10 pm (Saturday and Sunday to 9 pm) and charges US$4 per hour.

Café Online (Map 14; ☎ 634-28-12), in Plaza Minarete at Blvd Sánchez Taboada 4002 (look for Sam's Club), is good too, but, at US$5.50 per hour, more expensive; it's open daily 9 am to 9 pm. Finally, Tijuan@net Café (Map 15; ☎ 686-14-95), in Plaza Campestre at Blvd Agua Caliente 11300, across from the golf course, charges US$4 per hour and is open daily 10 am to 9 pm.

Phones in Tijuana and the rest of Mexico generally use US-style telephone sockets, so if you have a laptop you should carry a US RJ-11 telephone adapter that works with your modem. Some hotel rooms have direct-dial phones with data ports. Others have phone sockets that allow you to unplug the phone and insert a phone jack that runs directly to your computer. In some cases you're confronted with digital switchboard phone systems and/or a room phone with a cord wired directly into the wall, both of which make it difficult to get online. For tips on getting around this problem, see www.teleadapt.com.

If your laptop uses a PC-card modem, it may or may not work outside your home country – for a long stay the safest option is to buy a reputable 'global' modem or a local PC-card modem.

INTERNET RESOURCES

The World Wide Web is a rich resource for travelers. You can research your trip, find bargain airfares, book hotels, check on weather conditions and chat with locals and other travelers about the best places to visit (or avoid!).

There's no better place to start your Web explorations than the Lonely Planet Web site at www.lonelyplanet.com (see Internet Resources in the San Diego Facts for the Visitor chapter for details).

Here are a few other Web sites – all in English – with more or less accurate and up-to-date information about Tijuana.

Tijuana Tourism Trust Official tourism site, with comprehensive information about hotels, restaurants, sightseeing, events and services; www.seetijuana.com

BajaLife Online Commercial site with nightlife, restaurant and hotel listings as well as information about car insurance and other business services; www.bajaonline.com/tijuana

Tijuana.com Basic commercial site with information on hotels, attractions, nightlife; fairly up-to-date but not very comprehensive; www.tijuana.com

BOOKS
Lonely Planet
For· those planning on venturing beyond Tijuana and the border area, Lonely Planet's comprehensive *Baja California* guidebook is an excellent purchase. And if you're planning an extended tour of the entire country, the *Mexico* guidebook will be useful. A handy travel companion is Lonely Planet's *Latin American Spanish Phrasebook,* with practical, up-to-date words and expressions in Latin American Spanish.

Lonely Planet's *Read This First: Central & South America* offers tips on preparing for a trip to Mexico. The LP *World Food Mexico* is an intimate, full-color guide to every food or drink situation the traveler may encounter; it also plots the evolution of Mexican cuisine. Its useful language section includes a definitive culinary dictionary and practical phrases to help you on your eating adventure.

History & Politics
Tijuana: History of a Mexican Metropolis, by TD Proffitt, covers the city's history in a geographical, sociological and cultural context from prehistoric days to the early 1990s. Indigenous peoples, the Spanish mission period, migration and tourism are all addressed.

Rebellion in the Borderlands: Anarchism and the Plan of San Diego 1904–1923, by James A Sandoz, *The Desert Revolution,* by Lowell Blaisdell, and the newly published *Ricardo Flores Magón,* by Frank Ray Davis all deal with Magón's quixotic attempt to influence the Mexican Revolution from the Baja periphery.

Norris Hundley's *The Great Thirst: Californians and Water, 1770s–1990s* details the struggle between the US and Mexico over the Colorado River water supply.

Border Culture
Federico Campbell, a well-known and award-winning Tijuana-born journalist, deals with the problems facing his city in insightful narratives in two books. *Tijuanenses: Tijuana* looks at personages that shaped the city's history, while *Tijuana: Stories on the Border* is a collection of short stories that examines border life from several different viewpoints – from law student to gang member.

Beautiful Flowers of the Maquiladora: Life Histories of Women Workers in Tijuana (1997), by Norma Iglesias Prieto, is a haunting account of the struggles faced by maquiladora workers based on interviews with 50 women.

Ted Conover's *Coyotes* is a dated but compelling account of undocumented immigrants by a writer who befriended Mexican workers while picking fruit with them in the orchards of Arizona and Florida, lived among them in their own country and accompanied them across the desert border despite concerns about his (and their) personal safety at the hands of corrupt police and unsavory characters.

Similar themes appear in Luis Alberto Urrea's grim but fascinating *Across the Wire: Life and Hard Times on the Mexican Border,* which focuses on the problems of migrants and the shantytowns in a Tijuana that few visitors ever see. Urrea's recent *By the Lake of the Sleeping Children: The Secret Life of the Mexican Border,* produced with photographer John Lueders-Booth, deals with Tijuana's garbage pickers – the ultimate recyclers.

Rubén Martínez's collected essays about Mexican and Mexican-American culture in *The Other Side* include a lengthy piece on Tijuana. Oscar Martínez's *Troublesome*

Border deals with current issues such as population growth, economic development, ecology and international migration.

Alan Weisman's *La Frontera: The United States Border with Mexico* explores all aspects of border life and culture, from the shiny skyscrapers of San Diego and Tijuana to the poverty-stricken shantytowns.

Art

Numerous books deal with artistic cross-fertilization along the US-Mexican border. Two that stand out are *La Frontera – The Border: Art about the Mexico/United States Experience* (1993), by Larry T Baza and Hugh M Davies, and *The Fence and The River: Culture & Politics at the US-Mexico Border* (1999), by Claire Fox. Fox presents a sweeping 20th-century chronology of art – photography, novels, performance art, painting etc – dealing with issues and conflicts along the border.

FILMS

Depictions by early Hollywood directors of Mexican borderlands rife with casinos and prostitution were so insulting that Baja California's first cinematic production, the 1927 *Raza de Bronce* (Race of Bronze), was a nationalistic response to what director Guillermo Calles perceived as racist stereotyping.

Independent US director Jonathan Sarno's oddball romance *Ramona* (1992), which won several awards and is available on video, is set partly in Tijuana. In 1994, *El Jardín de Eden* (The Garden of Eden), a Mexican-Canadian coproduction directed by María Novaro, follows the lives of three women – one Mexican, one Chicana and one from the US – in their struggle to find themselves and a source of survival. The same year also saw the production of the avant-garde *Fronterilandia* (Frontierland) by Rubén Ortiz Torres and Jesse Lerner, who interweave interviews, performance art and dialogue in their exploration of border culture.

Less cerebral fare has been produced more recently not too far south of Tijuana, where 20th Century Fox custom built a

studio for the filming of James Cameron's epic *Titanic,* which is now the permanent Fox Baja Studios. See the Tijuana Excursions chapter for details.

Tijuana also hosts an annual film festival, usually in late April to early May, which brings top independent movies from around the world to the border town.

NEWSPAPERS & MAGAZINES

The most widely read daily newspapers in Tijuana are *La Frontera* and *El Mexicano. El Heraldo,* Baja California's first daily, dates from 1941, but is not as popular as it once was. *La Brújula* (The Compass) is a supplement to the Thursday edition of *La Frontera* and contains local entertainment news and an events schedule.

Zeta is a crusading weekly alternative to the generally conservative daily press. Its editor J Jesús Blancornelas received an International Press Freedom Award from the New York-based Committee to Protect Journalists for his exposés and candid criticisms of political and police corruption, drug lords, and the connections among them. Not everybody supports his efforts: in November 1997, Blancornelas survived an assassination attempt, presumably ordered by drug lords; his bodyguard died protecting him. *Zeta's* extensive readers' letters give a good sampling of the state's best articulated public opinion.

RADIO & TV

Canal 45, Telemundo (Canal 33), Televisa (Canal 12) and TV Azteca (Canal 27) are the four regional television stations operating in the border region; but US channels are also widely received, as are cable and satellite services. Televisa, the Mexican multinational TV network, maintains a large studio and production facilities in Tijuana.

Of the 41 radio stations in Baja California, 26 are on the AM band and 15 on FM. All are commercial except for four FM stations, mostly associated with the Universidad Autónoma de Baja California, that emphasize cultural programming. Several US stations can be received south of the border as well.

PHOTOGRAPHY & VIDEO

Print film is sold at supermarkets, drugstores and tourist shops, but for slide film you may need a photo processing place or large electronics store like Coppel. In any case, prices tend to be higher than in the US or other countries, so stock up before coming to Tijuana. Mexican customs allows the duty-free import of up to 12 rolls of film, but enforcement is lax. Don't buy film previously displayed in sun-exposed shop windows.

Processing a 36-exposure roll of print film costs about US$9. Dorian's department store (Map 13) on Avenida Niños Héroes between Calle 2a (Juarez) and Calle 3a (Carrillo Puerto) offers one-hour developing, as do Copy Pronto (Map 14; ☎ 684-96-77, 684-97-15) in Plaza Río and Star Photo Express (Map 13; Calle 3a 7978). Quality can be uneven, so if it's important wait till you get home.

For general tips on photography, see the Photography & Video section in the San Diego Facts for the Visitor chapter.

Photographing People

Mexicans are normally gracious about being photographed. No one seems to mind being in the shot in the context of an overall scene, but if you want a close-up, you should ask. Simply saying, *'Con su permisión?'* ('With your permission?') while pointing at the camera will usually result in broad smiles and generous posing.

Airport Security

See Airport Security in the San Diego Facts for the Visitor chapter.

TIME & ELECTRICITY

Tijuana is on the same time as San Diego and also uses the same electrical current. See the San Diego Facts for the Visitor chapter.

WEIGHTS & MEASURES

Mexico uses the metric system. In this book, temperatures, weights and liquid measures are given in both US units and their metric equivalents. There is a conversion table at the back of the book.

LAUNDRY

Coin-operated launderettes are a rarity in Tijuana. A central one is Lavamática Gota (Map 13), on Calle 3a (Carrillo Puerto) between Avenidas Martínez and Mutualísimo. You can either wash a load (US$3 to US$4, including dryer) yourself or leave it to the staff for a nominal surcharge.

TOILETS

Public toilets are virtually nonexistent, so take advantage of facilities in hotels, restaurants, bars and bus stations. Toilet paper may not always be available, so carry some with you. If there's a wastepaper basket beside the toilet, put paper, tampons etc in it – it's there because the drains can't cope otherwise.

HEALTH

Taking out travel health insurance to cover emergencies is just common sense. Residents of the US should check their policies to see if coverage extends to Mexico. For details see Travel Insurance earlier this chapter.

Immunizations

No vaccinations are required for Mexico travelers, but it's a good idea to be up to date on tetanus and diphtheria vaccines. If your travels include onward travel to rural areas in mainland Mexico, polio and typhoid shots are recommended. Also consider immunization against hepatitis A. Plan ahead: Some vaccinations require more than one injection, while some should not be given together. Seek medical advice at least six weeks before travel.

Medical & Dental Services

The quality of healthcare in Tijuana is high by Mexican standards, and all types of regular and advanced treatments are available; doctors often are trained in some of the finest universities in the US and elsewhere. Medical bills are comparatively low, but most hospitals and doctors require payment at the time of service; doctors usually insist on cash payment.

Hospitals are certainly dependable for non-life-threatening ailments, like diarrhea

TIJUANA

or dysentery, and minor surgery, such as stitches and sprains. If, however, you come down with a serious illness, you may feel more comfortable being treated in your home country, in which case adequate travel health insurance will prove especially useful.

Tijuana has a reputation for providing cheap, quality dentistry; and many Americans come here for the express purpose of having their teeth fixed. Savings can be substantial (30% to 70%), but obviously depend on the dentist and the type of treatment, which can range from simple cleanings to fillings to root canals and crowns.

There are dozens of dentists in downtown Tijuana alone. If you don't have a recommendation, pop into a few offices, talk with the staff and the doctors, and pick one that feels right.

Food & Water

Cooked food is generally safe, as long as you don't punish your stomach by consuming large portions immediately upon arrival. Avoid uncooked or unpasteurized dairy products, like raw milk and homemade cheeses. Dairy products from supermarkets are usually *pasteurizado,* but in restaurants you can't be sure.

Vegetables and fruits should be washed with purified water or peeled when possible. In tourist hotels and restaurants, salads are usually safe. If thoroughly cooked, meat, chicken and most seafood should not give you problems. Be careful with raw seafood such as oysters and sushi, and marinated but uncooked food like ceviche.

As a rule, clean-looking places packed with people are likely to be safe; food in busy restaurants is cooked and consumed quickly and is probably not reheated. Be suspicious of places without customers. Don't buy food from sidewalk carts, which have no proper refrigeration.

Some travelers recommend taking a preventive dose of Kaolin preparation (such as Pepto-Bismol) for the first two or three days to stave off stomach problems.

Tijuana's tap water is not safe to drink. If you are served water or water-based drinks in restaurants or bars, ask if it is *agua purificada* (purified water) and don't drink it if it isn't. Often the water will simply be *filtrado* (filtered), which does not remove harmful organisms. The same is true of ice cubes. Buy bottled water, available for a few pesos in supermarkets and liquor stores. If you're truly sensitive, also use bottled water for brushing your teeth.

Licuados con leche (milk shakes) from juice stands are usually safe because the government requires the use of pasteurized milk and purified water. Tea or coffee should also be OK, since the water should have been boiled.

Diarrhea

If you do consume contaminated food or water, you may come down with a case of diarrhea, popularly known as Montezuma's Revenge or *turista.* A few rushed trips to the toilet (with no other symptoms) are not indicative of a major problem, but if the condition persists, you could end up suffering dehydration. This is potentially serious, particularly for children or the elderly. To replace lost fluids keep drinking weak black tea *(té negro),* chamomile tea *(agua de manzanilla),* nonfizzy mineral water *(agua mineral)* or soft drinks allowed to go flat and diluted 50% with clean water. If symptoms persist beyond 48 hours, see a doctor.

Gut-paralyzing drugs such as loperamide or diphenoxylate often relieve symptoms but don't cure the problem. Note that these drugs are not recommended for children under 12.

WOMEN TRAVELERS

Tijuana is fairly cosmopolitan, and women using common sense should not encounter any serious problems, especially in the daytime. Along the tourist corridor from the border to Avenida Revolutión, non-Latinas without a male companion(s), however – whether alone or in groups – may attract attention, mostly in the form of catcalling, whistling and suggestive comments. You'll encounter the greatest concentration of such bottom-feeders on La Revo outside girlie clubs like Sans Souci and Bambi and for some reason, on the east side of La Revo between Calle 5a (Zapata) and Calle 6a (Flores Magón). Discourage attention by avoiding eye contact (sunglasses help) and acting aloof; if you ignore them, they'll usually lose interest after a while. Particularly slimy vendors may try to come on to you or touch you; avoid being in a store alone. Walking alone around the Zona Norte at any time of day and anywhere in town at night is not a good idea.

Going to a bar or nightclub alone is inviting trouble; even several women together should be careful and not allow anyone to become separated from the group. Limit your alcohol intake and avoid all drugs. As elsewhere in the world, use of the 'date rape' drug Rohypnol (aka 'roofies,' 'ruffies' or 'roche'), a tranquilizer, is not uncommon; keep an eye on your drink at all times. Don't walk back to your hotel or accept offers from people you just met to drive you there; cabs are cheap.

GAY & LESBIAN TRAVELERS
Homosexual sex is legal in Mexico, but gays and lesbians tend to keep a low profile. Tijuana has several bars and discos, mostly for gay men. Some cater primarily to locals, some have both local and foreign (mostly US) patrons. It helps to speak some Spanish, or you're unlikely to get beyond the 'hustle' stage. As elsewhere in the world, the lesbian scene is smaller, less active or visible, but does exist.

Tijuana has a number of activists and even a bimonthly publication, *La Frontera Gay* (www.fronteragay.com), which deals with discrimination, crime against homosexuals, HIV and AIDS and other hot-button issues. Other Web-based information is available from *The Gay Mexico Network* (www.gaymexico.net), the 'mother' of all Mexican gay Web sites; and *Sergay,* a Spanish-language magazine with a site at www.sergay.com.mx.

DISABLED TRAVELERS
Wheelchair-bound visitors will have a hard time in Tijuana, as Mexican law does not require businesses to be accessible to the mobility-impaired. With a few exceptions, hotels and restaurants are tough to enter without assistance. Local buses are hopeless, taxi drivers impatient, and even navigating around town is difficult because of preposterously high curbs and uneven, potholed sidewalks.

TIJUANA FOR CHILDREN
Mexicans as a rule like children, but there's not much for them to do in Tijuana. Some may enjoy browsing for exotic toys in markets and souvenir shops. The Museo de las Californias has some interesting exhibits, which may appeal to slightly older children. Nearby, Mundo Divertido may also keep kids busy for awhile. Parque Morales, Parque de la Amistad and Paraiso Azteca are all family-oriented places, but they're far from the center. The more central Parque Teniente Guerrero has a nice playground.

Children are likely to be more affected than adults by heat or disrupted sleep. They need time to acclimatize and extra care to avoid sunburn. Replacing fluids if a child gets diarrhea is essential (see the Health section earlier in this chapter). Diapers (nappies), creams, lotions, baby foods and familiar medicines are widely available. Many hotels and motels allow children under 12 (sometimes under 18) to share their parents' room at no additional charge. Larger hotels often offer a baby-sitting service or may be able to help with arrangements.

UNIVERSITIES
Tijuana has 10 public and private institutions of higher learning, with some 14,000 students. The largest and most respected is the public Universidad Autónoma de Baja California (UABC), which offers undergraduate, graduate and postgraduate programs in many majors. Also of note are the Centro de Enseñanza Técnica y Superior (CETYS), and the Colegio de la Frontera Norte (El COLEF), which specializes in border-related studies.

DANGERS & ANNOYANCES
Ain't no lie: Tijuana's air quality will knock a buzzard off a shit-wagon. The Mexican

TIJUANA

genius in the arts, astronomy and cuisine is only equaled by their unerring ability to disable any catalytic converter ever devised by humankind. Sleep well away from main traffic thoroughfares, and be aware that your migraine isn't solely due to last night's extra margarita.

The Zona Norte, Tijuana's seedy red-light district west of Avenida Revolución and north of Calle 1a (Artículo 123), is not recommended for foreigners lacking street savvy, especially after dark. City officials prefer not to dwell on its continued existence, but the area is still of sufficient economic importance that authorities cannot, or will not, eradicate it. Neon-lit Calle Coahuila is especially notorious for its street prostitution and hardcore clubs.

Car theft is a major problem in Tijuana. According to an August 2000 *La Frontera* article, an average of 75 cars are stolen each day throughout the state, most of them in Tijuana. The Zona Centro and the eastern suburbs of Mesa de Otay and La Mesa are particularly notorious. Don't leave anything valuable-looking in your car, and park it in a guarded garage or lot rather than on the street (even if you have a car alarm).

If you're concerned, you could check the Mexico travel advisories provided by your country's state department, which are also posted on the Internet. In the US, call ☎ 202-647-5225 or check http://travel.state.gov; in Canada it's ☎ 800-267-6788, 613-944-6788 and www.dfait-maeci.gc.ca; in the UK, it's ☎ 020-7238-4503, www.fco.gov.uk; and in Australia ☎ 02-6261-3305, www.dfat.gov.au.

Also see Legal Help later this chapter.

Scams

It's unfortunate, but chances are that you'll become the victim of one or several scams during your stay in Tijuana. Most are relatively harmless, but having to be on guard at all times can be extremely annoying.

One common problem is what might be called the 'gringo tax' – surreptitious bill padding that's especially prevalent in bars and nightclubs. Always ask your waiter about drink prices before ordering, then compare them with a price list, which must be posted somewhere in the establishment. Keep track of your consumption, and don't rely on the server to tell you what you owe. If possible, try to get an itemized bill. Bill-padding also occurs in restaurants and, to a lesser extent, in hotels: Check for charge for long-distance calls you've never made and minibar drinks you've never consumed.

Shortchanging is another common practice, especially when you're paying in dollars and getting change in pesos. If prices are given in pesos only, ask which exchange rate is used, then figure out the dollar amount you should be paying (carrying a pocket calculator helps).

When using credit cards, be sure you're being charged for the correct amount. If possible, watch the merchant swipe your card; some unscrupulous types swipe it twice, let you sign one receipt, then forge your signature on the second one.

When making purchases, be sure to get – and keep – the receipt in case you need to make an exchange. If a merchant refuses to exchange an item, contact the Tourist Assistance Office (☎ 688-05-55) for help.

EMERGENCIES

Tijuana's central police station (☎ 060 for emergencies) is at Avenida Constitución 1616, at the corner of Calle 8a (Hidalgo) in the Zona Centro (Map 13); the fire station (☎ 068) is next door. Also see Legal Help.

Tijuana's Hospital General (Map 14; ☎ 684-09-22), north of the Río Tijuana at Avenida Centenario 10851, is the most central medical center with an emergency room. For an ambulance, call the Cruz Roja (Red Cross; ☎ 684-8984).

LEGAL MATTERS

Mexico's judicial system is based on Roman, or Napoleonic, Law, which presumes an accused person guilty until proven innocent. There is no jury trial. To avoid getting into trouble with the law in the first place, keep in mind a few general rules of behavior, most of which are just common sense.

Drinking alcoholic beverages in public is forbidden, as is fighting, nudity, immoral conduct (like urinating in the street) and disturbing the peace. Always carry a valid ID. Don't drink and drive and always wear your seatbelt. The age of consent is 18, as is the legal drinking age. Drugs are illegal, and the minimum jail sentence for possession of anything more than a token amount of any narcotic, including marijuana and amphetamines, is 10 years; it may take up to one year before a verdict is reached. If you're purchasing legal drugs at a pharmacy, make sure to have a prescription if required (see the boxed text 'Drugs & the Letter of the Law' in the Tijuana Shopping chapter for details). Bringing in a firearm or ammunition (even unintentionally) is punishable by up to five years in prison, unless a permit was obtained in advance from a Mexican embassy or consulate.

In all but the most minor car accidents, everyone involved is liable and considered guilty until proven otherwise. Without car insurance, you will be detained until fault has been established. For more on the subject, see the boxed text 'In Case of a Car Accident' in the Tijuana Getting Around chapter.

Legal Help

If arrested, you have the right to notify your embassy or consulate. Consular officials can explain your rights and provide a list of local lawyers. They can also monitor your case, make sure you are treated humanely and notify your relatives or friends – but they can't get you out of jail. More Americans are in jail in Mexico than any other country except the US – about 450 at any one time.

If you encounter minor legal hassles with public officials or local businesspeople, you can contact the Tourist Assistance Office under the auspices of Secure. The numbers are:

Tijuana	☎ 688-05-05
Playas de Rosarito	☎ 612-02-00
Ensenada	☎ 172-30-22
Tecate	☎ 654-10-95

Each office has English-speaking aides and can help with complaints and reporting crimes or lost articles. The 24-hour national

hotline maintained by Secure (☎ 5-250-01-23, 01-800-903-92-00) also provides advice on tourist protection laws and where to obtain help.

If Mexican police wrongfully accuse you of an infraction, you can ask for the officer's identification or to speak to a superior *(jefe)* or to be shown documentation about the law you have supposedly broken. You can also note the officer's name, badge number, vehicle number and department (federal, state or municipal). Then make your complaint to Secure.

BUSINESS HOURS

Stores in the Zona Centro and larger malls such as Plaza Río are generally open 9 or 10 am to 9 pm Monday to Saturday, and to 7 or 8 pm Sunday. Smaller stores sometimes close earlier. Offices are usually open 9 am to 7 pm Monday to Friday; some observe a two- or three-hour lunch period. Most banks are open 9 am to 1:30 pm Monday to Friday only, and sometimes again from 4 to 6 pm.

PUBLIC HOLIDAYS & SPECIAL EVENTS

Tijuanenses observe all major national and Catholic holidays. Banks, post offices and government offices are closed these days.

January

Año Nuevo (New Year's Day) January 1

Día de los Reyes Magos (Three Kings' Day; Epiphany) January 6. Mexican children traditionally receive gifts this day rather than at Christmas.

February

Día de la Constitución (Constitution Day) February 5

Día de la Bandera (Flag Day) February 24

March

Día de Nacimiento de Benito Juárez (Anniversary of Benito Juárez' Birth) March 21

Semana Santa (Holy Week) – March/April. Starting on Palm Sunday, a week before Easter; business closures are usually from Good Friday to Easter Sunday.

May

Día del Obrero (Labor Day) May 1

Cinco de Mayo May 5. This one marks the anniversary of Mexican victory over the French at Puebla (1862).

Día de la Madre (Mother's Day) May 10

June

Día de la Armada (Navy Day) June 1

September

Día de la Independencia September 15 to 16. This day commemorates Mexican independence from Spain (1821). Tijuana hosts one of the biggest celebrations, with fireworks, horse races, folk dances and mariachi bands.

October

Día de la Raza (Columbus Day) October 12. This is the day for celebration of the country's Spanish heritage.

November

Día de Todos los Santos (All Saints' Day) November 1

Día de los Muertos (Day of the Dead) November 2. This is Mexico's most characteristic fiesta; the souls of the dead are believed to

return to earth this day. Families build altars in their homes and visit graveyards to commune with their dead on the night of November 1 and the day of November 2, taking garlands and gifts such as the favorite foods of the deceased; a happy atmosphere prevails. Festivities are especially colorful in Tijuana.

Día de la Revolución (Anniversary of the Mexican Revolution of 1910) November 20

December

Día de Nuestra Señora de Guadalupe (Festival of Our Lady of Guadalupe) December 12

Navidad (Christmas Day) December 25

WORK

Many non-Mexicans are employed in management positions at maquiladoras or as teachers and professors at the universities, but by law people who enter Mexico as tourists are not allowed to take up employment. Working in the country without proper papers and visas will subject you to fines and/or deportation.

Getting There & Away

Most visitors to Tijuana arrive by land. In fact, the San Ysidro border crossing is the busiest in the world. For travel between Tijuana and San Diego, see the boxed text 'Crossing the US-Mexican Border' in the San Diego Getting Around chapter.

AIR

Mexico's fourth-busiest airport, Aeropuerto Internacional Abelardo L Rodríguez (Map 12; ☎ 683-24-18), is right on the international border in the suburb of Mesa de Otay, 5 miles (8km) east of downtown. It is a popular departure and arrival point, but, despite the name, there are no international flights at this time.

The closest international airport is in San Diego. See the San Diego Getting There & Away chapter for details, as well tips and information about international air travel.

Departure Tax

In addition to the 10% value-added tax (IVA), air tickets are subject to a domestic tax of about US$12.50. Taxes are normally added to your quoted fare and paid when you buy the ticket.

Other Parts of Mexico

Aeroméxico (☎ 684-84-44, 683-80-46 at the airport, 01-800-021-40-00 in Mexico, 800-237-6639 in the US), along with its subsidiary Aerolitoral, is in Plaza Río. Aerolitoral flies to Tucson (Arizona) and La Paz via the Mexican city of Hermosillo (Sonora). Aeroméxico has one daily direct flight each to La Paz and to Mazatlán and up to 10 flights to Mexico City with connections to other Mexican destinations.

Aero California (☎ 684-28-76, 682-87-54 at the airport, 800-237-6225 in the US), also in Plaza Río, has daily service to La Paz and Los Cabos and also goes to the northern Mexican mainland.

Mexicana (☎ 634-65-45, 682-41-83 at the airport, 01-800-502-20-00 in Mexico, 800-531-7921 in the US) is at Avenida Diego Rivera 1511 in the Zona Río and directly connects Tijuana with Guadalajara, Zacatecas and Mexico City.

Aerolíneas Internacionales (☎ 684-07-27, 682-94-32 at the airport, 01-800-026-68-05 in Mexico), at Vía Poniente 4246 on the corner of Leona Vicario in the Zona Río, flies to Hermosillo, Culiacán, Guadalajara, Aguascalientes, Cuernavaca and Mexico City.

BUS
Other Parts of Mexico

Buses to the Baja peninsula and to the Mexican mainland depart from Tijuana. Major companies are ABC, Transportes de Sonora (TNS), Elite and Estrellas del Pacífico, all which operate fleets of modern, air-conditioned buses with on-board sanitary facilities (bring your own toilet paper) and amenities like videos, drinks and snacks. Elite offers first-class service on more comfortable, faster (but slightly more expensive) buses.

Tickets cannot be reserved, but you'll be assigned a seat at the time of purchase. To ensure passage, buy tickets a day or two before departure.

Tijuana has a bewildering number of bus stations and companies. Your choice of destination determines your station, although sometimes buses depart from more than one. For example, buses to Mexico City leave from both the Antigua Central Camionera in downtown and from the Central Camionera in La Mesa.

Terminal Turístico Tijuana (Map 13) From Friday to Sunday, Mexicoach's Rosarito Beach Express departs at 11 am and 1, 3 and 5 pm from this terminal on Avenida Revolución between Calle 6a (Flores Magón) and Calle 7a (Galeana). In Rosarito, buses stop at the Rosarito Beach Hotel. Round-trip fare is US$6.

Antigua Central Camionera (Map 13) The old main terminal (☎ 688-07-52) is at Avenida Madero and Calle 1a (Comercio) in

TIJUANA

the Zona Centro and offers services by Subur Baja to Tecate and Rosarito, Greyhound to the US, and Elite and TNS to the Mexican mainland. The terminal is a short taxi ride or about a 10-minute walk from the border and has telephones, fax and photocopy service as well as clean bathrooms (2 pesos).

destination	fare (US)	duration	frequency
Playas de Rosarito	$1	½ hr	29 daily
Tecate	$3	1 hr	44 daily
Mexico City	$120/140	44 hrs	4 daily

Central Camionera de la Linea The border bus terminal (☎ 683-56-81) is on the southeastern edge of Plaza Viva Tijuana. (See Border Crossing map in the San Diego Getting Around chapter.) From here, ABC operates buses to Ensenada, San Quintín and San Felipe, while Estrellas del Pacífico goes to Mexicali, Guadalajara, Mazatlán and other mainland Mexico destinations.

destination	fare (US)	duration	frequency
Ensenada	$8	1½ hrs	32 daily
Mexicali	$12	3 hrs	11 daily
San Felipe	$22	5 hrs	2 daily

Central Camionera de la Mesa Tijuana's main long-distance terminal (☎ 621-76-40) is about 5 miles (8km) southeast of the city center at Blvd Lázaro Cárdenas and Río Alamar. From here, ABC runs buses along the Baja peninsula, while Greyhound goes to California and to the rest of the US; Elite and TNS serve mainland Mexico.

To reach the terminal from downtown, take any 'Buena Vista,' 'Centro' or 'Central Camionera' bus (US 50¢) from Calle 2a (Juárez) east of Avenida Constitución; these buses also stop at the Central Camionera de la Linea. For a few pesos more, you can also take a brown-and-white route taxi (marked 'Mesa de Otay') from Avenida Constitución and Calle 3a (Carrillo Puerto); alternatively, flag one down along Paseo de los Héroes in the Zona Río. A regular cab costs about US$14 from the

border or US$10 from Avenida Revolución, although the actual fare will depend on your bargaining skills.

destination	fare (US)	duration	frequency
Tecate	$3.25	1½ hrs	hourly
Ensenada	$8	1½ hrs	hourly
Mexicali	$11	2½–3 hrs	hourly
San Quintín	$17	5–6 hrs	4 daily
San Felipe	$20	6 hrs	2 daily
Loreto	$59	20 hrs	4 daily
La Paz	$76	22–24 hrs	4 daily
Mazatlán	$102	26 hrs	hourly
Mexico City	$120/140	44 hrs	several daily

The USA

Greyhound Bus Lines (☎ 800-231-2222 in the US, www.greyhound.com) has service to Los Angeles at least hourly from the Central Camionera with a pickup stop at the Antigua Central Camionera. The trip takes from 3½ to 5¼ hours, depending on the number of stops, and costs US$15.50 one way. From the downtown LA terminal you can connect to other US destinations. For Greyhound service to and from San Diego, see the San Diego Getting There & Away chapter.

TRAIN & TROLLEY

Tijuana has no trains, but is connected to Amtrak's US rail network by the San Diego Trolley, which has its terminal just north of the San Ysidro border. For details see the boxed text 'Crossing the US-Mexican Border' in the San Diego Getting Around chapter, and the Train section in the San Diego Getting There & Away chapter.

CAR & MOTORCYCLE

Tijuana is the northwestern terminus of two major Mexican highways: México 1 (aka the 'Transpeninsular') snakes down the Baja peninsula for 1060 miles (1700km), all the way to Land's End in Cabo San Lucas. Between Tijuana and Ensenada it is paralleled by México 1D, a toll road. For more on this route, see the boxed text 'Traveling the Tijuana-Ensenada Corridor' in the Tijuana Excursions chapter.

ua Caliente racetrack, Tijuana

Huichol craftwork, Tijuana

ol fruits and juices, Tijuana

Tijuana hot rod

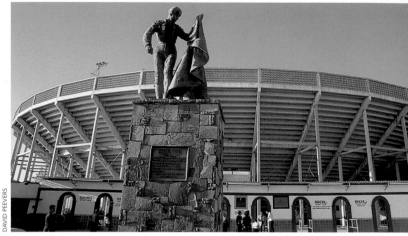

See a bullfight at Plaza Monumental, Playas de Tijuana.

'La Revo' Avenida Revolución, Tijuana

Tijuana sunshine

Theater, art and a giant golf ball at the Centro Cultural de Tijuana

Tijuana is also linked with Tecate, Mexicali and the Mexican mainland via the free México 2 and the toll road México 2D, which starts just east of the airport in Mesa de Otay. The latter is easier to find and faster once you're actually on it. The downside is the exorbitant fee of US$5.50 per vehicle for 20-mile (32km) stretch of road.

Coming from the US, I-5 and I-805 both end at the San Ysidro border. To get to the Mesa de Otay crossing, take Hwy 905 east off I-5 or I-805 to Hwy 125 south. Also see the boxed text 'Crossing the US-Mexican Border' in the San Diego Getting Around chapter.

Insurance

Mexican law recognizes only Mexican *seguro* (car insurance), so a US or Canadian policy won't suffice. Driving in Mexico without Mexican insurance is extremely foolish. Drivers who are involved in an accident – regardless of whose fault it is – can be jailed, or prevented from leaving the country until a bond has been posted, or even until all claims are settled; this could take months. A Mexican insurance policy is a guarantee that restitution will be paid and will expedite your release. At minimum, you should get liability insurance, although full coverage (collision, liability, fire, theft, glass, medical and legal) is advisable, especially given Tijuana's high rate of auto theft.

If you're entering Tijuana from San Diego, you'll find numerous insurance offices right at the Via de San Ysidro and Camino de la Plaza exits off of I-5. Some are open 24 hours and even offer drive-through insurance in five minutes or less. Several companies also issue policies via fax and the Internet. Rates are government controlled and fairly standard on both sides of the border. Most major US insurance companies and the American Automobile Association (AAA) can also arrange coverage.

Liability coverage runs about US$8 for the first day and US$2.50 each additional day. Be sure to clarify the extent of your coverage (US$50,000 is considered minimum). For full coverage, premiums depend on the age and make of your vehicle. For example, a car valued between US$5000 and US$10,000 costs about US$12 a day; those valued from US$15,000 to US$20,000 are US$16. In general, the longer your stay, the cheaper the per-day rate.

Below is a list of some US-based companies offering Mexican insurance policies. Insurance is also available from the Cotuco Tourist Office at the border (see the Tijuana Facts for the Visitor chapter for locations).

Baja Bound (☎ 619-437-0404, 888-552-2252, fax 888-265-7834, @ administrator@bajabound.com) 2222 Coronado Ave, Suite H, San Diego, CA 92154. Offers insurance in person, by fax or Internet; open 8:30 am to 4:30 pm Monday to Friday. Information-packed Web site: www.bajabound.com.

Instant Mexico Insurance Services (☎ 619-428-4714, 800-345-4701, fax 619-690-6533) 223 Via de San Ysidro, San Ysidro, CA 92173. Open 24 hours; also issues policies over the phone.

Mex-Insur (☎ 619-428-11-21) I-5 at Via de San Ysidro exit, San Ysidro, CA 92173, and (☎ 619-425-23-90) I-805 at F St & Bonito Rd, Chula Vista, CA 91910.

Sanborn's Insurance (☎ 956-686-3601, 800-222-0158, fax 956-686-0732, contact @ info@sanbornsinsurance.com) 2009 S 10th St, McAllen, TX 78503. Sells insurance via phone, fax, in person or at www.sanbornsinsurance.com.

Vehicle Permit

At the time of writing, you do *not* need a vehicle permit for travel in Tijuana or anywhere in Baja California. If you intend to take your car to mainland Mexico, check with a Mexican consulate or your local branch of the American Automobile Association (AAA) for information on how to obtain one.

Rental

Renting a car in Tijuana is expensive by US and European standards. You must have a valid driver's license (see the Tijuana Facts for the Visitor chapter for details), passport and major credit card and are usually required to be at least 23 (sometimes 25) years old. Some companies will also rent to 21-year-olds but require you to take out additional insurance.

In addition to the basic daily or weekly rental rate, you must pay for insurance, tax and fuel. Ask exactly what the insurance covers – sometimes the liability coverage amount is so ridiculously low (say, US$200) that you'd be in big trouble in an accident (also see boxed text 'In Case of a Car Accident' in the Tijuana Getting Around chapter). You may find it's wise to purchase additional liability insurance.

Most major international car rental agencies have offices in Tijuana. Sometimes you can get better rates by making reservations through toll-free telephone numbers than by walking into the office. On occasion, though, the local office may have special promotions not available through central reservations. It pays to compare.

The following are the major agencies represented in Tijuana.

Alamo (☎ 686-40-40, 683-80-84 at the airport) Blvd Sánchez Taboada 10285, Zona Río

Avis (☎ 683-06-03, 683-23-10, 800-288-88-88 in Mexico, 800-331-1084 in the US) Blvd Cuauhtémoc 406, Colonia Aeropuerto

Budget (Map 14; ☎ 634-33-04, 683-29-05 at the airport, 800-700-17-00 in Mexico, 800-472-3325 in the US) Avenida Paseo de los Héroes 77, Zona Río

Dollar (☎ 681-84-84, 800-800-4000 in the US) Blvd Sánchez Taboada 10285, Zona Río

Europcar (☎ 686-21-03, 800-003-95-00 in Mexico) Blvd Agua Caliente 5000

Hertz (Map 15; ☎ 686-12-12, 683-20-80 at the airport, 800-709-50-00 in Mexico, 800-654-3001 in the US) Blvd Agua Caliente 3402,

National (Map 15; ☎ 686-21-03, 800-227-7368 in the US) Blvd Agua Caliente 10598

ORGANIZED TOURS

For tours to Tijuana, see the San Diego Getting There & Away chapter.

Getting Around

Tijuana is not the easiest city in the world to get around, at least once you leave the central area. Drivers will encounter horrendous traffic and unorthodox driving styles. Public transportation is cheap, frequent and plentiful, but confusing. Many places described in this book, however, are relatively easy to reach on foot or without your own transportation.

TO/FROM THE AIRPORT

Traveling by cab between the airport and the border or downtown costs between US$10 and US$20, depending on your bargaining skills. Prices are per car, not per person. If you're starting at the border, note that the blue taxis – stationed behind the huge fleet of yellow cabs next to the Cotuco Tourist Office – are usually cheaper.

You can save by using public transportation. From the border, take any bus 'Aeropuerto' bus from the bus stop on the southeastern edge of Plaza Viva Tijuana. From downtown, buses to the airport depart from Avenida Constitución between Calle 4a (Díaz Mirón) and Calle 5a (Zapata). The fare is a reasonable 4.50 pesos (US 50¢).

PUBLIC TRANSPORTATION

Bus

From the San Ysidro border, take any bus marked 'Centro' to go downtown. Buses stop on the southeastern edge of Plaza Viva Tijuana; there's usually someone with a notebook to steer you toward the right bus to anywhere in town. The fare is 4.50 pesos (about US 50¢). Drivers have no change.

In the Zona Centro, buses in all directions stop between Avenida Revolución and Avenida Niños Héroes along either Calle 2a (Juárez), Calle 3a (Carrillo Puerto), Calle 4a (Díaz Mirón) or Calle 5a (Zapata).

Buses marked 'Centro-5 y 10' travel along Blvd Agua Caliente past the bullring, Chapultepec, Agua Caliente racetrack and Mercado de Todos as far as Plazas Carrousel & Las Brisas. Buses to the border are marked 'La Linea.' Buses to Playas de Tijuana travel west on Calle 3a (Carrillo Puerto); there are several stops along this road, including one at Avenida Constitución. There are no buses to the Zona Río; route taxis are your best option.

Route Taxis

Route taxis are station wagons that operate along designated routes – an efficient and inexpensive alternative to buses. You can board at their route terminus or by flagging them down. Since route taxis cater primarily to commuters, they're not set up to transport luggage (the trunk is converted into seats). If you have luggage, offer to pay double or triple the fare. Fares depend on the distance, but are usually 5 or 6 pesos (about US 60¢) per person. The driver will drop you off anywhere along the route.

From Avenida Constitución and Calle 3a (Carrillo Puerto), brown-and-white route taxis (marked 'Centro-Mesa de Otay' or 'Centro-Otay Mesa') go along Paseo de los Héroes to the Zona Río, then farther east to the Central Camionera de la Mesa and sometimes as far as the airport.

Red-and-black cabs travel along Blvd Agua Caliente to the El Toreo bullring, Chapultepec, the racetrack (Fracc Hipódromo), the Mercado de Todos and Plazas Carrousel and Las Brisas. They're usually marked 'Centro-Clínica 27' and may be hailed on Calle 4a (Díaz Mirón) between Avenidas Constitución and Niños Héroes.

Yellow-and-white taxis to Playas de Tijuana head west along Calle 3a (Carrillo Puerto) from Avenida Niños Héroes. There are two routes: to get to the beach or bullring, board a car saying 'Plaza Monumental'; the others go through central Playas.

Yellow-and-blue cabs to Rosarito depart from Avenida Madero near Calle 4a (Díaz Mirón); the fare is US$1.

CAR & MOTORCYCLE

If you plan on confining your Tijuana explorations to the border area – Zona Centro and Zona Río – you probably won't need a car. But since the rest of the city sprawls over a considerable area, tooling around with your own wheels is faster and more

In Case of a Car Accident

Two points cannot be stressed often enough:

• Do *not* drive in Baja California without Mexican insurance.

• Do *not* drive while drunk or under the influence of drugs.

Adhering to this advice will make your life less complicated if you are in an accident – regardless of whether you are at fault.

If you're in an accident, you and the other parties should wait until the police arrive. In case of minor damage, it's not likely that you'll be arrested and detained – unless you are intoxicated or without insurance! Ideally, the parties will be asked to arrive at a damage settlement, and you and your vehicle will be quickly released. Contact your insurance company before signing any agreement.

If a settlement cannot be reached, the damage is significant or there are injuries, you may be detained and your vehicle impounded while responsibility is assessed. When asked to make a statement, you can refuse to do so, but it's not a good idea. You should, however, ask for a lawyer to be present, as well as an interpreter. Under Mexican law, you have the right to both. If you don't know a lawyer, call your consulate for a referral.

Determining responsibility can take weeks or even months. Except in fatal cases, you should be released after posting a bond. What matters to the authorities is that you can guarantee restitution to the victims – plus fines, towing costs and other expenses – should you be found guilty. And yes, that's why getting insurance is so darned important! And, of course, if you were driving while intoxicated, being released on a bond is probably not going to happen.

For more on the Mexican justice system, see Legal Matters in the Tijuana Facts for the

convenient and comfortable than usin public transportation.

Driving in Tijuana poses special challenge (see Driving Conditions). Traffic can be ba any time of day, but tends to be especiall clogging in the morning and late afternoo Choose a hotel with a guarded parking lot o absent that, park in a secure garage or pay lo don't leave your car on the street overnigh Whatever you do – get Mexican car insu ance. See Insurance in the Tijuana Gettin There & Away chapter for details on ho and why – also for car rental information.

Driving Conditions

Driving in Tijuana is like Russian roulett on wheels and should not be attempted b the faint of heart. The rules you've learne at home don't apply in this city. The confu sion begins at the San Ysidro border cros ing, when drivers in all lanes of traffic mak a swerving mad dash for their road c choice. Take it slow, and try to get into th correct lane: 'Centro' for Avenida Revol ción and downtown, 'Zona Río' for Pase de los Héroes, 'Playas de Rosarito' c 'Scenic Road' (which bypasses the cit proper) for the fast road to Playas d Tijuana and the México 1D toll road.

Unless you're familiar with traffic circl (roundabouts), Tijuana's glorietas – whic abound along Paseo de los Héroes – coul give you nightmares. This is where, as wit the proverbial 'black holes,' all laws c physics break down in the *mano a man* pursuit of right-of-way. Do *not* cut acros lanes of onrushing traffic to exit these mad dening merry-go-rounds; if you can't mak it to your preferred exit, just take anothe turn around the circle and insinuate you self into a better orbit for the next pass.

Every taxi on the road should be r garded as a potential hazard, as cabbie have zero courtesy for any other drive who are not cabbies. They will skirt withi inches of your car, testing for weakness c resolve. Give them wide berth and don enter into their stupid – and dangerous games. Other pitfalls include obnoxiou one-way streets, omnivorous potholes an speeding, romping teenagers.

Remember: Courtesy counts for zip in Tijuana. Being a smart and aware driver is all that matters. And the smartest drivers are not on the roads at all, especially at night. For details on how to handle fender-benders, see the boxed text 'In Case of a Car Accident.'

TAXI

Tijuana's taxis lack meters, and cab drivers tend to overcharge gringos, especially for the five-minute trip from the border to Avenida Revolución – which should cost US$5 per car. Negotiate the price before getting into the taxi, and don't hesitate to walk away and try another cabbie if you don't like the price. Never agree to a per-person charge. The ride to Plaza Río from either the border or Avenida Revolución should cost about US$4, to the racetrack or the bullring US$5 or US$6. To Playas de Tijuana a fare of US$8 is reasonable, while an airport trip costs anything from US$10 to US$20. Tipping is not expected.

WALKING

Tijuana's downtown is compact and best explored on foot. Walking lets you experience the city at ground level and gives you a better sense of its quirks. The Tijuana Things to See & Do chapter has a self-guided walking tour of sights in the Zona Centro. Walking is also an option in the Zona Río, where you'll find some of the town's best shopping. That area's commercial heart, the Plaza Río mall, is a 20-minute walk from either Avenida Revolución or the border.

In the daytime, walking around is safe except in the red-light Zona Norte. The greatest danger comes from the uneven, and often unpaved, sidewalks and ridiculously high curbs, which require you to keep an eye out at all times. Don't walk around at night.

TIJUANA

Things to See & Do

ZONA CENTRO (MAP 13)

Tijuana's downtown is the city's most historical part, although most of its past has been obliterated by unimaginative storefronts, gaudy advertisements, and terrace bars enveloped in loud music and unfiltered car exhaust. Historical awareness has been nonexistent in this town, whose mostly migrant population has roots anywhere but Tijuana and little knowledge of – or interest in – preserving its former glories. Nowhere is this garish commercialism and utilitarian architecture more in evidence than on **Avenida Revolución**, downtown's main artery and tourist magnet.

Virtually every visitor has to experience at least a brief stroll up and down this raucous thoroughfare, popularly known as 'La Revo' – a noisy mishmash of nightclubs, bellowing hawkers outside seedy strip bars, brash taxi drivers, tacky souvenir stores, street photographers with zebra-striped burros, discount liquor stores and restaurants. Unfortunately, most people never venture beyond this cacophonous strip, returning to the border in the belief that they've 'done' Tijuana. Those who do make the effort will find a completely different reality – not beautiful, to be sure, but a glimpse into what makes this border metropolis tick. They'll even find a few survivors from Tijuana's past: singular, sometimes hidden, usually ignored, but not gone completely.

Walking Tour

Our walking tour begins on one of Tijuana's oldest streets and takes in all major sights in the downtown area. It covers 3 miles (4.5km) and can take from two hours to all day, depending on how long you spend lingering, breaking to eat and shopping. All places mentioned here are covered below in greater detail.

A good place to start is at the Secture Tourist Office on **Plaza Santa Cecilia**, right at the foot of Avenida Revolución. From here head south for one block to Calle 2a (Juárez), turn right (west) at the historic **Bital Bank Building** and walk one block to Avenida Constitución. Here, duck into the Antiguo Palacio Municipal and have a look at local talent in the **Galería Arte de la Ciudad**.

Continue west on Calle 2a, past the **El Reloj** clock and the entrance to the colorful **Pasaje Añagua** to the imposing **Catedral de Nuestra Señora de Guadalupe** at the intersection with Avenida Niños Héroes. Walk a few more blocks on Calle 2a, then turn south on Avenida Cinco de Mayo to emerge next to the **Iglesia de San Francisco**, which borders the popular **Parque Teniente Guerrero**.

Take a stroll around the park before backtracking east along Calle 3a (Carrillo Puerto) to Avenida Constitución, then turn right (south) and look for the entrance to a passageway halfway down the block's eastern side. Turn left into the passageway for a visit to the **Museo Foreign Club**. Exit this little alley on Avenida Revolución and turn right – you'll find yourself right at the legendary **Hotel Caesar's**, with its collection of bullfighting memorabilia.

Highlights

- Soaking up Baja history at the Museo de las Californias
- Catching a show of top-notch talent at the Centro Cultural de Tijuana
- Sampling local wine, brandy and tequila at Vinícola LA Cetto
- Browsing for crafts, unusual household items and produce at Mercado Hidalgo (see Tijuana Shopping)
- Wrapping up a day of discovery with sunset drinks in Playas de Tijuana
- Witnessing the pomp, pageantry and pathos of a bullfight at the Plaza Monumental
- Experiencing culinary greatness at Cien Años, Villa Saverio's or other top-rated restaurants (see Tijuana Places to Eat)

Farther south on La Revo you'll pass the **Frontón Palacio Jai Alai**. Turn right on Calle 10a (Sarabia), cross Avenida Huitzilao (the southern continuation of Avenida Constitución) and turn into Calle Cañon Johnson, where you can rest during a wine tasting at Tijuana's **LA Cetto** winery.

Backtrack to Avenida Huitzilao, then head uphill (south) to Parque 18 Marzo with its **Monumento a los Niños Héroes de Chapultepec** at the foot of a giant Mexican flag, the **Bandera Monumental**. Continue downhill along Calle Brasil to Blvd de los Fundadores and the **Torre de Tijuana**, where the tour concludes. The fastest way back to where you started is straight north on Avenida Revolución.

Plaza Santa Cecilia

Plaza Santa Cecilia is one of Tijuana's oldest streets and, at least in the daytime, a pleasant promenade peopled by souvenir vendors. A naive sculpture of its namesake, the patron saint of musicians, sits at the northern end. Cars were banished with the plaza's creation in 1981, partly with the help of the local Asociación de Mariachis. You can usually see a group of them hanging out, dressed in their finery, waiting for engagements. Unfortunately, the street attracts a less than salubrious element after dark.

Bital Bank Building

This beautifully restored 1929 structure at the corner of Avenida Revolución and Calle 2a (Juárez) is a rare oasis of elegance in this part of town and among the few surviving architectural gems of Old Tijuana. Previously a store, it is now a bank. The white facade is accented by solid marble and broken up into elegant arches separated by wrought-iron lamps. Especially ornate is the upper portion of the entrance, with its rounded corners, floral ornamentation, relief frieze and clock.

Antiguo Palacio Municipal

This building, at the corner of Avenida Constitución and Calle 2a (Juárez), was Tijuana's town hall from 1921 until 1986, when the city administration moved to a new, much larger

structure on Paseo de Tijuana (Avenida Centenario). At the building's entrance are two modest but interesting murals. The tranquil courtyard contains a library and a worthwhile bookstore and the Galería de Arte de la Ciudad (Municipal Art Gallery; ☎ 685-01-04), which plays host to important exhibits

---

Tijuana Galleries

Tijuana has a long list of accomplished artists, many of national and international renown (see Arts in the Facts about Tijuana chapter for details). Their work is on display at galleries and museums around town. To find out what's where, check with the tourist offices or get *La Brújula,* the Thursday entertainment supplement to the *La Frontera* newspaper. Most exhibits are free.

Galería de Arte de la Ciudad (Map 13; ☎ 685-01-04), Avenida Constitución at Calle 2a (Juárez), Zona Centro; open 9 am to 7 pm Monday to Friday

Casa de la Cultura de Tijuana (Map 13; ☎ 687-26-04), Calle París y Pompa Ibarra 5 Zona Centro; open 10 am to 7 pm Monday to Saturday

El Lugar del Nopal (Map 13; ☎ 685-12-64), off Calle 6a (Flores Magón) on Callejon 5 de Mayo 1328, Zona Centro; open from 5 pm Tuesday to Sunday

Sala de Exposiciones Comunitarias at Cecut (Map 14; ☎ 687-96-00), Paseo de los Héroes and Avenida Independencia, Zona Río; open 11 am to 8 pm daily

Multiforo del Instituto Cultural de Baja California (ICBC; Map 14; ☎ 683-59-22), Avenida Centenario 10151, Zona Río; open 9 am to 5 pm daily

Sala de Arte de la Universidad Autónoma de Baja California (☎ 624-11-00), Circuito Universitario, Mesa de Otay; open 9:30 am to 7 pm Monday to Friday

Galería de Arte at the Casa de la Cultura – Playas (Map 12; ☎ 630-18-25), Avenida del Agua 777, Playas de Tijuana

TIJUANA

showcasing local and regional talent (also see the boxed text 'Tijuana Galleries').

El Reloj

It's easy to walk right past one of the longest-lived vestiges of the old Tijuana: Neither a building nor a monument, it is…a clock. Anchored in the sidewalk on the south side of Calle 2a (Juárez), just west of the Antiguo Palacio Municipal, this ornate timepiece was built in Pennsylvania in the late 19th century. Resembling a giant single traffic light, it originally stood on historic Olvera Street in Los Angeles. In 1943 a wily Tijuana jewelry merchant installed it outside his store to attract customers. That store is still here, having changed owners twice, with each inheriting the clock, which, by the way, was still functional at the time of writing. Steps away is the colorful **Pasaje Añagua**, reputedly Tijuana's oldest market (see the Tijuana Shopping chapter).

Catedral de Nuestra Señora de Guadalupe

Tijuana's oldest church (☎ 685-30-26) evolved from an adobe chapel built in 1902. It sits smack-dab on one of the busiest intersections, Avenida Niños Héroes and Calle 2a (Juárez). The rectangular red and gray brick structure sports two towers topped by yellow and blue domes. The three-nave, barrel-vaulted interior is largely whitewashed, and accented with baroque-style gold leaf, stained glass in the central cupola and crystal chandeliers.

There are several chapels off to the right; the first is as busy as a dovecote. The main object of devotion is St Martín de Porres, a Dominican lay brother from Peru who is the patron of victims of racial injustice, the downtrodden and small animals. His figure is behind glass and further protected by iron grills. Most people finish up their prayer by smearing their fingers against the rather filthy glass; some try to make an even greater impression by leaving small chunks of chewed gum.

The church is open all day, and mass is held several times. Outside, vendors sell candles, rosary beads, framed pictures of the Virgin and other devotional kitsch.

Parque Teniente Guerrero

Named for a soldier who helped defend Baja California against the Magonistas in 1911 (see Revolution & Its Aftermath in the Facts about Tijuana chapter), this small, nicely landscaped park is one of the few green oases in central Tijuana. Kids squeal with delight while sliding, swinging and clambering around the well-kept playground, while young couples on benches whisper into each other's ears.

There are a couple of small ponds, an ornate bandstand and several statues, including one of Padre Miguel Hidalgo and another of Benito Juárez. The park has a reputation as a major after-dark cruising area for gay men.

On the east side of the park looms the twin-towered **Iglesia de San Francisco** (☎ 685-22-74), a single-nave church with an interesting star-vaulted ceiling, walls of modern stained glass and polished wood floors.

Museo Foreign Club

This haphazard collection of historical photographs and memorabilia is tucked away in an open arcade that boasts a huge Aztec calendar and is strewn with replicas of ancient Toltec and Olmec sculptures.

Founded by William McCain Clauson, an American who gained international fame as a singer of Mexican folk songs in the 1950s and '60s, the museum is operated on a shoe-string by Clauson and his director, Roberto Lango. This is one of the few permanent exhibits in town on the Tijuana of yore. Here are photographs of many long-demolished downtown landmarks, including the fort, the jail, the border crossing, the churches – even the first striped burros, a marketing idea born in 1954. Other exhibits deal with the Mexican Revolution and feature pictures of Emiliano Zapata and Pancho Villa. Upstairs is a small art gallery, as well as several classrooms where Clauson and Lango teach music, Spanish and English.

Somebody is usually at the museum (☎ 666-37-49) 7 am to 5 pm, though you may have to knock hard. Admission is free, but donations are welcome.

Hotel Caesar's

Built in 1930, the venerable – if somewhat worn – birthplace of the Caesar salad (see the boxed text 'All Hail Caesar's' in the Tijuana Places to Eat chapter) was once the favorite hotel of matadors and their entourages in town to fight the bulls at Tijuana's arenas. Some of their belongings have become memorabilia, enshrined behind glass in the hotel's lobby.

On view is the embroidered cape of Spanish bullfighter Manuel 'Manolete' Rodriguez. Manuel Capetillo and Joselito Huerta left their *trajes de luces* (suits of lights; the colorful and heavily ornamented outfits worn by toreros and matadors), as did Eloy Cavazos, who wore his in 1984 on the day of his first retirement (he's come back twice and was still fighting at the time of writing). You'll also see the mounted ears and tails of several vanquished bulls. There's more on Caesar's in the Tijuana Places to Stay chapter.

Frontón Palacio Jai Alai

An odd blend of Moorish and baroque architectural elements, this striking Tijuana landmark was begun in 1926 but not completed until 1947. For decades it hosted jai alai, the fast-moving game of Basque origin, which is kind of a hybrid of squash and tennis. Alas, poor attendance and the game's waning popularity forced its owner to close down in the late 1990s.

The future of the building, which takes up most of the block of Avenida Revolución between Calle 7a (Galeana) and Calle 8a (Hidalgo), is uncertain, but as of late it has hosted several smallish fairs and exhibitions. Outside is a sculpture of a *pelotari,* a jai alai player, striking a pose while balancing on the world. It's by local artist Eduardo Corrella, who used his son as a model.

Vinícola LA Cetto

LA Cetto (pronounced 'elle-a-TSCHE-to'), Mexico's largest winery, has opened its Tijuana branch to tours and tastings. Still operated by descendants of Italian immigrants who arrived in Baja California in 1926, it produces some 11 million gallons (50 million liters) annually, 30% of which is exported, mostly to Europe. There is a total of some 50 red and white varietals, including cabernet sauvignon, pinot noir, merlot and chardonnay, as well as sparkling wines, brandy and tequila.

The tour starts outside the main building, with its facade of planks from retired oak barrels. Inside, you'll see giant steel tanks that hold table wine and smaller oak casks used for aging the reserves. The tour passes the bottling facility before descending into the winery's inner sanctum – the musty, vaulted cellar where thousands of bottles of superior vintage reds are aged. Note that the bottles are stacked right on top of one another without racks.

The grapes are grown in vineyards in the fertile Valle de Guadalupe (see the Tijuana Excursions chapter). Tours are between 10 am and 5 pm Monday to Friday and to 4 pm on Saturday. The cost is US$2 and includes a sampling of two wines. Prices at the winery's store are 25% lower than around town and start at US$5 for a bottle of wine, US$6 for sparkling wine or brandy and US$12 for tequila.

Vinícola LA Cetto (☎ 685-30-31) is at Calle Cañón Johnson 8151, just southwest of Avenida Constitución.

Bandera Monumental

This giant Mexican flag, measuring 86 feet X 150 feet (28.6m X 50m) and inaugurated in 1997 by former president Ernesto Zedillo himself, is a source of great pride to locals. Easily spotted from throughout downtown, it's part of a military complex atop a hillside in Colonia Morelos, just past the southern end of Avenida Revolucíon.

It's adjacent to the smallish Parque de 18 Marzo and the **Monumento a los Niños Héroes de Chapultepec** (Monument to the Boy Heroes of Chapultepec). This rather bombastic piece of sculpture features a massive eagle clutching a tablet inscribed with the names of six young military cadets who died on September 13, 1847 in one of

TIJUANA

the final battles of the Mexican-American War. When their academy on Chapultepec Castle outside of Mexico City was attacked by an overwhelming contingent of US troops, the cadets leapt to their deaths rather than surrender. These 'Boy Heroes,' whose behavior was considered an act of supreme heroism, have become symbols of the injustices suffered by Mexico at the hands of the US.

Torre de Tijuana

Squatting in a pint-sized triangular park at the intersection of Blvd de los Fundadores and Blvd Agua Caliente, just southeast of Avenida Revolución, is this faithful replica of the original 'Tower of Tijuana,' built in 1928 as part of the Agua Caliente Casino & Spa complex. Destroyed by fire in 1956, it originally stood on the site of what is now a Pemex gas station, near where Blvd Salinas and Blvd Agua Caliente merge. In 1984 the Tijuana Lion's Club decided to resurrect this popular landmark; it was inaugurated four years later. The white square structure is supported by four arches and has a pagoda-esque, three-tiered top which rises 70 feet (22m).

Museo de Cera

Leave any expectations at the door and you might actually enjoy a visit to Tijuana's wax museum, strategically placed right along the walking route to downtown from the border at the corner of Avenida Madero and Calle 1a (Comercio). On view are 90 waxen figures from Mexican history (eg, Hernán Cortés, Emiliano Zapata), world politics (Ronald Reagan, Bill Clinton) and entertainment (Bill Cosby, Cantinflas), plus the obligatory House of Horrors. Speaking of horror, things start off rather gorily with an Aztec warrior triumphantly posing with the heart of his poor victim.

Controversial personalities include Iran's Ayatollah Khomeini and Cuba's Fidel Castro, complemented by crowd pleasers such as an uncanny Frida Kahlo, a really bad Elvis and Rita Hayworth, who was discovered in Tijuana. The most moving display depicts Juan Soldado; it has become a shrine

to the martyred young soldier (see the boxed text 'Juan Soldado: Virtuous Victim or Patron Saint of *Pollos*').

The museum (☎ 688-24-78) is open 10 am to 7 pm Monday to Friday; admission is US$1.40. Display captions are in Spanish and English.

ZONA RÍO (MAP 14)

East of the Zona Centro, Tijuana's modern 'New Town' has sprung up along the Río Tijuana. Bisected by large, modern boulevards, especially Paseo de los Héroes, this is an upscale, commercial area. Nearly all of Tijuana's luxury hotels, fine restaurants and nightclubs are here, as are some of the city's best sightseeing and non-souvenir shopping.

Centro Cultural de Tijuana (Cecut)

Tijuana's modern cultural center (☎ 684-11-11), at Paseo de los Héroes and Avenida Independencia, goes a long way toward undermining the city's reputation as a cultural wasteland and is a facility that would be the pride of any city of comparable size in the world. It's Tijuana's premier showcase for highbrow events – concerts, theater readings, seminars, conferences, dance recitals and so forth (see the Tijuana Entertainment chapter for details).

In front of the distinctive complex is a humongous cream-colored sphere – sort of a giant golf ball – known as La Bola (the ball), which was designed by noted architects Pedro Ramierez Vasquez and Manuel Rosen Morrison. Financed by the federal government, it opened in 1982 as the first in a string of planned regional cultural centers. It has lived on as the last, since an international oil crisis and the devaluation of the peso in 1982 forced the government into severe fiscal restraint. For once, Tijuana was lucky. More than 1.3 million people visit Cecut each year.

Museo de las Californias Since April 2000, Cecut has one more showpiece, a state-of-the-art museum that chronicles the history of Baja California from prehistoric times to the present. It provides an excellent introduction to the peninsula and belongs

Juan Soldado: Virtuous Victim or Patron Saint of *Pollos**?

Tijuana has precious little in common with Lourdes, in France, but both cities lay claim to being reliable sources for the performance of miracles. The author of the Tijuana variety of divine intervention is the spirit of Juan Soldado (Juan the Soldier), whose life was distinguished only by the circumstances of his death.

When a 12-year-old girl was raped and killed in the 1930s, the uniform of young Juan Castillo Morales was found covered with her blood. Apparently, a local mob demanded *la ley fuga* (the law of flight) be carried out by the military. This meant that the condemned man had to flee his tormentors and – in this 'escape attempt' – would then be shot in the back. Morales was thus executed and the mob's lust for blood quelled.

Twenty years later, the story goes, Juan's commanding officer revealed on his deathbed that it was he, not Morales, who killed the girl. Thus began Juan's unlikely ascent to popular sainthood.

The ashamed Tijuana people began to pray at Juan's grave, and before long he was doling out miracles to the faithful. The Catholic Church scoffs at the notion that Juan was anything other than a drudge in the army who had a very short run of bad luck. Indeed, they insist that the greatest 'miracles' he's ever performed are the answered prayers of those who'd like to see their loved ones sneak successfully across the border.

But whether Juan is saintly or silly, wherever you find his image you'll find letters, candles, flowers and personal objects left in hopes of piquing his interest in worldly intervention. A stuffed version of the soldier saint in the city's wax museum has been turned into such a shrine. The real thing lies in a Tijuana cemetery, where you're asked to respect his tomb as a place of somber worship. What the heck! Drop a knee here and say a little prayer – it couldn't hurt!

* Mexicans entering the US illegally are sometimes referred to as *pollos*.

- David Peevers

on everybody's must-see list. The exhibits were designed by Mario Vásquez, Mexico's top museum designer, who was also behind Mexico City's famous Museo Nacional de Antropología (National Anthropology Museum), one of the best museums of its kind in the world.

The exhibit kicks off with replica cave paintings, then moves on to important historical milestones, including the earliest Spanish expeditions under Hernán Cortés, the mission period, the Treaty of Guadalupe Hidalgo, the Chinese immigration, the irrigation of the Colorado delta and the advent of the railroad. Displays in glass cases are mixed with scale replicas of explorers' ships, models of missions, found objects, maps, paintings and photographs. All explanatory text is in English and Spanish, and there are touch-screen terminals for additional information. It's all presented along gentle ramps in an airy space without encumbering walls. The museum is open 9 am to noon and 2 to 5 pm Tuesday to Saturday, 10 am to 8 pm Sunday; admission is US$2.

Jardín Caracol This charming garden, laid out to resemble a snail (hence the name), often hosts free events and exhibits, many of them for children. The **Museo Jardín Caracol** has an exhibit of pre-Hispanic sculpture and is open Tuesday to Friday 9 am to 1 pm, weekends from noon to 5 pm; admission is US 80¢.

Monuments

The *glorietas* (traffic circles) along Paseo de los Héroes may be a motorist's worst nightmare, but the pompous statues that anchor them are a gallery of Mexico's 'Who's Who.' The monument closest to the border, where Paseo de los Héroes intersects Avenida

Independencia, is also the strangest. Consisting of two tall spikes, it is nicknamed 'Tijeras' (scissors), but is actually a stylized version of the letter 'M' for Mexico. In that sense, it is a monument to the Mexican people, a **Monumento México**.

At Avenida Cuauhtémoc is – surprise – a magnificent statue of **Cuauhtémoc**, the last emperor of the Aztecs, in full regalia with headdress, shield and weapon. Cuauhtémoc, whose name translates as 'Descending Eagle,' allegedly had his feet toasted by Hernán Cortés in a torturous attempt to extract information about the whereabouts of the legendary Aztec treasure. The emperor kept mum, and Cortés ended up killing him without ever finding out.

Farther southeast, the monument to **Abraham Lincoln**, at Avenida Diego Rivera, may at first seem out of place, but the 16th US president is in fact a much-revered figure throughout Mexico. The monument was an exchange between Tijuana and San Diego, which received a statue of Mexican president Benito Júarez, on view in Balboa Park. Mexican historians frequently draw parallels between the two contemporary statesmen, because both fought for justice, stability and the union of their countries.

At the intersection of Avenida Abelardo Rodríguez stands the equestrian statue of **General Ignacio Zaragoza**, who in 1862 defeated the French army led by Napoleon III at the city of Puebla – a victory that greatly boosted the Mexican soldiers' morale during the civil war. The national holiday Cinco de Mayo (May 5) still celebrates the victory.

Another trio of monuments is north of the Río Tijuana, along Paseo de Tijuana (also known as Avenida Centenario) in the city's government zone near the Palacio Municipal (City Hall) and the Gobierno del Estado (State Government).

Where the Paseo meets Avenida Cuauhtémoc looms the imposing figure of the modest **Padre Eusebio Kino**, an Italian missionary (1644–1711). Kino fell gravely ill in 1663 and vowed to become a missionary should he survive. He did, so he trained as a Jesuit and was sent to Mexico in 1681. In 1683 he

founded the first mission in Baja California, Misión San Bruno, just north of present-day Loreto in Baja California Sur. He left two years later when the local native peoples proved too obstreperous to convert. He discovered more friendly territory in Sonora, in northern Mexico, where he wound up founding 20 more missions.

At Avenida Independencia stands the figure of Mexican independence martyr **Padre Miguel Hidalgo**. A priest of the town of Dolores, he issued the now-famous call to rebellion against the Spanish – the *Grito de Dolores* – on September 16, 1810. Despite early advances, the rebels were eventually pushed back and, in 1811, Hidalgo and many of his cohorts were captured and killed.

The last monument, at Avenida Márquez de León, depicts the sole woman of the bunch, and she's not even a real person. **Diana Cazadora** (Diana, the Huntress), alleged sister of Apollo and in Roman mythology considered not just the goddess of the hunt but also of the moon, fertility and childbirth. The monument is a replica of the one in Mexico City designed by Fernando Olaquibel. Her connection with Tijuana? Hard to say.

Mundo Divertido

This cute amusement park, off Paseo de los Héroes at Avenida Jose Maria Velasco, features tame rides, including a tiny roller coaster, video games and minigolf, and should appeal mostly to the milk-teeth set. It's open noon to 8:30 pm Monday to Friday, 10 am to 9:30 pm Saturday and 11 am to 9:30 pm Sunday. There's no set admission, but you buy tokens to the various attractions.

Old Agua Caliente Casino & Spa

Almost nothing survives of the old spa hotel and casino, which once took up a huge area right where Blvd Sánchez Taboada merges with Paseo de los Héroes. Where sleek ladies and dapper gents used to hit the sheets, kids in uniform now hit the books at a huge complex of elementary, secondary and vocational schools.

The most visible remaining landmark is the 200-foot (66m) **minaret**, actually a former chimney for steam generated by the hot spring water. The school grounds are gated, and normally the security guards take great pleasure in turning tourists away. You could try sweet-talking one of them into letting you in, but there's not much more to see inside except a beautifully tiled arch that once formed part of the pool.

The castle-like edifice across the street at Paseo de los Héroes 18818 is a newish hotel

America's Deauville: Tijuana's Days of Glam

Long before the Agua Caliente Casino & Spa played host to Hollywood royalty and the merely moneyed in the late 1920s and early '30s, the soothing hot springs – buried beneath what is today the eastern part of the Zona Río – had for centuries drawn local indigenous tribes for ritual purification baths.

Commercial exploitation on a tiny scale had begun in 1889, but it wasn't until the late '20s that the dribble of visitors turned into a flood. In 1926, the Argüellos sold the part of the rancho that contained the springs to General Abelardo L Rodríguez, who served as president of Mexico from 1932 to 1934. Rodríguez, in turn, hooked up with a trio of Americans – Baron Long, Wirt G Bowman and James N Crofton – to seriously exploit the springs. On July 4, 1927, the quadriga formed the Compañía Mexicana de Agua Caliente in Mexicali. With some US$750,000 in capital to play with, they hired the architect couple of Wayne and Corinne McAllister and, less than a year later, on June 23, 1928, the grand Agua Caliente Casino & Spa was born.

By all accounts, it was a fairy-tale affair, incorporating several architectural styles, from Moorish to renaissance to Spanish Mission and Byzantine. The lavish hotel had 50 rooms, with a matching number of parking spaces – a revolutionary concept. Its Patio Andaluz restaurant served fine international cuisine, and the *Salón de Oro* (Golden Salon) dazzled with brocade-covered walls, sparkling chandeliers and other decorations fit for a palace.

With Prohibition raging in the US, Tijuana's spa resort – which advertisements touted as 'America's Deauville' in reference to the exclusive French spa town – quickly became the darling of the Hollywood crowd. People like Clark Gable, Jean Harlow, Johnny 'Tarzan' Weissmuller, Bing Crosby and Douglas Fairbanks flocked here; some of them, including Jimmy Durante, Buster Keaton, Charlie Chaplin and Rita Hayworth, came also as performers. For recreation guests could enjoy the large pool, different baths and spa treatments, the lushly landscaped gardens, a golf course where big purse tournaments were held, a dog-racing track, the casino and, later on, a horse track as well. The place even had its own radio station and a landing strip from which, on Sundays, tri-engine planes would shuttle famous visitors back to their homes in San Diego or Los Angeles. It was definitely the good life.

But, alas, the party had to end. It wasn't the 1933 repeal of Prohibition in the US that did in the Agua Caliente, but rather a law passed in Mexico: In 1935 President Lázaro Cárdenas declared casino gambling illegal. The complex closed immediately and began to restructure. When it finally reopened in 1937, its renaissance was short-lived: Its fickle clientele had moved on to the next 'hot' thing, and the place closed down indefinitely after only three months. Shortly thereafter it was expropriated by the government and became the property of the Ministry of Public Education.

By 1939 Tijuana's temple of entertainment had been converted into a high school, the Instituto Tecnológico Industrial Agua Caliente; over time it was remodeled beyond recognition. Hotel rooms became dormitories; the garage, workshops for carpenters, mechanics and electricians. The dog-racing track was turned into a sports field and the casino rooms were reborn as recreational areas. An era had come to an end.

currently called the Fiesta Inn (it seems to change names periodically; also see the Tijuana Places to Stay chapter). Built close to the site of the original resort, its Moorish arches and crenellated outlines are intended to mimic its predecessor but succeed only at parody – the gray concrete facade is about as glamorous as an elephant's butt.

The hotel sits atop sulphurous thermal springs with soothing powers you can sample during a visit to the elegant European-style **Vita Spa Agua Caliente** (☎ 634-69-25) on the 1st floor. The water, 150°F (65°C) hot when it emerges from the ground, must actually be cooled for you to enjoy it. The spa offers the gamut of hydrotherapeutic baths, including aroma, fango and sea salt (US$22), as well as massages (US$27 to US$54) beauty treatments like facials (US$27 to US$43), body wraps (US$27 to US$75) and waxing (US$7 to US$40). Even if spas don't do it for you, sneak a peek at the original's grandeur through a lobby display of historical photographs, menus and advertisements.

EASTERN TIJUANA

This section covers some of Tijuana's less-central sights and attractions in such districts as Chapultepec and Hipódromo as well as the outer suburbs, including Mesa de Otay.

Club Campestre

Tijuana's country club, at Blvd Agua Caliente 11311 in Chapultepec, is a semiprivate golf course founded in 1948 and designed by Allister McKenzie. It's an 18-hole, 6500-yard (5915m), par-72 course that's in decent shape. There's a pro shop and a restaurant and bar on the grounds.

Fees are US$30/40 weekdays/weekends including golf cart, or US$20/30 without. Reservations are recommended but only really necessary for decent tee times on Saturday. Call ☎ 681-78-55/6 or 888-217-1165 tollfree from the US.

Agua Caliente Racetrack

Horseracing became part of the Tijuana experience as early as 1909, when a small racetrack opened not far from the border. But it wasn't until the city's heyday, during US Prohibition, that the horses really took off. The Jockey Club – Hipódromo de Agua Caliente – opened as part of the Agua Caliente Spa & Casino in 1929 and continued operation long after the roulette wheels stopped spinning in 1935.

Since the Hipódromo's owner, controversial Tijuana multimillionaire Jorge Hank Rhon, refused to give in during a long labor dispute several years ago, the ponies no longer circle this landmark racetrack, and the place has literally gone to the dogs – greyhounds, that is. In fact, it would be more accurate to call it a *galgódromo*.

Meanwhile, white horse sculptures still greet visitors to this imposing complex on Blvd Agua Caliente, just east of the golf course, about 8 miles (12km) from the border. But the real surprise is a handful of live animals: Playful brown bears, a tiger and a lion are behind glass and wire mesh enclosures, ready for inspection.

For more on the racetrack, see the Tijuana Entertainment chapter.

Gran Monumento a Cristo Rey

In the suburb of Los Alamos is the Gran Monumento a Cristo Rey, Tijuana's answer to the giant Rio de Janeiro statue of Cristo Rendentor. From its perch above the Río Tijuana, a statue of Jesus lords over the city, arms slightly raised in a half embrace, wearing a gentle smile and a flowing robe. Built by Virginio Ramirez and his sons, it is made of fiberglass and resin, stands 72 feet (24m) tall and weighs 10 tons. It is the largest such statue in Mexico and the second largest in Latin America (after the one in Rio, which is nearly 120 feet – or 40m – tall).

The giant Jesus balances atop a vaulted chapel, still under construction at the time of research for this book. When finished, it will be surrounded by a semicircle of 28 angels and have stained-glass windows that tell the history of Baja California.

Iglesia de San Martín de Porres

The Cristo Rey monument is the brainchild of the priest of this adjacent parish church, one of Tijuana's nicest and, with a consecration date of 1985, newest. Built in baroque style, it sports two square towers topped by cupolas, and three larger domes, one above the apse and two above the transepts (side chapels). The whitewashed exterior is oddly accented with pink trim. As you enter, note the oak double door, intricately carved with floral motifs as well as depictions of St Peter (on the left) and St Martin. Above the entrance is a relief of the Last Supper.

The interior, too, has some interesting aspects, notably the stained-glass windows with tastefully rendered Biblical scenes such as the Annunciation, Jesus' birth and the Crucifixion. Of note too are the marble floors and frilly porcelain chandeliers above the central aisle, more typical of a palace than a house of worship.

Parks

Metropolitan Tijuana is largely devoid of open spaces, but does have a couple of parks on the outskirts where families flock on weekends. On Blvd Industrial, southeast of the airport in the suburb of Mesa de

---

La Mona! Will You Lose Your Lease-a?

You're driving along a twisted road on the edge of a canyon within which sprawls the fetid Tijuana neighborhood of Colonia Aeropuerto, a squalid collection of shacks nailed, chicken-wired and duct-taped together from automobile hoods, abandoned doors and old pizza boxes. Suddenly there arises – above the barely arrested avalanche of human debris – a 55-foot (22m), 20-ton (18.9-metric-ton) woman, buck naked, with defiant fist raised above the smoke and a pigeon coop stuck in her head.

Your brain screams: 'I *told* you not to eat the worm in that tequila!' But fear and loathe not: This is not a drug-addled vision of Hunter Thompson. Rather, it's the in-your-face vision of Tijuana's artistic scion and scourge Armando Muñoz-García, who sleeps – quite literally – within her ample bosom.

DAVID PEEVERS

The self-taught Muñoz – who once raved, 'Give me enough rebar and a torch and I'll line the whole border with giant, nude Amazons!' – began work on his massive maidenly muse in 1991 and built her entirely from scratch; and there ain't much 'scratch' in Tijuana art circles. Undeterred, Muñoz plunged ahead – with no commission or sponsorship – and built his brazen broad from the ground up. Her cardiovascular system includes all mod-cons: plumbing and electricity, TV and phones, bath, light, water and the aforementioned pigeons batting around in her belfry. Where lesser Mexican aesthetes wrung their hands, Armando damn well built (indeed, La Mona *is* damn well built)! But having thrown all of his fortune and energies into erecting the woman of his dreams, Armando – like Dr Frankenstein before him – now finds himself drained, broke and beleaguered by local 'critics' of his vision, including bankers who insist that such a protean figure should pay his bills. Imagine!

What is to become of La Mona and the genius she took to her bosom, so to speak? Will Armando end up behind bars? Or will he end up behind rebars of even more colossal proportions and pulchritude? I, for one, would like to see him provided with enough rebar and torches to…well. Amazons would surely beat the hell out of looking at the damn border fences.

- David Peevers

Otay, is the large **Parque de la Amistad**, which has shady trees conducive to picnicking. There are barbecue facilities, a children's playground and even a small lake with geese, ducks and swans; paddle boats are for rent as well. There are also paths for in-line skating and bicycling. Hours are daily 7 am to 8 pm; admission is free.

The largest park, which has various activities and attractions, is **Parque Morelos** (Map 12), at Blvd Insurgentes 16000 in La Mesa. It has clowns, a petting zoo, a fossil room and a fish pond, as well as a toy train for tots, a miniature golf course, an open-air theater and a botanical garden. You can also take a boat ride on a small lake. There's a small lake with little boats. There are also clowns, a petting zoo, a fossil room and a fish pond , as well as a toy train for tots, a miniature golf course, an open-air theater and a botanical garden. Admission is US 60¢; hours are 9 am to 5 pm Tuesday to Sunday.

Even farther east, across from the Hyundai plant at Km 21.5 on México 2 (the free road to Tecate), is **Paraiso Azteca** (☎ 672-45-95), a theme park-cum-funfair-cum-water park. While the little ones may enjoy tooling around on a toy train, getting lost in the house of mirrors, taking a gentle boat ride or spinning around on a carousel, older ones can take a sauna, listen to a concert featuring local talent or see collections of coins, weapons or antique cars. Snacks and drinks are available. It's open Saturday and Sunday only, 9 am to 8 pm. The cost depends on the number of attractions you use; the minimum is US$3 for an adult plus child. Call to confirm hours and prices.

PLAYAS DE TIJUANA

Popular with locals, Tijuana's beaches tend to get crowded. On some Sunday afternoons there's live entertainment on a stage above the sand. People swimming in the ocean are sadly oblivious to the high level of water contamination here, a result of raw sewage being discharged through the channelized Río Tijuana a few miles north near Imperial Beach.

A narrow walkway – *malecón* – parallels the sand and is popular with strollers and the occasional in-line skater, jogger and bicyclist. Up above, you'll find Avenida Pacífico is lined with small restaurants serving *antojitos,* fresh coconuts and drinks. Also along here you'll come across two sculptures: the 'arches,' which sort of symbolize the 'window to the Pacific,' and Oscar Ortega Corrall's *Ultima Oportunidad Para Ti Madre,* an arresting work of near Dali-esque surrealism.

The Border

Four years after the fall of the Berlin Wall, a different wall went up along the San Diego-Tijuana border, its construction a mandate of Operation Gatekeeper, the anti-illegal-immigration policy of the US government. Nowhere has the abruptness of this division had a greater visual impact than in Playas de Tijuana, where a rusted, corrugated metal fence extends through the sand and into the ocean. A historic obelisk-like border marker stands here as well, the last of 258 set up all along the US-Mexican border (the first one is in Matamoros).

On the Mexican side there are homes and restaurants. Children and couples on a beach outing rub shoulders with the border.

Families stand on the bluff, staring across into San Diego. Kids stick their hands through holes in the fence to touch the sand on the other side. On the 'other side' is Border Field State Park, heavily patrolled by armed US immigration officers.

Propped up against the fence on the beach is a list of names of those who have died between 1995 and 1999 attempting to cross the border – again, eerily evoking the ghosts of divided Berlin.

Plaza Monumental

Tijuana's famous bullring by the sea is also the world's only 'bullring on the border.' It seats up to 25,000 people on steep bleachers accessed through entrances bearing the names of famous matadors. In the parking lot outside the bullring are two sculptures. The one closer to the entrance is a likeness of the matador Rodolfo Gaona (1888–1975), nicknamed Califa de León and considered by many to be the best Mexican bullfighter ever. It's the work of Humberto Peraza, who also designed the Lincoln Monument and *El Charrito* at the Cortijo San José. The other monument, *El Encierro,* shows a herd of bulls following a man on horseback as they are led to the corral before the fight.

Cortijo San José

The Cortijo San José (☎ 630-18-25, Avenida del Agua 777), originally an arena primarily for *charreadas* (Mexican rodeo), is now often used as a general event space; the Casa de la Cultura – Playas is also here. *El Charrito,* a statue of a charreada rider, now proudly guards the entrance. This work wasn't always treated with such respect or accorded such dignity. Originally in the glorieta at Avenidas Independencia and Centenario, where Padre Miguel Hidalgo now holds court, it was taken down in 1988 and stored away. It resurfaced twice in different spots in eastern Tijuana before finally being assigned in the mid-1990s to its final and most logical location.

TIJUANA

Places to Stay

Tijuana has plenty of accommodations in all categories, from the really seedy to the world-class luxurious. Tourist authorities may try to steer visitors away from less-expensive but very acceptable lodging choices. Most budget hotels, which cater to visiting gringos, are in the Zona Centro along Avenida Revolución and its side streets. The Zona Río is the place for luxury digs, while most mid-range places are along Blvd Agua Caliente in the southeastern neighborhoods of Chapultepec and Hipódromo.

Prices

By US or European standards, Tijuana hotels are fairly affordable, although prices are higher here than elsewhere in Mexico. A few shoestring places rent doubles for as little as US$15, but for a room with a modicum of comfort you'll likely pay between US$35 and US$50. For slightly more you can often get more updated facilities and more amenities, like a pool or a gym. Tijuana's upscale hotels are equivalent to their US counterparts in comfort, facilities and service, but they are usually cheaper, with some special rates starting at US$80.

Room rates vary by type and location of room. Larger rooms, or those recently renovated or with amenities like kitchenettes, have higher prices. Rooms with a view cost more than those without. Some upscale hotels have special floors catering to business travelers, with a concierge and a variety of secretarial services.

While price differences between single and double occupancy are small, the number and size of beds does matter. *Cuarto sencillo* (single room) means a room with one double bed *cama matrimonial,* usually queen-size. One person can usually get such a room for less than two people. A *cuarto doble* has either one large (king-size) bed or two queen-size beds. The latter configuration sleeps up to four people – useful if you've brought the kids along – and children sometimes stay free in their parents' room. Some hotels allow up to four adults in such rooms, although a fee may be charged for the third and fourth person.

Note that room rates are fickle – especially in upscale hotels, where price and demand are intimately related. Unless a hotel is fully booked, it's usually possible to get a better-than-rack rate. Because the margin of profit is lower in budget and mid-priced hotels, their rates do not fluctuate as much.

Prices in this book are guidelines only. Where available, email addresses are listed. Inquiries made over the Internet, however, do not always get a response.

Taxes

The 10% value-added tax (IVA) is tacked on to hotel rates, as is a 2% 'lodging tax.' Budget hotels usually include taxes in their quoted prices; mid-range establishments sometimes do, but top-end ones usually don't. If in doubt, ask, '¿Están incluidos los impuestos?' ('Are taxes included?').

PLACES TO STAY – BUDGET
Camping

Metropolitan Tijuana does not have any campgrounds. The closest one is the hilltop *KOA Trailer Park/Campground* (☎ 631-33-05), about 8 miles (13km) south of town in the coastal village of San Antonio del Mar, reached via the toll road México 1D. Although it caters mostly to long-term residents, a few spaces for passing RVs (water and electric) are usually available, and it can also accommodate tents. Sites cost US$19 per night for two, US$1 for each additional person.

Zona Centro (Map 13)

Tijuana's cheapest beds are in the Zona Norte red-light district, but because many places here do double (or triple) duty as bordellos or safe houses for *pollos,* none are recommended.

The closest acceptable place is *Hotel San Nicolas* (☎ 688-04-18, *Avenida Madero*

768), which exudes a surprisingly artsy vibe, with Frida Kahlo posters decorating the hallways. Rooms are small, clean and have a phone (incoming calls only), but no air-con or TV; the cost is US$23/29 single/double.

Run by a gracious proprietor, *Hotel del Prado* (☎ 688-23-29, *Calle 5a 8163*) is decidedly no-frills, but clean as a whistle while dirt cheap. Shoebox-size rooms are US$14 with shared facilities, or US$17 with private bath. A room for up to four adults costs just US$24. This is a great place to crash if you came just for the day and end up too wobbly to make it back across the border.

Just a little more expensive, but a notch up in terms of comfort, is *Hotel Catalina* (☎ 685-97-48), on Calle 6a at Avenida Madero. They charge US$16/21 for rooms with a shower and WC, and those with TV are US$26; each extra person costs US$5. Owners of this family hotel stress security, and rooms are clean and tidy. You can even order room service from the cafeteria below.

A better bet for less money is *Hotel Colonial* (☎ 688-17-20, *Calle 6a 1812*), which is run by friendly folks and has clean if simple rooms with showers but no air-con. Rates are US$25 single or double. *Hotel Plaza* (☎ 638-43-55, 638-42-84, Calle 5a 8257) also offers acceptable rooms for US$20/30, with a US$5 charge per extra person.

Motel Plaza Hermosa (☎ 685-33-53, *Avenida Constitución 1821*), at Calle 10a (Sarabia), is less central, but quieter, and has secure parking. Singles/doubles cost US$24/30 Sunday through Thursday, US$30/35 Friday and Saturday.

Offering the best value in the budget category is *Hotel Lafayette* (☎ 685-39-40, *Avenida Revolución 325*). Well-maintained and spick and span, it charges US$20 to US$26 for singles/doubles with TV, phone and bath. Four people can share a room for US$30. It's a safe place, thanks to management's zero tolerance for riffraff – but do ask for a room facing away from La Revo.

The large *Motel Aragón* (☎ 685-26-88, *Avenida Negrete 1671*) offers basic but acceptable accommodations in a two-floor structure wrapped around a large courtyard with plenty of parking and good security.

The 70 rooms are a bit run-down but are clean and cost US$24/36/48 for two/three/four people without TV; doubles and triples with TV go for US$30/42.

Family-run *Villa Bonita* (☎ 685-90-30, *Calle 3a 7856*) may look foreboding, with the receptionist behind a security window, but the harsh first impression is tempered by a cozy flower-festooned courtyard. Rooms are OK; all have TV and some have kitchenettes. They cost US$28 single/double; larger units for up to four are US$42. Request a room in back to escape the street noise.

Colonias Cacho & América (Map 14)
Ample parking and a swimming pool are offered at *Motel La Sierra* (☎ 686-16-01, fax 686-15-77, *Blvd Cuauhtémoc Sur Oriente 2800*). Rooms are plain, but adequately furnished with TV, phone, air-con and heat. They cost just US$34 single/double.

Chapultepec & Hipódromo (Map 15)
Those in need of little more than a roof over their head could try *Motel Colonial* (☎ 686-34-70, *Blvd Salinas 11256*), practically across from the golf course entrance. Rooms give meaning to the term 'barebones,' and the mattresses probably date back to the disco era, but at US$13/16 you can't expect much. Consider it a 'cultural' experience….

A small step up is the nearby *Motel Golf* (☎ 686-20-18, fax 686-28-76, *Blvd Agua Caliente 11420*), almost as ancient and run-down. Rooms have TV, but the phones work only for incoming calls, and the lack of air-con can be a big problem in rooms facing the noisy boulevard. Rates are US$25/37.

PLACES TO STAY – MID-RANGE Zona Centro (Map 13)
An excellent downtown choice, *Hotel La Villa de Zaragoza* (☎ 685-18-32, fax 685-18-37, ✉ rey@telnor.net, *Avenida Madero 1120*) is quiet, yet just a block from Avenida Revolución. It has amenities more typical of a luxury hotel, including room service, dataport

TIJUANA

phones, 24-hour fax service and parking. Large rooms come with satellite TV, telephone, heat and air-con. Rates are US$43/53, including parking and local calls. Nonsmokers and the disabled can be accommodated, and small suites with kitchenettes are available for US$63. The restaurant-bar is popular with locals for breakfast and the lunchtime US$4 *comida corrida*.

Hotel Nelson (☎ 685-43-03, fax 685-43-04, *Avenida Revolución 721*) is a perennial favorite with gringos for its central location and 92 clean, carpeted standard-issue rooms. Inexpensive breakfasts and snacks are available in the coffee shop. Rooms with telephone, satellite TV and squeaky-clean bathrooms cost US$42.

Friendly *Hotel París* (☎/fax 685-30-23, *Calle 5a 8181*) has 40 raggedy and not overly clean rooms with telephone, color TV and air-con, from US$30 to US$47 singles/doubles. Nearby, *Motel León* (☎ 685-63-20, fax 685-40-16), on Calle 7a (Galeana) between Avenidas Revolución and Constitución, has worn rooms which are reasonably quiet because all face an interior corridor. Furnishings are close to monastic, and the TV and phone may or may not work. With rates of US$45/50 you can probably do better elsewhere.

If you want to stay in a landmark, check in at *Hotel Caesar's* (☎ 685-16-06, fax 685-34-92, *Avenida Revolución 1079*), at Calle 5a/Zapata, where historic bullfighting posters line the hallways, and some rooms are named after famous matadores. Its original restaurant created the Caesar salad (see the boxed text 'All Hail Caesar's!' in the Tijuana Places to Eat chapter). Singles/doubles/triples cost US$34/44/54.

Hotel América (☎ 688-27-11, fax 688-20-07, *Calle 4a/Díaz Mirón 8432*) is a bright spot in an otherwise rather bland part of downtown, where taquerías rub shoulders with little stores and auto repair shops. This clean and largely gringo-free establishment offers good value, with carpeted rooms, cable TV, phone and air-con. The cost is US$45 to US$50 for singles and US$66 for doubles sleeping up to four. There's a restaurant and parking.

Hotel Central (☎ 685-14-41/2/3/4/5, *Calle 7a/Galeana 8381*) is another good, inexpensive place with friendly staff. Rooms with telephone, TV, heat and air-con cost US$38/45, and there's free parking as well.

Zona Río (Map 14)
The well-run *Hacienda del Río* (☎ 684-86-44, fax 684-86-20, 800-026-69-99 in Mexico, ☎ 800-303-2684 in the US, ☻ bajainn@telnor.net, *Blvd Sánchez Taboada 10606*) is popular with business travelers. Its 131 large rooms are appointed with taste and have direct-dial phones, cable TV with CNN, air-con and heating. There's a restaurant-bar to tank up on energy and a heated pool and a gym where you can work it all off. Up to two children under 12 stay free in their parents' room. Rates range from US$64 to US$77 single/double. Rooms for nonsmokers are available.

Colonias Cacho & América (Map 14)
Recently remodeled, *Hotel Palacio Azteca* (☎ 681-81-00, fax 681-81-60, 800-026-66-60 in Mexico, ☻ palacio@telnor.net, *Blvd Cuauhtémoc Sur 213*) has a spacious, elegant lobby. Its 200 stylish, modern rooms come with satellite TV, air-con and phone. The gardens and pool area are anchored by a grove of palm trees, and there's a bar and restaurant as well. Rates are US$64/74.

Hotel Corona Plaza (☎ 681-81-83, fax 681-77-76, *Blvd Agua Caliente 1426*) is a modern glass tower near the bullring. It offers nicely appointed rooms with all the modern conveniences including data ports, as well as a restaurant, bar and off-street parking. Prices of US$56 single or double (US$67 for triple) are good value, although rates go up by US$10 Friday and Saturday night.

Chapultepec & Hipódromo (Map 15)
Tropical gardens and friendly, helpful staff make the 120-room *Hotel La Mesa Inn* (☎ 681-65-22, fax 681-28-71, 800-303-26-84 in Mexico, 800-303-2684 in the US, *Blvd Gustavo Díaz Ordaz 50*) one of the nicest properties in town. Modern, immaculate

rooms have satellite TV, telephone, air-con and bottled water. There's plenty of free parking, a nice swimming pool, free coffee all day and a small restaurant. Rates are a reasonable US$55/70. There's no extra charge for two kids under 12 staying in their parents' room.

Also pleasant is the ***Country Club Hotel*** (☎ 681-77-33, fax 681-76-92, 800-026-70-01 in Mexico, 800-303-2684 in the US, ✉ bajainn@ telnor.net, Tapachula 1), one of the most historic properties in this part of Tijuana and right next to the Agua Caliente racetrack. Most of the 135 spacious suites and rooms overlook the golf course and the city. All have air-con, cable TV, telephone, private bath and bottled water; some are set aside for nonsmokers. There's a swimming pool and Casa Dobson, a well-known restaurant popular with locals. Rates are US$63/75.

The Spanish colonial-style ***Hotel El Conquistador*** (☎ 681-79-55, fax 686-13-40, 800-662-7329 in the US, Blvd Agua Caliente 10750) has old-fashioned character coupled with a full range of modern amenities. Rooms are oversized and frilly. There's a small pool and Jacuzzi, as well as a sauna. The restaurant and bar are popular with locals and guests alike. Rates are US$67 single/double (US$73 on Friday and Saturday), extra persons are US$12.

The new and modern ***Motel Real Inn*** (☎ 686-64-38/45, Blvd Agua Caliente 11451) has 54 comfortable and clean rooms with cable TV, data port phones and air-con, as well as a pool, Jacuzzi and free parking. It's a bit low on charm but good value at US$49/54 single/double.

Playas de Tijuana (Map 12)

Right above the beach, ***Motel Jardines Monumental*** (☎ 680-67-75, 680-97-81, Avenida del Pacífico 109) offers great value. The comfortable rooms all have color TV, telephone, small stove and refrigerator, and some also have ocean-view patios. The good-natured staff speaks some English. Singles/doubles cost US$30/40 (US$5 more on Friday and Saturday).

Hacienda del Mar (☎/fax 630-8603, 888-675-2927 in the US, Paseo Playas No 116),

Find a bunk near the beach!

with buildings wrapped around an inner courtyard, is right next to the bullring. Rooms have all the trappings, from satellite TV to telephone, heating and air-con; junior suites have microwaves and coffeemakers. There's a small heated pool and a restaurant as well. Rates are US$50 (US$60 on Friday and Saturday) for rooms and US$60/70 for the small suites. Additional persons are US$10.

PLACES TO STAY – TOP END
Zona Río (Map 14)

Modern and efficient, ***Hotel Real del Río*** (☎ 634-31-00, fax 634-30-53, 800-026-66-77 in Mexico, 877-517-6479 in the US, ✉ realrio@ telnor.net, José María Velasco 1409) has an art deco-inspired lobby, parking, a swimming pool and a restaurant. Special touches include voice mail and 24-hour room service. Singles/doubles cost US$84/91.

The hulking ***Fiesta Inn*** (☎ 634-69-01, fax 634-69-12, 800-504-50-00 in Mexico, Paseo de los Héroes 18818) sits on the grounds of the former Agua Caliente Casino & Spa, but lacks its grand elegance. A modern spa on the 1st floor makes use of the ancient hot springs flowing from underneath the hotel. Otherwise, it's a modern hotel with respective amenities, including data port phones. The official rate is US$93 per room, but special deals are frequent. Nonsmoking and wheelchair-accessible rooms are available.

Despite its gaudy, candy-colored facade, the ***Hotel Camino Real*** (☎ 633-40-00, fax 633-40-01, 800-901-23-00 in Mexico,

TIJUANA

tij@caminoreal.com, Paseo de los Héroes 10305) is one of Tijuana's classiest hotels and a favorite among visiting dignitaries and international business travelers. The staff is professional, courteous and fluent in English. It offers a health club with gym, sauna and Jacuzzi, as well as two bars and a restaurant. Official rates range from US$130 to US$200 but discounts are common. Two children under 12 stay free with their parents. Nonsmoking and wheelchair-accessible rooms are available.

The resort-style *Hotel Lucerna* (☎ 633-39-00, fax 634-24-00, 800-026-63-00 in Mexico, 800-582-3762 in the US, *lucerna@telnor.net, Paseo de los Héroes 10902)* has elegant rooms and suites with all the trimmings: Many overlook the large heated pool framed by lush landscaping. There's also a gym, a business center, three restaurants and a nightclub. Rack rates are US$150/160.

The only luxury hotel close to the border, *Pueblo Amigo Inn* (☎ 683-50-30, fax 683-50-32, 800-026-63-86 in Mexico, 800-386-6985 in the US, *htlpuebl@telnor.net, Via Oriente 9211)* is a welcoming, US-style establishment, where special touches include a covered, heated pool, 24-hour room service, free valet parking and a free shuttle to the airport. There's race and sports booking on the premises. Rates start at US$150.

Chapultepec & Hipódromo (Map 15)

The 200-room, high-rise *Hotel Plaza Las Glorias* (☎ 622-66-00, fax 622-66-02, *plgtij@icanet.com.mx, Blvd Agua Caliente 11553)* looks a bit shabby on the outside but has a friendly atmosphere. Rooms have color TV, air-con and telephone, but are nothing special and so somewhat overpriced at US$90 single/double.

In a shiny, 23-story tower, *Grand Hotel Tijuana* (☎ 681-70-00, fax 681-70-16, 800-343-7825 in the US, *ghotel2@telnor.net,*

Blvd Agua Caliente 4500) is literally the city's most prominent hotel. Amenities include cable TV and minibars, and there's a heated pool, Jacuzzi and tennis court, as well as two restaurants and a cocktail bar. Rates start at US$70.

South of Tijuana

For those preferring a resort experience while staying close to the city, a couple of lodging options can be found on the coast along the toll road México 1D.

The *Real del Mar* (☎ 631-34-01, 631-36-70, 800-662-61-80, 800-803-8038 in the US, *rdelmarc@telnor.net),* at Km 19.5, is a full-service luxury resort with its own tennis courts, golf course (18-hole, par-72, 6400-yard), equestrian center, spa and gym, as well as swimming pool and Jacuzzi. The hotel is run by Marriott and is a nice, all-suites place, where rates are US$109/119 single/double, with one- or two-bedroom suites costing US$139/149. Prices include continental breakfast and a happy hour with complimentary wine and beer. Golf and spa packages are available.

At Km 25 is the Moorish architecture-inspired *Oasis Beach Resort & Convention Center* (☎ 631-32-50, fax 631-32-52, 800-818-3133 in the US), a luxurious beachfront hotel/RV-park resort. It has 55 paved sites with small patios, brick barbecues and full hookups, including cable TV. There's a tennis court, two pools and Jacuzzis, a ministore and a minigolf facility, as well as a clubhouse with bathrooms, sauna, TV, laundry and weight room. RV rates are US$49/59 per night midweek/weekend during peak periods for two people, US$10 more for each extra person. Its 100 spacious suites sleep up to four people with rates starting at US$109/119 (for two), US$15 more for each extra person. The resort's gourmet restaurant, La Perla del Nilo, serves top quality international fare at top pesos.

Places to Eat

Tijuana's cuisine scene is one of the city's big delights. Much more than tacos and burritos, it's full of regional differences and subtle surprises, due to most locals having migrated here from other parts of Mexico, bringing their cooking with them. In addition to Mexican fare, you'll find all sorts of international food.

Mexicans eat three meals a day: *desayuno* (breakfast), *comida* (lunch) and *cena* (dinner). When eating in a restaurant, note that servers will not bring the check until you ask for it. *El menú* can mean either the menu or the special fixed-price meal of the day. To make sure you get the menu, you need to ask for *la carta*.

FOOD

Mexican meals usually include one or more of the following:

tortillas – These are thin patties of pressed dough cooked on griddles, available as *harina* (flour) and the more traditional *maíz* (corn) tortillas.

frijoles (beans) – These staples come boiled, fried, refried, in soups, on tortillas or with eggs.

chilies – These vary in spiciness: *Habanero* and *serrano* are spicy hot; the *poblano* ranges from mild to riotous depending on when it was picked. Ask if the chili is *picante* (spicy hot) or *muy picante* (fiery hot). If you exceed your tolerance, ingest sugar, beer, milk or bread to extinguish the fire. Water, strangely but truly, exacerbates the pain.

For a full list of menu items with translations, see the Menu Translator at the back of this book.

Meals

Breakfast *(desayuno)* is generally eaten between 7 and 11 am. Although a traditional Mexican breakfast is more of the light, continental-style variety, with coffee, juice and a pastry, most Tijuana restaurants serve full, cooked breakfasts built around eggs and/or meat served with beans and tortillas. The cost runs US$3 on the low end to US$8 on the high end.

A caveat: When ordering eggs, never ask '¿*Tiene huevos?*' ('Do you have eggs?'), because *huevos* is slang for 'testicles' in this context. Instead, ask '¿*Hay huevos?*' ('Are there eggs?').

Some places also serve US-style breakfasts featuring eggs, hash browns, hotcakes, sausages and bacon. Granola, *ensalada de frutas* (fruit salad) and cereals are often available too.

Lunch *(la comida)* is the main meal of the day. Although most restaurants open for lunch at 11:30 am or noon, you'll find them practically empty until about 1:30 pm. Some offer special fixed-price menus called *comida corrida* or *menú del día*, which are great food bargains: For as little as US$3.50 you get soup or salad and a soft drink, in addition to the main course.

For many Mexicans, dinner *(la cena)* consists of just a snack or a light meal. During the work week, many either eat at home or grab a quick torta or taco on the road. Going out for dinner tends to be a social affair involving large gatherings of friends or family. Most restaurants are open nightly, but don't get busy until Friday and Saturday. Note that some close as early as 9 pm.

Typical Dishes

Fish *(pescado)* and seafood *(mariscos)* are available year-round, although choices depend on what's in season and/or what's been caught that day. Fish can be a *filete* (filet), *frito* (fried whole fish), or *al mojo de ajo* (fried in butter and garlic). One great delight is the fish taco *(taco de pescado)*, a piece of deep-fried fish you can dress up with a range of condiments, including salsa, raw or browned onions, white or red cabbage, limes and mayonnaise.

Ceviche, the popular Mexican cocktail, consists of raw fish and seafood (shrimp, oysters, scallops etc) marinated in lime and mixed with onions, chilies, garlic and tomatoes. There are other seafood *cocteles* (cocktails) as well. Unfortunately, seafood is also

Mexican 'Soul' Food

Antojitos, or 'little whims,' are traditional Mexican snacks or small meals. Mexicans eat them at any time of day, on their own or as part of a larger meal. Here are some of the more popular ones:

burrito – any combination of beans, cheese, meat, chicken and seafood, seasoned with salsa or chili and wrapped in a flour tortilla

chilaquiles – fried tortilla chips with scrambled eggs or sauce, often topped with grated cheese

chile relleno – poblano chili stuffed with cheese, meat or other ingredients, dipped in beaten egg, fried and baked in a sauce

enchilada – ingredients similar to the burrito, wrapped in a corn tortilla and then baked in a sauce

gordita – fried maize dough filled with refried beans, topped with sour cream, cheese and lettuce

guacamole – avocados mashed with onion, chili, lemon, spices and sometimes tomato

machaca – cured, dried and shredded beef or pork, reconstituted and mixed with eggs, onions, cilantro and chilies and fried

quesadilla – flour tortillas filled with melted cheese and sometimes other ingredients

sope – thick patty of corn dough lightly grilled then served with green or red salsa and frijoles, onion and cheese

taco – ingredients similar to the burrito, wrapped in a soft or crisp corn tortilla and then topped with a range of condiments (onion, chopped cilantro, tomato, mayonnaise, shredded cabbage etc)

tamale – corn dough stuffed with meat, beans or chilies, wrapped in corn husks and then steamed

torta – Mexican-style sandwich in a roll

tostada – flat, crisp tortilla topped with meat or cheese, tomatoes, beans and lettuce

a major source of intestinal problems, so check for cleanliness and freshness, especially with uncooked fare.

Meat dishes feature beef or pork. *Chorizo* is a spicy sausage, which is sometimes served scrambled with eggs for breakfast. *Machaca* is shredded, dried and cured beef reconstituted in a sauce. It's delicious in burritos *(burrito de machaca)* or with eggs *(huevos con machaca)*. *Carnitas* is a specialty dish from the state of Michoacán that involves slow-roasting an entire pig; portions are served by weight and eaten with a variety of side dishes and condiments. *Carne asada* is grilled meat, usually beef, often sliced thinly and used as stuffing for tacos, burritos and other *antojitos.*

Soup *(sopa)* does not figure big on Tijuana menus and is usually just broth with some noodles. *(Menudo)* is a hominy-based soup with some unusual animal parts (stomach, intestines), while its lighter version, *(pozole)*, may contain chicken and vegetables. Menudo is considered an excellent hangover antidote; in fact, many restaurants serve it only on Saturday and Sunday.

Most desserts *(postres)* are an afterthought, and the selection is usually limited to flan, ice cream *(helado)* or rice pudding *(arroz con leche)*.

DRINKS

Don't drink any water, or drinks served with ice cubes or made with water, unless you know the water has been purified (see the Health section in the Tijuana Facts for the Visitor chapter). Bottles of inexpensive purified or mineral water are available everywhere.

Nonalcoholic

Ordinary Mexican *café* is flavorful but often served weak. Those in need of stronger caffeine jolts should ask for 'Nescafe.' You'll be given hot water and a jar of granulated coffee, allowing you to make your drink strong enough to knock your socks off.

Gourmet coffees – espresso, latte, mocha, cappuccino etc – have recently become popular, although these are usually only served in dedicated coffeehouses (see the Tijuana Entertainment chapter).

Tea in Tijuana consists of a cup of tepid water with a tea bag next to it. If you want black tea, ask for *té negro*, because otherwise you'll invariably be given *té de manzanilla* (chamomile). If you want milk or lemon, request *té con leche* or *té con limón*.

Pure fresh juices *(jugos)* are readily available from street stalls and juice bars, where the fruit is normally squeezed before your eyes. *Licuados* are blends of fruit or juice with water and sugar. Other items can be added or substituted: raw egg, milk, ice and flavorings such as vanilla or nutmeg. Delicious combinations are practically limitless.

Aguas frescas are made by mixing fruit juice, or a syrup made from mashed grains or seeds, with sugar and water. Unusual, but delicious, choices include *agua fresca de arroz* (rice water), which has a sweet, nutty taste; it is also called *horchata*.

In restaurants, and at reputable chains like La Michoacana, aguas and licuados are made with purified water, although you shouldn't assume the same of street stalls.

Alcoholic

Late 19th-century German immigrants established the first breweries in Mexico. Several large companies now produce more than two dozen brands of beer *(cerveza),* many excellent. Tecate, Corona, Carta Blanca, Dos Equis and Sol Especial, all medium-bodied blond lagers, are popular. Beer lovers should not leave Tijuana without sampling the excellent fullbodied pilsner brewed at La Cervecería de Tijuana, Baja's first microbrewery, which opened in early 2000 (see the Tijuana Entertainment chapter for details).

Wine is less popular than beer, and is expensive. Most of Mexico's wine is grown and produced in the nearby Valle de Guadalupe (see the Tijuana Excursions chapter). One of the wineries, Vinícola LA Cetto, offers tours and tastings at its production facility in Tijuana (see the Tijuana Things to See & Do chapter).

Tequila enjoys great popularity in Tijuana, both with tourists and locals. The most popular Tequila-based cocktail is the margarita, a concoction that also contains sweet liqueur (such as Triple Sec, Grand Marnier or Controy, which is the Mexican version of Cointreau) and lime juice, blended with ice or served on the rocks, usually in a saltrimmed glass. (For more on tequila, see the boxed text 'Wasting Away: The Glorious & Sad Fate of Tequila,' later.) Other spirits and liqueurs, many made in Mexico, are inexpensive and widely available: Bacardi Rum, brandy, Controy, Kahlua (coffee liqueur) and Oso Negro vodka, to name a few.

PLACES TO EAT – BUDGET
Zona Centro (Map 13)

La Revo has numerous eateries serving Mexican food calibrated to tourist tastes. It's cheap, basic and often good – as long as you don't mind having it served with a serious helping of deafening rock music from speakers the size of god. A Mexican combo platter featuring something like one taco, one enchilada and one tamale can cost as little as US$4. Places include *Iguanas Ranas*, *Tilly's Fifth Avenue*, *Margarita's Village* and *El Torito Pub*, all of which turn into rowdy bars and dance clubs after dark and therefore are more thoroughly described in the Tijuana Entertainment chapter.

For a more authentic culinary experience, head to *Café La Especial* (☎ 685-66-54, *Avenida Revolución 718),* in the basement of the Pasaje Revolución shopping arcade. For decades local families and tourists have hunkered down at its wooden tables to dig into sizable portions of stickto-the-ribs Mexican fare. The hand-painted beamed ceiling is a pleasant touch, and roaming mariachis provide entertainment.

For a slice of Italy – or pizza, for that matter – stop in at *Vittorio's* (☎ 685-17-29), on La Revo at Calle 9a (Zaragoza), where the air is thick with garlic, tomato and oregano. The best value is the US$4 lunch special; otherwise, the 14-inch pizza (US$6 to US$10) easily feeds two, and there's pasta and salads as well.

Step one block east or west off Avenida Revolución and you'll find plenty more culinary candidates worthy of your attention.

TIJUANA

One of Tijuana's best values is the diner-style 24-hour *Tortas Ricardo* (☎ 665-40-31, 665-31-46, *Avenida Madero 1410*), at Calle 7a (Galeana), a bright and clean place in business since 1965. Breakfasts are excellent here, and the bulging tortas are among the tastiest in town. Nicotine-phobics can breathe a sigh of relief since Tortas Richardo is a rare smoke-free zone.

Tortas Chapultepec (☎ 685-14-12), on Avenida Constitución at Calle 6a (Flores Magón), is even older (1952) and just as good. The specialty is the torta stuffed with ham, pork loin and cheese for US$3; there are also superb aguas. Other good places for tortas are the tunnel-shaped *Tortas Tapatío* (☎ 685-37-49, *Avenida Constitución 821*), at Calle 2a (Juárez), and the hole-in-

Wasting Away: The Glorious & Sad Fate of Tequila

In the glory days of westerns, Clint or the Duke would lick the salt off a knuckle, throw back a grimy shot glass, bite the lime wedge and hiss loudly through clenched teeth. This was a *manly* ritual. You could feel their pain. *This* was tequila, *hombre*. The little bite of death. And generations of ill-prepared students have joined in this ritual only to find themselves 'hugging the bowl' and awaking to thoughts and sensations akin to those felt in the brain of a wolverine on angel dust.

Tequila, then as now, is not for the meek. But what began as the home brew of Mexican peasants ('Okay, we need to get drunk, so let's boil that blue agave over there and see what happens. Maybe toss a worm in it too, just for effect.') has steadily escalated in alcoholic lore to the point where its legendary qualities are threatening its existence.

Now found in every chic bar from Moscow to Melbourne, tequila has become the choice of connoisseurs whose tastes formerly ran to the dry martini or the ancient brandy. Whipping up a 'killer margarita' has made the reputation of many a trendy publican and resulted in a global gulping frenzy. Not bad for a spiky desert plant related to the lily family, you say? Sorry, but actually *es muy malo* for the Weber blue agave of Jalisco, the only plant authorized by the Mexican government for tequila production.

Global demand resulted in sales of US$296 million worth of tequila in 1998. But it takes this humble plant eight to 12 years to mature before its heart – in true Aztec fashion – is ripped out, mashed and distilled. And as the World Trade Organization has designated to tequila – like champagne – the unique status of a geographically distinct liquor, Jalisco is running out of…juice.

This has resulted in waves of agave smugglers harvesting inferior plants and pawning them off as the real deal. And the price for Jimmy Buffett's favorite vegetable has gone through the roof: The ton of agave that sold a year ago for US$40 now costs well over US$600. This means you'll be 'paying at the pump' as well, with a bottle of Herradura's Selección Suprema going for around US$500.

You can still get *mezcal* – tequila's bastard cousin – at a fair price, though you can't serve it at the yacht club. *Plata* tequila – the silver variety – is the most affordable legit stuff, but if you want to get toasty with a paramour, better shell out for a Reposada, aged in wood. And if you're asking for the hand of Don Jaime's lovely daughter, you'd best sell off your AT&T stocks and pony up with an *anejo* of 100% agave, if you know what's good for you, hombre.

- **David Peevers**

the-wall **Tortas Las Tortugas** (☎ 634-07-83, Avenida Ocampo 409), which even delivers.

You'll also fill up well and cheaply at **El Farolito**, on Calle 7a (Galeana) near Avenida Constitución, a little eatery decked out in a riot of color. You can watch the food being prepared in the open kitchen, and you'll spend less than US$3 for breakfast or US$6 for a fish-and-shrimp combination. The more conventionally decorated **Plata de Oro** (☎ 685-60-60, Avenida Niños Héroes 1151) is bigger, just as clean and a good value.

Religion and enchiladas seem to mix well at **Super Antojitos** (☎ 685-50-70, Calle 4a 1810), where a sculpture of the Virgen de Guadalupe keeps an eye on the cash register. Gut-busting combination platters are US$5, and three enchiladas for $1.50 will satisfy smaller appetites. Servers wear smiles and traditional garb, but there's no alcohol or smoking. It's open 7 am to 10 pm.

Tamalandia (☎ 685-75-62, Calle 8a 8374) is a cheery little place selling homemade tamales stuffed with beef, chicken or cheese, plus the dessert-like *dulce* (all US$0.75 each). Most people come for take-out, although there are a couple of tables as well.

Zona Río (Map 14)

The 24-hour **Tacos El Gordo**, on Blvd Sánchez Taboada at Calle Javier Mina next to Mercado Hidalgo, has cult status among night owls. The tacos (US$1 each) are definitely on the greasy side, and some of the offerings are perhaps a bit too adventurous, but in the wee morning hours crowds stack up three deep at this little stand.

Across the street, the newish **Taquería Franc**, at the corner of Calle 8a (Hidalgo), is giving El Gordo a run for the money (see map 13 for both of these). This large place, which has already developed a loyal following, has a few tables, which definitely cuts down on the taco-eating messiness.

A fun place to go after dinner – or anytime the sweet tooth calls – is **Tepoznieves** (☎ 634-65-32, Blvd Sánchez Taboada 4002) in Plaza Minarete (look for Sam's Club). It's famous for its hundreds of flavors of natural ice creams, frozen yogurts

and sorbets, including more unusual varieties like chili and hibiscus. This is not a place for the indecisive.

Colonia Cacho (Map 13)

Mariscos El Nuevo Anclote, at the corner of Avenidas Brasil and Batopilas, is a little shoebox of a restaurant specializing in seafood cocktails. Choose among three sizes, from US$3.50 for the *chico* (small) to US$7 for the grande (large), or fill up on ceviche tostadas for US$1 each.

Chapultepec & Hipódromo (Map 15)

El Rincón de Xochimilco (☎ 686-24-91, Privada Valencia Rivera 157) is a youthful family restaurant with a menu that runs the gamut of antojitos, including flautas, sopes, pozoles and gorditas, all prepared in the style of Mexico City, the owners' hometown. A huge plate of food, including rice and beans, costs about US$3. Leave room for the yummy flan.

The venerable **Carnitas Uruapán** (☎ 681-61-81, Blvd Agua Caliente 12650) has fed generations of Tijuanenses with its authentic carnitas served at garden patio-type wooden benches and tables. The pig is slow-cooked on the premises and served with rice, beans, guacamole, salsa and tortillas, often to the sound of live mariachis. Half a portion (US$6) is enough for one. Night owls are welcome – the place routinely stays open till 3 am.

Birria de chivo, a stew made from roasted baby goat, may be an acquired taste; a good place to start acquiring it is **Birriería el Cuerno de Chivo** (☎ 681-03-95, Blvd Díaz Ordaz 9), across from the Auditorio Municipal near the racetrack. Another place serving this kind of food is **Birriería Guanajuato** (Map 12; ☎ 626-23-24, Blvd Díaz Ordaz 15602), in Plaza Carrousel.

Self-Catering

The two largest supermarket chains are Gigante and Calimax, while the less common Comercial and Ley are more like superstores, mixing foodstuff with general household goods, clothing and automobile accessories. Branches are distributed all along Blvd Agua Caliente, Paseo de los Héroes and Blvd Sánchez Taboada.

Central outlets on Avenida Revolución (Map 13) include a Calimax branch at Calle 10a (Sarabia) and a Gigante in the small mall between Calle 2a (Juárez) and Calle 3a (Carrillo Puerto). Both are open 24 hours. In the Zona Río (Map 14), Calimax is on Paseo de los Héroes right at the Cuauhtémoc traffic circle, while Gigante is on Blvd Sánchez Taboada at Camino Nuevo. Comercial has an outlet in the Plaza Río mall.

For delicious baked goods, try *El Molino* *(Map 13; ☎ 684-90-40)*, at Avenida Quintana Roo and Calle 10a (Sarabia). In business since 1928, it makes everything from ordinary *bolillos* (typical Mexican bread) to fanciful wedding cakes. Another good place for fresh and amply stuffed pastries is *Pastelería/Panadería Ensenada* (Map 13) at Calle 3a (Carrillo Puerto) 1517, near the Parque Teniente Guerrero.

Cafe Français *(Map 14; ☎ 684-17-29)*, on Blvd Sánchez Taboada, is a tiny temple of tempting tarts and other French-style pastries and cakes. There's another branch on Calle 7a (Galeana), just off Avenida Revolución (Map 13). *La Sonrisa*, in Plaza Fiesta (Map 14), specializes in whole-grain breads and pastries and also makes sandwiches to go for under US$2. Next door, *Lo Ma' Bonita* stands out for its brightly pigmented facade and fruit display. This is a good place for aguas and licuados, although they also serve antojitos in their casual outdoor dining area.

PLACES TO EAT – MID-RANGE
Zona Centro (Map 13)

Regardless of the controversy around the Caesar salad (see the boxed text 'All Hail Caesar's!'), fact is, one of the best is still served at the 24-hour *Caesar's Sports Bar & Grill* *(☎ 688-27-94, 638-45-62)*, at Calle 5a (Zapata). You'll fill up for US$5 *and* get to watch your blue-haired waiter go through the ritual preparation right at your table. They also have heartier main courses for US$8 to US$12.

Up the street, next to the Frontón Palacio Jai Alai, is *Chiki Jai* *(☎ 685-49-55, Avenida Revolución 1388)*, which has been packed with patrons since 1947. In the golden days of jai alai (the 1950s and '60s), the most famous players used to hang out here,

All Hail Caesar's!

It has absolutely nothing to do with ancient Rome and even less with the gambling emporium in Las Vegas. The Caesar salad is a completely Tijuana concoction devised to elevate the lowly leaves of romaine lettuce to the status of haute cuisine. The secret, of course, is in the dressing: a combination of olive oil, garlic, Parmesan, Worcestershire sauce, black pepper, a raw or coddled egg and, sometimes, mashed anchovies.

The delicious dish gets its name from Caesar Cardini, the first owner of Hotel Caesar's at Avenida Revolución and Calle 5a (Zapata). It first appeared on the hotel's menu sometime in the late 1920s and was an immediate success copied by other restaurants around town. While Cardini is frequently given full credit for the salad's creation, many food historians believe that it was, in fact, his 18-year-old Italian immigrant chef, Livio Santini, who came up with the dressing.

To soothe his homesickness, Santini replicated a salad his mother had served back in the Old Country when he was growing up. As the story goes, a rich customer happened upon Livio eating his greens in the hotel kitchen, asked for a taste and – well, it was love at first bite. Cardini, ever the wise businessman, put the dish on the menu as the house salad, which is how it got its name.

Still today, at Caesar's Sports Bar & Grill, as the hotel's restaurant is now called, you can marvel at the tableside preparation of one of the world's great palate pleasers. And every year in mid-October, Tijuana honors its famous culinary creation with The World's Biggest Caesar's Salad Festival, on Avenida Revolución.

It's definitely a little *mordida* (bite) of Tijuana's storied past.

thanks, in part, to the consistently good Spanish/Basque food. The chef makes a mean paella for US$9. Come at lunchtime; in the evening doors close at 9 pm.

Attached to the department store of the same name, **Sanborn's** (☎ 688-14-62), on La Revo at Calle 8a (Hidalgo), is a coffee shop popular with locals. The food is solid but uninspired, and the service on the slow side. Still, it's clean, dependable, and the selection of dishes is enormous. The best meal is breakfast, which costs US$4 and includes a hot drink and juice. There are several other branches around town, mostly in large malls such as Plaza Río (Map 14: ☎ 684-89-58) and Plaza Las Brisas (Map 12).

Zona Río (Map 14)

Seafood is prepared in both traditional and unusual ways at **Mariscos Los Angulo** (☎ 634-60-27, Paseo de los Héroes 4449), a giant restaurant tented by the hugest and steepest palapa roof you may ever see. One favorite is fish fillet stuffed with a bonanza of shrimp, oysters and squid.

Asador Pamplona (☎ 681-88-88, Avenida Río Suchiate 9430), a favorite among local business and office folks, is owned by a former jai alai player and has some of the best Spanish food in town. It's a diminutive and welcoming space, where specialties include paella and fried pork loin. Everything is under US$10, and the wine list is excellent.

La Espadaña (☎ 634-14-88/89, Blvd Sánchez Taboada 10813) is in a mission building look-alike with tasteful, earth-tone art and decor. Mesquite-grilled meats are the specialty, as are updated versions of Mexican cuisine. Breakfasts are among the best in town, and at lunchtime the office crowd invades. You'll find that many main courses are under US$10.

If you're feeling tropical, head to **La Casa del Mole** (☎ 634-69-20, Paseo de los Héroes 1501) for Tijuana's best mole-based dishes served in a glass-roofed jungle environment centered around a giant rock fountain. A jazz pianist will sometimes serenade you with popular classics at lunchtime. You can eat and drink well here for under US$10. It's open 8 am to 8 pm daily.

The festively decorated **Guadalajara Bar & Grill** (☎ 634-30-65, Avenida Diego Rivera 19) is a dependable tourist favorite with an energetic vibe and good Mexican staples; the succulent fajitas are a specialty. This is also a good place just for drinks and appetizers. It's open noon to midnight.

California Restaurante (☎ 688-19-80), in Plaza Río, is a cafeteria-style restaurant popular for its all-you-can eat buffets (US$8.50 for breakfast or dinner, US$10 for lunch). There's a second branch on Blvd Agua Caliente at Calle Robirosa, across from the Grand Hotel.

Gypsy's (☎ 683-60-06), in the Pueblo Amigo mall, is a lively tapas bar and restaurant with decor inspired by Spanish artists Miró, Gaudí and Dalí. The tapas are winners, including the *calamari a la romana* (deep-fried calamari rings) and the *patatas bravas* (French friespotatoes with spicy tomato sauce). Of the main courses, only the paella ($7), almost big enough for two, passes muster, while everything else tends to be over salted. It's open noon to 1 am.

La Taberna Española (☎ 684-94-01), in Plaza Fiesta, presents some serious competition to Gypsy's, although the decor is more traditionally Iberian (painted tile and dark wood). The food here is great, especially the mushrooms swimming in a sea of garlic sauce, perfect for sopping up with some fresh bread.

Family-owned **El Faro de Mazatlán** (☎ 684-88-82, Blvd Sánchez Taboada 9542), in the back of Plaza Ejecutiva (also known as Plaza Financiera), is a trusty Tijuana standby, where owner Bernabé Bernal himself may welcome you with a smile and a handshake. Fish and seafood come charcoal-grilled, sautéed or baked and in combination with an appetizer, seafood soup, vegetables, rice and warm rolls. The wine list is above average. Hours are 11 am to 11 pm.

A decent mid-priced Chinese restaurant is **Dragon Plaza** (☎ 684-19-63, 684-23-56), inside Plaza Río, where huge portions fit in with the dining room's banquet-style seating (large, round tables for up to 10 people). Anything seafood is good here, and there's also a handful of tofu-based dishes.

TIJUANA

After a couple of surprisingly potent margaritas, the decor, especially the dragon heads peeking down from the ceiling, is definitely surreal. It's open 11 am to 11 pm.

Caesar's Restaurant may have invented it, but many Tijuanenses would give *Victor's* (☎ 634-33-09, *Blvd Sánchez Taboada 9848),* at Calle Joaquín Clausell, the honor of 'best Caesar salad' (here confusingly called Ensalada Victor's). It's cheaper in the restaurant's coffee shop section, but better in its steak house, where the dressing is made to order. The coffee shop also serves great breakfasts.

Colonias Cacho & América (Map 13)

The cheerfully tiled facade of *Paellas Toñico* (☎ 684-09-41, *Avenida Jalisco 2433)* sets the tone for this intimate restaurant, where eating feels like dining among friends. Red tablecloths beautifully set off the namesake dish, paella Valenciana, which at US$7 is a veritable steal. Other classic Spanish dishes include *jamón Serrano* (cured ham) and *tortilla española* (potato omelet).

Merlot Bistro (☎ 684-71-21, *Avenida Guanajuato 2585)* is ensconced in a rambling red-tile villa divided into several sections and fringed by a nice garden. The healthful menu features 10 salads, available in two sizes, for US$3.50 to US$5. In addition to appetizers and Mediterranean-style main courses, the Merlot Bistro offers build-your-own sandwiches for under US$7.

At *Tango y Bife* (☎ 684-74-76), a rustically elegant Argentine steakhouse at the corner of Avenidas Brasil and Fresnillo, the emphasis is on quality cuts of meat and efficient, unobtrusive service. The wine list is among the best in town, and prices are surprisingly civilized, with many dishes costing around US$10. Groups often order the *asado Argentina,* which feeds five carnivores for US$55. It's open 1:30 pm to midnight.

As if to make a point, *Vallarta Natural* (☎ 686-15-60, *Blvd Agua Caliente 1252),* one of the Tijuana's few vegetarian restaurants, is right across from the El Toreo bullring. The chef attacks meatless fare with a culinary vengeance to produce some tasty, fresh and healthy choices. The soy chorizo is delicious, and all breads are baked on the premises. Breathe deep – this is a smoking-free zone. It's open 8 am to 6 pm.

A perennial favorite, *La Fonda de Roberto* (☎ 686-46-87, *Blvd Cuauhtémoc Sur Oriente 2800)* is part of Motel La Sierra (see the Tijuana Places to Stay chapter). Specialties from around Mexico are prepared with panache and an inspired palette of ingredients and spices. A typical dish is *chilies en nogada* – stuffed poblanos chili, baked in a creamy sauce spiked with ground walnuts and topped with pomegranate seeds. It's open 9 am to 9 pm Tuesday to Sunday.

Chapultepec & Hipódromo (Map 15)

El Potrero (☎ 686-38-26, *Blvd Salinas 4700)* deserves attention not so much for its fairly straightforward Mexican food as for its oddball architecture: Its roof is literally in the shape of a classic Mexican sombrero. Around since 1934, it's a vestige of Tijuana's 1930's heyday and known to generations of locals as El Gorro Drive Inn. It shows up in many old-timey photographs.

Cafe Saverio's (☎ 686-15-64, *Avenida Sonora 3808)* is an airy bistro with a contemporary flair and young and fashionable crowds. The service can be mildly attitudinous, but the pizza, pasta and salads are solid. Prices are mostly under US$10.

El Rodeo (Map 12; ☎ 684-56-40, *Blvd Salinas 1647)* is a fine beef restaurant where you can watch your steak being prepared tableside. The decor is eccentric, to say the least, with antique gas pumps, Coke machines and a shrine to assassinated PRI presidential candidate Luis Donaldo Colosio. All meals come with appetizer, salad and dessert.

Playas de Tijuana (Map 12)

With a bright, vibrantly colored dining room overlooking the ocean, *La Fonda de las Delicias* (☎ 630-94-14, *Avenida Pacífico 640)* features traditional Mexican cuisine that goes beyond the staples. The chef is famous for chilies en nogada and *sopa de medulla* (bone-marrow soup), but also serves carne asada and *cochinita pibil* (spicy shredded pork); most dishes cost around US$8. It's open 9 am to 9 pm daily.

Teatro, right on the oceanside of Avenida Pacífico at Parque de México Sur, is a hip hangout for Tijuana trendoids. Food and drink are served in a mildy theatrical setting with panoramic windows perfect for watching the sun drop into the ocean, although the best views are from the large terrace. Pasta figures big on the small menu, which also features appetizers.

A few blocks inland, ***Barra Jaripea*** (*Avenida Parque México Norte 257*) has a woodsy Old-World ambiance and an emphasis on steaks and other meats. Across from the Plaza Monumental, it's at its liveliest when the aficionados gather after the Sunday afternoon corrida.

PLACES TO EAT – TOP END
Zona Centro (Map 13)

Locals and tourists give top marks to ***La Costa*** (*☎ 685-84-94, 685-31-24, Calle 7a 8131*), a classy and warmly lit seafood restaurant known for its consistently high quality. Fish fillets prepared in umpteen ways and served with various sauces cost US$10, but shrimp and other specialties start at US$16. All main courses come with soup, appetizer, salad, rice and coffee. It's open daily 10 am to midnight.

Of the venerable Tía Juana Tilly's, formerly in the Jai Alai Palace, only the cheerful ***Tía Juana's La Terraza*** (*☎ 685-60-24*), on Avenida Revolución at Calle 7a (Galeana), has survived. You'll have good views of the passing crowds, but the food's overpriced, with Mexican combination platters costing around US$10, and steaks US$13. At times, fairly low-key entertainment may accompany your meal.

Zona Río (Map 14)

Regarded by many as the city's finest restaurant, ***Cien Años*** (*☎ 634-30-39, 634-72-62, Avenida José María Velasco 1407*) is one of Tijuana's temples of *alta cocina* (haute cuisine). The chefs have dug deep into a box of ancient Mexican recipes, some going back to the Aztecs and Mayans. The adventurous could munch on *chiniquiles* (fried

maguey worms) or slurp the spinal-cord soup, but there's plenty of less palate-challenging fare as well. The selection of tequilas (more than 100) and Baja wines is impressive. It's a fairly formal place, so dress nicely. Reservations are recommended. It's closed Sunday night.

La Cava Cien Años (*☎ 634-30-39, Avenida José Clemente Orozco 2340*) is Cien Años' more casual sibling. It's an intimate place, with saffron-colored walls, framed paintings, polished plank floors and complexion-friendly lighting, and coming in here feels a bit like entering a friend's living room. Come for a drink and appetizer or a full dinner. Meals are built around chicken, beef and shrimp and start at US$10.

Homesick Americans might want to snare a seat on the covered terrace of ***El Zaguan*** (*☎ 634-67-81, Paseo de los Héroes 10501*), overlooking the Abraham Lincoln traffic circle. The food here, though, is distinctly Mexican. Unusual offerings include chicken breast stuffed with *huitlacoche*, a chewy black fungus that grows on corn cobs and has been known since Aztec times to have aphrodisiacal qualities. Mains start at US$10, and there's also a sushi bar. El Zaguan is open 7 am to midnight.

Chan's (*☎ 634-27-66, Blvd Sánchez Taboada 10880*) is Tijuana's best Chinese restaurant. The decor is uncluttered and elegant with white linen-covered tables and neatly folded napkins. You could try the fish in black-bean sauce, although the piéce de résistance is the Peking duck served mu shu-style with little thin pancakes/tortillas.

Easily winning the award for most visually stunning restaurant is ***Villa Saverio's*** (*☎ 686-65-02, Escuadrón 201*), behind Chan's, an exquisitely furnished food temple reminiscent of a sumptuous Tuscan villa. Sparkling oak floors, framed original art, cathedral ceilings and immaculate table settings form the backdrop to the accomplished Italian cuisine. Pastas cost from US$9 to US$15, and lobster can be had for about US$20. Swank, and worth it.

Tucked away in the serene courtyard of the Hotel Lucerna, with a view of the pool

TIJUANA

area, is ***Rivoli Brasserie*** *(☎ 633-39-00, Paseo de los Héroes 10902),* where chef Hector Kabande works his magic. The food is Mexican-Mediterranean with global touches. Fresh ingredients, both local and flown in from around the world, are combined in adventurous ways that almost always work well.

Chapultepec & Hipódromo (Map 15)

'Wine every day is like breathing' is the motto of Nelly Alonso Sieiro, owner of the sophisticated ***La Avenida*** *(☎ 681-83-53, Avenida Sonora 65).* Such dedication to the grape certainly explains why the dining room looks like a wine cellar. The menu changes seasonally but always features creatively prepared pastas, seafood, chicken and beef dishes from US$10 upward. It's open 1 to 10 pm.

The appropriately named ***La Escondida*** *(☎ 681-44-58, Santa Monica 1)* is indeed a bit hard to find, but worth seeking out if you want to lunch or dine with Tijuana's movers and shakers. Installed in an old hacienda, it offers refined dining – including outdoors in the garden or on the patio – often with live piano music. The food is upscale Mexican and international; the butter-soft chateaubriand for two is a good deal at US$24. Reservations are recommended, especially to dine on Friday and Saturday.

La Leña *(☎ 686-47-52, Blvd Agua Caliente 1191),* just east of the Grand Hotel Tijuana, serves some of the city's best wood-fired Sonoran beef; the carne asada is particularly good, as is the filet mignon. It's all served with steaming tortillas, which you can watch being made. The complimentary chips are served alongside several delicious salsas. Hours are noon to 11:30 pm.

Mirador, between Tijuana and Ensenada

Tall cold one, Playas de Tijuana

ural at Santo Tomás winery

Boulevard Costero, Ensenada

Ensenada's Riviera del Pacífico

Dali-esque sculpture by Oscar Ortega Corrall

Roadside art on the Transpeninsular

Entertainment

Tijuana has wide-ranging cultural, entertainment and nightlife offerings that go far beyond its stereotypical boozetown image. To be sure, those looking for cheap drinks and wild partying will have plenty of places to choose from. And the element interested in the tawdry sex trade won't have to go farther than the Zona Norte or the cheesy strip clubs on Avenida Revolución.

But aficionados of highbrow entertainment won't be disappointed either, as there are numerous sophisticated venues around town where classical music, theater and dance – some of it truly top-notch – are the order of the day.

The best source for 'whats-on' information is the Thursday supplement to the *La Frontera* newspaper called *La Brújula* (The Compass), which contains the most comprehensive and accurate events and entertainment schedule for the city. Distributed through the tourist offices, the university campuses and cafes is the student-oriented *En Tu Ciudad*, a free biweekly entertainment guide. Also check the Web site at www.entucd.com.

CULTURAL VENUES

Tijuana has a rich tapestry of cultural offerings – from experimental theater to modern dance to classical music concerts – that take place at several multi-use venues. For an introduction to the city's most important performers and artists, see the Arts section in the Facts about Tijuana chapter.

The most important venue is the *Centro Cultural de Tijuana* (Cecut; Map 14; ☎ 684-11-11), on Paseo de los Héroes at Avenida Independencia, where excellent events of all stripes are held in rooms and halls that can accommodate from 60 to 1100 people.

In any given month the menu may include experimental or classic theater, chamber, orchestral or pop music, symposia and lectures, puppet shows, seminars, folkloric dancing or even a hypnotist. Ticket prices vary but tend to be lower than north of the border; student discounts are usually available, and many events are free.

Tijuana also has city-sponsored venues that function as forums for local artists. The *Instituto de Cultura de Baja California* (ICBC; Map 14; ☎ 683-59-22, Avenida Centenario 10151) offers everything from film screenings to art exhibits to dance recitals.

Two more hotbeds of activity are the Casas de la Cultura. An imposing neoclassical-style brick building (in the former 1929 Escuela Alvaro Obregón) houses the *Casa de la Cultura – Altamira* (Map 13; ☎ 687-26-04, Calle París 5), about 1 mile (1.6km) west of Avenida Revolución. The other is the *Casa de la Cultura – Playas* (Map 12; ☎ 630-18-25, Avenida del Agua 777), in the Cortijo de San José complex in Playas de Tijuana. Both host art exhibits, dance and choral performances, and many other events, often for free or at low cost.

The theater troupe of the Universidad Autónoma de Baja California, called Taller Universario de Teatro de Tijuana, performs at the *Teatro UABC* (Map 12; ☎ 682-10-33 ext 5261) on campus. Theater productions also take place at the *Teatro IMSS* (Map 15; ☎ 686-42-52), at Blvd Salinas and Calle Cárdenas.

The most important private venue is the delightful *El Lugar del Nopal* (Map 13; ☎ 685-12-64, Callejon 5 de Mayo 1328), where art, poetry, acoustic music and other cultural fare is on the menu. This sophisticated cafe-bar, restaurant and cultural center energetically supports local artists. It is an enchanting place – especially the garden patio. It's tucked away in a residential area and a bit hard to find, but worth the effort. The entertainment starts around 9 pm.

Several of Tijuana's coffeehouses also have ambitious cultural agendas. See Cafes later this chapter for details.

BARS

Bars abound throughout Tijuana, but they're especially concentrated in three central areas: Avenida Revolución and – in the Zona Río – Plaza Fiesta and Pueblo Amigo. La Revo is the main stomping ground for tourists, many of them sailors on leave or young Mexican Americans, as well as US college kids too young to get into the bars north of the border (the legal drinking age in Mexico is 18, versus 21 in California). Testosterone levels are high, security is tight (purses and bodies are usually checked for weapons) and the ambiance a cross between a conga line and *Animal House*. By contrast, Plaza Fiesta and Pueblo Amigo draw mostly a local, somewhat older, clientele.

Although most places are open nightly, things are pretty dead from Sunday to Wednesday. The action starts heating up on Thursday, helped along by cheesy enticements like Ladies Night, when drinks for women are free. On Friday and Saturday, everyone kicks loose, and clubs and bars are often filled to capacity.

Avenida Revolución (Map 13)

The days when Carlos Santana played the strip clubs on Tijuana's most famous – and notorious – entertainment drag are sadly a thing of the past (see the boxed text 'Carlos Santana: From Tijuana's Mean Streets to Solid Gold'). Today Avenida Revolución mostly vibrates with venues featuring ear-splitting recorded music. Sidewalk hawkers try to lure you inside bars and clubs with two-for-one drink specials and other gimmicks, but don't expect real bargains: In most cases, margaritas here are a close relative of lemonade.

One of the most popular places is *El Torito Pub* (☎ 685-16-36), upstairs at No 643, where the most coveted seats are on the

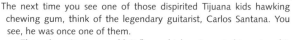

Carlos Santana: From Tijuana's Mean Streets to Solid Gold

The next time you see one of those dispirited Tijuana kids hawking chewing gum, think of the legendary guitarist, Carlos Santana. You see, he was once one of them.

These days, Santana couldn't fly any higher. A musical icon since his appearance at Woodstock in 1969, his recent album, *Supernatural*, sold nearly 30 million copies worldwide and won nine Grammy awards. But there was a time when the rocker found himself in a hard place: the streets of Tijuana.

Although it happened more than 45 years ago, Carlos' arrival in this city mirrors that of more recent newcomers. Born in 1948 in Autlán de Navarro in the state of Jalisco, he came with his family to Tijuana when he was eight years old, camping out in dilapidated Colonia Libertad, living without running water or electricity. His father, José, couldn't make ends meet and forced his young son to help pay the rent by shining shoes and selling gum.

But it was this hardship that spurred Carlos to take charge of his destiny. A talented musician, he soon was playing in Tijuana's tawdry nightclubs – in between striptease acts – with local legends like Javier Batiz, who became his mentor. If Hamburg was the musical cauldron that forged the Beatles, Tijuana did no less for the musician who almost single-handedly brought Latin music to the front of the world stage.

Since his first band performed in the San Francisco of the 1960s rock revolution, the Santana legend has soared. In October 2000, he was given the keys to the city and proclaimed its cultural ambassador – a bully pulpit from which he now advocates Mexican and American unity.

- David Peevers

terrace with a bird's-eye view of the action below. There's a large, circular dance floor, two pool tables and even a mechanical bull.

Nearby *Iguanas Ranas* (☎ 685-14-22), at Calle 3a (Carrillo Puerto), is similar, but is creatively decorated to resemble a circus. You enter through a candy-striped 'tent,' then advance to the main bar area to be greeted by sombrero lampshades and a mobile made of bras. You can sit inside a retired yellow school bus that's now part of the facade, but there's a terrace here as well. In the back is a large black-lit room, a disco/sports bar with pool tables.

Also popular is *Tilly's Fifth Avenue* (☎ 685-90-15), at Calle 5a (Zapata), a smaller, ground-floor establishment that's been around in one form or another since 1927. These days you'll imbibe your cerveza in a bizarre setting mixing Tiffany-type lamps with a hodgepodge of thrift-store items – old suitcases, ski boots, dolls etc – dangling from the ceiling.

Much in the same vein is *Margarita's Village* (☎ 685-38-62), at Calle 3a (Carrillo Puerto), a cheerfully decorated basement where the margaritas are strong and the mariachis roam.

The Tijuana branch of the ubiquitous *Hard Rock Café* (☎ 685-02-06), at No 520, has the standard collection of musicians' memorabilia and a bar shaped like a guitar. In the daytime the place crawls with culture-shocked gringos, but the Latin rock bands here Thursday to Saturday night always draw local fans.

Zona Río (Map 14)

Plaza Fiesta Most self-respecting Tijuana scenesters wouldn't be caught dead on La Revo. The Zona Río is where it's at for locals – in particular the village-style Plaza Fiesta, where the dozen or so bars, restaurants and coffeehouses draw a youthful party crowd. Come here to down a few cervezas, knock back some tequilas and hear the local rock talent thrash it out. Places seem to open and close continuously, but the ones listed here have demonstrated some staying power.

The most popular party haunt at the time of writing was *Monte Picacho* (☎ 634-16-40, 634-70-74), a smallish, L-shaped watering hole, which attracts a loud but friendly clientele. Next door, *Ah Jijo* (☎ 634-16-40, 684-70-74) mixes it up with mariachi on some nights and rock *en español* on others. The cheerfully hokey decor has a Mexican town plaza theme, complete with a plastic relief landscape and fake trees.

Across the way is the usually packed *Sótano Suizo* (☎ 684-88-34), meaning 'Swiss basement,' which may explain the vaguely ski lodge look and the menu featuring sauerkraut, sausages and cheese fondue. Happy hour is 5 to 7 pm, and Tuesday night is Ladies' Night.

Another mainstay is *Mi Barra*, a modern sports bar with floor-to-ceiling windows and really loud music, though not as loud as at *Porky's Place*, above La Taberna Española (see the Tijuana Places to Eat chapter), which draws attention to its upstairs location with deafening decibels. The crowd knocks back cerveza by the pitcher faster than you can say 'chihuahua,' and things do occasionally get rowdy. A quieter choice is the nearby *La Caja* (☎ 684-70-16), where mellow reggae rules.

Paseo de los Héroes Several bars along this major Tijuana boulevard cater to graduates from the drink-and-dance-til-you-drop set, but they're fun nevertheless.

One of oldest places, *Ochoa's Cocktail Lounge* (☎ 634-24-15, Paseo de los Héroes 10288) has lured a predominantly local crowd with strong, inexpensive cocktails and live music for 17 years; there's also a small dance floor and live music on some nights. Cover is US$4 on Friday, US$5 on Saturday, free other nights. Thursday is Ladies' Night, with free well drinks until 11 pm. The bar/restaurant in front serves mainstream Mexican fare delivered with a side dish of romantic songs by the resident pianist.

The Hotel Camino Real has two bars that attract a blend of hotels guests and Tijuana's moneyed elite. The *Lobby Bar* is a classy cocktail lounge where horseshoe-shaped armchairs orbit tiny cocktail tables. Live music – scheduled once or twice a week – tends to the subdued, mostly jazz and mellow pop that usually don't drown out

TIJUANA

TIJUANA

conversation. Adjacent is **María Bonita** (☎ 634-20-10), a comfortable cantina where tequila fans can indulge in a tasting frenzy, with more than 100 varieties to choose from.

Pueblo Amigo *Señor Frog's* (☎ 682-49-62, *Via Oriente 60*) is part of the Carlos & Charlie emporium known for its off-beat humor and upbeat fiesta feel. Downstairs is the restaurant and bar, but you'll have to navigate a steep flight of stairs to get to the upstairs bar and dance floor. During bull-fighting season, aficionados pack this place after the Sunday corrida to toast the brave matadors – and vanquished bulls.

Escenario (☎ 682-49-67), adjacent to El Rodeo (see Traditional Music later in this chapter), is the place go *cubano* to the sizzling sounds of live salsa and merengue Friday and Saturday nights (US$8 cover, free admission for women on Friday). Bands start playing around 10 pm, but the action doesn't really heat up until 11 or midnight.

El Perro Azul (☎ 634-16-40), which means 'blue dog,' might be called '*cielo azul*' (blue sky) because of the fake sky that's part of the decor. The smallish space spills out onto the walkway, with seating under a canopy of trees. Local bands occasionally heat up the stage, and there's DJ-dancing other nights. It's a nice place, which also hosts art exhibits and other cultural events, but unfortunately at least some of the waiters feel a need to pad the bill, so watch out.

CAFES

Tijuana has several comfortable coffee-houses delivering more than just a good cuppa. Many also offer regular programming, with anything from art exhibits to pop concerts to readings, drawing in a cultured crowd. Most also serve alcohol and snacks.

A relative newcomer – and the only cafe on Avenida Revolución – is **Pueblo Cafe Baja** (*Map 13*; ☎ 685-56-67), in the Frontón Palacio Jai Alai. There's indoor and outdoor seating, an occasional live performance, and a larger-than-usual menu featuring pastas, salads and sandwiches.

The crowd favorite at the time of writing was **Cafe del Mundo** (☎ 683-56-84), in the Pueblo Amigo. It's a classy candlelit cafe-bar where the mostly student-age crowd passes time chatting, playing cards or table games or listening to live concerts. Gourmet coffees, beer and wine, as well as snacks, are served. A tarot card reader sometimes comes in. It's open from 5 pm to 2 am, closed Monday.

Cafe La Estancia (*Map 14*; ☎ 634-33-09, *Blvd Sánchez Taboada 9848*), upstairs at Victor's (see Tijuana Places to Eat), is an old-fashioned coffeehouse with cream cakes and an eclectic musical schedule that might feature Yiddish sopranos one night and a Ukrainian jazz pianist another.

Plaza Fiesta has **Cinque Cafe-Bar** (*Map 14*; ☎ 634-16-40), a stylish place with some thought-provoking art by Tijuana's own Oscar Ortega. For sustenance, they serve snacks like cheese platters, crêpes and salads for less than US$5. Watch out for bill-padding.

For a respite from the rest of Plaza Fiesta's boisterous scene, duck into **El Callejón** (*Map 14*; ☎ 684-23-93), a quiet

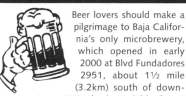

La Cervecería de Tijuana

Beer lovers should make a pilgrimage to Baja California's only microbrewery, which opened in early 2000 at Blvd Fundadores 2951, about 1½ mile (3.2km) south of downtown. It is the brainchild of José González Ibarra, whose vision it was to make a potent brew in the tradition of pilsner beer, which originated in Pilsen in the Czech Republic. Ibarra imported not only all the technology from that country but also a young Czech brewmaster, whose efforts have clearly paid off. Sold under the brand name Cerveza de Tijuana, this is a superior and full-bodied beer that easily measures up to some of Europe's finest. It's best enjoyed in the atmospheric timbered brewery-pub.

afe with updated country-style red-brick walls and wooden ceiling beams. The atmospheric lighting and original art are conducive to lingering, as are the delicious coffees and (nonalcoholic) drinks.

Chapultepec has a couple of establishments that fit perfectly into this upscale neighborhood. *Boga Cafe-Bar (Map 15; Avenida Sonora 3240)* is an artsy gathering place for Tijuana's young and beautiful. Large, glass-covered photographs behind the long bar, chairs with warped backs, and wacky metal-string lamps form part of the eccentric look. It's open from 6 pm Tuesday to Saturday and from 5 pm on Sunday (closed Monday).

Up the street, *Cafe de la Flor (Map 15; 686-29-76, Avenida Sonora 69)* is cozy, woodsy and festooned with white lilies reminiscent of Diego Riviera. This is a lovely place to hang and chat, sip cappucino or read a book. The cakes and pastries are killer (try the mango-and-cherry cheesecake), and they also serve cheese and wine.

DISCOS

Tijuana's discos are all upscale establishments that attract a young and high-flying clientele. Some open Friday and Saturday nights only (but check, this changes all the time). There's a dress code and dim doormen deciding who gets in and who doesn't. Purse and body checks are de rigueur. All also offer valet parking. Try to check not only cover charges but also drink prices before you enter a club.

At the time of writing, one of the hottest clubs in town was the Flintstone-esque *Baby Rock (Map 14; 634-24-04, 634-13-3)*, at the corner of Avenida Diego Rivera and Paseo de los Héroes in the Zona Río. It's a cavernous disco-bar with state-of-the-art sound and lighting. On Friday and Saturday night it gets Tijuana's trendy set going with its energetic vibe and alternative rock in English and Spanish. The cover charge is around US$10.

Across the street, the equally upscale *ZKA (Map 14; 634-71-40, 634-67-81, Paseo de los Héroes 10501)* is a modern

nightclub where '80s and '90s music dominates. Cover here is US$5.

In Pueblo Amigo, *Zoo'll (683-62-55 or 686-62-56)*, with industrial minimalist appeal, goes after the house and techno crowd and charges US$5 to US$10, depending on the night. It's open till 5 am; Thursday is Ladies' Night.

Cat's (Map 14; 638-85-59, Vía Poniente 4246), also in the Zona Río, is open Thursday, Friday and Saturday and sports sophisticated, modernist decor. Cover is US$8 to US$14.

In Playas de Tijuana, *Boomerang (Map 12; 630-99-98, Avenida del Pacífico 442)* predictably has an Australian theme and is the only place where you can dance the night away above the ocean. The crowd is young and hip, but the level of pretentiousness is tolerable and the music energetic. Happy hour runs from 4 to 7 pm, and Thursday is Ladies' Night.

TRADITIONAL MUSIC

The best place to catch live banda and norteña bands is *El Rodeo de Santa Fe (682-49-67)*, in Pueblo Amigo, which brings in some top names from around Mexico. After ascending a steep staircase worthy of a Mayan temple, you're plunged into a giant black-lit cavern that fills up with well-dressed locals, some in vaquero gear and white 10-gallon hats. A faux-rock wall complete with 'fossils' guides the way to a small rodeo arena behind the main stage. This is where semipros and courageous audience members test their macho-hood riding wild burros, a mechanical – and sometimes even a real – bull. Cover is US$8, or US$6.50 on Friday and Saturday night (women free on Friday) when it's DJ music only.

In business since 1988, *Las Pulgas (Map 13; 688-13-68, 685-95-94, Avenida Revolución 1501)*, Calles 7a (Galeana) and 8a (Hidalgo), has been around longer than El Rodeo and also attracts some top bands. It's rougher and not as sophisticated but equally popular. A huge place with several dance floors, its main bar section – with dozens of petite cocktail tables and incongruously frilly cushioned chairs – is open to the sidewalk.

TIJUANA

CINEMAS

Most of Tijuana's cinemas are modern multiplexes showing first-run Hollywood blockbusters either in the English original dubbed into Spanish or in English with Spanish subtitles. At some theaters, you'll also find the occasional Mexican, Latin American or European production thrown into the mix. Tickets cost about US$4, a bit less for shows before 6 pm.

The most central cinema is *Cinépolis Plaza Río (Map 14; ☎ 684-10-32, Paseo de los Héroes 9550),* in Plaza Río. A second theater in the mall, *Multicinemas Río (Map 14; ☎ 684-04-01)* was being remodeled at the time of writing, with no fixed reopening date scheduled (more often than not, places undergoing 'remodeling' never reopen, so keep Lonely Planet posted).

Nearby, still in the Zona Río, is *Cinemark 10 (Map 14; ☎ 634-74-30, Blvd Sánchez Taboada 4555)* with 10 screens, while *Cinema Las Torres Plus (Map 15; ☎ 686-55-70, Blvd Agua Caliente 4558),* inside one of the twin high-rises in Colonia Chapultepec, has two screens. Another double-screen theater is *Cinemas Gemelos (Map 15; ☎ 681-40-36),* in the dirt parking lot on Blvd Agua Caliente just southeast of the Agua Caliente racetrack.

The newest multiplexes are in the suburban malls, including the 10-screen *Cinépolis Plaza Carrousel (Map 12; ☎ 686-92-66, Blvd Díaz Ordaz 15-62)* in the mall of the same name in La Mesa. In Mesa de Otay, en route to the airport, you'll find *Cinema Star (Map 12; ☎ 624-33-91, Calzada del Tecnológico 2100),* which is in Plaza América and also has 10 screens; and the three-screen *Multicinemas Plaza Otay (Map 12; ☎ 623-13-70, Carretera Aeropuerto 1990),* in Plaza Gigante Otay.

Cine Planetario

Housed within Cecut's 'golf ball,' this popular Omnimax-style theater shows a changing roster of films – usually in Spanish – on a 180° screen. Admission is US$4.50, half-price for students.

Cineclubs

If mainstream movies don't do it for you, see what's on at Tijuana's *cineclubs,* which,

despite the name, don't require membership. Screenings take place, usually on a weekly schedule, at several cultural institutions and cost US$2 or US$3. Venues include the *Sala de Video* at Cecut, with screenings several times weekly (US$2); the *ICBC*, with free shows on Wednesday at 7:30 pm; the *Café Literario,* in the Casa de la Cultura – Playas, which has free screenings Wednesday at 7 pm; and *El Lugar del Nopal.* For addresses and phone numbers, see the Cultural Venues section earlier this chapter.

GAY & LESBIAN VENUES

Many of Tijuana's gay hangouts are seedy by American standards. An exception is Tijuana's oldest gay venue, *Emilio's,* a small cafe on Calle 3a (Carrillo Puerto) near Avenida Niños Héroes (Map 14; downstairs in the Parking América garage). It was founded more than 20 years ago by Emilio Velazquez, an activist and copublisher of the newspaper *La Frontera Gay.* This is a quiet, hustler-free zone that's also a good source for the latest news about the scene.

The place most heavily frequented by Americans is *Extasis (Map 13; ☎ 682-83-40),* a huge techno disco right across the border in Plaza Viva Tijuana. The place crawls with buff, pretty boyz showing off the results of endless hours in the gym. By all accounts, the male strippers are an eyeful, adding to the cruisy ambiance. It's open Thursday (Lesbian Night) to Sunday.

Tijuana's other bars and clubs have a decidedly local flavor. *Mike's Bar & Disco,* on La Revo near Calle 6a (Flores Magón), is popular for late-night partying and its drag shows (Map 13). *Los Equipales,* on Calle 7a (Galeana) just east of La Revo (Map 13), is another large Top-40 and Latin-music disco; it's open Wednesday through Sunday till the wee hours.

Ranchero replaces Top 40 in several cantinas where cowboy outfits are work clothes and not a fashion statement. *Noa Noa,* on Avenida Martínez near Calle 1a (Artículo 123), crawls with macho Mexican dudes but has a bit of a downtrodden vibe. *El Ranchero (Map 13; ☎ 685-28-00, Plaza Santa Cecilia 1914)* has cheap beers and even an pstairs balcony that's good for people vatching. The related **Villa Garcia**, a few loors down, is similar. Note that these bars re close to the Zona Norte and that patrons t both have reportedly been subjected to nuggings and beatings. If you must, come in he afternoon when the scene's safer.

PECTATOR SPORTS
Bullfights

Tijuana is recognized in Mexico as a major bullfighting venue and regularly draws ome of the best Latin American matadors s well as the occasional Spanish fighter.

Corridas take place Sunday at 4 pm every two or three weeks from the last weekend in April to late September/early October. Of the town's two bullrings, the larger, more spectacular is the **Plaza de Toros Monumental** *(Map 12;* ☎ *680-18-08, Avenida Pacíifico 1),* the renowned bullring-by-the-sea in Playas de Tijuana, right on the border fence. The other is **El Toreo de Tijuana** *(Map 14;* ☎ *686-12-19),* on Blvd Agua Caliente, halfway between the Zona Centro and the Agua Caliente racetrack.

Spring bullfights take place at El Toreo, which has room for 12,000 spectators. In

TIJUANA

Death in the Afternoon

To many people, a bullfight *corrida de toros* hardly seems to be sport or, for that matter, entertainment. Mexicans see it as both and more: It's as much a ritualistic dance as a fight. It's said that Mexicans arrive on time for only two events – funerals and bullfights.

The corrida begins promptly at 4, 4:30 or 5 pm on a Sunday. To the sound of music, usually a Spanish *paso doble,* the matador, in his *traje de luces* (suit of lights), and the toreros (his assistants) give the traditional *paseillo* (salute) to the fight authorities and the crowd. Then the first of the day's bulls (there are six in an afternoon) is released from its pen for the first of the ritual's three *suertes* (acts), or *tercios* (thirds).

The cape-waving toreros tire the bull by luring him around the ring. After a few minutes two *picadores,* on heavily padded horses, enter and jab long lances *(picas)* between the bull's shoulders. This is usually the most gruesome part of the whole process, as it instantly weakens the bull because of the sudden pain and blood loss.

After the picadores leave the ring, the *suerte de banderillas* begins, as two toreros take turns at sticking pairs of elongated darts into the bull's enormous neck muscles without getting impaled on his horns. After that the *suerte de muleta* is the climax: The matador has exactly 16 minutes to kill the bull. Starting with fancy cape work to further tire the animal, the matador then exchanges his large cape for the smaller *muleta* and takes the sword in hand, baiting the bull to charge before delivering the fatal *estocada* (lunge) with his sword. The estocada must be delivered from a position directly in front of the animal.

If the matador succeeds, the bull eventually collapses and dies. If the applause from the crowd warrants, the matador will be awarded an *oreja* (ear) or two and sometimes the tail. The dead bull is dragged from the ring to be butchered for sale.

A 'good' bullfight depends not only on the skill and courage of the matador but also on the spirit of the bulls. Animals lacking heart for the fight bring shame on the ranch that bred them. Very occasionally, a bull that has fought outstandingly is *indultado* (spared) – an occasion for great celebration – and then retired to stud.

Tijuana's two bullfighting arenas are the most famous in Baja California. The veteran Eloy Cavazos, from Monterrey, is often acclaimed as Mexico's best matador. Alfredo Lomeli and Eulalio López ('El Zotoluco') are younger stars. Bullfights featuring star matadors from Spain, such as Enrique Ponce, El Julí, José Tomás or El Cordobés, have spiced up the Tijuana bullfight scene as well.

July or August, corridas move to the ring in Playas, with a capacity of up to 25,000. Most matadors are Mexican; big names to look for are Eloy Cavazos, a 30-year veteran whose retirement may be imminent, and Eulalio 'El Zotoluco' López.

During the season tickets are available at the bullrings daily from noon to 6 pm and from 10 am on the day of the corrida. There's also a desk in the Grand Hotel (see the Tijuana Places to Stay chapter). In San Diego, contact Five Star Tours (☎ 619-232-5049, 800-553-8687, fax 619-232-7035), in the Amtrak station at Broadway and Kettner Blvd. Prices range from US$8 for general admission to US$45 for prime seats in the shade.

Greyhound Racing

Greyhound races with pari-mutuel wagering take place at the Agua Caliente racetrack at 7:45 pm daily and also at 2 pm weekends. Other sports bets include football, basketball, baseball, soccer, tennis, boxing and hockey – and there's bingo as well. Just beyond the Club Campestre golf course at Blvd Agua Caliente 12027, the track (☎ 633-73-00, 681-78-11) is open year-round; admission is free and parking is US$1.

Charreada

Related to the American rodeo, *charreadas* are demonstrations of superb horseman-

ship. A full charreada starts off with parade introducing the participants, the launches into 10 events, including mar roping *(los piales)*, head roping *(lazo d cabeza)* and the 'step of death' *(paso de l muerte),* in which the rider must jump fror a tame horse onto a wild one and ride i until it stops moving. Bull riding and ropin may also be part of the program.

In Tijuana, charreadas no longer tak place regularly but are occasionally held o Sunday afternoons between May and Sep tember. The most likely venue is the **Cortij San José** *(Map 12; ☎ 630-18-25, Avenida d Agua 777),* in Playas de Tijuana. The touri offices should know if something's schec uled during your stay.

Lucha Libre

Mexico's version of World Wrestlin Federation-style 'pro wrestling,' *lucha libr* (literally 'free fighting') is a hugely popula event, and nobody seems to mind that it more about showbiz than sport. Participan wear lurid masks and sport macho name like Bestia Salvaje, Shocker, Los Karate Bo and Heavy Metal. The governing body is th Consejo Mundial de Lucha Libre, founde in 1933. In Tijuana, the **Auditorio Municipe** *(Map 15; ☎ 681-64-74, Blvd Agua Calien 12421),* northeast of the Agua Caliente rac track, is the main address where you ca witness lucha libre live.

Shopping

Shopping is the favorite pastime of most Tijuana visitors, and for good reason. Prices here are low on everything from shoes to liquor to pharmaceuticals. In an age of 'mallification,' it's fun to look at items that are not available, hard to find or too expensive back home. This is especially true of the wide range of handicrafts and folk art, much of it handmade, from throughout Mexico. Shopping here also has an exotic feel, especially in the bazaar-like *mercados* (markets) where you can test your bargaining skills. And finally, shopping is also a window into another culture, telling you about local tastes, customs and preferences. You'll find every type of shopping experience in Tijuana, from ultramodern malls to hole-in-the-wall vendors, from chic boutiques to roadside hawkers.

Shops are generally open continuously Monday to Saturday from 9 or 10 am to 9 pm, to 8 pm Sunday. Some markets close around 6 pm, while many supermarkets are open 24 hours (see Self-Catering in the Tijuana Places to Eat chapter for details about the latter).

WHAT TO BUY
Quality Crafts

Bargain crafts abound in places like the Mercado de Artesanías and along Avenida Revolución, but, while these markets are fun to browse through, selections are repetitive and much of what's for sale is cheaply made and seriously kitschy. Not so in the following stores, which specialize in authentic crafts, albeit at higher prices. Also see the entry under Bazar de Mexico in the Where to Shop section later in this chapter.

H Arnold (Map 13; ☎ 685-56-60), Avenida Revolución 1068, has some classy decorative items, including painted clay sculptures from Oaxaca, colored glass vases in geometrical shapes, candlesticks, unusual furniture (you might like the Frida Kahlo-inspired chair) and brightly patterned Talavera ceramics. Its sister store, El Campanario (Map 13; ☎ 685-85-61), between Calle 3a (Carrillo Puerto) and Calle 4a (Galeana), has a similar selection.

In between the two, Casa de Ángel (Map 13; ☎ 685-10-44), Avenida Revolución 1026, has an eclectic assortment that includes Aztec and Mayan fertility figurines, Christmas ornaments, and Nativity scenes made from welded brass, tin and other materials.

The life-size papermâché animals, lacquered to look like porcelain, available at Tolan's (Map 13; ☎ 688-36-37), Avenida Revolución 1471, may not be everyone's idea of sophistication, but they are hugely popular with some designers. Tolan's also sells carved and painted tables and chairs, whimsical jewelry by Sergio Bustamante, as well as the usual pottery, pewter dishes and margarita glasses.

Casa Unibe (Map 13; ☎ 685-83-32), Avenida Revolución 1309, is a hangarlike space with helpful staff. It has an especially varied selection of chess sets – in wood, marble and malachite – as well as stone sculptures and rustic armoires.

Hand Art (Map 13; ☎ 685-26-42), Avenida Revolución 967, has sold embroidered, stitched, crocheted, knitted and sewn textiles – from blouses to table cloths, napkins to children's dresses – for more than 40 years. Goods come here from all over Mexico, including the Yucatán peninsula, Oaxaca and Jalisco.

Tear yourself away from La Revo to go where Tijuana's moneyed locals shop. One contender is La Casa del Ciruelo (Map 13; ☎ 684-07-00), Avenida Fresnillo 2361 in Colonia Cacho. Ensconced in a cute yellow cottage that doubles as a cafe, the store is owned by three charming sisters and their husbands, who are brothers. The women manage the business, and the men make the handsome furniture and home furnishings. Fluent English is spoken.

Also worth checking out is Centro Artesanal Tijuán (Map 14; ☎ 634-32-96), Blvd Sánchez Taboada in the Zona Río, which has lamps, wrought-iron, pewter, paintings, candles and other knickknacks in a cluttered setting.

Books

Sanborn's Department Store (Map 13; ☎ 688-14-62), at Avenida Revolución and Calle 8a (Hidalgo), is a venerable Mexican department store chain with a good book section and the city's best international newsstand. There's also a branch in Plaza Río in Zona Río (Map 14).

Librería El Día (Map 14; ☎ 684-09-08), Blvd Sánchez Taboada 10050 in the Zona Río, has books on Mexican history and culture, though none in English. In the Plaza Río, Librería de Cristal (Map 14; ☎ 634-10-18) also has a decent selection.

Shoes

Shoe fetishists will want to make a pilgrimage to Plaza Zapato (Shoe Plaza), a two-floor indoor mall with dozens of shops selling nothing but pumps, sandals, loafers, boots, sneakers and any imaginable kind of footwear for both men and women. It's next to Plaza Fiesta (Map 14) in the Zona Río. Leather accessories like wallets and handbags are available as well. Prices are good, but quality varies widely.

All of the malls mentioned under Where to Shop later in this chapter have at least one shoe store, but you'll also find a large concentration of them along Avenida Constitución and the parallel Avenida Niños Heroes between Calle 2a (Juárez) and Calle 3a (Carrillo Puerto).

Pharmaceuticals

Tijuana's pharmacies *(farmacias)* do box office, especially with US travelers, because many prescription drugs (including antibiotics, Viagra, antidepressants, high-blood pressure pills) are available over the counter here at considerable discounts. In fact, there's even a sort of 'drug tourism' among folks whose main reason for crossing the border is to stock up on medications. Savings can indeed be enormous, from 30% to 40% on the low end to up to 600% for certain brands of birth-control pills or

Renova, an antiwrinkle cream. Many medications are sold under a different name in Mexico, so bring along the box or accompanying leaflet that gives the drug's composition. For medications not available over the counter, you need to show a prescription, either from a US or a Mexican physician. Also see the boxed text 'Drugs & the Letter of the Law' for details about bringing back medications to the US. If you're returning to another country, check with customs about possible restrictions.

In recent years, pharmacies in Tijuana have proliferated faster than rabbits on

---

Drugs & the Letter of the Law

Under US Customs regulations, all medications purchased in Mexico must be declared when entering the US. If the drug requires a prescription in the US, you may be asked to produce one written in your name from either a US or a Mexican doctor.

Drugs that have not been approved by the Federal Drug Administration (FDA) may not be brought into the US, even if they're legal in Mexico and have been prescribed by a physician.

Under a fairly new ruling, US residents are legally allowed to bring back up to 50 dosage units of medications on the Drug Enforcement Agency's (DEA) controlled substances list, provided they have a prescription issued by a DEA-approved physician. Medications on this list include Valium and Librium, cough medicine with codeine, anabolic steroids and some barbiturates. For a full list, click on Travelers Information – Medications on the US Customs Web page (www.customs.usreas.gov/travel). Penalties for abuse are stiff.

If you purchase a controlled medication in Mexico, the pharmacy will need to keep the prescription, so be sure to make a copy to show to the customs inspector when re-entering the US. If you're buying noncontrolled medications, the pharmacy will let you keep the prescription.

Viagra. Staff in the ones in the Zona Centro, along Avenida Revolución and its side streets, are most likely to speak English. Two well-established chains are Farmacia Vida (Map 13; ☎ 681-74-02), Avenida Revolución 1651 at Calle 3a (Carrillo Puerto), and Farmacia Hidalgo (Map 13; ☎ 685-30-37), Calle 2a (Juárez) 1818, which has another location on Blvd Salinas at the corner of Calle Robirosa (Map 15; ☎ 686-44-24). Also well-respected, with some of the lowest prices, is Gusher (Map 14; ☎ 684-02-35/29), in Plaza Río, which has the added advantage of being open 24 hours. It's also famous for its *fuentes de sodas* (soda fountain), where delicious aguas and licuados are prepared on the spot. There's another branch in Plaza América (Map 12; ☎ 624-32-91/6).

Jewelry

All along La Revo and in the markets, you'll come across ambulatory vendors selling jewelry. The rings, bracelets and necklaces they sell are cheap and fun, but don't let anybody tell you they are silver. Most likely they're made from alpaca, which essentially means that they're silver-plated; real silver must be stamped '925.' Gold comes in 10, 14 and 18 karats, and stamps must indicate which quality it is. A 'CH' following the karat number means that the item is just gold-plated.

Los Castillo (Map 13; ☎ 638-46-91), in the Bazar de Mexico (see Where to Shop, below), is one of the most reputable stores, with pleasing, contemporary designs, some incorporating gemstones like onyx and turquoise. You may be able to get better prices – especially for gold – in stores away from Avenida Revolución, although styles here tend to be more traditional. Joyeria Durán (Map 13; ☎ 685-56-58), Avenida Constitución 943, is one such place worth checking out.

Designer Clothing

Varsity Club (Map 13; ☎ 685-16-95), Avenida Revolución 1184 at Calle 6a (Flores Magón), carries discounted clothing by Ralph Lauren, Calvin Klein and Tommy Hilfiger. Across the street at No 7727, Guess (Map 13; ☎ 685-25-33) has a smallish collection of what look like rejects from US stores. One block north at Calle 5a (Zapata) is Quicksilver (Map 13; ☎ 685-19-16), with surfer-inspired clothing. A popular outlet for casual wear is the Nautica Factory Store (Map 13), at the corner of Avenida Madero and Calle 7a (Galeana).

Car Body Work & Upholstery

Many US visitors take advantage of Tijuana's low-priced car body and upholstery repair shops, with prices typically less than half of those north of the border. Most places have English-speaking staff and do good work, but clarify your expectations beforehand, especially if you don't have a recommendation. Negotiate the price, get a written estimate before committing yourself and don't pay up front except for parts. Upholstery shops cluster on Avenida Ocampo and Avenida Pío Pico between Calle 3a (Carrillo Puerto) and Calle 8a (Hidalgo). Auto repair shops are mostly along Calle 2a (Juárez) between Ocampo and Madero. Some shops do both.

WHERE TO SHOP
Zona Centro

Avenida Revolución is Tijuana's main tourist-oriented shopping street. Souvenirs and handicrafts are plentiful, especially jewelry, wrought-iron furniture, baskets, silver, blown glass, pottery and leather goods; bargaining is the rule. Tequila, Kahlua and other liquors are also popular purchases, but you can save a couple of dollars by buying in supermarkets rather than liquor stores. For specific suggestions on where to buy what along here, see the What to Buy section earlier in this chapter.

Locals prefer to do their shopping along Avenida Constitución and Avenida Niños Héroes, just one and two blocks west of La Revo, respectively. The greatest concentration of shops is south of Calle 2a (Juárez), where the narrow sidewalks spill over with shoppers darting in and out of shoe stores, department stores, pharmacies, flower shops, jewelry stores and so on. Visitors who choose to join them will be rewarded with bargains galore offered at fixed prices.

TIJUANA

Markets

Mercado de Artesanias If you cross the border on foot, the first big market you'll encounter after you get off the second bridge is the Mercado de Artesanias (Artisans' Market), a large outdoor grid of alleyways. This is where you'll find the biggest concentration of souvenirs, crafts and curios, including wrought-iron chairs, earthenware pottery, wicker baskets, clay patio furnaces, blue-rimmed margarita glasses, plaster of Paris angel sculptures, striped woolen blankets. Bargain hard. Most shops are open till about 6 pm.

Bazar de Mexico The Bazar de Mexico (Map 13; ☎ 638-47-37), on Avenida Revolución at Calle 7a (Galeana), is an excellent showcase of quality arts and crafts from all around Mexico. You can watch some of the artisans at work, such as Alberto, a Zapotec Indian weaver, or a member of the Huichol tribe working on a colorful animal sculpture made from thousands of tiny pearls. Other products include wood masks from the state of Guerrero, crêpe flowers from Jalisco and silver from Taxco. Vendors will not hustle you and bargaining is OK. Quality is high and prices are not as inflated as in other tourist-oriented stores.

Pasaje Añagua By some accounts, Pasaje Añagua, on the south side of Calle 2a (Juárez) between Avenidas Niños Héroes and Constitución, is Tijuana's oldest market, with its origins in the early 20th century. In

Mercado Hidalgo – Up Close & Personal

For a taste of true Tijuana, be sure to visit Mercado Hidalgo, a wondrous cacophony of sounds and smells and impressions that will stay with you long after you've left town. This is where the locals shop for basics, and prices are accordingly low. Watch the grizzled old farmer free cactus ears from pesky prickers, his calloused hands immune to their sting. Wander by giant sacks spilling over with dried chilies or beans, lentils, garbanzos and other legumes. Be amazed at the many varieties of powdered chili – from pussycat mild to hellishly hot – heaped high in shiny tin buckets. Edge your way around tightly packed stalls selling tortilla presses, iron skillets, huge aluminum buckets, glazed earthenware and other household items. Watch the locals haggle over fruits, vegetables and spices, while a tired old parrot looks on from his cage. Pass underneath a flotilla of colorful piñatas – shaped like Pokemón, Mickey Mouse, Garfield or whatever character currently captures kids' imaginations – dangling from the ceilings like participants in some mad cartoon convention.

Mercado Hidalgo started in the mid-1950s in downtown at Calle 6a (Flores Magón) and Avenida Negrete and moved to its current spot in 1984. Many of the partially covered stalls, which wrap around a central parking lot, have been in the hands of the same family for generations. The market is run like a small village and even has elected officials and an organizational council. In December, members select one family's daughters to represent the market in the town's Christmas procession. And on April 2, the market's anniversary, there's a big celebration with free food and music.

Be sure to pop in at the small white structure topped with a blue-and-white dome in the middle of the parking lot, surrounded by smelly delivery trucks. This is the market chapel – *and* its public toilet. Birds, at least, don't seem to know the difference, for in order to ascend to the shrine, you must first hopscotch around their droppings. Upstairs awaits a charmingly pathetic display starring the Virgin in both paint and sculpture, along with a sea of plastic flowers and the Mexican flag. Piped-in pop music sometimes adds to the surreal ambiance. The market (Maps 13 & 14) is located between downtown and the Zona Río, on Blvd Sánchez Taboada between Avenida Independencia and Calle Javier Mina and is open 7 am to 6 pm (to 5 pm Sunday).

terms of offerings it's sort of a miniature Mercado Hidalgo (see the boxed text 'Mercado Hidalgo – Up Close & Personal'). Crammed into a covered passageway are dozens of stalls selling spices, sweets, dry legumes, chilies, piñatas and lots of other goodies.

Standouts include one store that sells a dozen different mole pastes, which must be diluted with water to create a creamy sauce served over chicken or other meats, and a large stall specializing in cheeses – ask for a taste before you buy and only get the pasteurized kind. In the center of the market is a small altar to the Virgen de Guadalupe.

Mercado Municipal Downtown, just north of the Catedral de Nuestra Señora de Guadalupe on Avenida Niños Héroes, this is another old-timey market, but owing to its proximity to the notorious Zona Norte, it's a rather seedy place. There are lots of *loncherías* (cafes) where you can have a snack, but the stifling air in this poorly ventilated space and the rather aggressive vendors may make you lose your appetite.

Mercado de Todos This swap meet on Blvd Agua Caliente, about 1 mile (1.6km) east of the Agua Caliente racetrack, is indeed a market for everything and for everyone. It's a huge, covered sprawl of bargains, where you'll find items like designer knock-off blue jeans, jogging suits and jackets, shoes, housewares, electronics, toys, leather goods and lots more. Expect to bargain, but prices are already low: In many if not all cases, so is quality. There's inexpensive parking in back; enter from Avenida F Gomez.

Shopping Malls
Entering Tijuana on foot, you'll automatically pass through Plaza Viva Tijuana (☎ 682-82-92), a large outdoor mall (see the San Ysidro Border Crossing map in the San Diego Getting Around chapter). Shops here sell the same curios and souvenirs offered elsewhere around town, but at higher prices. Bargain hard. There are also several pharmacies and a few mediocre restaurants, but large sections of the mall

stand empty as most people prefer just push on to more interesting shopping.

Tijuanenses do most of their shopping in modern malls; the most central is Plaza Río (Map 14; ☎ 684-04-02), on Paseo de los Héroes, a five-minute cab ride or 15- to 20-minute walk from the border. This pleasant, sprawling outdoor mall is anchored by the Comercial superstore and Dorian's. Other shops sell shoes, books, music, lingerie, computers, clothes and more. Prices here and in the following malls are fixed.

Smaller malls line Tijuana's major boulevards, including Paseo de los Héroes, Blvd Sánchez Taboada and Blvd Agua Caliente, but there are several new major ones in the eastern suburbs. In La Mesa, on Blvd Díaz Ordaz (the eastern continuation of Blvd Agua Caliente) are, side by side, Plaza Carrousel (Map 12; ☎ 626-12-10) and Plaza Las Brisas. Major stores in Plaza Carrousel are Smart & Final, Dorian's and Comercial. At Las Brisas, you'll find Waldo's $1 Mart, a Gigante supermarket and a huge Coppel electronics store.

North of here, on Carretera al Aeropuerto, the road to the airport, another pair of brand-new malls awaits: Plaza América (Map 12; ☎ 624-32-30) and Plaza Gigante Otay (Map 12; ☎ 623-15-90). Besides a bevy of nice restaurants, you'll find two state-of-the-art movie multiplexes, a huge Dorian's and a 24-hour pharmacy.

Department Stores
Sanborn's (Map 13; ☎ 688-14-62), on Avenida Revolución at Calle 8a (Hidalgo), has a smallish assortment but decent prices for shoes, electronic goods, crafts, handbags and other goods, plus an excellent international newsstand.

Dorian's has a bigger and more upscale selection. There are branches in the Zona Centro on Avenida Niños Héroes between Calle 2a (Juárez) and Calle 3a (Carrillo Puerto), in Plaza Río, in Plaza Carrousel and a huge one in Plaza Gigante Otay.

DAX is a warehouselike discount department store with a branch in Plaza Río and another next to Dorian's on Avenida Niños Héroes in downtown.

Excursions

This chapter begins by following the coastal highway México 1 (the Transpeninsular) south from Tijuana. Moving through fast-growing Playas de Rosarito to the bustling port town of Ensenada, it hits the famous blowhole of La Bufadora. From there it hooks back north to highway México 3 through Baja's wine country in the Valle de Guadalupe (before culminating in the pleasant border town of Tecate). This trip makes a perfect loop that can be easily traveled either under your own steam or by using public buses. (For more on route options, see the boxed text 'Traveling the Tijuana–Ensenada Corridor,' later.)

PLAYAS DE ROSARITO

Rosarito is a quickly expanding party town and a popular getaway for Southern Californians. From April to October it's often flooded with revelers on weekends and especially during US college spring break. Prices – and noise levels – skyrocket during those times, so avoid visiting unless you're a party animal yourself.

Until a dozen or so years ago, Rosarito was a modest fishing village with a single posh resort hotel, long sandy beaches and a few taco stands. Since the 1990s, its 'discovery' has fostered a busy commercial strip lined by hotels, crafts stores and fine restaurants. Its beaches, shopping, fishing, organized bicycle rides and horseback riding are the main attractions.

Rosarito's population nearly doubled in the '90s and, with a growth rate of more than 14%, it continues to be the fastest-growing community in Baja California. In recognition of the town's increased size and importance, the state government granted Rosarito *municipio* status in 1995. Both the municipio and the town are now known formally as Playas de Rosarito.

Orientation & Information

Rosarito's main artery, Blvd Juárez (which is a segment of México 1) is lined by hotels,

restaurants, shops and other businesses. On most weekends, it becomes a two-way traffic jam, as hordes of visitors stream in. On either side of this road is a maze of narrow streets, most of them still unpaved. A few of the cheaper hotels can be found in the area west of the boulevard.

Rosarito's 'downtown' is toward the southern end, around the Rosarito Beach Hotel. Most of the tourist-oriented places are here, while northern Rosarito has a more local flair.

Most business have street addresses, but the numbering system is maddeningly erratic. Adding to the confusion, outside of downtown most east-west streets crossing Blvd Juárez do not have signs. Locals often use landmarks such as the Rosarito Beach Hotel as points of reference. Whenever possible, this section uses cross streets to help locate a particular place, but you may still need to refer to the map a little more often than usual.

The local branch of Secture (☎/fax 6-612-02-00), the state-run tourist agency, occupies an office in the Plaza Villa Floresta, a minimall at Blvd Juárez 2000, at the far northern end of town. It has a few brochures and leaflets, along with recent issues of the *Baja Sun,* an English-language newspaper with tourist-oriented news and information. English-speaking staff can help with tourist hassles and try to answer questions. It's open 9 am to 7 pm Monday to Friday and 10 am to 4 pm Saturday and Sunday.

A bit more central is the Rosarito Beach Convention & Visitors Bureau (Cotuco; ☎ 6-612-03-96, 612-30-78, 800-962-2252 in the US), in the Oceana Plaza mall on Blvd Juárez at Encino. This office is usually open Monday to Friday 9 am to 6 pm and Saturday to 3 pm.

Museo Wa Cuatay

The name of Rosarito's small historical and anthropological museum, near the

Rosarito Beach Hotel, translates as 'place of the waters,' the native people's name for the area. The museum is lovingly maintained by Pedro Aries, who's also been a bartender at the hotel for the past four decades, and it offers a good introduction to the area from pre-Columbian times to the present. Subjects include the missions and the beginnings of tourism. Indigenous artifacts, good historical photographs and the occasional traveling show from mainland Mexico round off the exhibit. It's open 10 am to 4 pm Thursday to Sunday; admission is free.

Horseback Riding

Horses can be hired at several locations on the western side of the Transpeninsular in Rosarito and on the beach by the Rosarito Beach Hotel. The average rate is US$5 per hour. Bargain, if necessary.

Places to Stay

Because it's a resort town and so close to the border, Rosarito lacks consistent budget accommodations. Rates vary both seasonally and between 'weekdays' (Sunday to Thursday) and 'weekends' (Friday and Saturday). Given this fickle market, prices

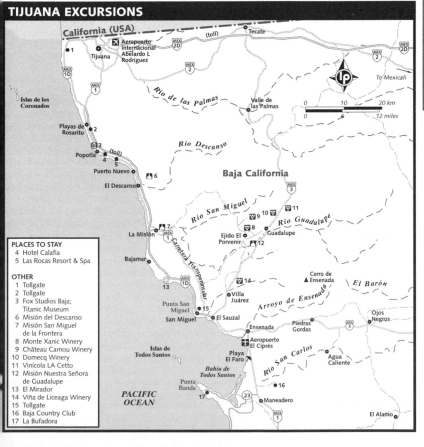

TIJUANA EXCURSIONS

PLACES TO STAY
4 Hotel Calafia
5 Las Rocas Resort & Spa

OTHER
1   Tollgate
2   Tollgate
3   Fox Studios Baja;
    Titanic Museum
6   Misión del Descanso
7   Misión San Miguel
    de la Frontera
8   Monte Xanic Winery
9   Château Camou Winery
10 Domecq Winery
11 Vinícola LA Cetto
12 Misión Nuestra Señora
    de Guadalupe
13 El Mirador
14 Viña de Liceaga Winery
15 Tollgate
16 Baja Country Club
17 La Bufadora

TIJUANA

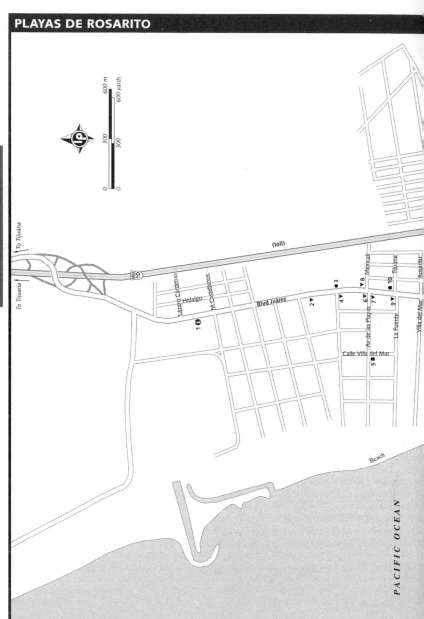

PLAYAS DE ROSARITO

TIJUANA

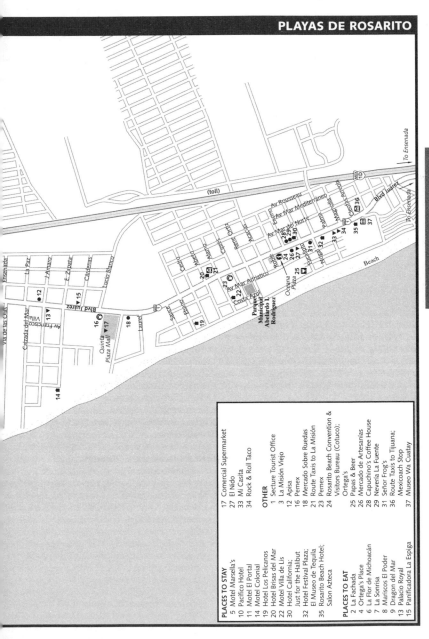

To Ensenada

(toll)

Av Rousseau
Av Enero
Av Mar Mediterráneo
Av Mar Adriático
Av Mar del Norte
Costa Azul
Parque Municipal
Abelardo L Rodríguez
Beach
Oceana Plaza

Blvd Juárez
To Ensenada

Quinta Plaza Mall

Villa Juárez
Blvd Juárez

Av Francisco
Av de las Olas
Calzada del Mar
Ensenada
La Paz
L Amaro
E Zapata
Cárdenas
Iturbi Blanco
Sánchez
Ébano
Cedro
Abeto
Alamo
René Ortiz
Laurel

PLACES TO STAY
5 Motel Marsella's
10 Pacífico Hotel
11 Motel El Portal
14 Motel Colonial
19 Hotel Los Pelícanos
20 Hotel Brisas del Mar
22 Motel Villa de Lis
30 Hotel California;
    Just for the Halibut
32 Hotel Festival Plaza;
    El Museo de Tequila
35 Rosarito Beach Hotel;
    Salón Azteca

PLACES TO EAT
2 La Fachada
4 Ortega's Place
6 La Flor de Michoacán
7 La Sonrisa
8 Mariscos El Poder
9 Dragon del Mar
13 Palacio Royal
15 Panificadora La Espiga

17 Comercial Supermarket
27 El Nido
33 Mi Casita
34 Rock & Roll Taco

OTHER
1 Secture Tourist Office
3 La Misión Viejo
12 Apisa
16 Pemex
18 Mercado Sobre Ruedas
21 Route Taxis to La Misión
23 Pemex
24 Rosarito Beach Convention &
    Visitors Bureau (Cotuco);
    Ortega's
25 Papas & Beer
26 Mercado de Artesanías
28 Capuchino's Coffee House
29 Nevería La Fuente
31 Señor Frog's
36 Route Taxis to Tijuana;
    Mexicoach Stop
37 Museo Wa Cuatay

listed in the following sections can give you only a rough guide of what to expect.

Budget The *Hotel California* (☎ 6-612-25-50, 800-399-2255 in the US, Blvd Juárez 32), right in downtown Rosarito, has comfortable rooms with cable TV for about US$40 to US$50. Quiet and clean, the sky blue *Motel Villa de Lis* (☎ 6-612-23-20, fax 613-16-51), on Alamo at Costa Azul, is a popular choice among budget travelers. Rooms have cable TV and cost US$32 midweek and US$42 on weekends, US$10 more for ocean views. Rates drop US$10 in winter.

Another good choice is the 24-room *Motel Marsella's* (☎ 6-612-04-68, Calle Villa del Mar 75), where clean, carpeted and spacious rooms with wood paneling, large beds and cable TV range from US$20 to US$40.

In the same general neighborhood, aging *Motel Colonial* (☎ 6-612-15-75), on Calle 1a at Mayo 71, has suites with separate living/dining areas, kitchenette, double bed and enough space for cots and sleeping bags. Prices start around US$25.

The best choice in northern Rosarito is the brightly painted *Motel El Portal* (☎ 6-612-00-50), on Blvd Juárez at Vía de las Olas, where singles/doubles cost US$31 to US$49; however, rates can plunge to as low as US$16 during lulls in visitor activity.

Mid-Range & Top End The newish *Pacífico Hotel* (☎ 6-612-25-16, fax 612-22-56, Blvd Juárez 286), between Calles Mexicali and Tijuana, has 47 comfortable rooms with cable TV, telephone, heat and air-con. Rates are a steal weekdays at US$45, but climb to US$95 to US$110 on weekends. Continental breakfast is included.

One of Rosarito's better values is the oceanside *Hotel Los Pelicanos* (☎ 6-612-04-45, Calle de Cedro 115). Basic singles or doubles cost US$38 to US$48, plus US$7.50 for each additional person. Rooms with ocean-view balconies cost US$60. There's also a good restaurant with a deck overlooking the beach.

Wedged in between the ocean and Blvd Juárez, the *Rosarito Beach Hotel* (☎ 6-612-11-11, fax 612-11-76, in the US ☎ 619-498-8230, 800-343-8582) opened during Prohibition in the late 1920s and quickly became a popular watering hole and gambling haven for Hollywood stars such as Orson Welles and Mickey Rooney. Facilities include two pools, a gym and two restaurants as well as a popular spa. The best rooms are suites in the new building closest to the beach. Summer rates range from US$89 to US$129 midweek and US$109 to US$179 on weekends single or double, including a welcome margarita and dinner.

The high-rise *Hotel Festival Plaza* (☎ 6-612-29-50, 800-453-8606 in the US), on Blvd Juárez just north of the Rosarito Beach Hotel, looks like a colorful children's playground – for adult 'children,' that is. This place is party central, and any illusions of a quiet night's sleep quickly disappear when you discover that all rooms face the outdoor plaza where live concerts take place! Some 10 clubs and restaurants, a tequila 'museum' and even a small Ferris wheel are part of the complex. Standard doubles cost about US$80 midweek and US$100 weekends in summer.

A bit removed from the action, *Hotel Brisas del Mar* (☎/fax 612-25-47, ☎ 888-871-36-05 in the US, Blvd Juárez 22), between Calles Alamo and Abeto, has 71 contemporary rooms with air-con, heat and cable TV. There's secure parking, a heated pool and volleyball courts. Rates range from US$45 to US$95 midweek and US$65 to US$95 weekends.

Places to Eat

To stock up on produce, cookies, drinks, cheese and the like, head to the giant *Comercial* supermarket in the Quinta Plaza shopping center. The best bakery is *Panificadora La Espiga*, with several branches around town, including one at Blvd Juárez and Calle Cárdenas. For delicious wholegrain pastries and breads, head to *La Sonrisa* (Blvd Juárez 285), next to the Dragon del Mar restaurant.

Central Rosarito Adjacent to the Hotel Festival Plaza, casual *Mi Casita* is the oldest *taquería* in town and, many say, the best. At

US 75¢ per taco and US$1.50 for a burrito, they'll definitely fill you up without breaking the bank. If you're in the mood for fish tacos, head across the street to *Just for the Halibut*, where you'll be given large chunks of deep-fried fish (or shrimp) to dress up with a wide range of condiments. Tacos are US$1 each.

Also nearby is *Rock & Roll Taco*, a full bar/restaurant that was allegedly a favorite hangout of Leonardo di Caprio and Kate Winslet during the filming of *Titanic*. It's built on the site of a former mortuary, which may explain the numerous skeletons in the splashy decor. This is more a place for drinking and partying than eating, but they do serve decent tacos and other *antojitos*.

For more substantial fare, one of the best downtown restaurants is *El Nido* (☎ 6-612-14-30, Blvd Juárez 67), which enjoys a good reputation for its prime cuts of meat as well as solidly prepared seafood dishes. *Salon Azteca* (☎ 6-612-01-44), inside the Rosarito Beach Hotel, is an all-gringo enclave with lavish weekend buffets (breakfast US$7.95, lunch US$10.95, dinner US$8.95).

Northern Rosarito Venerable *La Flor de Michoacán* (☎ 6-612-18-58, Blvd Juárez 291) specializes in authentic *carnitas,* served with rice, beans, guacamole, salsa and tortillas. Individual portions cost US$6, while pork tacos are US 80¢; it's closed Wednesday. Across the street is *Mariscos El Poder*, a simple stand that serves delicious fish tacos and other seafood fare for little money.

Upscale *La Fachada* (☎ 6-612-17-85, Blvd Juárez 317) gets rave reviews all around for its grilled steak and lobster. *Ortega's Place* (☎ 6-612-17-57, Blvd Juárez 200) also serves tasty lobster dinners; its weekly Sunday champagne brunch (US$8) is also a big attraction. Another *Ortega's* (☎ 6-612-27-91) is in the Plaza Oceana, Blvd Juárez at Roble.

Good Chinese restaurants are the *Palacio Royal* (☎ 6-612-14-12), found at the Centro Comercial Ejido Mazatlán, and the banquet-style *Dragon del Mar* (☎ 6-612-06-04, Blvd Juárez 283). Both have the usual wallet-friendly lunch specials.

Entertainment

College students, soldiers and young Mexican-Americans who've 'done' Avenida Revolución one too many times descend on Rosarito on weekends for a dose of serious partying. Many of the most raucous haunts are in or near the Hotel Festival Plaza complex, whose *El Museo de Tequila* (☎ 6-612-29-50) is one of several establishments around the country that claims to have the world's biggest tequila collection. There's often live mariachi music. Also here is *Rock & Roll Taco* (see the Places to Eat section), an imaginatively decorated bar that extends outdoors to a wooden deck and a small swimming pool. Next to the hotel, another party palace – *Señor Frog's* – offers much the same mix of music, drinking and dancing.

Behind the hotel, by the beach, is *Papas & Beer* (☎ 6-612-04-44), one of a chain of dedicated watering holes. A small cover is usually charged, and a hefty bouncer keeps rowdies, minors (under 18) and undesirables from entering this outdoor bar and its sandlot volleyball court.

A quieter crowd gathers at the Rosarito Beach Hotel for performances by mariachis, balladeers and gaudy cowboys doing rope tricks. Another subdued hangout is *Capuchino's Coffee House* (☎ 6-612-29-79, Blvd Juárez 890-3), between Calles Encino and Eucalipto, which makes good espresso drinks and pastries. Next door, *Nevería La Fuente* offers an excellent selection of fruit-flavored juices and ices.

Shopping

Rosarito has a reputation for being the best place in northern Baja for quality rustic furniture, which can be custom-made for a fraction of what it would cost in the US. Several businesses are on Blvd Juárez in Rosarito proper, but you'll find the biggest concentration – and lower prices – on the Transpeninsular a few miles south of town.

In downtown itself, the 150 stalls of the Mercado de Artesanías, at Blvd Juárez 306, offer a huge selection of curios, crafts and souvenirs. This is where you should haggle for *serapes* (blankets), wind chimes,

TIJUANA

hats, T-shirts, pottery and glass items. It's open 9 am to 6 pm daily.

For better quality and less generic items, you might want to browse the 18,000 sq feet of Apisa (☎ 6-612-01-25), at Blvd Juárez 2400 in northern Rosarito. It has a great assortment of colonial-style furniture, sculptures and crafts, though none of it is cheap. Prices are lower at La Misión Viejo (☎ 6-612-15-76, Blvd Juárez 139), the oldest of Rosarito's fine crafts stores, a bit farther north near Calle de Mexicali.

On Sunday, from early morning to late afternoon, the Mercado Sobre Ruedas, a produce/flea market, takes place near the Ejido Mazatlán mall in northern Rosarito.

Getting There & Around

From Friday to Sunday, Mexicoach operates its Rosarito Beach Express from the Terminal Turístico Tijuana, on Avenida Revolución between Calles 6a (Flores Magón) and 7a (Galeana). Buses to Rosarito depart at 11 am and 1, 3 and 5 pm and return at noon, 2, 4 and 8 pm. The fare is US$3 each way.

ABC buses between Tijuana and Ensenada stop at the tollgate at the southern end of Rosarito but do not enter the town itself. Southbound travelers may find it more convenient to take a route taxi (see below) to La Misión and flag down the bus there. Subur Baja comes through about every 30 minutes from 6 am to 8 pm and goes to Tijuana's Antigua Central Camionera for US$1.

Yellow route taxis leaving from a stand near the Rosarito Beach Hotel connect Rosarito with Tijuana (US$1). White taxis with yellow-green stripes run to points as far south as La Misión (see later in this chapter); they leave from the southern side of Hotel Brisas del Mar at Calle Alamo and Blvd Juárez. Because all cabs travel along Blvd Juárez, they are also a good way to get from one end of town to the other; you can simply flag one down.

ROSARITO TO ENSENADA
Popotla

Until 1996 Popotla, about 3 miles (5km) south of Rosarito, at Km 33 on the Transpeninsular, was nothing but a rustic fishing village. Then Fox Studios Baja moved in. Planned as a temporary facility built for the filming of *Titanic* (1997), the site has evolved into a permanent studio, its giant water tank having been used for scenes from several other movies, including *Tomorrow Never Dies* (1997) and *Deep Blue Sea* (1999). In 2000, parts of the movie *Pearl Harbor,* starring Ben Affleck, were filmed here.

No studio tours are available, but you can relive the epic during a visit of the **Titanic Museum,** open weekends from 10 am to 6 pm for US$6. You'll see a 25-minute video about the making of the movie before moving on to sets and props such as the First Class Smoking Lounge, the Palm Court Café, the First Class Dining Salon, the Boiler Room and the fireplace from Rose's (Kate Winslet) first-class cabin. The replica ship itself, alas, has been turned into scrap metal.

To Baja insiders Popotla was a favorite destination long before Hollywood arrived. The main attraction was – and still is – the super-fresh fish and seafood served here at prices much lower than in Rosarito, Ensenada or Puerto Nuevo. Most places are informal, family-run affairs that don't serve alcohol (bring your own), take only cash and are open for lunch only.

Places to Stay At Km 35.5 on the Transpeninsular, *Hotel Calafia (☎ 6-612-15-80, fax 612-02-96, ☎ 877-700-2093 in the US, @ calafia1@telnor.net)* is a curious open-air museum showcasing replicas of mission facades, and there's also a small exhibit about the making of *Titanic* inside the main building. The hotel itself has an attractive oceanfront setting. Summer rates are US$55/79 midweek/weekend for rooms with ocean or garden views and US$70/85 for oceanfront rooms with balcony. Prices include dinner for two. On weekends, the restaurant does a famous brunch for US$7.95; the best tables are right above the waves.

The nicest hotel along the Tijuana-Ensenada corridor is the Greek-Mediterranean-style *Las Rocas Resort & Spa (☎/fax 6-612-21-40, in the US ☎ 619-234-9810, 888-*

27-7622, *lasrocas@telnor.net)*, at Km 38.5. ts 34 luxury suites and 40 standard rooms ll have private, ocean-view balconies, atellite TV and telephones. Suites are appointed with stylish furniture and have microwaves, coffeemakers and fireplaces. Guests relax by the free-form 'infinity' pool or luxuriate at the first-rate hotel spa; he long menu of treatments ranges from your regular facial to the more exotic basalt-rock massage. Also popular are the private-tub baths in sun-flooded rooms vith views of the waves. Two restaurants, both with attentive service, serve delicious seafood and Mexican dishes.

Summer rates start at US$89 for the standard rooms, surging to US$169 for the deluxe suites. From October to April, midweek rates are US$65/119. Spa packages are available.

Puerto Nuevo

f tectonic uplift were not raising this section of the coastline from the sea, the village of Puerto Nuevo, at Km 44 on the Transpeninsular, might sink beneath the weight of its 35 or so seafood restaurants. They all specialize in lobster, usually cooked in one of two manners: *ranchera* (simmered in salsa) or *frito* (buttered and fried or grilled) and served with flour tortillas, beans, rice, butter, salsa, chips and limes. All have similar prices – about US$15 for a full lobster dinner and US$10 for a grilled fish dinner.

It was the Ortega family who opened the first lobster restaurant in Puerto Nuevo, and their restaurant, ***Ortega's Patio***, is one of the nicest places in town, especially if you get to sit on the outdoor terrace. They have several other branches here and two more in Playas de Rosarito. The ordinary-looking ***Miramar*** also serves good food.

For the best deals, go to the smaller places on the southern edge of the village; these get less foot traffic and often outdo each other with amazing specials. At the time of research, four half lobsters with all the fixings went for just US$12.

TIJUANA

Traveling the Tijuana-Ensenada Corridor

Free road or toll road? That's the question you'll have to ask yourself when driving south from Tijuana to Ensenada.

México 1D, the divided toll road, is the faster road, more easily accessed and offering spectacular coastal views over its entire length. From the border at San Ysidro simply follow the (slyly manipulative) 'Ensenada Scenic Road' signs along Calle Internacional. Paralleling the border fence, the road turns south in Playas de Tijuana just before plunging into the ocean. Here, it passes through the first of three tollgates.

Tolls for the entire 68-mile (110km) stretch, which takes about 1½ hours to drive, come to US 60¢ for an ordinary passenger vehicle or motorcycle and twice that for any larger vehicle. Onethird of the toll is charged at each of three gates – Playas de Tijuana, Playas de Rosarito and San Miguel – though there are several other exits along the route.

Two-lane, toll-free México 1 (the Transpeninsular) passes through equally spectacular scenery, but heavier traffic makes it slower. From the Tijuana border crossing, follow the signs to central Tijuana and continue straight (west) along Calle 3a (Carrillo Puerto), turning left (south) at Avenida Revolución. Follow Avenida Revolución to the end, where it veers left (east) and becomes Blvd Agua Caliente. Turn right just before the twin towers of the Grand Hotel Tijuana and head south.

México 1 hits the coast just north of Playas de Rosarito. From here, the free road and the toll road run parallel for several miles. At La Misión, the Transpeninsular turns inland and zigzags through the countryside for 21 miles (34km) before returning to the coast and crossing the toll road again near San Miguel. The toll road continues straight to Ensenada – this is the most spectacular stretch, with mostly unimpeded coastal views.

Misión del Descanso

The Dominican Misión del Descanso was one of the last missions founded in California. When Misión San Miguel, about 5 miles (8km) south, lost its irrigable lands to floods, Fray Tomás de Ahumada moved part of its operations north to this site around 1817. The two missions operated simultaneously for some time, but Descanso was also known as San Miguel Nuevo. As of the historian Peveril Meigs' visit in 1927, adobe ruins still existed; an apparent guardhouse overlooked the mission from a 150-foot (45m) slope on the southern side of the valley.

A large marker commemorates the original mission, but no ruins survive. Instead, another church built in the early 20th century occupies the site. An abandoned adobe house on a knoll to the east was once part of the 1827 Machado grant that assumed control of the mission lands.

The original boundary between the Dominican and Franciscan mission provinces, and thus between Baja and Alta California prior to the Treaty of Guadalupe Hidalgo, was just north of here but was later moved to Tijuana.

To get to the site, turn east onto a sandy road about 1½ miles (2.4km) south of Cantamar on the Transpeninsular (look for the Vivero La Central nursery's sign) that passes beneath the toll road and reaches the church after about half a mile (1km).

La Misión

The village of La Misión, on the Transpeninsular's inland turn, is most notable as the site of the Dominican **Misión San Miguel de la Frontera**, also known as San Miguel Encino and San Miguel Arcángel. Founded in 1787 at a site unknown today, the mission moved up the valley of the Río San Miguel when the spring it depended on dried up. This valley bisects a broad fault surface known locally as a mesa, which is surrounded by higher lava flows.

Fishing from balsa rafts, local indigenous peoples relied mostly on seafood for their subsistence, but the mission also grew wheat, maize, barley and beans and grazed more than 1600 head of cattle and 2100 sheep at its peak. The highest Indian population, about 400, was recorded in 1824; it was a fairly large number at this late date.

The few remaining ruins are behind the Escuela Primaria La Misión (the elementary school) at Km 65.5, about one mile (1.6km) south of the bridge over the Río San Miguel. They include the foundations and some adobe walls of the church and adjacent buildings.

El Mirador

El Mirador, a roadside viewpoint at Km 84 on México 1D, is spectacularly situated above the ocean. There are a few picnic tables and a children's playground, but food and beverage service had been discontinued at the time of research.

ENSENADA
• pop 350,000

Ensenada, about 75 miles (120km) south of Tijuana on Bahía de Todos Santos, is the most sophisticated and well rounded of the northern coastal towns. It's a fairly wealthy city with great civic pride. Several museums are dedicated to its history, and generously designed public areas – rather than hotels – line the waterfront. These include Plaza Cívica, known colloquially as Plaza de Las Tres Cabezas (Three Heads Plaza) for its massive busts of historical icons Benito Juárez, Miguel Hidalgo and Venustiano Carranza. The circular Plaza Ventana al Mar is anchored by a gigantic Mexican flag. Lining the harbor is a tranquil *malecón* (waterfront promenade), which culminates at the historic Riviera del Pacífico, perhaps the most beautiful building in northern Baja. Ensenada is also the capital of Baja's wine production and the gateway to the vineyards and wineries in nearby Valle de Guadalupe (see later in this chapter).

Orientation & Information

Most of Ensenada's hotels and restaurants line Avenida López Mateos (also known as Calle 1a), which is one block inland from the waterfront Blvd Costero, also known as Blvd Lázaro Cárdenas. Five blocks inland, Avenida Benito Juárez has shops and businesses

ENSENADA

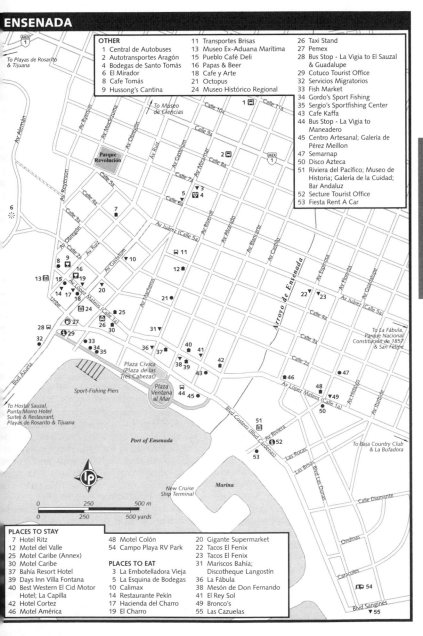

OTHER
1 Central de Autobuses
2 Autotransportes Aragón
4 Bodegas de Santo Tomás
6 El Mirador
8 Cafe Tomás
9 Hussong's Cantina
11 Transportes Brisas
13 Museo Ex-Aduana Marítima
15 Pueblo Café Deli
16 Papas & Beer
18 Cafe y Arte
21 Octopus
24 Museo Histórico Regional
26 Taxi Stand
27 Pemex
28 Bus Stop - La Vigia to El Sauzal & Guadalupe
29 Cotuco Tourist Office
32 Servicios Migratorios
33 Fish Market
34 Gordo's Sport Fishing
35 Sergio's Sportfishing Center
43 Cafe Kaffa
44 Bus Stop - La Vigia to Maneadero
45 Centro Artesanal; Galería de Pérez Meillon
47 Semarnap
50 Disco Azteca
51 Riviera del Pacífico; Museo de Historia; Galería de la Cuidad; Bar Andaluz
52 Secture Tourist Office
53 Fiesta Rent A Car

TIJUANA

PLACES TO STAY
7 Hotel Ritz
12 Motel del Valle
25 Motel Caribe (Annex)
30 Motel Caribe
37 Bahía Resort Hotel
39 Days Inn Villa Fontana
40 Best Western El Cid Motor Hotel; La Capilla
42 Hotel Cortez
46 Motel América
48 Motel Colón
54 Campo Playa RV Park

PLACES TO EAT
3 La Embotelladora Vieja
5 La Esquina de Bodegas
10 Calimax
14 Restaurante Pekín
17 Hacienda del Charro
19 El Charro
20 Gigante Supermarket
22 Tacos El Fenix
23 Tacos El Fenix
31 Mariscos Bahía; Discotheque Langostín
36 La Fábula
38 Mesón de Don Fernando
41 El Rey Sol
49 Bronco's
55 Las Cazuelas

catering more to locals. On the western edge of downtown is Ensenada's 'party district,' centered on Avenida Ruiz; legendary Hussong's Cantina (see Bars & Cantinas, later in this section) is here as well. Farther west, the hills of Colinas de Chapultepec are an exclusive residential zone.

If you're planning on traveling south of Ensenada and don't yet have a validated tourist card, you can pick one up the Servicios Migratorios (Immigration Office; ☎ 6-674-01-64), Blvd Azueta 101. It's open 9 am to 5 pm daily.

Ensenada's Cotuco office (☎ 6-178-24-11, fax 178-36-75), at Blvd Costero 540 across from the Pemex station, has a friendly, obliging and well-informed staff and lots of free maps and brochures. Hours are 9 am to 7 pm weekdays, 10 am to 6 pm Saturday and 11 am to 3 pm Sunday.

Secure (☎ 6-172-30-22, 172-30-81), at Blvd Costero 1477, is open 8 am to 5 pm weekdays, 10 am to 3 pm weekends. The Tourist Assistance Office, which can help with tourist hassles and legal problems, is here as well.

El Mirador

Atop the Colinas de Chapultepec, El Mirador offers panoramic views of the city and Bahía de Todos Santos. Climb or drive up Avenida Alemán from the western end of Calle 2a in central Ensenada to the highest point in town.

Bodegas de Santo Tomás

Founded in 1888 near the vineyards of the Valle de Santo Tomás south of Ensenada, Santo Tomás is one of Baja's premier vintners. Varietals include pinot noir, chardonnay and cabernet; up to 120,000 cases are shipped annually throughout Mexico and to Western Europe, but not to the US.

At Avenida Miramar 666, Santo Tomás (☎ 6-178-33-33, 178-25-09) offers daily 30-minute tours at 10 and 11 am, noon, 1 and 3 pm for US$2, including tasting of four wines. For US$5 you can sample up to 15 wines and get to keep the souvenir glass.

Riviera del Pacífico

An extravagant waterfront complex with Spanish-Moorish architectural touches, the Riviera del Pacífico opened in 1930 as the Playa Ensenada Hotel & Casino. The second casino in Northern Baja (after the Agua Caliente in Tijuana), this lavish facility was once the haunt of Hollywood figures such as ex-Olympic swimmer Johnny Weissmuller ('Tarzan'), Myrna Loy, Lana Turner and Ali Khan. Briefly managed by US boxer Jack Dempsey, the facility closed in 1938 after President Lázaro Cárdenas outlawed casino gambling. The building was rescued from the wrecking ball in the early 1990s and reborn as a center for cultural events, weddings, conventions and meetings.

Open to the public, the Riviera – framed by splendid gardens – is well worth exploring. The lobby (entered from the Jardín Bugambillias courtyard on the parking lot side behind the building) contains an impressive **relief map** of the mission sites throughout Baja and Alta California. Most rooms feature carved and painted ceilings, elaborate tile work, giant wrought-iron chandeliers and creaky plank floors. The Dining Room and the circular Casino Room are especially impressive, as is the elegant Bar Andaluz (see Entertainment later in this section) with its arched wooden bar.

The complex's **Museo de Historia** traces northern Baja history from settlement by the indigenous natives to the mission period. A new wing features changing themed exhibits and an art gallery. The museum is open 9 am to 2 pm and 3 to 5 pm daily (Monday from 10 am); entry costs US$1. On the building's basement level is the **Galería de la Cuidad**, with monthly exhibits featuring regional artists. It's open 9 am to 6 pm weekdays only and is free.

Museo Histórico Regional

This modest exhibit about the 'People and Cultures of Meso-America' is housed in 1886 military barracks that served as the city's jail until as recently as 1986. Perhaps more intriguing than the exhibit is the cell block where several of the tiny, windowless concrete cubicles sport some rather accomplished murals by the former inmates. Staying in one of these 'private' cells was actually a privilege that had to be paid for; the

ternative was the crammed and explosive
eneral holding cell. Apparently, this prac-
ce is still common in many Mexican
risons. The museum (☎ 6-178-25-31), on
venida Gastelum near López Mateos, is
pen from 10 am to 5 pm Tuesday to
unday; a donation is requested.

Museo Ex-Aduana Marítima
uilt in 1887 by the US-owned International
Company of Mexico, the former Marine
Customs House, Avenida Ryerson 99 at
Uribe, is Ensenada's oldest public building.
. houses rotating exhibitions with a cultural
r historical angle. It's open 10 am to 5 pm
uesday to Sunday; a donation is requested.

Museo de Ciencias
Ensenada's science museum, Avenida
Obregón 1463 between Calles 14a and 15a,
orth of downtown, contains exhibits on
oth the natural and physical sciences,
tressing marine ecology along with endan-
ered species and habitats. It's open 9 am to
pm Tuesday to Friday and noon to 5 pm
n Saturday; a donation is requested.

Fish Market
ight by the sportfishing piers is the colorful
ish Market, where you can admire – and
urchase – the day's catch daily between
:30 am and 7 pm. The taquerías in the
arket area, though, do not have a very
ood reputation.

Fishing
Among the popular species found in north-
rn Baja are albacore, barracuda, bonito,
alibut, white sea bass and yellowtail, de-
ending on the season. Most people join an
rganized fishing trip for about US$40 per
erson. The two main operators are
Gordo's Sport Fishing (☎ 6-178-35-15, fax
78-04-81) and Sergio's Sportfishing Center
☎/fax 6-178-21-85, @ sergios@telnor.net),
oth with offices right next to the sport-
shing piers near the Fish Market. Orga-
ized trips leave year-round at 7 am and
eturn at 2:30 pm.

Everyone on board (whether fishing or
ot) must have a Mexican Fishing License.

These are available from Semarnap (☎ 6-
176-38-37), with an office on Calle 2a at
Avenida Guadalupe.

Whale-Watching
Between December and March, California
gray whales pass through Bahía de Todos
Santos on their way to calving sites in
southern Baja.

Both Gordo's and Sergio's (see Fishing,
above) operate four-hour whale-watching
trips for about US$20. The Museo de Cien-
cias also organizes tours that are accompanied by a – usually – bilingual guide and also
cost about US$20.

Golf
Two golf courses are within easy reach from
Ensenada. About 10 miles (16km) to the
south is the 18-hole Baja Country Club (☎ 6-
177-55-23), at the end of a canyon; it's open
7 am to 7 pm daily. Greens fees are US$35/45
weekdays/weekends, including the golf cart;
equipment may be rented for US$12.

The other golf course, on the ocean and
generally considered nicer, is at Bajamar,
about 22 miles (35km) north of town at Km
77.5. There's an 18-hole course and a newer
nine-holer. Both are open to the public;
greens fees are US$65 for 18 holes midweek
and US$80 weekends. After 4 pm, rates
drop to US$33/40. Club rentals are US$30.
An expensive hotel flanks the course, and
packages are available.

Places to Stay
Although Ensenada has many hotels,
demand can exceed supply at times. On
weekends and in summer, reservations are
advisable. Unless there's a special event,
weekday accommodations are not a
problem, but as in Playas de Rosarito, rates
vary both seasonally and between weekdays
and weekends, making it difficult to catego-
rize hotels by price.

Budget At the southern end of downtown,
at Blvd Las Dunas and Sanginés, *Campo
Playa RV Park* (☎ 6-176-29-18) has 90
small, grassy campsites with shade trees for
pitching a tent or parking a camper or

motor home. Fees are US$18 for rustic camping and US$20 with hookups, both including access to hot showers.

One of the few hostels in northern Baja, **Hostal Sauzal** *(☎ 6-174-63-81, 344 Avenida López Mateos 628)* is a friendly, alcohol-free place in the suburb of El Sauzal, about 6 miles (10km) north of Ensenada. Bunks in four-person ocean-view dorms cost US$10, including breakfast. To get there, take the local 'El Vigia' bus from the corner of Costero and Gastelum (near the Cotuco tourist office); the fare is US 50¢.

Central Ensenada's best bargain is **Motel Caribe** *(☎ 6-178-34-81, Avenida López Mateos 628)*, whose clean rooms cost US$25, US$30 with TV. Larger ones are US$5 to US$15 more. In the **annex** across the street, considerably less comfortable rooms cost just US$15.

Another good choice is **Motel América** *(☎ 6-176-13-33, Avenida López Mateos 1309)*, which has clean, simple singles/doubles with kitchenette for US$22/33. **Motel Colón** *(☎ 6-176-19-10, fax 176-47-82)*, at López Mateos and Guadalupe, is similar and charges the same.

A step up is the **Hotel Ritz** *(☎ 6-174-05-01, fax 178-32-62, Calle 4a 381)*, a remodeled downtown hostelry that has managed to retain some character. Rates are US$25/35 for carpeted rooms with cable TV and telephone.

Those who can afford a little more may like the modern, well-kept **Motel del Valle** *(☎ 6-178-22-24, Avenida Riveroll 367)*. Its 21 carpeted rooms with cable TV cost US$38 to US$47, but rates may rise after the completion of a new annex.

Mid-Range Many places in this category flank Avenida López Mateos, the main tourist drag. Ask for a room away from the street if you're not part of the party crowd.

Those looking for character and comfort should encamp at the venerable **Hotel Cortez** *(☎ 6-178-23-07, fax 178-39-04, ☎ 800-303-2684 in the US, Avenida López Mateos 1089)*. Rooms spread out over three structures and come with air-con, heat and color TV. Free coffee, newspaper, bottled water and room service are available as

well. Rates range from US$55 for standard rooms to US$70 for small suites. This is popular place; it's often booked solid o summer weekends, so make reservations.

Another favorite is **Bahía Resort Hote** *(☎ 6-178-21-03, fax 178-14-55, ☎ 888-308 9048 in the US, @ htlbahia@telnor.net), a* Alvarado. Its 64 clean, carpeted single and doubles with balcony, heater an small refrigerator range in price from US$35.50 to US$65.

Renovated and upgraded, **Days In Villa Fontana** *(☎ 6-178-34-34, 800-422-520 in the US, Avenida López Mateos 1050)* ha a bar, coffee shop, swimming pool, Jacuzz and parking. Comfortable singles an doubles with full carpeting, air-con, cabl TV and balcony cost US$50 to US$60.

The **Best Western El Cid Motor Hote** *(☎ 6-178-24-01, fax 178-36-71, ☎ 800-352-430 in the US, @ info@hotelelcid.com, Avenid López Mateos 993)* has rooms from US$50 t US$70 during the week and US$75 t US$100 on weekends. Facilities include swimming pool, a good restaurant and secur parking.

Top End The **Punta Morro Hotel Suite** *(☎ 6-178-35-07, fax 174-44-90, ☎ 800-520 6676 in the US)* is a stylish, quiet and relaxin oceanside resort at Km 106, about 1½ mile (2.4km) north of Ensenada. Beautifully ap pointed suites have equipped kitchens an terraces with views of the waves. The restau rant is among the best in the area (see th Places to Eat section). Rates are US$80 130/175 for suites with one/two/three bed rooms, dropping by about 20% from Sunda to Thursday.

Places to Eat

As a popular tourist spot, Ensenada ha eateries ranging from street taquerías an basic restaurants offering antojitos to place serving seafood, Chinese and sophisticate French cuisine.

Large supermarkets in the downtown are include a branch of **Gigante**, on Gastelur between Avenida López Mateos and Call 2a, and a **Calimax**, one block north on th same street.

eafood For the city's best fish tacos, head ▸ *Tacos El Fénix*, two stands at the corner ◻ Avs Juárez and Espinosa. A local institu-on, it's clean, fresh and friendly. Each taco ɔsts US 60¢; shrimp tacos are US 90¢.

Mariscos Bahía (Avenida Riveroll 109), tfers generous portions, reasonable prices nd friendly service. There's a nice sidewalk ɛrrace from which to observe the action.

For a special treat, book a table at the iffside *Punta Morro Restaurant (☎ 6-178-5-07),* at Km 106 on the Transpeninsular, ɔout 1 mile (1.6km) north of Ensenada. ɔu'll be seated above crashing waves that ill compete for your attention with the im-ɛccably prepared and tasty seafood and ɪeat dishes (about US$20). This classy es-ɪblishment is also part of a resort complex ɛee the Places to Stay section earlier in this ɪapter).

Mexican Though it serves standard antoji-ɔs, *Las Cazuelas (☎ 6-176-10-44, Blvd anginés 6)* has a chef whose repertoire is ɪore creative than most. Choices may ɪclude stuffed squid, quail in orange sauce nd abalone with lobster sauce, all at fairly ɛasonable prices. It's also famous for its reakfast omelets.

At *Bronco's (☎ 6-176-49-00, Avenida ópez Mateos 1525),* vaquero culture is ive in the decor as well as in the hearty nd humongous fare coming from the ɛamy kitchen. Its mesquite-grilled steaks ɛe top quality, and it's open for breakfast, ɪnch and dinner.

Tourist-oriented *Mesón de Don Fer-ando (☎ 6-174-01-55, Avenida López lateos 627)* has adequate, if slightly pricey, ɪre. The best deal is the weekday breakfast ɪffet for US$5. Otherwise, a good reason ɔ come is for the excellent margaritas, best ɪjoyed on the sidewalk terrace.

For marinated Mexican-style chicken, ɪilled or roasted over an open flame, try *ʼacienda del Charro (☎ 6-178-40-45, venida López Mateos 454).* Freshly made ɔrtillas, salsa and other condiments accom-ɪny all orders, many of which cost around ɪS$5. Related *El Charro* across the street is ɪore casual but has the same food.

International The Santo Tomás winery complex, on Avenida Miramar between Calles 6a and 7a, features two outstanding dining establishments. *La Esquina de Bodegas (☎ 6-178-75-57)* is worth a look for its decor alone. Metamorphosed from a former brandy distillery, it integrates the ancient drums, vats and pipes into a hip in-dustrial environment. En route to the dining area, you'll pass a wine boutique and an art gallery. The menu is Mediterranean with Mexican inflections and runs from US$7.50 for pasta to about US$40 for a seven-course gourmet meal.

The more formal *La Embotelladora Vieja (☎ 6-174-08-07),* where the culinary focus is Spanish-Mexican, is an ambiance-laden wine cellar decorated with wooden casks and other wine-making implements. The weekday set lunch (three courses and a glass of wine) is an excellent value at US$10. Dinners run about US$20 to US$30. It's closed Tuesday.

One of Baja's finest dining experiences, venerable *El Rey Sol (☎ 6-178-23-51, Avenida López Mateos 1000)* is an elegant but relaxed French-Mexican restaurant. Full dinners start at US$35, but if you pick carefully, you can get away with less. Leave room for the killer pastries.

Families flock to *Restaurante Pekín (☎ 6-178-11-58, Avenida Ruiz 98),* an established Chinese favorite where you can fill up for as little as US$3.

Entertainment

Bars & Cantinas Potent, tasty and inex-pensive beer, margaritas and other liquors are prime attractions for gringos, especially those under the US California drinking age of 21. On weekends most bars and cantinas along Avenida Ruiz, which might more ac-curately be called Avenida Ruido (Noise Avenue), are packed from midday to the early morning hours.

The spit-and-sawdust *Hussong's Cantina (☎ 6-178-32-10, Avenida Ruiz 113)* is proba-bly the best-known watering hole in the Californias – though its namesake beer now comes from Mazatlán. After arriving from Germany in the late 19th century, the

TIJUANA

Hussong family used their knowledge of traditional German brewing to establish one of Ensenada's first cantinas in 1892. Initially a stagecoach stop frequented by miners and ranchers, it later hosted Hollywood glam queen Marilyn Monroe, rough rider Steve McQueen and a bunch of other celebs. These days it's the 'mecca of margaritas and mariachis' for a motley crowd of college students, tattooed bikers, retirees and honeymooning cruise-ship couples. It's open from 10 am to 1 am, but tables – and even spots at the bar – are often at a premium after midafternoon.

Nearby **Papas & Beer** (☎ 6-174-01-45, *Avenida Ruiz 102*) caters mostly to rowdy college students, and a small army of bouncers keeps things under control. Roaring music drowns out conversations, but the

margaritas are sweet and fruity; hours a 10 am to 3 am.

For a complete change in ambiance, vis the cultured **Bar Andaluz** (☎ 6-177-17-3 inside the Riviera del Pacífico, where havir a drink is an exercise in nostalgia. You ca almost visualize Lana Turner sipping martini at the polished walnut bar.

Nightclubs Above the Mariscos Bah restaurant, **Discotheque Langostín** (☎ 174-03-18, *Avenida Riveroll 109*) is whe low-key locals take to the dance floor t disco, banda and rock, depending on th night. Up the street, the trendy **Octopi** caters to a younger (18 to 25) crowd. Bot places have live music on weekends.

Another popular haunt for the mid-20 and-up crowd is **Disco Azteca** (☎ 6-176-1 01 ext 257, *Avenida López Mateos 1534* inside the Hotel San Nicolás. It also puts c Latin and tropical tunes nightly, with liv bands on weekends. Smallish **La Capil** (☎ 6-178-24-01, *Avenida López Mateos 993* inside El Cid Motor Hotel, is also popula

Coffeehouses For a cuppa with characte head to **Cafe Kaffa**, on López Mateo between Castillo and Blancarte, or **Ca Tomás**, in the Plaza Hussong mall farthe west. Nearby, **Pueblo Café Deli** (☎ 6-17 80-55, *Avenida Ruiz 96*) serves pasta, sala and sandwiches (under US$10) in additic to delicious coffee drinks. At **Cafe y A** (*Avenida López Mateos 496*) most of th decoration is also for sale.

Shopping

Many items sold in Tijuana are also avai able here, sometimes at slightly lowe prices, but the overall selection is smaller.

Stores along Avenida López Mateos a tourist-oriented but fairly classy. Most se crafts from throughout Mexico, includir woven blankets, leather goods, wood car ings, wrought-iron candlesticks, margari glasses etc. Los Castillo, with sever branches along López Mateos, is a rep utable store selling silver jewelry.

Galería de Pérez Meillon (☎ 6-174-03-94 in the Centro Artesanal, Blvd Costero 109

In Search of the Best Margarita

Hordes of gringos descend on Ensenada in search of the perfect margarita, and many become derailed as a result – the victims of their successful 'research.' Solely as a service to you, dear readers, we undertook this most grueling sort of legwork, put our bodies – and brains – on the line, and narrowed down the choices. Here's our top three 'Margie' list, as far as we can recall…

Margaritas at **Hussong's Cantina** look small and innocent but pack a mean and sneaky punch. They're also good value at US$2.50. At **Mesón de Don Fernando** you'll need both hands to hoist the 'bird-bath' glasses – ask for 'on the rocks' and expect to fork over about US$5. Another convincing contender is **Bar Bahía**, inside the Bahía Hotel, where heady concoctions keep the karaoke crowd howling like demented coyotes in heat. So pick your poison and, if memory serves you, let us know about your favorite 'cactus cocktail.'

Please note: Lonely Planet accepts no responsibility for the behavior of those who wake up with racy tattoos or lost articles of intimate apparel.

ells first-rate indigenous pottery and folk art from Baja California's local peoples, as well as the famous Mata Ortiz pottery from mainland Mexico.

Getting There & Away

Bus Ensenada's Central de Autobuses is at Avenida Riveroll 1075, at the corner of Calle 1a, 10 blocks north of Avenida López Mateos. ABC buses heading north to Tijuana and Playas de Rosarito come through every half-hour; the trip to either takes about 1½ hours and costs US$8. Buses to Tecate pass through the Valle de Guadalupe, with departures at least three times daily. Note that Tijuana-bound buses drop Rosarito passengers at the tollgate rather than in Rosarito proper.

Between 6 am and 7 pm, Autotransportes Aragón, Avenida Riveroll 861 at Calle 8a, just south of the main bus terminal, goes hourly to Tijuana (US$8) and every other hour to San Quintín (US$10).

Getting Around

Local bus service is provided by La Vigia's blue-and-white minibuses and by Transportes Brisas (☎ 6-178-38-88), whose buses are yellow. Both travel within Ensenada and as far as outlying farming communities such as El Sauzal or Guadalupe to the north and Maneadero to the south. There are several stops along Blvd Costero, Avenida Reforma and Blvd Azueta. The destination usually appears on the windshield. Transportes Brisas also has a terminal at Calle 4a 771. The fare is about US 50¢.

Taxis are available 24 hours a day at several corner stands along Avenida López Mateos – one major stand is at the corner of Avenida Miramar.

AROUND ENSENADA
La Bufadora

La Bufadora is a tidal blowhole that spews water and foam through a V-shaped notch in the headlands of the Punta Banda peninsula. Arrive on a day when the sea is rolling heavily and you'll see a spectacle. Other times, the blowhole just sits and puffs. Nevertheless, it remains the area's most popular weekend destination for tourists and locals alike.

La Bufadora has undergone recent improvements: The endless souvenir stands are tidier than before, there's regular trash collection and the public toilets (US 50¢) at the otherwise empty exhibition center (now the site of a small cactus garden) are adequately clean.

BCN-23, the paved road to La Bufadora and Punta Banda, leaves the Transpeninsular at Maneadero and passes several campgrounds and roadside stands that sell chili peppers and olives. Beyond the Baja Beach Resort are a few isolated campsites and, past a gaggle of taco stands and dozens of souvenir stalls at the end of the road, La Bufadora itself roars – or sighs tiredly.

Probably the best reason to visit the area, Dale's La Bufadora Dive Center (☎ 6-174-29-92) offers underwater excursions to view sea anemones, sea urchins, sponge colonies, nudibranchs and dozens of fish species. The Canadian operator has three boats and charges US$20 to US$35 per person, depending on the number of people in the boat. Full sets of dive/snorkeling gear cost US$35/20. Tanks are US$7 each. Dale also rents single/tandem kayaks at US$20/30 for a half-day and US$30/40 for a full day. Oceanside camping is possible too.

Places to Eat Many stalls at La Bufadora serve fish tacos, shrimp cocktails and *churros* (deep-fried dough sticks dipped in sugar and cinnamon). There are also seafood restaurants with lower prices and better ocean views than those in Ensenada. *Los Panchos* has served tourists and locals for three decades; the octopus in ranchero sauce is a popular dish. It's open 9 am to sunset Friday to Wednesday.

Near the entrance to Rancho La Bufadora is *Los Gordos*, where photographs, memorabilia and graffiti exude an Old Baja ambiance. The bar is a favorite watering hole for US expatriates.

Celia's has a Sunday breakfast buffet for just US$3.50, while *El Dorado*, with its palapa-covered patio, is the place for a romantic seafood dinner.

Getting There & Away Cab rides to La Bufadora from downtown Ensenada cost about US$8. Transportes Brisas, at Calle 4a 771 in Ensenada, offers regular bus service as far as Maneadero; from the turnoff to La Bufadora you can probably hitch a ride. Several Ensenada travel agencies offer package tours by van or bus on weekends.

Maneadero

The farm settlement of Maneadero, on the Transpeninsular about 10 miles (16km) south of Ensenada and just beyond the turnoff to Punta Banda, contains little of note except a military guns-and-drugs checkpoint south of town that also checks for tourist cards; if yours are not in order, you'll have to return to Ensenada. Some travelers without proper ID have used *la mordida* (a bribe) to get past the police in the past, but the military is a different matter.

WINE COUNTRY

Northeast of Ensenada, along México 3, lies the Valle de Guadalupe, Mexico's largest wine-growing region. Some 95% of all wines produced in the country are grown in this valley, where arid, scrubby hills alternate with the lush green of the vineyards. Its location inland from the ocean and sheltered by the coastal mountains creates a favorable climate of cool nights and warm days that's conducive to growing top-quality grapes.

The Dominicans began cultivating grapes for sacramental wine here in the late 18th century. Abandoned after secularization in 1832, the vineyards were bought in 1888 by two Spaniards who founded Bodegas de Santo Tomás, Mexico's oldest winery (see Ensenada, earlier in this chapter).

In the valley itself, commercial wine production started up again in earnest in the 1980s. About half a dozen wine estates operate along here. Collectively, they produce some 80 generic and varietal wines. The most notable reds are cabernet sauvignon, merlot and pinot noir, while best-known whites include chardonnay, sauvignon blanc and chenin blanc. Quality varies from drinkable generics to vintages with complexity and finesse. Rarely exported to the US, Mexican wines are served in Baja's better restaurant and may also be tasted – and bought – at the wineries themselves.

The two largest – Domecq Winery and Vinícola LA Cetto – don't require appointments for their tours and tastings and are easily accessible from the highway. **Domecq** (☎ 6-155-22-49, fax 155-22-59), a subsidiary of the big Spanish brandy and wine company, offers tours of its facility at Km 73, followed by a tasting, from 10 am to 4 pm weekdays and to 1:30 pm Saturday (US$1). Nearby, at Km 73.5, **Vinícola LA Cetto** (☎ 6-155-22-64, fax 155-22-69) is open for free tours and tastings 9 am to 5 pm daily. LA Cetto also has an outfit in downtown Tijuana; see the Tijuana Things to See & Do chapter.

Other wineries may be visited by appointment only. Coming from Ensenada, the first one is **Viña de Liceaga** (☎ 6-684-11-84, fax 684-02-82), at Km 93 in the village of San Antonio de las Minas. Founded in 1982, it's still small (1200 cases a year) but may be toured for free, usually on Saturdays at 1 pm. The signature wine is merlot.

If you've got the time and your own set of wheels, don't miss the top-notch **Monte Xanic** winery (☎ 6-174-70-55, fax 174-68-48). Coming from Ensenada, drive about 25 minutes until you cross a bridge and reach the turnoff to the village of Francisco Zarco. Turn left and drive for about 2 miles (3.2km). The winery is open for tours and wine tastings 9 am to 4 pm weekdays (US$5). One of their specialties is a late-harvest chenin blanc, a complex dessert wine.

Nearby, **Château Camou** (☎ 6-177-22-21, fax 176-06-76), founded only in 1995, employs wine makers trained in Bordeaux, France and has already produced some award-winning wines. Tours are offered 10 am to 2 pm weekdays and to noon Saturday for US$2.

In August the Fiesta de La Vendimia (Wine Harvest Festival) takes place at several of the valley's wineries.

Guadalupe

The village of Guadalupe is at Km 78, about 20 miles (32km) northeast of Ensenada, in the heart of Baja's wine country. Settled by Molokans, members of a Russian sect, in the early 20th century, it also contains ruins of the Dominican **Misión Nuestra Señora de Guadalupe**, the last mission built in Baja California. Founded in 1834, it was destroyed by Indians only six years later. Set in a fertile zone perfect for grain farming and grazing, it was a powerful and important mission during its brief existence. Pictographs by indigenous people adorn a huge granite boulder known as Ojá Cuñúrr, where the canyon of the Río Guadalupe narrows, but almost nothing remains of the mission itself.

The Russians, pacifist refugees from the area of present-day Turkey, first arrived in Los Angeles but found the lands not to their liking and chose to head south across the border in 1905. Initially they lived in Indian dwellings known by their Kumeyaay name of *wa,* but they soon built adobe houses that the Kumeyaay later emulated. Across from the site of the former Dominican mission are the arches of the former Russian school, demolished some years ago. The nearby Russian cemetery still contains headstones with Cyrillic inscriptions.

Museo Comunitario de Guadalupe Only a handful of families of demonstrably Russian descent remain in the area. The private Museo Comunitario keeps alive their heritage with photographs and artifacts such as samovars, a Russian Bible and traditional clothing. In addition to the interior exhibits, antique farming machinery and a wa dwelling decorate the museum grounds.

Part of the house is still inhabited by the family of Franziska San Marín, herself married to a descendant of the early Russian settlers (ask to see the authentic sauna in the back of the house). In the attached 'restaurant,' her young daughter serves Russian dishes on weekends. To reach the museum (coming from Ensenada), turn left off México 3 onto the paved lateral at the town's Pemex station; bear to the right at the fork and follow the dirt road to the museum. Hours are 10 am to 6 pm Tuesday to Sunday; a donation is requested.

Museo Histórico Opposite the Museo Comunario is this INAH-maintained facility, which tells the story of the local mission and also has an exhibit about the Russian settlers. It's open 10 am to 5 pm Tuesday to Friday, and a donation is requested.

Getting There & Away

ABC buses from Ensenada to Tecate (and vice versa) will drop passengers at any place along México 3.

MAP 12 TIJUANA

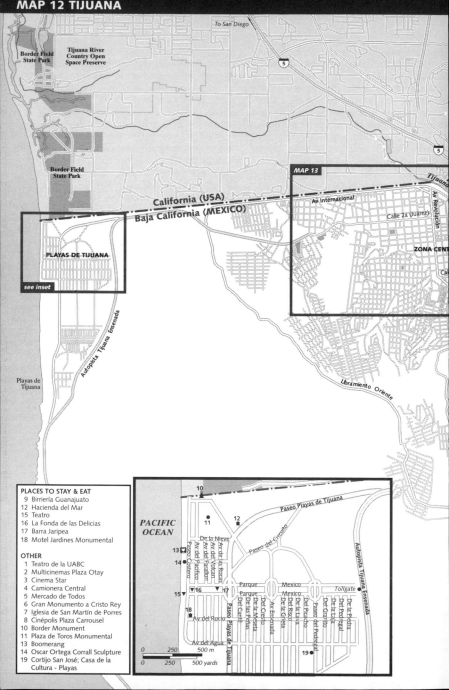

To San Diego

Border Field State Park

Tijuana River Country Open Space Preserve

Border Field State Park

California (USA)

Baja California (MEXICO)

MAP 13

Av Internacional

Calle 2a (Juárez)

ZONA CENT

PLAYAS DE TIJUANA

see inset

Autopista Tijuana Ensenada

Playas de Tijuana

Libramiento Oriente

Tijuana

Av Revolución

PLACES TO STAY & EAT
9 Birriería Guanajuato
12 Hacienda del Mar
15 Teatro
16 La Fonda de las Delicias
17 Barra Jaripea
18 Motel Jardines Monumental

OTHER
1 Teatro de la UABC
2 Multicinemas Plaza Otay
3 Cinema Star
4 Camionera Central
5 Mercado de Todos
6 Gran Monumento a Cristo Rey
7 Iglesia de San Martín de Porres
8 Cinépolis Plaza Carrousel
10 Border Monument
11 Plaza de Toros Monumental
13 Boomerang
14 Oscar Ortega Corrall Sculpture
19 Cortijo San José; Casa de la Cultura - Playas

PACIFIC OCEAN

10
11
12
Paseo Playas de Tijuana
De la Nieve
Paseo del Circuito
13
14
Parque
Mexico
15 16 17
Parque Mexico
Tollgate
18
Av del Rocio
Av del Agua
Paseo Playas de Tijuana
Autopista Tijuana Ensenada
Paseo del Pedregal
19

0   250   500 m
0   250   500 yards

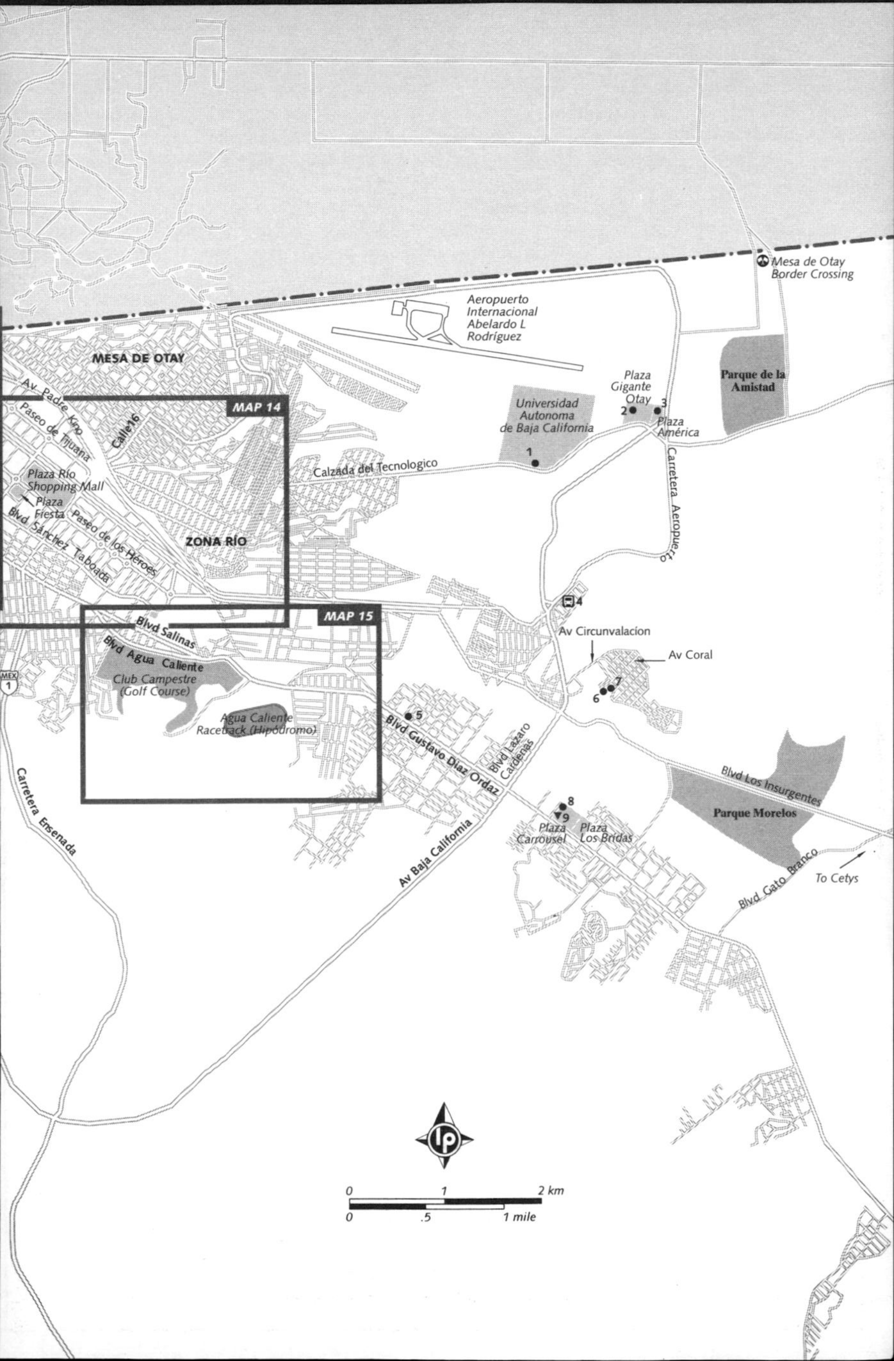

Mesa de Otay
Border Crossing

MESA DE OTAY

Aeropuerto
Internacional
Abelardo L
Rodriguez

Parque de la
Amistad

Plaza
Gigante
Otay

Universidad
Autonoma
de Baja California

Plaza
América

Av. Padre Kino

Paseo de Tijuana

Calle 16

Plaza Río
Shopping Mall

Plaza
Fiesta

Blvd Sánchez Taboada

Paseo de los Héroes

ZONA RÍO

Calzada del Tecnologico

Carretera Aeropuerto

Blvd Salinas

Blvd Agua Caliente

Club Campestre
(Golf Course)

Agua Caliente
Racetrack (Hipódromo)

Av Circunvalacion

Av Coral

Blvd Gustavo Diaz Ordaz

Blvd Lazaro Cardenas

Blvd Los Insurgentes

Parque Morelos

Plaza
Carrousel

Plaza
Los Bridas

Av Baja California

Blvd Gato Branco

To Cetys

Carretera Ensenada

MAP 14

MAP 15

MEX
1

0   1   2 km

0   .5   1 mile

MAP 13 ZONA CENTRO

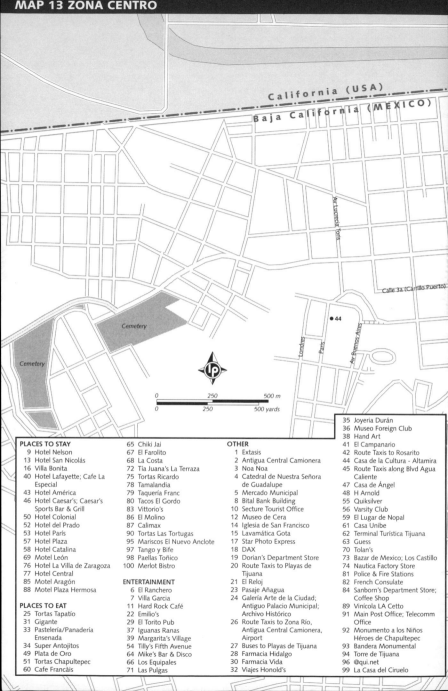

California (USA)

Baja California (MEXICO)

Av. Lucrecia Toris

Calle 3a (Carrillo Puerto)

Cemetery

Cemetery

● 44

Londres

París

Av. Buenos Aires

0   250   500 m
0   250   500 yards

PLACES TO STAY
9   Hotel Nelson
13 Hotel San Nicolás
16 Villa Bonita
40 Hotel Lafayette; Cafe La
    Especial
43 Hotel América
46 Hotel Caesar's; Caesar's
    Sports Bar & Grill
50 Hotel Colonial
52 Hotel del Prado
53 Hotel París
57 Hotel Plaza
58 Hotel Catalina
69 Motel León
76 Hotel La Villa de Zaragoza
77 Hotel Central
85 Motel Aragón
88 Motel Plaza Hermosa

PLACES TO EAT
25 Tortas Tapatío
31 Gigante
33 Pastelería/Panadería
    Ensenada
34 Super Antojitos
49 Plata de Oro
51 Tortas Chapultepec
60 Cafe Francàis

65 Chiki Jai
67 El Farolito
68 La Costa
72 Tía Juana's La Terraza
75 Tortas Ricardo
78 Tamalandia
79 Taquería Franc
80 Tacos El Gordo
83 Vittorio's
86 El Molino
87 Calimax
90 Tortas Las Tortugas
95 Mariscos El Nuevo Anclote
97 Tango y Bife
98 Paellas Toñico
100 Merlot Bistro

ENTERTAINMENT
6   El Ranchero
7   Villa Garcia
11 Hard Rock Café
22 Emilio's
29 El Torito Pub
37 Iguanas Ranas
39 Margarita's Village
54 Tilly's Fifth Avenue
64 Mike's Bar & Disco
66 Los Equipales
71 Las Pulgas

OTHER
1   Extasis
2   Antigua Central Camionera
3   Noa Noa
4   Catedral de Nuestra Señora
    de Guadalupe
5   Mercado Municipal
8   Bital Bank Building
10 Secture Tourist Office
12 Museo de Cera
14 Iglesia de San Francisco
15 Lavamática Gota
17 Star Photo Express
18 DAX
19 Dorian's Department Store
20 Route Taxis to Playas de
    Tijuana
21 El Reloj
23 Pasaje Añagua
24 Galería Arte de la Ciudad;
    Antiguo Palacio Municipal;
    Archivo Histórico
26 Route Taxis to Zona Río,
    Antigua Central Camionera,
    Airport
27 Buses to Playas de Tijuana
28 Farmacia Hidalgo
30 Farmacia Vida
32 Viajes Honold's

35 Joyeria Durán
36 Museo Foreign Club
38 Hand Art
41 El Campanario
42 Route Taxis to Rosarito
44 Casa de la Cultura - Altamira
45 Route Taxis along Blvd Agua
    Caliente
47 Casa de Ángel
48 H Arnold
55 Quiksilver
56 Varsity Club
59 El Lugar de Nopal
61 Casa Unibe
62 Terminal Turística Tijuana
63 Guess
70 Tolan's
73 Bazar de Mexico; Los Castillo
74 Nautica Factory Store
81 Police & Fire Stations
82 French Consulate
84 Sanborn's Department Store;
    Coffee Shop
89 Vinícola LA Cetto
91 Main Post Office; Telecomm
    Office
92 Monumento a los Niños
    Héroes de Chapultepec
93 Bandera Monumental
94 Torre de Tijuana
96 @qui.net
99 La Casa del Ciruelo

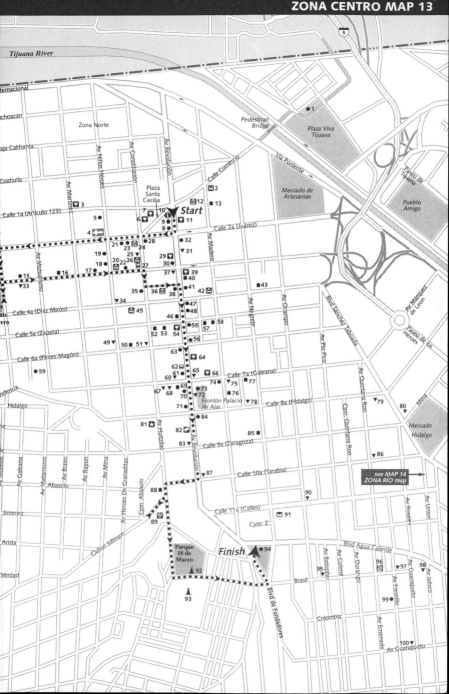

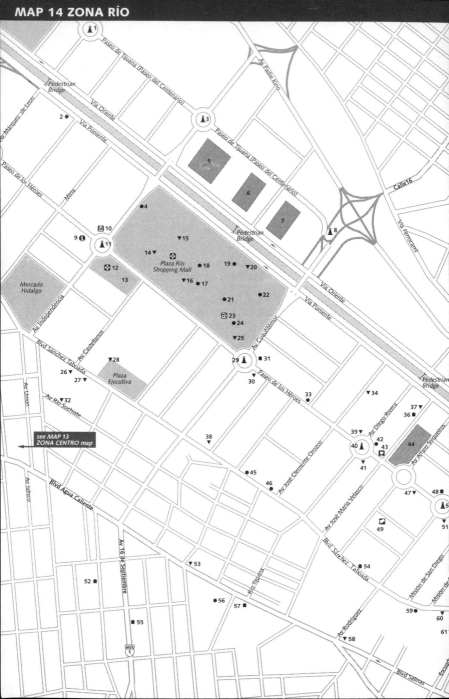

MAP 14 ZONA RÍO

PLACES TO STAY

31 Hotel Camino Real; Lobby Bar;
    Cantina María Bonita;
    Viajes Honold's
36 Hotel Real del Río
48 Hotel Lucerna; Rivoli Brasserie
52 Hotel Palacio Azteca
54 Hacienda del Río
55 Motel La Sierra; La Fonda de
    Roberto
57 Hotel Corona Plaza
63 Fiesta Inn

PLACES TO EAT

14 Comercial
15 Sanborn's Department Store
16 California Restaurante
20 Dragon Plaza
25 Sanborn's
26 Cafe Français
27 Gigante
28 El Faro de Mazatlán
30 Calimax
32 Asador Pamplona
34 La Cava Cien Años
37 Cien Años
38 Victor's; Cafe La Estancia
39 Guadalajara Bar & Grill
41 El Zaguan; ZKA
47 Mariscos Los Angulo
51 La Casa del Mole
53 Vallarta Natural
58 El Rodeo
60 Chan's
61 Villa Saverio's
62 La Espadaña
67 Tepoznieves

OTHER

1 Monument to Diana Cazadora
2 Cat's
3 Monument to Padre Miguel
    Hidalgo
4 Aero California
5 Palacio Municipal
6 Instituto Cultural de Baja
    California (ICBC); Main Public
    Library
7 Gobierno del Estado
8 Monument to Padre Eusebio
    Kino
9 Cotuco Head Office
10 Centro Cultural Tijuana (Cecut);
    Museo de las Californias;
    Museo Jardín Caracol; Cine
    Planetario; Sala de Exposiciones
    Comunitarias; Sala de Video
11 Monumento México
12 Plaza Fiesta: La Sonrisa, Lo Má
    Bonita, La Taberna Española,
    Porky's Place, Monte Picacho,
    Ah Jijo, El Callejon, Mi Barra,
    Cinque Cafe-Bar, Sótano Suizo,
    La Caja
13 Plaza Zapato
17 Gusher
18 Librería de Cristal
19 Multicinemas Río
21 Dorian's
22 Cinépolis Plaza Río
23 The Net; Copy Pronto
24 Aeroméxico
29 Monument to Cuauhtémoc
33 Budget Rent-a-Car
35 Hospital General
40 Monument to Abraham Lincoln
42 Baby Rock
43 Ochoa's Cocktail Lounge
44 Mundo Divertido
45 Librería El Día
46 Viajes Carrousel; Amex
49 Canadian Consulate
50 Monument to General
    Ignacio Zaragoza
56 El Toreo de Tijuana
59 Centro Artesanal
64 Site of Old Agua Caliente
    Casino & Spa
65 Cinemark 10
66 Agua Caliente Minaret
68 Cafe Online

Carretera Aeropuerto

To Airport

Defensores de Baja California

Av Padre Kino

Loreto

Pedestrian
Bridge

Av La Paz

Blvd Misión de la Paz

Blvd Sánchez Taboada

Paseo de los Héroes

63 ■

● 64

65 ●

Plaza
Minarete

● 66

▼ 67

68

see MAP 15
CHAPULTEPEC &
HIPÓDROMO map

0   250   500 m
0   250   500 yards

MAP 15 CHAPULTEPEC & HIPÓDROMO

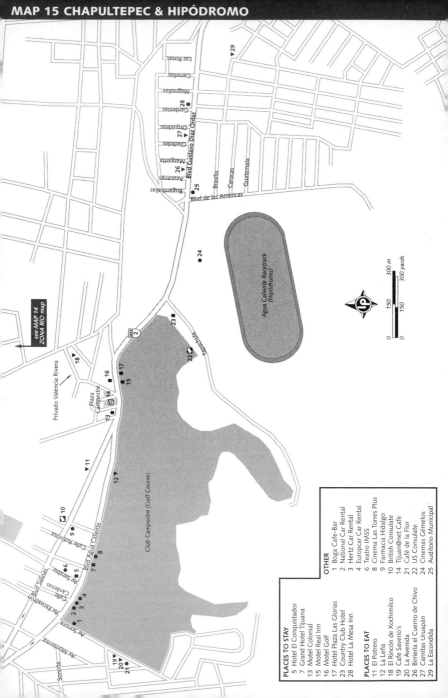

PLACES TO STAY
5 Hotel El Conquistador
7 Grand Hotel Tijuana
13 Motel Colonial
15 Motel Real Inn
16 Motel Golf
17 Hotel Plaza Las Glorias
23 Country Club Hotel
28 Hotel La Mesa Inn

PLACES TO EAT
11 El Potrero
12 La Leña
18 El Rincón de Xochimilco
19 Cafe Saverio's
20 La Avenida
26 Birriería el Cuerno de Chivo
27 Carnitas Uruapán
29 La Escondida

OTHER
1 Boga Cafe-Bar
2 National Car Rental
3 Hertz Car Rental
4 Europcar Car Rental
6 Teatro IMSS
8 Cinema Las Torres Plus
9 Farmacia Hidalgo
10 British Consulate
14 Tijuan@net Cafe
21 Café de la Flor
22 US Consulate
24 Cinemas Gémelos
25 Auditorio Municipal

see MAP 14
ZONA RÍO map

Agua Caliente Racetrack
(Hipódromo)

Club Campestre (Golf Course)

Plaza
Campestre

Privado Valencia Rivera

Blvd Gustavo Díaz Ordaz

Blvd de las Américas

Las Rosas
Camelias
Magnolias
Gardenias
Orquídeas
Gladiolas
Margarita
Azucenas
Bugambilias

Brasilia
Caracas
Guatemala

Av Monterrey
Av Escondida
Blvd Salinas
Calle Cárdenas
Av Sanabria
Av Sonora
Blvd Agua Caliente
Calle Robinosa

Sonalta

0   150   300 m
0   150   300 yards

Menu Translator

antojito – 'little whim,' a traditional Mexican snack or small meal that can be eaten at any time, on its own or as part of a larger meal

Sopa (Soup)
birria – a spicy-hot soup (almost a stew) of meat, onions, peppers and cilantro, served with tortillas
caldo – broth *(caldo tlalpeño)*, a hearty chicken, vegetable and chili variety
gazpacho – chilled vegetable soup spiced with hot chilies
menudo – tripe soup made with the spiced entrails of various four-legged beasts
pozole – rich, spicy stew of hominy (large maize kernels) with meat and vegetables
sopa de arroz – not a soup at all, but just a plate of rice, commonly served with lunch
sopa de pollo – chicken soup in broth

Huevos (Eggs)
huevos cocidos – hard-boiled eggs (specify the number of minutes if you're in doubt)
huevos fritos (con jamón/tocino) – fried eggs (with ham/bacon)
huevos mexicanos – eggs scrambled with tomatoes, chilies and onions (representing the red, green and white of the Mexican flag)
huevos poches – poached eggs
huevos rancheros – fried eggs on tortillas, covered in salsa

Pescado & Mariscos (Fish & Seafood)
abulón – abalone
almejas – clams
atún – tuna
cabrilla – sea bass
callos – scallops
camarones – shrimp
camarones gigantes – prawns
cangrejo – large crab
ceviche – raw seafood marinated in lime and mixed with onion, chile, garlic and tomato
filete de pescado – fish fillet
huachinango or *pargo* – red snapper
jaiva – small crab

jurel – yellowtail
langosta – lobster
lenguado – flounder or sole
mariscos – shellfish
ostiones – oysters
pescado al mojo de ajo – fish fried in butter and garlic
pez espada – swordfish
sierra – mackerel
tiburón – shark
trucha de mar – sea trout

Carnes & Aves (Meat & Fowl)
asado – roast
barbacoa – barbecued by placing under hot coals
biftec – beefsteak
cabra – goat
carne – meat
carne al carbón – charcoal-grilled meat
carne asada – grilled beef
chicharrones – deep-fried pork rinds
chorizo – pork sausage
chuletas de cerdo – pork chops
cochinita – suckling pig
conejo – rabbit
cordero – lamb
cordoniz – quail
costillas de puerco – pork ribs or chops
hígado – liver
jamón – ham
milanesa – breaded beefsteak
patas de puerco – pig's feet
pato – duck
pavo or *guajolote* – turkey
pollo – chicken
pollo asado – grilled chicken
pollo frito – fried chicken
tocino – bacon or salt pork

Frutas (Fruit)
coco – coconut
dátil – date
fresa – strawberry; often used to refer to any berry
guayaba – guava
higo – fig

limón – lime or lemon
naranja – orange
piña – pineapple
plátano or *banana* – banana
toronja – grapefruit
uva – grape

Verduras (Vegetables)

aceituna – olive
aguacate – avocado
calabaza – squash or pumpkin
cebolla – onion
chícharo – pea
ejote – green bean
elote – corn on the cob
jícama – root crop, resembling potato or apple, eaten with chile and salt
lechuga – lettuce
papa – potato
papitas fritas – potato chips
zanahoria – carrot

Dulces (Desserts)

flan – custard
helado – ice cream
nieve – flavored ice; Mexican equivalent of US 'snow cone'
paleta – flavored ice on a stick; equivalent to US popsicle, Australian icy-pole or UK ice-lolly

pan dulce – sweet roll
pastel – cake
postre – dessert

Other Foods

azúcar – sugar
bolillo – French-style bread rolls
crema – cream
leche – milk
mantequilla – butter
mole – sauce made from unsweetened chocolate, chile and many spices, often served over chicken or turkey
pimienta negra – black pepper
queso – cheese
sal – salt
salsa – sauce made from chile, onion, tomato, lemon or lime juice and spices

At the Table

cuchara – spoon
cuchillo – knife
cuenta – bill
menú – menu
plato – plate
propina – tip, usually 10% to 15% of the bill
servilleta – napkin or serviette
taza – cup
tenedor – fork
vaso or *copa* – glass

Glossary

For a list of Spanish food and drink terms, see the Menu Translator.

agave – century plant
agua purificada – purified water
alto – stop; also means 'high'
Apdo – abbreviation of *Apartado* (Box); in addresses, stands for 'Post Office Box'
asentamientos irregulares – shantytowns of Tijuana, Mexicali and other border towns
asistencia – in colonial times, a way station between missions
avenida – avenue

bajacaliforniano – resident of Baja California
ballena – whale; also a colloquial term for a liter-size bottle of Pacífico beer
banda – style of dance music
béisbol – baseball
bolillo – typical Mexican bread
bracero – literally, 'farmhand'; used to describe work program established by the US and Mexican governments during WWII that allowed Mexicans to work north of the border to alleviate labor shortages in the US

cabina – phone booth
calle – street
cambio or **casa de cambio** – currency exchange house
campanario – bell tower
Canaco – Cámara Nacional de Comercio (National Chamber of Commerce)
charreada – rodeo, frequently held during fiestas and other special occasions; particularly popular in northern Mexico
charro – Mexican cowboy or horseman; mariachi bands often dress in gaudy charro clothing
chilango – native or resident of Mexico City; depending on context, the term can be very pejorative
cholismo – rebellious youth movement, akin to punk, that has had some influence on the visual arts in Baja California
colonia – neighborhood in Tijuana or other large city; literally, 'colony'

corrida de toros – bullfight
corrido – folk ballad of the US-Mexico border region; corridos often have strong but subtle political content
Cotuco – Comité de Turismo y Convenciones (Committee on Tourism & Conventions)
coyote – smuggler who charges up to US$2000 to spirit illegal immigrants across the US-Mexican border
Cruz Roja – Red Cross

ejido – cooperative enterprise, usually of peasant agriculturalists, created under the land reform program of President Lázaro Cárdenas (1934–40); ejidos also participate in economic activities such as mining, ranching and tourism

fianza – bond posted against the return of a motor vehicle to the US
fraccionamiento – synonym for colonia (see above)
fronterizo – an inhabitant of the US-Mexico border region
frontón – venue for jai alai

glorieta – city traffic circle
gotas – water purification drops
gringo – term describing any light-skinned person, but most often a resident of the US; often but not always pejorative
güero – 'blond,' a term often used to describe any fair-skinned person in Mexico

hielo – ice
hipódromo – horseracing track

indígena – indigenous person
IVA – *impuesto de valor agregado,* or value-added tax

jai alai – game of Basque origin resembling squash
Judiciales – Mexican state and federal police

Ladatel – *Larga Distancia Automática,* or Automatic Long Distance phones

La Frontera – the area where Dominican priests built their missions in colonial times (from 1774); it extends from immediately south of present-day San Diego (mainland California) as far as El Rosario, at about the 30th parallel

librería – bookstore

licorería – liquor store; also called *vinos y licores*

llantera – tire repair shop, common even in Baja's most out-of-the-way places

lonchería – casual eatery, often a counter in markets, serving breakfast and lunch only

machismo – an exaggerated masculinity intended to impress other men more than women

Magonistas – followers of the exiled Mexican intellectual Ricardo Flores Magón, who attempted to establish a regional power base in the towns of northern Baja California during the Mexican Revolution

maguey – any of several species of a common Mexico fiber plant (*Agave* spp), also used for producing alcoholic drinks like tequila, mescal and pulque

malecón – waterfront promenade

maquiladora – industrial plant in Tijuana, Mexicali or another border town that takes advantage of cheap Mexican labor to assemble US components for re-exportation to the north

matador – bullfighter

mestizo – person of mixed Indian and European heritage

mordida – bribe; literally, 'the bite'

municipio – administrative subdivision of Mexican states, roughly akin to a US county

NAFTA – North American Free Trade Agreement, a pact between the US, Canada and Mexico that reduces or eliminates customs duties and other trade barriers

neophyte – a new convert (in this book, an indigenous person made Catholic by the missionaries)

ofrenda – offering given to a saint in exchange for a wish or wishes granted

ola – wave

palapa – palm-leaf shelter

pastillas para purificar agua – water-purification tablets

peatonal – pedestrian walk

peligro – danger

Pemex – Petróleos Mexicanos, the Mexican government oil monopoly

piñata – papier-mâché animal full of candy, broken open by children at celebrations like Christmas and birthdays

plaza de toros – bullring

pollero – synonymous with 'coyote'; a smuggler of undocumented immigrants (*pollos,* or 'chickens') into the US

Porfiriato – de facto dictatorship of Porfirio Díaz, who held Mexico's presidency from 1876 until the Revolution of 1910; under his rule, much of Baja California was granted to foreign companies for ambitious colonization projects, most of which soon failed

posada – at Christmas, a parade of costumed children reenacting the journey of Mary and Joseph to Bethlehem

presidio – during colonial times, a military outpost

PRI – Partido Revolucionario Institucional, the official party of government in Mexico from 1929 until 2000

propina – tip, at a restaurant or elsewhere

pueblo – town

ranchería – subsistence unit of hunter-gatherers in the contact period with Europeans, or, later, units associated with missions; implies a group of people rather than a place

rancho – tiny rural settlement, ranging from about 20 to 50 people

recinto fiscal – official vehicle-impound lot

Secture – Secretaría de Turismo del Estado (State Tourism Office)

Semarnap – Secretaría de Medio Ambiente, Recursos Naturales y Pesca, the Mexican government's primary conservation agency

Servicio Postal Mexicano – the Mexican national postal service

Servicios Migratorios – Immigration Office
SIDA – AIDS (Acquired Immune Deficiency Syndrome)
s/n (sin número) – street address without a specific number

todo terreno – mountain bike
tope – speed bump
tortillería – tortilla factory or shop
turista – tourist; also a colloquial name for diarrhea contracted by tourists

vaquero – Mexican cowboy

yodo – iodine, sold in pharmacies for water purification

zócalo – central plaza, a term more common in mainland Mexico than in Baja California
zona de tolerancia – in border cities, an area in which prostitution and related activities are concentrated
zona hotelera – hotel zone

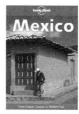

Index

Bold indicates maps.

San Diego Places to Stay

San Diego Places to Eat

Tijuana Places to Stay

Tijuana Places to Eat

Boxed Text

MAP LEGEND

ROUTES

City · Regional

- ....Freeway
- ....Toll Freeway
- ....Primary Road
- ....Secondary Road
- ....Tertiary Road
- ....Dirt Road
- ....Pedestrian Mall
- .... Steps
- .... Tunnel
- ....Trail
- .... Walking Tour
- ....Path

ROUTE SHIELDS

- **80** Interstate Freeway
- **MEX 2** Mexico Highway
- **G4** County Road
- **101** US Highway
- **95** State Highway
- **1** California State Highway

TRANSPORTATION

- ....Train
- ....Metro
- .... Bus Route
- .... Ferry

HYDROGRAPHY

- ....River; Creek
- ....Canal
- ....Lake
- ....Spring; Rapids
- ....Waterfalls
- ... Dry; Salt Lake

BOUNDARIES

- ..... International
- .... State
- ....County
- .... Disputed

AREAS

- ....Beach
- ....Building
- ....Campus
- .... Cemetery
- ....Forest
- ....Garden; Zoo
- .... Golf Course
- ....Park
- ....Plaza
- ....Reservation
- ....Sports Field
- ...Swamp; Mangrove

POPULATION SYMBOLS

- **◎ NATIONAL CAPITAL** ...National Capital
- **◉ State Capital** ....State Capital
- **● Large City** ....Large City
- **● Medium City** .... Medium City
- **● Small City** ....Small City
- **● Town; Village** .... Town; Village

MAP SYMBOLS

- ▲ .... Place to Stay
- ▼ ....Place to Eat
- ● ....Point of Interest

- ....Airfield
- ....Airport
- .... Archeological Site; Ruin
- ....Bank
- ....Baseball Diamond
- ....Beach
- ....Bike Trail
- .... Border Crossing
- .... Bus Station, Terminal
- ....Bus Stop
- ....Cable Car; Chairlift
- ....Campground
- ....Castle
- ....Cathedral
- ....Cave

- ....Church
- ....Cinema
- .... Embassy; Consulate
- .... Ferry Terminal
- ....Footbridge
- ....Fountain
- ....Garden
- .... Gas Station
- .... Golf Course
- ....Hospital
- ....Information
- ....Internet Café
- ....Lighthouse
- ....Lookout
- ....Mine

- ....Mission
- ....Monument
- ....Mountain
- ....Museum
- ....Oasis
- ....Observatory
- ....Park
- .... Parking Area
- ....Pass
- ....Picnic Area
- .... Police Station
- ....Pool
- ....Post Office
- ....Pub; Bar
- ....RV Park

- .... Shopping Mall
- ...... Skiing - Downhill
- .... Stately Home
- ....Surfing
- ....Synagogue
- ....Taxi
- ....Temple
- ....Theater
- .... Toilet - Public
- ....Trailhead
- ....Train Station
- ....Tram Stop
- ....Transportation
- ....Winery
- ....Zoo

Note: not all symbols displayed above appear in this book

LONELY PLANET OFFICES

Australia
Locked Bag 1, Footscray, Victoria 3011
☎ 03 8379 8000 fax 03 8379 8111
email talk2us@lonelyplanet.com.au

USA
150 Linden Street, Oakland, California 94607
☎ 510 893 8555, TOLL FREE 800 275 8555
fax 510 893 8572
email info@lonelyplanet.com

UK
10a Spring Place, London NW5 3BH
☎ 020 7428 4800 fax 020 7428 4828
email go@lonelyplanet.co.uk

France
1 rue du Dahomey, 75011 Paris
☎ 01 55 25 33 00 fax 01 55 25 33 01
email bip@lonelyplanet.fr
www.lonelyplanet.fr

World Wide Web: www.lonelyplanet.com *or* AOL keyword: lp
Lonely Planet Images: lpi@lonelyplanet.com.au